D0699873

HISTORICAL DICTIONARIES OF U.S. HISTORICAL ERAS

Jon Woronoff, Series Editor

1. *From the Great War to the Great Depression*, by Neil A. Wynn, 2003.
2. *Civil War and Reconstruction*, by William L. Richter, 2004.
3. *Revolutionary America*, by Terry M. Mays, 2005.
4. *Old South*, by William L. Richter, 2006.
5. *Early American Republic*, by Richard Buel Jr., 2006.
6. *Jacksonian Era and Manifest Destiny*, by Terry Corps, 2006.
7. *Reagan–Bush Era*, by Richard S. Conley, 2007.
8. *Kennedy–Johnson Era*, by Richard Dean Burns and Joseph M. Siracusa, 2008.
9. *Nixon–Ford Era*, by Mitchell K. Hall, 2008.
10. *Roosevelt–Truman Era,* by Neil A. Wynn, 2008.

Historical Dictionary of the Roosevelt– Truman Era

Neil A. Wynn

Historical Dictionaries of
U.S. Historical Eras, No. 10

The Scarecrow Press, Inc.
Lanham, Maryland • Toronto • Plymouth, UK
2008

SCARECROW PRESS, INC.

Published in the United States of America
by Scarecrow Press, Inc.
A wholly owned subsidary of
The Rowman & Littlefield Publishing Group, Inc.
4501 Forbes Boulevard, Suite 200, Lanham, Maryland 20706
www.scarecrowpress.com

Estover Road
Plymouth PL6 7PY
United Kingdom

British Library Cataloguing in Publication Information Available

Library of Congress Cataloging-in-Publication Data

Wynn, Neil A.
    Historical dictionary of the Roosevelt-Truman era / Neil A. Wynn.
        p. cm. -- (Historical dictionaries of U.S. historical eras ; no. 10)
    Includes bibliographical references and index.
    ISBN-13: 978-0-8108-5616-5 (hardcover : alk. paper)
    ISBN-10: 0-8108-5616-6 (hardcover : alk. paper)
    1. United States—History—1933–1945—Dictionaries. 2. United States—
History—1945–1953—Dictionaries. 3. United States—Politics and
government—1933–1945—Dictionaries. 4. United States—Politics and
government—1945–1953—Dictionaries. 5. United States—Biography—
20th century—Dictionaries. I. Title.
E806.W96 2008
973.91703—dc22

                                                        2008004628

∞ ™ The paper used in this publication meets the minimum requirements of
American National Standard for Information Sciences—Permanence of Paper
for Printed Library Materials, ANSI/NISO Z39.48-1992.
Manufactured in the United States of America.

In Memory of
Hilda Wynn
(1912–2006)

Contents

Editor's Foreword

The United States has rarely had to face more serious challenges than in the two decades from 1933 to 1953. The three most daunting ones were the Great Depression, World War II, and the Cold War, but many others tested two exceptional presidents, Franklin D. Roosevelt and Harry S. Truman. More forceful and flamboyant, FDR reacted with a first and then a second round of New Deal measures, introducing some of the most far-reaching reforms ever seen. Harry S. Truman, not initially voted into the job and coming toward the end of the world war, nonetheless grew into the presidency and prepared the country for another phase of conflict—not always a shooting war but still one that could destroy the United States and the rest of the world. On this background, partially spawned by it, a continuing series of reforms was adopted that revamped the economy and created the welfare state and also improved the situation of racial minorities, especially African Americans, women, and working people in general. This all took place within the framework of wider changes in society and culture, with the emergence of radio, television, and cinema and flourishing of literature and the arts.

Historical Dictionary of the Roosevelt–Truman Era is thus a crucial volume, for it shows how the United States was transformed, changing from a country in which government played a minor role to one where it was the major player, and also from a world in which the United States was just another nation to one in which it was the leader of the "free world." This transformation can most readily by grasped by tracing the many often fateful events in the chronology. Just how these events came about and how they relate to one another is examined in the introduction. The details are set forth in several hundred dictionary entries on significant people—not only figures in government or the military, but also in the economy, society, and culture—and entries on the more noteworthy events—whether on the home political scene or abroad, as well as more general entries on major trends and some lesser fashions. Meanwhile, the list of acronyms helps navigate the alphabet soup of new agencies and organizations. The bibliography, a rather comprehensive yet selective one, allows readers to follow up on specific aspects.

This book is written by Neil A. Wynn, which is fortunate for two reasons. He is one of the leading authorities on the period, having taught history and American studies of the 20th century first at the University of Glamorgan in Wales and more recently at the University of Gloucestershire. During his more than 30 years as an academic, he has written numerous articles and chapters, as well as several books, and edited or coedited two other works, the most relevant being *The Afro-American and the Second World War* (1976) and *America's Century: Perspectives on U.S. History since 1900* (1993). He has also already written a book in the Historical Dictionaries of U.S. Historical Eras series, *Historical Dictionary from the Great War to the Great Depression* (2003). This gives him a better understanding of how the earlier period impacted the latter and also permits a more seamless connection between the two. In addition, together these two books offer readers a broader and deeper view of an often troubled period in American history and one that pointed the United States in directions it is still following today.

Jon Woronoff
Series Editor

Preface

It would be hard to imagine two decades more filled with major events and developments than the 1930s and 1940s, so much so that I was reluctant to take on the task of compiling this dictionary. Having done so, I found my worst fears justified as it became a work that required twice as much time to complete as originally anticipated. That the book was finished at all was due to Jon Woronoff's patience and also that of my long-suffering wife, Regina, who was forced to spend many an evening and weekend alone while I labored on the task. The work was to some extent made possible by the support allowed by the Department of Humanities at the University of Gloucestershire, through the provision of time to spend in the libraries. Despite this, I still suspect one volume cannot do full justice to these two decades. I discovered many gaps in my own knowledge, and in making inevitable choices about what or whom to leave out, I am sure that I will disappoint many experts in the field. This is particularly likely to be true in the sphere of culture and entertainment, as these were enormously creative years. In the end, even with having been granted extra space, I was forced to include only those I thought were the most significant figures or developments in these fields; however, I hope I have managed to give a sense of the key changes in those areas while concentrating on the major political and international developments. I dedicate this dictionary to the memory of my mother, Hilda Wynn, who lived through all the decades I have written about but sadly did not survive to see this book completed.

Neil A. Wynn
University of Gloucestershire

Acronyms and Abbreviations

AAA	Agricultural Adjustment Administration
ACC	Allied Control Council
ACLU	American Civil Liberties Union
ADA	Americans for Democratic Action
AEC	Atomic Energy Commission
AFBF	American Farm Bureau Federation
AFC	America First Committee
AFL	American Federation of Labor
AFL-CIO	American Federation of Labor-Congress of Industrial Organizations
ALP	American Labor Party
AMA	American Medical Association
ANZUS	Australia-New Zealand-United States Alliance
BSCP	Brotherhood of Sleeping Car Porters
CAA	Civil Aeronautics Authority
CBS	Columbia Broadcasting System
CCC	Civilian Conservation Corps
CEEC	Committee for European Economic Cooperation
CENTO	Central Treaty Organization
CIA	Central Intelligence Agency
CIO	Congress of Industrial Organizations
COINTELPRO	Counter Intelligence Program
COMECON	Committee for Mutual Economic Assistance
COMINFORM	Communist Information Bureau
CORE	Congress of Racial Equality
CPA	Civilian Production Administration
CPUSA	Communist Party of the United States of America
CWA	Civil Works Administration
DAR	Daughters of the American Revolution

ECA	Economic Cooperation Administration
EEC	European Economic Community
ERP	European Recovery Program
FBI	Federal Bureau of Investigation
FCA	Farm Credit Administration
FCC	Federal Communications Commission
FDIC	Federal Deposit Insurance Corporation
FEPC	Fair Employment Practices Committee
FERA	Federal Emergency Relief Administration
FHA	Federal Housing Administration
FPHA	Federal Public Housing Authority
FRB	Federal Reserve Board
FRG	Federal Republic of Germany
FSA	Farm Security Administration
FWA	Federal Works Agency
GATT	General Agreement on Tariffs and Trade
GDR	German Democratic Republic
GNP	gross national product
HOLC	Home Owners' Loan Corporation
HUAC	House Un-American Activities Committee
ILGWU	International Ladies Garment Workers Union
IMF	International Monetary Fund
IWW	Industrial Workers of the World
MOWM	March on Washington Movement
NAACP	National Association for the Advancement of Colored People
NAM	National Association of Manufacturers
NASA	National Aeronautics and Space Agency
NATO	North Atlantic Treaty Organization
NBC	National Broadcasting Corporation
NDAC	National Defense Advisory Commission
NFU	National Farmers' Union
NHA	National Housing Agency
NIRA	National Industrial Recovery Act
NLB	National Labor Board
NLRB	National Labor Relations Board
NNC	National Negro Congress
NRA	National Recovery Administration

NRPB	National Resources Planning Board
NSC	National Security Council
NSC-68	National Security Council Report 68
NWLB	National War Labor Board
NYA	National Youth Administration
OAS	Organization of American States
OCD	Office of Civilian Defense
OES	Office of Economic Stabilization
OFF	Office of Facts and Figures
OPA	Office of Price Administration
OPM	Office of Production Management
OPS	Office of Price Stabilization
OSRD	Office of Scientific Research and Development
OSS	Office of Strategic Services
OWI	Office of War Information
OWM	Office of War Mobilization
PAC	Political Action Committee
PHA	Public Housing Administration
PWA	Public Works Administration
RA	Resettlement Administration
RAF	Royal Air Force
REA	Rural Electrification Administration
RFC	Reconstruction Finance Corporation
SALT	Strategic Arms Limitation Talks
SCLC	Southern Christian Leadership Conference
SDF	Social Democratic Federation
SEATO	Southeast Asia Treaty Organization
SEC	Securities and Exchange Commission
SHAEF	Supreme Headquarters of the Allied Expeditionary Force
SHAPE	Supreme Headquarters Allied Powers Europe
SLP	Socialist Labor Party
SNCC	Student Nonviolent Coordinating Committee
SPA	Socialist Party of America
START	Strategic Arms Reduction Talks
STFU	Southern Tenant Farmers' Union
SWOC	Steel Workers' Organizing Committee
TVA	Tennessee Valley Authority

UAW	United Automobile Workers
UMW	United Mine Workers
UMWA	United Mine Workers of America
UN	United Nations
UNESCO	United Nations Educational, Scientific, and Cultural Organization
UNRRA	United Nations Relief and Rehabilitation Administration
USES	United States Employment Service
USHA	United States Housing Authority
USO	United Service Organizations
USSR	Union of Socialist Soviet Republics (Soviet Union)
USWA	United Steel Workers of America
V-E	Victory Europe
V-J	Victory Japan
WACS	Women's Army Corps
WASPS	Women's Air Force Service Pilots
WAVES	Women Appointed for Voluntary Emergency Service
WFB	War Food Administration
WIS	Women in Industry Service
WLB	War Labor Board
WMC	War Manpower Commission
WPA	Works Progress Administration
WPB	War Production Board
WRA	War Relocation Authority
WRB	War Refugee Board
WSA	War Shipping Administration
WSB	Wage Stabilization Board
YMCA	Young Men's Christian Association
YWCA	Young Women's Christian Association

Chronology

1933   23 January: The Twentieth Amendment to the Constitution advancing the start of congressional sessions and moving the presidential inauguration from March to January, thus ending the so-called "lame duck" sessions, passed by Congress on 2 March 1932, is ratified. **30 January:** Nazi leader Adolf Hitler becomes chancellor of Germany. **20 February:** The Twenty-First Amendment to the Constitution is passed in Congress repealing the Eighteenth Amendment that introduced prohibition in 1920. **4 March:** Franklin D. Roosevelt is inaugurated as president. In his inaugural address Roosevelt tells the American people that "the only thing we have to fear is fear itself" and calls for sweeping powers to tackle the problems of the Great Depression. **5 March:** President Roosevelt calls Congress to convene in an emergency session to address the immediate problems of the Great Depression following the Wall Street Crash of 1929. **6 March:** President Roosevelt declares a national bank holiday to halt the bank crisis. **9 March:** Congress meets in emergency session and passes the Emergency Bank Act formalizing the bank holiday and giving the president power to control the movement of gold and issue new Federal Reserve notes. **20 March:** Congress passes the Economy Act cutting the wages of federal government employees and government spending to finance other New Deal measures. **22 March:** The Beer Act, repealing the Volstead Act (1919) and allowing the manufacture and sale of alcohol and allowing revenue to be raised by taxation on alcohol, is passed. **27 March:** Executive Order 6084 is issued establishing the Farm Credit Administration to provide loans to farmers. **5 April:** The Civilian Conservation Corps is established by executive order to provide employment for young unemployed people in land conservation programs. **12 May:** The Agricultural Adjustment Act is passed to tackle the crisis in farming by encouraging farmers to reduce crop and livestock production to raise prices. The Emergency

Farm Mortgage Act is passed the same day. The Federal Emergency Relief Act is also passed to provide $500 million in relief payments for the unemployed and establish the Federal Emergency Relief Administration. An international economic conference was convened in London to address the international crisis. **17 May:** The Tennessee Valley Authority is established to provide hydroelectric power and water irrigation along the Tennessee River. **27 May:** The Securities Act requiring full disclosure of information relating to securities is passed. **13 June:** The Home Owners' Loan Act is passed enabling the government to underwrite defaulted mortgages and thus avoid foreclosures. **16 June:** The Banking Act (Glass-Steagall Act) establishing the Federal Deposit Insurance Corporation (FDIC) and a federal guarantee of bank deposits is passed. The Farm Credit Act making provision of loans for farmers on a short-term basis is passed. The National Industrial Recovery Act (NIRA) is passed setting up the Public Works Administration (PWA) to provide work relief programs and the National Recovery Administration (NRA) to establish codes of fair competition, wages, and prices to encourage industrial recovery. **5 August:** The National Labor Board is established to resolve issues arising from section 7(a) of the NIRA recognizing the rights of organized labor. **9 November:** The Civil Works Administration is established by executive order to provide a speedy program of work relief over the winter months. **5 December:** The Twenty-First Amendment to the Constitution is ratified.

1934 1 January: Dr. Francis E. Townsend announces his Old Age Revolving Pension Plan. **30 January:** The Gold Reserve Act setting the value of the dollar in relation to gold introduced as a way of controlling prices is passed. **24 March:** Congress passes the Tydings-McDuffie Act granting the Philippines independence but only after a 10-year period for constitutional development. **21 April:** The Bankhead Cotton Control Act, a measure to control cotton production, is passed. **6 June:** President Roosevelt signs the Securities Exchange Act establishing the Securities and Exchange Commission to ensure that new regulations of the securities markets are enforced. **18 June:** Congress passes the Indian Reorganization Act initiating the "Indian New Deal." **21 June:** Railway Labor Act according railworkers the same rights granted other workers under the NIRA is passed. **28 June:** President Roosevelt signs the National Housing Act establishing the Federal Housing Administration to insure loans made to homeowners to buy or improve their homes. **6 August:** U.S. Marines leave Haiti.

1935 4 January: In his State of the Union address to Congress, President Roosevelt outlines his plans to provide for the better use of the land's natural resources, for a system of social security, and for the provision of decent homes. **19–20 March:** A race riot in which three people are killed breaks out in the African American community in Harlem, New York, following an incident involving a black youth and a white policeman. **8 April:** The Emergency Relief Appropriation Act providing $4.8 billion for work relief programs is passed. **30 April:** The Resettlement Administration is established by executive order to help resettle displaced farmers. **6 May:** The Works Progress Administration is created by executive order to provide work relief programs. **11 May:** The Rural Electrification Administration is set up by executive order to encourage provision of electric power to rural areas. **27 May:** In *Schechter Poultry Corporation v United States* the Supreme Court rules the NRA unconstitutional. **26 June:** The National Youth Administration (NYA) is established by executive order. **14 August:** The Social Security Act providing the first federal unemployment and old age insurance for many Americans is passed. **23 August:** The Banking Act strengthening the role of the governors of the Federal Reserve System and requiring all large state banks to come under their jurisdiction is passed. **30 August:** The Revenue Act, sometimes known as the Wealth Tax Act because it increased taxes on the wealthy and on businesses, is passed. **31 August:** The first of several Neutrality Acts is passed imposing an embargo on the export of implements to belligerent powers and forbidding U.S. vessels from carrying munitions to nations at war. **10 September:** Louisiana Senator Huey Long dies after being shot two days earlier on the steps of the state capitol. **21 December:** The NRA is terminated by executive order.

1936 6 January: In *United States v. Butler et al* the Supreme Court declares the Agricultural Adjustment Administration unconstitutional. **29 February:** A second Neutrality Act is passed extending existing provisions to include loans. The Soil Conservation Act is passed to provide support for farmers who switched to soil conserving crops. **8 March:** The Federal Dance Project is established. **25 March:** The

Second London Naval Treaty between the United States and Great Britain is signed providing for the exchange of information about naval building programs. **20 April:** The Rural Electrification Act is passed. **19 June:** African American heavyweight boxer Joe Louis is knocked out by the German Max Schmeling in round 12 of their fight. **22 June:** A Flood Control Act authorizes studies of flood prevention methods on the Mississippi River. **29 June:** The Merchant Marine Act is passed to provide financial support and encourage the building and development of the U.S. Merchant Marine. **18 July:** The Spanish Civil War begins. **1 August–16 August:** The XIth Olympic Games take place in Berlin, Germany. African American track athlete Jesse Owens wins four gold medals. African American athletes win a total of seven gold, three silver, and two bronze medals, an achievement seen by many as undermining Nazi racial ideologies. **3 November:** Roosevelt is reelected president in a landslide victory, defeating Republican candidate Alf Landon with 60.8 percent of the vote to Landon's 36.5 percent. **25 November:** Members of the Abraham Lincoln Brigade sail from New York to fight for the republican cause in the Spanish Civil War. **30 December:** Workers in several General Motors (GM) plants in Flint, Michigan, led by Walter Reuther and other officials of the United Auto Workers, stage sit-down strikes to secure union recognition.

1937   20 January: Roosevelt is inaugurated for his second term as president. In his inaugural address he says that the nation should continue the reforms in place as he still saw millions suffering and "one third of a nation ill-housed, ill-fed, and ill-nourished." **February:** GM agrees to union recognition. **7 February:** President Roosevelt sends the Court Reorganization Bill to Congress in an attempt to change the composition of the Supreme Court, which ruled several New Deal measures unconstitutional. The president's proposals are not accepted, but the court begins to uphold New Deal measures. **29 March:** In *West Coast v. Parrish* the Supreme Court upholds a Washington state minimum wage law, suggesting a change in direction with regard to welfare legislation. **12 April:** In *National Labor Relations Board v. Jones & Laughlin Steel Corp.* the Supreme Court upholds the constitutionality of the National Labor Relations Act. **6 May:** Thirty-six people die when the airship *Hindenburg* explodes while trying to dock at the Lakehurst Naval Base in New Jersey. **30 May:** Ten people are shot and killed by police in the

Memorial Day Massacre when striking workers attempt to establish picket lines outside Republic Steel in South Chicago. **22 June:** Black boxer Joe Louis knocks out James Braddock in the eighth round to become world heavyweight champion. Louis holds the title for 12 years. **29 June:** The Emergency Relief Appropriation Act reducing spending on relief is passed. The cutback contributed to the recession that year. **7 July:** Following a clash at the Marco Polo Bridge near Peiping, China, Japanese forces invade China threatening the "Open Door" agreed with the United States and central to U.S. foreign policy in Asia. **22 July:** The Bankhead-Jones Farm Tenancy Act providing low-interest loans to tenant farmers, sharecroppers, and farm laborers is passed. The Emergency Relief Appropriations Act passes the same day introducing cuts in relief spending and contributing to the downturn in the economy. **17 August:** The Miller-Tydings Act allowing price maintenance agreements between manufacturers and retailers is passed. **26 August:** The Revenue Act taxing corporations that hold onto profits rather than paying them in dividends is passed. **1 September:** The Farm Security Administration is established to oversee provision to farmers under the Resettlement Administration and Bankhead-Jones Farm Tenancy Act. It also includes the Photographic Division, under the direction of Roy Stryker, responsible for recording many images of rural life in the Depression.

1938 3 February: The Housing Act establishes the Federal Public Housing Authority to encourage slum clearance. **16 February:** The second Agricultural Adjustment Act is passed to provide payment to enable farmers to store surplus crops in good years. Payment is to be made out of general taxation rather than a processing tax, the issue on which the previous Agricultural Adjustment Act had been declared unconstitutional. **22 June:** In a highly symbolic contest, Joe Louis wins a smashing victory in his second fight with the German boxer Max Schmeling, knocking out his opponent in under three minutes. **23 June:** The Civil Aeronautics Act providing for the regulation of all air services is passed. **25 June:** The Fair Labor Standards Act is passed establishing minimum wage and maximum hour levels for many workers. The act also effectively prohibits the employment of children under the age of 16 in industrial and manufacturing businesses. **30 October:** The radio broadcast of *War of the Worlds* by Orson Welles creates panic among listeners who think it was a real, live event. **8 November:** The Republican Party gains six Senate seats and 71 seats in the House of Representatives in the midterm elections following the president's attempt at "court packing" and the onset of the "Roosevelt recession." **12 December:** In *Missouri ex rel. Gaines v. Canada* the Supreme Court rules that a state has to provide in-state education facilities for African Americans, even though separate, and cannot rely on out-of-state provision. **31 December:** The U.S. ambassador to Japan protests against the Japanese breach of the "Open Door" policy.

1939   28 March: The fall of Madrid to Franco's forces signals the end of the Spanish Civil War. **9 April:** African American singer Marian Anderson performs on the steps of the Lincoln Memorial to a crowd of 75,000 after being denied the use of Constitution Hall by the Daughters of the American Revolution. **16 May:** The Food Stamp Program is introduced to enable poor families to purchase foodstuffs at lower prices. **1 July:** A number of agencies are established under the reorganization of the executive branch of the federal government. The Federal Loan Agency is established to coordinate and supervise all federal lending agencies. The Federal Security Agency is established to bring together the work of the Social Security Board, Public Health Service, Civilian Conservation Corps (CCC), and NYA, among others. The Federal Works Agency brings together the activities of agencies dealing with the upkeep, maintenance, and construction of public buildings and of federal housing programs. A National Resources Planning Board is established to consider plans for the development and exploitation of national resources. This increasingly focused on resources necessary for wartime. **21 August:** The Nazi-Soviet Nonaggression Pact is signed. **1 September:** German armies invade Poland, starting World War II. **4 November:** The Neutrality Act of 1939 amends existing laws to allow the sale of materials to belligerent powers on a "cash and carry" basis.

1940   2 September: The "Destroyers-for-Bases" Agreement, in which the United States exchanged several out-of-date battleships with Great Britain in return for the use of naval bases in the Caribbean, is finalized. **4 September:** The America First Committee, an organization supporting isolationism, is established. **16 September:** The Selective Service Act is introduced, the first time conscription was adopted in the United States during peacetime. **16 October:** A total embargo is imposed on the export of iron and steel scrap to Japan. **5 November:** Roosevelt wins an unprecedented third term by defeating Republican

Wendell Willkie with 54.8 percent of the popular vote to Willkie's 44.8 percent and by 449 electoral college votes (38 states) to 82 (10 states). **29 December:** In a "fireside" chat broadcast on radio President Roosevelt says the United States should be "the arsenal of democracy."

1941   6 January: President Roosevelt outlines the "four freedoms" on which the future world should be based in his State of the Union Address to Congress. **7 January:** The Office of Production Management (OPM) is established to supervise the production and allocation of raw materials for national defense production. **20 January:** Roosevelt is inaugurated as president. **1 March:** The Senate establishes a special Senate Committee to Investigate the Defense Program chaired by Senator Harry S. Truman. **11 March:** The Lend-Lease Act enabling the United States to "lend or lease" necessary goods and materials to the warring democracies is passed. **21 May:** A German U-boat sinks the U.S. freighter *Robin Moor*. **22 June:** Hitler launches an attack on the Soviet Union, and as a result the USSR begins to receive Lend-Lease aid from the United States. **25 June:** President Roosevelt issues Executive Order 8802 establishing a Fair Employment Practices Committee to ensure an end to discrimination in employment in defense industries and so averts the March on Washington called by A. Philip Randolph scheduled for 1 July. **26 July:** The United States freezes Japanese assets and suspends diplomatic relations with Japan. **14 August:** Roosevelt and Churchill issue the Atlantic Charter outlining their vision for the postwar world. **31 October:** USS *Reuben Jones* is sunk by a German U-boat. **November:** Respective proposals regarding the conflict in Asia are exchanged between Japan and the United States. **27 November:** U.S. Pacific commands are warned of the likelihood of war. **7 December:** Japanese aircraft attack the U.S. fleet in Pearl Harbor. Japanese troops also invade Malaya. **8 December:** The United States and Great Britain declare war on Japan. **11 December:** Germany and Italy declare war on the United States in support of Japan. **18 December:** The first War Powers Act is passed enabling the government to pass powers to war agencies.

1942   1 January: The United Nations Declaration is signed by 26 governments during the Arcadia conference in Washington. **16 January:** The War Production Board (WPB), under Donald Nelson and empowered to oversee the production and distribution of raw materials and manufactured goods and award contracts, replaces the OPM. **26**

January: The first U.S. troops begin to arrive in Britain. **19 February:** President Roosevelt issues Executive Order 9066 authorizing the establishment of exclusion areas on the West coast and the relocation of people deemed a threat to security. **27 February:** Combined U.S., British, and Dutch forces are defeated in the battle of the Java Sea. **18 March:** The War Relocation Authority is established to oversee relocation of Japanese Americans. **27 March:** The second War Powers Act is passed extending the power of the WPB. **9 April:** U.S. forces on Bataan are forced to surrender. **18 April:** The Doolittle raid is launched by U.S. aircraft against targets in Japan. **3 May:** General John DeWitt orders all people of Japanese ancestry to gather at assembly centers prior to their relocation to camps in various remote parts of the country. More than 112,000 Japanese Americans are placed in relocation camps. **4–8 May:** The battle of the Coral Sea halts the Japanese fleet and thus prevents a possible invasion of Australia. **3–6 June:** In the battle of Midway, the U.S. Pacific fleet inflicts a defeat on the Japanese navy that enables the United States to take the offensive. **13 June:** The Office of War Information is established. **4 July:** The first U.S. air force bombing raids in Europe begin. **4 August:** The Bracero program, allowing the temporary importation of Mexican workers to the United States, is signed. **7 August:** U.S. troops land on Guadalcanal. **3 November:** The Republican Party makes gains in the congressional elections, but the Democratic Party maintains control of both House and Senate. **8 November:** In Operation Torch, 65,000 U.S. troops land in Casablanca, Algiers, and Oran in North Africa. **16 November:** U.S. forces land on New Guinea in the Pacific.

1943   14–24 January: Allied leaders Winston Churchill and Franklin D. Roosevelt meet in Casablanca, Morocco, to agree on military strategy and plan the invasions of Sicily and Italy. They call for the unconditional surrender of the Axis powers. **8 February:** U.S. forces defeat the Japanese on Guadalcanal. **30 May–7 June:** For nearly a week, conflict between servicemen and Mexican American youths erupts in racial violence in Los Angeles. The riot is known as the "zoot suit riot" because of the style of clothing worn by the Mexican Americans. **20–24 June:** Following a clash between blacks and whites, race rioting erupts in Detroit, where 34 people—25 of them black—are killed before peace is restored. **21 June:** The Supreme Court upholds the conviction of a

Japanese American for breaking the curfew imposed in defense areas on the west coast in *Hirabayashi v. United States*. **25 June:** The War Labor Disputes (Smith-Connally) Act is passed over the president's veto. **9 July:** In Operation Husky, Allied forces begin the invasion of Sicily. **1–2 August:** An incident between a white policeman and black soldier sparks a riot in Harlem, New York, in which five people are killed and millions of dollars worth of damage is done in attacks on largely white-owned property. During the summer, riots and racial conflicts occur in more than 240 towns and cities, including Mobile, Alabama, and Beaumont, Texas. **3 September:** Allied troops land in Italy. **8 September:** Italy surrenders, although control of the northern areas remains in German hands. **23–26 November:** Churchill and Roosevelt meet with Chinese leader Chiang Kai-shek to agree on postwar policies in Asia and call for the unconditional surrender of Japan. **28 November–1 December:** The three Allied leaders, Churchill, Roosevelt, and Stalin, meet in Tehran for the first time to agree on the final military strategy of the war, including the dates for the invasion of Europe by Britain and the United States.

1944 11 January: President Roosevelt outlines his proposals for an Economic Bill of Rights in his State of the Union address to Congress. **22 January:** Allied troops land at Anzio, a town south of Rome, in an attempt to break the military deadlock in Italy. The German forces are not defeated until late May. **22–23 February:** President Roosevelt vetoes the Revenue Bill after Congress refuses to include all his requests to raise taxes; however, Congress passes the bill over the president's veto. **3 April:** The Supreme Court rules that the all-white Democratic Party primary in Texas is unconstitutional in *Smith v. Allwright*. **4 June:** Allied troops enter Rome. **6 June:** One hundred thirty thousand Allied troops land on five beaches in Normandy during the D-Day invasion of Europe. **19–20 June:** The Japanese navy suffers a further defeat in the battle of the Philippine Sea. **22 June:** The Selective Serviceman's Readjustment Act, or G.I. Bill of Rights, is passed to ease the transition of ex-servicemen from military to civilian life. **1–22 July:** More than 700 delegates from all 45 Allied nations meet at Bretton Woods, New Hampshire, and agree to establish a World Bank and International Monetary Fund. **19–21 July:** The Democratic Party National Convention is held in Chicago where President Roosevelt is overwhelmingly nominated as their presidential candidate. Senator Harry S. Truman is chosen as the vice presidential candidate. **21 July:** U.S. forces land on Guam. **26–29 July:** The Republican Party National Convention is held in Chicago where Governor Thomas E. Dewey of New York is nominated as their presidential candidate over Wendell Willkie. **21 August–7 October:** Representatives of the Allied Powers (Great Britain, China, the Soviet Union, and the United States) meet at Dumbarton Oaks in Washington, D.C., to discuss the structure of the United Nations (UN). **11 September:** The first U.S. troops cross German borders. **7 November:** Roosevelt is reelected president, defeating the Republican Dewey by 53.5 percent of the popular vote to 46 percent and 432 electoral college votes to 99. **22 October:** Under the command of General Douglas MacArthur, U.S. forces return to the Philippines. **23–26 October:** The Japanese navy is defeated in Leyte Gulf during their attempt to halt U.S. landings in the Philippines. **24 November:** The first U.S. air raids on Tokyo are launched from the Marianas Islands. **16 December:** The "Battle of the Bulge" begins after German armies launched a counteroffensive in the Ardennes. **18 December:** In *Korematsu v. United States* the Supreme Court rules that the need for security in wartime overrides the rights of individuals, and it upholds the government's decision to intern Japanese Americans in relocation centers.

1945   20 January: Roosevelt is inaugurated as president for an unprecedented fourth term. In his brief message, the president urges Americans to work for a "just and honorable peace, a durable peace." **4–11 February:** Churchill, Roosevelt, and Stalin meet at Yalta in the Crimea and reach a broad agreement on the future of postwar Germany. **16 February:** U.S. troops land on the island of Corregidor in the Philippines. **19 February:** The U.S. landings on the island of Iwo Jima begin. **4 March:** Manila, capital of the Philippines, is liberated. **16 March:** The defeat of Japanese forces on Iwo Jima is completed. **1 April:** U.S. landings on Okinawa begin. **12 April:** Vice President Harry S. Truman is sworn in as president following President Roosevelt's sudden death in Warm Springs, Georgia. **15 April:** Following a memorial service in the White House the previous day, Roosevelt is buried at his home in Hyde Park, New York. **25 April–26 June:** The conference in San Francisco to establish the UN takes place. **30 April:** Adolf Hitler commits suicide. **7 May:** The German surrender is signed by Admiral Dönitz. **8**

May: VE (Victory Europe Day) is declared. **21 June:** Fighting in Okinawa comes to an end. **26 June:** The UN Charter is signed. **16 July:** The first test explosion of the atomic bomb takes place in Alamogordo, New Mexico. **17 July–2 August:** The leaders of the Grand Alliance meet in Potsdam, Germany, following Germany's surrender to consider the postwar division of their former enemy. President Truman informs Stalin of the acquisition of a new powerful weapon—the atomic bomb. Stalin agrees to enter the war against Japan. **6 August:** The first atomic bomb is dropped on the Japanese city of Hiroshima. **8 August:** The USSR enters the war against Japan. **9 August:** A second atomic bomb is dropped on the Japanese city of Nagasaki. **14 August:** Japanese armies surrender. **15 August:** VJ (Victory Japan) Day is declared. **28 August:** The first U.S. troops land on mainland Japan. **2 September:** Representatives of the Japanese government sign the formal terms of surrender onboard the USS *Missouri*. **6 September:** In his first address to Congress, President Truman outlines a wide-ranging program of reform measures indicating a wish to continue the New Deal. **20 November:** War crimes trials of leading Nazi officials begin in Nuremburg, Germany. **14 December:** General George C. Marshall is sent to attempt to mediate in the civil war in China.

1946   24 January: The first meeting of the UN General Assembly takes place in London, England. **9 February:** Stalin announces the need for a new Five-Year Plan in the USSR in light of the incompatibility of the communist and capitalist systems and the likelihood of conflict with the West. **22 February:** George F. Kennan sends his "Long Telegram" to the State Department outlining the inevitability of conflict with the USSR and the need for a policy of "containment." **5 March:** Winston Churchill speaks of an "Iron Curtain" falling across eastern Europe in his address at Westminster College in Fulton, Missouri. **1 April:** Miners begin a strike that is followed shortly after by workers in several other industries as strikes reach a new level. **17 May:** Faced by a national rail strike, President Truman threatens to take over the rail system, but the dispute is settled and confrontation is avoided. **20 May:** The threat earlier of a miners' strike brings further strong action from President Truman, who secures a court order against the miners. **3 June:** In *Morgan v. Virginia* the Supreme Court rules that segregation in interstate transport is unconstitutional. **4 July:** The Philippines gain independence from the United States. **6 November:** The Republican Party wins control of both the House of Representatives and Senate in the congressional elections. **9 November:** President Truman lifts all but a few controls on prices.

1947 1 January: The British and U.S. zones in Germany are united to form the economic unit Bizonia. **12 March:** In an address to Congress President Truman announces the Truman Doctrine of support to democratic governments threatened by subversion and specifically calls for aid for Greece and Turkey. **21 March:** The Twenty-Second Amendment to the Constitution limiting the number of times a person could be elected as president to two and preventing any person who has been president for more than two years of a term from being elected more than once is passed. **22 March:** President Truman issues Executive Order 9835 establishing federal loyalty boards to investigate federal employees accused of disloyalty. **15 April:** Jackie Robinson becomes the first African American in 60 years to play for a Major League Baseball team when he makes his first appearance for the Brooklyn Dodgers. **5 June:** Secretary of State George C. Marshall calls for a program of aid for Europe in his speech at Harvard University. This leads to the Marshall Plan and the establishment of the European Recovery Program. **20 June:** President Truman vetoes the Taft-Hartley Act intended to regulate trade unions. **23 June:** The Taft-Hartley Act is passed over President Truman's veto. **1 July:** Kennan's article outlining the need for "containment" is published in the journal *Foreign Affairs* under the pseudonym "X." **18 July:** President Truman signs the Presidential Succession Act, placing the speaker of the house and Senate president pro tempore next in line of succession after the vice president. **26 July:** President Truman signs the National Security Act establishing the Department of Defense, National Security Council (NSC), and Central Intelligence Agency. **2 September:** The United States signs a pact of mutual assistance with Latin American nations in Rio de Janeiro, Brazil. **21 September:** The House Un-American Affairs Committee (HUAC) issues subpoenas to 43 workers in the film industry. **October:** In the course of the hearings on communist influences in Hollywood before HUAC, 10 of those called refuse to answer questions and are charged with contempt. The "Hollywood Ten" are subsequently sentenced to terms in jail and blacklisted by the industry. **25 November:** Several heads of film studios meet at the Waldorf Astoria in New York City and agree to implement a blacklist of suspected communists.

1948   12 January: In *Sipuel v. Board of Regents of the University of Oklahoma* the Supreme Court rules that the Oklahoma University Law School can not deny entry to students simply on the grounds of race nor can they provide separate facilities that are inadequate. **2 February:** President Truman sends a package of civil rights measures to Congress. **2 April:** Congress approves the Marshall Plan. **30 April:** Twenty-one nations sign the charter of the Organization of American States in Bogota, Colombia. **3 May:** In *Shelley v. Kraemer* the Supreme Court declares that restrictive housing covenants on grounds of race cannot be enforced. **3 May:** The Supreme Court rules in favor of the government in *United States v. Paramount Pictures, Inc. et al* in declaring that the Hollywood studios' control of movie theaters constitutes a monopoly. Thereafter the theaters showed films from whichever studio they wished. **14 May:** President Truman recognizes the state of Israel. **11 June:** The Senate approves the Vandenberg Resolution authorizing alliances with other countries to oppose communism. **18 June:** Britain, France, and the United States announce the introduction of a single common currency in the western zones of Germany and Berlin. **19 June:** Selective service is reintroduced for men between the ages of 19 and 25. **21–25 June:** The Republican Party National Convention meets in Philadelphia and nominates Governor Thomas E. Dewey of New York as their presidential candidate over Senator Robert A. Taft and Governor Harold E. Stassen. **24 June:** The Soviet Union imposes a land blockade on the western Allied sectors of Berlin provoking an airlift to keep the city supplied. **12–14 July:** The Democratic Party National Convention gathers in Philadelphia and nominates Harry S. Truman as their presidential candidate with Alben W. Barkley as the vice presidential candidate. The adoption of a strong civil rights platform leads to the walk out of southern delegates who formed a States' Rights Party. **17 July:** The States' Rights Party holds its convention in Birmingham, Alabama, and nominates South Carolina Governor Strom Thurmond as their presidential candidate. **23–25 July:** The Progressive Party holds its national convention in Philadelphia and selects former vice president Henry A. Wallace as their presidential candidate. **26 July:** President Truman issues Executive Order 9981 initiating the start of the desegregation of the U.S. armed forces. **3 August:** Whittaker Chambers testifies before HUAC that he spied for the Soviet Union in the 1930s. He also names Alger Hiss, a former senior government worker, as a spy. **2 November:** In a remarkable upset, Truman wins the presidential election, beating Dewey with 49.5 percent of the vote to Dewey's 45.1 percent and carrying 28 states with 303 electoral college votes to Dewey's 16 states with 189 electoral college votes. The States' Rights candidate, Strom Thurmond, receives 2.4 percent of the vote and 39 electoral college votes from four southern states, while the Progressive Party candidate, Henry Wallace, has the same percentage of the popular vote but no electoral college votes. **15 December:** HUAC indicts Hiss for perjury.

1949   5 January: President Truman outlines his "Fair Deal" program in his State of the Union Address to Congress. **20 January:** In his inaugural address Truman outlines his "Point Four" program for peace and freedom. **4 April:** The North Atlantic Treaty is signed in Washington, D.C., establishing the North Atlantic Treaty Organization, including the United States, Belgium, Canada, Denmark, France, Great Britain, Iceland, Italy, Luxemburg, the Netherlands, Norway, and Portugal. **8 May:** The Federal Republic of Germany is established in western Germany with its capital in Bonn. **12 May:** The Soviet blockade of Berlin ends. **10 August:** A unified Department of Defense is established. **29 August:** The Soviet Union successfully tests its first atomic bomb. **1 October:** The People's Republic of China is officially established under the leadership of communist Mao Zedong. **7 October:** The communist German Democratic Republic is formally established in East Germany with its capital in East Berlin. **14 October:** Eleven leaders of the Communist Party of the United States are convicted under the Smith Act (1940) for advocating the overthrow of the government.

1950   21 January: After a second trial, a grand jury finds Alger Hiss guilty of perjury for concealing his membership to the Communist Party. He is sentenced to five years in jail. **9 February:** In a speech to a meeting of Republican women in Wheeling, West Virginia, Senator Joseph McCarthy claims to have a list of 205 names of people in the State Department who are known to be members of the Communist Party. This initiates a wave of accusations and investigations known as

"McCarthyism" and often described as a "witch hunt." **14 February:** The Soviet Union and the People's Republic of China sign a mutual defense treaty. **14 April:** NSC briefing paper NSC-68 outlining the need for increased military spending to maintain the policy of containment is issued. **5 June:** In *McLaurin v. Oklahoma State Regents* the Supreme Court rules that black students admitted to the previously all-white Law School cannot be segregated. In *Sweatt v. Painter* on the same day, the court also rules that the creation of separate facilities in a new segregated law school are unequal to those in the Texas Law school and the black plaintiff, Herman Sweatt, should be admitted to the white institution. **25 June:** The Korean War begins when troops from North Korea cross the 38th parallel into South Korea. By 28 June the northern forces take the southern capital of Seoul. **27 June:** The UN votes to send forces to defend South Korea under U.S. leadership. **20 July:** The Senate committee headed by Millard Tydings dismisses Senator McCarthy's charges of communist infiltration of the State Department but with little effect. **15 September:** UN forces land at Inchon behind the North Korean lines and push back northern forces, liberating Seoul. **23 September:** The McCarran Internal Security Act to control subversive activities is passed over the president's veto. Among its provisions is the requirement that communist organizations register with the Justice Department. **7 October:** UN forces cross the 38th parallel into North Korea. **25 October:** In response to UN forces approaching the Yalu River, the Chinese Army invades Korea, forcing UN armies back toward South Korea. By March 1951 the war reached a stalemate along the 38th parallel. **1 November:** Two Puerto Rican nationalists fire on the White House. One of the attackers and a police officer are killed.

1951 **8 February:** President Truman orders the seizure of the nation's railways to prevent a strike. **27 February:** The Twenty-Second Amendment to the Constitution limiting the number of presidential terms to two is ratified. It did not apply to President Truman. **6 March:** The trial of Ethel and Julius Rosenberg begins. **29 March:** Ethel and Julius Rosenberg are found guilty for spying. **5 April:** Ethel and Julius Rosenberg are sentenced to death. **11 April:** President Truman fires General Douglas MacArthur, the U.S. commander of UN forces in Korea, after he publicly threatened an invasion of China. MacArthur is replaced by General Matthew Ridgway. **19 April:** MacArthur criticizes the administration's policies in Korea when he addresses a joint session of Congress before retiring. **1 September:** The Australia-New Zealand-United States Alliance (ANZUS) mutual defense treaty between the United States, Australia, and New Zealand is signed. **16 October:** The long-running television series *I Love Lucy* begins on CBS.

1952   29 March: President Truman announces that he will not seek reelection. **8 April:** Faced with the threat of a national steel strike, President Truman nationalizes all steel mills. **28 April:** U.S. occupation of Japan formally ends with the signing of the Treaty of San Francisco. **2 June:** In *Youngstown Sheet & Tube Co. v Sawyer* the Supreme Court rules to restrict the president's power to seize private property without congressional approval. The case was brought in response to the takeover of the steel mills in April. **27 June:** The McCarran-Walter (Immigration and Nationality) Act lifting racial immigration restrictions but allowing exclusion and deportation for subversive activities is passed over the president's veto. **7–11 July:** The Republican Party Convention gathers in Chicago and nominates Dwight D. Eisenhower as their presidential candidate over Senator Robert A. Taft. Richard M. Nixon is chosen as the vice presidential candidate. **21–26 July:** The Democratic Party Convention meets in Chicago and nominates Governor Adlai Stevenson of Illinois as the presidential candidate over Estes Kefauver and Richard Russell. John J. Sparkman becomes the vice presidential candidate. **25 July:** Puerto Rico becomes a self-governing commonwealth of the United States. **1 November:** The United States successfully detonates its first hydrogen bomb. **4 November:** Eisenhower defeats Adlai Stevenson in the presidential election by a margin of 55 percent to 44 percent of the popular vote, carrying 39 states with 442 electoral college votes. Stevenson wins in only nine states with 89 electoral college votes.

1953   20 January: Dwight D. Eisenhower is inaugurated as the 34th president of the United States. President Truman retires to his home in Independence, Missouri. **5 March:** Joseph Stalin dies. **19 June:** Ethel and Julius Rosenberg are executed by the electric chair for spying. **27 July:** A cease-fire comes into force in Korea.

Introduction

It is hard to think of two more significant decades in U.S. history than the 1930s and 1940s. During these 20 years, the United States suffered the worst ever economic collapse during the Great Depression; underwent major political reform under the New Deal; survived and emerged victorious in a world war that brought enormous change, not least in America's world role; went through postwar reconstruction at home; and entered into an international struggle that became the Cold War that was to last 40 years.

For many people, the Depression that followed the Wall Street Crash of 1929 threatened the very existence of liberal capitalism. In Europe it led to the rise of new ideological groups on both the right and the left, posing the alternative visions of Soviet communism or the fascism of Italy and Nazi Germany. Although some Americans turned to one ideology or another for answers, the economic crisis produced instead one of the greatest periods of political, social, and economic reform under Franklin D. Roosevelt, who went on to become the longest-serving president in U.S. history. Roosevelt's New Deal reshaped the very nature of the American state and established the basis of the modern welfare system while preserving the democratic form of government. In the process, the makeup of the major political parties, particularly the Democratic Party, changed, and the political agenda for much of the rest of the century was established.

Historians have debated the exact nature of these changes ever since. While the New Deal was so complex and lacking in coherence that it is difficult to define, for some writers it represented a definite period of revolutionary change; for others it has been seen as neither revolutionary nor even particularly new. Some writers traced the roots of the New Deal to progressivism and others to the experience of World War I; revisionists reevaluating the career of Herbert Hoover argued that the

1

foundations of much of the reform had already been laid before 1933. Historians, often on the left, have pointed to the many shortcomings of the New Deal: the failure to change capitalism rather than save it, the omission of certain groups such as African Americans or women from the reform agenda, and the failure to redistribute wealth. All the major pieces of legislation have been picked over and their weaknesses revealed. Most of all, every writer recognizes that the Roosevelt administration failed to end the blight of mass unemployment that still affected the country by the end of the decade; however, there is now recognition that the New Deal avoided the worst alternatives, that working through the various constraints in the democratic system, it was still able to provide hope and restore faith in the U.S. government—a point reinforced at the polls.

The Depression and New Deal were followed by U.S. entry into World War II, a cataclysmic event that, as its name suggests, resulted in worldwide change. The war raged across virtually the whole of Europe, most of Asia and the Pacific, and large parts of Africa. It left 50 million people dead and millions displaced or homeless; it saw the collapse of empires and brought about major changes in the balance of power across the globe. It will forever be associated with the unspeakable horrors of the Holocaust. However, for the United States, the war brought economic recovery and ended the "hungry thirties"; it also reinforced the central role of the federal government in the lives of all Americans either through the introduction of Selective Service and the service of 15 million men and women in the armed forces, or through the many war agencies established as "Dr. Win-the-War" replaced "Dr. New Deal." The war confirmed Roosevelt's reputation as one of the greatest presidents of all time. Unlike World War I or the Vietnam War, few Americans subsequently doubted the justice of the country's role in World War II. Although an isolationist element had been evident in the 1930s, the Japanese attack on Pearl Harbor appeared to unite the nation. Many would later look back nostalgically to the "Good War" or remember those who had served as "the greatest generation."

While the military events of the war were well known, it was not until the 1960s and 1970s that historians focused on the home front. Initially, the positive elements of the war's impact were recognized—the achievements of U.S. industry and resilience of the economy that provided full employment, gains for minority groups, advances for women, the rewards for service for veterans, and the continuation of social welfare provision during and after the war. However, it also became apparent that unity was not total. The war witnessed considerable labor strife, the persistence of racism and race violence, and the survival of gender discrimination that was only too evident in postwar lay-offs. That said, there is little doubt that the war, combined with the events of the previous decade, had an enormous effect and helped to shape the country's development for the next 20 or 30 years in countless ways, political, economic, social, and cultural.

One of the most obvious consequences of the defeat of Germany and Japan was the presence of U.S. armies in Europe and Asia, but also of an enormous power vacuum with the collapse of the former leading world powers, particularly Great Britain and France. In part, to fill this gap and prevent further conflicts, the United States recognized the need for an international body to supplant the moribund League of Nations. The United States thus took much of the initiative in creating and committing itself to the United Nations (UN); however, the defeat of fascism not only brought the automatic rise of the left in Europe, it also saw the presence of Soviet forces across the length and breadth of Central and Eastern Europe. Competing visions of postwar settlement combined with ideological differences and a history of suspicion led to the breakup of the wartime Grand Alliance and a steady slide into opposition that became the Cold War, a conflict that spread to Asia with the triumph of the communists led by Mao Zedong in 1949.

This conflict may have been inevitable given the differences of outlook and experience of the respective countries involved in the Cold War, but it has been the subject of much debate. Some commentators immediately suggested that Roosevelt had been too conciliatory to the Soviets during the war and had conceded too much; others argued instead that his successor, Harry S. Truman, had been too uncompromising or lacked the experience to deal with the enormity of the postwar crisis. Truman, already viewed critically by some historians for approving the use of the atomic bomb in 1945, has often been seen as overly belligerent in his relations with the Soviet Union; however, since the collapse of the communist regime in the late 1980s and the full recognition of the many failings of the Soviet system, there has been a sense that Truman's position and actions were justified at the time and ultimately successful in the long run. There is though still the possibility that things might have been different from the start given a different approach.

Truman's reputation has gone through a considerable sea change. Becoming president by virtue of a predecessor's death in office is bad enough at the best of times. To do so in such a period of worldwide turmoil and to succeed one of the most revered presidents in history was an enormous burden. As Truman honestly said after learning of Roosevelt's death, he felt as if, "the moon, stars and all the planets had fallen" upon him. Lacking the charisma and refinement of Roosevelt, who after all came from the east coast elite, the former haberdasher from Missouri also lacked a clear political mandate. His critics both then and later charged him with letting down the New Deal legacy, unleashing the atomic age, initiating the Cold War and setting a foreign policy agenda that dominated the next 40 years (and some said led inevitably to the disaster that was Vietnam), and laying the groundwork for the period of political hysteria at home known as McCarthyism. His period in office ended with the war in Korea that was only brought to a conclusion by his Republican successor, Dwight D. Eisenhower.

However, just as Truman's position with regard to the Cold War is now often seen as understandable, if not justifiable, so too he has been recognized for his achievements. It has been pointed out that under Truman the country made the transition from wartime to peacetime production with only a brief period of dislocation and that the feared return to the Depression did not materialize. And despite the lack of a strong political base, Truman continued some elements of the New Deal in his own Fair Deal program. If his accomplishments were limited, it is suggested that the conservative opposition had much to do with it, and after almost 15 years of war and economic and political upheaval, the American people did not want further drastic change, a view supported by Truman's remarkable upset victory in the election of 1948. Equally, a number of writers have pointed to some considerable achievements, particularly in the area of civil rights. In setting a tone of honesty and plain speaking with the motto "the buck stops here" firmly located on his desk, Truman established standards against which some of his successors have been judged—and failed. As a result he is now often ranked alongside Theodore Roosevelt and Woodrow Wilson by historians and only two or three places below Franklin D. Roosevelt himself.

POLITICAL DEVELOPMENTS

The election of Democratic candidate Franklin D. Roosevelt in 1932 and his inauguration on 4 March 1933, marked the end of a period of Republican "ascendancy." Having suggested to the American people in his 1928 inaugural address that they would soon "be in sight of the day when poverty will be banished from this nation," Herbert Hoover was himself a victim of the economic collapse that led to an unemployment rate of 25 percent by 1933. Roosevelt's vague promise of a "New Deal" secured an overwhelming victory by a margin of more than 57 percent of the vote to Hoover's less than 40 percent and by 472 electoral college votes to 59. However, the president-elect declined to cooperate with the outgoing president during the interregnum, and it was not until after his inauguration that the nature of the New Deal became clear.

Suggesting, in words that were soon on many lips, that the only thing the country had to fear was "fear itself," Roosevelt called for broad executive power to wage war against the emergency and summoned Congress into special session. Roosevelt also brought people from diverse backgrounds into government to create a Brain Trust of advisors. They helped shape the program that the president described during a radio broadcast in June 1934 as one providing relief, recovery, and reform. In the "first one hundred days," a benchmark against which all subsequent administrations were to be assessed, Congress passed an unprecedented number of bills to put this into effect.

The country's basic financial institutions were stabilized by declaring an immediate bank holiday to stop further bank collapses and by passing legislation providing federal guarantees of deposits in the Banking Act (1933). When banks reopened, customers began to deposit rather than withdraw their funds. The problems of falling farm prices and incomes were addressed in part through the Agricultural Adjustment Act in May 1933, which created the Agricultural Adjustment Administration (AAA) to pay farmers not to produce by reducing acreage and output. Subsequently declared unconstitutional by the Supreme Court, a second Agricultural Adjustment Act was passed in 1938. Farmers were also provided assistance with mortgages through the Farm Credit Administration and later, in 1937, through the Farm Security Administration (FSA). Help was provided for some of those displaced from the land through the Resettlement Administration established in 1935.

Relief for the unemployed came through the Federal Emergency Relief Administration, which provided additional federal funds to support state relief spending. More significant was the creation of work relief programs through the Public Works Administration (PWA) under Harold Ickes, which ultimately created more than 2 million jobs. When that proved too slow to take effect, the Civil Works Administration (CWA) was established and headed by Harry Hopkins to provide work for 4 million during the winter of 1933–1934. A Civilian Conservation Corps (CCC) was created to provide good, wholesome work on reforestation and irrigation schemes for young people (primarily men) between the ages of 17 and 25.

Industrial recovery was the focus of the National Industrial Recovery Act that set up the National Recovery Administration (NRA) to enable businesses to agree on codes of fair practice, setting prices and wages, and providing for recognition of trade unions. The program was supported by massive publicity under the "Blue Eagle" symbol and the slogan "We Do Our Part." Although there were more than 500 codes involving 2 million employers, the NRA was never very successful in terms of union recognition, and it became caught up in political conflict and personal scandal surrounding its head, Hugh Johnson. Like the AAA, it too was declared unconstitutional by the Supreme Court.

Another major measure aimed at providing work, tackling soil erosion, and encouraging industrial development in what became known as the "First New Deal" was the creation of the Tennessee Valley Authority (TVA). The TVA was a massive program to build more than 20 hydroelectric plants on the Tennessee River and its tributaries. The TVA provided electricity for an area covering seven states and a population of more than 2 million people; it also opened up these parts of the country for industrial development.

During the brief lull after this wave of legislation, Roosevelt faced criticism on a number of fronts. The Louisiana governor, now Senator Huey Long, called for more radical programs of redistribution to "Share Our Wealth," while the radio priest Father Charles Coughlin demanded nationalization of banks and suggested that the New Deal was in the hands of both bankers and communists. Dr. Francis Townsend meanwhile attracted a great deal of support with his revolving pension plan to help the elderly. Left wing groups, members of the Communist Party of the United States of America (CPUSA) and the Socialist Party of America, also called for more radical action.

Faced with these challenges and the persistence of the Depression itself, a "Second New Deal" began in 1935, with a greater emphasis on reform, suggesting that it had moved further to left. First an even greater program of work relief was initiated with the Emergency Relief Appropriation Act in 1935 creating the Works Progress Administration (WPA) under Hopkins. Reform came in the form of the Social Security Act, which provided a federal-state system of old age and unemployment insurance. The measure did not include all workers, excluding self-employed, agricultural, and domestic employees. Nonetheless it laid the foundations of the modern U.S. welfare system.

In 1935 the New Deal also passed the National Labor Relations Act, although in reality this was largely the work of New York Senator Robert Wagner. The act outlawed unfair labor practices and recognized the worker's right to join trade unions and benefit from free collective bargaining. The political impact of these measures was clear. In 1936 Roosevelt trounced Republican candidate Alf Landon, gaining almost 61 percent of the vote. The Democratic Party now increasingly had the support of the urban immigrant communities, organized labor, African Americans, and other underprivileged groups, as well as the traditional support of the South. The fact that the number of votes for the communist and socialist candidates was even less in 1936 than in 1932 revealed the New Deal's appeal to the have-nots in society.

Further reform came with the National Housing Act in 1937, which provided federal mortgage support for homeowners and built low-cost public housing. In 1938 the Fair Labor Standards Act finally prohibited the employment of children under the age of 16 and established a basic minimum wage and maximum of work hours of 44 per week, falling to 40 by 1940. Again this legislation did not apply to agricultural or domestic workers.

Events in the late 1930s effectively brought the New Deal legislative program to a close. First, having seen the Supreme Court undermine crucial legislation and facing the possibility that it would do the same with the labor relations and social security acts, Roosevelt called for the reorganization of the court early in 1937. Proposing to add one additional justice for each over the age of 70, the president was accused of attempted "court packing" and faced criticism inside Congress and beyond. Although confrontation was avoided when the court began to approve new pieces of legislation and Roosevelt was able gradually to appoint his own justices as members retired, the damage had been done.

When the economy took a downturn in 1937–1938, Roosevelt was held responsible. To make matters worse, in the run-up to the 1938 congressional elections the president tried to purge conservative Democrats from the party. He failed in all but one case. Not only were the conservative Democrats returned, but for the first time Republicans made gains in both houses. A conservative bloc now appeared in Congress restricting the opportunity for further reform, but by then foreign affairs were also beginning to dominate politics.

The last years of Roosevelt's second administration were dominated by the mounting crisis in Europe and the growing conflict with Japan. Many Americans were anxious to avoid being needlessly sucked into another European conflict, and from 1935 on Congress passed a series of Neutrality Acts to prevent trade or loans to belligerent powers or travel on the ships of belligerents. Although the isolationist lobby, spearheaded by the America First Committee, remained strong, in 1940 preparations were made for the nation's self defense, and in October 1940 Congress approved an increase in defense spending and the introduction of the first peacetime draft in U.S. history.

In 1940 Roosevelt, arguing against change amid the mounting international crisis, stood for an unprecedented third term. He defeated Republican candidate Wendell Willkie by a margin of 54.8 percent of the vote to 44.8 percent. A decisive moment in the campaign was Roosevelt's declaration that American "boys are not going to be sent into foreign wars"; however, when the Japanese attacked Pearl Harbor on 7 December 1941, the Senate responded to the president's request for a declaration of war with a unanimous vote in favor. The House of Representatives voted in favor by 388–1, with Jeanette Rankin of Montana casting the single vote against.

Entry into the war had a huge impact on the U.S. political system. The president's power and authority was immediately increased by virtue of his position as commander in chief but also because of his role in negotiating with the leaders of the other Allied powers. The War Powers Acts of 1941 and 1942 extended his authority to allocate priorities and resources without consulting Congress. To manage the war effort, more than 30 war agencies were created. The Office of Production Management (OPM), created in January 1941, was replaced in 1942 by the War Production Board (WPB), a supreme agency to have oversight of industry, allocate raw materials, and set quotas. The allocation of manpower was handled by the War Manpower Commission (WMC); the Office of Price Administration (OPA) was established to manage prices, rents, and rationing; the Office of Civilian Defense enlisted 10 million people in preparation for a possible attack and later in conserving scarce materials; the Office of War Information (OWI) dealt with propaganda; and a National War Labor Board was established in 1942 to adjudicate in labor disputes and set wage levels. An Office of War Mobilization was set up in 1943 to balance the demands of the other war agencies.

By the end of the war, the number of people working in federal government had risen from less than 1 million to 3.8 million, and the federal budget had increased from $9.4 billion in 1939 to $95.2 billion in 1945. Although this development has been described as "state-managed capitalism," it still relied a great deal on voluntary cooperation. While the war effort saw the return of many businessmen to positions of influence within government and the inclusion of labor leaders in a number of agencies, plans to implement the central direction of labor through national service or to conscript women were resisted. Rationing, too, varied from state to state and was never total. Despite this, although the New Deal agencies now disappeared, the war served to confirm the centrality of the federal government in the everyday life of U.S. citizens.

Although the role of Congress was limited during the war, to some extent politics continued as usual. Talk of suspending elections or adopting a national government was overruled in favor of continuing to demonstrate the strength of American democracy. Congressional elections were held in 1942 and saw a considerable swing to Republicans as the Democrats lost 45 seats in the House and nine in the Senate. Democrats still had a majority in both houses, but the conservative bloc was strengthened. Congress provided scrutiny of executive action, legitimized presidential decisions, and in some cases limited wartime measures. The abolition of New Deal agencies was largely initiated by Congress; congressional criticism led to the limitation of OWI's functions, the War Labor Disputes Act was passed over the president's veto in 1943, and Roosevelt's attempt to raise taxes on incomes more than $25,000 was thwarted. Nonetheless, Roosevelt was reelected for the fourth and final time in 1944 despite concerns for his health. The liberal vice president Henry A. Wallace was dropped in favor of Harry S. Truman. Roosevelt's margin of victory over Republican Thomas E.

Dewey was reduced from 53.5 percent to 46 percent, but the Democrats regained many of the lost seats in the House of Representatives while the position remained unchanged in the Senate.

Having taken over as president following Roosevelt's death on 12 April 1945, Truman had the task of managing the transition to peacetime at home. Shortly after the surrender of Japan, Truman seemed to signal a continuation of the New Deal when he outlined a 21-point legislative program including action to ensure full employment, the expansion of social security benefits, housing reform, and a permanent Fair Employment Practices Committee (FEPC). However, the rapid demobilization of the armed forces (from 12 million to 1.5 million in a year), conversion of war industry to peacetime production, and the lifting of some government controls led to inflation and labor-management conflict. Congressional opposition limited the powers of the OPA, and it came to an end in 1946. Truman was also forced to compromise on the 1946 Employment Act, and in dealing with the industrial disputes he managed to anger both sides. In 1946 the Republicans, whose campaign slogan was simply "Had Enough?" won control of both the Senate and the House of Representatives for the first time since 1928.

Truman and the conservative-dominated 80th Congress were in conflict over a number of issues. The Taft-Hartley Act aimed at limiting the power of labor was passed over the president's veto; congressional attempts to reduce taxation were twice vetoed by Truman. However, Truman did secure support for his foreign policy initiatives and for the National Security Act (1947) establishing a new cabinet office of secretary of defense with separate departments of army, navy, and air force; a National Security Council (NSC); and a Central Intelligence Agency. Nonetheless, Truman appeared to face overwhelming defeat in the 1948 election. His support for civil rights with the appointment of a civil rights commission that reported in 1947 and his order initiating the process of military desegregation in 1948 led to the defection of southern Democrats behind the States' Rights candidate Strom Thurmond; Truman's strong stand against the Soviet Union alienated liberals who turned to the Progressive Party behind Wallace. Dewey, once again the Republican candidate, seemed a certain victor; however, Truman followed a determined election strategy that targeted key groups—labor groups, African Americans, the Jewish community, and those living in small-town America—in a remarkable old-fashioned whistle-stop tour across the country. The result was an upset victory in which he won 49.6 percent of the vote to Dewey's 45.1 percent, with Wallace and Thurmond both securing 2.4 percent each. In an indicator of what was to come in the future, Thurmond carried four southern states.

Buoyed by his victory, in January 1949 Truman announced his Fair Deal containing many of his earlier proposals: civil rights reform, housing reform, national health insurance, and further extensions to social security. He managed to achieve only the extension of social security benefits to include another 10 million workers, some limited housing reform, and the raising of minimum wage levels. Reform was less likely in the conservative mood brought about by McCarthyism. The attack on the Democratic administration launched by Senator Joseph McCarthy in 1950 dominated politics for the next three years as he hurled one accusation of communist infiltration after another. Finally, in 1954 he went too far and turned on members of the armed forces, but he left a damaging legacy of loyalty oaths, blacklists, fear, and suspicion that reached from federal to state and local levels.

Apart from fending off charges of communist subversion at home, the president and country were increasingly concerned with foreign affairs, particularly with the onset of the Korean War in 1950. In 1952 Truman chose not to seek reelection (he was exempted from the Twenty-Second Amendment ratified in 1951 limiting presidents to two terms). Instead the Democrats chose Adlai Stevenson as their candidate to face the Republican candidate, former commander in chief of the Allied forces, Dwight D. Eisenhower. The war hero won an overwhelming victory with 55.1 percent of the vote to Stevenson's 44.4 percent. The Republicans were back in the White House after an absence of 20 years; however, despite this apparent change in direction, there were already signs of an emerging political consensus involving an acceptance of basic New Deal welfare reforms and continued international involvement focused particularly against communism. The debates now centered on how far policies would be pursued in either area.

ECONOMIC AND SOCIAL TRENDS

The period from 1933 to 1953 can be divided into two in terms of economic development: the 1930s, during which the country struggled to free itself from the grips of the Great Depression, and the years from 1940 onward when a war-induced boom brought massive growth to the economy and launched a boom that, with the exception of a brief downturn at the end of World War II, continued into the 1950s and laid the basis for the "Affluent Society." That said, there were some elements of continuity, as the 1930s were not without their positive developments. The process of modernization continued as such new industries as electrical, plastics, aircraft continued to grow during the Depression years. Popular entertainment continued to grow as movies and radio became even more significant forms of media. Second, the central role of the federal government, albeit in very different circumstances, was a common feature of both decades. Nonetheless, the predominant feature of the 1930s was a struggling economy.

The Wall Street Crash of 1929 revealed the flaws in the apparent boom of the 1920s. Between 1929 and 1932 some 5,000 banks failed; 90,000 businesses collapsed; 250,000 people lost their homes; and between 12 and 17 million people, 25 percent of the labor force, were out of work. By 1933 industrial production was less than 50 percent of 1929 levels.

Farm income, already one-third lower in 1929 than in 1920, fell from $6.2 billion to $2 billion in 1932 as a consequence of the catastrophic decline in world prices and the collapse of export markets. To make matters worse for farmers, a series of long, hot summers were followed by high winds blowing down from Canada across the Midwest creating a Dust Bowl of massive proportions. Driven out by the weather, foreclosures, and bank seizures, 170,000 people left Oklahoma alone, and the total number of farms declined by almost 200,000 during the decade. By 1940 farming accounted for only 18 percent of the labor force, a drop from 21 percent in 1930.

The New Deal set out to address many of these issues. Financial institutions were stabilized through banking legislation and regulation of Wall Street. Industrial recovery was encouraged by the NRA, which suspended antitrust legislation to allow businessmen to agree on production levels, prices, and wages. At the same time, huge public works programs were intended to act as a primer for the economy by injecting money at the bottom and increasing purchasing power. The NRA achieved only limited success before it was declared unconstitutional by the Supreme Court in 1935. The notion of central national economic planning and business self-regulation was less significant thereafter. Instead the emphasis appeared to be more on using federal spending through even greater work relief programs and the protection of workers' rights through labor legislation to increase demand via consumer spending.

Labor clearly benefited from New Deal policies, and against all the odds in a period of high unemployment trades, unions went through a period of rapid growth. The conservative policies of the old American Federation of Labor (AFL) were challenged in the 1930s by the new Congress of Industrial Organizations (CIO). Encouraged by the promise of recognition in New Deal legislation, industrial unions began to organize using new tactics such as the sit-down strike to unionize first car workers and then major sections of the steel industry. By 1941 union membership had almost doubled.

The problems of agriculture were tackled through a combination of programs establishing government-supported production quotas (planned scarcity), price support loans, and financial assistance with mortgages as well as some assistance in resettlement. Through production divisions of the AAA, agricultural output was reduced—initially through the destruction of crops and slaughter of livestock—and price levels agreed. When the Supreme Court declared the AAA unconstitutional in 1936, it was replaced by a second Farm Act in 1938, which introduced the system of surplus commodity storage and a system of price parity that remained in place more or less into the 1970s.

The reform measures tended to benefit larger farmers, and little was done for the tenant farmers or sharecroppers, many of whom left the land. Resettlement provided aid for less than 10 percent of those who needed it; however, the New Deal did improve life for those who remained on the land, particularly through the rural electrification schemes. In 1930 only 13 percent of farms had electricity; by 1940 this had risen to more than 33 percent; by 1950 it was more than 90 percent.

Despite the limitations of the New Deal measures, agriculture did undergo something of a recovery with farm prices rising by some 50 percent and farm income doubling to $4.6 billion by 1939. How much this was due to the federal programs and how much to the effects of shortages brought about by farm failures and natural disasters is hard to gauge, and paradoxically, soil conservation and irrigation schemes only served to increase production and encourage a return to crops that would later be the victims of dust storms in the 1950s. Overall, however, the New Deal's economic success was qualified. Between 1933 and 1937 the gross national product (GNP) grew at about 10 percent per year, and industrial output and real income levels had both reached those of 1929 by 1937. Unemployment fell from 25 percent to 14 percent. As a result, Roosevelt cut federal spending, the money withheld from wages to fund social security reduced spending, and work relief. All combined to increase unemployment back to 19 percent or around 10 million. If by 1938 the New Deal had adopted aspects of the deficit spending theories of British economist John Maynard Keynes, Roosevelt was clearly only a reluctant and late convert. Ultimately, it was World War II that ended the Depression, not the New Deal.

The war saw an enormous growth in industrial output and revealed the underlying strength of the U.S. economy. In 1940 the GNP was approximately $99 billion; by 1942 it had risen to $150 billion, and by the end of the war was more than $200 billion. This was achieved through the massive injection of $186 billion in federal spending on war production combined with the prodigious efforts of U.S. industry. In 1939, for example, 2,500 airplanes were produced a year. By 1941 that number was produced in a single month, and the total aircraft production in 1944 was 100,000. More new plants were built during three years of war than in the previous 15 years as huge new factories like the Ford plant at Willow Run outside Detroit were built. Mass production techniques were introduced, even in shipbuilding, and production of Liberty ships increased from one every six months to one every 20 days. In addition to supplying the needs of their own armed forces, U.S. industries also supplied 40 percent of all Allied war materials.

Farming output increased during the war by 30 percent, despite a fall in farm labor as almost 3 million people left the land. Production increased as a result of mechanization of farm production as the tractor forever replaced the horse during World War II. Fertilizer was used more extensively, and farming modernized and moved to large-scale production as family farms increasingly disappeared. Farm income rose by 200 percent, closing the gap that had existed between the agricultural and industrial sectors.

The wartime boom saw businessmen back in favor. Not only were they incorporated into war agencies, they also benefited from the suspension of antitrust legislation and from federal payments on the basis of "costs plus" guarantees of profits and the promise they could keep new plants after the war. Larger companies tended to benefit most from government spending as the top 100 companies like Lockheed, Douglass, Ford, and others accounted for 70 percent of production. This development tended to continue after the war and led to the formation of what became known as the "military industrial complex."

While the rich undoubtedly grew richer during the war, there was some narrowing of inequality as incomes for the bottom fifth of society rose by 70 percent compared to a 23 percent rise for those at the top. Wage levels virtually doubled, and even allowing for inflation, the increase was significant. Equally, with 15 million people in the armed forces, full employment was achieved, although not until well into the war. Although this gave people money to spend, there was less to spend it on given wartime shortages. The 1942 Revenue Act extended income tax so that, coupled with the rising the wage levels, almost all Americans came into the tax system. Taxes and war bonds not only helped fund the war, they also helped to control consumer demand. By the war's end, Americans had $146 billion in savings, and the pent-up consumer demand was to be unleashed in the 1950s. Wartime shortages, however, encouraged the development of such substitutes as synthetic rubber, nylon, and plastics; frozen and dehydrated food processes were also given a boost, as was research that aided the later development of television, transistor radios, and such key medicines as penicillin.

Full employment and the inclusion of union leaders in government agencies further added to the membership of trade unions, and by the end of the war union membership stood at almost 15 million. One drawback to this growth was that union officials now seemed more remote from their members and, with the exception of the miners' leader John L. Lewis, had lost some of their militancy. The unions also had to accept restrictions. Limits on the working week were lifted, and a virtual wage freeze was imposed in 1943. In 1943, faced with rising prices, many workers went on strike, and as a result Congress passed the War Labor Disputes Act in an attempt to curb shop-floor union militancy. Although not terribly effective, this legislation provided the basis for the postwar Taft-Hartley Act, also aimed at restricting the right to strike.

Labor unrest was just one indicator of wartime social tensions. The war triggered a massive movement of people as almost 15 million people moved out of state, mostly heading to northern and western centers of defense production. More than 1.4 million people entered California alone during the war, flooding into San Francisco and Los Angeles. Seattle, Washington, Detroit, Michigan, and Chicago, Illinois, all faced huge population increases necessitating further federal housing provision and OPA controls on rent. Another feature of the wartime dislocation was, inevitably, the absence of male heads for many families. The family unit, already disrupted by the impact of the Depression, suffered further strain during the war. Divorce rates rose, but so too as servicemen returned from war, did marriage rates. The increase in marriages led to a boom in births, and birthrates rose from 19.4 per 1,000 people in 1940 to 24 per 1,000 in 1946. Whereas the population had only grown slowly in the 1930s (by 8.9 million), in the 1940s it doubled to 19 million.

The end of the war saw a rush to domesticity reflected in homemaking and the baby boom. This was made possible in part by the Selective Servicemen's Readjustment Act, or GI Bill, which provided $13 billion to assist veterans make the transition to peacetime by financing the purchase of homes and businesses and a return to college. By 1950 almost one-third of the nation had benefited from one aspect or another of this scheme, and nearly 8 million ex-service personnel returned to school or college between 1945 and 1952. Another 4.5 million took advantage of home loans. Truman's continuation of social welfare policies also helped maintain economic growth, as did the sustained federal spending on defense during the Cold War.

The postwar housing boom and pent-up demand eased the transition from wartime to peacetime production. Although there was a period of some dislocation as workers were laid off and servicemen returned, there was no return to Depression conditions that many people feared. There were labor conflicts in 1946 and 1947 leading both to the threat of takeover by the president and the passage of the Taft-Hartley Act by Congress, but this was relatively short-lived. The unions themselves seemed to grow more conservative with the onset of the Cold War, and by 1948 inflation was coming under control, and the economy was resuming an upward trend. By 1952 the GNP had risen to $347 billion, and the Affluent society was already emerging. While this affluence was evident in the rise of auto registrations from 26 million in 1945 to 40 million in 1950, two developments also indicated the new direction the country was taking. By 1950 there were already 8 million homes with televisions, and in 1952 Quaker produced the first TV dinner.

WOMEN AND RACIAL AND ETHNIC MINORITIES

The experiences of women in the 1930s and 1940s seemed very different from those of other underprivileged groups. While it is possible, for example, to see both decades as ones in which African Americans made discernable progress toward the goal of equality, the same could not be said for women. Instead there seemed to be quite contradictory developments.

The Depression revealed how little had been gained since women won the vote in 1920, and it revealed how far they were from achieving economic equality. With the rapid rise in unemployment there was strong pressure for women to give up their jobs for men. The 1932 Economy Act, for example, specified that the federal civil service should only employ one spouse from each family, and by 1933 1,500 married women had been dismissed. Elsewhere many schools refused to appoint women, and others dismissed those existing female teachers who were married. Not until 1937 was legislation passed prohibiting discrimination on the grounds of marital status. Because of such prejudices and the fact that women were concentrated in vulnerable, low-paid, unskilled manufacturing jobs and domestic service, unemployment among women rose at a quicker rate than among men. But economic necessity often forced women to seek work, and as a result their proportion in the labor force rose from 24.3 percent in 1930 to 25.1 percent in 1940, and the percentage of women workers who were married actually rose from less than 30 percent to 35 percent.

Women gained some recognition from the New Deal, most famously with the appointment of Frances Perkins as secretary of labor. Many women played key roles in New Deal agencies or in the Democratic Party organization. An Emergency White House Conference on the Needs of Women at least recognized that there was an issue, even if it did little in practical terms. Also significant was the role of Eleanor Roosevelt, who as an active first lady did much to give women a positive role model. Although women benefited from the Fair Labor Standards Act, New Deal agencies themselves often discriminated in terms of rates of pay or participation rates, and in many ways the New Deal, both through legislation and cultural reference, placed an emphasis on the ideal of the nuclear family with women and children supported by male breadwinners. In part this was a response to the notion that the Depression broke up families. The marriage rate and birthrate dropped, and although divorce levels remained fairly constant, it was clear that many men deserted their families during the Depression years "looking for work."

World War II brought about a dramatic change in women's positions. As labor shortages surfaced there was a drive to recruit female workers—married and single—to join "Rosie the Riveter" and fill the gaps in defense industries. Three million women who would normally have stayed at home went to work as the number of females in the labor force rose from 12 to more than 16 million, and the proportion of women in the labor force rose from 25 percent to 36 percent. Several thousand more women joined auxiliary branches of the various armed services. Although it appeared that women had made a major breakthrough, there were signs that this was not so. Women were promised equal pay for equal work, but in fact earnings lagged 40 percent behind men's; women occupied few senior posts and were discriminated against by fellow workers and trade unions. Most significant of all was the pressure to leave work with the war's end, and as some 2 million women were laid off, their representation in the labor force fell back to 29 percent; however, this was still higher than before the war, and by the early 1950s the number was back above 30 percent.

In reality, women's employment increased, but the 1950s were years in which women faced enormous pressures to remain at home and rear children. In films, television series, women's magazines, and even Cold War propaganda, domesticity was the goal presented for women to aim for. Betty Friedan's revolutionary book *The Feminine Mystique* (1963) was a call to arms based on a critique of these years.

The experience of African Americans in the 1930s and 1940s was also mixed, but for many historians these decades are now seen as vital in paving the way for the explosion of civil rights in the 1950s and 1960s. The immediate impact of the Depression on African Americans was entirely negative as the old adage "last hired, first fired" resulted in unemployment rates often twice those of whites. With more than 75 percent of the black population concentrated in the South—many still as sharecroppers—the collapse in agricultural prices, particularly of cotton, was catastrophic. After a period of decline, there was a sudden rise in the incidence of lynching in the 1930s as blacks became victims of white resentment.

Unlike previous decades, however, violence and discrimination against African Americans was now the subject of protest. The case of the Scottsboro boys—nine African American teenagers accused, tried, and convicted of raping two young white women in Alabama—became an international cause célèbre that was fought throughout the 1930s by the National Association for the Advancement of Colored People (NAACP) and the CPUSA and eventually resulted in the death penalties being overturned. In the North, African Americans in Harlem, New York, rioted in 1935; elsewhere they organized "Don't Buy Where You Can't Work Campaigns." During the 1930s the NAACP began to prepare legal cases to challenge segregation, particularly in education. The organization also had greater access to the White House through New Dealers and the good offices of Eleanor Roosevelt. The New Deal employed enough African Americans in key posts for there to be a "Black Cabinet," and this influence produced results in terms of benefits from legislation

However, President Roosevelt failed to speak out on race issues, and New Deal agencies were operated at state level where local prejudices applied. WPA relief payments were lower for blacks than white, and the CCC was segregated and initially only admitted African Americans in limited numbers. Despite this, there were sufficient positive developments for African Americans to switch political allegiance. African Americans went from voting 70 percent Republican in 1932 to 70 percent Democrat by 1936.

World War II brought the issue of race into sharp focus. Rather than a sense of national unity, the war illuminated some differences. Shortly after Pearl Harbor, despite there being no evidence of disloyalty, 112,000 Japanese Americans were placed in relocation camps in 1942 and lost an estimated $400 million worth of property and possessions in the process. Not until many years later did they receive an apology and full compensation for their losses.

Facing segregation and discrimination in both military institutions and defense industries, black Americans protested as early as 1939 and continued to argue for democracy at home and abroad during the war.

Such protest brought some concessions in military policies in 1940, and A. Philip Randolph's threat of a march on Washington won a major victory in 1941 with the executive order that outlawed discrimination in defense industries and established a Fair Employment Practices Committee (FEPC). The combined effects of FEPC, and more importantly increasing labor shortages, led to opportunity. Almost 1 million African American workers entered the labor force, and the numbers of black skilled and semiskilled workers doubled. There was change in employment patterns for black women as many left domestic service for factory work.

The migration of African Americans that had begun with World War I but slowed during the 1930s resumed as 500,000 people (17 percent of black southerners compared with only 3 percent of whites) left the South. Tensions over housing, competition over jobs, and the stresses of wartime led to a rise in racial tension and outbreaks of violence. In 1943 there were more than 240 racial incidents in 47 different towns and cities ranging from full-scale riots in Detroit, Harlem, and Los Angeles, to industrial conflicts—"hate strikes"—in places like Mobile, Alabama. Lynching occurred in a number of different states.

There were some changes in military policies during the war, and while segregation continued, all branches of the services were gradually opened to African Americans. More than 1 million African Americans served during the war. Black service personnel still experienced discrimination and prejudice in and around southern training camps and within the military itself. As a result, black servicemen not only protested against discriminatory practices during active duty, but they were also found among the black political activists at the war's end. Many left the South after the war, and the continued demographic changes increased the political influence of African Americans in northern states and undoubtedly contributed to Harry S. Truman's decision to call for an end to segregation in the armed forces and civil service just before the 1948 election.

The experiences of Mexican Americans in the 1930s and 1940s were very much shaped by the different economic trends of the respective decades. During the Depression years Mexican workers were no longer welcome, and about one-third were deported or encouraged to return to Mexico. The Mexican American population fell from 617,000 in 1930 to 377,000 in 1940; however, wartime labor shortages once again encouraged migration, and in 1942 the government reinstituted the Bracero program to import temporary workers from across the border. About 200,000 people entered the country legally and perhaps another 200,000 illegally during the war. Because they were excluded from the provisions of the draft, many Americans viewed the migrants as draft dodgers, and in Los Angeles resentment against Mexican American youths dressed in zoot suits led to a major riot in 1943. However, Mexicans continued to enter the country after the war, and the Bracero program was used again during the war in Korea. Although these new arrivals were mainly concentrated in the southwest and California, some began to migrate to such larger northern cities as Chicago and Detroit. They were among the largest group of the growing postwar Hispanic population.

FOREIGN AFFAIRS

The 1930s and 1940s were crucial in shaping the foreign policy of the United States. Initially, the impact of the Great Depression was to reinforce the nationalism that underlay the strong isolationist mood that had shaped much of U.S. foreign policy in the 1920s. Thus attempts to reach international agreements at the London Economic Conference in 1933 were rejected in favor of the domestic interests of the New Deal. However, a "Good Neighbor" Policy was adopted with regard to Latin American countries promising that the United States would not intervene in the internal affairs of other countries, and the remaining American troops were withdrawn from Dominica and Haiti. Relations with Cuba and Mexico survived changes in government that threatened U.S. interests, and the "Good Neighbor" Policy also enabled beneficial trade agreements to be reached.

The possibility of trade was perhaps one factor that led President Roosevelt to recognize and reestablish diplomatic relations with the Soviet Union in November 1933; however, the main threat to U.S. isolationism appeared to come from Europe, where the rise of the new right-wing ideologies of fascism and Nazism threatened peace. The Spanish Civil War (1936–1939) pitted left against right as the Soviet Union backed the republican government against General Franco's forces, which were supported by Adolf Hitler's Germany and Mussolini's Italy. Although some U.S. volunteers joined the conflict in Spain,

Congress was determined that the country would not be dragged into another European war. Neutrality Acts passed from 1935 onward were strengthened and extended to include Spain; however, when Japan attacked China in 1937, Roosevelt avoided the Neutrality Laws by claiming that neither side had declared war and so was able to continue to support the Chinese. On 5 October 1937, the president suggested that aggressor nations should be "quarantined," but it was not clear how this should be done. In January 1938, following a direct appeal from Roosevelt who was alarmed by the possible limits to presidential power, the House of Representatives narrowly rejected the proposed Ludlow Amendment that would have required a national referendum on any declaration of war.

Support for the Ludlow Amendment increased following the sinking of the USS *Panay* by Japanese aircraft in December 1937 amid fears that the incident could lead to war. It was, however, because of events in Asia that the United States became involved in World War II. Although the Roosevelt administration responded to the outbreak of war in Europe by lifting the arms embargo in 1939, agreeing on a Destroyers-for-Bases Agreement with Great Britain in 1940, providing aid through the Lend-Lease Act in 1941, and drawing up an Atlantic Charter with Prime Minister Winston Churchill in August 1941, this still stopped short of war with Germany. Instead, the administration responded to the Japanese expansion of the war in Asia by first restricting exports to Japan in 1940, and in August 1941 imposing a total trade embargo and freezing Japanese assets. Facing the likelihood of a military response from the United States if they pushed further into Asia to obtain oil and other necessary resources, the Japanese attacked the U.S. fleet at Pearl Harbor on 7 December 1941. The United States declared war on 8 December, and Germany and Italy declared war on the United States on 11 December.

American isolationism effectively ended as World War II ushered in what Henry Luce described as "the American century." Alongside Britain and the Soviet Union, the United States was the leading Allied power, providing much-needed aid to both partners. In the course of meetings between war leaders in Casablanca, Morocco; Cairo, Egypt; Tehran, Iran; and Yalta, Ukraine, they agreed not only on the military strategy of the war and the future of postwar Europe, but also on the establishment of a UN, agreed on in detail at the San Francisco Conference in April 1945. Plans for postwar international economic cooperation were reached at the Bretton Woods Conference in 1944. Harry S. Truman, the new president who succeeded Roosevelt after his death, continued the commitment to internationalism backed by the Republicans, led by Arthur H. Vandenberg; however, disagreements with the Soviet Union began to appear in Truman's first and only meeting with Stalin at Potsdam in July–August 1945, and this deterioration continued after the war had come to an end.

Buoyed perhaps by the possession of the atomic bomb, Truman adopted a fairly aggressive tone with Soviet representatives regarding perceived failures to honor agreements about Poland and East Germany reached at Yalta. In 1946 the American chargé d'affaires in Moscow, George F. Kennan, sent a telegram to Washington outlining the inevitability of conflict between the USSR and calling for a policy of containment. Winston Churchill encouraged the growing mood of pessimism when he said in a speech in Fulton, Missouri, that an "iron curtain" had fallen across Eastern Europe. Influenced by these views and responding to the call for aid to Greece, in March 1947 the president announced the Truman doctrine effectively putting containment into effect and committing the United States to a worldwide struggle. This was followed by the Marshall Plan to provide economic aid to European nations struggling to recover from the war and facing a variety of left-wing challenges. The Cold War had begun.

The Soviet response to these actions was to tighten control in Poland, Hungary, and Czechoslovakia. When the Western powers seemed to be moving to unite West Germany, Stalin responded by imposing a blockade on the divided city of Berlin in June 1948. For almost a year the Western powers mounted the Berlin airlift of materials to support the western sectors until the blockade was lifted in May 1949. Although the West had won in this confrontation, fear of further Soviet expansion led to the formation of the North Atlantic Treaty Organization (NATO), a military alliance committing the United States to support European nations against possible aggression. General Dwight D. Eisenhower was appointed supreme commander of NATO forces, and four U.S. army divisions were located in Europe.

The Cold War spread to Asia following the victory of Chinese communists led by Mao Zedong in 1949. The United States refused to recognize the new government, instead continuing to back Chiang Kai-shek in Taiwan. In response to the "loss of China" and the successful atomic test by the Soviet Union in 1949, the NSC produced a review of defense policy, NSC-68, calling for a massive increase in military spending. Not acted upon immediately, it soon became government policy after forces in North Korea crossed into South Korea in June 1950. Viewed as another case of communist expansion, Truman secured UN backing for a military response and sent U.S. forces to take the lead in the Korean War that lasted until 1953. Containment was furthered through the Australia-New Zealand-United States Alliance treaty, the South Pacific equivalent of NATO. The Korean War encouraged an increasing anticommunist hysteria at home and provided the basis for McCarthyism; it also brought to an end the Democratic Party's control of the presidency.

CULTURAL CHANGES: LEISURE AND ENTERTAINMENT

The decades of the 1930s and 1940s have often been seen as significantly different in cultural terms, one being marked by pessimism induced by the Depression and the other characterized by a more positive mood following victory in the war and the economic recovery that followed. However, there are probably much stronger elements of continuity as film, literature, and the arts were all marked by a mixture of anxiety and optimism throughout both periods. It can even be argued that it was the 1930s that were optimistic and the 1940s that pointed to "an age of doubt" and anxiety.

One feature of the 1930s was a return not just to a focus on things American but also to ordinary Americans and their values. This could be seen in the painting of the American regionalists and their celebration of the American landscape, in sharp contrast to the bleak black and white photographs of rural poverty and soil erosion produced by the FSA and the more ambiguous paintings of Edward Hopper. Faith in the land and the ability of the American people to survive was also evident in the work of composer Aaron Copland and in two literary classics of the decade, Margaret Mitchell's *Gone With the Wind* and John Steinbeck's *The Grapes of Wrath*, both of which were made into successful movies. Optimism too was the outstanding feature of *The Wizard of Oz*, while a belief in fundamental political values was central to the films of Frank Capra. A much darker view, however, was presented in Mervyn

Leroy's *I Am a Fugitive from a Chain Gang*, and there was even a sense of darkness beneath the surface of the Marx Brothers' zany escapist comedies.

However, if overall a distinctive and often celebratory American culture emerged from the Depression years, this was not necessarily the case with the war and postwar years. Despite the apparent unity and economic and military achievements of the "Good War," the horrors of the war and the reality of the Holocaust, coupled with the tension of the ever-present atomic threat during the Cold War, often seemed to bring a sense of doubt and uncertainty to the arts. The attacks on intellectuals, writers, and filmmakers during the McCarthy era only served to increase this mood. Such new writers as Saul Bellow, Norman Mailer, and playwright Arthur Miller in *Death of a Salesman* and *The Crucible* were perhaps the most obvious voices of this changed climate, but the popular thirties' detective fiction of Hammett and Chandler also lent itself to the bleak atmosphere in the film noir of the 1940s. Similarly, one of the postwar film classics, *High Noon*, captured much of the oppressive and critical feeling of the times. On the other hand, Broadway offered a rather different view particularly with the success of the Rogers and Hammerstein musicals, from *Oklahoma* (1943) and *Carousel* (1945) to *Guys and Dolls* (1949), *South Pacific* (1950), and *The King and I* (1951)—all films suggesting a more upbeat frame of mind.

The history of Hollywood in many ways charts the complexities of these two decades. The period from 1930 to the start of the 1950s began with movies experiencing a decline brought about by the initial effects of the Great Depression and ended with a drop in popularity brought about by the rise of new forms of entertainment and political challenges. In between, movies experienced something of a golden period in terms of film content and audience size. Movie attendance reached roughly 80 million per week by the end of the 1930s and 90 million weekly by the end of the war. Hollywood was credited with providing alternatives to revolution during the Great Depression and helping to maintain national morale during the war; however, beginning with the House Un-American Affairs Committee hearings in 1947, the movies were accused of procommunist influences and subjected to investigations and blacklists. In 1948 the power of the film studios was weakened following the Supreme Court's ruling preventing their monopolistic control of film theaters and film distribution. Perhaps more importantly, with the rise of the suburban family and the "baby boom," audiences now stayed at home where the rapid rise of television provided an alternative form of visual entertainment with an altogether more optimistic content. With these developments, movie audiences were halved between 1946 and 1953.

Television, suburbia, and the rise in automobile ownership all pointed to the positive achievements of the U.S. economy as it moved toward the affluent society that was to emerge in the 1950s. While materialism fueled by the release of pent-up consumer demand was one of the dominant characteristics of the postwar years, Americans also sought spiritual reassurance. Inspired no doubt by Billy Graham's religious revival that began in 1949, and by such popular religious novels as *The Robe* (1942) and *The Big Fisherman* (1948)—both later made into films—church attendance soared, rising from 64 million in 1940 to 114 million in 1960. As a result of the 1930s and 1940s, Americans increasingly looked to the federal government in times of need, but they still clearly turned elsewhere amid the uncertainties of the modern world.

The Dictionary

– A –

ACHESON, DEAN GOODERHAM (1893–1971). Born to a privileged family in Middletown, Connecticut, Dean Acheson attended Groton, Yale, and Harvard Law School, where he graduated in 1918. He served briefly in the navy in 1918, and after working as a clerk to **Supreme Court** Justice **Louis Brandeis**, he joined a Washington law firm in 1921 and practiced until 1941.

A conservative **Democrat**, Acheson joined **Franklin D. Roosevelt**'s administration in 1933 as undersecretary of the treasury but resigned quietly that same year in disagreement over monetary policy. With the onset of war in Europe, he became a fervent interventionist and pushed for measures supporting Great Britain and provided an important legal brief in support of the **Destroyers-for-Bases Agreement** in 1940. Named assistant secretary of state for economic affairs in 1941, he played a significant role at the **Bretton Woods Conference** in 1944, which established the **International Monetary Fund** and the World Bank.

Acheson was undersecretary of state from 1945 to 1947, and in 1949 President **Harry S. Truman** appointed him secretary of state. He served until 1953, helping shape U.S. policies in the early **Cold War**, including the **Truman Doctrine** and the **Marshall Plan**. He was one of the leading architects of the political, economic, and military structures to contain the **Soviet Union**—a Cold War strategy codified in **National Security Council Report 68** in 1950. The **North Atlantic Treaty Organization**, the decision to build the hydrogen bomb, the U.S. military response to North Korean aggression, the substantial defense build-up, and the incorporation of West **Germany** and **Japan** into the Western Alliance all reflected his influence. Despite his anticommunist policies and convictions, Acheson was subjected to merciless criticism by the right wing of the **Republican Party**, especially Senator **Joseph McCarthy**, particularly over failures in Asia—the "loss of **China**" and the **Korean War**—but also for refusing to turn his back on **Alger Hiss**. He dismissed such criticism as the work of "primitives." His tailored suits, neat moustache, and fastidious attention to appearance led to him being accused of pomposity and snobbery. He did, however, retain the support of President Truman.

Acheson returned to his law practice in 1953 but remained involved in **foreign policy** issues and vigorously defended the strategy of **containment** he had helped implement. When Presidents John F. Kennedy and Lyndon B. Johnson sought his advice, he consistently supported a tough line until 1968, when he abruptly urged U.S. disengagement from the Vietnam War. His aptly titled memoir, *Present at the Creation*, won the Pulitzer Prize in 1970.

AFRICAN AMERICANS. The African American population (11.8 million in 1930) felt the impact of the **Great Depression** and **World War II** as much as their white counterparts, but those effects were reflected through a prism of continuing racial prejudice and discrimination. As the economy failed, black Americans were "last hired, first fired" and experienced unemployment at more than twice the rate of white workers. In 1935, 30 percent—approximately 4 million—African Americans were on relief. More than 75 percent were still located in the South, where falling farm prices meant that black sharecroppers were further impoverished and were often evicted from the land and their homes by landlords or banks. The number of black sharecroppers fell by almost 100,000 during the 1930s.

The economic crisis increased feelings of racial prejudice. One slogan demanded "No Job for Niggers until Every Whiteman Has a Job." Racial hatred was evident too in the continued lynching of African Americans—about 20 per year for most of the decade, except for 1932, 1938, and 1939, when the number dropped to single figures. While attempts to secure the passage of **antilynching** legislation in Congress gained publicity from these atrocities, southern congressmen were always able to prevent the passage of such measures.

African Americans responded to discrimination in a variety of ways. They took enormous pride in the sporting achievements of **Joe Louis** and **Jesse Owens**, who both undermined theories of white racial superiority. Some African Americans responded at a practical level. In the South, blacks joined white tenant farmers to form the **Southern Tenant Farmers' Union (STFU)** in 1934. The vice president of the STFU was an African American, O. H. Whitfield, and the approximately 25,000 black members constituted about one-third of the total. In the North too, African Americans organized in the form of "Don't Buy Where You Can't Work" boycotts and protests in New York, Chicago, and Washington, D.C. The **National Association for the Advancement of Colored People (NAACP)**, led by **Walter White**, was also more conspicuously active in campaigning for **civil rights** during this period. However, anger could also surface, and in March 1935, for example, **Harlem**, the black community in New York City where 100,000 people were on relief, erupted in a two-day explosion of frustration directed at the largely white-owned stores and buildings, inflicting more than $2 million in damage.

The Depression years appeared to bring to an end the literary and artistic movement of the 1920s known as the "Harlem Renaissance," but black writers such as **Langston Hughes** and **Zora Neale Hurston** continued to produce during the 1930s and 1940s, while newcomer **Richard Wright** made a considerable impact with his work in the 1940s.

Like Wright, a small number of African Americans looked to left-wing groups for support. The **Communist Party of the United States of America (CPUSA)** did win some backing among African Americans for its role in the **Scottsboro** case and that of Angelo Herndon, an African American found guilty in 1933 of organizing insurrection in Atlanta, Georgia, where he had organized a demonstration of unemployed black and white workers. After five years, the **Supreme Court** overthrew his 18-year sentence. An African American, James W. Ford, was the vice presidential candidate for the CPUSA in 1932, 1936, and 1940. Although it failed to attract many votes, black or white, the CPUSA worked with the **National Negro Congress** and the Southern Negro Youth Congress, formed in 1937. However, what little support the party had among African Americans was lost following the Nazi-Soviet Pact in 1939 and even more so after 1941, when it opposed civil rights protests that might threaten the war effort.

While President **Franklin D. Roosevelt** did not speak out on race relations himself, the presence of white progressives in his administration helped bring about greater recognition for African Americans in and by the federal government. The appointment of several leading African Americans, including **Mary McLeod Bethune** to the **National Youth Administration, William Hastie** to the Department of the Interior, and **Robert C. Weaver** to the **Federal Housing Administration**, led to talk of a **Black Cabinet**. As a consequence of this and the benefits from some of the **New Deal** measures, there was a dramatic change in black voting. Whereas in 1932, 70 percent of black votes were cast for the **Republican Party**, by the end of the decade this was reversed with 70 percent of votes going for the **Democratic Party**. This allegiance was to continue well into the late 20th century. **Arthur W. Mitchell** became the first black Democrat elected to Congress in 1934. In 1942, Republican **William Dawson** and Democrat **Adam Clayton Powell** were also elected to the House.

Although African Americans did benefit from a number of political developments, the local operation of most New Deal agencies ensured that they also experienced a considerable amount of discrimination. The **National Recovery Administration** was known among the black community as "Negroes Ruined Again" because of the agency's discrimination and because increases in wage levels meant it was now cheaper to mechanize such industries as tobacco producing rather than employ African American workers. Similarly, the **Agricultural Adjustment Administration**'s policies to reduce farm production to raise prices often encouraged southern landlords to simply evict their black tenants. Many African Americans were excluded from **Social Security** legislation because of their concentration in agricultural work or domestic service. Relief payments were also significantly lower for black families than for whites. Although African Americans constituted 11 percent of the workforce of the **Tennessee Valley Authority**, they received only 9 percent of the wages. Black Americans did, however, make up a considerable proportion of the people put to work by the **Works Progress Administration** and those provided federal housing by the **Federal**

Housing Administration. Despite early discrimination and the continuation of segregation, the percentage of black Americans among the workforce of the **Civilian Conservation Corps** rose from 3 to 8 percent.

African Americans were significantly affected by **World War II**. The war against Nazism and for the "**four freedoms**" had a particular resonance for an underprivileged minority. African Americans demanded inclusion from the start in **A. Philip Randolph**'s **March on Washington Movement** and later in the *Pittsburgh Courier*'s "Double V" campaign for victory at home and abroad. The combined challenge of war and black protest brought some change in military policies. More than 1 million African Americans served in the armed forces, including 4,000 black **women**. Half a million African Americans saw service overseas, the majority in service of supply regiments. While military segregation remained intact other than for an exceptional period during the **Battle of the Bulge** in 1944, access to military service widened to include all branches of the services by the end of the war, including the air force and marines, from which they had previously been excluded. **Benjamin O. Davis Sr.** became the first black general in 1940, and his son, **Benjamin Davis Jr.**, became the highest ranking black officer in the air force.

Initially the navy confined African Americans like **Dorie Miller** to service in the kitchens, galleys, or boiler rooms, but they were gradually admitted to all branches in auxiliary vessels. In total, 150,000 served in the navy, and 20,000 served in the marines. Beginning in 1941, African Americans were admitted into the air force, and almost 600 pilots trained at Tuskegee Institute after 1941 and served in most theaters of the war.

During the war, the newly-established **Fair Employment Practices Committee** and more significantly mounting labor shortages ensured greater employment of African Americans. An additional 1 million black workers joined the labor force, and the number of African Americans in skilled and semiskilled occupations doubled by 1945. There was also an increase in the number of African Americans employed by the federal government during the war. Increased employment opportunities in war industries located in the North and West encouraged more than a million African Americans to leave the South. While they found work in defense plants, they also encountered resistance from white workers. When black streetcar workers were upgraded from porters to drivers in Philadelphia in August 1944, a transit strike necessitated the use of military force to persuade white employees back to work. In the South, conflict over the upgrading of black workers to the position of welders in the Alabama Drydock and Shipping Company was followed by a riot in 1943, a year when conflict over jobs, housing, and public transportation, heightened by wartime anxieties, led to an outbreak of more than 240 riots and racial incidents across the country, the worst occurring in **Detroit**. Other major outbreaks took place in **Los Angeles** and **Harlem**.

At the war's end, there was some fear that returning black service personnel would face the racial violence they had encountered in the aftermath of World War I, and there were some incidents in which black servicemen were the targets of racial hatred. There were also outbreaks of racial violence in Athens, Alabama; Columbia, Tennessee; Philadelphia; and Chicago. However, such events were not on the scale of the "Red Summer" of 1919. They were relatively few in number and were met with widespread condemnation, including that of President **Harry S. Truman**. Truman also took significant steps to bring greater equality in the federal civil service and to end segregation in the armed forces. The latter neared completion during the **Korean War** when more than 600,000 African American served in the military, many in integrated units.

Other significant breakthroughs came in sports, where **Jackie Robinson** became the first African American to play for a white baseball team in the major leagues. The Supreme Court also issued a number of significant rulings against segregation in the immediate postwar years. However, while the **Cold War** may have encouraged the federal government to insist that America practiced what it preached, it also discouraged radical protest for fear of being labeled "communist." The black singer and civil rights campaigner **Paul Robeson** and former civil rights leader W. E. B. Du Bois both had their passports withheld in 1950 and 1951 because of their association with left-wing groups. Despite such actions, African Americans found encouragement in developments at home during the 1940s and early 1950s and also in the growing process of decolonization abroad. *See also* AMOS 'N' ANDY; ANDERSON, EDWARD LINCOLN (EDDIE, "ROCHESTER"); ANDERSON, MARIAN; ARM-

STRONG, LOUIS; BUNCHE, RALPH JOHNSON; ELLINGTON, EDWARD KENNEDY ("DUKE"); HAYES, ROLAND; HOUSTON, CHARLES HAMILTON; MARSHALL, THURGOOD; *MISSOURI EX REL. GAINES V. CANADA*; RED BALL EXPRESS; ROOSEVELT, (ANNA) ELEANOR; *SHELLEY V. KRAEMER*.

AGEE, JAMES RUFUS (1909–1955). A Pulitzer Prize-winning novelist, journalist, and film critic, James Agee was born in Knoxville, Tennessee. Following his father's death in a road accident, he was educated at several boarding schools before attending Harvard University, where he became editor of the *Harvard Advocate*. Following his graduation he wrote for *Fortune*, *Time*, *The Nation*, and *New Masses*. His book of poetry, *Permit Me Voyage*, was published in 1934.

In 1936 Agee, together with photographer **Walker Evans**, spent several weeks among the white sharecroppers of Hale County, Alabama, working on an assignment for *Fortune*. The material was not published by the magazine, but it appeared in book form in 1941 as *Let Us Now Praise Famous Men*. Not a best seller in its day, it is now recognized as a classic of the Depression years, documenting the poverty and hardship of rural life with a combination of photographic images and a literary reporting style.

During **World War II**, Agee was the film critic for *Time* and *The Nation*. He became a freelance writer in 1948 and also wrote film scripts, two of which, *The African Queen* (1951) and *The Night of the Hunter* (1955) (although there is some question about the authorship of this work), became major successes of the 1950s. *A Death in the Family*, a novel published in 1957, won Agee a posthumous Pulitzer Prize the following year. Several pieces of his film criticism were published as *Agee on Film* (1960). *See also* GREAT DEPRESSION; LITERATURE AND THEATER.

AGRICULTURAL ADJUSTMENT ACT, 1933. Passed on 12 May 1933, the Agricultural Adjustment Act was intended to tackle the plight of farmers in the **Great Depression** and to raise the prices of wheat, corn, cotton, and other crops and livestock and return the farmers' purchasing power to pre-World War I levels. The act was based on ideas developed during the 1920s, particularly the "domestic allotment plan" involving acreage reduction by government allotment. The act designated "basic commodities" that would be covered by "marketing agreements" in which farmers would agree to reduce their output. They would be compensated with funds raised by a processing tax levied on the first domestic processing of the commodity. The act was to be administered by the **Agricultural Adjustment Administration**. Initially some crops had to be plowed under and livestock, including 6 million piglets, were slaughtered, but by 1934, 40 million acres had been withdrawn from production. Amendments to the act extended it to include cattle, sugar cane, and sugar beets in 1934. However, in *United States v. Butler* in 1936, the **Supreme Court** ruled that the act was unconstitutional. It was later superseded by the **Agricultural Adjustment Act** of 1938. *See also* AGRICULTURE; BANKHEAD COTTON ACT; BANKHEAD COTTON CONTROL ACT; EMERGENCY FARM MORTGAGE ACT.

AGRICULTURAL ADJUSTMENT ACT, 1938. Replacing the first **Agricultural Adjustment Act** of 1933 and supplementing the **Soil Conservation and Domestic Allotment Act** of 1936, the 1938 act established a "granary" principle setting marketing quotas, crop insurance, and parity price payments. This system paid farmers to store surplus commodities produced during good years so that they could be released during lean years. The funds were raised out of general taxation. *See also* AGRICULTURE.

AGRICULTURAL ADJUSTMENT ADMINISTRATION (AAA). The AAA was established in 1933 to implement the **Agricultural Adjustment Act** and was headed by **George N. Peek**. However, the AAA was criticized because of the decision to destroy millions of acres of crops already in production and to slaughter 6 million piglets and 200,000 sows. Moreover, Peek proved a controversial figure, and his refusal to accept the principle of crop reduction rather than the purchase and export of surpluses led to his resignation in December 1933. He was succeeded by **Chester Davis**. Although the Agricultural Adjustment Act was declared unconstitutional by the **Supreme Court** in 1936, the AAA continued to administer the **Soil Conservation and Domestic Allotment Act, 1936**, and then the second **Agricultural Adjustment Act, 1938**. In 1942, the AAA became the Agricultural Adjustment Agency, and its chief function was to encourage maximum production for wartime. In 1945, the AAA was taken over by the Production and Marketing Administration. *See also* AGRICULTURE.

AGRICULTURE. Perhaps no area was affected by the changing trends of the decades of the 1930s and 1940s as much as agriculture. Although for much of its history the United States was a predominantly agrarian economy, by the end of the 19th century, farmers were displaced socially and politically and experienced increasing economic problems due to overproduction and worldwide competition that resulted in falling prices. In the late 19th century, the anger of farmers—often directed at banks, railroads, and middlemen—found expression in the Populist movement that became incorporated into the **Democratic Party**.

While some of the farmers' demands were met during the progressive presidencies of Theodore Roosevelt and Woodrow Wilson, it was rising farm prices that brought relief—albeit temporary—to the farmers' plight. World War I brought a boom in agriculture as world trade was limited. The demand for grain and food to feed both the U.S. and **Allied** armies brought an expansion in farm acreage and output. Mechanization and the use of tractors contributed further to farm efficiency. After the war, however, world competition resumed, and the artificially high commodity prices fell. American farmers once again struggled to pay off their debts, and many lost their farms. The farm population, which was more than 32 million in 1910, was 31.9 million in 1920 and had fallen to 30.5 million by 1930. As a proportion of the total population, this represented a drop from more than 30 percent to just under 25 percent.

Attempts in the 1920s to secure federal legislation to relieve the farmers' situation largely failed, and the **Great Depression** only worsened the situation as agricultural prices collapsed after 1929. By 1932, the average farm income had dropped by two-thirds. With many farmers unable to meet mortgage repayments, almost a million farms were repossessed between 1930 and 1934. The drought and dust storms of the 1930s only added to the misery. Desperate farmers declared "farm holidays" in which they withheld their produce from the market or dumped it in the roads. Farm sales following evictions were often blocked, and farmers demonstrated in neighboring towns. By 1940, the number of farms had dropped from 6.3 million in 1930 to 6.1 million. President **Herbert Hoover** responded by signing the Agricultural Marketing Act in 1929 and attempted to stabilize prices through Federal Farm Boards. However, this had little immediate effect, and it was not until the coming of the **New Deal** that farming began to experience a recovery.

Tackling the problem of agricultural overproduction and falling farm incomes was a major priority for **Franklin D. Roosevelt**'s administration. Loans were quickly provided to farmers through the **Farm Credit Act** in 1933. Under the **Agricultural Adjustment Administration (AAA)** established that year, a system of domestic allotments was created for wheat, cotton, corn, hogs, rice, tobacco, and dairy products under which farmers were given cash subsidies to cut production. These payments were financed by a processing tax. By 1934, 40 million acres had been withdrawn from production, and although the AAA was declared unconstitutional by the **Supreme Court**, these measures, combined with the impact of the droughts and floods that hit parts of the country in the mid-1930s, led to a 50 percent rise in farm income. A second **Agricultural Adjustment Act** was introduced in 1938 establishing a system of parity price payments and production quotas. Soil conservation schemes were introduced through the **Tennessee Valley Authority**, the **Soil Conservation and Domestic Allotment Act** of 1936, and the work of agencies like the **Civilian Conservation Corps**. Farmers also benefited from the **Rural Electrification Administration**, which assisted farmers in establishing cooperatives among themselves to bring electric power to their properties. In 1935, only 10 percent of farms had electricity. By 1940 this had risen to 40 percent, and by 1950 it was 90 percent. The **Farm Security Administration**, established in 1937, assisted displaced farm workers through the **Resettlement Administration** and provided further financial aid to farmers.

With the coming of **World War II**, American agriculture faced further change. The migration from the land continued during the war as people moved to take advantage of work in war industries across the nation. By 1950, the number of farmers had fallen again from 30.84 million in 1940 to 25 million, and the number of farms fell from 6.1 million to 5.3 million. While there were fewer farms, they tended to be larger. Shortages of farm labor were met by importing Mexican workers (***braceros***) and by the increased use of mechanization. Despite labor shortages, farm output per laborer increased by 36 percent as machines replaced horse-driven or man-powered equipment and as the number of tractors increased by almost 1 million between 1940 and 1945. Farm income rose by an estimated 250 percent during the war. After the war, various proposals were made to maintain the farmers' position, the most radical being the **Brannan Plan** involving direct income-maintenance payments. However, after some debate in Congress, the **American Farm Bureau Federation**'s proposal to continue price supports was adopted. *See also* ANDERSON, CLINTON PRESBA; BANKHEAD COTTON ACT; BANKHEAD COTTON CONTROL ACT; BRANNAN, CHARLES FRANKLIN; EMERGENCY FARM MORTGAGE ACT; FARM CREDIT ACT; FARM CREDIT ADMINISTRATION (FCA); FARM-LABOR PARTY; PEEK, GEORGE NELSON; WALLACE, HENRY AGARD.

ALIEN REGISTRATION ACT. *See* SMITH ACT.

ALLEN, GRACIE (1895–1964). Grace Ethel Cecile Rosalie Allen was born in San Francisco, California. She first appeared on stage at the age of three as a dancer and with her three sisters appeared as an Irish singer and dancer in local vaudeville theaters before touring on the east coast. Failing to get work on her own, Allen enrolled in secretarial school in New York, but in 1923 she met **George Burns**, and they established a comedy routine together in which Allen assumed the comic role to Burns's straight man. Allen established a persona of "Dizzy Dora," who despite her lunacy, somehow made sense. The partnership quickly became successful, and she and Burns married in 1926. In 1930, they appeared in vaudeville on Broadway for a run of 17 weeks and shortly thereafter made their debut on American **radio**. In 1933, they began their own show on CBS, originally called "The Adventures of Gracie" and later named "The George Burns and Gracie Allen Show." It was a favorite of U.S. listeners through 1950.

Allen and Burns made a number of movie shorts for Paramount between 1929 and 1931, followed by several feature films, including *Six of a Kind* (1934) with **W. C. Fields**. Allen did not enjoy making movies, and her last was *Two Girls and a Sailor* (1944). In 1950, Burns and Allen successfully moved to **television**. Their show ran until June 1958, when Allen insisted on retiring to spend more time with her adopted children and grandchildren. She suffered a serious heart attack in 1961 and died in Hollywood three years later. Although he provided most of their material, Burns always insisted that Allen "was the whole show" and that it was her comic timing and delivery that made them a success. *See also* CINEMA.

ALLIED CONTROL COUNCIL (ACC). The ACC was created on 5 June 1945 to oversee the postwar occupation of **Germany**. It consisted of representatives from **Great Britain**, France, the **Soviet Union**, and the United States. The ACC ceased to exist after the withdrawal of the Soviet representative in March 1948 and was replaced in West Germany by the **Allied High Commission**.

ALLIED COUNCIL FOR JAPAN. In August 1945, the victorious **Allied powers** established the Allied Council under the command of General **Douglas MacArthur** to oversee the occupation of **Japan**. The council consisted of representatives from the United States, the **Soviet Union**, **China**, Australia, and the Philippines.

ALLIED HIGH COMMISSION. Following the breakdown of relations with the **Soviet Union** and the withdrawal of their representative on the **Allied Control Council** in 1948, an Allied High Commission consisting of the United States, **Great Britain**, and France was established to run West **Germany** and West **Berlin**. The commission was disbanded when West Germany became independent as the **Federal Republic of Germany**.

ALLIED POWERS. Initially, the Allied powers in **World War II** were **Great Britain** (and the Commonwealth countries, including Canada, New Zealand, Australia), France, and Poland, brought together in defense of the latter following the attack by Nazi **Germany** on 1 September 1939. In 1940, they were joined by Belgium, Norway, and the Netherlands; by the **Soviet Union** following the Nazi invasion of Russia in June 1941; and by the United States and **China**

after the Japanese attack on **Pearl Harbor**. Other nations, particularly in Latin America, subsequently joined, and the Allied powers also became known as the **United Nations** with the Declaration of the United Nations on 1 January 1942. Their opponents were the **Axis powers** and their allies. *See also* JAPAN.

AMERASIA **CASE.** In January 1945, an article that seemed to be based on classified State Department papers appeared in *Amerasia*, a journal of Far Eastern affairs. Acting without a warrant, officers of the **Federal Bureau of Investigation (FBI)** broke into the journal's offices, where they found classified documents. The editor of the journal, Russian-born Phillip Jaffe, a State Department worker and naval intelligence officer, were arrested, as was **John Stewart Service**. Charges against Service were thrown out by a grand jury and, as there was no evidence that material had been passed to any enemy state, the other three accused were charged with illegal possession of government documents. Rather than proceed with the trial and reveal the FBI's illegal actions, a deal was struck in which Jaffe pleaded guilty, the State Department member pleaded no contest, and charges against the naval officer were dropped. Despite this, the case was later referred to by **Joseph McCarthy** when he claimed that communist sympathizers were present in government.

AMERICA FIRST COMMITTEE (AFC). The AFC was formed in September 1940 in response to the outbreak of war in Europe in 1939. It quickly became the most influential voice of isolationism in the United States. The original members were Robert E. Wood, **Charles A. Lindbergh**, and **John T. Flynn**. The AFC's policies were to encourage preparedness through the creation of a powerful U.S. defense to deter any foreign attack and to keep out of the European conflict. It opposed **Franklin D. Roosevelt**'s policy of "all aid short of war" and **Lend-Lease**. By 1941, the AFC had an estimated membership of more than 800,000 and 450 local chapters. It ceased to operate four days after the attack on **Pearl Harbor**.

AMERICAN CIVIL LIBERTIES UNION (ACLU). The ACLU was founded in 1920 by social reformers, including Roger Baldwin,

Jane Addams, Crystal Eastman, and Clarence Darrow. It was established to preserve civil liberties guaranteed under the Bill of Rights of the Constitution, namely, freedom of speech, press, and religion. During the 1920s, the ACLU supported John Scopes in the famous "Scopes Money Trial" (1925) and also Italian anarchists Ferdinando Nicola Sacco and Bartolomeo Vanzetti (1927). It was involved in the defense of the **Scottsboro Boys** in the 1930s. In 1933, the ACLU played a significant role in the case permitting James Joyce's book *Ulysses* to be allowed into the United States.

From 1936 to 1943, the ACLU provided assistance to the Jehovah's Witnesses in their campaign to allow children to be exempted from saluting the national flag on religious grounds. The **Supreme Court** found in favor of the flag salute requirements in 1940 but reversed itself in *West Virginia State Board of Education v. Barnette* in1943. During **World War II**, the ACLU helped represent the **Japanese Americans** challenging wartime internment in the cases of *Korematsu v. United States* and *Hirabayashi v. United States*.

During the **Cold War** years, the ACLU challenged the **federal loyalty program** and led the opposition to loyalty oaths in a number of states. However, the organization was divided during this period, with some members, including one of its founders, Roger Baldwin, supporting anticommunist measures.

AMERICAN FARM BUREAU FEDERATION (AFBF). Established in 1919 as a federation of state bureaus, the AFBF represented 36 states and developed from the farm extension programs established during World War I to disseminate more widely scientific and technical advances in **agriculture**. It established lobbies at state and federal levels to promote agricultural interests and by 1930, with a membership of 163,000, it was the most important farm organization. It was to have considerable influence on the **New Deal**. The aim of the AFBF was to achieve "parity," meaning restoring the purchasing power of farmers to pre-World War I levels. It supported the **Agricultural Adjustment Act** of 1933 and again in 1938. However, it tended to argue that the Department of Agriculture should work primarily in the interests of farmers rather than for the greater good of the country as a whole. By the end of the 1940s, membership in the AFBF had risen to 1.3 million.

AMERICAN FEDERATION OF LABOR (AFL). A federation of autonomous, craft-based **trade unions** formed in 1886 by Samuel Gompers and Adolph Strasser, the AFL was conservative and non-political in outlook and largely excluded unskilled immigrant and black workers. Nonetheless, by 1910 it was established as the leading union organization and had a membership of more than 2 million. Although membership doubled during World War I, the organization was unable to consolidate upon wartime advances in the face of employer resistance in the more conservative 1920s. Following a series of defeats, union membership declined once more and by 1933 was only 2.3 million.

The AFL maintained its conservative outlook with regard to unskilled and immigrant workers, and this approach continued when **William Green** succeeded Gompers in 1924. The continued reluctance to organize industrial workers led the industrial-based unions headed by **John L. Lewis**, **Sidney Hillman**, and **David Dubinsky** to form the Committee of Industrial Organizations in 1934. In 1938, they broke away to form the **Congress of Industrial Organizations (CIO)**. As a consequence of both organizing drives and the recognition afforded by the **National Labor Relations Act**, AFL membership increased. With full employment achieved during **World War II** and the "maintenance of membership" agreement, the AFL increased in membership and by 1945 had more than 6 million members. Although stronger and more closely associated with the **Democratic** administrations during and after the war, it was not able to prevent the passage of the **Taft-Hartley Act** in 1947. During the **Cold War**, it was staunchly anticommunist and assisted in establishing noncommunist organizations in postwar Europe. Green was succeeded after his death in 1952 by George Meany, and three years later the AFL merged with the CIO to form the AFL-CIO.

AMERICAN LIBERTY LEAGUE. An anti-**New Deal** organization, the American Liberty League was formed in August 1934 by conservative politicians and businessmen, including **John Jakob Raskob**, **Jouett Shouse**, and the Du Pont family. **Alfred E. Smith** was also a supporter. The league had a membership of about 125,000, but it faded after **Franklin D. Roosevelt**'s election success in 1936 and was dissolved in 1940.

AMERICAN SCENE. The "American Scene" was the name given to the artistic movement of the 1920s and especially the 1930s that saw a concentration on American themes and subjects rather than European modernist images. It included **regionalist** painters **John Steuart Curry, Thomas Hart Benton**, and **Grant Wood**, as well as such social realists as **Edward Hopper** and **Ben Shahn**. *See also* BURCHFIELD, CHARLES EPHRAIM.

AMERICANS FOR DEMOCRATIC ACTION (ADA). The ADA was a liberal political lobbying group, formed in January 1947 by people who opposed communism but wished to support a reform agenda. Included among the founders were **Hubert Humphrey, Reinhold Niebuhr, Walter Reuther, Eleanor Roosevelt**, and **Arthur Schlesinger Jr**. They supported **Harry S. Truman**'s **Fair Deal** program and helped ensure the inclusion of a **civil rights** plank in the **Democratic Party** platform in 1948.

AMOS 'N' ANDY. The longest-running **radio** program in broadcast history, at the height of its success in the 1930s *Amos 'n' Andy* attracted audiences of 30 to 40 million and was aired six times a week. The show was written and first performed in 1928 in Chicago by two white actors, Freeman Gosden and Charles Correll, playing the roles of **African Americans** in the style of old blackface comedy. It was broadcast nationally by NBC beginning in 1929 and by CBC beginning in 1939. The show moved to television in 1951, where it became the first **television** program with an all-black cast. However, its portrayal of demeaning racial stereotypes always attracted criticism, first from the *Pittsburgh Courier* and other black newspapers in the 1930s, and later from the **National Association for the Advancement of Colored People**. The protests helped bring the program to an end in 1953.

ANDERSON, CLINTON PRESBA (1895–1975). Clinton Anderson was born in South Dakota. He attended Dakota Wesleyan University until 1915 and the University of Michigan at Ann Arbor until 1916 but did not graduate from either institution. When he discovered he was suffering from tuberculosis in 1917, Anderson moved to Albuquerque, New Mexico. There he became a newspaper reporter and editor before turning to insurance in 1922. Anderson was also active in public affairs and was executive secretary of the New Mexico Public Health Service in 1919 and later chair of the state **Democratic Party**. During the 1930s, he worked for the New Mexico Relief Administration and later as a field representative for the **Federal Emergency Relief Administration (FERA)**. In 1940, he was elected to the federal House of Representatives, where he served until 1945 when he was appointed secretary of **agriculture** by President **Harry S. Truman**.

As secretary of agriculture from 1945 to 1948, Anderson helped establish the **Famine Emergency Committee** under President **Herbert Hoover** and also addressed the problem of farm prices in the Agricultural Act in 1949 maintaining the price support system rather than the **Brannan Plan**. In 1948, Anderson was elected to the Senate for New Mexico, and he held his seat until he retired in 1973. His most notable achievement was in support of the space program as chair of the Senate Committee on Aeronautical and Space Science from 1963 to 1973.

ANDERSON, EDWARD LINCOLN (EDDIE, "ROCHESTER") (1905–1977). **African American** entertainer Eddie Anderson was born in Oakland, California, and joined his brother in vaudeville performances in the 1920s before moving to Hollywood. His first film acting performance was in *What Price Hollywood* (1932), but his first significant role was in *Green Pastures* (1936). He also appeared in *Show Boat* (1936) and *Gone with the Wind* (1939). Anderson continued to play roles in films until the 1960s. It was on radio that he finally became a national star, playing the part of the butler "Rochester" on the "**Jack Benny** Show" from 1937 until 1955. He was so successful that he was once the highest-paid African American performer. Anderson appeared on the televised version of the Benny show until 1965, but the stereotyped character eventually grew unpopular. *See also* CINEMA; TELEVISION.

ANDERSON, MARIAN (1897–1993). Born in Philadelphia, Pennsylvania, **African American** contralto Marian Anderson became a national and international concert and opera singer, beginning with her first performance with the New York Philharmonic in 1925. She first sang in Europe in 1930 and established her reputation touring over the next five years. When the Daughters of the American Revolution refused to allow her to perform in Constitution Hall in Washington, D.C., in 1939, **Harold Ickes**, supported by **Eleanor Roosevelt**, organized a public performance on the steps of the Lincoln Memorial before an audience of 75,000. Anderson became the first black singer to perform at the Metropolitan Opera in New York in 1955. She began her farewell tour in 1965 with a performance at Constitution Hall.

Anderson was awarded the **National Association for the Advancement of Colored People**'s Spingarn Medal in 1938 and the Presidential Medal of Freedom by Lyndon Johnson in 1965. She also received the **United Nations** Peace Prize in 1972.

ANDERSON, MARY (1872–1964). Swedish-born Mary Anderson moved to the United States in 1889. After working in a boardinghouse, she moved to West Pullman, Illinois, and found work in the garment industry and then in a shoe factory. Anderson became an active **trade unionist** and was the only **woman** to sit on the executive board of the International Boot and Shoe Workers' Union. She joined the Women's Trade Union League in 1905 and became a full-time organizer with the league in 1911. In 1918, she became assistant director of the government's newly created Women in Industry Service (WIS), and in 1919 she became director. The following year the WIS became the Women's Bureau within the Department of Labor. In 1933, Anderson was appointed by **Franklin D. Roosevelt** to head the U.S. delegation to the International Labour Organization and as an adviser to the U.S. delegate at an international conference on the textile industry. During **World War II**, the Women's Bureau was active in aiding the employment of women in war industries and campaigning for equal pay for equal work. The bureau issued several reports on women's working conditions during the war. Anderson retired in 1944 but continued to campaign for equal pay for women into the 1950s.

ANTILYNCHING BILL. A bill to outlaw lynching was first introduced to Congress by Indiana **Republican** senator Leonidas Dyer and Republican congressman Charles Curtis of Kansas in 1921. It passed in the House of Representatives but failed to pass in the Senate in 1921 and 1923. The **National Association for the Advancement of Colored People** drafted a new **Federal Antilynching Bill** in 1933, and it was presented to Congress by Democratic senators Edward P. Costigan from Colorado and **Robert F. Wagner** from New York. Having failed to make progress, it was reintroduced in 1935 and passed by the House in 1937 but abandoned following a filibuster in the Senate in 1938. Wagner and Republican congressman Joseph Gavagan from New York, introduced yet another bill in 1940, but it too met the same fate.

ANZIO. In the operation code-named "Shingle," on 22 January 1944, U.S. and British troops landed on the beaches at Anzio, Italy, cutting the German lines between Rome and Cassino in an attempt to break the stalemate between **Allied** and Nazi forces. Although unopposed, U.S. forces failed to take advantage, and German forces regrouped and counterattacked. They were not defeated until May 1944, by which time the Allied forces had suffered heavy losses.

ARCADIA CONFERENCE, 1941–1942. Arcadia was the code name given to the meeting between British prime minister **Winston Churchill** and President **Franklin D. Roosevelt** and their respective military staffs in Washington, D.C., from 22 December 1941 to 14 January 1942, during which they agreed on their joint strategy for **World War II**. A unified command was established with a Combined Chiefs of Staff with a supreme military commander in each theater of war. The Allies also agreed that a "**Germany** first" policy would be pursued, while in the Pacific the first objective would be to prevent further Japanese expansion. The meeting also led to the issuing of the Declaration of the **United Nations** on 1 January 1942 that committed its signatories to uphold the principles of the **Atlantic Charter** and not to conclude any separate peace agreement with the **Axis powers**.

ARMSTRONG, LOUIS (1901–1971). Born in New Orleans, the great jazz trumpeter and singer Louis Armstrong, also known as "Satchmo" or "Pops," was placed in a Colored Waifs' Home for Boys at the age of 12. He began his career as a professional musician in 1918, playing the cornet in clubs and on Mississippi River paddle steamers. In 1922, Armstrong moved to Chicago to play second cornet in Joe "King" Oliver's Creole Jazz Band. He made his first recordings between 1923 and 1924 with Oliver, including "Riverside Blues," "Snake Rage," and "Dipper Mouth Blues." He moved to New York City to join Fletcher Henderson's orchestra in 1924. It was this new band that developed the jazz style known as "swing." Armstrong made a number of records playing trumpet with Henderson, including "One of these Days," "Copenhagen," and "Everybody Loves My Baby," and he also recorded with Clarence Williams' Blue Five, a group featuring Sydney Bechet and singers Ma Rainey and Bessie Smith. Armstrong returned to Chicago in 1925 and began to lead his own groups, the Hot Five and the Hot Seven, with whom he made some classic recordings of traditional jazz, including "Cornet Chop," "Gut Bucket Blues," and "Heebie Jeebies."

Armstrong and his band moved to New York in 1929 and made several records on which he sang, often using his improvised "scat" singing. He achieved great success with "I Can't Give You Anything but Love" and "Ain't Misbehavin'," recorded in 1929. From 1930 through the 1940s Armstrong played with a number of big bands and returned to small combos after **World War II**. Between 1932 and 1965 he also appeared in nearly 50 movies, including *Pennies from Heaven* (1936), *High Society* (1956), and *Hello Dolly* (1969). Armstrong's song "Hello Dolly" had already reached number one on the popular **music** charts in 1964. Through his long and successful career from the days of the Harlem Renaissance through to the post-civil rights period of the 1960s, Armstrong was one of the most significant figures in jazz music. *See also* AFRICAN AMERICANS; CINEMA.

ART. The visual arts captured and reflected the effects of the **Depression** in a number of ways, sometimes paradoxical. While photographers, particularly those working for the **Farm Security Administration**, depicted the poverty and suffering brought about by the economic crisis or the devastation of the land during the **Dust Bowl** in countless black and white images, painters often seemed to look back to the American past as a symbol of hope for the future. **Regionalists** and others like **Grant Wood** and **Thomas Hart Benton** concerned with the **American scene** painted rich, lush, colorful landscapes. Some working in the **Federal Art Project** painted murals celebrating American achievements and workers, while others, like **Ben Shahn** provided some bleaker images of the Dust Bowl in federal posters and adverts. **Edward Hopper** produced bright, cheerful images of the New England coast but at the same time dark views of urban loneliness and alienation. During **World War II**, a number of artists like Shahn were employed to produce posters for the **Office of War Information**. **Norman Rockwell**'s **Four Freedoms** series also appeared as covers for the *Saturday Evening Post*. By the end of the war, a new school of abstract expressionism—perhaps influenced by the many European exiles—was appearing and was best represented by **Jackson Pollock** and Mark Rothko. Both of these artists were among those exhibited at Peggy Guggenheim's Art of the Century gallery in New York City in October 1942. *See also* AGEE, JAMES RUFUS; BURCHFIELD, CHARLES EPHRAIM; EVANS, WALKER; LANGE, DOROTHEA; LEE, RUSSELL WERNER; ROTHSTEIN, ARTHUR; SHAHN, BEN; STRYKER, ROY EMERSON.

ASTAIRE, FRED (1899–1987). The son of Austrian immigrants, Fred Astaire was born in Omaha, Nebraska, and began dancing in vaudeville with his sister in 1906 at the age of seven. In 1917, they moved to stage performances, appearing on Broadway and in London in George and Ira Gershwin's *Lady, Be Good!* (1924) and *Funny Face* (1927). In 1932, he starred on his own in **Cole Porter**'s *The Gay Divorcée*. Astaire began appearing in movies in 1933 and made the first film with **Ginger Rogers**, a version of *The Gay Divorcée*, in 1934. A number of successful films cemented their on-screen relationship and ensured box office success, most notably *Top Hat* (1935), *Follow the Fleet* (1936), *Shall We Dance* (1937), and *The Story of Vernon and Irene Castle* (1939). Following a dispute over fees, Astaire left Rogers to work on his own. Among others, he also appeared in *Broadway Melody of 1940* (1940), *Holiday Inn* (1942), and *Ziegfeld Follies* (1945–1946).

After a brief period in retirement, Astaire returned to make 10 more films between 1948 and 1957. He had a major hit with **Judy Garland** in *Easter Parade* (1948) and made successful films with Cyd Charisse, Leslie Caron, and Audrey Hepburn (*Funny Face*

[1957]). Astaire made a number of very successful **television** shows, including four musical specials between 1958 and 1968. His last musical film was *Finian's Rainbow* (1968), but he also had several nondancing, nonmusical roles in *On the Beach* (1959), *The Pleasure of His Company* (1961), *The Notorious Landlady* (1962), *The Midas Run* (1969), and *The Towering Inferno* (1975). He also had dramatic roles in a number of television specials and series. *See also* CINEMA; MUSIC.

ATLANTIC CHARTER, 1941. As U.S. assistance to **Great Britain** increased following the **Lend-Lease Act**, President **Franklin D. Roosevelt** and British prime minister **Winston Churchill** met in Argentia Bay off Newfoundland in August 1941 to agree on common principles. On 14 August, they issued a joint declaration known as the Atlantic Charter listing eight principles that they hoped to see applied to better the future of the postwar world. These principles were 1) a declaration that signatories intended to make no territorial gains from the present conflict; 2) that any territorial changes should only be made in line with the wishes of the peoples concerned; 3) that the principle of self-determination should be applied; 4) that trade barriers should be lowered; 5) that global economic cooperation should be applied; 6) that there should be freedom from want and fear; 7) that there should be freedom of the seas; and 8) that there should be the disarmament of aggressor nations. In September 1941, representatives of the governments of Belgium, Czechoslovakia, Greece, Luxemburg, the Netherlands, Norway, Poland, the **Soviet Union**, Yugoslavia, and the Free French signed the statement. The Atlantic Charter paved the way for the **United Nations Charter**.

ATOMIC BOMB. The atomic bomb was a weapon made using enriched uranium, which on detonation caused a chain nuclear reaction involving the fission of atomic particles. Development of the atomic bomb in the United States began after **Albert Einstein** wrote to **Franklin D. Roosevelt** in August 1939 informing him of the early discoveries in atomic science and the potential to create a powerful bomb based on nuclear fission and warning of the need to develop such weaponry before Nazi **Germany**. In 1942, the government established the **Manhattan Project** under the leadership of General

Leslie R. Groves, and on 16 July 1945 the first bomb was tested in Alamogordo, New Mexico. The first bomb was used during **World War II** when it was dropped on **Hiroshima**, Japan, on 6 August 1945. A second bomb was dropped on 9 August on **Nagasaki**. Both bombs had devastating effects, and shortly afterward proposals were drawn up in an effort to prevent the proliferation of atomic weapons. These proposals were put to the **United Nations** in the **Baruch Plan** but were rejected by the **Soviet Union**. With the onset of the **Cold War** and the testing of an A-bomb by the Soviet Union in 1949, the threat of nuclear war became a real possibility. In 1952, the atomic bomb was superseded by the **hydrogen bomb**, a more powerful weapon based on nuclear fusion rather than fission. *See also* ATOMIC ENERGY ACT.

ATOMIC ENERGY ACT, 1946. The Atomic Energy Act, or Mc-Mahon Act (named after **Democratic** senator Brien McMahon from Connecticut, who proposed the act), passed in August 1946, established civilian control of the development of atomic energy in the United States under the U.S. **Atomic Energy Commission**. It also controlled the release of information about atomic research. *See also* ATOMIC BOMB; BARUCH, BERNARD MANNES.

ATOMIC ENERGY COMMISSION (AEC). The AEC was a five-man board established by Congress in 1946 under the **Atomic Energy Act** to oversee the development and control of atomic energy. The commission took over control from the military and supported research in universities and industry on the use of radioactive material in all aspects, industrial and medical as well as military. The commission was first chaired by **David E. Lilienthal**, who was succeeded by Gordon Deans in 1950. The committee was supported by an advisory group and ran into some controversy when **J. Robert Oppenheimer** was suspended in 1953 as a security risk. The AEC ceased to exist in 1974, and its role was eventually taken over by the U.S. Department of Energy.

AUSTRALIA-NEW ZEALAND-UNITED STATES SECURITY TREATY (ANZUS). The ANZUS was a mutual defense security treaty agreed upon on 1 September 1951 and put into effect on 29

April 1952. It stated that an attack on any one of the countries—Australia, New Zealand, or the United States—would be regarded as an attack on them all. The treaty reflected both the close cooperation between the three nations during **World War II** and the impact of the **Cold War** in the Pacific following the communist takeover in **China**. However, the treaty came under strain in 1985 when New Zealand objected to nuclear testing in the Pacific by the United States and refused to allow nuclear vessels into its ports. The United States abrogated the treaty with regard to New Zealand in 1986, but New Zealand has not formally withdrawn from the agreement. Both Australia and New Zealand supported the United States in the war against the Taliban in Afghanistan following the 1991 attack on the World Trade Center in New York City.

AVERY, SEWELL LEE (1874–1960). Businessman Sewell Avery was born in Saginaw, Michigan. He attended Michigan Military Academy and the University of Michigan Law School, where he graduated in 1894. He became the manager of a plaster works in Alabaster, Michigan, which later became part of U.S. Gypsum. Avery became president of the company in 1905 and held that position until 1937. Under his leadership, U.S. Gypsum became the nation's biggest supplier of building materials. In 1931, Avery became chair of the Montgomery Ward mail-order company and once more led the company to success. However, during **World War II** he was in constant dispute with the **National War Labor Board** over its "maintenance of membership" policy, which strengthened **trade union** organization. In April 1944, Avery was physically removed from his office by soldiers, and the military took over the company in 1944 and 1945. After the war, Montgomery Ward's success declined, and Avery's high-handed management led shareholders to force his resignation in 1955.

AXIS POWERS. The primary Axis powers were **Germany**, Italy, and **Japan**. The Axis developed in 1936 from a Treaty of Friendship between **Adolf Hitler**'s Nazi Germany and Mussolini's fascist Italy. It became a formal alliance between the two nations in 1939, and Japan joined with the Tripartite Treaty on 27 September 1940. Hungary, Rumania, Slovakia, and Bulgaria joined in 1940. The Axis powers were opposed during **World War II** by the **Allied powers**. The Axis effectively ended with the surrender of Germany on 8 May 1945.

AZERBAIJAN. This northernmost region of Iran was occupied by the **Soviet Union** during **World War II**. The Russians had indicated, both at the **Tehran Conference** and the **Potsdam Conference**, that they would withdraw at war's end. However, in response to growing U.S. interest in the Iranian oilfields and separatist movements in the region, in December 1945 they established pro-Soviet provincial governments in Azerbaijan and neighboring Kurdistan. The crisis helped to convince President **Harry S. Truman** that the Soviets were intent on a policy of expansionism that should be resisted. Accordingly, the United States exerted diplomatic pressure both directly and through the **United Nations** and also increased the U.S. naval presence in the eastern Mediterranean. Faced with this opposition and promised oil concessions in Iran, Soviet forces withdrew in April 1946. Following this crisis, the policy of **containment** was extended to the Near East, and aid given to the Iranian government enabled them to regain control of the northern provinces.

– B –

BABY BOOM. The end of **World War II** and the return of service personnel from abroad saw a sudden increase in marriage and consequently births. Marriage rates (per 1,000 unmarried women over the age of 15) rose from 73.0 in 1939 to 118.1 in 1946. In 1946, the birth rate (number of live births per 1,000 people) rose from under 20 in the late 1930s to 26.6 in 1947. In 1946, 3.4 million babies were born, and in 1947 the number was 3.8 million. Between 1948 and 1953 more babies were born than in the preceding 30 years. The long-term effect was felt in the 1960s when these children came of age and were a dominant social and cultural force.

"BABY FACE" NELSON (LESTER JOHN GILLIS) (1908–1934). The notorious bank robber and murderer was born Lester John Gillis in Chicago, but by 1931 he had assumed several aliases, including George Nelson. Because of his size (5'4" tall) and youthful appearance, he was known as "Baby Face." Nelson was a juvenile delinquent who was first sent to a boy's home in 1922. He was jailed for bank robbery in 1931 but escaped while being transferred between jails in 1932. After taking part in a number of robberies in which people were killed, Nelson joined up with **John Dillinger** in 1934. When Dillinger was shot dead in April of that year, Nelson replaced him as the **Federal Bureau of Investigation**'s "Public Enemy Number One." Cornered by agents in Barrington, Illinois, near Chicago, in November 1934, Nelson killed two lawmen and escaped, though he was badly wounded. He died several hours later.

BACALL, LAUREN (1924–). Born Betty Joan Perske in New York city, Lauren Bacall trained as an actor at the American Academy of Dramatic Arts and had a number of acting and modeling roles before she appeared on the cover of *Harper's Bazaar* in March 1943 and was cast by the film producer **Howard Hawks** in *To Have and Have Not* with **Humphrey Bogart** in 1944. The film was a great success, and Bacall went on to star in several more thrillers alongside Bogart, who she married in 1945, including *The Big Sleep* (1946), *Dark Passage* (1947), and *Key Largo* (1948), also starring **Edward G. Robinson**. Bacall also played lighter roles in *Bright Leaf* (1950) with **Gary Cooper** and in *How to Marry a Millionaire* (1953) with Marilyn Monroe and **Betty Grable**. After Bogart's death in 1957, her film career declined, and she turned to Broadway, where she won Tony Awards for her roles in *Applause* (1970) and *Woman of the Year* (1981). She appeared in films in the 1960s and 1970s and achieved some success in *Shock Treatment* (1964) and *Murder on the Orient Express* (1974). *See also* CINEMA.

BAER, MAX (1909–1959). Born Maximilian Adelbart Baer Cussen to German immigrant parents in Omaha, Nebraska, boxer Max Baer developed his strength and physique working on cattle ranches in Colorado. This power gave him a devastating right-hand punch and a fearsome reputation in the ring. He turned professional in 1929. In 1930, he was charged with manslaughter when his opponent Frankie Campbell died after Baer knocked him out. Although cleared, he was suspended for a year. Baer, who always indicated his Jewish origins with a Star of David on his trunks, knocked out the German boxer Max Schmeling in 1933, and the following year he felled the giant Italian **Primo Carnera** 11 times before finally knocking him out in the 11th round to become world heavy weight champion. In June 1935, he lost the title to the "Cinderella Man," **Jim Braddock**, but he continued fighting until 1941. He was twice beaten by **Joe Louis**.

Baer acted in a number of films, usually playing the role of a boxer, as in *The Prizefighter and the Lady* (1933) and *The Harder They Fall* (1956).

BALDWIN, RAYMOND EARL (1893–1986). Born in Rye, New York, Raymond Baldwin moved to Middletown, Connecticut, as a child, and it was in that state he made his political career. After being educated at Wesleyan University and serving in the U.S. Navy during World War I, he graduated from Yale Law School in 1921. He established a law practice in Bridgeport and New Haven, Connecticut. A **Republican**, Baldwin served as town prosecutor (1927–1930) and judge (1931–1933) in Stratford, and also sat as a representative in the Connecticut General Assembly (1930–1935). In 1938, he was elected state governor and, although defeated in 1940, he was reelected again in 1942 and 1944. As governor Baldwin was responsible for a wave of reform, including labor reform, the introduction of workmen's compensation, comprehensive pensions for state employees, and the creation of an Interracial Commission. In 1946, he was elected to the U.S. Senate but resigned in 1949 to become a justice on the Connecticut **Supreme Court**. He became chief justice of the court in 1959 and served until 1963.

BANKHEAD, JOHN HOLLIS (1872–1946). Born in Lamar County, Alabama, John H. Bankhead graduated from the University of Alabama in 1891, and from Georgetown University Law School in 1893. He and his brother **William B. Bankhead** established their own law company in 1905. A **Democrat**, from 1903 to 1907 John Bankhead was a member of the Alabama state legislature. In 1930, he was elected to the U.S. Senate—a position he held until 1946. Bankhead drafted several pieces of legislation relating to **agriculture**, particularly cotton, and he was coauthor of the revised **Agricultural**

Adjustment Act of 1938. *See also* BANKHEAD COTTON ACT; BANKHEAD COTTON CONTROL ACT.

BANKHEAD, WILLIAM BROCKMAN (1874–1940). Born in Lamar County, Alabama, William B. Bankhead graduated from the University of Alabama in 1893, and from Georgetown University Law School in Washington, D.C., in 1895. He practiced law in Huntsville, Alabama, where he became city attorney from 1898 to 1901. A **Democrat**, he was elected to the state House of Representatives in 1900 and 1901, and to the national House of Representatives in 1916. He served until 1940 and was majority leader from 1935 to 1937 and speaker of the House from 1935 to 1939. With his brother, **John H. Bankhead**, he was associated with legislation to aid cotton and tobacco farmers. *See also* AGRICULTURE; BANKHEAD COTTON ACT; BANKHEAD COTTON CONTROL ACT.

BANKHEAD COTTON ACT, 1934. The Bankhead Cotton Act was a supplement to the **Agricultural Adjustment Act** of 1933 introduced by **William B. Bankhead** and passed in 1934 to establish a national quota of cotton production in order to raise prices and to establish a tax to be imposed on any cotton produced in excess of individual quotas by licensed growers. A similar measure was introduced for tobacco. The act was repealed in 1936 after the **Supreme Court** had declared the Agricultural Adjustment Act of 1933 unconstitutional. *See also* AGRICULTURE.

BANKHEAD COTTON CONTROL ACT, 1934. Drafted by **John H. Bankhead** and **William B. Bankhead**, the Bankhead Cotton Control Act of 1934 supplemented the provisions of the **Agricultural Adjustment Act** of 1933 by taxing those farmers who produced excess cotton to limit production. When the Agricultural Adjustment Act of 1933 was declared unconstitutional in 1936, the act was repealed. *See also* AGRICULTURE.

BANKHEAD-JONES FARM TENANCY ACT, 1937. The Bankhead-Jones Farm Tenancy Act was an act passed in 1937 to help tenant farmers buy their own land, animals, and feed by providing low-interest federal loans over a three year period. The act was drafted by

Senator **John H. Bankhead** of Alabama and representative **Marvin Jones** of Texas. Under the legislation, Congress was also empowered to purchase land that was no longer capable of maintaining a sufficient living standard for farm families. The **Farm Security Administration** was set up by **Henry A. Wallace** to administer the program. The funding of $85 million proved inadequate, and few of the impoverished sharecroppers benefited. *See also* AGRICULTURE.

BANKING. Historically, banking in the United States was a complex political and economic issue. Opposition to a strong centralized government led to the demise of the National Bank in 1836. Although national banking was restored with the banking acts of 1863 and 1864, the banking system was complicated and inclined to instability. A three-tier system of national banks chartered by the federal government, state banks chartered by individual states, and local banks, all of which remained independent and essentially local businesses, existed. Lack of regulation and the impact of local events, such as problems in **agriculture**, often resulted in bank collapses. Bank panics—the worst being in 1907—and the 19th-century crisis in farming led to demands for regulation that resulted in the creation of the **Federal Reserve** in 1913. While this brought some stability, it did not solve all the problems as only about one-third of all banks registered with the Federal Reserve. Between 1921 and 1928 5,000 banks were forced to close.

With the collapse in investors' confidence following the **Wall Street Crash**, a further 1,345 banks failed in 1930 alone. Banking failure contributed enormously to the coming of the **Great Depression** as credit shrank and business loans and mortgages on homes and farms were called in. While President **Herbert Hoover** attempted to tackle the problem with a number of measures, many banks remained closed on the eve of **Franklin D. Roosevelt**'s inauguration. It was only with the banking reforms of the **New Deal**, beginning with an **Emergency Banking Act** of 9 March 1933, closing all the nation's banks temporarily in a "bank holiday," and then with the **Banking Acts** of 1933 and 1935, that some semblance of order and stability returned. In the process, some 1,000 banks were liquidated.

BANKING ACTS, 1933, 1935. The 1933 Banking Act, known as the Glass-Steagall Act, passed on 16 June 1933, restricted the use of the Federal Reserve for speculative purposes and established a **Federal Deposit Insurance Corporation** to insure money deposited by approved banks. The 1935 act reorganized the Federal Reserve Bank, reducing the Federal Reserve Board of governors. The act also strengthened the board's powers to limit speculation and required all large state banks to join the Federal Reserve system by 1942. *See also* BANKING.

BARKLEY, ALBEN WILLIAM (1877–1956). 35th vice president of the United States, 1949–1953. The son of poor tenant farmers, Alben Barkley was born and raised in Kentucky. After schooling in Kentucky, Barkley went to Emory College in Georgia, and then the University of Virginia Law School. He was admitted to the bar in 1901 and practiced law in Paducah, Kentucky, where he became prosecuting attorney and then judge of McCracken County Court, from 1909 to 1913. A **Democrat** and Woodrow Wilson supporter, he was elected to the House of Representatives in 1913 and held his seat until he became a U. S. Senator in 1927. He was reelected three times and served as Democratic majority leader in the Senate from 1937 to 1947 and minority leader from 1947 to 1949. A supporter of **Franklin D. Roosevelt**, in 1944 Barkley resigned when the president rejected the tax bill he had brokered; Roosevelt backed down and Barkley was reelected majority leader.

An effective public speaker and a popular senator acceptable to the South, Barkley ran successfully as vice presidential candidate with **Harry S. Truman** in 1948, despite his age. Referred to as "Veep," Barkley supported the treaty that created the **North Atlantic Treaty Organization**, involvement in the **Korean War**, and the dismissal of General **Douglas MacArthur**. After serving as vice president, he was regarded as too old to be the presidential candidate in 1952, but he was reelected to the Senate and served from 1955 until his death in 1956.

BARTON, BRUCE FAIRCHILD (1886–1967). Born in Tennessee, Bruce Barton graduated from Amherst College in 1907. After a series of jobs in newspaper and magazine journalism, he became assistant sales manager for the publisher Colliers in 1912 and then editor of *Every Week* in 1914, where he developed the skill of writing inspirational articles. He became a regular contributor of such work to the *American Magazine, McCall's, Collier's, Good Housekeeping*, and *Reader's Digest*. Several volumes of his writings were published between 1917 and 1924.

During World War I, Barton worked as publicity director for the United War Work Agencies. In 1919, he joined Roy S. Durstine and Alex F. Osborne to form an advertising agency that by 1928 was the fourth largest in the United States. In 1925, Barton published the best-selling *The Man Nobody Knows*, in which he portrayed Christ as "the world's greatest salesman." He also wrote a study of the Bible in a similar vein, *The Book Nobody Knows* (1926), and a portrait of St. Paul, *He Upset the World* (1932).

A **Republican**, Barton supported and wrote speeches for Calvin Coolidge. In 1937, he was elected to fill an unexpired term in Congress as a representative for New York. He won a full term in 1938. He campaigned against the **New Deal**, and together with **Joseph Martin** and **Hamilton Fish**, was ridiculed by **Franklin D. Roosevelt** as one of "Martin, Barton & Fish" during the 1940 election campaign. He failed to win election to the Senate in 1940 and returned to his advertising company. Barton continued to advise Republican politicians, including **Thomas E. Dewey** and **Dwight D. Eisenhower**.

BARUCH, BERNARD MANNES (1870–1965). Born in South Carolina, after graduating from City College in New York, Bernard Baruch became a financier and successful Wall Street broker and investor. He supported Woodrow Wilson in 1912 and was appointed to the Advisory Commission to the Council of National Defense in 1916. In 1918, he became chairman of the War Industries Board, where he directed the industrial war effort. He helped formulate the economic provisions of the Versailles Treaty. Baruch was less in the public eye during the 1920s and 1930s. His plans for wartime industrial mobilization were presented to the Senate Military Affairs Committee in 1937. As special "park bench" adviser to **Franklin D. Roosevelt**'s administration during **World War II**, he chaired the Rubber Survey Committee that drafted an influential report on rubber rationing, and he also authored a report on postwar conversion. In 1946, President **Harry S. Truman** named the 70-five-year-old Baruch to present the U.S. plan for the international control of atomic energy drafted by

Dean Acheson and **David E. Lilienthal**, but known as the **Baruch Plan**, to the **United Nations**. Despite a dramatic opening speech by Baruch, the negotiations came to naught due to a veto by the **Soviet Union**. Baruch's influence subsequently declined.

BARUCH PLAN, 1946. The Baruch Plan was the proposal to control the use of atomic power presented to the **United Nations Atomic Energy Commission** in 1946 by **Bernard Baruch**. It called for the information about nuclear power to be made open, the implementation of international controls to ensure the peaceful use of atomic power, the elimination of atomic weapons, and a system of international inspection to ensure compliance. The proposal was rejected by the **Soviet Union** because it opposed the principle of external inspectors, which it saw as a threat to its national sovereignty. *See also* ATOMIC BOMB; HYDROGEN BOMB.

BASTOGNE. A key battle in the **Battle of the Bulge** during **World War II**, Bastogne was a village in Belgium where several important roads converged and where U.S. forces held the attacking German army between December 1944 and January 1945. Offered the opportunity to surrender, the U.S. commander simply replied "Nuts," and General **George S. Patton**'s forces relieved the siege and the Germans were pushed back.

BATAAN. Bataan is the peninsula on the island of Luzon in the Philippines where General **Douglas MacArthur** took a stand against the advancing Japanese army in January 1942. While MacArthur withdrew in March to head the buildup of U.S. forces elsewhere, together with Filipino troops, U.S. forces held out in Bataan for three months before being forced to surrender in April. Some 75,000 prisoners were then force-marched more than 100 miles in a week to camps, enduring harsh treatment and high temperatures en route. Almost 10,000 soldiers died as a result. The battle had, however, significantly slowed the Japanese advance and gave U.S. forces a chance to regroup in the Pacific. Bataan was liberated from the Japanese by U.S. forces in February 1945. *See also* JAPAN; WORLD WAR II.

BATTLE OF THE BULGE. In December 1944, German forces launched a strong counteroffensive against U.S. forces in the Ardennes region of Europe, forcing them back a distance of 60 miles and creating a huge bulge in **Allied** lines. Two entire U.S. regiments were forced to surrender. However, a successful counteroffensive was launched, and the German armies were pushed back by the end of January 1945. Although U.S. losses numbered almost 40,000, the Germans lost more than 200,000, and this was their last offensive effort of **World War II**.

BEER AND WINE REVENUE ACT, 1933. Passed on 22 March 1933 the Beer Act repealed the Volstead Act of 1919 and confirmed the end of prohibition under the **Twenty-First Amendment** to the Constitution. It permitted the manufacture and sale of alcohol, as well as raising revenue by taxing alcoholic beverages.

BENNY, JACK (1894–1974). Comedian Jack Benny was born Benjamin Kubelsky to a Russian immigrant father and Lithuanian mother in Chicago. He began his career in vaudeville at the age of 18 as Ben K. Benny. During World War I, Benny served in the navy and perfected his comedy routine performing to naval audiences. After the war, he took the name Jack and presented himself as a "monologist." In 1926 Benny performed on Broadway in the musical revue *The Great Temptations*, and his success led to a film contract with Metro-Goldwyn-Mayer (MGM) film studios. After appearing in a number of films, including *Hollywood Revue of 1929* (1929), *Chasing Rainbows* (1930), and *The Medicine Man* (1930), Benny returned to the stage to do a musical revue. This led to a radio performance and the beginning of a radio show that ran from 1932 until 1955. More than a series of jokes, Benny's program involved a narrative of regular characters, most notably "Rochester," played by **Eddie Anderson**.

Benny continued to appear in movies, most famously *To Be or Not to Be* (1942). Others included *George Washington Slept Here* (1942), *The Meanest Man in the World* (1943), and *The Horn Blows at Midnight* (1945). In 1948, Benny switched from NBC to CBS, and his radio program ran on the CBS network until 1955 when it transferred to **television**. After a slow start, the television program established itself and ran until 1965. Benny continued to appear in nightclub shows and gave "musical" performances with his violin for charitable causes almost until his death. *See also* CINEMA.

BENTON, THOMAS HART (1889–1975). Born in Neosho, Missouri, Thomas Hart Benton briefly attended military school before going to study at Chicago Art Institute in 1906 and then in Paris from 1908 to 1911. In 1913, he moved to New York City, where he had his first successful show in 1916 as part of a modernist collection in the Forum exhibition. He served in the navy during World War I and afterward abandoned modernism in favor of the **American scene** and the rural emphasis associated with **regionalism** during the 1930s. During the 1920s, he completed 18 works as part of *The American Historical Epic*, and in 1930 he produced a series of murals entitled *America Today*. The vibrant colors and depictions of ordinary working people led some critics to compare him to both right- and left-wing art. His Indiana murals painted in 1933 to mark a *Century of Progress* and those in *The Social History of the State of Missouri* in the state capitol in Jefferson, Missouri, celebrated American settlement but also depicted scenes of racism and violence. Nonetheless, Benton made the cover of *Time* magazine in December 1934 and was regarded as one of the country's leading artists.

The richness of color and content in Benton's voluptuous rural scenes, such as *Cradling Wheat* (1938) and *Threshing Wheat* (1939), were in stark contrast to the arid landscapes of the **Dust Bowl** recorded by the photographers of the **Farm Security Administration**. His autobiography, *An Artist in America*, appeared in 1937. From 1935 to 1941 Benton taught at the Kansas City Art Institute, where one of his students was **Jackson Pollock**, and during **World War II** he produced several paintings of Nazi atrocities. Although his style went out of fashion in the 1940s and 1950s, in 1961 he completed another mural depicting historical scenes, *Independence and the Opening of the West*, in the **Truman** library in Independence, Missouri.

BENTON, WILLIAM BURNETT (1900–1973). Born in Minneapolis, Minnesota, and educated at Shattuck Military Academy and Carleton College in Northfield, Minnesota, William Benton graduated from Yale University in 1921 and entered advertising. In 1929, he established Benton & Bowles with **Chester Bowles**. In 1937, he became vice president of the University of Chicago and in 1943 was instrumental in the university's acquisition of *Encyclopedia Britannica*, which he managed and later purchased. Benton served as assistant secretary of state from 1945 to 1947, and although a **Democrat**, was appointed to the U.S. Senate for Connecticut in 1949 to fill the post following the resignation of **Republican** incumbent **Raymond Baldwin**. Benton was an outspoken critic of **Joseph McCarthy**, who in turn labeled the Connecticut senator a communist sympathizer. As a result, Benton failed to win the election in 1952. He then concentrated on his publishing business, which expanded in 1964 when he took over *Webster's Dictionary*. From 1963 until 1968 Benton was U.S. ambassador to the **United Nations Educational, Scientific, and Cultural Organization** in Paris.

BERKELEY, BUSBY (1895–1976). Born Busby Berkeley William Enos in Los Angles, California, the film choreographer and director attended military school and was first employed in entertainment by the army in France during World War I. After the war, he worked as an actor and stage manager. Berkeley's first dance directing was in the musical *A Connecticut Yankee* (1927). After a series of successful Broadway musicals including *Street Singer* (1929), Berkeley went to Hollywood and staged the dances in *Whoopee* starring **Eddie Cantor** in 1930. In 1933, he had three big hits with Warner Brothers' film musicals, *42nd Street*, *Gold Diggers of 1933*, and *Footlight Parade*, that established his trademark style of lavish singing and dancing routines with large numbers of chorus girls performing eye-catching routines in geometric formations often shot to appear in kaleidoscopic images.

After leaving Warner Brothers for Metro-Goldwyn-Mayer (MGM), Berkeley provided choreography and direction for a number of movies starring **Judy Garland** and **Mickey Rooney**, including *Babes in Arms* (1939), *Strike Up the Band* (1940), *Babes on Broadway* (1941), and *Girl Crazy* (1943). He also worked on *The Gang's All Here* (1943), memorable for even more elaborate sets and costumes. After the war, Berkeley directed *Take Me Out to the Ball Game* (1949) and choreographed *Million Dollar Mermaid* (1952) and *Easy to Love* (1953). His last film was *Jumbo* in 1962. *See also* CINEMA; LITERATURE AND THEATER.

BERLE, ADOLF AUGUSTUS (1895–1971). Born in Boston, Massachusetts, Adolph Berle was a child prodigy who graduated with a B.A. and M.A. in history, a law degree, and passage to the bar all by the age of 21. Although a pacifist, he served in the Signal Corps during World War I and then attended the Paris Peace Conference as a delegate in 1918 but resigned over the terms of the Versailles peace treaty. He became professor of corporate law at Columbia Law School in 1927 and held the post until he retired in 1963. Berle wrote several major books on law, including, with Gardiner C. Means, *The Modern Corporation and Private Property* (1932), *The 20th Century Capitalist Revolution* (1954), and *Power without Property* (1959).

In the 1930s Berle became a member of President **Franklin D. Roosevelt**'s "**Brain Trust**" and also an adviser to Mayor **Fiorello La Guardia** of New York. During **World War II**, Berle was appointed assistant secretary of state for Latin affairs, and from 1945 to 1946 he was ambassador to Brazil. In 1961, Berle was one of the advisers who helped shape President John F. Kennedy's Alliance for Progress Policy for Latin America. His book, *Latin America: Diplomacy and Reality*, was published in 1962.

BERLIN. This capital of **Germany** was overrun by the Red Army in 1945, bringing an end to **World War II**. Under the **Potsdam** Agreement, the city was divided between east and west, with the three **Allied powers**—the United States, **Great Britain**, and France—each holding a sector in the west, and the **Soviet Union (USSR)** holding the east. However, the city became the focus of growing disagreements about the postwar future of Germany and the payment of reparations. When the Allies proposed unifying the sectors and introduced a common currency in 1948, the USSR imposed a land blockade. The Allies responded with the **Berlin airlift**. Berlin remained divided; in April 1961, a wall symbolizing the divisions between East and West in the **Cold War** was built on the East German side. It remained in place until November 1989, when its destruction indicated the collapse of the communist regime and end of the Cold War.

BERLIN, IRVING (1888–1989). Born Israel Isidore Baline in Russia, Berlin's family moved to the United States in 1893 and settled in New York's Lower East Side. He was forced to work from an early age and did a variety of casual jobs, including being a singing waiter. However, Berlin began writing songs. His first published song in 1907 included a misprint of his name, which he then changed to Irving Berlin. From 1908 to 1911 he mainly wrote lyrics for other people's music, but in 1911 he achieved his first major success with "Alexander's Rag-time Band." Berlin entered the army during World War I and staged the revue *Yip Yip Yaphank*. Following the war he wrote for the *Ziegfeld Follies* before establishing his own theater, The Music Box. After moderate success, he went through a fairly unproductive period from 1927 to 1932, although one of his hit songs was "Blue Skies" performed by Al Jolson in the movie *The Jazz Singer* (1927). He began to write hit songs again with **Rudy Vallee**'s "How Deep Is the Ocean" (1932) and then had a string of hits with the Broadway revue *As Thousands Cheer* (1933), including the songs "Easter Parade," "Harlem on My Mind," and "Heat Wave." He also wrote the music for the movie *Top Hat* (1935), starring **Fred Astaire** and **Ginger Rogers**, and won an Oscar for the song "Cheek to Cheek."

Berlin's film success continued during the war with *Holiday Inn*, featuring **Bing Crosby** singing "White Christmas"—the song that became the most played Christmas song—and the reprise of *Yip Yip Yaphank* retitled *This is the Army* (1943) based on the revue that had first been staged in 1942. It now included "God Bless America," a song first performed by Katie Smith in 1938, which was so popular during the war it almost became the nation's anthem. His contribution to the nation was recognized by President **Harry S. Truman** with the award of the Medal of Merit in 1945.

Berlin was a huge success after the war with one of his greatest musicals, *Annie Get Your Gun* (1946), produced by **Richard Rodgers** and **Oscar Hammerstein**, including the songs "There's No Business Like Show Business" and "Anything You Can Do." The musical was made into a film in 1950. The movie *Easter Parade* appeared in 1948. However, Berlin's subsequent productions, *Miss Liberty* (1949) and *Mr. President* (1962), were regarded as flops, and he largely retired thereafter. He did, however, write "I Like Ike," the campaign song for **Dwight D. Eisenhower** in 1952. Berlin is remembered as one of greatest songwriters. *See also* CINEMA; LITERATURE AND THEATER.

BERLIN AIRLIFT. Following the imposition of a land blockade on **Berlin** by the **Soviet Union** in April 1948, the United States and **Great Britain** began to fly in food, fuel, and other necessities to sustain the population in the **Allied** sectors of the city. The blockade was finally lifted at the end of September 1949, by which time the Allies had flown in more than 2 million tons of supplies in Operation Vittles. In maintaining their control in West Berlin the Allies had won a major victory in the newly begun **Cold War**.

BETHUNE, MARY MCLEOD (1875–1955). Born one of 17 children to former slave parents in South Carolina, Mary McCleod Bethune attended a one-room schoolhouse before gaining a college education. She taught in Georgia and South Carolina and then established the Daytona Normal and Industrial Institute for Negro Girls in Florida in 1904, which became the Bethune-Cookman College in 1929. An active member and later vice president of the **National Association for the Advancement of Colored People (NAACP)**, Bethune was also a leader in the organization of black **women**'s clubs and president of the National Association of Colored Women from 1924–1928. From 1936 to 1950 she was president of the Association for the Study of Negro Life and History.

Bethune took part in the National Commission for Child Welfare during the administration of **Herbert Hoover**, and in 1936 **Franklin D. Roosevelt** appointed her director of Negro Affairs in the **National Youth Administration (NYA)**. She was the first black woman to hold such a high-ranking federal position. Her role made her an important member of the **Black Cabinet**. She returned to teaching when the NYA came to an end in 1943 but advised the War Department on the appointment of black women army officers for the **Women's Army Corps**. In 1945, Bethune was one of several black advisers to attend the **United Nations** meetings in San Francisco, California. Her work in race relations was recognized with awards from several African countries in addition to the NAACP's Spingarn Medal and numerous honorary degrees. *See also* AFRICAN AMERICANS.

BIDDLE, FRANCIS BEVERLEY (1886–1968). Born in Paris, France, to a wealthy American family, Francis Biddle graduated from

Groton in 1905 and Harvard Law School in 1911 and was employed as a secretary to **Supreme Court** Justice Oliver Wendell Holmes. Having failed to get elected to the Pennsylvania state senate in 1912, Biddle began a private law practice. He was assistant U.S. attorney for the Eastern District of Pennsylvania from 1922 to 1926, but during the 1930s he changed allegiance from the **Republican Party** to the **Democratic Party**. In 1935, **Franklin D. Roosevelt** appointed Biddle as chair of the **National Labor Relations Board (NLRB)**. He resigned in 1935 when the NLRB was declared unconstitutional but was appointed judge on the U.S. Circuit Court of appeals for the Third Circuit in 1939. In 1940, Biddle became U.S. solicitor general and then attorney general in 1941. He was responsible for the implementation of the internment of **Japanese Americans** during the war, an act he subsequently regretted. He was also responsible for the removal of **Sewell Avery** from his office in 1944. Biddle resigned as attorney general in 1945 when **Harry S. Truman** became president and was one of the four judges at the **Nuremberg War Trials** from 1945 to 1947. From 1950 to 1953 he was head of the liberal **Americans for Democratic Action**. Biddle was a writer as well as lawyer, and among his publications were a novel, *Llanfear Pattern* (1927), a biography of Oliver Wendell Holmes, *Mr. Justice Holmes* (1942), a critique of **McCarthyism**, *Fear of Freedom* (1951), and his own memoirs, *A Casual Past* (1961) and *Brief Authority* (1962).

BILBO, THEODORE GILMORE (1877–1947). Born in Juniper Grove, Mississippi, Theodore Bilbo attended Peabody College in Nashville from 1897 to 1899 but left without graduating. After teaching briefly, he also attended Vanderbilt Law School in 1905 but again left without graduating. Nonetheless, he was admitted to the bar in 1907 and, a **Democrat**, he was elected to the state senate in 1907 but expelled in 1910 for his involvement in an election scandal. In 1911, Bilbo was elected lieutenant governor, and in 1915 he became governor despite further charges of political corruption. He was a progressive governor who raised taxes and increased appropriations for education and a state highway system. He failed to win reelection in 1923 but was successful in 1927. Bilbo was elected to the U.S. Senate in 1934, where, unlike many other southern Democrats and, although an outspoken racist, he remained a staunch supporter of

Franklin D. Roosevelt and the **New Deal**. He was reelected in 1946 but was denied his seat by the Senate because of charges that he had advocated violence against black veterans who tried to register to vote. He died of cancer shortly after.

BLACK, HUGO LAFAYETTE (1886–1971). One of the longest-serving **Supreme Court** justices, Hugo Black was born near Ashland, Alabama. Educated at Ashland College, he graduated from Alabama Law School in Tuscaloosa in 1906 and practiced law in Birmingham. Black joined the army in 1917 and became a captain in the artillery but did not see action. He was elected to the U.S. Senate in 1927 and served until 1937. From 1935 he chaired the Senate Committee on Education and Labor and supported the initial legislation to introduce minimum wages and maximum hours that eventually became the **Fair Labor Standards Act**.

In 1937, President **Franklin D. Roosevelt** nominated Black to succeed **Willis Van Devanter** on the Supreme Court. In the furor following Roosevelt's attempted "**court packing**," the nomination was referred to the Judiciary Committee before going before the Senate for approval. Questions were asked both about the constitutional issue of appointing someone still sitting in Congress and about Black's past connections with the Ku Klux Klan, which Black denied. The nomination was approved, but when the **African American** newspaper the *Pittsburgh Courier* revealed that he had defended a Klansman for murder in 1921 and been a Klan member himself from 1923 until 1925, Black was forced to broadcast a retraction of his denial on radio, and he indicated that his membership had been brief and insignificant. His subsequent career in the court, with a commitment to upholding the Bill of Rights, often demonstrated sympathy for **civil rights** causes and decisions affecting African Americans, such as *Shelley v. Kraemer* and later *Brown v. Board of Education of Topeka*.

Although an advocate of the literal reading of the Constitution, Black supported the expansive use of federal power in matters of commerce and supported decisions to uphold **New Deal** legislation. With **William O. Douglas**, Black dissented from the decisions upholding convictions of members of the **Communist Party of the United States of America (CPUSA)** under the **Smith Act**. He also argued for strict separation of church and state. However, he wrote the majority opinion upholding the government's decision to intern **Japanese Americans** in *Korematsu v. United States*, argued in favor of the use of wiretapping, and argued against the notion of constitutional guarantees to rights of privacy. Although a supporter of the principle of free speech, Black distinguished between "speech" and "action" and dissented when the court ruled to allow flag burning or wearing obscene slogans in 1969 and 1971, respectively. He also did not agree that the Constitution prohibited use of the death penalty. He retired shortly before his death.

BLACK CABINET. The Black Cabinet was an informal network of the more than 40 **African Americans** appointed to positions in various federal agencies by the **New Deal** by 1936. It included **Mary McLeod Bethune**, **Ralph Bunche**, **William H. Hastie**, and **Robert C. Weaver**. This black presence in government contributed significantly in the switch in political allegiance of black voters from the **Republican Party** to the **Democratic Party** in the 1930s.

BLACKLIST. Following the citation of the **Hollywood Ten** for contempt in 1947, leaders of the major Hollywood film studios met in New York City in 1947 and agreed that the 10 and any other known communists or communist sympathizers should not be employed in the film industry. The Motion Picture Association of America endorsed the decision in November 1947, and the blacklist operated until 1960. *See also* CINEMA; MCCARTHYISM.

BLOCK, HERBERT (1909–2001). Better known as Herblock, Herbert Block was a political cartoonist. He began work with the *Chicago Daily News* but moved in the 1930s to Newspaper Enterprises, where he became known as a supporter of **Franklin D. Roosevelt** and the **New Deal**. He joined the *Washington Post* in 1946 and stayed there for the remainder of his career. Known for his liberal views, Herblock was critical of **Joseph McCarthy** and coined the phrase "**McCarthyism**." He was awarded the Pulitzer Prize for his cartoons in 1942, 1954, and 1979, and the Presidential Medal of Freedom in 1994.

BLUE EAGLE. A blue American eagle was the symbol of the **National Recovery Administration** and was used in advertising and posters with the slogan "We Do Our Part" to demonstrate that the company or employer had signed up to the codes of fair competition, wages, and prices.

BOARD OF WAR COMMUNICATIONS. The Board of War Communications was a federal agency established by executive order on 24 September 1940 to coordinate the use of the **radio**, telegraph, and telephone during a war emergency. After **Pearl Harbor**, the board, composed of the chair of the **Federal Communications Commission**, the chief of the Army Signal Corps, the director of Naval Communications, and representatives from the State Department and Treasury, was empowered to establish priorities and use, control, or close any communications service deemed necessary for the war effort. It ceased operation in 1947. *See also* WORLD WAR II.

BOGART, HUMPHREY DEFOREST (1899–1957). Born into a wealthy family in New York City, Humphrey Bogart served in the navy during World War I and then held a variety of jobs before finding work in the theater in the 1920s. In 1931, he signed a contract with Fox but was not particularly successful until he appeared in *The Petrified Forest* in 1936. Rather than being conventionally handsome, his rugged looks suited him for parts as a well-worn, world-weary character like those described in the novels of **Dashiell Hammett** and **Raymond Chandler**. Bogart appeared as the hero in both *The Maltese Falcon* (1941) and *The Big Sleep* (1946). Among his best films are *High Sierra* (1941), *Casablanca* (1942), *To Have and Have Not* (1944) with **Lauren Bacall**, *The Treasure of the Sierra Madre* (1948), *Key Largo* (1948) with Bacall and **Edward G. Robinson**, *The African Queen* (1951), *The Caine Mutiny* (1954), and *The Desperate Hours* (1955). He won Academy Awards for both *The African Queen* and *The Caine Mutiny*. Bogart actively campaigned against the **House Un-American Activities Committee**'s investigations of Hollywood in 1947 and the introduction of the **blacklist**. However, faced with criticism in the press, he did not pursue this position. Bogart died of cancer in 1957.

BOHLEN, CHARLES EUSTIS (1904–1974). Born in New York, raised in South Carolina, and educated in Massachusetts, Charles Bohlen graduated from Harvard University in 1927 with a specialization in European history. He entered the Foreign Service in 1929 and after serving in Prague and Paris in 1934 was posted to the embassy in Moscow. After a brief return to Washington, D.C., Bohlen was back in Moscow in 1938 and then Tokyo in 1940. He was interned after the attack on **Pearl Harbor** but returned to the United States in 1942. Bohlen's experience and knowledge of Russia made him a key adviser on **Soviet** affairs, and he acted as interpreter to President **Franklin D. Roosevelt** at the **Tehran Conference**, the **Yalta Conference**, and to President **Harry S. Truman** at the **Potsdam Conference**. Bohlen also attended the **San Francisco Conference** and was an adviser to Secretaries of State **James F. Byrnes, George C. Marshall**, and **Dean Acheson**. He was nominated to become ambassador to the **Soviet Union (USSR)** in 1953 and was approved by the Senate despite criticism from **Joseph McCarthy** because of his sympathetic attitude toward the USSR. From 1957 to 1959 Bohlen was ambassador to the Philippines, until he became principal adviser to Secretary of State Christian Herter. From 1962 until 1968 he was ambassador to France. He was also an adviser to President John F. Kennedy. Bohlen wrote two books, *The Transformation of American Foreign Policy* (1969) and *Witness to History* (1973).

BONUS ACT, 1936. Passed in January 1936 over President **Franklin D. Roosevelt**'s veto, the Bonus Act authorized the immediate payment of the bonus due to veterans of World War I. The payment had been due to be paid in 1945, but protests from veterans, such as the **Bonus Army**, forced Congress to bring the payment forward.

BONUS ARMY. In 1932, unemployed veterans of World War I organized a Bonus Expeditionary Force to march on Washington to petition for early payment of bonuses approved in 1924 and due to be paid in 1945. The Bonus Army of 15,000 to 20,000 men established a camp on the Anacostia Flats in Washington, D.C. A Bonus Bill was approved by the House of Representatives but rejected by the Senate in June 1932. Many of the marchers left the capital, and in July the administration of **Herbert Hoover**, fearing the possibility of violence, ordered the eviction of the remaining individuals. A military force, including tanks, led by General **Douglas MacArthur**, used teargas and bayonets to drive out the veterans and their families before setting fire to the camp. One veteran was shot dead by police during the confrontation. The images of the veterans fleeing in the face of troops with bayonets drawn and the burning camp against the backdrop of the Capitol buildings were widely shown on newsreels and in newspapers and contributed to the growing unpopularity of President Hoover. *See also* BONUS ACT, 1936.

BORAH, WILLIAM EDGAR (1865–1940). After a limited education in Kansas, William Borah passed the bar examinations in law in 1887 and practiced for three years before moving to Idaho. Having stood unsuccessfully for the U.S. House of Representatives as a **Democrat** in 1896, Borah turned to the **Republicans** as a candidate for the Senate in 1902. Unsuccessful again, he was eventually elected in 1906. Borah served six successive terms and was known for his oratory and political independence. In domestic matters, he had progressive tendencies, supporting antitrust legislation, the income tax, popular election of senators, and prohibition. On issues of **foreign policy**, he was one of the leading opponents of the Versailles Treaty and League of Nations, but he supported the Washington Conference from 1921–1922. As chairman of the Foreign Relations Committee from 1924 to 1933, he helped secure ratification of the Kellogg-Briand Pact in 1928.

During the 1930s, Borah departed from his own party line to support such **New Deal** measures as the **Social Security Act** and the **National Labor Relations Act**, but he also disapproved of other **New Deal** measures, like the **National Industrial Recovery Act**. In 1936, he attempted to win the Republican presidential nomination but was unsuccessful. He was, however, able to use his position on the Senate Judiciary Committee to help block President **Franklin D. Roosevelt**'s attempt at "**court packing**." As a leading isolationist, Borah supported the **Neutrality Acts** but was unable to prevent Roosevelt's revision of them.

BOULDER DAM. *See* HOOVER DAM.

BOURKE-WHITE, MARGARET (1904–1971). Margaret White (she later added her mother's name) was born in New York City. She studied at the University of Michigan and Cornell University, where she graduated with a degree in biology in 1927. She had already begun to develop her skill as a photographer, and her work photographing the steel mills of Cleveland brought her to the attention of **Henry Luce**, who offered her a position as associate editor and photographer at *Fortune* magazine in 1929. She remained there until 1933. In the meantime, Bourke-White produced *Eyes on Russia* in 1931. She joined *Life* magazine in 1936 and worked there until 1957, continuing to contribute even after her retirement. During the 1930s, Bourke-White, like **Dorothea Lange**, documented the plight of those hit by the **Dust Bowl**. She also collaborated with **Erskine Caldwell** (to whom she was briefly married) on *You Have Seen Their Faces* (1937), *North of the Danube* (1939), and *Russia at War* (1942). During **World War II**, Bourke-White was accredited with the U.S. Air Force. She was later in Moscow during the attack by the Nazi forces, and in 1945 she was present when General **George S. Patton** liberated Buchenwald concentration camp. After the war, she went on photojournalist assignments in India from 1946 to 1949 and South Africa from 1949 to 1950. She was in Korea in 1952 during the **Korean War**.

BOWLES, CHESTER BLISS (1901–1986). Born in Springfield, Massachusetts, Chester Bowles attended Choate Rosemary Hall School in Connecticut and then went to Yale University, where he graduated with a B.S. in science in 1924. After working as a journalist, he became an advertising copywriter, and in 1929 he established his own advertising agency with **William Burnett Benton**. He sold his share in 1941 and became director of the Connecticut **Office of Price Administration (OPA)** in 1942. He was appointed director of the national OPA in 1943 and held the position until 1946, when he was appointed director of the **Office of Economic Stabilization**. He also attended the **United Nations Educational, Scientific, and Cultural Organization** conference in Paris as one of the U.S. delegates and served briefly as a special adviser in the **United Nations**. In 1948, Bowles was elected governor of Connecticut, but his liberal policies (including desegregating the state national guard) cost him reelection in 1950.

From 1951 until 1953, Bowles was U.S. ambassador to India. He was elected for one term to the House of Representatives in 1958 and failed on several attempts to become a senator for Connecticut. John F. Kennedy appointed him as a **foreign policy** adviser, and in 1961 he became undersecretary of state but lost the position because of his opposition to the Bay of Pigs attack on Cuba. After serving as an ambassador at large, he was again appointed ambassador to India in 1963, a position he held until 1968. Bowles was the author of several books dealing with different aspects of his career, among them *The Conscience of a Liberal* (1962) and *Promises to Keep: My Public Life* (1971).

BRACEROS. *Braceros* (meaning "open arms") were Mexican workers imported into the United States by agreement with the Mexican government in 1942 to fill labor shortages during **World War II**, particularly in **agriculture**. It is estimated that some 200,000 workers entered the United States under this agreement, mostly to work in southern California, New Mexico, and Texas; another 200,000 Mexican workers probably entered the country illegally. *See also* HISPANIC AMERICANS; LOS ANGELES RIOT.

BRADDOCK, JAMES WALTER (1906–1974). Born in New York City but raised in Guttenberg, New Jersey, Jim Braddock began boxing as a teenager and turned professional in 1926. Fighting as a light heavyweight, he fought for the title in 1929 but lost to the holder, Tommy Loughran. Following the **Wall Street Crash**, Braddock's investments were lost when his taxicab company failed. He fought 33 fights between 1929 and 1933 and lost all but 10. He also suffered a broken hand and was forced to work as a stevedore. In 1934, he made a comeback as a heavyweight, defeating John Griffin in three rounds. After two more successful bouts, he was matched against heavyweight champion **Max Baer** on 13 June 1935. Although considered the underdog, Braddock defeated Baer and earned the nickname "Cinderella Man." He held the title until June 1937, when **Joe Louis** finally knocked him out in the eighth round. He retired after one more successful fight. During **World War II**, Braddock enlisted in the army and rose to the rank of captain. After the war, he found successful employment as a marine equipment operator and supplier. *See also* SPORT.

BRADLEY, OMAR NELSON (1893–1981). Born in Missouri, Omar Bradley graduated from West Point Military Academy in 1915, a contemporary of **Douglas MacArthur**, **Dwight D. Eisenhower**, and **George S. Patton**. Bradley served in the infantry on the Mexican border in 1915 before being posted to service in Montana during World War I. After the war, he taught at West Point; served in Hawaii; attended General Staff School at Fort Leavenworth, Texas; and in 1938 joined the War Department. During **World War II**, he served under Patton in North Africa in 1942 and took part in the invasion of Sicily in 1943. He was given command of the U.S. First Army in June 1944 and commanded the **Normandy landings** at **Utah Beach** and **Omaha Beach**. Known as the "the soldiers' general," it was Bradley who successfully planned and led the **Allied** breakout from Normandy in "Operation Cobra" and almost achieved a smashing victory at Falaise. Bradley also commanded U.S. troops during the **Battle of the Bulge**; later it was his forces that crossed the Rhine and captured the crucial bridge at Remagen and in April 1945 met **Soviet** troops on the Elbe, effectively bringing the war in Europe to an end.

In 1945, Bradley returned to Washington, D.C., as head of the Veterans' Administration rather than being sent to **Japan**. In 1945, he became chief of staff and in 1949 chair of the Joint Chiefs of Staff. The following year Bradley was made general of the army and chair of the **North Atlantic Treaty Organization** committee. In this capacity, he resisted MacArthur's attempts to expand the war in **Korea** into open conflict with **China**, saying it would be "the wrong war, at the wrong place, at the wrong time, and with the wrong enemy." He retired in 1953. Bradley's memoirs, *A Soldier's Story* and *A General's Story*, were published in 1951 and 1983, respectively.

BRAIN TRUST. Sometimes known as the "Brains Trust," this group of academic advisers was formed by President **Franklin D. Roosevelt** in March 1932 to help plan the **"First Hundred Days"** of the **New Deal**. The group initially consisted of three professors from Columbia University, **Raymond Moley**, **Rexford Tugwell**, and

Adolph Berle, but they were joined by Basil O'Connor, Samuel I. Rosenman, Hugh Johnson, Robert Lovett, and Frances Perkins. Named the Brains Trust by *New York Times* reporter James M. Kiernan, the group was often attacked in the press for their idealism. Although the original group ceased after 1933, Roosevelt continued to draw upon academics and lawyers for advice and to help write speeches on a number of issues.

BRANDEIS, LOUIS DEMBITZ (1856–1941). The son of Austrian immigrants, future **Supreme Court** Justice Louis Brandeis was born in Louisville, Kentucky. After traveling in Europe and studying in Dresden, Germany, Brandeis returned to the United States in 1875 and entered Harvard Law School. He graduated in 1877 with the highest grades ever achieved. Brandeis practiced law briefly in St. Louis and then returned to Boston. He gradually developed a reputation as a progressive lawyer who favored equal protection of **trade unions** in their relations with business and who opposed monopoly. In the landmark case of *Muller v. Oregon* (1908), Brandeis used statistical and other information rather than legal precedent to establish that long hours of work were potentially harmful to **women** and persuaded the Supreme Court to uphold Oregon's laws limiting the hours of work for females. He also supported the prohibition of child labor and laws introducing unemployment and old-age insurance. He backed the candidacy of Woodrow Wilson, who, in turn, appointed Brandeis to the Supreme Court in 1916.

As a Supreme Court justice, Brandeis argued for the qualification on the principle of "clear and present danger" established by Justice Oliver Wendell Holmes in upholding wartime espionage legislation in *Schenck v. United States* (1919), arguing in 1920 and 1927 that the danger had to be "serious" and "imminent." In 1928 he argued that wiretapping was a violation of the Fourth Amendment. He was sympathetic to much of the **New Deal** but opposed what he saw as excessive centralization. Although with **Benjamin Cardozo** and **Harlan Stone** Brandeis was regarded as one of the "liberal" bloc, he voted with the rest of the Court on "Black Monday" to declare the **National Industrial Recovery Act** unconstitutional. The oldest justice at the time, Brandeis was personally offended by President

Franklin D. Roosevelt's "**court packing**" proposals. In the end, he was forced to retire because of ill health in 1939. Brandeis University was named after him.

BRANNAN, CHARLES FRANKLIN (1903–1992). Harry S. Truman's secretary of agriculture, Charles F. Brannan was born in Denver, Colorado. He earned his degree in law from the University of Denver in 1929 and began work in the **New Deal** as an assistant regional attorney for the **Resettlement Administration** from 1935 to 1937, and then as regional attorney for the Department of **Agriculture**. From 1941 to 1944 Brannan worked for the **Farm Security Administration** and became assistant secretary of agriculture in 1944 and secretary of agriculture in 1948. His proposals to maintain farm income and consumer prices, as outlined in the **Brannan Plan**, were rejected. After leaving office, he was general counsel to the Farmers' Union from 1953 until 1990. He was also vice president of the Harry S. Truman Library Institute for National and International Affairs. *See also* AGRICULTURE.

BRANNAN PLAN, 1949. In April 1949, Secretary of Agriculture **Charles F. Brannan** called upon Congress to expand the agricultural support program to maintain farm income and low food prices through subsidies. The plan proposed to limit the amount of subsidy available to the largest farms. It was rejected by the **Republican**-dominated Congress. *See also* AGRICULTURE.

BRETTON WOODS CONFERENCE, 1944. Following discussions led by U.S. Assistant Secretary of the Treasury Harry Dexter White and the British Treasury representative **John Maynard Keynes** about ways to ensure postwar economic stability and prevent another **Great Depression**, representatives of 45 nations met in Bretton Woods, New Hampshire, in July 1944. The **International Monetary Fund** and the International Bank for Reconstruction and Development, or World Bank, sprang from the agreements reached and established, among other things, the principles of international monetary exchange with currencies fixed on the gold standard. This provided the basic framework for much of the Western industrial world until the 1970s.

BRIDGES, HARRY (1901–1990). Born in Australia, militant trade unionist Alfred Renton Bridges became known as Harry after he had come to the United States in 1920. He joined the Industrial Workers of the World in 1921 and later became an active **trade union** organizer within the International Longshoremen's Association (ILA) among the dockworkers and longshoremen of San Francisco, California. In May 1934, he led the West Coast Longshore Strike. In 1935, he was elected president of the pacific coast district of the ILA. The pacific branch left the ILA in 1937 to form the International Longshoremen's and Warehousemen's Union and affiliated with the **Congress of Industrial Organizations**. Attempts to deport Bridges in 1938 on the grounds of his supposed membership in the **Communist Party of the United States of America** failed in 1939. A second attempt in 1941 also failed, and the **Supreme Court** overturned the attorney general's attempts to insist on deportation in 1945. In 1949, Bridges was tried for perjury because of his denial of Communist Party membership when he sought naturalization, but the conviction was also overturned by the Supreme Court in 1953. The government's attempts to revoke Bridges's citizenship—granted in 1945—in the civil courts finally ended in 1954. He was, however, jailed briefly for making critical comments about the **Korean War**. He retired from union work in 1977.

BROWDER, EARL RUSSELL (1891–1973). Born in Wichita, Kansas, Earl Browder joined the Socialist Party in 1906, and in 1914 he formed the League for Democratic Control to oppose U.S. entry into World War I. In 1917, he was jailed for two years for draft evasion. Browder joined the **Communist Party of the United States of America (CPUSA)**, went to Moscow in 1921, and was editor of the *Labor Herald* until 1926. He went to **China** in 1926 to organize communist **trade unions**. Upon his return in 1929, he joined the ruling council of the CPUSA and in 1934 became general secretary. He led the call for a united front against fascism, and in 1935 at Moscow's behest, this became the more inclusive Popular Front. Browder ran in the presidential election of 1936 but obtained a mere 80,159 votes. The Popular Front came to a rapid end when the **Soviet Union** signed a nonaggression pact with Nazi **Germany** in August 1939. Browder and the party opposed any involvement in the conflict in Europe, until 1941 when they became committed to all-out support. These swings in position did nothing to enhance support for the CPUSA, and in the election of 1940 Browder's vote was down to 46,251. In 1941, Browder was jailed for 18 months for passport fraud, but his sentence was commuted in the interests of national unity. In 1944, he declared the Communist Party no longer necessary and replaced it with the Communist Political Association. He was expelled from the CPUSA and replaced by **William Z. Foster** in 1945.

BUCK, PEARL SYDENSTRICKER (1892–1973). Best-selling author Pearl S. Buck was born in West Virginia, but her missionary parents moved to **China** in 1892. Buck returned to the United States in 1910 to attend Randolph-Macon Women's College in Virginia, where she graduated in 1914. She returned to China and taught at Nanking University but came back to the United States to study at Cornell University, where she got her M.A. in 1926. She and her husband finally left China in 1934. Although some of Buck's novels dealt with pioneer life in the United States, China provided the inspiration for most of her writing, and her first book was *East Wind: West Wind* (1930). Her second, *The Good Earth* (1931), won the Pulitzer Prize in 1932 and the William Dean Howells Medal in 1935. In 1938, she became the first **woman** to be awarded the Nobel Prize for **Literature**. During **World War II**, Buck often spoke in defense of China against **Japan**'s aggression. She wrote almost 100 books, the last, *The Three Daughters of Madame Liang*, appearing in 1969.

Buck was also active in **civil rights** and humanitarian concerns and in 1949 established the Welcome House Inc., an interracial adoption agency. In 1960, she also set up the Pearl S. Buck Foundation, and although this was later involved in some controversy regarding its management, it too helped orphaned Amerasian children.

BUENOS AIRES CONFERENCE, 1936. Concerned about the possible impact of conflict in Europe on the western hemisphere, **Franklin D. Roosevelt** called for an Inter-American Conference for the Maintenance of Peace, which met in Buenos Aires, Argentina, at the Buenos Aires Conference in December 1936. In his speech at the conference, Roosevelt reaffirmed the **"Good Neighbor" Policy** outlined in his inaugural address and underlined the end of United

States's unilateral action in the region with a promise that the nations of the western hemisphere would consult with one another for their mutual safety and good. His attempts to reach agreement not to support fascism failed, as Argentina had strong links with the **German** regime. Participants did agree on a common policy of neutrality in the event of conflict between any two of them.

BULLITT, WILLIAM CHRISTIAN (1891–1967). William C. Bullitt began work as a writer for the *Philadelphia Public Ledger* from 1915 to 1917 but joined the State Department in 1917. In 1919, he was sent to Moscow to report on the Bolshevik government, and he recommended recognition of the Soviet regime. When this was rejected, he became disaffected and spoke against acceptance of the Versailles Treaty.

Bullitt was recalled from relative obscurity by **Franklin D. Roosevelt**, who sent him on two private fact-finding tours of Europe in 1932. Bullitt mistakenly reported that **Adolf Hitler** had little political future. He was appointed ambassador to the **Soviet Union** from 1933 to 1936. While in Moscow, he abandoned his previous procommunist outlook and became increasingly critical of **Joseph Stalin**. He continued to express these views during **World War II**, and many of his views were summed up in his book *The Great Globe Itself* (1946). Some of these ideas clearly influenced **George F. Kennan** and helped shape the policy of **containment** that emerged during the **Cold War**.

From 1936 to 1941, Bullitt was ambassador to France. He became a special assistant to the secretary of the navy in 1942, but he vacated the position following a dispute with **Sumner Welles** to serve as an officer in the Free French Army from 1944 to 1945. He continued to write articles on foreign issues for *Life* magazine and other publications after World War II had ended.

BUNCHE, RALPH JOHNSON (1903–1971). Born in Detroit, Ralph Bunche moved first to Albuquerque with his family in 1914, and then to Los Angeles. He graduated from the University of California in Los Angeles in 1927 with a major in international relations. Bunche undertook postgraduate research at Harvard University and while there in 1934 produced the first political science dissertation by an **African American**—a prize-winning study—and went on to research in anthropology at Northwestern University, the London School of Economics, and Capetown University in South Africa. He was chair of the Department of Political Science at Howard University in Washington, D.C., from 1928 to 1950. In 1938, Bunche joined the research team directed by Gunnar Myrdal that produced *An American Dilemma* (1944), the classic study of black life and conditions. He was also a member of the **Black Cabinet** consulted by the administration of **Franklin D. Roosevelt** on racial matters.

During **World War II**, Bunche worked first in the **Office of Strategic Services** and then in the African section of the State Department. He became one of the organizers of conferences leading to the organization of the **United Nations (UN)**. He was a member of the U.S. delegation to the General Assembly and in 1946 was placed in charge of the Department of Trusteeship by UN Secretary General Trygve Lie. He then became undersecretary general of the UN and was involved in the mediation between Palestine and **Israel** from 1947 to 1949. Bunche took over the role of chief mediator following the assassination of Count Folke Bernadotte in 1948 and was successful in negotiating an armistice and peace settlement.

Bunche was subsequently involved in the peacekeeping efforts following the Suez Crisis in 1956 and the conflict in the Belgian Congo (Zaire) in 1960. In addition to the Nobel Peace Prize awarded in 1950 for his work in the Middle East, Bunche was awarded the **National Association for the Advancement of Colored Peoples'** Spingarn Medal, the Presidential Medal of Honor in 1963, and the U.S. Medal of Freedom in 1963. He continued to work at the UN until shortly before his death.

BURCHFIELD, CHARLES EPHRAIM (1893–1967). Born in Ohio, Charles Burchfield trained at the Cleveland School of Art, and after graduating in 1916, he briefly attended the New York Academy of Design. He served in the army from 1918 to 1919 and then returned to Salem, Ohio. In 1912, he was employed as a wallpaper designer for a company in Buffalo, New York. The focus of much of his painting in the 1920s was on towns and cities, as evident in *Old Tavern at Hammondsville* (1926–1928), *Rainy Night* (1928–1930), and *Black Iron* (1935). While most of his work was done in watercolors,

Burchfield did do some work in oil, including his *November Evening* (1931–1934). Later he produced such fantasy works as *The Sphinx and the Milky Way* (1946) and toward the end of his career *Orion In Winter* (1962), but Burchfield is remembered for his depiction of nature and the urban landscape as "a recorder of the **American scene**." *See also* ART.

BUREAU OF THE BUDGET. Established in 1921 under the Budget and Accounting Act, the Bureau of the Budget was headed by the director of the budget with the primary function of preparing the annual executive budget. The bureau was also responsible for the supervision of the administrative management of executive agencies, the improvement of federal statistical services, and the promotion of economic and efficient government running. President **Franklin D. Roosevelt** reinvigorated the bureau in 1933 and appointed Lewis Douglas, a former **Democratic** congressman, as director. Roosevelt initially aimed to reduce expenditure and balance the budget, but as the **New Deal** developed, the policy was abandoned, and Douglas resigned in 1934, to be replaced by Daniel W. Bell from the Treasury Department. By 1938, the bureau was effectively reviewing the financial implications of all legislation, and in 1939 it was transferred from the Treasury to the Executive Office. Harold D. Smith, formerly director of the Michigan state budget, was appointed director. During the war, the bureau grew in size and importance, reflecting the increase of its role in the federal government and federal spending.

BURNS, GEORGE (1896–1996). Born Nathan Birnbaum, comedian George Burns was one of 12 children brought up in poverty in Lower East Side, Manhattan. Burns left school after failing fifth grade and worked various odd jobs but struggled to enter the world of entertainment. He became a song-and-dance man in vaudeville but did not achieve success until he teamed up with **Gracie Allen** in 1923. Together they formed a comedy partnership in which she delivered the jokes he wrote, and he played the straight man.

Burns and Allen married in 1926, became successful in the theaters of New York, and toured Europe in 1930. They made their **radio** debut in England and then established "The Burns and Allen Show," which ran for 26 years, on the radio in the United States. Burns's career seemed to come to an end after Allen's death in 1964, but in 1975 he won an Oscar for Best Supporting Actor in *The Sunshine Boys*. He had several other movie roles and also starred in several **television** specials. Burns authored a number of books, including *I Love Her, That's Why* (1955), about Allen, and the autobiographical or semiautobiographical *The Third Time Around* (1980), *How to Live to Be 100—or More* (1983), *Wisdom of the 90s* (1991), and *100 Years, 100 Stories* (1996). *See also* CINEMA.

BURTON, HAROLD HITZ (1888–1964). Born in Massachusetts, Harold Burton graduated from Bowdoin College in 1909 and Harvard Law School in 1912. He established a practice in Cleveland, Ohio, and in 1914 went to Salt Lake City, Utah, to work for the Utah Power and Light Company. In 1917, he joined the infantry, and after the war he returned to Cleveland, where he established his own law firm in 1925. In 1927, Burton was elected to the East Cleveland Board of Education, and in 1928, as a **Republican** in the Ohio House of Representatives. From 1929 until 1932, Burton was Cleveland's director of law. He returned to his private practice in 1932 but was elected mayor of Cleveland in 1935. In 1940 he was elected to the U.S. Senate. In 1945, President **Harry S. Truman** appointed him to succeed Justice **Owen Roberts** on the **Supreme Court**. Burton served until 1958, taking a generally centrist position and supporting the federal government in most areas except the extension of powers in commercial fields. After he retired, he served on the U.S. Court of Appeals for Washington, D.C., until 1962.

BUSH, VANNEVAR (1890–1974). Engineer and physicist Vannevar Bush was born in Massachusetts. He graduated from Tufts University in 1913 and worked for General Electric from 1913 to 1914. He attended Clark University briefly in 1915 and took on a teaching position at Tufts. Bush completed a doctorate in engineering at Massachusetts Institute of Technology/Harvard University in 1916 and resumed his teaching position in electrical engineering at Tufts. During World War I, Bush was a consultant with the American Research and Development Corporation, and he designed devices for locating submarines. In 1919, he joined the faculty at MIT, and in 1931 he became vice president and dean of engineering. He also continued to work with industry and was linked to a number of inventions, most notably a differential analyzer. He also began work on the idea for a system of storing information that he called the "memex," a forerunner of the Internet. His proposal for a method to store fingerprints on film was turned down by the **Federal Bureau of Investigation**.

In 1938, Bush became president of the Carnegie Institution of Washington (CIW), one of the largest research organizations of the day. From 1939 to 1941 he chaired the National Advisory Committee for Aeronautics, and he continued to serve on the committee during **World War II**. However, his most significant role came in June 1940 when President **Franklin D. Roosevelt** responded to his suggestion and created a National Defense and Research Committee with Bush as its chair. In 1941, this became the **Office of Scientific Research and Development**. After the war, Bush called for the creation of a National Research Foundation in his report *Science, the Endless Frontier* (1945), and this eventually emerged as the **National Science Foundation** in 1950. Bush returned to CIW, where he worked until retiring in 1955. He was chair of the MIT Corporation from 1957 to 1959 and director of American Telegraph and Telephone from 1947 to 1962. He was awarded the Medal of Merit by President **Harry S. Truman** and the National Medal of Science by President Lyndon Johnson in recognition of his contributions to scientific research and development.

BUTLER, PIERCE (1866–1939). The son of Irish immigrants, Pierce Butler was born in Northfield, Minnesota. He was admitted to the Minnesota bar in 1888. He was briefly assistant county attorney and was elected county attorney in 1892 and 1894. In 1908, he was chosen as president of the Minnesota State Bar Association. A **Democrat**, Butler narrowly lost election to the state senate in 1906, but he continued to advise state governors. As a member of the Board of Regents of the University of Minnesota during World War I, he supported the dismissal of professors who expressed pacifist or radical opinions. In 1922, President Warren Harding nominated him to the United States **Supreme Court**, and he served until 1939. He was generally conservative, committed to principles of laissez faire, and opposed to any expansion of the power of the federal government and voted against almost every **New Deal** measure. Butler was also conservative on issues of civil liberties and **civil rights**, and he opposed the rejection of the conviction of the **Scottsboro Boys** in 1932, and dissented from the decision against the white primaries in Texas that year. After President **Franklin D. Roosevelt**'s failed attempt at "**court packing**" in 1937, Butler was one of the conservative minority. *See also* MCREYNOLDS, JAMES CLARK; ROBERTS, OWEN JOSEPHUS; SUTHERLAND, (ALEXANDER) GEORGE; VAN DEVANTER, WILLIS.

BYRD, HARRY FLOOD (1887–1966). Although a **Democrat**, one of the **New Deal**'s staunchest critics, Harry Byrd was born in Martinsburg, West Virginia, and began working for the family newspaper in Winchester, Virginia, at the age of 15. He eventually became a newspaper publisher and businessman, and he served in the Virginia state senate from 1915 to 1925, and as state governor from 1926 to 1930. He gained a reputation as a progressive governor, streamlining the state administration and making it more efficient. He also encouraged industrial development and investment in the state. However, at the national level he was a conservative. In 1933, he was appointed to replace Senator Claude Swanson, whom President **Franklin D. Roosevelt** had appointed secretary of the navy. A defender of states' rights and fiscal conservatism, Byrd opposed the **National Industrial Recovery Act** and the **Agricultural Adjustment Act** and was incensed by the president's attempt at "**court packing**" in 1937. He opposed Roosevelt's renomination in 1940. His criticism of federal spending continued after the war, and he opposed the **Marshall Plan** and the **Truman Doctrine**. In the 1950s, he led the massive resistance to the desegregation of the schools following the 1954 *Brown v. Board of Education of Topeka* decision, and he consistently opposed the **civil rights** reforms of the 1960s. In every way, Byrd was representative of the old-fashioned, traditional southern Democrats.

BYRNES, JAMES FRANCIS (1882–1972). Born in Charleston, South Carolina, James F. Byrnes left school early, lied about his age (claiming to have been born in 1879), and was employed as a court stenographer. He passed the South Carolina bar exam in 1903. Byrnes was elected to the House of Representatives in 1911 and served until 1924. He failed to win election to the Senate in 1924, but he was successful in 1930 and was reelected in 1936. An old friend of **Franklin D. Roosevelt**'s, he helped see much of the early **New Deal** legislation through Congress. However, by 1937 he believed the worst of the **Great Depression** was over and became increasingly conservative. Nonetheless, in 1941 Roosevelt appointed him to the **Supreme Court**, but he resigned in 1942 to head the **Office of Economic Stabilization**, later the **Office of War Mobilization**. This office was effectively the most powerful of all the war agencies, and Byrnes was regarded by some as "assistant" president. It was widely accepted that he would be Roosevelt's running mate in 1944, but his segregationist background was seen as a handicap, and instead the position of vice president went to **Harry S. Truman**. Nevertheless, Byrnes was involved in major decision making at home and abroad, and he accompanied Roosevelt to the **Yalta Conference**.

In 1945, Truman made Byrnes secretary of state. Although not afraid of hard decisions (he supported the use of the **atomic bomb**), Byrnes was accused by **Republican** critics of being "soft" on the **Soviet Union**, and he resigned in 1947. He was governor of South Carolina from 1951 to 1955 and led the massive resistance to school desegregation after the 1954 *Brown v. Board of Education of Topeka* decision. In 1952, he declared his support for **Dwight D. Eisenhower** and in 1960 abandoned his **Democratic** affiliation to support **Richard M. Nixon** and in 1964 Barry Goldwater, neither of whom were successful.

– C –

CAGNEY, JAMES FRANCIS (1899–1986). Actor James Cagney was born in New York City. After high school, he briefly attended Columbia University before his father died in 1918, forcing him to find work. Cagney began to appear in vaudeville as a song and dance man and achieved success on Broadway in 1920 in *Pitter Patter*. He continued a successful stage career with several Broadway hits before he appeared in the film *Sinner's Holiday* (1930) for Warner Brothers. He made a great impact as a gangster in *Public Enemy* in 1931. Often remembered for his gangster or hard-man roles, as in *Smart Money* (1931) with **Edward G. Robinson**; *Angels with Dirty*

Faces (1938), for which he was nominated for an Oscar; and *White Heat* (1949), Cagney had as much success in comedy and musicals, like *Footlight Parade* (1933), which included tributes to the **New Deal** and the **National Recovery Administration** and also starred Jean Blondell. Equally successful were the romantic comedies *Here Comes the Navy* (1934) and *Yankee Doodle Dandy* (1942), for which Cagney won an Oscar for his role as songwriter George M. Cohan.

In 1940, Cagney was called before the **House Un-American Activities Committee** to answer allegations about supposed left-wing associations. Cagney was cleared, and he continued to make such well-received films as *City of Conquest* (1941), *Johnny Come Lately* (1943), and *Blood on the Sun* (1945). His film career continued through the postwar years, and his final role before retiring was in *One, Two, Three* (1961), a comedy that received several Academy nominations. Cagney was given the first Lifetime Achievement Award by the American Film Institute in 1974. He came out of retirement to appear in the well-received *Ragtime* in 1981 and in a number of television roles. He was awarded the Medal of Freedom in 1984. *See also* CINEMA.

CAIRO CONFERENCE, 1943. In November 1943, President **Franklin D. Roosevelt** met British prime minister **Winston Churchill** and Premier **Chiang Kai-shek** of China in Cairo, Egypt, to agree on their postwar Asia policy. Their statement declared that in the event of an **Allied** victory, all islands seized by **Japan** would be freed, and all Chinese territories occupied by the Japanese would return to the Republic of **China**. It was also agreed that **Korea** would become a free and independent state.

CALDWELL, ERSKINE (1903–1987). Born in White Oak, Georgia, best-selling writer Erskine Caldwell attended Erskine College and the University of Virginia for a number of years and worked as a journalist before moving to Maine in 1926 to concentrate on writing fiction. His first novel, *The Bastard*, appeared in 1929, and his collection of short stories, *American Earth*, in 1931. However, it was with his portrayal of the life and loves of southern sharecroppers in *Tobacco Road* (1932) and then *God's Little Acre* (1933) that he achieved critical acclaim and some notoriety. *God's Little Acre* was the subject of an obscenity trial, which Caldwell won. Both books were huge best sellers, and both were made into films, *Tobacco Road* in 1941 and *God's Little Acre* in 1958.

Caldwell went to Hollywood as a screenwriter in 1933, but he continued as a prolific author. *Kneel to the Rising Sun* appeared in 1935, as did his documentary work *Some American People*. He produced a number of photographic essays with **Margaret Bourke-White** (to whom he was briefly married), including *You Have Seen Their Faces* (1937) and *Russia at War* (1942). Another collection of short stories, *Georgia Boy*, appeared in 1943. Caldwell's novels about poor southern life continued, although less successfully, with *A House in the Uplands* (1946), *The Very Earth* (1948), and *Place Called Estherville* (1949). Caldwell wrote several novels in the 1950s and turned to racial issues in the 1960s in *Jenny by Nature* (1961) and *Summertime Island* (1968). He also produced nonfiction with *In Search of Bisco* (1965) and *Deep South* (1968). His last novel was *Annette* in 1971. *See also* LITERATURE.

CANTOR, EDDIE (1892?–1964). Entertainer Eddie Cantor was born Israel Iskowitz in New York City and raised by his grandmother after his parents died when he was three. He changed his name to Cantor in 1911 when he began working as a singer and comedian in vaudeville. After success in musical comedy in 1916, he joined the *Ziegfeld Follies* between 1917 and 1919. He played an important part in the strike in 1919 that led to the Actors' Equity Association gaining a foothold on Broadway. He later became president of the Screen Actors' Guild, the American Federation of Radio Artists, and the American Guild of Variety Artists.

After appearing in various Broadway musicals and revues, he achieved great success in *Kid Boots*, one of the longest running musicals of the 1920s. He starred in the silent film version in 1926. Bankrupted by the **Wall Street Crash** in 1929, Cantor was successful once more in 1930 with *Whoopee*, which was also made into a film. He was one of the first stars from Broadway to have a weekly **radio** show. He was on the "Chase and Sanborn Hour" from 1931 until the end of 1934, but continued on other radio shows throughout the decade. He also stared in a number of successful films, including *Palmy Days* (1931), *The Kid from Spain* (1932), *Roman Scandals*

(1933), *Kid Millions* (1934), *Forty Little Mothers* (1940), and continued appearing in movies like *If You Knew Susie* (1948). He recorded the soundtrack to *The Eddie Cantor Story* in 1953. Cantor made a few television appearances but had to retire following a heart attack in 1957.

As well as his **trade union** activities, Cantor was involved in a number of social causes supporting needy children and assisting Jewish children who fled the Nazi regime in **Germany** and elsewhere. He was also the founder of the March of Dimes, established to combat polio. He was awarded the Medal of Freedom by Lyndon Johnson in 1964. *See also* CINEMA; LITERATURE AND THEATER.

CAPRA, FRANK (1897–1991). Frank Capra was born in Sicily, and his family moved to Los Angeles, California, in 1903. Capra obtained a degree in chemical engineering from Throop college of Technology in 1918, and served briefly in the army until the end of World War I. He began to direct silent movies in the early 1920s, and moved to Hollywood in 1923, where he directed a number of Harry Langdon films. In 1928, Capra began working for Columbia Pictures. After a number of average successes, he achieved a major breakthrough with *It Happened One Night* (1934), starring Claudette Colbert and **Clark Gable**. The film won five Oscars, including best director. In 1936, *Mr. Deeds Goes to Town* with **Gary Cooper** was another prize winner, with an Oscar for best direction. More awards and nominations came for *You Can't Take It with You* (1938) and *Mr. Smith Goes to Washington* (1939).

Following the attack on **Pearl Harbor**, Capra volunteered for service in the army and became head of the Army Pictorial Service. He directed and produced the propaganda series *Why We Fight*, and one of the films, *Prelude to War*, won the Oscar for Best Documentary in 1942. Capra was awarded the Distinguished Service Medal, Order of the British Empire, and French Legion of Merit in recognition of his services.

In 1947, Capra produced and directed *It's A Wonderful Life* (1947), starring **James Stewart**. Although not an immediate success, the film became recognized as a classic and is shown regularly at Christmas on **television** across the world. After a number of unnoteworthy films and television documentaries, Capra made *A Hole in the Head* with

Frank Sinatra in 1959. His last film, *Pocketful of Miracles* (1961), was neither a commercial nor critical success, and Capra retired in 1966. He was awarded a Lifetime Achievement Award by the American Film Institute in 1982. *See also* CINEMA.

CARAWAY, HATTIE OPHELIA WYATT (1878–1950). Hattie Caraway graduated from Dickson Normal College in Tennessee in 1896. She married Thaddeus Caraway in 1902, and they settled in Arkansas, where she raised three children. Thaddeus Caraway served first in the United States House of Representatives from 1912 and then in the United States Senate from 1921. When he died in 1931, Hattie Caraway was appointed to fill his vacant seat. She then became the first **woman** ever elected to the Senate when, supported by the Arkansas **Democratic** Party, she won a special election. In 1932, Hattie Caraway defeated six challengers in the Democratic primary and was reelected in her own right in 1932. Caraway won election again in 1938 and went on to become the first woman to preside over the Senate, first to conduct a Senate committee hearing, first to chair a committee, and first senior senator. She cosponsored the Equal Rights Amendment in 1943. She was defeated in the Democratic primary in 1944 by J. William Fulbright, who went on to win her seat. Caraway subsequently served on the Employees' Compensation Commission and Employees' Compensation Appeals Board.

CARDOZO, BENJAMIN NATHAN (1870–1938). Supreme Court Justice Benjamin Cardozo was born in New York City and educated at home. He attended Columbia College and then Columbia Law School. After leaving law school in 1889 without graduating, he passed the bar exams and practiced law in New York City. He served as a justice of the Supreme Court of New York from 1913 to 1914, when he moved to the New York Court of Appeals. He became chief judge in 1926 and moved to Albany, New York. He also published a number of legal texts and was founder and vice president of the American Law Institute.

In 1932, President **Herbert Hoover** nominated Cardozo to succeed Oliver Wendell Holmes on the Supreme Court. Cardozo demonstrated a liberal inclination in generally supporting **New Deal** legislation, upholding federal regulation of the economy and arguing strongly in favor of sociological jurisprudence. He was also active in a number of Jewish organizations.

CARNERA, PRIMO (1906–1967). Six-foot–seven-inch Italian-born boxer Primo Carnera left home to work in France in various laboring jobs and found work in a circus as a boxer, weight lifter, and wrestler. He became a professional boxer in 1928 and won several fights by fair means or foul—several fights were fixed by his manager Léon Sée. In 1930, Carnera came to the United States and again fought in some contests in which the outcome seemed to be predetermined. However, after one bout, his opponent Ernie Schaaf died of brain damage.

In 1933, Carnera knocked out heavyweight champion Jack Sharkey in the sixth round. After twice defending his title, Carnera was mercilessly beaten by **Max Baer** in 11 rounds. In 1935, he was knocked out by **Joe Louis**, and he returned to Italy where he became a film actor from 1940 to 1942. He returned to the United States in 1946 as a wrestler and became a U.S. citizen in 1953. He also appeared in several films, including *On the Waterfront* (1954). *See also* SPORT.

CASABLANCA CONFERENCE, 1943. President **Franklin D. Roosevelt** became the first president to leave the United States in wartime and the first to visit Africa when he traveled to newly liberated Casablanca, Morocco, to meet the British prime minister **Winston Churchill** and other **Allied** leaders in 1943. The Soviet leader, **Joseph Stalin**, was unable to attend due to the war situation in the **Soviet Union (USSR)**. During this first wartime conference, which lasted from 14 to 24 January, the Allies agreed that their objective should be the unconditional surrender of **Germany**, Italy, and **Japan**. They also agreed that there should be an invasion of Italy.

CENTRAL INTELLIGENCE AGENCY (CIA). The CIA developed from the wartime **Office of Strategic Services** and was established under the **National Security Act** of 1947 at the start of the **Cold War**. The purpose of the CIA was to gather foreign intelligence, direct propaganda, and organize such covert acts as necessary. The 1949 Central Intelligence Agency Act exempted the agency from the normal limitations on expenditure. The first director of the CIA was Rear Admiral Roscoe H. Hillenkoetter (1897–1982), who served from 1947 until 1950. He was succeeded by General Walter Bedell Smith (1895–1961), who served from 1950 until 1953, when the first civilian director, Allen Dulles (1893–1963), was appointed.

CHAMBERS, (DAVID) WHITTAKER (1901–1961). Born Jay Vivian Chambers in Philadelphia, Pennsylvania, Whittaker Chambers worked a number of different jobs under different names before enrolling at Columbia University in 1919. He left without graduating in 1923. In 1925, Chambers joined the **Communist Party of the United States of America** and worked as a journalist for the *Daily Worker*, and in 1931 he became editor of the *New Masses*. In 1933, he and his wife went to Moscow, where he was trained as a spy. By the late 1930s, Chambers appeared to have defected from the party and was attempting to expose communists working in the United States to government officials. He began working for *Time* magazine in 1939 and became an editor. In August 1948, he appeared before the **House Un-American Activities Committee** and gave evidence accusing a former State Department official, **Alger Hiss**, of passing secret material to him in the 1930s. Challenged to produce evidence, Chambers revealed to an investigating committee led by Congressman **Richard M. Nixon** microfilmed papers incriminating Hiss that had been hidden in a pumpkin at his farmhouse. Following Hiss's conviction, Chambers left *Time*, and after writing his autobiography *Witness* in 1952, he joined the *National Review* in 1957 as a senior editor. While for defenders of Hiss he remained a liar and fraud, for others he was an American hero. In 1984, President Ronald Reagan awarded him a posthumous Medal of Freedom.

CHANDLER, RAYMOND THORNTON (1888–1959). A writer of detective fiction who, with **Dashiell Hammett**, was to establish an American literary genre that produced new cinematic forms (the film noir) and influenced popular language in the 1930s and 1940s, Raymond Chandler was born in Chicago but educated largely in England. Until 1912 he worked in the British Admiralty, but he returned to United States and established a home in Los Angeles, California. In 1917, Chandler joined the Canadian army and saw action in Europe. Returning to Los Angeles, he worked at an oil company until he was sacked in 1932 due to his drinking and womanizing. He turned instead to writing, selling his first short story to *Black Mask* in 1933. More short stories followed, and in 1939 his first novel, *The Big Sleep*, was published, followed by *Farewell, My Lovely* (1940), *The High Window* (1942), and *The Lady in the Lake* (1943). In these stories, his cynical, world-weary hero, Philip Marlowe, countered corruption and violence with resignation while maintaining his own personal integrity. As well as seeing his own books turned into films, Chandler began work on Hollywood scripts, including *Double Indemnity* (1944) and *The Blue Dahlia* (1946). After writing *The Little Sister* (1949), Chandler's last Philip Marlowe novel was *The Long Goodbye* (1953). His last book was *Playback* (1958). In addition to novels, Chandler wrote articles for *Atlantic Monthly* and a brilliant essay on detective fiction, "The Simple Art of Murder" (1944). *See also* CINEMA; LITERATURE AND THEATER.

CHAPLIN, CHARLES (CHARLIE) SPENCER (1889–1977). One of the greatest performers in silent films, Charlie Chaplin was born in London, England, where he performed in music halls and plays in his early teens. In 1913, he signed a contract with the Keystone Studios in the United States. Chaplin first appeared in a motion picture in 1914, and he made 35 films with Keystone and 14 with Essanay before moving to the Mutual Film Corporation in 1916. He quickly established his film persona in such movies as *The Tramp* (1915), *The Vagabond* (1917), and *The Immigrant* (1917). As the little tramp with his distinctive walk, little moustache, bowler hat, and large shoes, Chaplin effectively combined slapstick with pathos. By 1917, he was a huge star and had signed a 1-million-dollar contract with the First National Exhibitors' Circuit to make eight films. In 1919, he joined Mary Pickford, Douglas Fairbanks, and D. W. Griffith to establish United Artists to produce their own films. Chaplin scored critical and box office success with *The Kid* (1921) and *The Gold Rush* (1925). His first sound film was *City Lights* (1931), which had a musical score but no dialogue. Chaplin turned to social comment in the 1930s again without dialogue in *Modern Times* (1936), and in his first real dialogue film, *The Great Dictator* (1940), Chaplin parodied **Adolf Hitler**.

During the 1940s, Chaplin's reputation was damaged by revelations concerning his personal life and charges of immorality following a paternity suit and possible charges under the Mann Act. His marriage to 17-year-old Oona O'Neill in 1943 further tarnished his name. Chaplin's support for the **Soviet Union** during and immediately after **World War II** also led to criticism from conservative groups. He was called to appear before the **House Un-American Activities Committee** in 1947, but the hearings were cancelled. His next two films, *Monsieur Verdoux* (1947) and *Limelight* (1952), did badly. In 1952, Chaplin, still a resident alien, applied for a reentry permit to the United States prior to a visit to Europe. Shortly after he set sail, his permit was revoked, and it was announced that he would not be readmitted until he answered questions about his political views and moral behavior. Chaplin then took up permanent residence in Switzerland. He made only two more films, one of which, *A King in New York* (1947), was a satirical comment on **McCarthyism** and his recent experiences in the United States. Despite the objections of **J. Edgar Hoover**, he was able to return to the United States in 1972 when he was awarded a special Oscar for his contribution to film. Queen Elizabeth II knighted him in 1975. He died in Switzerland. *See also* CINEMA.

CHAPULTEPEC AGREEMENT, 1945. In February 1945, the United States and all Latin American countries other than Argentina signed an agreement at the Inter-American Conference in Chapultepec, Mexico, providing for close military and naval cooperation to prevent aggression from outside the western hemisphere. The United States and Canada subsequently signed a separate agreement.

CHIANG KAI-SHEK (1887–1975). Chiang Kai-shek, also known as Jian Jieshi, was a Chinese soldier and politician who assumed control of the Republic of **China** in 1928 as leader of the Nationalist Party (Kuomintang). As well as trying to unify and modernize China, Chiang was involved in a long war with communist forces led by **Mao Zedong**, even after the Japanese invasion of Manchuria in 1931 and the war with **Japan** that began in 1937. After **Pearl Harbor**, Chiang was included among the "Big Four" **Allied** leaders and attended the **Cairo Conference** in 1941. Although he agreed to cooperate with the communist armies, open conflict soon resumed once the Japanese were defeated. However, the nationalists were defeated and forced to withdraw to **Taiwan** (Formosa), where Chiang established the Republic of China based in Taipei and ruled until his death.

CHINA. U.S. interests in China developed through the late 19th century following trading agreements in the 1840s. Concern that China might fall victim to European partition in the late 1890s led Secretary of State John Hay to send out "Open Door" notes to various powers indicating U.S. commitment to the preservation of Chinese territorial integrity and a policy of equal trade access. This position was reaffirmed in the Treaty of Portsmouth in 1905 and the Nine Power Treaty at the Washington Conference in 1921–1922. The Japanese invasion of Manchuria in 1931 was denounced in the **Stimson** Doctrine, and the United States refused to recognize the creation of Manchukuo under Japanese control. Thus for the U.S. administration, China became the equivalent of Poland for the British government, and there was increasing conflict over Japanese expansionist policies that led to **Pearl Harbor** and U.S. entry into **World War II**.

During the war, two groups fought the Japanese: nationalists led by **Chiang Kai-shek** and communist forces led by **Mao Zedong**. With the defeat of **Japan** in 1945, the future of China became a major issue for the administration of **Harry S. Truman**. In November 1945, General **George C. Marshall** was sent as a special envoy to determine whether China could be reestablished as a strong, united, independent, **democratic** country. In February 1946, Marshall announced that agreement had been made to establish a government including both major groups, but the subsequent failure to include the communists led him to denounce the nationalists as "reactionaries" in January 1947. As a result all U.S. agencies and armed forces were withdrawn from China. Aid to the nationalists ceased in 1949.

When the communists triumphed in 1949, **Republicans** in Congress formed the **China lobby** and denounced Truman's policies as a failure and betrayal. On 5 August 1949, the State Department issued a White Paper absolving the United States from responsibility in the defeat of the nationalists, but the "loss of China" became a major focus for **McCarthy** and his followers. The United States refused to recognize the People's Republic of China established on 1 October

1949 and instead backed the nationalists now established as the Republic of China on Taiwan (Formosa). Diplomatic relations were not reestablished with the communists until 1979, and U.S. forces fought Chinese communists in the **Korean War**. The Chinese also later supported the North Vietnamese against the United States in Vietnam.

CHINA LOBBY. Organized support for the Chinese nationalists began following the nationalist revolution of 1925–1928. Subsequently, these elements called for a firm U.S. response to Japanese aggression against China from 1931 onward. The Price Committee, led by Frank and Harry Price, was able to enlist the support of **Henry Stimson** and through him had some influence on **Franklin D. Roosevelt's** policies. During **World War II**, support for China was mainly in the form of financial aid coordinated by the United China Relief group. However, with the triumph of the communists in 1949, the China lobby was primarily concerned with organizing support for the Republic of China, keeping the Peoples' Republic of China out of the **United Nations**, and directing criticism against the administration of **Harry S. Truman**, particularly Secretary of State **Dean Acheson**. The leading figures in this group were **Henry Luce**, Alfred Kohlberg, Frederick C. McKee, and in Congress Representative Walter H. Judd, and Senators William F. Knowland, **Karl Mundt**, and **Joseph McCarthy**. The lobby continued as a force in various forms until the 1970s, when the communist regime was finally recognized. *See also* COLD WAR.

CHURCHILL, WINSTON LEONARD SPENCER (1874–1965). British statesman, prime minister, and wartime leader Winston Churchill was born in Blenheim Palace, England. He served in the army in Egypt and South Africa before becoming a Conservative member of parliament in 1900. Churchill later became a member of the Liberal Party and held various Cabinet positions, including home secretary and first lord of the Admiralty. In 1917, he became minister of munitions. After the war, he served as secretary of state for war, and then, having rejoined the Conservatives, was chancellor of the exchequer from 1924 to 1929. Out of office during the 1930s, with the start of **World War II** in 1939, Churchill returned to the Admiralty, and in 1940 he became leader of the coalition wartime government.

Churchill proved himself to be one of Britain's greatest leaders, mobilizing the people with stirring speeches, articulating courage and determination to fight, and determining strategy. He worked closely with President **Franklin D. Roosevelt**, and together they issued a joint statement of principles in the **Atlantic Charter** of 1941. He also put aside his anticommunist feelings to work with **Soviet** leader **Joseph Stalin**, with whom he reached agreement at the **Moscow Conference** (1943) about the spheres of influence in the Balkan regions after the war. He was unsuccessful persuading Roosevelt that a rapid advance on **Berlin** was necessary to limit Soviet power in Europe, and during the **Potsdam Conference**, Churchill suffered electoral defeat at home and was succeeded by Labour leader Clement Attlee. After the war, in a speech in Fulton, Missouri, Churchill declared that an "**iron curtain**" had fallen across Eastern Europe, and he encouraged President **Harry S. Truman** to take a strong anti-Soviet position.

Churchill became prime minister once again in 1951 but was forced to pass over power to Anthony Eden in 1955 due to ill-health. *See also* TEHRAN CONFERENCE; YALTA CONFERENCE.

CINEMA. The 1930s and 1940s are often regarded as Hollywood's "Golden Age." Cinema was as significant as **radio** during this period. The initial impact of the **Great Depression** caused a decline in the movie-going audience, and with the closure of more than one-third of movie theaters by 1933, the future of some of the major film studios seemed in doubt—indeed Paramount and Fox went bankrupt. However, numbers gradually started to climb, with eventually 60 to 75 million people—60 percent of the population—going to the cinema at least once a week. Cinema offered an escape from the harsh economic realities of the outside world, and it has been suggested that this escapism helped sustain the population through hard times. Walt Disney's cartoons, like Mickey Mouse, who first appeared in *Steamboat Willie* in 1928; *The Three Little Pigs* (1933); and the first full-length cartoon, *Snow White and the Seven Dwarves* (1937), seemed like childish entertainment, but the songs "Who's Afraid of the Big Bad Wolf," "Heigh–Ho," and "Whistle While You Work" clearly had a morale-boosting impact. Even **Busby Berkeley**'s *Gold Diggers of 1933*, with its focus on a play about the Depression, had the uplifting song "We're in the Money," although it ended with the haunting "My Forgotten Man." Another musical featuring Berkeley's choreography and with a similar storyline, *42nd Street* (1933), was reputed to have saved the Warner Brothers' film studio from bankruptcy. One of the most famous musical films was the fantasy *The Wizard of Oz* (1939) set in **Dust Bowl** Kansas and starring **Judy Garland** singing, among other optimistic songs, "Somewhere over the Rainbow." Optimism too perhaps underlay the success of the epic film version of **Margaret Mitchell**'s Civil War novel *Gone with the Wind* (1939), ending with the immortal words, "After all, tomorrow is another day."

Escapism also came in the form of the adventure *King Kong* (1933), in which the giant ape was finally shot down from the Empire State Building, or in the zany comedies of the **Marx Brothers** and in **Charlie Chaplin**'s humorous critique of factory life, *Modern Times* (1936). The 1930s also saw the emergence of a new genre—the crime thriller. This led to the film noir, first with the classic gangster films, starring **Edward G. Robinson** as *Little Caesar* (1930) and **James Cagney** in *Public Enemy* (1931), and then with **Humphrey Bogart** as the private eye in several films of the novels of **Dashiell Hammett** and **Raymond Chandler**, including *The Maltese Falcon* (1941). During the 1930s and 1940s, America's western heritage also became the backdrop for the classic films of **John Ford**, starring **John Wayne**, while **Frank Capra** focused on traditional small-town values and beliefs and the strength of ordinary people in 20th century America in *Mr. Deeds Goes to Town* (1936) and *Mr. Smith Goes to Washington* (1939).

Not all film was about escapism or nostalgia. One of the major successes was Ford's powerful film of the **John Steinbeck** novel dealing with the plight of the **Okies**, *The Grapes of Wrath* (1940), starring **Henry Fonda**. Even more bleak was Mervyn LeRoy's *I Am a Fugitive from a Chain Gang* (1932), starring **Paul Muni**. Another great film classic, **Orson Welles**'s *Citizen Kane* (1941), used a montage of newsreel intercut with studio scenes to reveal the life of a newspaper magnate. Realism also featured in the documentary films made for the **New Deal** by **Pare Lorentz** and others. These films dealt with problems of soil erosion and the need for conservation.

During **World War II**, Hollywood was recognized as an important medium for "informing and entertaining," and although affected by wartime shortages and limited in terms of the amount spent producing each film, it escaped direct government control over content. The number of films released fell from 533 in 1942 to 377 in 1945. Many in the industry enlisted in the war effort, and directors like Capra and Ford were among those who made films for the army or the government outlining "Why We Fight" or depicting some of the major battles of the war, like *The Battle of Midway* (1942). Several of the major stars joined the military during the war, among them **Clark Gable**, Henry Fonda, and **James Stewart**. Countless others in the industry contributed to **War bond** drives and morale-boosting performances for the **United Service Organizations**, including the servicemen's pin ups, **Betty Grable**, **Rita Hayworth**, and **Dorothy Lamour**.

Despite an initial drop in audiences immediately after **Pearl Harbor**, cinema attendance soon rose, and during the war about 60 million people went to the movies once a week. Among the feature films were war films celebrating American heroism either in World War I, as in *Sergeant York* (1941), or in World War II, as in *Bataan* (1943) or *Objective Burma* (1945), a picture starring **Errol Flynn** in a far-fetched role that offended the British. More realistic was a film version of **Ernie Pyle**'s reports, *The Story of G.I. Joe* (1945) and various wartime documentaries, like *Memphis Belle* (1944), the story of a B-17 Flying Fortress bomber. **Women** too featured in patriotic roles as nurses on **Bataan** in *So Proudly We Hail* (1943) and in the Philippines in *Cry Havoc* (1943). The shift from detached noninvolvement to commitment by an American was famously captured in *Casablanca* (1942), starring Bogart with Ingrid Bergman. American home life was celebrated in Welles's *The Magnificent Ambersons* (1942), *Holiday Inn* (1942), and the nostalgic *Meet Me in St. Louis* (1944), while the lighthearted musical *Going My Way* (1943), starring **Bing Crosby**, swept the Oscars in 1944. Rather less cheerful was *The Best Years of Our Lives* (1946), dealing with the plight of returning servicemen and their problems readjusting after 1945.

After the war, Hollywood was affected by the **Cold War** in a number of ways. First, Hollywood became the focus of investigations by the **House Un-American Activities Committee (HUAC)**, and some writers and directors, like the **Hollywood Ten**, were blacklisted. Others were excluded after being listed in *Red Channels* and after 48 leading executives from the film business had agreed in November 1947 to keep out any individuals identified as possible "subversives." Second, films sometimes dealt directly with the supposed threat of subversion, either directly in *I Married a Communist* (1950), *I Was a Communist for the FBI* (1951), or *Big Jim McLain* (1952), starring John Wayne as a HUAC investigator, or indirectly in the later science fiction film *Invasion of the Body Snatchers* (1956). Despite this there were still great moments in cinema: Capra's *It's A Wonderful Life* (1948), starring James Stewart, quickly established itself as a perennial Christmas classic. **Bob Hope** and Bing Crosby continued their successful formula in the *Road* films with *Road to Utopia* (1946), *Road to Rio* (1947), and *Road to Bali* (1952), and Ford continued to mine the American Western heritage in *Fort Apache* (1948), *She Wore a Yellow Ribbon* (1949), and *Rio Grande* (1950). Stewart also appeared in one of the first postwar Westerns to present a sympathetic view of **Native Americans** in *Broken* Arrow (1950). Other notable films of the period were *The African Queen* (1951), an adventure with Humphrey Bogart and **Katherine Hepburn**; the musical starring **Gene Kelly**, *An American in Paris* (1951); the Western Cold War allegory with **Gary Cooper**, *High Noon* (1952); another musical with Gene Kelly, *Singin' in the Rain* (1952); *Shane* (1953), a Western starring **Alan Ladd**; and *The Wild One* (1953), a film about motorcycle gangs starring the young Marlon Brando and signaling the rise of the teenager as a media phenomenon. However, cinema audiences, which reached a height of 90 million a week in 1946, began to decline thereafter as the **baby boom** forced people to stay home and as the new domestic entertainment, **television**, began to replace film. In 1953, 50 million people watched an episode of the TV series *I Love Lucy*, while only 45 million went to the cinema. *See also* ASTAIRE, FRED; BACALL, LAUREN; BURNS, GEORGE; DAVIS, BETTE; DIETRICH, MARLENE; FIELDS, WILLIAM CLAUDE (W. C.); GARBO, GRETA; HAWKS, HOWARD WINCHESTER; KARLOFF, BORIS; LAKE, VERONICA; LOMBARD, CAROLE; RAFT, GEORGE; ROGERS, GINGER; ROONEY, MICKEY; SELZNICK, DAVID O.; SINATRA, FRANCIS (FRANK) ALBERT; SKEL-

TON, ("RED") RICHARD BERNARD; WEST, MAE; WYLER, WILLIAM; ZANUCK, DARRYL FRANCIS.

CIVIL AERONAUTICS ACT, 1938. The Civil Aeronautics Act of 1938 established a Civil Aeronautics Authority (CAA) to regulate air mail, passenger, and freight services. The CAA was initially empowered to regulate airline rates and schedules, designate new airways, and oversee airline companies. It included an Air Safety Board to establish safety rules and investigate air accidents. In 1940, the CAA was located within the Department of Commerce.

CIVIL DEFENSE ACT, 1951. Passed by Congress on 2 January 1951, the Civil Defense Act was intended to provide for the country's defense in the event of atomic attack. It initiated a three-year program of building bomb shelters and provided for the coordination of state, local, and national civilian defense by the Civil Defense Administrator.

CIVIL RIGHTS. The modern civil rights movement had its origins in organizations formed early in the 20th century and in developments in the 1930s and 1940s. The leading black civil rights organization, the **National Association for the Advancement of Colored People (NAACP)**, was established in 1909 by white progressives and black leaders. By the early 1920s, it had begun a largely black-led organization with an influential journal edited by **African American** educator and spokesman W. E. B. Du Bois. In the 1930s, the NAACP, led now by **Walter White**, had some success gaining access to the White House, particularly through the good offices of **Eleanor Roosevelt**. With or without President **Franklin D. Roosevelt**'s blessing, she spoke frequently on behalf of racial equality. In 1939, when the Daughters of the American Revolution refused to allow black singer **Marian Anderson** to perform in Constitution Hall, Mrs. Roosevelt publicly resigned her membership, and with Secretary of the Interior **Harold Ickes**, she helped organize a performance for Anderson at the Lincoln Memorial.

However, the **New Deal**'s impact on African Americans was mixed. Roosevelt was reluctant to take any action that would jeopardize the support of the southern **Democrats** in Congress for his general reform program and so failed to speak out against race discrimination and violence. Nonetheless, the NAACP continued lobbying the government on behalf of **antilynching** legislation, continued working with trade unions, and in 1930 it was one of several groups to help block the confirmation of John J. Parker to the **Supreme Court** on grounds of his record on race and labor unions. The NAACP also helped defend the **Scottsboro Boys**, a case that became something of an international cause célèbre, but their involvement was always complicated by their relationship with other defending groups, like the **Communist Party of the United States of America**.

From the start of **World War II**, black organizations campaigned to ensure a double victory at home and abroad. As the United States began to prepare for the possibility of war, African American leaders lobbied to end segregation and discrimination in the U.S. armed forces and for greater inclusion in the expanding defense industries. The demand for equal opportunity in defense industries brought the threat of a **March on Washington** organized by **A. Philip Randolph** in 1941. The possibility of such an event led Roosevelt to issue Executive Order 8802 in June ordering the end of discrimination in defense industries and establishing a **Fair Employment Practices Committee (FEPC)** to ensure its implementation. Although the FEPC had limited impact, it had enormous symbolic and psychological importance, and a number of cities and states also established similar bodies during the war. The possibility of mass, nonviolent protest signaled by the March on Washington Movement (MOWM) was also an important precedent for future years. Another significant development was the formation in Chicago in 1942 of the Congress of Racial Equality (CORE), an organization that rose to prominence in the 1960s.

The MOWM continued in existence during the war, but its activities were limited. However, black leaders and newspapers continued to press for greater inclusion in the military, and although segregation continued, African Americans were included in all branches of the military during the war. Attention returned to this issue with the reintroduction of the draft in 1947, and when A. Philip Randolph responded with the threat of a campaign of mass civil disobedience, it appeared to have considerable support among African Americans of military service age. In part as a response to this threat and in part in line with his developing policy, and also in a crucial election year, in

1948 President **Harry S. Truman** issued an executive order requiring an end to discrimination in the federal civil service and another order initiating the process of desegregation in the armed forces.

The increasing demand for equality after **World War II** was evident in the number of black voter registration drives, often led by African American veterans. Voter registration in the South rose from 150,000 in 1940 to 1.2 million in 1952, from 5 percent of the voting age population to 25 percent. The increased expectations among African Americans were also evident in the rise in NAACP membership from 50,000 in 1939 to 400,000 in 1945. In 1947, CORE mounted its first "Freedom Ride" to test Supreme Court decisions on segregation in interstate transport in Virginia, North Carolina, and Kentucky. Although it attracted little attention and less success, it too was a precedent for the future.

African Americans were encouraged in their hopes for change after the war by the unprecedented action on civil rights by President Truman. Addressing the NAACP from the steps of the Lincoln Memorial on 29 June 1947 in a nationally broadcast speech, Truman called for an end to racial violence and said the federal government should lead the way. In 1946, he had established the President's Committee on Civil Rights and its report, *To Secure These Rights*, published in 1947, set out an agenda for racial equality across all aspects of American life. Truman began implementing some of this with the desegregation of the U.S. armed forces. He also addressed black audiences in Harlem in the election campaign of 1948 and again in 1952, and the black vote significantly contributed to his surprise election victory.

Although Truman's actual achievements in civil rights were perhaps more symbolic than real, the Supreme Court issued a number of significant decisions in the 1940s and 1950s undermining the practice of racial segregation and exclusion. In *Smith v. Allwright* in 1944, they ruled against the white primary; in *Morgan v. Commonwealth of Virginia* in 1946, they ruled against segregation in interstate transport; in *Shelley v. Kraemer* in 1948, they outlawed restrictive housing covenants; and in *Sipuel v. Oklahoma Board of Regents* in 1948, *McLaurin v. Oklahoma State Regents* in 1950, and *Sweatt v. Painter* in 1950, they issued a number of rulings challenging segregation in education that paved the way for the 1954 landmark decision of

Brown v. Board of Education of Topeka. See also BETHUNE, MARY MCLEOD; HASTIE, WILLIAM HENRY; HOUSTON, CHARLES HAMILTON; MARSHALL, THURGOOD.

CIVIL WORKS ADMINISTRATION (CWA). Established by executive order on 9 November 1933, the CWA was created to provide immediate employment during the winter months. Headed by **Harry Hopkins** and run as an entirely federal program, the CWA recruited more than 4 million unemployed people to work on relief projects. The administration built 40,000 schools, 469 airports, and improved thousands of miles of roads. It also employed people on such less essential tasks as preserving historic sites or funding touring opera singers. In many respects, when it ended in 1934, it had established the precedent for the later **Works Progress Administration**.

CIVILIAN CONSERVATION CORPS (CCC). Created on 31 March 1933, during the "**First Hundred Days**" of the **New Deal**, the CCC was a program that aimed to tackle the problems of unemployed youth and at the same time rectify some of the causes of soil erosion through reforestation, irrigation, and flood and fire control schemes. Young men (**women** were only included at **Eleanor Roosevelt**'s insistence and some 8,500 participated) between the ages of 17 and 25 were recruited for a six month period from the relief rolls by the Department of Labor and transported to one of 2,600 camps. After protests by black leaders, **African Americans** were included in proportion to their numbers in the population (about 11 percent) and some 200,000 participated but in segregated camps.

Supervised by the Department of Agriculture and the Department of the Interior and coordinated by **Robert Fechner** and the CCC staff, workers were involved in conservation projects like the planting of 200 million trees in the reforestation of 17 million acres of land. Workers were paid $30 per month, $25 of which was sent home. By the time the scheme came to an end in 1943, the CCC had employed more than 3 million single men.

CIVILIAN DEFENSE. *See* OFFICE OF CIVILIAN DEFENSE (OCD).

CIVILIAN PRODUCTION ADMINISTRATION (CPA). Created in November 1945, the CPA took over the functions of the **War Production Board** and was intended to manage the orderly transition to full peacetime industrial production. The CPA had the authority to expand production of needed materials, limit production of unnecessary products involving scarce resources, and prevent hoarding. It operated primarily through committees and conferences rather than direct control. The CPA ceased operation in 1947.

CLARK, TOM CAMPBELL (1899–1977). Born in Dallas, Texas, Tom Clark briefly served in the Texas National Guard in 1918 before attending the University of Texas. He graduated from law school in 1922 and practiced law in Dallas until 1927, when he became the city's district attorney. In 1937, he joined the U.S. Department of Justice, where he held various posts, including handling the legal aspects of the relocation of **Japanese Americans** in 1941. In 1943, he became assistant to Attorney General **Francis Biddle**, and in 1945 he himself was appointed attorney general by President **Harry S. Truman**. As attorney general, Clark was active in **civil rights**, providing amicus curiae briefs in *Shelley v Kraemer* and supporting the **Federal Bureau of Investigation**'s investigation of lynchings. Clark also presented 160 antitrust suits. He offended liberals by drawing up a list of dangerous organizations, mostly left-wing, and approving the use of wiretaps and the prosecution of members of the **Communist Party of the United States of America**. Despite some opposition, he was confirmed as a **Supreme Court** justice in 1949 following **Frank Murphy**'s death. In his new role, he earned Truman's ire by voting to declare the president's seizure of the steel mills unconstitutional in *Youngstown Sheet & Tube Co. v. Sawyer* in 1952, having previously advised the president that such action was legal.

Clark took a generally conservative position in the court and supported anticommunist measures, but he also was an advocate of civil rights and voted with the majority to declare school segregation unconstitutional in *Brown v. Board of Education of Topeka* in 1954. He also wrote the majority decision against daily school Bible readings. He resigned in 1967 when his son, Ramsey Clark, was appointed attorney general by Lyndon Johnson.

CLAY, LUCIUS DUBIGNON (1898–1978). Born in Marietta, Georgia, Lucius Clay graduated from West Point in 1918 and was commissioned in the Engineers Corps. In the interwar years, he served at a number of schools and colleges and in the Rivers and Harbors Section of the Office of the Chief of Engineers. As the Chief of Engineers spokesman to congress, Clay assisted with several programs in the **Works Progress Administration**. From 1937 to 1938 he was chief of staff for General **Douglas MacArthur** in the **Philippines**. After returning to the United States, he was assistant administrator with the Civil Aeronautic Authority and was responsible for improving and building airfields for military uses. He held a number of wartime posts involving production and procurement of military supplies and in 1944 took command of supplying the **Allied** forces in **Normandy**. At the end of the year, he became aide to **James F. Byrnes** in the Office of War Mobilization and Reconversion before returning to Europe to assist in the military occupation of **Germany**.

Clay was appointed deputy military governor of the American zone from 1945 to 1947 and military governor from 1947 to 1949. He advocated an element of German reconstruction prior to payment of reparations to the **Soviet Union** and in May 1946 broke off negotiations concerning reparations from the American zone. Clay also worked to unite the British and American zones with a common economic policy in the Bizone on 1 January 1947. Following the French entry into the agreement and the establishment of a common currency in January 1948, the Soviets imposed the **Berlin** blockade. Clay proposed smashing the blockade by force but was overruled by President **Harry S. Truman**. Instead, Clay directed the **Berlin Airlift** that eventually helped bring about the lifting of the blockade. He returned home to the United States and received a ticker-tape welcome in New York City. After his retirement in 1950, Clay was chair of the Continental Can Company until 1962 and a senior partner in Lehman Brothers investment bankers from 1963 to 1973. He also acted as a special advisor in Berlin from 1961 to 1962 following the construction of the Berlin Wall.

CLAYTON, WILLIAM LOCKHART (1880–1966). Born in Mississippi, Will Clayton left school at the age of 13 and held a number of secretarial posts before joining the American Cotton Company in

1896. He later became manager of the Texas Cotton Products Company and in 1904 established his own brokerage company, which was eventually extremely successful. During World War I, he served on the War Industries Board. Clayton was an active supporter of U.S. intervention in **World War II** and from 1942 to 1944 was assistant secretary of commerce and member of the **Office of War Mobilization**. He was appointed special advisor on economic affairs in 1944 and attended the **Potsdam Conference** in 1945. Concerned by **Soviet** expansion, Clayton advocated U.S. economic aid to preserve liberal democracy in Western Europe after the war. He was a representative to the **United Nations Relief and Rehabilitation Administration**, helped negotiate loans to **Great Britain**, and drew up the plans to assist Greece and Turkey as laid out in the **Truman Doctrine** in 1947. Clayton also had considerable influence on the **Marshall Plan** and assisted with creating the **General Agreement on Tariffs and Trade** in 1947 before retiring from public service.

CLIFFORD, CLARK MCADAMS (1906–1998). Clark Clifford was born in Fort Scott, Kansas, attended Washington University law school, and ran his own law practice from 1928 to 1943. He served in the navy from 1944 to 1946 and was assistant naval aide and then special counsel to President **Harry S. Truman**. He helped to negotiate settlements in the rail and mining strikes in 1946 but was also influential in **foreign policy** matters. He helped draft the speech outlining the **Truman Doctrine** advocating support for the policy of **containment**. Clifford also played a significant role in planning Truman's successful election strategy in 1948 before returning to his private law practice in 1949. In 1960, he returned as an advisor on defense matters and foreign intelligence in the administration of John F. Kennedy and in 1968 was appointed secretary of defense by Lyndon Johnson. He left office in 1968 and advocated the withdrawal from Vietnam. He was awarded the presidential Medal of Freedom in 1969 and served as an emissary to India and Cyprus for President Jimmy Carter in 1980.

COHEN, BENJAMIN VICTOR (1894–1983). The son of Polish immigrants, Benjamin Cohen was born in Muncie, Indiana. He earned a degree in philosophy and doctorate in jurisprudence from the University of Chicago and graduated from Harvard Law School in 1916. Cohen was secretary to a federal circuit judge, attorney for the U.S. Shipping Board, and corporate lawyer in New York City from 1922 onward. In 1933, he was brought to Washington, D.C., by **Felix Frankfurter** and provided legal advice as a general counsel in a variety of government departments and agencies. With **Thomas Corcoran**, Cohen helped to draft the **Securities and Exchange Act** of 1934 and later the legislation establishing the **Federal Housing Administration**, **Tennessee Valley Authority**, and several other **New Deal** agencies. He advised on the **Lend-Lease Act**, in 1941 was counsel to the ambassador to **Great Britain**, and from 1943 to 1945 was general counsel to the **Office of War Mobilization**. In 1945, he was appointed general counsel in the State Department and was an assistant to **James F. Byrnes**. Having been involved in the **Dumbarton Oaks Conference**, Cohen was a member of the U.S. delegation to the **United Nations** from 1948 to 1952. After retiring from public service, he frequently acted as a voluntary and unofficial adviser on many issues.

COHN, ROY MARCUS (1927–1986). Born in New York City, Roy Cohn graduated from Columbia Law School in 1947 and became an assistant U.S. attorney in 1948. He rose to prominence as one of the prosecutors involved in the case of **Ethel** and **Julius Rosenberg** in 1951 and three years later became special counsel to **Joseph McCarthy**'s Senate Committee on Government Operations. He and his friend David Schine notoriously toured State Department offices in Europe and removed what they classified as procommunist literature from the libraries, including books by **John Steinbeck** and **Dashiell Hammett**. Cohn was forced to resign his position when it was revealed during the army hearings that he had tried to use his influence to have Schine exempted from military service. He established a law practice and established a reputation as powerbroker with links to the media. However he was also involved in unproved charges of jury tampering and later of tax avoidance. He died from an Aids-related illness.

COLD WAR. The Cold War was the term coined by American columnist **Walter Lippmann** in 1947 to describe the deterioration of relations between the communist **Soviet Union** and the capitalist

Western democracies, principally the United States, **Great Britain**, and their allies. It effectively dominated world politics until its end in 1989 and 1990 and had an enormous impact on the domestic affairs of all participants.

The growing conflict between the former **Allied powers** developed as differences about the nature of the postwar settlement, centered initially on Poland and **Germany**, became increasingly viewed as a struggle between rival ideologies. These ideological differences, evident since the Russian Revolution of 1917, had been papered over while the two sides made common cause against Nazi Germany and **Japan** during **World War II**. Although relations were generally amicable during the war and agreements were reached at the various wartime conferences, most notably **Yalta** and **Potsdam**, there was always an element of fear and suspicion on both sides. While Soviet fears were heightened due to delays in opening a Second Front against the Nazi armies, Western alarm rose when Soviet armies proceeded to establish left-wing regimes wherever they pushed back the German forces in Eastern Europe. With the end of the war and sudden cutting of **Lend-Lease**, such issues as the reparation payments and the economic future of Germany became vital.

The situation in Europe deteriorated rapidly. Speaking in Fulton, Missouri, in 1946 former British prime minister **Winston Churchill** warned that an **"iron curtain"** had descended in Europe from "Stettin in the Baltic to Trieste in the Adriatic." Alarmed too by the apparent failure of the Soviets to honor agreements made at Yalta concerning Poland and by the rise of left-wing parties in France, Italy, and more especially Greece where civil war erupted, President **Harry S. Truman** presented a vision of a world divided between the forces of democracy and dictatorship when he announced the **Truman Doctrine** in March 1947. Influenced by **George F. Kennan**'s view of irreconcilable differences between East and West, Truman accepted the principles of **containment**. These principles were extended with the **Marshall Plan** in 1947, and following the imposition of a communist government in Czechoslovakia and the **Berlin** blockade in 1948, they were also furthered with the creation of the **North Atlantic Treaty Organization (NATO)** in 1949. In 1950, the **National Security Council Report 68** called for massive rearmament to meet the Soviet challenge.

Apprehension about the communist threat escalated rapidly in 1949 with the testing of the Soviet **atomic bomb** and the "fall" of **China** to the communist forces of **Mao Zedong** the same year. These communist successes inspired a crisis at home as the political opponents of the **Democratic** administration leveled charges of failure and even betrayal against the government. The hunt for communist sympathizers within began with the investigations of the **House Un-American Activities Committee** but reached its height during the **Korean War** with Senator **Joseph McCarthy**'s campaign to find communist supporters and spies in the State Department and other branches of government.

Although **McCarthyism** came to an end in 1954, the Cold War continued unabated under the **Republican** administration of **Dwight D. Eisenhower**, even though **Joseph Stalin**'s death in 1953 brought a change of leadership to the Soviet Union. In 1955, the Soviet-led Warsaw Pact was formed to meet the challenge posed by NATO forces in Western Europe with the rearmament of the **German Federal Republic**, and in 1956 Soviet troops crushed an uprising in Hungary. In 1961, Berlin was divided by the erection of the Berlin Wall to prevent the exodus of Germans from the east.

The 1950s and 1960s were marked by an arms race as each side tried to match and outdo the other's military capacity. During the 1950s, the Third World increasingly also became the focus of Cold War rivalries as both sides tried to gain influence and control of rich natural resources like oil. Tensions between the East and the West did not decline significantly until the 1980s, but it was the breakup of the Soviet Union that finally led President George H. W. Bush to meet with Premier Gorbachev and officially declare the Cold War over in 1989. *See also* ACHESON, DEAN GOODERHAM; CLAY, LUCIUS DUBIGNON; VANDENBERG, ARTHUR HENDRICK.

COLLIER, JOHN (1884–1968). Born in Atlanta, Georgia, John Collier was educated at Columbia University and the College de France. In 1907, he became secretary of the Peoples' Institute in New York City, working with immigrants. He left in 1919 to become director of adult education in California, and when that job collapsed, he went to New Mexico, where he lived for some time with the Pueblo Indians. In 1922, he became a research agent for the Indian Welfare

Committee of the General Federation of Women's Clubs. In 1923, he became the executive director of the American Indian Defense Association, working to preserve Native American lands and culture. In 1933, Collier was appointed commissioner of Indian affairs in the Department of the Interior and launched what became known as "the Indian New Deal."

Through Collier, the government provided compensation to the Pueblo Indians for lost lands, established relief programs for destitute Indians, and cancelled Indian debts for road building. The **Indian Reorganization Act** of 1934 ended the previous policy of land allotments established under the Dawes Act and restored surplus lands to the tribes. It also provided the basis for tribal self-government. However, many tribes did not accept the act, and it was only a limited success. Many of the programs introduced by Collier came to an end in 1939 with financial cuts and particularly with the coming of war in 1941. Critics point out that Collier did not appreciate the complexity of **Native American** tribal systems nor did he seriously challenge their segregation from the rest of society. He resigned in 1945 and began teaching at the City College of New York.

COLUMBIA RIVER PROJECT. Established by Congress in September 1933, the Columbia River Project created a Columbia River Authority, like the **Tennessee Valley Authority**, to provide hydroelectric power and irrigation to surrounding states in the Pacific Northwest (Washington, Oregon, and Idaho) through the building of the Bonneville Dam, completed in 1937, and **Grand Coulee Dam**, completed in 1942.

COMMUNIST PARTY OF THE UNITED STATES OF AMERICA (CPUSA). Communism was established in the United States in 1919 with the creation of the Communist Party and Communist Labor Party, which had been formed by elements of the **Socialist Party of America** and others, following the 1917 Bolshevik Revolution and the launching of the Third International, or Comintern, in March 1919. The two groups merged in 1921 to become the Workers' Party of America. In 1928, it was again renamed the Communist Party. The party always remained a minority party with a large foreign-language and immigrant membership. Its greatest electoral support came during the **Great Depression** when it secured 102,991 votes in the 1932 presidential election. Following the launching of President **Franklin D. Roosevelt**'s **New Deal** program, the party's membership fell to only 26,000 in 1934. Under the leadership of **Earl Browder**, the party began to change direction and support the New Deal and from 1935 on began to talk of a popular front in the struggle against fascism. As a result Browder received 80,869 votes in 1936, and membership rose to 100,000 again by 1939.

However, the CPUSA, loyal to the **Soviet Union**, abruptly changed again after the Nazi-Soviet Nonaggression Pact that year abandoned the popular front and increasingly spoke out against any possible involvement in war with **Germany**. But when the Germans invaded the Soviet Union in 1940, yet again the party abandoned its previous policy in favor of all out support of war. This continued to such an extent after the United States entered **World War II** in 1941 that Browder even suggested that the CPUSA was no longer necessary, and he was expelled from what was left of the organization and replaced by **William Z. Foster**. The party continued to decline during the **Cold War**, and by 1955 party membership was less than 5,000, one-third of whom were said to be **Federal Bureau of Investigation** agents. However, in 1948 the Truman administration prosecuted 11 CPUSA leaders under the terms of the **Smith Act**, and in 1949 they were sentenced for terms of one to five years in prison. As the Cold War progressed and events such as the Soviet suppression of the rising in Hungary in 1957 occurred, membership fell even further and was a mere 3,000 by 1958. The collapse of the Soviet Union in 1989 brought yet another decline, and the party barely continued to exist.

CONGRESS OF INDUSTRIAL ORGANIZATIONS (CIO). Faced with declining **trade union** membership following the onset of the **Great Depression** and with members facing reduced hours or wages, in 1934 elements within the **American Federation of Labor** (**AFL**), led by **John L. Lewis** of the Mineworkers Union, began to call for the organization of unskilled workers on an industrial basis. Lewis was joined by of the Amalgamated Clothing workers union, **David Dubinsky** of the International Ladies Garment Workers, and others in 1935 to form the Committee for Industrial Organizations which, in 1938, became the **Congress of Industrial Organizations**

(CIO). Encouraged by **New Deal** legislation, first in the **National Industrial Recovery Act (NIRA)** and then in the **National Labor Relations Act** that recognized the right to free collective bargaining, the CIO began the struggle to organize steelworkers in 1936. The **Steel Workers' Organizing Committee (SWOC)**, led by **Philip Murray**, overcame the traditional ethnic and racial divisions among the workforce and won recognition from the U.S. Steel Corporation in 1937. In 1936 the United Automobile Workers began **sit-down strikes** to secure recognition in the auto industry, and in 1937 General Motors conceded defeat. Although **Henry Ford** and the "Little Steel" companies still refused recognition, by 1940 CIO membership had outstripped that of the AFL.

Lewis was replaced by Philip Murray as leader of the CIO in 1940 when the mine workers leader endorsed **Wendell Willkie** rather than **Franklin D. Roosevelt**. During the war, the CIO supported the no-strike pledge in 1941, although the extent of wartime strikes in 1943 was sufficient to lead to the passage of the **War Labor Disputes Act**, a forerunner of the postwar **Taft-Hartley Act** limiting union freedom of action. Nonetheless, CIO membership rose to about 5 million during **World War II**. In addition, the CIO became more closely associated with the **Democratic Party** through the Political Action Committee established by **Sidney Hillman** and Philip Murray in 1943 to bypass the restrictions on political activities imposed by the wartime labor legislation.

After the war, the CIO attempted to continue the working relationships established with the government and business during the war, but this was undermined by the outbreak of strikes in 1946 and the later Taft-Hartley Act. Attempts to organize southern textile workers in Operation Dixie were a complete failure. The **Cold War** also had an impact as left-wing groups and individuals like **Harry Bridges** were expelled from the organization. When **Walter Reuther** succeeded Murray as president in 1952, he began to lead the CIO toward cooperation with the AFL, and the two finally merged in 1955.

CONGRESSIONAL REORGANIZATION ACT, 1946. Introduced by **Robert M. La Follette Jr.**, the Congressional Reorganization Act streamlined the legislative process by reducing the number of standing committees from 48 to 19 in the House and from 33 to 15 in the Senate. It provided a staff to assist committees, an improved reference service, and a legislative budget. In addition, it increased congressional salaries from $10,000 to $12,500 and provided a tax-exempt allowance.

CONNALLY, THOMAS (TOM) TERRY (1877–1963). Texan politician Tom Connally was a graduate of Baylor University in 1896 and the University of Texas Law School at Austin in 1898. He was admitted to the bar and established a law practice in Waco, Texas. During the Spanish-American War, Connally joined the volunteer infantry but did not see service overseas, nor did he see combat during World War I, although he was a captain in the infantry. A **Democrat**, Connally served in the Texas House of Representatives from 1901 until 1905. In 1917, he was elected to the U.S House of Representatives, and he held his seat until 1929 when he entered the U.S. Senate. He supported most of President **Franklin D. Roosevelt's New Deal**, with the exception of the **National Recovery Administration**. However, he was opposed to the president's attempt at "**court packing**" and mobilized opposition against it.

Connally was chair of the Senate Committee on Foreign Relations from 1941 to 1947 and again from 1949 to 1953. He helped to secure the approval of the **United Nations Charter** in 1945 and attended the first assembly meeting as a U.S delegate in 1946. Connally also backed President **Truman's Cold War** policies and the president's decision to commit U.S. troops to the **Korean War**. He chose not to seek reelection in 1953 and established a law practice in Washington, D.C.

CONSCIENTIOUS OBJECTORS. The **Selective Service Act** of 1940 exempted from combatant service in **World War II** any individual who objected "by reason of religious training and belief . . . to participation in war in any form." This excluded those who objected on nonreligious, moral grounds. Of the 34.5 million men registered for the draft, 72,354 applied for conscientious objector status, mainly from the traditional peace churches—the Quakers, Mennonites, and Brethren. Of these, 25,000 accepted military service in noncombatant roles, primarily in the medical corps. Another 12,000 accepted alternative service in civilian public service camps, many of them former

Civilian Conservation Corps camps, and worked in conservation, forestry, firefighting, and other tasks. They had to pay the federal government for their room and board and relied on the churches for financial support. About 500 of these men took part in medical experiments as guinea pigs.

Almost 6,000 conscientious objectors were "absolutists" who refused to support the war in any way, directly or indirectly, and were sentenced to jail. Almost three-quarters were Jehovah's Witnesses. Among those who refused to accept military service were members of the Nation of Islam, or Black Muslims, several hundred of whom, including their leader Elijah Muhammad, were jailed for their opposition on a mixture of religious and racial grounds. During the **Korean War**, 4,300 people were conscientious objectors.

CONTAINMENT. The term "containment" was coined by **George F. Kennan** in his "long telegram" in 1946 and in his article written under the name "X" in *Foreign Affairs* in July 1947 to describe his recommended response to real or perceived expansion by the **Soviet Union**. The policy implicitly accepted the presence of Soviet forces in the areas of Eastern Europe occupied after pushing back and defeating the German armies but outlined a constant policy of resistance, primarily by economic means, to any further spread of communist influence. If contained in this fashion, Kennan believed that the Soviet Union would collapse due to internal forces.

Kennan's ideas were largely accepted by President **Truman** in his speech to Congress in March 1947 asking for aid for Greece and Turkey, in which the president enunciated what became known as the **Truman Doctrine**. This was followed in 1948 by the **Marshall Plan** providing economic assistance for Western Europe. However, containment took on a more military aspect as a result of the **Berlin** blockade in 1949 and the creation of the **North Atlantic Treaty Organization** in 1949. After the fall of **China** in 1949, the policy extended to Asia and the development of a series of regional alliances (the Southeast Asia Treaty Organization in 1954 and the Central Treaty Organization in 1959), but it led to U.S. involvement in war after the North Korean invasion of South Korea in 1950, and ultimately it can be argued that it saw the growing commitment to resist communism in Vietnam that led to greater conflict in the 1960s.

See also COLD WAR; KOREAN WAR; NATIONAL SECURITY COUNCIL REPORT 68 (NSC-68).

COOPER, GARY (1901–1961). Born Frank James Cooper in Helena, Montana, the movie star was educated in England and was 21 when he went to Grinnell College in Iowa. In 1924, he began work as a cowboy in Tom Mix Westerns. He changed his name in 1926 and finally achieved some recognition in *The Winning of Barbara Worth* (1926). He starred with Clara Bow in several films and gradually made the transition to talkies with the lead role in *The Virginian* (1929), *The Texan* (1930), *Morocco* (1930), and others. In 1932, he starred in the lead role in the film version of **Ernest Hemingway**'s *A Farewell to Arms*, and in 1933 he partnered with Joan Crawford in *Today We Live*. In 1936, his portrayal of the simple idealist in **Frank Capra**'s *Mr. Deeds Goes to Town* had enormous appeal to **Great Depression** audiences.

By the 1940s, Cooper was the highest paid star in Hollywood, and he had big hits with *Meet John Doe*, *Sergeant York*, and *Ball of Fire*, all made in 1941. He won an Oscar for his part in *Sergeant York*, the story of the World War I pacifist turned war hero. He also had huge box office success in the film of Hemingway's story of an American in the **Spanish Civil War**, *For Whom the Bell Tolls* (1943), where again quiet, unassuming idealism marked the hero's role. Increasingly, however, Cooper's work seemed outdated, and it appeared that his career was in terminal decline until he appeared as the main character in the **Cold War** allegory *High Noon* in 1952, and won a second Oscar. He continued to make films throughout the 1950s despite his obvious declining health. He died of cancer and was mourned by millions. *See also* CINEMA.

COPLAND, AARON (1900–1990). The son of Russian Jewish immigrants, Copland was one of America's greatest modern composers. His work combined the influences of Igor Stravinsky with that of jazz and American folk melodies. He wrote for **radio**, theater, and movies, and his first major piece was *Symphony for Organ and Orchestra*, composed in 1924. During the 1920s, Copland was very much part of the avant-garde and contributed articles to the new journal *Modern Music*. He established the American Festivals of Contemporary Music at Saratoga Springs in 1932. His *El Salon Mexico* (1936) was influenced by visits to South America and Central America. He is best known for his later ballets celebrating American themes, *Billy the Kid* (1938), *Rodeo* (1942), and A*ppalachian Spring* (1944), and for the patriotic pieces written in 1942, *A Lincoln Portrait* and *Fanfare for a Common Man*. Copland wrote many famous film scores, including those for *Of Mice and Men* (1939) and *Our Town* (1940), and in 1949 he won an Oscar for his music for the movie *The Heiress*. During the period of **McCarthyism** in the 1950s, Copland was investigated for his supposed communist sympathies, and he testified before Congress in 1953. *See also* CINEMA.

CORCORAN, THOMAS ("TOMMY") GARDINER (1900–1981). Born in Pawtucket, Rhode Island, Thomas ("Tommy") Corcoran went to Brown University and Harvard Law School, where he graduated in 1926. Supported by **Felix Frankfurter**, he became clerk to Oliver Wendell Holmes for a year before practicing law on Wall Street. In 1932, Corcoran joined the **Reconstruction Finance Corporation** and remained there until 1940. Again through his links with Frankfurter, Corcoran became an unofficial member of the **New Deal** and assisted with drafting important legislation, including the act establishing the **Tennessee Valley Authority** and **Fair Labor Standards Act**. He also wrote several speeches for President **Franklin D. Roosevelt** and was an active member of the election campaign team in 1940. However, when he failed to receive any public appointment, he left government to resume his private law practice. He remained an influential figure in Washington, D.C., and in 1941 was accused of "influence peddling." Although never formally charged, such accusations continued for much of his career.

COSTIGAN-WAGNER BILL. *See* FEDERAL ANTILYNCHING BILL.

COUGHLIN, CHARLES EDWARD (1891–1979). The man who became the **"radio** priest," Charles Coughlin was born in Ontario, Canada. He was ordained as a priest in 1916, and in 1923 he moved to Detroit, Michigan, and in 1926 he established a parish, the Shrine of the Little Flower, where he remained the rest of his life. Coughlin began broadcasting his sermons in 1926, and his success led CBS radio to broadcast his hourly service every week from 1930 to 1931. When CBS failed to renew his contract, he established his own radio network.

As the impact of the **Great Depression** grew, Coughlin, an outspoken critic of **Herbert Hoover**, began to attack bankers and financiers in his sermons and call for control of the money supply. He initially supported President **Franklin D. Roosevelt** and the **New Deal**, but by 1934 he was becoming critical of the administration, even though he still said the people faced a choice of "Roosevelt or ruin." But in November 1934 Coughlin established his own National Union for Social Justice, calling for the nationalization of banks and public utilities and fairer taxation, and he began to establish links with **Huey Long** and Dr. **Francis Townsend**. In May 1936, Coughlin, together with Long and Townsend's successor, **Gerald K. Smith**, set up the **Union Party** with **William Lemke** as its presidential candidate, but following an abysmal performance that attracted only 900,000 votes, Coughlin disbanded his organizations and announced his retirement from politics. However, he still continued to express his views via the airwaves and in his publication *Social Justice*. He spoke and wrote in defense of **Adolf Hitler** and supported Nazi **Germany** in its opposition to the communist **Soviet Union**. He also appeared to be increasingly anti-Semitic in his views. He supported American isolationism and described Roosevelt as a "war monger." His radio broadcasts were suspended in 1940, and in 1942 the Postal Service refused mailing rights for *Social Justice*. Denied a voice, Coughlin concentrated on his parish activities until his retirement in 1966. *See also* WORLD WAR II.

"COURT PACKING" BILL. Following a succession of decisions by the **Supreme Court** striking down key measures in the **New Deal**, including the **National Industrial Recovery Act** and **Agricultural Adjustment Act**, President **Franklin D. Roosevelt** was anxious to ensure support for subsequent reform measures. In 1937, he presented a court reorganization act before Congress, making it possible to increase the number of justices from nine to 15 on the basis of a new appointment for any judge over the age of 70 who did not retire. The bill was met by considerable congressional and public protest and rejected by the Senate Judiciary Committee. While Roosevelt tried to win over public opinion in a "**fireside chat**" in March 1937, the Court itself responded with the "switch in time that saved nine" and on March 29 reversed an earlier decision against minimum wage legislation. It went on to uphold both the **Social Security Act** and **National Labor Relations Act**. Additionally, as justices, beginning with **Willis Van Devanter**, began to retire, Roosevelt was able to appoint replacements more sympathetic to the New Deal. As a result, the proposed bill was replaced with one incorporating minor reforms of lower court procedures. Nonetheless, the "court packing" incident was important as it demonstrated the limits to which the New Deal could go. It was also significant in encouraging opposition from conservative **Democrats** and thus weakening the president's power base in Congress. *See also* BORAH, WILLIAM EDGAR.

CROSBY, BING (1903–1977). One of the most successful singers and film stars in history, Bing Crosby was born Harry Lillis Crosby in Tacoma, Washington. He was educated at Gongaza High School in Spokane, Washington, and attended Gongaza University from 1921 to 1925. With his singing partner Al Rinker, Crosby joined the Paul Whiteman band in 1926 in Chicago. They were joined by Harry Barris to form the Rhythm Boys, but Crosby soon went solo and had a hit with "Ol' Man River" in 1928. With regular **radio** broadcasts and best-selling records, Crosby achieved one hit after another in the 1930s with his relaxed "crooning" style. Between 1935 and 1946 he starred on *Kraft Music Hall* and was a top-rated radio performer through the 1960s. Crosby also began to appear in films in the 1930s with *Reaching for the Moon* and *King of Jazz* in 1930, being the first of 20 or more movie appearances in that decade alone. Crosby appeared in more than 70 films during his career. In 1940, he began his famous film partnership with comedian Bob Hope in the first of the Road series, *The Road to Singapore*. The last was *The Road to Hong Kong* in 1962. He was enormously popular during **World War II** both for his broadcasts to troops in Europe and also for his appearance in the movie *Holiday Inn* in 1942 and the hit record, "White Christmas," which sold more than 40 million copies. It was one of several Crosby songs to win an Academy Award, and he won an award for acting in *Going My Way* in 1944. He achieved another big success with *Bells of St. Mary's* in 1945 and in *High Society* in 1956. In addition to his film roles, he also starred in **television** shows throughout the 1950s and 1960s, including the *Bing Crosby Show* in 1954 and again in 1964–1965. *See also* CINEMA.

CURRY, JOHN STEUART (1897–1946). Born in Kansas, John Steuart Curry studied **art** at Kansas City Art Institute in 1916, the Art Institute of Chicago from 1916 to 1918, and Geneva College in Pennsylvania from 1918 to 1919. He worked as an art teacher and illustrator for magazines and novels in New York City and spent a year in Paris in 1926. In 1937, Curry became artist in residence at the University of Wisconsin, Madison. One of the **regionalists**, much of Curry's work depicted American landscapes and themes in U.S. history, like his *Baptism in Kansas* (1928), *Tornado over Kansas* (1929), and *Wisconsin Landscape* (1937–1938). In 1934, Curry completed several murals in public buildings for the **Federal Art Project**. In 1937, his murals in the Kansas statehouse, showing an angry figure of John Brown, and also including members of the Ku Klux Klan, were regarded as controversial, and he did not complete the projected four panels.

– D –

DAVIS, BENJAMIN OLIVER, JR. (1912–2002). Born the son of the U.S. Army's first black general, Benjamin O. Davis Jr. attended the University of Chicago before he became the first **African American** in the 20th century to graduate from West Point Military Academy in 1936. He was only the second black officer at the time, his father, **Benjamin O. Davis Sr.**, being the other. Although he wanted to serve in the Army Air Corps, Davis was excluded on grounds of color. He was stationed at Fort Benning, Georgia. However, he was subsequently posted to Tuskegee Institute, where he was among the first black pilots to get their wings in 1942. In 1943, as lieutenant colonel, he was given command of the all-black 99th Pursuit Squadron and posted to North Africa. He subsequently went to Italy in command of the 332nd Fighter Group. He flew more than 60 missions and in 1944 was awarded the Distinguished Flying Cross.

After **World War II**, Davis was involved in devising plans for the integration of the air force, and he commanded a fighter group during the **Korean War**. He was promoted to lieutenant general in 1965, and in 1967 he became chief of staff of U.S. forces in Korea. Davis retired from the army in 1970 and in 1971 was assistant secretary of transportation. He retired in 1975. In 1998, President Bill Clinton awarded him a fourth star to make him a full general.

DAVIS, BENJAMIN OLIVER, SR. (1880–1970). The first **African American** general in the U.S. Army, Benjamin O. Davis Sr. was born in Washington, D.C., where he attended high school and took part-time classes at Howard University. In 1898, he joined the 8th Volunteer Infantry and served for a year in Georgia before mustering out. He rejoined the 9th Cavalry (one of four black regular regiments established by Congress after the Civil War). He rose through the ranks and became a first lieutenant in 1905. After a posting in the Philippines from 1901 to 1905, Davis took a position as professor of military science at Wilberforce University in Ohio. He was posted as the U.S. military attaché to Liberia from 1909 to 1912. He was posted back to the Philippines in 1917 and returned to the United States in 1920 as a lieutenant colonel. During the 1920s, Davis held different teaching positions at Tuskegee Institute and Wilberforce University. He made brigadier general in 1940 and retired in 1941 but was recalled following U.S. entry into **World War II**. During the war, he toured U.S. bases and the European Theater of Operations as an "adviser on Negro Problems." He reported on conditions and the morale of African American servicemen, but most of his recommendations were ignored. His primary role was to act as a morale-boosting model for black Americans. He retired in 1948. Davis was awarded the Bronze Star and the Distinguished Service Medal. He is buried in Arlington National Cemetery.

DAVIS, BETTE (1908–1989). Future movie star Bette Davis was born Ruth Elizabeth Davis in Lowell, Massachusetts. She worked as a secretary before turning to acting in the late 1920s. Her first Broadway role was in 1929. She joined Universal Studios in 1930 and appeared in *The Bad Sister* in 1931. She moved to Warner Studios and achieved a breakthrough with *The Man Who Played God*, followed by *Of Human Bondage*, both in 1934. Davis won an Academy Award for her role in *Dangerous* (1935) and appeared with **Humphrey Bogart** in *The Petrified Forest* (1936). Her second Academy Award came for her acting in *Jezebel* (1938). Not a conventional star, Davis appeared onscreen and offscreen as a liberated, independent **woman**. This involved her in some conflict with the studio, and her contract ended in 1949. Nonetheless, she made a number of successful film appearances, including *Dark Victory* (1939), *Watch on the Rhine* (1943), and *Mr. Skeffington* (1944).

During **World War II**, Davis made several public appearances to raise **war bonds**, and in 1942 she was one of several Hollywood stars to established the Hollywood Canteen to cater for servicemen in Los Angeles, California. She was awarded the Distinguished Civilian Service Medal in 1980 for her war work. Although her career faltered in the late 1940s, Davis received Academy nominations for her role in *All About Eve* (1950) and *The Star* (1952). A major success came later with *Whatever Happened to Baby Jane?* (1962). Awarded a Lifetime Achievement Award in 1977, she made her last film appearance in 1987. *See also* CINEMA.

DAVIS, CHESTER CHARLES (1887–1975). Born in Iowa, Chester Davis graduated from Grinnell College in 1911. After working as a journalist, he became editor of *The Montana Farmer* in 1917. In 1921, he became the state commissioner of **agriculture** and labor for Montana, and in 1925 he was appointed director of grain marketing for the Illinois Agricultural Association. Davis was an outspoken supporter of the McNary-Haugen Plan to maintain farm prices by government purchase of surpluses for export, and in 1928 he helped persuade the **Democratic Party** convention to adopt the proposal.

In 1933, **George N. Peek** appointed Davis as director of the division of production within the **Agricultural Adjustment Administration (AAA)**. When Peek resigned later that year, Davis succeeded him as head of the AAA. Internal differences within the AAA, particularly over the issue of protection for tenant farmers, eventually led Davis to resign in 1936. He joined the board of governors of the **Federal Reserve Board**, a position he held until 1941 when he became president of the Federal Reserve Bank of St. Louis. Davis was an associate director of the Ford Foundation in the early 1950s.

DAVIS, ELMER HOLMES (1890–1958). Author, journalist, and **radio** broadcaster Elmer Davis was born in Aurora, Indiana. He graduated from Franklin College in 1910 and was awarded a Rhodes Scholarship to Oxford. Davis returned to the United States in 1913 and began working as a journalist in New York City. In 1914, he was hired as a reporter for the *New York Times*. He became a freelance reporter in 1923, and he published fiction and nonfiction articles in a number of well-known journals. He also published popular novels. In 1939, he was appointed as a news analyst at CBS, and his subsequent wartime reports were heard by millions and made him as famous as his colleague, **Edward R. Murrow**.

In June 1942, **Franklin D. Roosevelt** appointed Davis head of the newly created **Office of War Information (OWI)**. His aim was to let the people have as much information about the war as possible, but this proved difficult given the reluctance of the military to release details. Davis was also accused of running a propaganda agency for the president. He continued as director of the OWI until it ceased operation in September 1945. In the postwar years, Davis was a critic of **Joseph McCarthy** in both his radio broadcasts and his writing.

DAVIS, JOHN WILLIAM (1873–1955). Born in Clarksburg, West Virginia, John Davis qualified in law in 1895 and went into practice with his father. Although a conservative on issues like **women**'s suffrage, he supported Woodrow Wilson and was appointed solicitor general in 1913. He held the position until 1918, when he became ambassador to **Great Britain**. He returned to legal practice on Wall Street in 1921.

In 1924, because of the deadlock between Senator William McAdoo and Governor **Alfred E. Smith**, Davis was nominated as the **Democratic** presidential candidate on the 103rd ballot. In the election, Davis received less than 8 million votes, while the Republican Calvin Coolidge won 16 million. In 1928, Davis supported Smith's campaign, and in 1932 he backed **Franklin D. Roosevelt**. However, he opposed much of the **New Deal** and joined Smith and other conservatives in forming the **American Liberty League**. After the war, he also opposed **Harry S. Truman**'s **Fair Deal** program. A successful appellate lawyer, he argued 141 cases before the **Supreme**

Court, most notably in *Youngstown Sheet & Tube Co. v. Sawyer* in 1952, when he argued against President Truman's takeover of the steel industry. He also served as counsel to **J. Robert Oppenheimer** when he was accused of being a security risk in 1954.

DAWSON, WILLIAM LEVI (1886–1970). African American politician William Dawson was born in Albany, Georgia. He graduated from Fisk University in Nashville in 1909, and in 1912 he moved to Chicago. In 1917, he joined the infantry and served as a first lieutenant in France during World War I. After the war, he went to Northwestern University Law School and was admitted to the bar in Chicago. A **Republican**, Dawson was elected to Chicago City Council. He unsuccessfully challenged **Arthur W. Mitchell** in 1938 and switched to the **Democratic Party** in 1939. He succeeded Mitchell when Mitchell was elected to the House of Representatives in 1942. At the time, he was the only African American in the House. In 1949, Dawson became the first African American to chair a congressional committee when he headed the Committee on Government Operations. He was a staunch party member, mobilizing black support for both city and national administrations, even during the Vietnam War. In 1966, when Martin Luther King came to Chicago to protest black poverty and poor housing, Dawson criticized him as an outsider. He remained in office until his death.

D-DAY, 1944. D-Day was the name given to the start of the **Allied** invasion of **Normandy** (code named "Overlord") in **World War II**. Initially planned for 5 June 1944, it was delayed by bad weather and finally took place on 6 June. It involved the successful landing of 130,000 troops on five beaches—Gold, Juno, and Sword (British and French) and **Utah** and **Omaha** (American).

DEMOCRATIC PARTY. The Democratic Party is one of the two major political parties in the United States, the other being the **Republican Party**. After a number of years in the 1890s as the second party, the Democrats gained control first of Congress and then of the White House with the election of Woodrow Wilson in 1912. They held a majority in both the Senate and the House of Representatives from 1913 to 1917 and maintained a majority in the Senate from 1917 to

1919. However, after 1919 the Democrats were divided on the issues of prohibition, the League of Nations, and ethnic and racial issues and lost the presidency in 1920, 1924, and 1928 to overwhelming defeats. The divisions between rural and urban areas and the South and North persisted throughout much of the 1920s, and the party was not able to unite again until the election of 1932 when, in the face of the **Great Depression**, they unified behind **Franklin D. Roosevelt** and recaptured control of both the House with 310 seats and the Senate with 60. Their control of Congress increased with larger majorities in both houses in 1934, and again in 1936 (331 in the House, 76 in the Senate).

Under Roosevelt's **New Deal**, the Democratic Party moved away from its traditional laissez faire position and notions of limited federal intervention to one of support for economic regulation and federal provision of social welfare for the unemployed and elderly. The party was increasingly identified with the urban, ethnic, and immigrant population; **African Americans**; **women**; and **trade unions**. It also continued to be the party of the South, and with this combined strength it was able to dominate both houses in Congress until the election of the postwar 80th Congress in 1946, and again with the 83rd Congress in 1952. However, following the "**court packing**" attempt in 1937 and the further recession that year, from 1938 the southern element often combined with Republicans to form a "conservative coalition" and block reforms, and the divisions became increasingly strained on issues of civil rights. In a foretaste of things to come in the 1960s, in 1948 the **Dixiecrats** bolted from the party because of **Harry S. Truman**'s creation of a Committee on Civil Rights and his subsequent order to begin the desegregation the armed forces. Although they returned to the fold after the election, the fragile structure disintegrated in the 1970s and 1990s with further political realignments along regional and ideological lines.

DENNIS V. UNITED STATES **(341 U.S. 494 1951).** Eugene Dennis was general secretary of the **Communist Party of the United States of America** and was one of 11 communists convicted under the **Smith Act** in 1949. The **Supreme Court** upheld the charges in this decision.

DESTROYERS-FOR-BASES AGREEMENT, 1940. The Destroyers-for-Bases Agreement was an agreement signed in September 1940 by President **Franklin D. Roosevelt** and British prime minister **Winston Churchill** granting the United States 99-year rent free leases on naval and air bases on British possessions in the Caribbean in return for 50 out-of-service destroyers. The agreement indicated the growing support for Britain by the Roosevelt administration and angered some isolationists. It was justified on the grounds that it strengthened U.S. security.

DETROIT RACE RIOT, 1943. One of the major centers of war production during **World War II**, Detroit, Michigan, attracted an influx of more than 500,000 people, of whom some 60,000 were **African American**. This rapid increase in population put a huge strain on housing and transportation. For African Americans, the situation was particularly acute as they tended to be restricted to existing black areas. The attempt to provide public housing with the Sojourner Truth Project led to violent confrontations in 1942. There were strikes in automobile plants when black workers were promoted. On 20 June 1943, a confrontation between blacks and whites in the amusement park on Belle Isle quickly escalated into a full riot. As mobs of white people hunted down black workers and pulled them from trams and buses, African Americans responded by attacking white-owned property. The riot was finally brought under control after three days with the arrival of 6,000 federal troops. By then, 34 people were dead, 25 of them black. More than 1,000 people were injured, and almost 2,000 were arrested. *See also* HARLEM RACE RIOT, 1935; HARLEM RACE RIOT, 1945; LOS ANGELES RIOT.

DEWEY, THOMAS EDMUND (1902–1971). Born in Owosso, Michigan, Thomas E. Dewey studied music and law at the University of Michigan and graduated in 1923. He graduated from Columbia Law School in 1925 and began working on Wall Street. He also became active in the **Republican Party**. In 1931, Dewey was appointed assistant U.S. district attorney for New York's Southern District, and in 1933 he became district attorney. He was appointed special prosecutor to deal with organized crime and in 1936 secured the conviction of the New York Mafia leader Charles ("Lucky") Luciano. His success led him to become the first Republican to be elected district attorney for New York County (Manhattan) in 1937. He narrowly lost the election for state governor in 1938, losing to **Herbert Lehman**. However, he won the election in 1942 and was reelected in 1946 and 1950. As governor he introduced antidiscrimination laws in 1945, established New York's state university system in 1947, approved the building of the New York State Thruway, developed public health programs, and balanced the state's budget.

Dewey's undoubted achievements led to his nomination as the Republican presidential candidate in 1944 and 1948. Although he was quite easily defeated by the incumbent, **Franklin D. Roosevelt**, in 1944, in 1948 he was regarded as the favorite against **Harry S. Truman** and a divided **Democratic Party**. Dewey did not campaign very effectively, and Truman pulled out a famous upset. Dewey did not stand again in 1952, but he supported the nomination of **Dwight D. Eisenhower** for the presidency and **Richard M. Nixon** for the vice presidency. He retired from the governorship of New York in 1955 and took up private law practice in New York City.

DEWITT, JOHN LESESNE (1880–1962). Born in Nebraska, John DeWitt entered the U.S. infantry in 1898. He served in France during World War I and was awarded the Distinguished Service Medal. After the war, he served in the War Department with the General Staff as quartermaster general, and he served briefly in the Philippines. DeWitt was attached to the U.S. Army War College from 1937 to 1938 and in 1939 was made head of the West Defense Command. Following the attack on **Pearl Harbor** in 1941, DeWitt strongly advocated the relocation of **Japanese Americans** on the grounds that they posed a threat of subversion and sabotage. He argued that the fact that no such acts had been carried out only indicated that they were likely in the future. After President **Franklin D. Roosevelt** had approved the relocation in 1942, DeWitt had charge of the exclusion of Japanese Americans from West Coast areas and their removal to relocation camps. He became commandant of the Army and Navy College in 1943 and remained there until he retired in 1947. In 1954, Congress made DeWitt a general.

DEWSON, MARGARET WILLIAMS ("MOLLY") (1874–1962).
Born in Quincy, Massachusetts, Molly Dewson graduated from
Wellesley College in 1897 and joined the Women's Educational and
Industrial Union in Boston. She became an active campaigner to
establish a minimum wage for **women** in Boston. From 1919 until
1924 Dewson was the research secretary for the National Consumers'
League and worked with **Felix Frankfurter** in preparing arguments
in favor of minimum wages for women in the 1920s. From 1924
until 1931 she was president of the New York Consumers' League,
and through her activities she befriended **Eleanor Roosevelt**. She
supported **Alfred E. Smith**'s campaign in 1928 and **Franklin D.
Roosevelt** in 1932. As head of the Women's Division of the Democratic National Committee from 1933 until 1937, Dewson worked to
increase the representation of women in the **Democratic Party** and
did much to mobilize support among female voters. She also supported the appointment of **Frances Perkins** as secretary of labor and
was involved in drafting the **Social Security Act**. In 1937, Dewson
became a member of the Social Security Board but retired in 1938
due to ill-health.

DIETRICH, MARLENE (1901–1992). The German-born actress and
singer was born Maria Magdalena Dietrich in Berlin, **Germany**,
but she adopted Marlene as her stage name. She made a number of
successful films in Germany before moving to Hollywood in 1930.
There she made *Morocco* (1930), *Dishonored* (1931), *Shanghai
Express* (1932), *Scarlet Empress* (1934), and *The Devil Is a Woman*
(1935) and became one of the highest-paid actors. After a lull, her
career picked up in 1939 with the Western *Destry Rides Again*. Having refused to return to Germany, Dietrich became a U.S. citizen in
1939, and during the war she worked tirelessly in bond drives and
in 1943 gave up making films to work with the **United Service Organizations** to entertain troops in the United States and Europe. She
was awarded the Medal of Freedom and the French Legion of Honor
for her war services.

Dietrich returned to her film career after the war and made several
films in the late 1940s and 1950s. She also developed a singing career. In the late 1950s, she appeared in *Witness for the Prosecution*
(1958), *Touch of Evil* (1958), and *Judgment at Nuremberg* (1961).

Her last film appearance was in *Just a Gigolo* (1978). *See also* CINEMA.

DILLINGER, JOHN HERBERT (1903–1934). Notorious bank robber John Dillinger was born in Indianapolis, Indiana. He joined the U.S. Navy in 1923 but deserted, received a dishonorable discharge, and returned to Indiana. In 1924, he was jailed for robbery. He was released in 1933 and jailed again shortly afterward in Lima, Ohio, but escaped. Captured again in Tucson, Arizona, Dillinger was in Crown Point jail in Indiana when he escaped in March 1934, and he began robbing banks in the Midwest while on the run. His gang, including **"Baby Face" Nelson**, was responsible for 10 deaths during robberies and encounters with the law. Despite this, Dillinger was regarded as a "Robin Hood" character by some people for his attack on banks and several jailbreaks. Having crossed state lines, he became "Public Enemy Number One" for the **Federal Bureau of Investigation (FBI)**. In April, surrounded after a tip-off, Dillinger and his gang made yet another escape, killing an FBI agent in the process. On 22 July 1934, Dillinger was finally cornered coming out of a movie theater in Chicago and was shot dead. After his death, some doubt was cast on whether it was in fact Dillinger who had been killed, but fingerprints and other evidence pointed to him. *See also* HOOVER, JOHN (J.) EDGAR.

DIMAGGIO, JOSEPH (JOE) PAUL (1914–1899). The son of Sicilian immigrants, Joe DiMaggio was born Giuseppe Paolo DiMaggio in California. He dropped out of high school and in 1932 joined the San Francisco Seals minor league baseball team rather than fish with his father. In 1934, he was sold for $25,000 and five players to the New York Yankees, although he played the 1935 season with the Seals because of a knee injury. The Yankees won the World Series in each of his first four seasons. DiMaggio played for the Yankees until his retirement in 1951 and was one of the outstanding baseball players of the century. Known for his grace both on and off the field, he was a stylish player renowned for his fielding and hitting. He hit 28 home runs in his first season, and upon retirement he had the fifth most career home runs, with a total of 361. In 1941, his 56-gamehitting streak gripped the nation, and he became known as "Joltin' Joe" and the

"Yankee Clipper." In February 1942, asking for no special treatment, DiMaggio enlisted in the U.S. Army Air Force and served as a physical education instructor and played exhibition games for the troops through **World War II**. He resumed his baseball career in 1946 and led the Yankees to four more victories in the World Series.

Although he won his third title as most valuable player in 1947 and was the first player to earn $100,000 in 1949, DiMaggio retired when he felt his game begin to decline. In 1954, he married movie star Marilyn Monroe, but they were divorced after less than a year. It seemed that they were planning to reconcile just before her suicide in 1962. DiMaggio was elected to the Baseball Hall of Fame in 1955 and in 1969 was named the greatest living baseball player. He is remembered in several songs, most notably Simon and Garfunkel's "Mrs. Robinson." His brothers Vince and Dominic were also successful baseball players, Vince with the Cincinnati Reds and Pittsburgh Pirates and Dom with the Boston Red Sox. *See also* SPORT.

DIXIECRATS. The Dixiecrats were members of the States' Rights Party formed by southerners who bolted from the **Democratic Party** convention in 1948 due to the adoption of a strong **civil rights** plank and following **Harry S. Truman**'s call for the beginning of desegregation in the U.S. armed forces. With the slogan "Segregation Forever," they nominated **Strom Thurmond**, governor of South Carolina, as their presidential candidate. In the election, they carried Louisiana, Mississippi, Alabama, and South Carolina, and won 39 Electoral College votes. Despite this and defections to the liberal **Progressive Party**, Truman won the election. The Dixiecrats reappeared as the American Independent Party behind the candidacy of Governor George Wallace of Alabama in 1968 in what led to a realignment of political party structures in the United States.

DONOVAN, WILLIAM (BILL) JOSEPH (1883–1959). William (Bill) Donovan was born in Buffalo, New York. He attended St. Joseph's Collegiate Institute, Niagara University, and Columbia University, where he graduated with an A.B. in 1905 and an LL.B. in 1907. He initially worked as a lawyer in Buffalo. In 1912, he formed and led a cavalry unit that served in the border action in Mexico in

1916, and during World War I he served with the 69th Infantry and was wounded several times and awarded the Medal of Honor and Distinguished Service Cross for his bravery.

After the war, Donovan resumed his legal practice but in 1922 was appointed U.S. attorney general for New York's Western District. He campaigned unsuccessfully as the **Republican** candidate for lieutenant governor of the state. He was also unsuccessful when he ran for the governorship in 1932. In 1924, Donovan was appointed assistant attorney general, a post he held until 1929 when he began to practice law in New York City. In 1940, he was sent to England by **Frank Knox** to report on **Great Britain**'s ability to continue to fight against Nazi **Germany** in **World War II**. In July 1941, he was appointed as coordinator of information to gather intelligence, and on 13 June 1942 this became the **Office of Strategic Services** with Donovan as its head. Donovan was influential in the decision to establish the **Central Intelligence Agency** in 1947. In 1953, Donovan was appointed as ambassador to Thailand, but he was forced to resign due to poor health in 1954.

DOOLITTLE RAID. On 18 April 1942, 16 twin-engine B-25 bombers led by Colonel James H. Doolittle took off from the aircraft carrier USS *Hornet* in the Pacific and flew some 600 miles to bomb Tokyo, **Japan**. Although the physical damage to Japan was slight, the attack had great psychological significance, boosting morale in the United States and embarrassing the Japanese naval command. Their determination to keep the U.S. Navy from mounting further attacks led to the Battle of **Midway** in June 1942 and a major Japanese defeat.

Fifteen of the U.S. bombers involved in the raid made it to **China**, and most of the crew survived. However, eight were captured by the Japanese, three were executed, one died, and four were freed at the end of the war. *See also* WORLD WAR II.

DOUGLAS, HELEN GAHAGAN (1900–1980). Born Helen Gahagan in New Jersey, Helen Douglas (she married actor Melvyn Douglas in 1931) attended Barnard College before starting an acting career in 1922. She was well-known for theater and opera performances on Broadway, including *Fashions for Men* (1922), *Chains* (1923), and *Young Woodley* (1925); made several tours of Europe;

and appeared in one film, *She*, in 1935. Having moved to California, Douglas became involved in **Democratic Party** politics. She served on the National Advisory Committee to the **Works Progress Administration** and also with the **National Youth Administration** and was a Democratic National Committee member from 1940 to 1944. She was elected to the House of Representatives in 1944 and served until 1951. In 1950, she stood for election to the Senate but was defeated by **Republican Richard M. Nixon**, who accused her of being "pink down to her underwear." She continued to be active in politics speaking and giving lectures and in 1952 appeared again on Broadway in *First Lady*. She also authored a book, *The Eleanor Roosevelt We Remember* (1963).

DOUGLAS, WILLIAM ORVILLE (1898–1981). The longest-serving justice on the **Supreme Court**, William Douglas was born in Maine, Minnesota, but his family moved to Washington, where he attended Whitman College. After briefly teaching in high school, he went to Columbia Law School, where he graduated in 1925. Douglas practiced law for a short time before accepting a teaching position at Yale law school. In 1934, he joined the **Securities and Exchange Commission (SEC)** and became chairman in 1937. In 1939, he succeeded **Louis D. Brandeis** on the Supreme Court, where he became a strong defender of First Amendment rights of free speech. With **Hugo Black**, he opposed several decisions upholding convictions against left-wing groups during the **McCarthy** period. In 1953, he granted a stay of execution for **Ethel** and **Julius Rosenberg** on a technicality relating to their sentence. However, his decision was overruled by **Frederick Vinson**, and there was a short-lived attempt to impeach Douglas for his action.

Douglas did not have the impact on the court that he might have because, with Black, he was generally in the minority, and his dissenting opinions were often too hastily written to be memorable. In the 1960s, he found more liberal support in the court, but his colorful personal life (he was divorced three times), support for radical causes, and involvement in a private foundation led to a further but unsuccessful attempt to impeach him in 1970. He was a strong supporter of environmental causes, and in one case he held that inanimate objects such as trees had rights. He retired in 1975.

DUBINSKY, DAVID (1892–1982). Born David Dobnievski in Poland, Dubinsky was imprisoned in Siberia for his early **trade union** activities. He immigrated to the United States in 1911, found work as a cutter in the garment industry, and joined the International Ladies Garment Workers Union (ILGWU) and the **Socialist Party of America**. He became secretary-treasurer of the union in 1929 and president in 1932. He held the position until 1966. In 1934, he became vice president of the **American Federation of Labor (AFL)** but left to help form the **Congress of Industrial Organizations (CIO)** in 1936. He was one of the leading trade union supporters of **Franklin D. Roosevelt** and the **New Deal**, and in 1936 he left the Socialist Party to help found the American Labor Party (ALP). He left the CIO in 1938, and the ILGWU was independent until 1945 when it rejoined the AFL. Dubinsky left the ALP in 1944 and was one of the founders of the Liberal Party. He was also active in **Americans for Democratic Action**, formed in 1947 to oppose communism. After the war, Dubinsky was involved in combating racketeering in the unions and was a member of the American Federation of Labor-Congress of Industrial Organizations Committee on Ethical Practices.

DUMBARTON OAKS CONFERENCE, 1944. Dumbarton Oaks is a residence in Georgetown, Washington, D.C., that was the location of the meeting between representatives of the United States, **Great Britain, China**, and the **Soviet Union** between 21 August and 7 October 1944 that established the principles on which to create a **United Nations (UN)** organization. It led to the calling of a further conference of all **Allied** nations at the **San Francisco Conference** in April 1946 to establish the UN.

DUST BOWL. The Dust Bowl was the title given to an area of the United States plagued first by drought in 1930 through 1933 and then hit by a series of high winds that swept away the topsoil from 1933 through 1937 and exacerbated the plight of many Midwestern farmers during the **Great Depression**. Although it covered a huge area across the Great Plains, from the Canadian border southward, its worst effects were concentrated in Kansas, Oklahoma, New Mexico, Arkansas, and Texas, and the circumstances led to the displacement of thousands of migrants, often referred to as **"Okies."** Government soil conservation and reforestation schemes under the **New Deal** were implemented to tackle the problems of soil erosion that caused the Dust Bowl. *See also* AGRICULTURE; STEINBECK, JOHN ERNST.

– E –

ECCLES, MARRINER STODDARD (1890–1977). Born in Utah and a graduate of Brigham Young College in 1909, Marriner Eccles took over his family's businesses following his father's death in 1912. Together with his brother and other associates, he created the Eccles-Browning Bank in 1924 and the First Security Corporation in 1928. Established as a successful and influential banker, Eccles helped to draft the **Emergency Banking Act** of 1933 and joined the Treasury as an assistant to **Henry Morgenthau** in 1934. In 1935, he became chair of the **Federal Reserve**. In this capacity, Eccles encouraged the application of the theories of **John Maynard Keynes**. He continued to have a significant influence throughout **World War II** and afterward took part in the discussions at the **Bretton Woods Conference** that led to the creation of the **International Monetary Fund** and World Bank in 1946. Eccles also urged support of the **Marshall Plan** in 1947. Although he was not reappointed as chair of the Federal Reserve, he stayed on as vice chairman until 1951. Afterward, he returned to his private business and established the Marriner S. Eccles Library and Fellowship in Political Economy at the University of Utah. The Federal Reserve Building in Washington, D.C., is named in his honor.

ECONOMIC BILL OF RIGHTS. In his State of the Union Address to Congress on 11 January 1944, President **Franklin D. Roosevelt** called for measures to provide a second bill of rights offering U.S. citizens economic security in the postwar world. The principles he outlined included the right to employment and a living wage; the right to a fair and adequate return for farmers; freedom from unfair competition for businessmen; the right to a decent home; and medical care, education, and economic security against the risks of unemployment, accident, and old age. One measure enacted in line with these proposals was the **Employment Act** of 1946. **Harry S. Truman**'s **Fair Deal** also included some of these proposals.

ECONOMIC STABILIZATION ACT, 1942. Passed on 2 October 1942, the Economic Stabilization Act (sometimes known as the Antiinflation Act) was intended to control the cost of living. It increased the power of the **Office of Price Administration** to include rationing and gave the **National War Labor Board** power to control wages by limiting all increases to the 15 percent established in the **"Little Steel" formula** in 1942.

ECONOMY ACT, 1933. Passed on 20 March 1933, the Economy Act was outlined by President **Franklin D. Roosevelt** in his second message to Congress at the start of the **New Deal** and was passed in only two days. The act cut the pay of workers in federal government and the armed forces by 15 percent and cut spending in government departments by 25 percent. It also cut payments to veterans. The measure was intended to help balance the budget and allow spending on New Deal programs.

EINSTEIN, ALBERT (1879–1955). Born in Ulm, **Germany**, and educated in Munich and Zurich, Switzerland, Albert Einstein developed the theory of relativity published in a series of articles in the *Annals of Physics* in 1905. This was the most revolutionary development in physics since Sir Isaac Newton's theory of gravity in the 17th century. From 1913 until 1933 Einstein was the director of the Kaiser Wilhelm Institute of Physics in Berlin, Germany. He was awarded the Nobel Prize in 1919 and published *The Principle of Relativity* in 1923.

Jewish by origin and a committed pacifist, Einstein was forced to emigrate when **Adolf Hitler** came to power in 1933, and he secured an appointment at the Institute for Advanced Study at Princeton. In 1939, he wrote to **Franklin D. Roosevelt** expressing his concern that Germany might develop nuclear weapons first and urging the president to ensure that the United States prevented such an act. This provided the incentive for the **Manhattan Project** and the development of the **atomic bomb** in the United States. Einstein spent the rest of his career trying to establish the relationship between gravitation and electromagnetism.

EISENHOWER, DWIGHT DAVID ("IKE") (1890–1969). 34th president of the United States. Born in Denison, Texas, Dwight D. ("Ike") Eisenhower graduated from West Point Military Academy in 1915 and was commissioned in the infantry. During World War I, Eisenhower remained in the United States in charge of training camps. After the war, he served in Panama and attended the General Staff School at Fort Leavenworth, Texas, and the Army War College in Carlisle, Pennsylvania. After serving as General **Douglas MacArthur**'s chief of staff and a term in the Philippines, Eisenhower was appointed head of the War Plans Division in Washington, D.C., in December 1941. In May 1942, he was given command of U.S. troops in **Great Britain**, and in July he was appointed to lead the **Allied** invasion of North Africa in November. He led the invasion of Sicily on 10 July 1943 and the invasion of Italy on 9 September 1943. In December 1943, President **Franklin D. Roosevelt** appointed Eisenhower as supreme allied commander with the responsibility of leading the invasion of Europe in June 1944.

Although sometimes criticized for his caution, Eisenhower was an excellent strategist, and he managed to get the best out of British General Bernard Montgomery and American **George S. Patton**. However, Eisenhower's insistence that fighting be continued on a broad front meant that supplies were spread thinly, and it left Allied forces vulnerable to counterattack, which occurred during the **Battle of the Bulge** in December 1944. Nonetheless, Eisenhower was able to turn the tide by his effective use of manpower and the support for the forces holding **Bastogne**, Belgium. Once the Germans were forced back, Eisenhower continued the broad front strategy rather than letting either Montgomery or Patton move on to **Berlin**. Instead, he left it to the **Soviet** army to take the German capital. In November 1945, Eisenhower replaced General **George C. Marshall** as the U.S. Army's chief of staff. Eisenhower retired in 1948 and produced his war memoir, *Crusade in Europe*, that year.

After leaving the army, Eisenhower became president of Columbia University in New York City. He resisted overtures from both political parties to run on the presidential ticket in 1948. In 1951, he became first Allied supreme commander in Europe, and he provided military leadership for the newly formed **North Atlantic Treaty Organization**. However, in 1952 he was persuaded to run as the **Re-**

publican presidential candidate, and he defeated Senator **Robert A. Taft** to win the party's nomination. He easily defeated **Democratic** candidate **Adlai Stevenson** and went on to win a second term in 1956, again defeating Stevenson.

As president, Eisenhower practiced what he called "dynamic conservatism," or "moderate progressivism," meaning that he was liberal on social issues but conservative on economic matters—his was a "middle way." He distanced himself from **Joseph McCarthy** and disapproved of the worst excesses of **McCarthyism**. Abroad, Eisenhower brought the **Korean War** to an end and refused to commit U.S. troops to the war in Vietnam following the French defeat in 1954. He did, however, sanction the overthrow of an apparently left-wing government in Iran in 1953 and Guatemala in 1954. During the 1950s, the United States became increasingly involved in the Middle East, sending troops to the Lebanon in 1958 but refusing to support the British and French in the Suez Crisis of 1956. In 1959, Eisenhower approved preparations by the **Central Intelligence Agency** for an invasion of Cuba to overthrow the new regime of Fidel Castro. Those plans led to the failure in the Bay of Pigs in 1961.

At home, Eisenhower accepted the basic reform initiatives of the **New Deal**, extending **Social Security** and raising minimum wage levels. His administration also approved the construction of the St. Lawrence Seaway and embarked on a massive road-building scheme with the 1956 Federal Highways Act. Following the Soviet success in launching Sputnik, an unmanned satellite, in 1957, Eisenhower established the National Aeronautics and Space Agency (NASA) in 1958 and provided federal funding for scientific research through the National Defense Education Act. Although as a fiscal conservative he aimed for a balanced budget, he only achieved that balance on two occasions. However, he supported such probusiness policies as the reduction of corporation taxes and increased tax relief. He refused to support any expansion of the **Tennessee Valley Authority** or federal control of atomic energy. Moreover, Eisenhower only reluctantly acted on **civil rights** issues, disapproved of the **Supreme Court**'s decision in *Brown v. Board of Education of Topeka*, and used federal troops in Little Rock, Arkansas, to enforce desegregation of the public schools only when forced to by Governor Orval Faubus. Although he took a strong position against the Soviet Union when they shot down a U-2 U.S. spy plane in 1960, when Eisenhower left office he warned against the dangers of a growing "military-industrial complex." He retired in Abilene, Kansas.

EISENHOWER, MILTON STOVER (1899–1985). The younger brother of **Dwight D. Eisenhower**, Milton Eisenhower was also born in Abilene, Kansas. He studied journalism at Kansas State College in Manhattan, Kansas, where he then taught. He served briefly in the U.S. Consulate in Edinburgh, Scotland, before becoming assistant to William Jardine, Calvin Coolidge's secretary of agriculture. In 1928, Eisenhower became director of information in the Department of **Agriculture**, a position he held until 1941. In 1942, he was appointed to head the **War Relocation Authority** responsible for the supervision of the camps established to house the interned **Japanese Americans** during **World War II**. His attempts to provide reasonable conditions in the camps were to some extent limited due to the resistance he encountered from politicians and military officials. He later regretted his involvement in the relocation. After only 90 days, Eisenhower moved to the **Office of War Information**, where he became assistant to **Elmer Davis**.

In 1943, Eisenhower left government service to become president of Kansas State College, a position he held until 1950 when he became president of Pennsylvania State University. In 1956, he moved to become president of Johns Hopkins University. He retired in 1967 but took the position again briefly from 1971 until 1972.

During his brother's presidency, Eisenhower acted as adviser, speechwriter, and special representative. He also assisted President John F. Kennedy and was chair of President Lyndon Johnson's National Commission on the Causes and Prevention of Violence. His political memoir, *The President is Calling*, was published in 1974.

ELLINGTON, EDWARD KENNEDY ("DUKE") (1899–1974). The **African American** jazz musician and composer was born Edward Kennedy Ellington but acquired the nickname "Duke" as a schoolboy in Washington, D.C. Ellington did not have professional musical training, but he learned how to play from other black musicians. He formed his first group in 1917, and in 1923 he and several band members moved to Harlem, New York, where they found work in clubs. In 1924, Ellington became the bandleader and developed an improvisational style of composition. In 1926, the Ellington band recorded "East St. Louis Toodle-Oo," followed in 1927 by "Birmingham Breakdown" and "Black and Tan Fantasy." It was in 1927 that the group became the resident band at Harlem's famous Cotton Club. Over the coming years, Ellington and his band composed and recorded the jazz classics "Creole Love Call" (1927), "Mood Indigo," (1930) "Sophisticated Lady" (1932), "Solitude" (1934), and many more. With successful recording and live **radio** broadcasts from the Cotton Club from 1931 onward, Ellington became a major figure in popular **music**. In 1933, he made his first visit to London and other European locations.

Ellington continued to produce great jazz hits through band and record label changes. After moving from Columbia to Victor in 1940, the band recorded "Take the 'A' Train," "Cotton Tail," and "Ko-Ko." He also began to produce symphonic pieces, like "Black, Brown, Beige," in 1943, and extended pieces, like "Harlem," in 1948. After a brief lull in their success, the Ellington band had a revival of fortunes following a performance at the Newport Jazz Festival in 1956, and they continued to perform throughout the 1950s and 1960s, as well as provide film scores and music for theater. Before he died, Ellington had been awarded honorary degrees, membership in the American Institute of Arts and Letters, the French Legion of Honor, and the Presidential Medal of Freedom.

EMERGENCY BANKING ACT, 1933. Faced with the collapse of the country's financial institutions in the aftermath of the **Wall Street Crash** and onset of the **Great Depression**, newly elected president **Franklin D. Roosevelt** convened a special session of Congress to enact the emergency **Banking Act** on 9 March 1933. It formalized the bank holiday already declared by the president and implemented procedures to protect banks from further collapse, including action by the **Reconstruction Finance Corporation** to relieve banks of debts. These measures originated from earlier proposals under the administration of **Herbert Hoover**. *See also* BANKING.

EMERGENCY FARM MORTGAGE ACT, 1933. An amendment to the **Agricultural Adjustment Act** of 1933 providing for refinancing of farm mortgages through the purchase of tax exempt bonds. It also provided $200 million in loans to enable farmers to redeem land already lost through foreclosure. *See also* AGRICULTURE.

EMERGENCY PRICE CONTROL ACT, 1942. Passed in January 1942 to control inflation during **World War II**, the Emergency Price Control Act reorganized the **Office of Price Administration** to give it more power under a single administrator and the authority to fix prices or rents, commodities, and services.

EMERGENCY RELIEF APPROPRIATIONS ACT, 1935. Passed on 8 April 1935, the Emergency Relief Appropriations Act of 1935 provided $4.8 billion for work relief programs to alleviate unemployment. This was the largest peace-time appropriation up to that point. It led to the creation of the **Works Progress Administration** on 6 May 1935.

EMERGENCY RELIEF APPROPRIATIONS ACT, 1937. Concerned about the continuing cost of relief and the need to balance the federal budget, President **Franklin D. Roosevelt** asked for only $1.5 billion in relief spending for 1937–1938. The Emergency Relief Appropriations Act of 1937, passed on 22 July 1937, also excluded aliens not in the process of becoming citizens from work relief programs. The resulting cuts in spending are thought to have contributed to the "Roosevelt Recession" that year.

EMPLOYMENT ACT, 1946. The Employment Act of 1946, passed on 20 February 1946, created the Council of Economic Advisers as part of the White House staff, whose duty was to "formulate and recommend national economic policy" that would further the national goal of "maximum employment, production, and purchasing power." The act was intended to address the fear among many Americans that the mass unemployment of the **Great Depression** might return after **World War II** and to provide for economic growth.

The idea for the bill emerged from the **National Resources Planning Board**, the **New Deal**'s official planning agency, which in the early 1940s promoted the idea of "full employment" as a postwar goal. It also reflected President **Franklin D. Roosevelt**'s call in 1944 for an "**economic bill of rights**," which included "the right to a useful and remunerative job." Progressive labor and farm groups were also actively lobbying for legislation to promote government-guaranteed full employment, as were leading economists influenced by **John Maynard Keynes**. When the bill was introduced in Congress in January 1945, it was titled the Full Employment Bill. It called for the president to adopt economic policies that would create jobs for anyone who wanted them by using compensatory federal spending to create jobs if the private sector appeared unlikely to generate enough employment. President **Harry S. Truman** supported the measure after Roosevelt's death, as did most New Dealers in Congress. However, after the mid-term elections in 1946, not enough New Dealers remained to enact the original bill.

After strenuous opposition from employers, who feared that a full employment economy would drive up labor costs, conservatives in Congress diluted the legislation, and the phrase "full employment," disappeared from both the title and body of the bill, as did all the specific policy requirements that gave the phrase meaning. However, the act did require that the president issue an annual economic report indicating the state of the economy and outlining the government's economic goals and means of achieving them. The Council of Economic Advisers did at times encourage presidents to choose policies that promoted economic growth. Thus, while the Employment Act did not guarantee full employment, it did help make fiscal policy an important element of economic planning and indicated that the federal government would continue to have a central role in ensuring the nation's economic well-being in the postwar era.

***ENDO V. UNITED STATES* (323 U.S. 283 1944).** Mitsuye Endo was a **Japanese American** native of California, who in 1942 applied for a writ of habeas corpus challenging the legality of her internment in a relocation center during **World War II**. Her case eventually reached the **Supreme Court**, which ruled unanimously on 18 December 1944 that the government had no right to hold citizens whose loyalty they had conceded. On the basis of this decision, the **War Relocation Authority** gradually began to release the inmates of the camps back into society.

ENOLA GAY. The name given to the B-29 bomber from which the first **atomic bomb** was dropped on the Japanese city of **Hiroshima** on 6 August 1945.

ENTERTAINMENT, ARTS, AND LEISURE. *See* ART; CINEMA; LITERATURE AND THEATER; RADIO; SPORT; TELEVISION.

EUROPEAN RECOVERY PROGRAM (ERP). Popularly known as the **Marshall Plan**, the ERP was intended to help contain communism abroad by rebuilding the economies of postwar Europe and averting a return to the conditions that brought about the **Great Depression** and **World War II**. The program of aid was announced by Secretary of State **George C. Marshall** at Harvard University on 5 June 1947. Following a conference in Paris in July through September, a four-year recovery plan was agreed on, and President **Harry S. Truman** approved the first appropriation bill in April 1948.

Between 1948 and 1952, $13 million of aid in different forms was provided to participating Western European countries (and the western zone of **Germany**) through the Committee for European Economic Cooperation and the U.S. Economic Cooperation Administration. The resultant move to unify the economy of West Germany led to the **Berlin** Blockade in 1948 and the formation of a Soviet-led economic bloc in Eastern Europe, the Committee for Mutual Economic Assistance or COMECON. The Marshall Plan prevented the economic collapse of Western Europe and spurred economic recovery and the move toward economic integration. *See also* COLD WAR.

EVANS, WALKER (1903–1975). Famous photographer Walker Evans was born to a wealthy family in St. Louis, Missouri, and educated in private schools and at Williams College. He lived for a time in Paris, where he developed an interest in photography. Evans's first photographs were published in 1930, and in 1935 he joined the **Farm Security Administration**, where he worked until 1938. In 1935, he took leave to visit Alabama with **James Agee**, producing the study of sharecropping families that was published as *Let Us Now Praise Famous Men* (1941). The Museum of Modern Art held an exhibition of Evans's work in 1938, the first time an exhibition had been devoted to a single photographer. In 1943, Evans became a contributing editor at *Time* magazine, and in 1945 he moved to *Fortune* magazine, where he remained as an editor until 1965 when he took up the position of professor of graphic design at the Yale School of Art and Architecture. *See also* ART.

EVIAN CONFERENCE, 1938. As growing numbers of Jewish refugees fled from Nazi persecution in **Germany**, representatives from 32 countries met at the nine-day Evian Conference held in the French town of Evian in July 1938, called largely at the instigation of President **Franklin D. Roosevelt**. The U.S. representative was not a member of the administration, but a businessman friend of the president, Myron C. Taylor. The conference proved ineffectual and failed even to issue a statement condemning the situation in Germany. The United States failed to raise the quota of Germans and Austrian immigrants in order to admit Jewish refugees, and on some occasions ships bearing Jews were turned away from U.S. ports. Between 1939 and 1945 only 250,000 Jews were admitted to the United States.

– F –

FAHY, CHARLES (1892–1972). Born in Rome, Georgia, and educated at Notre Dame University and Georgetown University Law School, Charles Fahy qualified as a lawyer in 1914. After serving as a navy pilot during World War I, he practiced law in Washington, D.C., until 1924, and then in Santa Fe, New Mexico. In 1933, he became assistant solicitor in the Department of the Interior; in 1935 general counsel to the **National Labor Relations Board**; in 1940 assistant U.S. solicitor general; and in 1941 solicitor general, a position he held until 1945. After holding several other government appointments, including legal adviser to the American Military Government in Germany, in 1949 he was appointed chair of the President's Committee on Equality of Treatment and Opportunity in the Armed Services established by President **Harry S. Truman**'s Executive Order 9981 in 1948, with responsibility for overseeing the desegregation of the U.S. armed forces. In 1949, he was appointed to the U.S. Court of Appeals on the D.C. circuit and later took senior status as a federal judge.

FAIR DEAL. The title given to President **Harry S. Truman**'s program announced in his State of the Union Message to Congress in January 1949, after he said, "Every segment of our population, and every individual, has a right to expect from his government a fair deal." The Fair Deal included **civil rights**, repeal of the **Taft-Hartley Act**, income support for farmers, federal education reform, a housing bill, and national health insurance. Although there was some progress in housing reform and civil rights, the program amounted to very little due to the conservative opposition and **Republican** domination of Congress or because of the influence of powerful lobbying groups like the American Medical Association, which labeled national health insurance "socialized medicine."

FAIR EMPLOYMENT PRACTICES COMMITTEE (FEPC). The FEPC was established by President **Franklin D. Roosevelt** by Executive Order 8802 on 25 June 1941. The order was issued in response to the threat of a **March on Washington** by **African Americans** led by **A. Philip Randolph** to protest the discrimination in defense industries, scheduled for July 1. The president ordered an end to discrimination and established the FEPC to oversee the order. Although limited in size and funding, the FEPC held a series of widely-publicized hearings on discrimination in Los Angeles, Chicago, New York, Birmingham, Washington, D.C., Philadelphia, and Portland. The hearings in Birmingham, Alabama, angered southern politicians, and the FEPC was transferred to the **War Manpower Commission** in July 1942. A further Executive Order 9346 enlarged the committee and its field staff in 1943. In 1946, Congress failed to approve further appropriations for FEPC due to a southern filibuster in the Senate, and the committee came to an end. It had heard more than 6,000 cases of discrimination and brought almost 2,000 cases to a satisfactory conclusion. Influenced by the federal initiative, a number of states and cities established their own fair employment practice bodies during **World War II**.

FAIR LABOR STANDARDS ACT, 1938. Becoming law on 25 June 1938, the Fair Labor Standards Act was one of the major reform measures of **Franklin D. Roosevelt**'s **New Deal**. Minimum wage provision had originally been included in the **National Industrial**

Recovery Act of 1933, but when the act was declared unconstitutional by the **Supreme Court**, it was clear that further measures were necessary. The Fair Labor Standards Act set a minimum wage of 25 cents per hour in 1938, increased to 30 cents in 1939, and a maximum working week of 44 hours, reduced to 40 by 1940, for all workers engaged in interstate commerce. Agricultural workers, domestic servants, seamen, fishermen, and street rail workers were excluded.

FAMINE EMERGENCY COMMITTEE. The Famine Emergency Committee was established by President **Harry S. Truman** in February 1946 in response to the food crisis that affected Europe in the immediate aftermath of **World War II**. In addition to issuing conservation orders diverting grain and dairy products to famine relief, Truman established a committee headed by former president **Herbert Hoover** to assess the situation and recommend solutions. In keeping with his approach to previous problems, Hoover believed that the main role of the committee was to "educate and inform," and he did so mainly through personal visits to Asia, Europe, and Latin America. Bonus payments to farmers for wheat increased production and made it possible to ship 6 million tons to Europe by the summer of 1946. *See also* AGRICULTURE.

FARLEY, JAMES ALOYSIUS (1888–1973). Born in Grassy Point, New York, James Farley was employed in the family businesses before qualifying as a bookkeeper. He worked for the Universal Gypsum Company in a variety of capacities until 1926. Farley entered politics in 1912 as town clerk for Stony Point, New York, and became involved in the **Democratic Party**. He was a supporter of **Alfred E. Smith** in the gubernatorial contest in 1918, and he held a number of party positions in the early 1920s before being elected to the State Assembly in 1922. Farley voted against prohibition and was defeated in 1924. In 1925, Smith appointed him to the State Boxing Commission. He also established his own General Building Supply Company in 1926 and was its president until 1933. In 1928, Farley helped manage **Franklin D. Roosevelt**'s gubernatorial campaign and provided crucial support for his presidential nomination in 1932. When Roosevelt was elected, Farley was appointed postmaster general. He was also chair of the Democratic National

Committee, and he managed Roosevelt's 1936 campaign. Farley was not one of Roosevelt's inner circle of advisers, by 1940 he was opposed to the president seeking a third term. He put his own name forward for nomination but was easily defeated by Roosevelt. Shortly afterward Farley resigned from the cabinet and from his position in the Democratic Party. He made two unsuccessful attempts to win the New York gubernatorial nomination in 1958 and 1962. He became chair of the Coca-Cola Export Corporation, a position he held until 1973.

FARM CREDIT ACT, 1933. The Farm Credit Act was passed on 16 June 1933 to make loans to farmers available through production credit corps, and it established the **Farm Credit Administration** to oversee its operation. *See also* AGRICULTURE.

FARM CREDIT ADMINISTRATION (FCA). Established by executive order in March 1933 and confirmed by the Federal Credit Act on 16 June1933 as part of the legislation introduced in the "**First Hundred Days**" of the **New Deal** to tackle the agricultural crisis, the FCA established a central bank for cooperatives and 12 regional banks that could make loans to provide production credit, refinance farm mortgages, and repurchase properties. By 1940, the agencies supervised by the FCA had lent some $6.87 million. In 1939, the FCA was transferred to the Department of **Agriculture**.

FARM SECURITY ADMINISTRATION (FSA). Established by Secretary of **Agriculture Henry A. Wallace** in 1937, the FSA was to supervise the work of the **Resettlement Administration** and programs established under the **Bankhead-Jones Farm Tenancy Act**. The FSA provided funds for rural rehabilitation loans, grants to those affected by natural disasters, and loans to establish farm cooperatives. Between 1937 and 1947 the administration made loans of $293 million to 47,104 farmers. It also established almost 100 camps for migratory workers and medical cooperatives for the rural poor. In 1946, the Farmers Home Administration took over the FSA programs and began to terminate loans and other obligations.

An important aspect of the FSA's work was to continue collecting the photographic material for the Historical Section directed by

Roy Stryker. Some 77,000 photographs were made available to the press or used in exhibitions to publicize the plight of the rural poor. *See also* AGRICULTURE; DUST BOWL; EVANS, WALKER; LANGE, DOROTHEA; LEE, RUSSELL WERNER; ROTHSTEIN, ARTHUR ; SHAHN, BEN.

FARMING. *See* AGRICULTURE.

FARM-LABOR PARTY. The Farm-Labor Party was a third party formed in 1919 by John Fitzpatrick and members of the Committee of Forty-Eight, a group of progressives led by Amos Pinchot in an attempt to unite farmers and the labor movement under a reform program. The party first nominated **Robert M. La Follette Jr.** as their presidential candidate, but when he rejected the nomination, the party turned to Parley P. Christensen of Utah. In the 1920 election, he received 260,000 votes. In 1924 the Farm-Labor Party supported La Follette's Progressive Party. By the mid-1920s, the party was only the Minnesota Farm-Labor Party, and in 1930 their candidate, Floyd Olson, was elected state governor. The party supported the **New Deal** and defeated the local **Republicans** until 1938. In the 1940s, the Minnesota party merged with the **Democrats** to form the Democratic-Framer-Labor Party of Minnesota.

FAULKNER, WILLIAM CUTHBERT (1897–1962). William Faulkner was one of the greatest southern writers of the 20th century. Born William Cuthbert Faulkner in Mississippi, he had a desultory education, worked in the family bank, and spent some time at the University of Mississippi. Rejected by the U.S. Army, Faulkner joined the British Royal Air Force in Canada in 1918. After the war, he studied at the University of Mississippi from 1919 to 1921 and published various poems and reviews. He earned a living as postmaster at the University until 1924. His first book, *The Marble Faun*, was published that year and was followed by many others, including *Soldier's Pay* (1926), *Sartoris* (1929), *The Sound and the Fury* (1929), *As I Lay Dying* (1930), *Sanctuary* (1931), *Light in August* (1932), *Absalom, Absalom!* (1936), *Intruder in the Dust* (1948), *Requiem for a Nun* (1951), and *The Reivers* (1962). In many of his novels, he traced the decline of the Old South through the stories of fictional families in "Jefferson," a composite Mississippi town in the mythical county of Yoknapatawpha.

Despite his prodigious output, Faulkner was not widely known for some time but regarded as a southern "regional" writer. He supplemented his income from royalties by writing film scripts, contributing to the **Howard Hawks**'s movies *To Have and Have Not* (1944) and *The Big Sleep* (1946). The publication of *The Portable Faulkner* in 1946 brought him to a wider audience. He was awarded the Nobel Prize for **Literature** in 1950 "for his powerful and artistically unique contribution to the modern American novel." *A Fable* (1954) was awarded the Pulitzer Prize in 1955, and *The Reivers* received the same award in 1963.

FECHNER, ROBERT (1876–1939). The first director of the **Civilian Conservation Corps** (**CCC**), Robert Fechner was born in Chattanooga, Tennessee, and educated in Georgia. He became an apprentice on the Georgia Central Railroad in 1892, joined the army in 1898 but did not see action, and later worked in mining in Mexico and Central and South America. He returned to Georgia in 1905 and became a labor organizer. From 1913 to 1933 he was executive officer of the International Associations of Machinists. During World War I, he served as an adviser on labor policy, where he met **Franklin D. Roosevelt**, then as assistant secretary to the navy. In 1933, President Roosevelt made him head of the CCC. Fechner rejected proposals that the corps become an educational program, and he also resisted the implementation of military training in the camps. He was reluctant to include **African Americans**, particularly as officers. As a consequence, there were only two officers in the CCC, and African Americans were segregated. Fechner died of a heart attack in 1939 and was succeeded by James J. McEntee.

FEDERAL ANTILYNCHING BILL. Drafted by the **National Association for the Advancement of Colored People** (**NAACP**) in 1933 in response to the increasing number of lynchings after 1930, and presented by Republican congressman Edward Costigan from Colorado and Senator **Robert Wagner**, the bill failed in 1934. It was reintroduced in 1935 following the widely publicized lynching of Rubin Stacy in Fort Lauderdale, Florida, in July. In the face of southern opposition, and lacking the support of President **Franklin D. Roosevelt**, who did not wish to jeopardize other reform measures, pressure in support of the bill decreased, and it was abandoned in 1938. *See also* ANTILYNCHING BILL.

FEDERAL ART PROJECT. The Federal **Art** Project was established as part of the **Works Progress Administration** under **Federal One** to provide work for artists. By 1936, it employed 6,000 people, more than half of them directly producing works of art, including more than 42,000 paintings and 1,000 murals on public buildings. Among those employed at different times were **Ben Shahn**, **John Steuart Curry**, and **Grant Wood**.

FEDERAL BUREAU OF INVESTIGATION (FBI). The FBI began in 1908 as a corps of special agents within the Department of Justice to investigate crime at a federal level. In 1909, it was named the Bureau of Investigation. Following U.S. entry into World War I, the bureau became responsible for investigating violations of the Selective Service Acts, Espionage Act, and Sabotage Act. The Justice Department widened its brief with the creation of a General Intelligence Division headed by **J. Edgar Hoover**. The Federal Bureau was created in 1924 to investigate violations of federal law with Hoover as its head, a position he held until his death in 1972.

During the 1930s, the FBI grew in national prominence following the implementation of an anticrime program to combat the apparent rise in gangsterism publicized by such people as **John Dillinger**, George "Machine Gun" Kelly, Charles "Pretty Boy" Floyd, and Bonnie and Clyde (Bonnie Parker and Clyde Barrow), criminals who were often seen as "Robin Hood" figures by the public. Justice Department media campaigns showed FBI agents ("G-men"), including Hoover, in action against "public enemies." By the end of the decade the bureau had more than 750 agents and offices in 42 cities and a budget that had doubled to more than $6 million. In 1935, it was officially named the Federal Bureau of Investigation.

With the rise of Nazism in Europe and the approach of **World War II**, the powers of the bureau were extended to provide surveillance of subversive organizations and after 1941 to safeguard against acts of espionage and sabotage. The FBI was responsible for the apprehension of eight Nazi saboteurs who landed in 1942, and they were also involved in the internment of **Japanese Americans**, a policy Hoover disagreed with.

During the **Cold War**, the bureau was involved in the investigation of communist subversion at home, including the breaking and entering into the offices of the journal *Amerasia*. Agents arrested six people in 1945, providing material for the **House Un-American Activities Committee** hearings and later for **Joseph McCarthy** and in the trials of **Whittaker Chambers**, **Alger Hiss**, and **Ethel** and **Julius Rosenberg**. The concern for security led to the agency's expansion, and by 1952 the FBI had a force of more than 7,000 agents.

In later years, the FBI was involved in surveillance of civil rights leaders, including Martin Luther King Jr.; antiwar demonstrators and their supporters during the war in Vietnam; and organized crime. The agency's reputation was increasingly tarnished by revelations of illegal activities, institutional racism, and conservatism, and in the mid-1970s it was increasingly subjected to congressional oversight. It was further damaged following the terrorist attacks on the World Trade Center in New York City on 11 September 2001, and the subsequent discovery that the bureau had failed to coordinate with other agencies or follow up on reports from its own field agents of suspicious activities that might have prevented the attacks. Nonetheless, at the start of the 21st century it remains the most important federal domestic investigative branch of the Department of Justice, with a staff of more than 10,000 agents and a budget of almost $3 billion.

FEDERAL COMMUNICATIONS COMMISSION (FCC). Established by the Communications Act in June 1934, the FCC replaced the Federal Radio Commission (1927) and consisted of seven commissioners who were empowered to regulate interstate and international **radio**, wire, telephone, telegraph, and cable communication (later extended to **television**) in the national interest. It was able to issue or withdraw licenses for broadcasting, allocate wave lengths, and oversee the communications industry.

FEDERAL DANCE PROJECT. The Federal Dance Project was one of the projects funded under **Federal One** to provide employment for out-of-work dancers. It established three dance units in 1936 to employ 185 dancers. Despite its many internal and external difficulties, the project did bring dance performance to a wider public and also provided dance lessons for many people. Charges of left-wing sympathies led to the end of the project in 1940.

FEDERAL DEPOSIT INSURANCE CORPORATION (FDIC). Created under the **Banking Act** of 1933, the FDIC was established to insure deposits of member banks in the Federal Reserve System and restore public confidence in the **banking** system. By 1935, 14,400 banks had joined, and the number of bank failures was more than halved in two years.

FEDERAL EMERGENCY RELIEF ACT, 1933. Part of the first program of the **New Deal** to bring relief to the approximately 17 million unemployed, the Federal Emergency Relief Act of 1933 established the **Federal Emergency Relief Administration** with a budget of $500 million for national emergency relief. This work came to an end with the **Social Security Act** of 1935.

FEDERAL EMERGENCY RELIEF ADMINISTRATION (FERA). Established in May 1933 by the **Federal Emergency Relief Act**, FERA was empowered to distribute $500 million in relief, matching every $3 of local money with $1 of federal funds. Headed by **Harry Hopkins**, FERA established a Works Division with federal work programs that gave work directly to more than 2 million people, distributed funds, and provided for rural rehabilitation. By 1935, FERA had distributed more than $2 billion in relief. However, it was viewed by many as extravagant, a threat to the authority of the states, and an encouragement for the idle. Increasingly seen as a political liability, FERA came to an end in 1935, but some of its functions were later taken over by the **Works Progress Administration**.

FEDERAL HOUSING ADMINISTRATION (FHA). The FHA was established with the **National Housing Acts** of 1934 and 1937. The intention of the legislation was to provide work for unemployed building workers by tackling problems of poor housing. The administration was empowered to provide loans to banks for relending to individuals to build or repair homes and to provide insurance for lending institutions. Limited leadership initially restricted the amount of assistance for poorer areas, but amendments to the original act in 1938 led to a doubling of the number of new homes financed. By 1939, 275,000 small homes had been constructed with FHA financing, and more than 1.5 million homes had been repaired or improved.

FEDERAL LOAN AGENCY. Established in 1939, the Federal Loan Agency replaced various existing temporary loan agencies to "supervise and coordinate the functions and activities" of all federal lending bodies, other than those in **agriculture**. The agencies covered included the **Reconstruction Finance Corporation, Federal Housing Administration, Home Owners' Loan Corporation**, and others.

FEDERAL LOYALTY PROGRAM. In response to **Republican** charges that the **Democrats** were "soft on communism," in November 1946 President **Harry S. Truman** established a Temporary Commission on Employee Loyalty. Following their recommendations, Truman issued Executive Order 9835 on 21 March 1947 establishing a Federal Loyalty Program. The program was intended to remove "any disloyal or subversive person" from the federal civil service. Disloyal activities were listed as including sabotage, espionage, treason, sedition, the advocacy of revolution or violent overthrow of government, passing secret information to another party, and "membership, affiliation, or sympathetic association with" any group or organization "designated as totalitarian, fascist, communist, or subversive." These organizations were listed by the attorney general and included the **Communist Party of the United States of America**, Socialist Workers' Party, Ku Klux Klan, National Negro Congress, Silver Shirts, and various groups involved in the **Spanish Civil War**.

The Civil Service Commission was required to establish a Loyalty Review Board, and federal workers were vetted through federal loyalty boards. Almost 3 million people were checked during the Truman administration, and between 400 and 1,200 were dismissed (precise figures are unclear) and between 1,000 and 6,000 resigned rather than face investigation. The process continued under President **Dwight D. Eisenhower**, and the definition of disloyal was widened to include "security risk" from 1953 onward. Rather than silence the attacks from conservatives as intended, information from the Loyalty Review Board was used by Senator **Joseph McCarthy** and others to demonstrate that there was indeed a threat of subversion. In this respect, the loyalty program was a precursor to **McCarthyism**.

FEDERAL MARITIME BOARD. Established within the Department of Commerce in 1950 to replace the **U. S. Maritime Commission**, the Federal Maritime Board was to regulate shipping and provide subsidies for the construction of merchant shipping, maintain the National Defense Reserve Fleet, and direct merchant shipping in wartime. It was abolished in 1961.

FEDERAL MUSIC PROJECT. The Federal Music Project was created in 1935 under the provisions of **Federal One** in the **Works Progress Administration (WPA)**. It provided work for more than 15,000 unemployed musicians who gave thousands of live concerts, performances, and radio broadcasts, as well as more than 1.5 million **music** classes. It subsequently became the WPA Music Project and lasted until 1943.

FEDERAL ONE. Federal One was the name for a group of projects created by the **Works Progress Administration** to provide work for those unemployed in the **arts**. The projects included the **Federal Art Project, Federal Dance Project, Federal Music Project, Federal Writers' Project, Federal Theater Project**, and Historical Records Survey.

FEDERAL POWER COMMISSION. Under the Federal Power Act of 1935 the authority of the Federal Power Commission, which had been created in 1920 to manage hydroelectric power, was amended to enable it to regulate all electric energy no matter how it was generated. This power was further increased in 1938 when it was extended under the Natural Gas Act to include natural gas production. In 1977, the Federal Power Commission became the Department of Energy.

FEDERAL PUBLIC HOUSING AUTHORITY. The Federal Public Housing Authority was created within the **National Housing**

Agency in 1942 and replaced the **United States Housing Authority**. Its function was to fund slum clearance and encourage the building of low-cost public housing, particularly during the war emergency. It built a total of 840,000 homes at a cost of $2.3 billion. *See also* FEDERAL HOUSING ADMINISTRATION (FHA).

FEDERAL REPUBLIC OF GERMANY (FRG). *See* GERMANY, FEDERAL REPUBLIC OF (FRG).

FEDERAL RESERVE BOARD (FRB). First established under the Federal Reserve Act of 1913, the Federal Reserve was a system of 12 regional Federal Reserve Banks that could hold cash reserves for national banks, state banks, and trust companies that entered the system. However, the FRB had limited powers and exercised little monetary control. The **Banking Act** of 1935 provided more centralized control through the board of governors of the Federal Reserve, particularly with regard to interest rates and credit management and the ability to buy or sell government securities. *See also* BANKING.

FEDERAL SAVINGS AND LOAN INSURANCE CORPORA-TION. Established under the provisions of the **National Housing Act of 1934**, the Federal Savings and Loan Insurance Corporation provided insurance for loans and the equivalent security as that offered to **banks** through the **Federal Deposit Insurance Corporation (FDIC)**. It offered insurance on individual accounts of up to $5,000 and by 1940 had insured more than 2,000 accounts. The corporation went insolvent during the savings and loans crisis of the 1980s and was incorporated into the FDIC.

FEDERAL SECURITIES ACT. *See* SECURITIES ACT (FEDERAL SECURITIES ACT).

FEDERAL SECURITY AGENCY. Established under the Reorganization Plan of 1939, the Federal Security Agency brought a number of agencies, including the Social Security Board, Public Health Service, U.S. Office of Education, **National Youth Administration**, **Civilian Conservation Corps**, and U.S. Employment Service, together under one body, headed by **Paul V. McNutt**. In 1953, the Federal

Security Agency was subsumed within the cabinet-level Department of Health, Education, and Welfare.

FEDERAL SURPLUS COMMODITIES CORPORATION. The Federal Surplus Commodities Corporation was created in 1935 and replaced by the Farm Surplus Relief Corporation established in 1933 to purchase surplus farm produce to distribute among the needy. By 1940, 3 million families had received food through this assistance program.

FEDERAL THEATER PROJECT. Created under the **Works Progress Administration (WPA)** in 1935, the Federal Theater Project, led by Hallie Flanagan of the experimental theater at Vassar College, was established to provide employment for those in theater. At its height, the project employed almost 13,000 people nationwide. The biggest concentration, with 31 production units, was in New York City, but plays and broadcasts were put on in almost all parts of the country. In total, 250,000 performances were given in 110 cities to audiences totaling 150 million people. Among the most famous productions was the 1936 Negro Peoples' Theater version of *Macbeth* directed by **Orson Welles** and set in Haiti. The *Living Newspaper* provided dramatic comment on current events and developments. The production of Sinclair Lewis's antifascist play *It Can't Happen Here* was shown successfully in 22 cities. Always controversial, the project was often attacked by its critics as an extravagant, left-wing organization, and it was finally ended by Congress in 1939. *See also* FEDERAL ONE; LITERATURE AND THEATER.

FEDERAL WORKS AGENCY (FWA). The FWA was established in 1939 to supervise the care and maintenance of public buildings and coordinate federal housing projects. Among others, it brought together the activities of the **Works Progress Administration**, the **Public Works Administration**, and the **United States Housing Authority**. The FWA was abolished in 1949 and replaced by the General Services Administration.

FEDERAL WRITERS' PROJECT. Created in 1935 as part of **Federal One**, the Federal Writers' Project provided work for some 6,600 unemployed writers, including Nelson Algren, Saul Bellow, John Cheever, Ralph Ellison, Studs Terkel, and **Richard Wright**. The writers produced local histories and 48 state guides as part of the "American Guide Series" between 1935 and 1943.

FIELDS, WILLIAM CLAUDE (W. C.) (1880–1946). Vaudeville film and radio comedian W. C. Fields was born William Claude Dukenfield in Philadelphia, Pennsylvania. His early theatrical career began as a juggler, and in the 1890s through 1915 he toured America and Europe. In 1915, Fields joined the *Ziegfeld Follies* on Broadway and appeared in a successful Broadway musical, *Poppy*, from 1923 until 1924. The film version of *Poppy*, *Sally of the Sawdust* appeared in 1925 (and in sound in 1936), and Fields also appeared in numerous other silent movies in the 1920s developing his comic persona as the con man or harassed husband, both with a strong disliking for children and a liking for alcohol. In the 1930s, he moved to Hollywood, where he wrote scripts and starred in several films, including *It's a Gift* (1934), *David Copperfield* (1935), and *The Bank Dick* (1940). Other successful films included *You Can't Cheat an Honest Man* (1939), *Never Give a Sucker an Even Break* (1941), and *My Little Chickadee* (1940), which also starred **Mae West**. Fields also had a successful **radio** career on *The Chase & Sanborn Hour* starting in 1937. In 1940, he authored a spoof political campaign program, *Fields for President*. His last film was *Sensations* in 1945, released shortly before his death. *See also* CINEMA.

FIRESIDE CHATS. On 12 March 1933 President **Franklin D. Roosevelt** addressed the nation in a **radio** broadcast to explain why he declared a **bank** holiday. It was the first of his presidential "fireside chats," a term used by the head of CBS in Washington to describe Roosevelt's second address on 7 May 1933. Roosevelt used the radio while governor of New York to talk to his constituents in an informal fashion, and now, sometimes speaking to the audiences as "my friends" and always speaking in a personal tone, he used the same method to good effect as president. Estimates of his audience ranged from 25 percent to almost 40 percent of the American population. Altogether Roosevelt gave 28 "fireside chats," 30 including recordings of addresses to Congress. The last broadcast was on 12 June 1944 to launch the fifth War Loan Drive.

FIRST HUNDRED DAYS. The first three months of President **Franklin D. Roosevelt**'s **New Deal** from 9 March to 16 June 1933, known subsequently as the "First Hundred Days," began with Congress being called into emergency session and ended with an unprecedented 15 major pieces of new legislation being passed to tackle the problems of the **Great Depression**. The "First Hundred Days" was a defining moment in the New Deal that set a benchmark of achievement against which all subsequent presidencies were to be judged.

FIRST NEW DEAL. From about the mid-1930s on, the **New Deal** was often seen in two parts, the First New Deal and the **Second New Deal**. Although the lines of demarcation are not precise, the First New Deal is generally seen as covering the period 1933 to 1934—the "**First Hundred Days**" and beyond. The primary focus of the First New Deal was tackling the immediate problems of the **Great Depression** and providing relief and stimulating recovery. It came to an end in 1934 and 35 with mounting criticism from both left and right and with the **Supreme Court**'s decision to invalidate early legislation, like the **National Industrial Recovery Act**.

FISH, HAMILTON STUYVESANT (1888–1991). Born in Putnam County, New York, and educated at Geneva and Harvard University, where he graduated in 1909, Hamilton Fish followed in his father's footsteps and served as a **Republican** in the House of Representatives from 1920 until 1945. Prior to this he worked in insurance before entering politics as a supporter of Theodore Roosevelt and the Progressive Party. Fish served in the New York State Assembly from 1914 to 1916. A member of the New York National Guard, he became an officer of the 369th U.S. Infantry Regiment, the all-black unit known as the "Harlem Hellfighters." After the war, Fish was active in the formation of the American Legion and introduced the resolution providing for the Tomb of the Unknown Soldier at Arlington National Cemetery in Washington, D.C.

As a firm isolationist, Fish opposed the Versailles Peace Settlement and U.S. membership of the League of Nations. In 1939, he met and was entertained by various German Nazi officials and as a result was accused of being both pro-Nazi and anti-Semitic in the United States. He helped to establish the Committee to Keep America Out of Foreign Wars and spoke in support of the **America First Committee**. Fish opposed any modification of the **Neutrality Acts** and also resisted the introduction of **Selective Service** in 1940. Although he had been a long-time friend of **Franklin D. Roosevelt**, he became an outspoken critic of the **New Deal**, particularly of the **Works Progress Administration** and the attempted "**court packing**." As a result, he was listed in a chant by the president with **Bruce Barton** and **Joseph Martin** as "Barton, Martin, and Fish" in the 1940 election campaign. However, he held onto his seat until 1945. During the war, he called for the full utilization of **African Americans** in all branches of the military. After the war, he continued his many business interests but also spoke and wrote in opposition to communism.

FLOOD CONTROL ACTS, 1936, 1944. Following a series of major floods, including one in Mississippi in 1927 and Ohio in 1933, and concern about soil erosion, flooding was recognized as a national issue requiring federal involvement. This led to the passage of the Flood Control Act in 1936 authorizing studies in water control. Further amendments in the 1930s required state and local flood control measures. The Flood Control Act of 1944 established the Missouri River Basin Project, a series of 112 dams and hydroelectric plants serving 10 states. The program is ongoing.

FLYNN, EDWARD JOSEPH (1891–1953). Born in New York City, Edward Flynn became a major political figure in the city. After graduating from Fordham University Law School in 1912, he was admitted to the bar and practiced law for five years. He was elected to the New York State Assembly in 1918 and in 1921 was elected sheriff of Bronx County. Flynn was also chair of the Bronx County **Democratic** Committee. In 1926, he was elected chamberlain of New York City, and in 1929 he became secretary of New York. As a major political boss, Flynn had considerable influence. He was also a personal friend of President **Franklin D. Roosevelt** and a supporter of the **New Deal**. Roosevelt appointed Flynn as regional administrator to the **National Recovery Administration**. From 1940 to 1942, Flynn was chair of the Democratic National Committee, replacing **James A. Farley**. In 1943, Roosevelt nominated Flynn as minister to Australia, but charges of corruption over a minor issue forced him to withdraw and resign. Nonetheless, he accompanied the president to the **Yalta Conference** in 1945, and he continued to be influential during the administration of **Harry S. Truman**.

FLYNN, ERROL (1909–1959). Born Errol Leslie Thomson Flynn in Hobart, Tasmania, the future movie star worked as a lifeguard, model, boxer, miner, and sailor before entering acting in London, England, in 1933. After playing roles in theater and small films in **Great Britain**, Flynn came to the United States in 1934. His breakthrough came in *Captain Blood* (1935), which established him as a swashbuckling romantic hero. Flynn went on to make 60 films, the most successful produced between 1935 and 1942. He starred in *The Charge of the Light Brigade* (1936), *The Prince and the Pauper* (1937), *The Adventures of Robin Hood* (1938), *Sea Hawk* (1940), and *They Died with Their Boots On* (1942). He became an American citizen in 1942, and in the same year he was charged with statutory rape for having sexual relations with two underage girls. The trial pushed the war off the front pages. Flynn was acquitted, but his career never recovered. He made several war films, including *Dive Bomber* (1941) and *Objective Burma* (1945). After the war, he had some success with *Don Juan* (1948), but his performances were increasingly affected by alcoholism and poor health. He starred in *The Sun Also Rises* in 1957, based on the **Ernest Hemingway** novel, and he made only two other films before his death.

FLYNN, JOHN THOMAS (1882–1964). John Flynn was born in Maryland. After studying law at Georgetown University in Washington, D.C., he became a journalist, first with the *New Haven Register*, and after moving to New York City in 1920, with the *New York Globe*. From 1923 onward, Flynn was a freelance journalist and became a well-know political commentator through his articles in the *New Republic*, *Harper's Magazine*, and *Collier's Weekly*. Many of his articles were critical of bankers and industrialists, and

Flynn was initially a strong supporter of **Franklin D. Roosevelt** and the **New Deal**. However, in 1934 he became an adviser to the **Nye Committee**, and his work on the links between the munitions industry and American involvement in World War I made him an outspoken isolationist. He was critical of the president's attempts to involve the United States in European affairs and was one of the founders of the **America First Committee**. With American entry into **World War II** in 1942, Flynn became increasingly unpopular, a trend that continued with his critical study of Roosevelt, *As We Go Marching* (1944). After the war, he supported claims that the New Deal had been soft on communism, and his book, *The Roosevelt Myth* (1948), suggested that communists had been included in the Roosevelt administration. He developed this position further in supporting **Joseph McCarthy** and in his publications, *The Road Ahead: America's Creeping Revolution* (1949), *While You Slept* (1951), and *The Lattimore Story* (1953). Other targets for Flynn's attacks included the **United Nations** and even President **Dwight D. Eisenhower**. Eventually he alienated even fellow conservatives, and he retired from public life in 1960.

FONDA, HENRY (1905–1982). Born in Grand Island, Nebraska, Henry Fonda abandoned study at the University of Minnesota to become an actor. After working in **theater** in Omaha, he moved to New York and through the 1920s performed in a variety of roles in productions with the University Players Guild Falmouth and the National Junior Theater. His first appearance on Broadway was in 1929, but his first major role was in *The Farmer Takes a Wife* in 1934, and he starred in the film version the following year. Fonda subsequently combined theater and movie acting and in 1939 starred to some acclaim in **John Ford**'s *Mr. Lincoln*. This was followed by *Drums along the Mohawk*. It was, however, as Tom Joad in the film version of **John Steinbeck**'s powerful novel about the "**Okies**," *The Grapes of Wrath* (1940), that Fonda was nominated for an Academy Award.

Fonda made a number of films for 20th Century Fox in the early 1940s, perhaps most notably *The Ox Bow Incident* in 1943. He then enlisted in the navy and resumed his acting career in 1946 with the film *My Darling Clementine* and *The Fugitive* in 1947. His theater performance in *Mr. Roberts* in 1955 won him a Tony Award, and he was also praised for his performance as a juror in the film *12 An-*

gry Men in 1957. Fonda won an Oscar for his last film, *On Golden Pond*, made in 1981. The Academy of Arts awarded him a Lifetime Achievement Award in 1978, and he was given a special Tony Award in 1979 for his contribution to theater. *See also* CINEMA.

FOOD STAMPS. In 1939, the **Federal Surplus Commodities Corporation** introduced a system than enabled people on relief to purchase stamps that could be used to buy surplus food stuffs. Introduced first in Rochester, New York, by 1940, 100 cities were included in the program, and by the time it ended in 1943, 20 million people had benefited. A similar program was established in 1961.

FORD, HENRY (1863–1947). Synonymous with the development of the automobile from the first appearance of his mass-produced Ford Model T in 1909, Henry Ford was a major figure in American industry and politics from World War I through **World War II**. Ford built his first car in 1896 and in 1899 established the Detroit Automobile Company. For a time, he concentrated on building race cars, and his company became the Cadillac Motor Car Company in 1902.

Ford returned to automobile manufacturing when he established the Ford Motor Company in 1903. He first began production of the Model T in 1909 using the concept of mass-produced standardized parts and developed it further at his new Highland Park factory in 1910. In 1913, Ford developed the moving assembly line method of production enabling an enormous increase in production. In 1914, he introduced a profit sharing scheme and a five-dollar, eight-hour work day for his employees and later the five-day week. However, he also attempted to control workers through a personnel department that implemented mandatory English lessons for immigrant workers and a no smoking, no drinking, nonunion policy.

Ford personally funded a "peace ship," *Oscar II*, in 1915 in an attempt to end World War I, but once America entered the conflict, the Ford Company turned to producing engines, tractors, and vehicles for the government. Ford opened the world's largest single manufacturing plant at River Rouge, Dearborn, near Detroit, in 1916. Such was Ford's public stature that in 1916 he won the **Republican** presidential primary in Michigan without campaigning. In 1918, he was persuaded by Woodrow Wilson to run for the Senate but was defeated.

There were attempts to persuade him to stand for the presidency in 1920 and 1923, but Ford supported Warren Harding and Calvin Coolidge. During the early 1920s, Ford's magazine, the *Dearborn Independent*, published a series of anti-Semitic articles, and in 1938 the German Nazi government honored him.

Ford expanded his operation after World War I to develop luxury cars and airplanes. In 1927, he ceased production of the out-of-date Model T and began producing the Model A. Sluggish sales of the new car are seen by some economists as a contributory factor leading to the **Great Depression**. Certainly unemployment was exacerbated in 1931 when Ford began to layoff workers to retool for the new V-8 engine. In March 1932, 3,000 unemployed workers marched on the Dearborn plant protesting wage cuts and unemployment. They met a violent response from the police and Ford Company security, who fired into the protestors killing four and wounding 60. The company also held out against the **trade union** drives of the 1930s, and when **Walter Reuther** led a rally of United Automobile Workers outside the Dearborn plant in 1937, they too were met with violence, although there were no fatalities. Union recognition was only granted in 1941.

During World War II, the Ford Company converted entirely to war production and built a huge aircraft production plant at Willow Run outside Detroit. Ford himself was increasingly unwell, and in 1945 he passed control to his grandson, Henry Ford II, who was company president until 1960. The company continued to grow and by the 1960s was a multinational organization.

FORD, JOHN (1895–1973). Born Sean Aloysius O'Fearna (or Feeney) in Maine, the famous movie director was the son of Irish immigrants. After brief attendance at the University of Maine, he joined his brother in California and took the name Ford while working as a film extra. He starred in *The Tornado* (1917), which he also wrote and directed. He began listing himself as John Ford in movie credits beginning with the much-acclaimed film *The Iron Horse*. He made several more successful silent movies and then did equally well in the medium of sound with *Men without Women* (1930), *Arrowsmith* (1932), and *The Lost Patrol* (1934). In 1935, he won an Academy Award for Best Director for *The Informer*. A succession of major films followed including, *Young Mr. Lincoln* (1939), *Drums along the Mohawk* (1939), and *The Long Voyage Home* (1940). Four of his films won him Oscars: *Stagecoach* in 1939, starring **John Wayne**; *The Grapes of Wrath* based on **John Steinbeck**'s major novel of the **Great Depression** and starring **Henry Fonda** in 1940; *How Green Was My Valley* in 1941; and *The Quiet Man*, again with Wayne, in 1952.

During **World War II**, Ford joined the navy and became chief of the Field Photographic Branch of the **Office of Strategic Services**. He was wounded at the Battle of **Midway**, and his film, *The Battle of Midway*, won an Oscar for Best Documentary in 1942. He won another award for the propaganda film, *December 7th*. He was awarded the Purple Heart, Legion of Merit, and Air Medal for his war services.

Returning to Hollywood in 1946, Ford made a succession of Westerns that became classics in the genre: *My Darling Clementine*, (1946), *Fort Apache* (1948), *She Wore a Yellow Ribbon* (1949), *Rio Grande* (1950), *The Searchers* (1956), and *The Man Who Shot Liberty Valance* (1962). Other films included *They Were Expendable* (1945), *What Price Glory* (1952), the Academy Award-winning *The Quiet Man* (1952), and *Mr. Roberts* (1955). Many of these also starred Wayne.

His later films in the 1960s were not as successful, but his previous movies were "rediscovered," and in 1973 the American Film Institute awarded Ford its first Lifetime Achievement Award. He was also awarded the Medal of Freedom by President **Richard M. Nixon**. *See also* CINEMA.

FOREIGN POLICY. The 1930s and 1940s witnessed the final resolution of the struggle between internationalism and isolationism that had been the dominant motif of U.S. foreign relations since World War I. Having struggled and failed to keep out of the developing world conflict that developed in the late 1930s, the United States became the leading partner in the Grand Alliance with **Great Britain** and the **Soviet Union** in the war against **Germany** and **Japan**. Furthermore, having rejected participation in the League of Nations in 1919, the United States now led the way in establishing a **United Nations** organization. The onset of the struggle to combat the spread of Soviet-inspired communism in the **Cold War** after 1945 led to the total abandonment of George Washington's advice to avoid "entangling alliances" as the United States became a member of the **Organization of American States** in 1948, the **North Atlantic Treaty Organization** in 1949, the **Australia-New Zealand-United States Alliance** in 1951, and later a party to both the South East Asia Treaty Organization (SEATO) in 1954 and the Central Treaty Organization (CENTO) in 1955. By the mid-1950s, America's role not just as a world power but as the leading world power was firmly established in terms of military and economic might and political influence.

The **Great Depression** had an enormous impact on international relations, increasing nationalism and bringing new elements to power in Germany and Japan that destabilized the existing world order. Economic nationalism was evident at the **London Economic Conference of 1933** in **Franklin D. Roosevelt**'s refusal to have the United States remain on the gold standard. Economic interest was undoubtedly partly behind Roosevelt's reiteration of **Herbert Hoover**'s **"Good Neighbor" Policy** with Latin American countries that led to trade agreements and a trebling of U.S. exports to Latin America in the 1930s. Trade agreements were also reached with the newly recognized Soviet Union.

While such measures helped improve international relations, the United States maintained its essentially isolationist position during much of the 1930s. Convinced that entry into World War I had been a mistake, many Americans supported the passage of **Neutrality Acts** from 1935 onward, imposing first a trade embargo with belligerent powers, then prohibiting the travel by U.S. citizens on belligerent vessels and forbidding loans to belligerent powers. In 1937, the laws were extended to include nonmilitary goods that could be sold to belligerent nations only on a "cash and carry" basis. These laws were applied during the **Spanish Civil War** in 1936, even though it was not a conflict involving warring nations. However, Roosevelt refused to invoke the legislation when Japan attacked **China** in 1937, instead calling for aggressor nations to be quarantined. His speech angered isolationists and following the Japanese sinking of the USS *Panay* on the Yangtze River in 1937, support grew for an amendment requiring a declaration of war to be subject to national referendum. The resolution was only narrowly defeated in Congress in 1938.

In Europe, the reluctance of Great Britain, France, and the United States to risk war enabled **Adolf Hitler** to reoccupy the Rhineland, forcibly establish a union with Austria, and in 1938 acquire the Sudetenland from Czechoslovakia. German troops occupied the remainder of Czechoslovakia in 1939. However, when Hitler next demanded territory from Poland, the British and French guaranteed their support to the Polish government, and when Hitler invaded on 1 September 1939, **World War II** began.

Although support among the American people was overwhelmingly behind the **Allies**, this backing was outweighed by the desire to avoid direct involvement in the war. The Neutrality Acts were amended to allow the sale of munitions, but only on the cash and carry basis. Nothing was done to stop the German armies from overrunning Denmark, Norway, the Netherlands, Belgium, and most of France, but in the summer of 1940 Roosevelt established a **Destroyers-for-Bases** Agreement with Britain to strengthen U.S. security in exchange for outdated ships. In the election campaign of 1940, Roosevelt still promised that American males would not be sent into foreign wars, but having secured reelection, he bypassed the restriction on loans to belligerents with the passage of the **Lend-Lease Act** of 1941. When the Germans began to sink British ships carrying much-needed supplies, Roosevelt extended the American security zone into the mid-Atlantic and provided U.S. naval support. When Germany attacked the Soviet Union in June 1941, lend-lease was extended to the Russians. Not only was this short of war, but in August 1941 Roosevelt agreed on the principles on which a postwar world should be based in the **Atlantic Charter** signed with **Winston Churchill** in August 1941.

Despite increasing U.S. involvement in the conflict in Europe, American entry into World War II came in Asia. As Japan continued its aggression against China, the Roosevelt administration responded by placing embargoes on iron, steel, copper, and brass products in 1940 and 1941. Following the breakdown of negotiations and further Japanese moves against Indo-China and the Dutch East Indies in the spring and summer of 1941, the United States stopped all oil shipments to Japan and froze Japanese assets in America. Japanese requests to pursue their expansionist policy and for the restoration of trade were met with proposals for a resumption of trade in return for a withdrawal. Reluctant to withdraw and needing to expand to secure raw materials, the Japanese anticipated war with a preemptive strike on the U.S. Pacific fleet in **Pearl Harbor** on 7 December 1941, a day which, Roosevelt said, would "live in infamy." On 8 December the United States declared war on Japan, and Germany and Italy declared war on the United States in line with their agreements with Japan.

With Great Britain and its Allies, together with the Soviet Union, the United States was now part of the Grand Alliance. While the Soviet Union called for an early second front to relieve the pressure caused by the German invasion of Russia, Britain and the United States wanted to delay an invasion of Europe until they had sufficient personnel and material. Instead, in November 1942 an invasion was launched in North Africa to divert German troops and open up the Mediterranean and provide a base for an attack on Europe's "soft underbelly." Having successfully defeated German and Italian forces in Africa by spring 1943, the invasion of Sicily was launched on 10 June 1943, and on 8 September Italy surrendered. However, the campaign on the Italian mainland continued until the war's end in 1945.

The **Allied** invasion of northern Europe began on **D-Day** on 6 June 1944, when British, Canadian, and U.S. troops landed on five beaches in **Normandy**. The German forces were pushed back, and, despite a counteroffensive in the **Battle of the Bulge** in December 1944, the Allies crossed the Rhine into Germany in March 1945. Meanwhile, Soviet forces, having defeated German armies at Stalingrad in 1943, had been steadily driving forward from the east and entered **Berlin** in April 1945. Hitler committed suicide in his bunker, and the German forces surrendered on 8 May.

In the Pacific, the seemingly inexorable Japanese advance was finally halted following naval battles in the Coral Sea and **Midway** in May through June 1942. With Australia secure, U.S. forces were able to begin their "island hopping" campaign, taking New Guinea in January 1943, **Guadalcanal** in February 1943, the Marianas in June 1944, **Iwo Jima** in March 1945, and **Okinawa** in June 1945. From these positions, the U.S. Air Force was able to launch bombing attacks on mainland Japan. Rather than a costly invasion of Japan, President **Harry S. Truman** approved the dropping of the new **atomic bomb** on **Hiroshima** on 6 August 1945 and a second on **Na-**

gasaki three days later. The Japanese agreed to U.S peace terms on 14 August and formally surrendered on 2 September 1945.

During the war, the Allied leaders held several meetings to discuss military strategy and plan for the future. Roosevelt and Churchill met in Washington, D.C, in 1942 and Casablanca, Morocco, in January 1943. They met with the Chinese leader **Chiang Kai-shek** in **Cairo**, Egypt, in November 1943 before meeting the Soviet leader **Joseph Stalin** in **Tehran**. The next and most crucial meeting took place between the Big Three at **Yalta** in the Crimea in February 1945. There agreements were reached about the future military occupation of Germany, the issue of reparations to the Soviet Union, and the future of Poland, although these were vague on certain aspects that were to be problematic once the war was over. Agreement was reached about Soviet entry into the war against Japan. The final meeting took place in **Potsdam**, Germany, in July 1945. By then, Truman had succeeded Roosevelt, and Churchill was replaced during the conference by Clement Attlee. While Truman was happy that Stalin reaffirmed his intention to enter the war against Japan and agreement was reached on the new frontiers of Poland and the denazification of Germany, there was only vague agreement on the issue of reparations payments to the Soviets, and questions about the composition of the Polish government remained unresolved. There was also disagreement about the nature of the Soviet-imposed governments in Bulgaria, Hungary, and Rumania.

In January 1942, plans to establish a **United Nations (UN)** organization to replace the League of Nations had been approved, and details were further agreed on by the wartime leaders at the **Dumbarton Oaks Conference** in 1944. The UN was formally established at a conference in **San Francisco** in April 1945. However, the UN was unable to prevent the growing conflict between the Soviet Union and its former Allies as relations quickly deteriorated. Stalin's declaration to the Russian people in February 1946 that capitalism and communism faced inevitable conflict was countered on the U.S. side by **George F. Kennan**'s analysis that accepted the premise of inevitable conflict and called for a policy of **containment**.

Encouraged by Churchill's statement in 1946 that an "iron curtain" had fallen across Eastern Europe, and in response for requests for aid to resist left-wing elements in a civil war in Greece, Truman adopted Kennan's position in announcing the **Truman Doctrine** to a joint session of Congress on 12 March 1947. This was reinforced shortly afterward with the introduction of the **Marshall Plan** to provide economic assistance in rebuilding Western Europe. For the Western powers, Germany was central to economic recovery. As they moved toward unifying the West German currency, the Soviet Union responded by imposing a blockade on Berlin, the jointly occupied capital, in June 1948. The challenge was met by a combined U.S. and British airlift that kept the city supplied for almost a year before the blockade was lifted, but the fear of future Soviet aggression led to the creation of the **North Atlantic Treaty Organization (NATO)** in April 1949. Under NATO, U.S. troops now committed to the defense of Europe.

The Cold War, as the struggle between the United States and the Soviet Union came to be known, was increasingly played out on many different fronts as the respective rivals competed for influence in different parts of the world. The **Cold War** was a major factor leading to the continuation of the "Good Neighbor" Policy and the hemispheric defense treaty agreed on with Latin American countries in the **Rio Pact** in 1947. This was followed by the formation of the **Organization of American States** at Bogota in 1948. In 1949, the conflict spread to Asia when **Mao Zedong**'s communist forces defeated Chiang Kai-shek, who was forced to relocate to the island of **Taiwan**. The United States withheld recognition from communist China until 1978. Following the loss of China, in April 1950 the **National Security Council** produced **National Security Council Report 68** (NSC-68), arguing that given the clear intention of the Soviet Union to expand in Europe and Asia, the United States should build up its military strength through increased defense spending. This argument was strengthened when North Korean forces crossed into South Korea on 25 June 1950.

Korea had been annexed by Japan in 1910, but following its defeat, Soviet troops had occupied the northern areas, while U.S. troops were based in the south. A temporary divide was established along the 38th parallel, and following the creation of separate governments, Russian and U.S. troops withdrew. Believing that the invasion was Soviet-inspired, Truman secured a UN resolution calling for members to resist the attackers. Without benefit of a declaration of war,

Truman committed U.S troops to what he called a "police action." When the U.S.-dominated UN forces pushed toward the border with China in November 1950, the Chinese sent troops to aid North Korea, and the war settled into a stalemate that lasted until 1953.

The **Korean War** cost the United States the lives of 34,000 men. It contributed to rise of **McCarthyism** and the defeat of the **Democrats** in the 1952 election. In the long run, it also confirmed U.S. commitment to the policy of containment in Asia, ultimately leading to the tragic involvement in Vietnam. *See also* ACHESON, DEAN GOODERHAM; AMERICA FIRST COMMITTEE (AFC); BYRNES, JAMES FRANCIS; CHAPULTEPEC AGREEMENT; EVIAN CONFERENCE; HULL, CORDELL; ISRAEL; STETTINIUS, EDWARD REILLY, JR.; VANDENBERG, ARTHUR HENDRICK.

FORMOSA. *See* TAIWAN.

FORRESTAL, JAMES VINCENT (1892–1949). James Forrestal was born in New York and attended both Dartmouth College and Princeton University but left without graduating. He found work on Wall Street as a bond salesman and during World War I worked in the Office of the Chief of Naval Operations in Washington, D.C. After the war, he resumed work on Wall Street and became a successful executive. In 1940, Forrestal was appointed as an assistant to President **Franklin D. Roosevelt** and then became undersecretary of the navy with responsibility for procuring and distributing raw material. In 1944, he was appointed secretary of the navy after the death of **Frank Knox**. He was a firm supporter of the policy of **containment** and advocated sending the U.S. fleet to the eastern Mediterranean during the crisis in **Azerbaijan** in 1946. In 1947, he was appointed the first secretary of defense under the terms of the **National Security Act**. Forrestal faced criticism for some of the problems in the new department and also for his perceived pro-Arab and anti-Israeli views. In 1949 President **Harry S. Truman** asked for his resignation. Suffering from depression, Forrestal committed suicide shortly afterward.

FOSTER, WILLIAM ZEBULON (1881–1961). Born in Taunton, Massachusetts, William Foster grew up in poverty in Philadelphia,

Pennsylvania. Having traveled the country as an itinerant worker, he joined the **Socialist Party of America** in 1901 but left to join the Industrial Workers of the World (IWW). Foster gradually gravitated away from the IWW in favor of converting existing **trade unions** to syndicalism. In 1912, he established the Syndicalist League of North America, which became the Independent Trade Union League in 1914. During World War I, he helped mobilize the meatpacking workers. The **American Federation of Labor** then appointed him to lead the drive to unionize the steel industry in 1919. The resultant strike ended in defeat, partially because Foster's past affiliations were used to brand the strikers as revolutionaries. Foster converted to communism in the early 1920s and was the candidate for the **Communist Party of the United States of America (CPUSA)** in the 1924, 1928, and 1932 presidential elections.

As leader of the demonstration in New York's Union Square in March 1930, which turned into a riot, Foster was jailed for six months. The jailing did not stop him from running for president, and in 1932 he won more than 100,000 votes. He resumed leadership of the CPUSA following the ideological differences between the established executive led by his long-time rival, **Earl Browder**, and Moscow in 1945. In 1948, Foster was one of 11 communist leaders indicted by the government under the **Smith Act** of 1940. He was not jailed due to his ill health, but his codefendants were. Foster, who was unswervingly loyal to the **Soviet Union**, died in Moscow and received a state funeral there before his ashes were flown back to the United States.

FOUR FREEDOMS. Preparing the nation for the future possibility of war, in his State of the Union Address on 6 January 1941, President **Franklin D. Roosevelt** said that the United States should "look forward to a world founded upon four essential human freedoms." These four freedoms were freedom of speech and expression, freedom of worship, freedom from want, and freedom from fear. Artist **Norman Rockwell** was so influenced by the speech that he produced four paintings illustrating the freedoms that were used as cover illustrations for the *Saturday Evening Post* (20 and 27 February and 6 and 13 March, 1943). The paintings were exhibited by the **Office**

of War Information and turned into war posters to raise money for **war bonds**.

FRANKFURTER, FELIX (1882–1965). Born in Austria, Felix Frankfurter's family moved to the United States in 1894. Frankfurter gained a law degree at City College of New York and went on to Harvard University, where he graduated in 1906. He practiced briefly in New York and then became an assistant to **Henry Stimson**, a U.S. attorney in New York. Frankfurter became a professor at Harvard Law School in 1914, a position he held until 1939. During World War I, he became assistant secretary of labor and served as secretary for the President's Mediation Commission that investigated the labor unrest in the West in 1917. In 1916, Frankfurter headed the investigation into the convictions of Tom Mooney and Warren Billings, labor leaders sentenced to death for a bombing in San Francisco in which 10 people were killed. Frankfurter reported that there were several grounds for a retrial, and as a consequence, the death sentences were commuted. In 1918, he was appointed to chair the War Labor Policies Board to unify labor standards used by federal agencies.

After the war, Frankfurter called for recognition of the Bolshevik regime in Russia, joined the **American Civil Liberties Union**, defended immigrant members of left-wing groups against deportation, and called for a retrial in the case of Ferdinando Nicola Sacco and Bartolomeo Vanzetti. Frankfurter was a close friend of **Franklin D. Roosevelt** and influential in drawing up various pieces of **New Deal** legislation. Many of his students went to work in New Deal agencies. In 1938, Roosevelt nominated him to the **Supreme Court**, where he served until 1962. Frankfurter was not consistently "liberal" as a justice but believed in "judicial restraint" and the importance of precedent. He is most remembered for his majority opinion in *Minersville School District v. Gobitis* in 1940 and his dissents in *West Virginia State Board of Education v. Barnette* in 1943 and *Baker v. Carr* in 1962. In the first case, he ruled that the children of Jehovah's Witnesses could be expelled from school for refusing to salute the flag. When this was over-turned in *West Virginia State Board of Education*, he rejected the argument that the First Amendment barred mandatory flag salutes. In *Baker v. Carr*, he rejected any judicial remedy for malapportioned legislatures.

Frankfurter also upheld the government's actions in interning **Japanese Americans** during the war in cases like *Korematsu v. United States*. He was, however, conspicuous in his support of **African Americans**, and he wholeheartedly supported the decision against segregated schools in *Brown v. Board of Education of Topeka* in 1954. He did not, though, support picketing by African Americans to secure employment in supermarkets (*Hughes v. Superior Court of California for Contra Costa County*, 1950), nor did he approve of sit-ins or other militant tactics. Frankfurter retired in 1962. He was awarded the Presidential Medal of Freedom in 1963.

FROST, ROBERT LEE (1875–1963). Perhaps the greatest American poet of the 20th century, Robert Frost was born in San Francisco, California, but brought up in New Hampshire after his father's early death. He was educated in Lawrence, Massachusetts, and went to Dartmouth College in 1892. He did not complete his university education but for a while divided his time between farming, teaching, and writing poetry. In 1912, he sold his farm and moved to England, and in 1913 he published his first collection of verse, *A Boy's Will*. His second collection, *North of Boston*, was published in 1914. Having achieved some critical success, Frost and his family returned to the United States in 1915. *Mountain Interval* was published in 1916, and Frost was appointed to a teaching post at Amherst. He left his post in 1920, established a summer study program at Middlebury College, and was "poet in residence" at Ann Arbor. In 1923, *Selected Poems* and *New Hampshire* appeared. *New Hampshire* won the first of four Pulitzer Prizes that Frost was awarded. For the rest of his career, he divided his time between teaching appointments at different colleges.

Frost produced several more volumes of poetry. His *Collected Poems* (1930), *A Further Range* (1936), and *The Witness Tree* (1942) were awarded Pulitzer Prizes, but the 1930s were marked by personal tragedy with the deaths of his daughter and wife and suicide of his son. Although not particularly politically engaged, Frost was fairly critical of **Franklin D. Roosevelt** and the **New Deal**. After **World War II**, he wrote two plays in blank verse, *A Masque of Reason* (1945) and *A Masque of Mercy* (1947). Comparatively, he wrote very little after 1948. His last collection of poems, *In the Clearing* (1962), was well received. He was appointed as consultant on poetry at the Library of Congress from 1958 to 1959, and in 1961 he read one of his poems, "The Gift Outright," at President John F. Kennedy's inaugural and was awarded the Congressional Medal. Frost is remembered for his variations on blank verse and use of rural images and references to New England in a language easily accessible to the layperson. *See also* LITERATURE AND THEATER.

FUCHS, KLAUS (1911–1988). Klaus Fuchs was a German-born nuclear physicist who fled Nazi **Germany** in 1933 and worked in British universities before moving to the United States in 1943 to join the **Manhattan Project**. Named as a spy by a **Soviet** defector in 1945, he confessed to espionage in 1950 and was sentenced to 14 years in jail in **Great Britain**. His information led to the convictions of **Ethel** and **Julius Rosenberg** in the United States. Fuchs was released in 1959 and returned to the **German Democratic Republic**.

FULBRIGHT, JAMES WILLIAM (1905–1995). J. William Fulbright was born in Missouri, but he was raised in Arkansas and graduated from the University of Arkansas in 1925. He then studied at Oxford University, England, as a Rhodes Scholar until 1928. Upon his return to the United States, he taught at George Washington Law School and the University of Arkansas. In 1939, he became president of the University of Arkansas and the youngest college head in the country. In 1942, Fulbright began his political career when he was elected as a **Democrat** to the U.S. House of Representatives. In 1944, he was elected to the Senate and joined the Foreign Relations Committee. A committed internationalist, he supported the **United Nations (UN)** and in 1946 sponsored the educational exchange program, which was named after him. He also supported the **Truman Doctrine** and **Marshall Plan**. Fulbright was a critic of **Joseph McCarthy** and right-wing groups like the John Birch Society. However, he opposed racial integration and in 1956 signed the Southern Manifesto against the **Supreme Court**'s decision in *Brown v. Board of Education of Topeka*, and he took part in the filibuster that tried to prevent passage of the 1964 Civil Rights Act.

As chair of the Senate Foreign Relations Committee from 1959 until 1975, Fulbright was an influential voice on **foreign affairs**.

Although he initially supported the Tonkin Resolution granting President Lyndon Johnson the power to increase U.S. involvement in the war in Vietnam, he subsequently came to regret it and wrote a critical study of U.S. policy in Asia, *The Arrogance of Power*, published in 1967. Fulbright supported the passage of the War Powers Act in 1973 limiting presidential war-making powers. He lost his seat in 1974 and worked in a law firm in Washington, D.C., also traveling and speaking widely on foreign affairs. In 1993, President Bill Clinton awarded him the Medal of Freedom in recognition of his work.

– G –

GABLE, (WILLIAM) CLARK (1901–1960). Actor Clark Gable was born in Cadiz, Ohio. He left home to tour with an acting troupe in 1917 and then worked as a lumberjack and a telephone lineman before returning to **theater** in 1924. After several minor parts on Broadway, he made his first appearances in movies as an extra. After some success on the stage in *The Last Mile* in 1930, he signed a contract with Metro-Goldwyn-Mayer. After appearing in a number of films with leading female stars, including *Strange Interlude* (1932), *Polly of the Circus* (1932), *Hold Your Man* (1933), and *Dancing Lady* (1933), he won an Oscar for his role in *It Happened One Night* (1934) and was the star in such films as *Mutiny on the Bounty* (1935), *China Seas* (1935), *San Francisco* (1936), and several others. His standing as one of the world's leading actors was confirmed in his iconic performance as Rhett Butler in *Gone with the Wind* (1939) and the immortal line, "Quite frankly my dear, I don't give a damn!"

Following the outbreak of **World War II**, Gable enlisted in the army air corps and won the Distinguished Flying Cross for his bravery in combat. He returned to Hollywood after the war and successfully resumed his career making several more films, his last being *The Misfits* with Marilyn Monroe in 1960. *See also* CINEMA.

GARBO, GRETA (1905–1990). Movie star Greta Garbo was born Greta Lovisa Gustafsson in Stockholm, Sweden. Her work as an advertising model in a department store led to a career in film beginning with *Peter the Tramp* (1920). From 1922 to 1924, Garbo studied at the Royal Swedish Dramatic Theater, and she acquired her stage name and reputation as an actress in *The Story of Gosta Berling* (1924). Following her success in Sweden, she moved to Hollywood in 1925, where her beauty and husky voice enabled her to play roles of sexual passion. Garbo made a total of 24 films in Hollywood. Her films, in which she often played the tragic heroine, included *Flesh and the Devil* (1927), *Love* (1927), *The Kiss* (1929), *Anna Christie* (1930), *Romance*, (1930), *Mata Hari* (1932), *Grand Hotel* (1932), *Anna Karenina* (1935), *Camille* (1936), and *Ninotchka* (1939). The attempt to change her screen image in *Two-Faced Woman* in 1941 was not a success, and Garbo did not make another movie. She retired aged 36 and moved to New York City to live a secluded life. During her career, she received four Academy Award nominations for Best Actress for *Anna Christie*, *Romance*, *Camille*, and *Ninotchka*. Famous for the "Garbo mystique" that she deliberately fostered, she was given a special Oscar in 1954 for her unforgettable performances. *See also* CINEMA.

GARLAND, JUDY (1922–1969). Film star and singer Judy Garland was born Frances Ethel Gumm in Grand Rapids, Minnesota, to a theater family. In 1926, the family moved to California, where Frances appeared with her sisters in a theater managed by their father. In 1934, they performed in Chicago as the Garlands, and in 1935 Frances was given a contract and a further name change by Metro-Goldwyn-Mayer (MGM). Judy Garland's first film was *Every Sunday* (1936). She made several more films and sang the hit song, "You Made Me Love You" in *Broadway Melody of 1938* (1937), before achieving her major breakthrough in *The Wizard of Oz* (1939), particularly with the hit song "Somewhere over the Rainbow." Further hits followed when she paired with **Mickey Rooney** in *Babes in Arms* (1939), *Strike Up the Band* (1940), *Babes on Broadway* (1941), and *Ziegfeld Girl* (1941), and with **Gene Kelly** in *For Me and My Gal* (1942). However, none of these matched *Meet Me in St. Louis* (1944). Her film performances varied, often due to her addiction to barbiturates and troubled personal life. However, Garland had another major success with **Fred Astaire** in *Easter Parade* and the song "We're a Couple of Swells" (1948). Although she made a considerable number of other films of varying quality, MGM fired her in 1950. In 1951, she was greeted with great acclaim following a series of performances at the London Palladium in England, and she had further film success in *A Star is Born* (1954).

Although she made several more films, Garland concentrated on her stage shows. After a physical collapse in 1959, she made another comeback in 1960 achieving an enormous hit with her performance at the Carnegie Hall in April 1961. Her final film was *I Could Go on Singing* in 1963. An unsuccessful television series in 1963, *The Judy Garland Show*, was followed by an overseas tour in 1969. She died in London after an overdose of barbiturates. *See also* CINEMA.

GARNER, JOHN NANCE (1868–1967). 30th vice president of the United States. John Nance Garner was born in a log cabin in Texas and after limited schooling he briefly attended Vanderbilt University, studied law, and qualified for the bar in 1890. Garner practiced law in Uvalde, Texas, where he became county judge from 1893 to 1896. He was elected as a **Democrat** to the state house of representatives in 1898 and to the U.S. House of Representatives in 1903. Garner served until 1933. He was not a conspicuous legislator. It was eight years before he made his first speech, but he gained power by virtue of seniority. Garner eventually became Speaker of the House from 1931 until 1933, when he was elected vice president to **Franklin D. Roosevelt**. His experience gave him a crucial role as liaison with Congress, and the Texas connection gave him influence with a number of key figures, and he was reelected in 1936. He has been described as the "most powerful vice president in history." Initially a supporter of the **New Deal**, Garner was increasingly unhappy with the social welfare and prolabor aspects of Roosevelt's program. He became openly hostile when Roosevelt attempted to alter the composition of the **Supreme Court** in 1937 and stood against FDR for the nomination in 1940. When he was unsuccessful, Garner left politics and retired to his ranch in Uvalde.

GENERAL AGREEMENT ON TARIFFS AND TRADE (GATT). The GATT was signed by 23 countries on 1 January 1948 following the preliminary agreement reached in Havana, Cuba, the previous

year. Intended to prevent the economic competition that had contributed to the **Great Depression** in the 1930s, the agreement was an
attempt to reduce international trade barriers by removing tariffs and
established "favored nation" status between participating nations.
Further reductions in tariff barriers were reached in 1949, 1951, and
1955.

GERMAN DEMOCRATIC REPUBLIC (GDR). On 7 October
1949, **Soviet** occupation forces in East **Germany** established the
GDR in response to the earlier creation of the **Federal Republic of
Germany (FRG)** in West Germany. It was governed by the communist Socialist Unity Party and joined the Soviet-led economic bloc,
COMECON, in 1950 and the Warsaw Pact in 1955. The imposition
of Soviet-style institutions and a police state led many people to flee
West until the border was closed in 1952. A workers' uprising in East
Berlin was brutally suppressed in 1953, and the continued flow of
refugees through West Berlin led to the building of the Berlin Wall
in 1961. Improved relations with the FRG led to mutual recognition
in 1972 and the inclusion of both states in the **United Nations** in
1973. Popular unrest continued, however, and in 1989 mass demonstrations brought about the collapse of the communist regime, the
disassembling of the Berlin Wall, and paved the way to reunification
in 1990.

GERMAN-AMERICAN BUND. An organization of German Americans sympathetic to **Adolf Hitler** and Nazi **Germany**, the German-
American Bund had its origins in the Friends of New Germany and
the National Socialist German Workers' Party in 1933. A German
naturalized as a U.S. citizen in 1924, Fritz Kuhn took over its leadership in 1936. At most, the Bund attracted approximately 25,000
members but also had supporters in **William Dudley Pelley**'s Silver Shirts. Some 20,000 supporters gathered at a rally in Madison
Square Garden in New York City on 19 February 1939 and heard
Kuhn attack **Franklin D. Roosevelt** and the **New Deal** as a Jewish
conspiracy. The Bund was outlawed once the United States entered
World War II, and many of its members, including Kuhn, were interned. Kuhn was deported to Germany after the war.

GERMANY. Following the defeat in World War I and the abdication of Kaiser Wilhelm II in November 1918, a new German Federal Republic, the Weimar Republic was established. The war officially ended with the signing of the Versailles Treaty in June 1919. However, because the treaty provided for the establishment of a League of Nations, it was rejected by the U.S. Congress. Formal hostilities between Germany and the United States were ended by a two-nation agreement in 1921. The Versailles Treaty also imposed huge reparation payments on Germany that, combined with the economic disruption brought about by the war, caused considerable instability in the German economy. Economic collapse in 1922 and 1923 led to a renegotiation of reparations under the Dawes Plan (1924) and again in 1929 under the Young Plan. Having survived the economic crises and an attempted putsch led by **Adolf Hitler** in Munich in 1923, the Weimar Republic appeared to have achieved some stability until it was hit by the effects of the **Great Depression.** By 1931, 6 million workers—30 percent of the labor force—were unemployed, and the country was plunged into economic and political chaos. Hitler and the Nazi (National Socialist) Party capitalized on this crisis and made major gains in the elections of September 1930. In the July 1932 elections, the Nazis emerged as the largest single party and were able to capture power by forming a coalition with conservative groups. On 30 January 1933, Hitler became chancellor and was granted virtually unlimited power in March. Following the death of President Paul von Hindenburg in 1934, Hitler became the Reich's führer.

Under Hitler's leadership, Germany embarked on a program to restore the economy through a program of public works and rearmament and to restore national pride by overturning the Versailles Treaty and regaining lost territory. At the same time, the anti-Semitic and anticommunist policies of the Nazis were implemented, and Jews and political opponents were placed in labor and concentration camps or executed. The attacks on Jews came to a climax in November 1938 when in "Kristallnacht" (Night of Broken Glass), homes, shops, and businesses were attacked and looted. Many Jews sought to flee the persecution, and some 60,000 found refuge in the United States between 1933 and 1938. However, members of the **Evian Conference** failed to agree on a response to the deepening refugee crisis among other nations, and many were unable to escape.

In 1936, German troops reoccupied the Rhineland, and the search for lebensraum in the east led to the Anschluss with Austria in 1938 and the annexation of the Sudetenland from Czechoslovakia in 1938 and of Czechoslovakia itself in March 1939. Finally, on 1 September 1939 German armies invaded Poland. As **Great Britain** and France had guaranteed Polish sovereignty, this attack led to the outbreak of **World War II**. The attack on Poland was preceded by the signing of the Nazi-Soviet Pact with the **Soviet Union** on 28 August 1939 that guaranteed the neutrality of either party in the event of war. It also included agreed spheres of influence that led to the Soviet occupation of eastern Poland as well as Estonia, Latvia, and Lithuania. Germany had also concluded agreements with fascist Italy and **Japan** in 1936, and these were further strengthened in the Tripartite Agreement of September 1940.

After their speedy occupation of Poland, in April 1940 the German armies turned to Western Europe, quickly overrunning Denmark and Norway and then invading Belgium and the Netherlands in May. French and British forces were defeated, and the remnants of the British armies were forced to withdraw at Dunkirk. France surrendered on 22 June 1940. The German air force launched bombing raids on Britain but was halted in the "Battle of Britain." German U-boats began to attack U.S. ships, providing **Lend-Lease** supplies to the British, but Hitler did not declare war on the United States until after the Japanese had attacked **Pearl Harbor** in December 1941. However, the British and Americans were not able to launch their invasion of Europe until **D-Day 1944**, and it was in the east that Germany first faced defeat. Ignoring the nonaggression pact, on 22 June 1941 Hitler launched an invasion of Soviet Russia to garner oil and food supplies, overthrow communism, and gain more living space. Initially successful, German armies became bogged down in the Russian winter and were halted at Moscow in 1942 and Stalingrad in 1943. They were forced to retreat, and faced with the combined **Allied** forces on two fronts, were forced to surrender on 8 May 1945.

As agreed at the **Potsdam Conference**, following its defeat, Germany was divided into four occupation zones, with the Soviet Union in the East and Britain, France, and the United States in the West. **Berlin** was also divided between the four victorious powers. Mounting disagreement between the former Allies led the United States,

Britain, and France to agree to the creation of a West German state on 31 May 1948, complete with a new currency. The USSR responded by imposing a blockade on Berlin. On 21 September 1949, the **Federal Republic of Germany** came into being, with its capital in Bonn. On 7 October 1949 the **German Democratic Republic** was established in the east under Soviet control, with its capital in East Berlin. The state of war with Germany was ended by the Western Allies in 1951, and complete sovereignty was granted to West Germany in May 1955. German membership to the **North Atlantic Treaty Organization** enabled British and U.S. troops to remain present in the country. Economic assistance through the **Marshall Plan** contributed to the "German economic miracle," which saw West Germany become an increasingly powerful economy in the 1950s. Germany continued to be a source of tension between the East and West until the end of the **Cold War** and the reunification of the country in 1990. *See also* BERLIN, BERLIN AIRLIFT.

GERMANY, FEDERAL REPUBLIC OF (FRG). Established on 23 May 1949 and known as West **Germany**, the FRG consisted of the nine regions or states occupied by British, French, and U.S. forces after **World War II**. This was a consequence of economic unification to facilitate administration of the **Marshall Plan**. The move to statehood accelerated following the **Berlin Airlift**. In 1949, parliamentary elections were held and a new federal government under Konrad Adenauer established. In response to the creation of the FRG, Soviet forces of occupation in the east established the **German Democratic Republic (GDR)** in October 1949, and the divided Germany remained at the center of the **Cold War**. In 1954, the FRG joined the **North Atlantic Treaty Organization**. Improved relations with the **Soviet Union** and more especially with the GDR in the 1960s led to mutual recognition of the two states in 1972 and their admission to the **United Nations** in 1973. The collapse of the GDR led to reunification in 1990.

GERSHWIN, GEORGE (1898–1937). Born Jacob Gershvin, George Gershwin became one of America's most famous composers of orchestral works, popular songs, jazz, and musical comedies. He worked as a pianist for a **music** publisher from 1914 to 1917, when he became a theater pianist. In 1919, he achieved his first hit with "Swanee," later recorded by Al Jolson. From 1920 on, Gershwin composed musical reviews, Broadway plays, and orchestral pieces. His best-known works were *Rhapsody in Blue* (1923), *Piano Concerto in F* (1925), *An American in Paris* (1928), and the opera written with Ira and based on the novel by DuBose Heyward, *Porgy and Bess* (1935), all notable for their combination of jazz and orchestral music.

Together with his brother **Ira Gershwin**, George Gershwin composed many hit songs for musicals. Among the best-known songs in these were "Fascinating Rhythm," "Someone to Watch over Me," "'S Wonderful," "Embraceable You," and "I got Rhythm." In 1936, the Gershwins went to Hollywood, where they wrote the music for *Shall We Dance?* (1937). Starring **Fred Astaire** and **Ginger Rogers**, the movie included such hits as "Let's Call the Whole Thing Off" and "They Can't Take That Away from Me." The Gershwins provided the music for two more movies, *A Damsel in Distress* (1937) and *The Goldwyn Follies* (1938), before George's death. Gershwin's music was incorporated into a number of films after his death, most notably *Rhapsody in Blue* (1945), *An American in Paris* (1951), and *Manhattan* (1979). In 1998, Gershwin was awarded a posthumous Pulitzer prize for his contributions to musical writing. *See also* CINEMA.

GERSHWIN, IRA (1896–1983). Born Israel Gershvin, Ira was the brother of **George Gershwin**. Ira provided the lyrics for many of George's compositions including the songs for the musicals *Lady Be Good* (1924), *Tip-toes* (1925), *Oh Kay!* (1926), *Funny Face* (1927), *Strike Up the Band* (1927), and the Pulitzer Prize-winning *Of Thee I Sing* (1931). From 1936 Ira provided the lyrics for George's **music** in a number of Hollywood movies. Following George's death, Ira wrote the lyrics for composer Kurt Weill's *Lady in the Dark* (1940), and Jerome Kern's *Cover Girl* (1944), as well as *The Firebrand of Florence* (1945), *Park Avenue* (1946), *The Barkleys of Broadway* (1949), *A Star is Born* (1954), and *The Country Girl* (1954). In addition to further collaboration with Weill, Ira also completed film scores based on George's notebooks for *The Shocking Miss Pilgrim* (1946) and *Kiss Me, Stupid* (1964). He was involved in the making of *An American in Paris* (1951) which incorporated some of his and George's earlier work and which won an Academy Award. His annotated collection of more than 100 lyrics, *Lyrics on Several Occasions* (1959) was widely acclaimed. *See also* CINEMA; HARBURG, EDGAR YIPSEL.

G.I. BILL OF RIGHTS. *See* SELECTIVE SERVICEMEN'S READJUSTMENT ACT.

GLASS, CARTER (1858–1946). Carter Glass left school at the age of 14 and held various types of employment before becoming a reporter in Virginia in 1880. He eventually became a newspaper editor and owner. He served in the state senate from 1899 to 1903 as a **Democrat** and then represented Virginia in the U.S. House of Representatives from 1902 to 1919 and in the U.S. Senate from 1920 until his death. An advocate of **banking** reform, he sponsored the Federal Reserve Act in 1913 and was secretary of the Treasury between 1918 and 1920. Glass was a member of the Democratic National Committee from 1916 to 1928 and, unusual for a southerner, he supported **Alfred E. Smith** in 1928. In 1932, with Representative Henry Steagall, he cosponsored the act that kept the United States on the gold standard. In 1933 he cosponsored the Glass-Steagall Act that established the **Federal Deposit Insurance Corporation.** Increasingly, however, as an advocate of states' rights, Glass opposed the **New Deal.** He did support President **Franklin D. Roosevelt's foreign policy** and opposed isolationism.

GLASS-STEAGALL ACT. *See* BANKING ACT, 1933.

GOLD RESERVE ACT, 1934. Intended as an inflationary policy, the Gold Reserve Act of 1934 enabled the president to authorize the purchase of U.S. minted gold at prices to be determined by him and to establish it as a reserve for paper currency. Gold was to be impounded in the Treasury. President **Franklin D. Roosevelt** set the price of gold at $35 per ounce, 59 percent of its pre-1933 level.

"GOOD NEIGHBOR" POLICY. In his inaugural address on 4 March 1933, President **Franklin D. Roosevelt** announced that in **foreign affairs,** the United States should be committed to "the policy of the good neighbor." This was confirmed by **Cordell Hull** at the meeting of American states in Montevideo in December 1933, when he declared that "no state has the right to intervene in the internal or external affairs of another." While to some extent this was a continuation of the policy initiated by **Herbert Hoover**, it officially was only ratified in the Senate in 1934. In 1934 a treaty was also signed with Cuba abrogating the amendments to the Cuban constitution imposed under the Platt Amendment of 1902. The U.S. marines were withdrawn from Haiti, and in 1936 the United States abandoned the right to intervene in Panama. Reciprocal trade agreements were also reached with a number of Latin American countries. *See also* CHAPULTEPEC AGREEMENT; ORGANIZATION OF AMERICAN STATES (OAS); RIO PACT.

GOODMAN, BENNY (1909–1986). The man who was to become "the King of Swing" was born Benjamin David Goodman to Jewish immigrant parents in Chicago, Illinois. Goodman began studying the clarinet at the age of 10 and left school at 14 to begin playing professionally. In 1925, he joined Ben Pollack's orchestra, and he made his first recording in 1926. Goodman began performing as a solo artist and with different ensembles in 1929, making a number of **radio** broadcasts and recordings. In 1934, he formed his own band in New York City, and his was one of three bands to play on the three-hour National Biscuit Company radio program *Let's Dance*. His band included drummer Gene Krupa and pianist and arranger Fletcher Henderson, and they had a number of hit records, including, *Stompin' at the Savoy* (1935) and *Don't Be That Way* (1938).

In 1935, the Goodman band began a national tour. It was not successful until August of that year when a performance at the Palomar Ballroom in Los Angeles provoked an enthusiastic response from the audience who began jitterbugging in the aisles. Goodman began to add black musicians to the lineup, including pianist Teddy Wilson, trumpeter Cootie Williams, and guitarist Charlie Christian. Their hits included "Bugle Call Rag," "One O'Clock Jump," and "Sing, Sing, Sing." After playing to packed houses at the Paramount Theater in New York in 1937, Goodman and his band appeared at Carnegie Hall in 1938 in what is regarded as a historic concert marking the pinnacle of the swing era. During the war years, the popularity of swing began to decline, and it was difficult to maintain big band performances or produce records. Goodman gave the occasional concert and recorded V-discs for the troops. From 1942 to 1944, he appeared in a number of films, including *The Powers Girl* (1943) and *The Gang's All Here* (1943). He also played and recorded a number of classical pieces. In 1948, he appeared in the movie *A Song Is Born* with Tommy Dorsey, Lionel Hampton, and **Louis Armstrong**.

During the 1950s, Goodman performed widely and took part in a number of international tours, some sponsored by the State Department. The film *The Benny Goodman Story* appeared in 1955. In 1961, he toured Latin America for the first time, and in 1962 he visited the **Soviet Union**. He even publicly debated with Soviet premier Nikita Khrushchev about the merits of jazz. Goodman continued performing and recording until the end. He put on his final concert in 1986 just days before his death. He received numerous awards and titles in recognition of his contribution to **music**. *See also* CINEMA.

GRABLE, BETTY (1916–1973). The serviceman's favorite pin-up girl during **World War II** was born Elizabeth Ruth Grable in St. Louis, Missouri. She began her film career in blackface in *Happy Days* in 1929 and had small roles in several films throughout the 1930s before achieving some success in *Dubarry Was a Lady* in 1939. She signed a contract with 20th Century Fox and starred in more than half a dozen films during World War II. In 1943, she posed in a bathing costume for a photograph that became iconic. It was named as one of 100 photos that changed the world by *Life* magazine. The best-paid female star, Grable's legs were reputedly insured for $1 million each. One of her wartime movies was appropriately entitled *Pin Up Girl* (1944). She made several more films after the war, including *Lady in Ermine* (1948), *My Blue Heaven* (1950), and her last film, *How to Marry a Millionaire* (1953). *See also* CINEMA

GRAND COULEE DAM. Construction of the Grand Coulee Dam on the Columbia River in Washington began in 1933 and was completed in 1942 as part of the Columbia River Reclamation Project. At the time, it was the largest concrete dam in the world and provided power and irrigation for 11 western states. *See also* COLUMBIA RIVER PROJECT.

GREAT BRITAIN. Along with **Germany**, France, and Spain, Great Britain was one of the leading Western European nations at the end of the 19th century and a major imperial power. However, although victorious in 1918, following the devastating effects of World War I, Great Britain suffered from political instability and uneven economic development. While such new industries as chemicals, electrical goods, and automobiles began to grow, particularly in the 1930s, such older staple industries as coal mining, steel, and shipbuilding were in decline. Unemployment never fell below 10 percent in the 1920s, and with the onset of the **Great Depression** after 1929, the rate rose to more than 20 percent. The nation was also beset by labor conflict, with major strikes occurring in 1919 and the General Strike in 1926. After 1920, political power shifted from the centrist Liberal Party to the Conservative Party, with a brief minority Labour Government in 1924. Labour again regained power as a minority government in 1929, but faced by the economic crisis, it collapsed in 1932 to be replaced by a National Government consisting of some Labour MPs, Conservatives, and Liberals. Leadership passed from Ramsay Macdonald (Labour) to Stanley Baldwin (Conservative) and finally in 1937 to Neville Chamberlain (Conservative).

The National Government was increasingly forced to respond to the rise of **Adolf Hitler** and the Nazi Party in Germany, and the Chamberlain administration was generally associated with the policy of appeasement that allowed Hitler to rearm and embark on expansion, first into the Rhineland, then Austria, and then Czechoslovakia between 1936 and 1939. Following the meeting between German, French, and British representatives at Munich in September 1938 in which the Sudetenland was ceded to Hitler, Chamberlain claimed to have achieved "peace with honor" and "peace in our time." However, when it became clear that Germany next threatened Poland, the British and French issued guarantees that they would maintain Polish independence. Thus when German armies invaded Poland on 1 September 1939, Britain and France declared war on 3 September, and **World War II** had begun.

After a period known as the "Phoney War," in which all sides prepared their forces, in 1940 German armies quickly overran Denmark and Norway and in May launched their assault on Belgium and the Netherlands. Faced with these setbacks, Chamberlain was forced to resign and was replaced as prime minister by **Winston Churchill**. Promising nothing more than "blood, toil, tears, and sweat," Churchill proved an inspirational wartime leader with his famous "V sign" gesture for victory—the personification of British resistance. That resistance was evident during the Battle of Britain, in which the Royal Air Force overcame the German Luftwaffe's attempts to gain air superiority over Great Britain in July through October 1940, prior to a possible invasion. The British people also demonstrated a dogged determination in response to the "Blitz," the German bombing of major towns and cities between September 1940 and May 1941 that claimed more than 43,000 civilian lives. These events were reported on by American reporters like **Edward R. Murrow** and **Ernie Pyle**, and Great Britain increasingly began to receive aid from the United States. Having secured a **lend-lease** agreement in March 1941, Churchill met with President Franklin D. Roosevelt in August and agreed on a common vision for the postwar world based on the Atlantic Charter.

Once the United States entered the war in 1941, cooperation between the two major **Allies** was established and a common strategy agreed upon at the **Arcadia Conference**. Other wartime meetings between British, U.S., and **Soviet** leaders and representatives took place at **Casablanca**, **Tehran**, **Moscow**, **Yalta**, and **Potsdam**. Although there were strategic differences between the British and Americans, for example concerning the invasion of North Africa (**Operation Torch**) and then Sicily (**Operation Husky**), the two nations generally worked closely together. Beginning in 1942 U.S. forces were based in Great Britain, leading to the buildup of **D-Day** and the invasion of **Normandy**. U.S. wartime aid and military presence helped to cement the "special relationship," which Churchill referred to after the war. Although Churchill was defeated in the elections of July 1945 and a Labour Government under Clement Attlee came to power, the relationship grew stronger when Great Britain, already impoverished by the war, faced economic crisis during the winter of 1946 and 1947. The British government indicated that it could no longer carry the burden of supporting royalist forces against left-wing groups in Greece and called upon the administration of **Harry S. Truman** for assistance. The response was the **Truman Doctrine** and the **Marshall Plan**, providing military and economic aid to European countries.

As one of the four occupying powers in postwar Germany, Great Britain worked closely with the United States during the **Berlin Airlift** in 1948. The British were also instrumental in securing the U.S. military commitment to the security of Europe in the establishment of the **North Atlantic Treaty Organization**, and from 1948 onward, U.S. Air Force bombers were located on British airfields. Britain actively supported the United States during the **Cold War** and committed 63,000 troops to the **United Nations** forces in the **Korean War**. However, British power was much diminished, and as parts of its empire gained independence, it could no longer claim to be a superpower. The Suez Crisis in 1956, in which Great Britain and **Israel** attacked Egypt, weakened its influence in the Middle East and strained relations with the **Dwight D. Eisenhower** administration. Great Britain increasingly favored Europe, joining the European Economic Community (EEC) in 1973. Nonetheless, relations with the United States continued to be strong, particularly during the presidencies of Ronald Reagan and George W. Bush and prime ministers Margaret Thatcher and Tony Blair, respectively.

GREAT DEPRESSION. The Great Depression was the worldwide economic crisis that followed the **Wall Street Crash** and the Depression that began in the United States in 1929. The calling in or cessation of foreign loans and the imposition of high tariffs led to a shrinking in international trade. As prices fell and trade shrank, the number of unemployed workers worldwide was estimated to be more than 30 million by 1933, with two-thirds of those in **Germany**, **Great Britain**, and the United States.

The Wall Street Crash was not the cause of the collapse but merely the trigger that revealed the underlying weaknesses of international markets and the U.S. economy in particular. The apparent prosperity of the "Roaring 1920s" masked a number of flaws, including the maldistribution of incomes, overproduction and buildup of inventories, falling farm prices, instability of banks, and imbalances in the international economy. The breakdown of financial institutions in the United States led to the failure of more than 5,000 banks between

1929 and 1932, and as money and credit dried up, businesses also reduced output or failed completely. Workers found their wages or hours of work cut, and many were laid off altogether. By 1933, industrial production in the United States had fallen to less than 50 percent of its 1929 levels. The automobile industry that had played such a key part in the prosperity of the 1920s was operating at 20 percent of its capacity.

Unemployment reached an estimated 17 million people, or 25 percent of the labor force. Farmers, already suffering in the 1920s, saw their situation further deteriorate as commodity prices fell by 55 percent between 1929 and 1932. Almost a quarter of farmers lost their property through foreclosures, and others were driven out by drought and dust storms in the early 1930s, joining the thousands of migrants—**"Okies"** and "Arkies,"—heading West. Urban workers too took to the road as 250,000 families lost their homes and jobs. Many men abandoned their families, and the number of female-headed households increased. Many **women** were forced to seek work, but gender-based discrimination increased as priority was often given to men. Similarly, **African Americans** found themselves "last hired, first fired," and black unemployment rates were twice as high as those of whites. Prejudice against **Hispanic Americans** forced half a million to return to Mexico in the 1930s.

Many Americans began to protest as their economic plight worsened. Farmers destroyed produce or poured milk into the road, foreclosures were prevented by mob action, and unemployed workers marched in protests sometimes organized by socialists or communists. In 1932, veterans of World War I marched on Washington, D.C., as part of a **Bonus Army** calling for payment of war bonuses. Their forcible removal from the capital was the last nail in the political coffin of President **Herbert Hoover**, whose name had become synonymous with the Depression. Hoover's inability to abandon a commitment to limited federal action led to his political defeat by **Franklin D. Roosevelt** in the election of 1932. Roosevelt promised the nation a "**New Deal**," and the 1930s witnessed a series of programs aimed at bringing "relief, recovery, and reform." The result of this political change was the transformation of U.S. politics and the beginning of a welfare state. However, although the situation was considerably alleviated by the New Deal, it was the expansion of industry that came with the **World War II** that finally ended the Depression. That was in part a result of the economic and political problems caused by the Great Depression in Europe and elsewhere.

GREEN, WILLIAM (1870–1952). William Green was born in Coshocton, Ohio. He left school at the age of 16 and became a coal miner and active trade unionist. From 1912 to 1914, Green was secretary-treasurer of the **American Federation of Labor**, and he became vice president in 1913. In 1924, he succeeded Samuel Gompers as president and continued his predecessor's conservative and rather undynamic approach. He opposed strikes, instead preaching the need for cooperation with business and management. Although Green agreed with industrial **trade unions**, having been an officer in the United Mine Workers of America, he resisted those people who founded the Committee of Industrial Organizations and the **Congress of Industrial Organizations** when it was formed in 1938, and he was highly critical of **sit-down strikes**.

Green supported much of the **New Deal** and served on the President's Committee on Economic Security, **National Recovery Administration**, Management-Labor Policy Committee of the **War Production Board**, Economic Stabilization Committee in the **Office of Economic Stabilization**, and Office of War Mobilization and Reconversion. During **World War II**, Green firmly supported the no-strike pledge. After the war, he mobilized opposition to the **Taft-Hartley Act** and disavowed any links with communism and established an International Confederation of Free Trade Unions. Such policies were supportive of President **Harry S. Truman**'s **Cold War** initiatives, like the **Marshall Plan**.

GROVES, LESLIE RICHARD (1896–1970). Born in Albany, New York, to a military family, Leslie Groves went to the University of Washington, Massachusetts Institute of Technology, and finally West Point, where he graduated in 1918. He was commissioned into the Army Corps of Engineers. He held a series of positions during the 1920s before joining the Office of Engineers in Washington, D.C., in 1931. Groves was involved in overseeing the construction of the Pentagon building for the War Department in 1941. In 1942, he was appointed brigadier general and military director of the **Manhattan**

Project. It was Groves who selected **J. Robert Oppenheimer** to head the Los Alamos National Laboratory. In 1945, Groves recommended that the **atomic bomb** be dropped on **Japan**, and he played a part in choosing the targets. He was appointed chief of the Armed Forces Special Weapons Project in 1945. He retired in 1948 and became vice president of the Sperry Rand Corporation until 1961. His account of the Manhattan Project, *Now It Can Be Told*, was published in 1962.

GUADALCANAL. Guadalcanal, one the larger Solomon Islands, was attacked by the U.S. Navy and Marines on 7 August 1942 to prevent **Japan** from building an airfield enabling attacks on Australia during **World War II**. The assault was followed by a series of naval battles before U.S. forces achieved control of the island in February 1943. From there the United States was able to continue their "island hopping" campaign against Japanese forces.

GUTHRIE, WOODROW WILSON ("WOODY") (1912–1967). Born in Okemah, Oklahoma, in 1927 Woody Guthrie moved to Pampa, Texas, where he learned to play the guitar and developed his skill as a singer/songwriter. He moved to California in 1937 and had his own **radio** show on KFVD in Los Angeles. Two years later, Guthrie was in New York, where he recorded songs and comments for the Library of Congress Archive of American Folk Song and also made his first commercial collection, *Dust Bowl Ballads*. It was in these songs, including "Hard Travellin'" and "I Ain't Got No Home in This World Anymore," that he captured the experiences of the "**Okies**"—the migrant families displaced from the Midwest states and the **Dust Bowl**.

In 1941, Guthrie worked for the Department of the Interior, but he left to become a merchant seaman. He was drafted near the end of the war and spent a year in the army. After the war, he briefly joined Pete Seeger and the Almanac Singers, who popularized songs of his, like "Good Night, Irene." After spending time traveling across the United States, Guthrie returned to New York, where he was hospitalized with Huntington's disease. During his career, he wrote more than 1,000 songs, including "This Land Is Our Land," and he was an inspiration to his own son, Arlo Guthrie, as well as for many other singers in the 1960s, including Bob Dylan and Phil Ochs. *See also* MUSIC.

– H –

HAMMERSTEIN, OSCAR, II (1895–1960). Born in New York City to a theatrical family, Oscar Hammerstein went to Columbia University, where he met **Richard Rodgers**. In 1918, Hammerstein became a stage manager for his uncle, and in 1920 he wrote the play *Always You*. With Otto Harbach, he wrote *Wildflower* (1922), *Rose-Marie* (1924), *Sunny* (1925), *Song of the Flame* (1925), and *The Desert Song* (1926). In 1927, he wrote *Show Boat* with Jerome Kern, which included "Ol' Man River." He was less successful in the 1930s, and in 1943 he began to work with Rodgers. They wrote nine musicals together, including the enormously successful *Oklahoma!* (1943), *Carousel* (1945), *South Pacific* (1949), *The King and I* (1951), and *The Sound of Music* (1959). *See also* LITERATURE AND THEATER; MUSIC.

HAMMETT, (SAMUEL) DASHIELL (1894–1961). Born in Maryland, Dashiell Hammett had a perfunctory education, and after a series of clerical jobs, in 1915 he found work with the Pinkerton National Detective Agency in Baltimore. In 1918, Hammett joined the army and served for a year. After the war, he moved to San Francisco, where he worked briefly as a Pinkerton agent once more. However, he also began to write short detective stories, which helped establish a genre in American fiction. In his stories of the "Continental Op" published in *Smart Set* and *Black Mask* and the novels *Red Harvest* (1929) and *The Dain Curse* (1929), Hammett introduced the cynical hero without illusions who reached his most developed form as Sam Spade in *The Maltese Falcon* (1930). Cool detachment of a more sophisticated style was the characteristic of Nick Charles in *The Thin Man* (1934).

From the mid-1930s onward, Hammett wrote mainly for Hollywood and with his partner, Lillian Hellman. He also became involved in various left-wing causes. In 1942, despite his age and health problems (he had bronchial problems after a bout of influenza in

1918 and 1919), Hammett joined the army in 1942 and served until 1945. In 1951, he refused to give information about donors to a bail fund established to aid political defendants charged under the loyalty laws and was jailed. In 1953, he was called to give evidence before **Joseph McCarthy**'s Senate Subcommittee on Investigations, and in 1955 he also had to give evidence before the New York State Joint Legislative Committee with regard to groups with supposed communist sympathies. For most of these years, Hammett was deprived of income due to action by the Internal Revenue Service to reclaim unpaid back taxes and forced to depend on the charity of friends. Because of his political views, some of his books were withdrawn from public libraries, but his work continued to be popular in Europe and was rediscovered by American readers in the 1970s and 1980s. *See also* LITERATURE AND THEATER.

HARBURG, EDGAR YIPSEL ("YIP") (1896–1981). The son of Jewish Russian immigrants, Yip Harburg was born Isidore Hochberg in New York City. He graduated from the City College of New York in 1917 and traveled and worked in Latin America before returning to New York, where he helped establish an electrical supply business in 1920. The company failed following the **Wall Street Crash**, but Harburg was already writing songs and in 1932 scored a major success with "Brother, Can You Spare a Dime?" He also wrote, with Vernon Duke, "April in Paris" (1932), and, with Harold Arlen, "It's Only a Paper Moon" (1932). He worked with **Ira Gershwin** on the review *Life Begins at 8:40* in 1934, and again with Arlen on the movie *The Wizard of Oz* (1939). One of the songs for which he provided the lyrics in *The Wizard of Oz* was "Somewhere over the Rainbow," which won an Academy Award. He and Arlen also wrote songs for the film *Cabin in the Sky* (1943). Harburg's greatest success came after the war with the stage musical *Finian's Rainbow* (1947) and his hit songs "How Are Things in Glocca Mora?" and "Old Devil Moon." However, in the 1950s Harburg was **blacklisted** because of his membership in organizations sympathetic to the **Soviet Union** in the 1940s. Unable to work in Hollywood, he returned to writing for Broadway and was successful with Arlen once more with *Jamaica* in 1957. His later work was not as well received. *See also* MUSIC.

HARLEM RACE RIOT, 1935. Harlem, in New York City, is an area a few blocks north of 125th Street bounded by Seventh Avenue and Lenox Avenue that became the center of the city's **African American** population from the early 1900s onward. In 1914, the black population was estimated to be 50,000. This number increased dramatically following the Great Migration of African Americans from the South during World War I. By 1930, Harlem was almost an entirely black community numbering more than 200,000, and it had become the cultural capital for African Americans—the center of the Harlem Renaissance in the 1920s. The migration of black Americans into New York continued during the 1930s, and by 1940 the total black population of the city was 458,000, of which about 300,000 lived in Harlem.

Conditions in this ghetto were deplorable, with many families crammed into tenement buildings, sharing toilet facilities, and in some cases lacking such amenities all together. Thousands lived in cellars and basements. Much of the property and businesses in Harlem were white-owned, while African Americans worked low-paying jobs, often as menials. As black unemployment soared during the **Great Depression**, resentment against the discrimination and prejudice increased until finally, following an incident involving a black youth in a white-owned store, the anger exploded into a riot on 19 March 1935. After two days of chaos, primarily directed at property, three African Americans were dead, 30 people had been injured, and more than $2 million worth of property had been damaged. *See also* DETROIT RACE RIOT; HARLEM RACE RIOT, 1943.

HARLEM RACE RIOT, 1943. Following an incident involving an **African American** soldier and a white police officer in which the soldier was shot and wounded, rioting broke out among the black community in Harlem—the black ghetto in New York City—on 1 August 1943. Angered by this and similar reported incidents, as well as the continued discrimination against black New Yorkers and African Americans in the armed forces, hundreds of Harlemites attacked white-owned shops and property, creating an estimated $5 million worth of damage. After three days of rioting, five African Americans had been killed, 500 wounded, and another 500 arrested. *See also* HARLEM RACE RIOT, 1935.

HARRIMAN, (WILLIAM) AVERELL (1891–1986). Born to a wealthy New York City family, Averell Harriman was educated at Groton and Yale. In 1941, he was appointed by President **Franklin D. Roosevelt** to supervise the **Lend-Lease** program to **Great Britain**. In 1943, he became ambassador to the **Soviet Union** and in 1945 ambassador to Britain and then administrator of the **Marshall Plan**. In 1952, he announced his intention to run for the **Democratic** presidential nomination, but he lost to **Adlai Stevenson**. In 1954, Harriman was elected governor of New York, where he worked to improve **civil rights** and extend antipoverty programs. He failed to get reelected in 1958, losing to **Republican** Nelson Rockefeller. He spent the rest of the 1950s speaking on **foreign policy** issues. In 1968, Harriman was chosen by President Lyndon Johnson to head the U.S. delegation in peace talks with North Vietnam, a position he relinquished when **Richard M. Nixon** took office.

HART, LORENZ MILTON (1895–1943). Broadway lyricist Lorenz Hart was born in New York City and educated at Columbia Grammar School and Columbia University's School of Journalism. Shortly after World War I, Hart met **Richard Rodgers**, and the two formed a songwriting partnership and began to write for Broadway. Their first success was in writing for the revue *The Garrick Gaieties* in 1925, which included their first hit, "Manhattan." A string of successful stage productions followed, and in the early-1930s Hart and Rodgers moved to Hollywood and scored immediate hits with *Love Me Tonight* (1932), *The Phantom President* (1932), and *Hallelujah, I'm a Bum* (1933). They also wrote "Blue Moon" for **Bing Crosby** in 1934.

Hart and Rodgers returned to Broadway in 1935, where they wrote numerous hit songs for stage musicals. Among their best known songs are, "The Most Beautiful Girl in the World" (*Jumbo* [1935]), "It's Got to Be Love" (*On Your Toes* [1936]), "My Funny Valentine" (*Babes in Arms* [1937]), "Falling in Love with Love" (*The Boys from Syracuse* [1938]), and "I Could Write a Book" (*Pal Joey* [1940]). Hart's final collaboration with Rodgers was the musical *By Jupiter* in 1942. He gradually succumbed to alcoholism and ill-health but did provide some of the lyrics for *A Connecticut Yankee* in 1943. *See also* LITERATURE AND THEATER; MUSIC.

HASTIE, WILLIAM HENRY (1904–1976). Born in Knoxville, Tennessee, William Hastie graduated from Amherst College in 1925 and Harvard Law School in 1930. Having passed the bar exams, he practiced law in Washington, D.C., with **Charles H. Houston** and also taught at Howard University. He obtained his doctorate in judicial science from Harvard Law School in 1933 and joined the faculty at Howard, where he remained until 1946. Hastie also worked for the **National Association for the Advancement of Colored People** with **Thurgood Marshall** and notably helped argue the cases *Smith v. Allwright* (1944) and *Morgan v. Commonwealth of Virginia* (1946).

In 1933, Hastie joined the **New Deal**'s **black cabinet** when he became an assistant solicitor in the Department of the Interior. He became the first **African American** appointed to the federal bench when he became judge of the U.S. District Court for the Virgin Islands in 1937. He returned to the United States in 1939 to become dean of Howard Law School. From 1940 to 1943 Hastie was civilian aide to Secretary of War **Henry Stimson**, but he resigned in frustration with the lack of progress in the racial policies of the military, particularly the Army Air Force. In 1946, he was appointed governor of the Virgin Islands and in 1949 judge of the U.S. Court of Appeals, Third Circuit. He subsequently became chief justice and served until 1971.

HAUPTMANN, BRUNO RICHARD (1899–1936). Born in Germany, Bruno Hauptmann served in the German army in World War I. After the war, he became a small-time criminal. He twice attempted to enter the United States illegally, finally succeeding in 1923. He married and settled down as a carpenter in New York City. In September 1934, he was arrested for the kidnapping and murder of **Charles Lindbergh**'s infant son in March 1932. Notes traceable as part of the ransom money were found in Hauptmann's possession. The trial, described by the journalist H. L. Mencken as "the greatest story since the Resurrection" and regarded at the time as "the trial of the century," lasted from 2 January to 13 February 1935. Found guilty on circumstantial evidence, Hauptmann was electrocuted on 3 April. Despite some inconsistencies in the evidence, it seems likely that he was guilty.

HAWKS, HOWARD WINCHESTER (1896–1977). Born in Goshen, Indiana, film director, producer, and writer Howard Hawks grew up in a wealthy family that moved to California while he was young. He attended Throop Polytechnic Institute, Phillips Exeter Academy, and Cornell University, where he graduated in 1918. Hawks briefly served in the U. S. Army Air Service, and after a number of jobs he moved to Hollywood and began work in the film industry in 1924. He wrote his first screenplay, *Tiger Love*, in 1924 and directed his first film, *The Road to Glory*, in 1925. Hawks made a number of classic films across different genres. In 1932 he directed *Scarface*, based on the life of the gangster Al Capone, and starring **Paul Muni**. In 1938 he had success with the comedy, *Bringing Up Baby*, starring **Katherine Hepburn** and Cary Grant. His film based on the life of World War I hero *Sergeant York* won **Gary Cooper** an Academy Award for Best Actor. In 1944, Hawks directed the first film coupling **Humphrey Bogart** and **Lauren Bacall**, *To Have and Have Not*, based on the novel by **Ernest Hemingway**. Bogart and Bacall also starred in Hawk's *The Big Sleep*, a **Raymond Chandler** novel. Hawks also made a few classic Westerns, most notably *Red River* (1948) and *Rio Bravo* (1959). His *Gentlemen Prefer Blondes* (1953) starred Marilyn Monroe. Hawks last film was *Rio Lobo*, made in 1977. He was given a lifetime achievement award by the Academy of Arts in 1975. *See also* CINEMA.

HAYES, ROLAND (1887–1977). African American singer and composer Roland Hayes was born the son of former slaves in Georgia but moved with his family to Chattanooga, Tennessee, in 1898. He studied at Fisk University, where he joined the Jubilee Singers in 1911. After touring nationally, Hayes traveled to London in 1920, and following a royal command performance, he toured throughout Europe performing a mixture of classical music with spirituals and other folk music and establishing his international reputation as the foremost black performer. He returned to the United States in 1923, became the first black singer to perform at the Carnegie Hall, and was awarded the **National Association for the Advancement of Colored People**'s Spingarn Medal in recognition of his achievements in 1924. In 1931, he sang at Constitution Hall in Washington, D.C., although his insistence on performing before an integrated audience apparently led to the subsequent all-white policy that led to his protégé **Marian Anderson**'s exclusion in 1939.

In 1942, Hayes and his wife were involved in a confrontation with police officers in Rome, Georgia, when the singer refused to accept segregation. He was beaten by the police and subsequently moved out of Georgia. He continued to give limited performances up until and through to the 1960s, and his farewell concert at Carnegie Hall took place in 1962. *See also* MUSIC.

HAYS, ARTHUR GARFIELD (1881–1954). Born in Rochester, New York, Arthur Hays graduated in law from Columbia University and became a successful corporate lawyer. He became counsel to the **American Civil Liberties Union** and was involved in the Scopes Trial (1925) and the defense of the Italian anarchists Ferdinando Nicola Sacco and Bartolomeo Vanzetti (1927). In 1931, he was briefly involved in the case of the **Scottsboro Boys** but refused to accept the restrictions imposed by the International Labor Defense team. In 1933 Hays helped represent Georgi Dimitrov, one of the people accused of setting the Reichstag fire in **Berlin**. He wrote *Let Freedom Ring* (1928), *Democracy at Work* (1939), and his autobiography, *City Lawyer* (1942).

HAYWORTH, RITA (1918–1987). Born Margararita Carmen Cansino in Brooklyn, New York, to parents who were both dancers, future movie star Rita Hayworth moved to California with her family in 1927. From 1936, she appeared in several films as Rita Cansino, but from 1937 onward she used the name Rita Hayworth. Like **Betty Grable**, Hayworth primarily appeared in musicals as a dancer. Her early successes were in *Only Angels Have Wings* (1939) and *Blood and Sand* (1941). She also appeared with **Fred Astaire** in *You'll Never Get Rich* (1941) and *You Were Never Lovelier* (1942). Also like Grable, Hayworth became a pin-up girl for servicemen during **World War II** and appeared on the cover of *Life* magazine. She was also an active fundraiser for the war effort. Appropriately, she starred in *Cover Girl* in 1944. After the war, Hayworth received considerable acclaim for her performances in very different roles in *Gilda* (1946) and *The Lady from Shanghai* (1948). Although she continued to appear in movies through 1971, including *Salome* (1953), *Miss Sadie*

Thompson (1953), and *Pal Joey* (1957), she was increasingly in the news for her stormy personal life. Hayworth was married five times, and her husbands included **Orson Welles** and Prince Aly Khan, head of the Shia Muslims. Her later performances were also affected by the early stages of Alzheimer's disease. *See also* CINEMA.

HEARST, WILLIAM RANDOLPH (1863–1951). Future news magnate William Randolph Hearst was born in San Francisco, California. After studying at Harvard University from 1882 until 1885, he began a career as a journalist and gradually built up a newspaper empire, acquiring ownership of the *San Francisco Examiner*, *Chicago American*, *New York Journal-American*, and *Daily Mirror*. Hearst also owned several magazines, including *International-Cosmopolitan*, *Harper's Bazaar*, and *Good Housekeeping*, and he created nationwide news syndicates. His papers became known for their sensationalism that earned the description "yellow journalism." They were also known for their nationalism. He was reported to have said to artist Frederic Remington, who was in Cuba in 1898, "You furnish the pictures, and I'll furnish the war."

Hearst entered politics as a **Democrat**, becoming a member of the U.S. House of Representatives from 1903 to 1907. He failed in his bid to become mayor of New York City in 1905 and 1909 and also in his attempt to become governor of New York in 1906. In 1908, he created his own Independence League in another attempt to win the gubernatorial race but failed again.

During World War I, Hearst's press adopted a passionately anti-British line that was abandoned once the United States entered the conflict. Hearst strongly opposed the League of Nations and U.S. participation in the Permanent Court of International Justice. He continued to be an influential voice during the 1920s, supporting **Republican** Calvin Coolidge. However, in 1932 the Hearst press initially backed Democrat **John Nance Garner** for the presidency but was persuaded to switch support to **Franklin D. Roosevelt**. Hearst gradually turned against the **New Deal** because of its regulation of business and taxation policies. In 1934, he visited Nazi **Germany** and returned as a committed crusader against communism. In 1936, he supported the candidacy of **Alf Landon**, but following Roosevelt's victory he seemed to lose interest in politics. His newspapers continued to back the Republican candidates in 1940, 1944, and 1948.

The Hearst empire was badly hit by the **Great Depression**, and he was forced to surrender control in 1937. Nonetheless, the company emerged from the crisis as the biggest publishing organization in the United States. Hearst's great wealth was evident in the huge art collection he amassed at his home in San Simeon, California, and he provided the model for the fictional character in **Orson Welles**'s *Citizen Kane* (1941).

HEMINGWAY, ERNEST MILLER (1899–1961). Born in Oak Park, Illinois, Ernest Hemingway was arguably the most significant voice of the "lost generation" of alienated Americans after World War I. He did not go to college, but in 1917 he began work as a reporter for the Kansas City *Star*. In 1918, Hemingway went to Italy as a volunteer ambulance driver for the American Red Cross. He was wounded and hospitalized shortly after his arrival. In 1920, he found work with the Toronto *Star*, and he continued to submit articles first from Chicago and then after 1922, from Paris, France.

Hemingway published a number of short stories while he was in Paris, where he became one of a group of expatriate writers and artists. His first collection of stories, *In Our Time* (1925), was followed by *The Sun Also Rises* (1926), *Men without Women* (1927), and *A Farewell to Arms* (1929). It was in the latter that he famously wrote that after the war "all gods were dead."

Hemingway returned to America in 1928 and settled in Key West, Florida, where he wrote a study of bullfighting, *Death in the Afternoon* (1932), followed by *Winner Take Nothing* (1933) and *Green Hills of Africa* (1935). He also published short stories and magazine articles. In 1937, Hemingway went to Spain to report on the civil war. His book *To Have and Have Not* was published the same year.

In 1939, Hemingway went to Havana, where he wrote his novel about the **Spanish Civil War**, *For Whom the Bell Tolls*, published in 1940. He wrote little of substance after this point, but he went to Europe as a war reporter for *Collier's* in 1944 and took part in the **D-Day** landings. Another novel set in Italy, *Across the River and into the Trees*, appeared in 1950. In 1952, *The Old Man and the Sea* was published to considerable acclaim, and Hemingway was awarded the Pulitzer Prize for Fiction in 1953. In 1954, he was awarded the Nobel Prize for **Literature**. Despite these successes and twice surviving airplane crashes in Africa in 1954, Hemingway increasingly suffered from depression, and in 1961 he committed suicide.

HENDERSON, LEON (1895–1986). Born in Millville, New Jersey, Leon Henderson enrolled in Swarthmore College in 1915 but left in 1917 to serve in the U.S. Army. He returned to college in 1919, and following his graduation in 1920, he studied economics at the University of Pennsylvania until 1922. He taught economics at the Carnegie Institute of Technology until 1925, when he became an assistant to Governor Gifford Pinchot. After two years, Henderson became director of consumer credit research at the Russell Sage Foundation. He was particularly involved in research in loans and loan-sharking.

In 1934, he was appointed director of the Research and Planning Division of the **National Recovery Administration (NRA)** by **Hugh Johnson**, and he became a considerable influence in the **New Deal**. When the NRA was declared unconstitutional by the **Supreme Court** in 1935, Henderson became economic adviser to the Senate Committee on Manufacturers and in 1936 served as adviser to the **Democratic Party**'s National Committee. That same year he was appointed to the **Works Progress Administration**, and he became an advocate of deficit spending and antimonopoly legislation. Following the "**Roosevelt Recession**," Henderson helped persuade **Franklin D. Roosevelt** to increase federal spending and establish the Temporary National Economic Committee to examine the issue of monopoly. Henderson served as the executive director of the committee from 1938 to 1941. He was also appointed to the **Securities and Exchange Commission** in 1939, and in 1940 he served on the **National Defense Advisory Commission**.

In 1941, Henderson was placed in charge of the Office of Price Administration and Civilian Supply, which once America entered **World War II** became the **Office of Price Administration**. Because of the criticism of the price controls, particularly from farmers, Henderson resigned in 1942 and became head of Civilian Supply for the **War Production Board (WPB)**. After the war, he became president of the International Hudson Corporation, chair of the **Americans for**

Democratic Action, and chief economist for the Research Institute of America.

HENDERSON, LOY WESLEY (1892–1986). Loy Henderson was born in Arkansas. He entered Denver Law School in 1915 but left to serve in the Red Cross during World War I. He remained with the Red Cross in Europe until 1921 when he joined the U.S. Consular Service in 1922. After two years in Ireland, Henderson joined the Eastern European Affairs section of the State Department and in 1927 was posted to Riga, Latvia, and in 1934 he went to Moscow, where, with fellow officers like **George F. Kennan** and **Charles Bohlen**, he was able to observe developments in the **Soviet Union**. Henderson returned to Washington in 1937 and was given responsibility for Eastern European Affairs. He was an expert advisor to U.S. and British diplomats during the **Moscow Conference** in 1943 but was reassigned to become minister to Iraq. In 1945, he became director of the division for Near Eastern Affairs, and he helped formulate the policies in response to the Soviet threat in **Azerbaijan** and Turkey and assisted in drafting aspects of the **Truman Doctrine**. However, in 1948, Henderson objected to the division of Palestine to create the independent state of **Israel** and was assigned first to Nepal and then as ambassador to India in 1948. His critical view of India's recognition of the communist People's Republic of **China** led to his transfer to Iran in 1951. While there, he assisted with the overthrow of Mohammed Mossadegh and the return of the shah in 1953. Henderson returned to Washington in 1954 and was undersecretary of state until his retirement in 1961. *See also* COLD WAR; FOREIGN POLICY.

HEPBURN, KATHERINE (1907–2003). Born in Hartford, Connecticut, and educated at Bryn Mawr College, Katherine Hepburn began her acting career in 1928 and made her debut on Broadway in 1932 in *The Warrior's Husband*. Not particularly successful in **theater**, she made her first film, *A Bill of Divorcement* (1932), and was an immediate hit. In 1933, she won an Academy Award for Best Actress for her role in *Morning Glory*. She also starred in *Little Women* (1933) and *Alice Adams* (1935). After a decline in popularity due to her high-handed attitude, Hepburn returned to Broadway in 1939 in

The Philadelphia Story. Both her regal bearing and strong personality came through in roles that portrayed strong, independent **women**.

In the 1940s, Hepburn starred in a number of films with her long-time lover, Spencer Tracy, most notably the comedies W*oman of the Year* (1942) and *Pat and Mike* (1952). She also appeared again on Broadway in *As You Like It* (1950) and *The Millionairess* (1952). One of her most successful films was *The African Queen* (1951), in which she costarred with **Humphrey Bogart**. Hepburn went on to win three Oscars for Best Female Actor in *Guess Who's Coming to Dinner* (1967) (Tracy's last film), *The Lion in Winter* (1968), and *On Golden Pond* (1981), with **Henry Fonda**. Throughout her career, Hepburn received 12 Academy nominations, making her one of the most successful female stars. *See also* CINEMA.

HICKOK, LORENA ALICE ("HICK") (1893–1968). Born in East Troy, Wisconsin, Lorena Hickok had an unhappy childhood and a broken education. She became a reporter in 1913 and worked for a succession of newspapers, including the *Milwaukee Sentinel, Minneapolis Tribune,* and *New York Daily Mirror.* In 1932, while covering the election campaign of **Franklin D. Roosevelt**, Hickok met **Eleanor Roosevelt**, with whom she formed a close long-term, and possibly even sexual, friendship. Among the more than 2,000 letters from the First Lady to Hickok in the library at the Roosevelt's home in Hyde Park are some that point to a romantic and physical relationship. From 1933 to 1936 Hickok was sent as an investigator for the **Federal Emergency Relief Administration** to report back to **Harry Hopkins** on conditions in the country and the public's response to the **"First Hundred Days"** of the **New Deal**. Her reports helped persuade the administration of the need for more relief and led to the creation of the **Civil Works Administration**. Hickok left the New Deal after Roosevelt's reelection in 1936 to become a publicist for the New York World's Fair, but she returned in 1940 and lived in the White House for four years. She joined the **Democratic** National Committee as executive secretary for the Women's Division. She resigned in 1945 due to ill-health and became a writer. She wrote books based on her knowledge of politics, including *The Story of Franklin D. Roosevelt* (1956), *The Story of*

Eleanor Roosevelt (1959), and *Reluctant First Lady* (1962). During her later years, she lived in a cottage on the Roosevelt estate, where she died.

HILLMAN, SIDNEY (1887–1946). Sidney Hillman was born in Lithuania. He came to the United States in 1907 after being arrested for his labor activities, and he found work in the clothing industry in Chicago, Illinois. In 1915, he became president of the newly created Amalgamated Clothing Workers Union. During the 1920s, Hillman espoused a New Unionism, which stressed cooperation with employers and workers' educational, social, and welfare programs. Hillman supported **Franklin D. Roosevelt's New Deal** during the **Great Depression** and had some influence on aspects of the **National Industrial Recovery Act**. He was a member of the board of the **National Recovery Administration** and worked with other unionists to secure Roosevelt's reelection in 1936. In 1935, Hillman was a cofounder of the **Congress of Industrial Organizations (CIO)** and became one of its vice presidents. In 1936, he helped found the American Labor Party, a left-wing group based in New York. During **World War II**, he headed the labor section of the **Office of Production Management** and then was vice chairman of the **War Production Board**. He established the **Political Action Committee** within the CIO to support Roosevelt. *See also* TRADE UNIONS.

HIRABAYASHI V. UNITED STATES **(320 U.S. 81 1943).** Gordon Kiyoshi Hirabayashi was a **Japanese American** student born in Seattle, Washington, who was convicted in 1942 of breaking the curfew and evading the internment of Japanese Americans during **World War II**. On 21 June 1943, the **Supreme Court** unanimously upheld his conviction for breaking the curfew but did not rule on the legality of internment. Hirabayashi was sentenced to 90 days in prison. When historical research subsequently made clear that there was no evidence to suggest that the Japanese Americans posed any military threat—the basis on which the relocation order had been justified—Hirabayashi's convictions were overturned by a court in Seattle in 1987. *See also ENDO V. UNITED STATES*; *KOREMATSU V. UNITED STATES*.

HIROSHIMA. The first **atomic bomb** was dropped on Hiroshima, a Japanese naval and military center, on 6 August 1945. More than 60 percent of the city was destroyed, and 80,000 people were killed immediately. Many more died later as a result of radiation sickness. The city was largely rebuilt after the war, but its name is a constant reminder of the danger of nuclear weapons. *See also* NAGASAKI.

HISPANIC AMERICANS. Hispanic Americans were the more than 2 million Spanish-speaking Mexican, Puerto Rican, and other people from Latin America living in the United States in 1930. The largest group was the Mexican American population, mainly concentrated in the southwest, while Puerto Ricans were located primarily in New York City. Long welcomed as a source of cheap **agricultural** labor but despised for their ethnic difference, during the **Great Depression** they faced increasing resentment from poor or unemployed white Americans. Many Mexican laborers were displaced by the "**Okies**," and approximately 500,000 of them returned to Mexico either voluntarily or as a result of expulsion by local officials. Those who remained worked for meager wages, and when they attempted to organize to protest in strikes in California in 1935 and 1936, they were easily defeated by the powerful fruit growers' and farmers' organizations.

Large numbers of Mexican Americans, displaced from the land, moved to cities looking for work, particularly Los Angeles. During **World War II**, this urban population increased as new workers, "*braceros*," were imported to work on the land. In Los Angeles, ethnic tension focused on Mexican youths wearing "**zoot suits**," and in June 1943 they were subjected to physical attacks by resentful white servicemen. Despite the discrimination, some 350,000 Mexican Americans served in the armed forces, and a disproportionate number won awards for their courage. More than 50,000 Puerto Ricans also served in the military, the majority either in the Puerto Rico National Guard or in the predominantly Puerto Rican 65th Infantry Regiment. During the war, the number of Puerto Ricans living on mainland America rose, and by 1950 this number had risen from about 70,000 in 1940 to 300,000. Like Mexican Americans, they too suffered discrimination and segregation, most living in the barrio of East Harlem in New York City.

HISS, ALGER (1904–1996). Born and educated in Baltimore, Maryland, Alger Hiss went to Powder Point Academy, Johns Hopkins University, and graduated from Harvard Law School in 1929. He worked briefly as a clerk for **Supreme Court** Justice Oliver Wendell Holmes before joining a Boston law firm in 1930. In 1933, he became an attorney with the **Agricultural Adjustment Administration** and then with the Justice Department before joining the State Department in 1936. Working with **Dean Acheson** and **Edward Stettinius Jr.**, Hiss was executive secretary at the **Dumbarton Oaks Conference** in 1944, became director of the Office of Special Political Affairs in 1945, attended the **Yalta Conference**, and was secretary general at the **United Nations** organizing conference in 1945. In 1947, he became president of the Carnegie Endowment for International Peace, a body that exemplified the liberal establishment targeted by Senator **Joseph McCarthy** and his allies.

In 1948, in testimony before the **House Un-American Activities Committee (HUAC)**, *Time* magazine editor and former communist **Whittaker Chambers** accused Hiss of having been a member of the **Communist Party of the United States of America**. In a dramatic HUAC appearance, Hiss confronted Chambers and denied the charges. Hiss sued Chambers for libel, and Chambers further accused him of passing secret documents to the **Soviet Union** during the 1930s. Chambers produced microfilms that he had concealed in a pumpkin on his Maryland farm that included State Department material written or copied by Hiss. Because of the three-year statute of limitation on espionage, Hiss was indicted by a grand jury in December 1948, not for spying but for perjury during HUAC testimony. His first trial in July 1949 resulted in a hung jury. A second trial in January 1950 resulted in conviction. His appeal failed, and he was imprisoned from 1950 to 1954.

Hiss's conviction was enormously damaging to **Harry S. Truman**'s administration and the **Democratic Party**. While senior politicians like Acheson and Supreme Court Justice **Felix Frankfurter** stoutly defended him, **Republican** politicians like freshman congressman and HUAC member **Richard M. Nixon** insisted on pursuing the charges and in doing so helped raise his own national profile. The outcome of the trial helped lend sustenance to the charges later made by McCarthy and cast doubt on the loyalty of a generation of politicians. Although Hiss continued to protest his innocence, evidence from the Soviet archives after the end of the **Cold War** convinced many historians that he had indeed committed espionage.

HITLER, ADOLF (1889–1945). German Nazi leader Adolf Hitler was born in Austria. After serving in the army in World War I, he joined the right-wing National Socialist German Workers' Party in 1919 and quickly assumed leadership. Jailed following a failed putsch in Munich in 1923, he and the Nazi Party later rose to prominence when **Germany** was hit by the effects of the **Great Depression**. On 30 January 1933, he was appointed chancellor of Germany and was able to establish a one-party state. On 2 August 1934, Hitler was proclaimed führer. His regime was marked by virulent anti-Semitism and racism that led to the persecution and eventual attempted extermination of the Jews, Gypsies, and other groups regarded as inferior. Intent on overturning the Versailles Treaty of 1919, Hitler built up the German armed forces, established an **Axis** with Mussolini's fascist Italy, and in 1938 began a policy of territorial expansion. German forces occupied Austria followed by Czechoslovakia. His attack on Poland led to the outbreak of **World War II** in September 1939. Easily victorious in the west, with only **Great Britain** remaining undefeated, Hitler attacked the **Soviet Union** in June 1940. When the United States declared war on **Japan** following the attack on **Pearl Harbor**, Hitler declared war on the United States on 11 December 1941. By 1945, Germany was under attack on two fronts, and as the **Allies** closed in on **Berlin**, on 30 April 1945 Hitler shot and killed himself. Only with his defeat did the full horror of Nazi rule and the Holocaust become known. Some of Hitler's closest associates stood trial and were executed following the **Nuremberg War Crimes Trials** after the war.

HOLLYWOOD TEN. The Hollywood Ten were a group of 10 scriptwriters and producers in the film industry who were cited for contempt of Congress in 1947 when they refused to answer the question "Are you now or have you ever been a member of the Communist Party?" before the **House Un-American Activities Committee (HUAC)**. HUAC called some 41 people, but only 10 refused to respond, appealing instead to the First and Fifth Amendments. The 10 individuals included Dalton Trumbo, Alvah Bessie, Herbert Biverman, Lester Cole, Edward Dmytryk, Ring Lardner Jr., John Howard Lawson, Albert Maltz, Samuel Ornitz, and Adrian Scott. They were each fined and sentenced to jail and served their sentences in 1950. They were subsequently **blacklisted** by the film industry and unable to work under their own names. Several adopted pseudonyms or worked abroad. The blacklist lasted until 1960. *See also* CINEMA; COMMUNIST PARTY OF THE UNITED STATES OF AMERICA (CPUSA).

HOME OWNERS' LOAN ACT, 1933. Passed in June 1933, the Home Owners' Loan Act enabled the **Home Owners' Loan Corporation** to offer government bonds to lenders to cover defaulted mortgages, preventing foreclosure and loss of homes.

HOME OWNERS' LOAN CORPORATION (HOLC). Established under the **Home Owners' Loan Act** in 1933, HOLC was created by the Federal Home Loan Bank Board set up by **Herbert Hoover** in 1932 to provide loans to enable homeowners to pay mortgages or secure advances for home repair. By 1936, when HOLC ceased giving loans, almost 1 million loans totaling $3 billion had been made, covering almost one-fifth of all mortgaged homes. Operations finally came to an end in 1951.

HOOVER, HERBERT CLARK (1874–1964). 31st president of the United States. Born in West Branch, Iowa, Herbert Hoover was orphaned at the age of nine. He grew up with relatives and went on to qualify in geology at Stanford University in 1895. Hoover became a millionaire working as a mining engineer in various western states and in Australia and **China** between 1895 and 1913. In 1914, he became chair of the American Relief Commission in London and from 1915 to 1919 chair of the Commission for Relief in Belgium. In 1917, Hoover rose to national prominence when Woodrow Wilson appointed him to head the United States Food Administration. He launched a massive national effort to maximize production and minimize private consumption through a program of propaganda that encouraged voluntary controls. Such was his public appeal that both political parties considered him as a potential presidential candidate in 1920, but he declined to run. President Warren Harding appointed

Hoover as secretary of commerce in 1921, and he was reappointed by Calvin Coolidge in 1924.

As secretary of the Department of Commerce, Hoover modernized the department and made it one of the most important federal agencies of its day. Hoover was in many ways progressive in that he hoped to bring about economic and social improvement through programs of education and voluntarism. He chaired the unemployment conference in 1921 to encourage business and local voluntary initiatives to counter the postwar recession. In 1921, he helped persuade United States Steel to accept the eight-hour work day. Hoover also backed the postwar "Own Your Own Homes" campaign and the Better Homes of America organization. He supported children's concerns and was president of the American Child Health Association from 1923 to 1935. He is generally credited with drawing up the Children's Bill of Rights in 1923 that was later incorporated in the 19-point Children's Charter drawn up at the White House Conference on Child Health and Protection in 1930.

In 1927, Hoover led the mobilization of relief following the Great Mississippi Flood. Again relying on voluntary and charitable relief, he raised $17 million in assistance for the thousands affected and further enhanced his reputation. When Calvin Coolidge declined to stand for reelection in 1928, Hoover won the **Republican Party**'s nomination and defeated **Democrat Alfred E. Smith** by a massive margin of 58 percent to 41 percent of the vote, carrying 40 states to Smith's eight. While awaiting his inauguration, Hoover embarked on a six-week "good will" tour of Latin America and laid some of the foundations for **Franklin D. Roosevelt**'s **"Good Neighbor" Policy**.

Upon taking office, Hoover's activity contrasted with his predecessor's inertia. He supported labor legislation that resulted in the Norris-La Guardia Antiinjunction Act of 1932, set limits on oil drilling and withdrew all federally held oil lands from further leasing, and ordered all large government rebates on income, estate, and gift taxes to be made public. The new president took action against corrupt patronage practices, supported land conservation, and attempted to win the support of black voters with his "southern strategy." However, Hoover's administration fell victim to the **Wall Street Crash** of 1929 and was quickly overwhelmed by the **Great Depression** that followed.

Hoover attempted to address some of the economic problems facing the United States early in his administration. In an effort to deal with the problems of **agriculture**, he called a special session of Congress that passed his Agricultural Marketing Act in 1929. A second special session was called to revise the 1922 tariff to help farmers. After 14 months of deliberation, the result was the Hawley-Smoot Tariff that in the end proved counterproductive.

Following the Wall Street Crash, Hoover held a series of conferences at the White House with industrialists, representatives of agriculture, and **trade union** leaders to try to ensure the maintenance of production, employment, and wage levels by voluntary action. The president called upon state and city officials to increase public works expenditure, and in 1930 he secured federal appropriations of $150 million for river and harbor improvement, new public buildings, and the building of the Boulder Dam (*see* HOOVER DAM). The federal government spent an unprecedented $700 million on public works, but Hoover insisted that there would be no direct federal relief. Publicly Hoover tried to restore confidence with comments like the forecast in March 1930 that, "the worst effects on unemployment will have passed in the next 60 days." In May he observed, "we have now passed the worst," and later remarked, "at least no one has starved." All of these statements came back to haunt him as the Depression deepened.

In 1931, Hoover attempted to ease the international economic crisis by declaring a moratorium on the payment of reparations and **Allied** debts. At home, the earlier President's Emergency Committee for Unemployment in 1931 became the President's Organization for Unemployment Relief, but this proved increasingly ineffectual given the lack of resources at state level. More effective were the Federal Home Loan Banks and the passage of the Glass-Steagall Act stabilizing credit and banking passed with Hoover's support in 1932. Equally significant was his approval of the Emergency and Relief Construction Act in 1932, which appropriated $2 billion for public works and $300 million for direct loans to states for relief purposes. However, he also called for increased taxation to balance the budget and the 1932 Revenue Act, which raised taxes by one-third, further restricting consumption.

In 1932, Hoover established the **Reconstruction Finance Corporation** to lend money to banks, industries, and railroads to stimulate the economy, but this had a limited effect and was seen by many Americans as a "rich man's dole." As discontent increased across the country, Hoover's name became synonymous with the Depression. Tramps lived in shanty towns often referred to as "Hoovervilles" and the newspapers they covered themselves with for warmth were "Hoover blankets." When the **Bonus Army** was driven out of Washington, D.C., in 1932 Hoover's popularity plummeted even further. Despite this, an unenthusiastic Republican Party renominated him for the presidency. The outcome of the election in 1932 confirmed the voters' disapproval. **Franklin D. Roosevelt** gained 22.8 million votes to Hoover's 15.7 million, and Hoover won only 59 Electoral College votes from six states.

After his defeat, Hoover dropped from the public's view for two or three years. However, from 1935 onward, he was openly critical of the **New Deal**. He tried to win the Republican nomination in 1940 but lost to **Wendell Willkie**. Hoover was a critic of U.S. **Cold War** policies. He opposed the formation of the **North Atlantic Treaty Organization** in 1949 and involvement in the **Korean War** from 1950 until 1953. However, President **Harry S. Truman** utilized the former president in several roles. In 1946, he chaired the **Famine Emergency Committee**, and in 1949 he was appointed chair of the **Hoover Commission** on Organization of the Executive Branch of Government. Many of his recommendations were implemented by Truman's administration.

HOOVER, JOHN (J.) EDGAR (1895–1972). J. Edgar Hoover was born in Washington, D.C. He earned his law degree from the National University Law School (now George Washington University) night school in 1916 and in 1917 joined the staff of the Alien Enemy Bureau in the Justice Department, where he was active in the campaign against radicals during and after World War I. As head of a newly created Radical Division, Hoover played a leading role in the postwar "Red Scare," planning and directing the raids in November 1919 and January 1920 that resulted in the arrest and deportation of suspected revolutionaries. In 1921, he became assistant director of the Bureau of Investigation, which later became the **Federal Bureau of Investigation (FBI)**.

As director of the Bureau of Investigation and then the FBI from 1924 until his death, Hoover achieved enormous power. During the

1930s, he became a national figure in leading the attack on organized crime and against such infamous criminals as **John Dillinger** and "**Baby Face**" **Nelson**. Hoover was also involved in the investigation and trial of American Nazis after 1938 and German saboteurs in 1942. An adept self-publicist, Hoover encouraged the Public Relations Department to publicize the role of the FBI through the making of films like *G-Men* (1935) and *The FBI Story* (1959), a book titled *The FBI in Peace and War* (1943), and a **television** series, *The FBI*, which ran from 1965 to 1974.

Hoover played a key role in postwar anticommunist campaigns and provided evidence for the prosecution of leaders of the **Communist Party of the United States of America** in 1949. He worked closely with the **House Un-American Activities Committee** and Senator **Joseph McCarthy** and was also involved in the spy investigations that led to the trial and execution of **Julius** and **Ethel Rosenberg** in 1953. Hoover authored a book about the communist threat entitled *Masters of Deceit* in 1958. In the late 1950s, he developed a Counter Intelligence Program (COINTELPRO) that was used successively against communist groups, the Ku Klux Klan, and in the 1960s against black organizations. Hoover personally led investigations to undermine the position of the **civil rights** leader Dr. Martin Luther King Jr. and even threatened him with blackmail. In the 1970s, Senate investigations produced a report highly critical of Hoover, his failure to tackle organized crime (the Mafia), and many of the FBI's domestic activities, but such was his power that no president was able to remove him from office. Since his death, he has been the subject of several critical studies, including, among other things, revelations about his sexuality.

HOOVER COMMISSION. Established in June 1947 by Congress, the Commission on the Organization of the Executive Branch of Government took its name from its chair, former president **Herbert Hoover**. The aim of the commission was to improve the efficiency of the Executive Office, and when the 12-man body reported in 1949, it made a total of 274 recommendations. More than 100 were enacted by 1951, many as a result of the Reorganization Act of 1949. Among the recommendations were appointing a staff secretary, establishing an Office of Personnel within the Executive Office, replacing the Council of Economic Advisers with an Office of the Economic Adviser, and transferring various financial bodies to the Treasury Department. It also proposed reorganizing various departments, including the Department of Agriculture, Department of Commerce, and Department of the Interior. A second Hoover Commission sat during the administration of **Dwight D. Eisenhower** from 1953 to 1955.

HOOVER DAM. Formerly known as the **Boulder Dam**, construction of the Hoover Dam on the Colorado River in Black Canyon between Arizona and Colorado began in 1931 and was completed in 1936. It created one of the largest artificial lakes, Lake Mead, and provided power to several southwestern states, including southern California and the city of Los Angeles. Planning for the dam began in the 1920s, but it was named after **Herbert Hoover** in 1931 as the sitting president. However, it was referred to as the Boulder Dam after 1933 until its original name was reconfirmed by Congress in 1947.

HOPE, BOB (1903–2003). Famous actor and comedian Bob Hope was born Leslie Townes Hope in England. His family immigrated to the United States in 1907 and settled in Cleveland, Ohio. Hope found a variety of casual jobs after leaving high school but turned to performing in vaudeville in 1921. He formed various partnerships and appeared on Broadway before he went solo and took the name "Bob" in 1928. He appeared in *Ballyhoo* on Broadway in 1932 and had success with the musical *Roberta* in 1933. He went on to appear in *Say When* in 1934 and in the *Ziegfeld Follies* in 1936. Hope's first major film appearance was in *The Big Broadcast of 1938* (1938), which included the song that was to become his trademark, "Thanks for the Memories." In 1940 Hope appeared in the first of the successful series of comedy films with **Bing Crosby** and **Dorothy Lamour**, *The Road to Singapore*. He went on to star in more than 50 films, including *Lemon Drop Hit* (1951), which included the hit song with Marilyn Maxwell, "Silver Bells." *The Road to Hong Kong* (1962) was his last Road series film, but he also appeared in *The Muppet Movie* (1979) and *Spies Like Us* (1985). Hope received two honorary awards from the Film Academy, including a Lifetime Achievement in Award in 1965.

Hope's **radio** career lasted from 1937 through 1956. He also made more than 500 **television** appearances, beginning with his first major appearance in 1950. Hope was also famous for his role in **United Service Organizations** shows to entertain U.S. troops overseas. He began the performances in 1941, and from 1943 onward many of his radio broadcasts came from military bases. Beginning in 1943 he toured installations in **Great Britain**, Africa, and Sicily. In 1948, Hope gave the first of many Christmas shows for troops when he performed in **Berlin**. His contribution was recognized when Congress made him an Honorary Veteran in 1997. In 1998, Queen Elizabeth gave Hope, who became a U.S. citizen in 1920, an honorary knighthood. *See also* CINEMA.

HOPKINS, HARRY LLOYD (1890–1946). Famous **New Deal** administrator Harry Hopkins was educated at Grinnell College. In 1912, he moved to New York City, where he became a social worker. He became executive secretary of New York's Board of Child Welfare and during World War I was involved in civilian relief for the families of servicemen for the Red Cross. In 1923, Hopkins became president of the American Association of Social Workers and in 1924 director of the New York Tuberculosis Association. In 1931, he was appointed by Governor **Franklin D. Roosevelt** to direct New York's Temporary Emergency Relief Administration and then in 1933 to head the **Federal Emergency Relief Administration**, which spent $1 billion in two years providing jobs for the unemployed.

When initial relief measures proved too slow, Roosevelt put Hopkins in charge of the **Civil Works Administration**, which employed 4 million people in six months working on public building projects. From 1935 to 1940 Hopkins directed the **Works Progress Administration**, which put more than 8 million workers on the federal payroll and spent $10.5 billion. He became secretary of commerce in 1938 and considered running for the presidential nomination in 1940. However, ill health forced him to abandon such ambitions, and he supported Roosevelt before resigning from the administration.

During **World War II**, Hopkins became a diplomat. He was first sent as a special envoy to **Great Britain** in 1941 and then to the **Soviet Union**. He organized **Lend-Lease** to the Allies before the United States entered the war and after 1941 headed the Munitions

Assignments Board to allocate war material to different **Allied powers**. Hopkins continued to work in the war administration despite poor health and the death of a son in combat. He was an influential figure at the **Tehran Conference** in 1943 and the **Yalta Conference** in 1945, and he played a part in ensuring Soviet participation in the **San Francisco Conference** that established the **United Nations** in 1945. That same year Hopkins resigned from government and was awarded the Distinguished Service Medal.

HOPPER, EDWARD (1882–1967). Born in Nyack, New York, Edward Hopper attended **art** school in New York City and then the New York School of Art in 1906. That year he made his first visit to Paris, where he would return again in 1909 and 1910, but he ultimately rejected European painting styles. He initially struggled as an artist, but in 1918 he won a prize from the U.S. Shipping Board for his poster *Smash the Hun*. In the 1920s, he worked on etchings and had a successful exhibition of water colors, and his *House by the Railroad* (1925) brought him some acclaim. Like **Charles Burchfield**, Hooper developed as a contributor to the "**American Scene**," and his work can be divided into landscapes and seascapes from the Maine coast and Cape Cod, where he established his home and studio, and his urban paintings, ranging from *Automat* (1927) to *Chop Suey* (1929) to *Nighthawks* (1942). His work captured the sense of alienation and isolation in modern society, yet also the beauty of buildings and locations using bold color and a uniquely American style.

HOUSE UN-AMERICAN ACTIVITIES COMMITTEE (HUAC). HUAC had its origins in a House committee formed in 1934 by John W. McCormack, a Democrat from New York, and Samuel Dickstein, a Democrat from Massachusetts, to investigate the influence of Nazi propaganda in the United States. It was reestablished in 1938 by Martin Dies, a Republican from Texas, ostensibly to investigate Nazi influences and the role of the Ku Klux Klan. However, it was dominated by conservative opponents of President **Franklin D. Roosevelt**'s **New Deal**, some of whom were themselves Klan members or sympathizers, who, finding no evidence relating to the Ku Klux Klan, instead charged that federal agencies, particularly the **Works Progress Administration** and the **Federal Theater Project**, were dominated by communist sympathizers. Such charges helped contribute to the **Republican Party**'s resurgence in the 1938 mid-term elections, and the charges reappeared after **World War II**.

In 1946, HUAC became a permanent committee, and in 1947 it began to investigate communist influence in the film industry, issuing 43 subpoenas to a variety of people working in Hollywood. The subsequent Hollywood hearings resulted in the jailing of 10 screenwriters and directors, known as the **Hollywood Ten**, for contempt and led to a **blacklist** of more than 300 people in show business. During the course of the hearings, **Whittaker Chambers** named former State Department official **Alger Hiss** as a former **Soviet** agent. The investigation and trial resulted in Hiss being jailed for perjury, brought **Richard M. Nixon**, a committee member, to national attention, and contributed to the rise of **McCarthyism**. Later investigations into **trade unions** and atomic scientists did not attract as much interest, and in 1969 the committee was renamed the Committee on Internal Security. It was finally abolished in 1975.

HOUSING ACT, 1949. The 1949 Housing Act extended federal mortgage insurance for low-cost rural housing and provided mortgage insurance for cooperative housing projects. It increased housing loans for **World War II** veterans and provided financial assistance for student and faculty housing at colleges and universities. *See also* HOUSING ACTS, 1934, 1937.

HOUSING ACTS, 1934, 1937. The Housing Act established the **Federal Housing Administration** to encourage banks and building loan associations to provide loans for home building and repairs. The second act in 1937 established the U.S. Public Housing Authority to encourage slum clearance by providing loans to local authorities to build public housing. *See also* HOUSING ACT, 1949.

HOUSTON, CHARLES HAMILTON (1895–1950). Born in Washington, D.C., Charles Houston graduated from Amherst in 1915 and taught literature at Howard University before joining the artillery and serving as an officer in France during World War I. After the war, he went to Harvard Law School and became the first black editor of the *Harvard Law Review*. He graduated in 1922 and became the first **African American** to obtain the doctorate in judicial science at Harvard in 1923. From 1924 until 1950 Houston practiced law in Washington, D.C., and taught at Howard Law School from 1924 to 1936. He became head of the law school in 1929. In 1935, he became special counsel for the **National Association for the Advancement of Colored People**, and it was Houston who devised the long-term legal strategy of challenging the 1896 *Plessy v. Ferguson* decision that underpinned the system of segregation in the South. Although suffering from ill-health, he assisted his successor as chief counsel, **Thurgood Marshall**, in a number of cases that culminated in the *Brown v. Board of Education of Topeka* decision in 1954.

HOWE, LOUIS MCHENRY (1871–1936). The "devoted friend, adviser, and associate" of **Franklin D. Roosevelt**, Louis Howe was born in Indianapolis, Indiana. He worked as a journalist beginning at age of 17 and joined the staff of the *New York Herald* in 1906. It was in this role that he met Roosevelt, and in 1912 he became his manager. When Roosevelt became assistant secretary of the navy, Howe joined him as his chief of staff and helped manage patronage appointments. He was Roosevelt's campaign manager in the vice presidential campaign of 1920 and also advised **Eleanor Roosevelt**. Howe continued as Roosevelt's manager through the gubernatorial campaign in 1928 and presidential campaign in 1932. He lived in the White House until 1935 when he was moved to the hospital due to failing health. When he died, he was given a state funeral in the White House.

HUGHES, CHARLES EVANS (1862–1948). The future associate justice of the U.S. **Supreme Court** from 1910 to 1916, secretary of state from 1921 to 1925, and chief justice of the U.S. Supreme Court from 1930 to 1941 was born in Glen Falls, New York. Hughes attended Madison University (now Colgate University) and then Brown University before graduating from Columbia Law School in 1884. He practiced law in New York City and served as counsel for the New York State Legislature's committee investigating gas companies in 1906. He achieved national prominence when, as counsel for a similar committee investigating insurance companies in 1905 and 1906, he exposed corrupt practices. In 1906, Hughes defeated

William Randolph Hearst to become the **Republican** governor of New York. He established the public service commission and introduced insurance law reforms and several pieces of labor legislation. From 1910 he served as associate justice to the U.S. Supreme Court until 1916, when he stood as the Republican presidential candidate. He lost the election to **Democrat** Woodrow Wilson by one of the narrowest margins in history.

Hughes was appointed secretary of state by President Warren Harding and President Calvin Coolidge from 1921 to 1925. In 1926, he became a member of the Hague Tribunal and also a judge on the Permanent Court of Internal Justice from 1928 to 1930. He was appointed chief justice of the U.S. Supreme Court by **Herbert Hoover** in 1930. As chief justice, Hughes generally held a moderately conservative position. He ruled in favor of the **Scottsboro Boys** in 1932 in the decision that those tried in capital cases were entitled to proper counsel, and again in 1935 against trials in which black people had been systematically excluded as jurors. However, Hughes had a mixed record with regard to the **New Deal**. In 1935, he led the majority decisions in three crucial cases against New Deal measures: *Schechter Poultry Corp. v. United States* against the **National Industrial Recovery Act**, *Louisville Joint Stock Land Bank v. Radford* against relief for farm debtors; and *Hopkins Federal Savings & Loan Assn. v. Cleary* against the **Home Owners' Loan Act**. In *United States v. Butler* in 1936, Hughes joined with **Owen J. Roberts**, and the four consistently conservative justices, **Willis Van Devanter**, **James McReynolds**, **George Sutherland**, and **Pierce Butler**, in declaring the **Agricultural Adjustment Act** unconstitutional.

When President **Franklin D. Roosevelt** attempted what was seen as "**court packing**" with a proposed Court Reorganization Plan in 1937, Hughes publicly and crucially criticized the president's argument and contributed to the act's defeat. However, he was aware that the court needed to respond to the times, and in 1937 he led the "switch in time that would save nine" in heading the decision to sustain minimum wage laws (*West Coast Hotel Co. v. Parrish*) and later in approving the **National Labor Relations Board** (*National Labor Relations Board v. Jones and Laughlin Steel Corp.*). He also voted with the majority in subsequent decisions approving the **Social Security Act**, the revised **Agricultural Adjustment Act**, and the

Fair Labor Standards Act. He retired from the Supreme Court in 1941 after a life of public service.

HUGHES, (JAMES MERCER) LANGSTON (1902–1967). Prolific black poet and writer, Langston Hughes was born in Joplin, Missouri, raised in Lawrence, Kansas, and later moved to Lincoln, Illinois, and then Cleveland, Ohio, where he went to high school. He entered Columbia University in 1921 but left to find work as a merchant seaman in 1922. After a brief stay in Paris, he returned to the United States in 1924. His first significant poem, "The Negro Speaks of Rivers," was published in 1921. In 1925, "The Weary Blues" won first prize in *Opportunity* magazine's literary contest. His collection *The Weary Blues* was published to some acclaim in 1926. He entered Lincoln University in 1926 and graduated in 1929.

An established part of the Harlem Renaissance, in 1927 Hughes published *Fine Clothes for the Jew* and began his relationship with Charlotte Mason, a wealthy, elderly white widow who was his patron for the next three years. His first novel, *Not without Laughter*, was published in 1930 and won the Harmon Gold Medal for **Literature**.

During the 1930s, Hughes visited Cuba, Haiti, and the **Soviet Union**, and the communist influence was apparent in some of his writing of the period. His collection of short stores, *The Ways of White Folks*, was well received when it was published in 1934. He also wrote several plays, including *Mulatto*, which opened on Broadway in 1935. Hughes continued to travel and was a reporter during the **Spanish Civil War** in 1937, and Paris in 1938. His autobiography, *The Big Sea*, appeared in 1940, and in 1942 another volume of poetry, *Shakespeare in Harlem*, was published. During the 1940s, he began to publish his popular Jesse B. Semple stories in newspapers (they were later produced in edited collections in the 1950s) and continued to write poetry and plays. His musical *Street Scene* was a financial success on Broadway in 1947, and the opera *The Barrier*, written with Jan Meyerowitz, was produced with mixed success in 1950. More poetry appeared in *Montage of a Dream Deferred* in 1951, and *Fight for Freedom*, the history of the **National Association for the Advancement of Colored People**, was published in 1962. Hughes also wrote several other works of nonfiction and numerous children's stories. He is regarded as one of the most significant black writers of the 20th century. Despite this, his work was often criticized by **African American** intellectuals because of its use of the folk, blues idiom and his honest portrayals of ordinary black life. His left-wing political sympathies led to investigations by the **House Un-American Activities Committee** and the **Federal Bureau of Investigation**. His work won various prizes and awards, and in 1966 he toured various African countries for the State Department.

HULL, CORDELL (1871–1955). Born near Byrdstown, Tennessee, Cordell Hull attended Cumberland Law School and was admitted to the bar in 1892. He practiced law until 1903 when he became a circuit judge. A **Democrat**, Hull was elected to the state legislature in 1893. In 1906, he was elected to the U.S. House of Representatives and was a supporter of Woodrow Wilson. Defeated in the elections of 1920, he served as chair of the Democratic National Committee and then returned to Congress in 1922. In 1933, **Franklin D. Roosevelt** appointed Hull as secretary of state, despite his lack of experience with **foreign policy**. He attended the abortive **London Economic Conference** in 1933 but was able to assert his authority over the president's personal adviser, **Raymond Moley**, who was forced to resign as assistant secretary of state. Later in 1933 Hull became the first secretary of state to attend an inter-American conference when he went to the meeting of American States in Montevideo, where the United States announced a future policy of nonintervention in Latin America.

A long-time advocate of tariff reduction, Hull was able to secure the passage of a Reciprocal Trade Agreement Act in 1934, which enabled the president to grant "most favored nation status" to trading partners and agree on tariff reductions without consulting Congress. In 1936, Hull attended a second inter-American meeting at the **Buenos Aires Conference**.

Hull contended with continued intervention in foreign policy matters by the White House, particularly by **Sumner Welles**. Hull considered running for the presidency for some time. However, he continued in his position and urged restraint with regard to the growing conflict between **Japan** and **China**, and he held many secret meetings with Japanese envoys but could not prevent the coming of war.

The conflict between Hull and Welles continued, and eventually Hull successfully demanded the removal of the undersecretary on grounds of his sexual proclivities. Although active in the **Dumbarton Oaks Conference** in 1944, Hull's health was deteriorating, and he resigned in November that year. He was too ill to travel to Oslo, Norway, to accept the award of the Nobel Peace Prize in 1945.

HUMPHREY, HUBERT HORATIO (1911–1978). 38th vice president of the United States. Born in South Dakota, Hubert Humphrey attended the University of Minnesota but left before graduating and worked as a pharmacist from 1933 to 1937. He completed his degree in 1939, and after further study at Louisiana State University, he taught at the University of Minnesota. During **World War II**, Humphrey was state director of public war service and assistant director of the state War Manpower Commission. He also taught political science from 1943 to 1944. Active as a **Democrat** in state politics, Humphrey helped bring about the merger of the Democratic Party and **Farm-Labor Party** in Minnesota. From 1945 to 1948, he was mayor of Minneapolis, where he had already begun to establish his liberal credentials. At the Democratic National Convention in 1948 Humphrey urged the adoption of a strong **civil rights** plank, asking the party to "get out of the shadow of states rights." In 1948 he was elected to the U.S. Senate, and he held his seat until 1964 when he became vice president.

Humphrey was a liberal but anticommunist. He was one of the founders of **Americans for Democratic Action**. He also tried unsuccessfully to defeat the **Taft-Hartley Act**. In 1964, he was chosen by Lyndon Johnson as his vice presidential running mate. Although he initially disagreed with Johnson about Vietnam, Humphrey remained loyal and later supported the escalation of the war. However, when Johnson indicated that he would not seek reelection in 1968, and following the assassination of Robert F. Kennedy, Humphrey became the Democratic presidential candidate, promising to end the war. He was defeated by **Republican Richard M. Nixon**. After briefly teaching political science at Macalester College and the University of Minnesota, in 1970 he was reelected to the Senate. He was given the specially created post of deputy president pro tempore of the Senate in 1977 not long before he died of cancer. Humphrey was awarded the Congressional Gold Medal in 1979 and the Presidential Medal of Freedom in 1980.

HURSTON, ZORA NEALE (1891–1960). Born in Alabama, **African American** novelist, folklorist, and anthropologist Zora Neale Hurston grew up in Florida in a community she later turned into a subject of her writing. Hurston attended Howard University from 1919 to 1923 and then Barnard College in New York City where she studied with anthropologist Franz Boas. She later began but did not complete a Ph.D. at Columbia University. Joining the growing literary movement of the Harlem Renaissance, Hurston published a number of short stories in magazines like *Opportunity* and several pieces on southern folklore based on her fieldwork in Florida and other parts of the South. Her first novel, *Jonah's Gourd Vine*, was published in 1934. Her second book, *Mules and Men* (1935), is based on her field trips. Hurston's most acclaimed novel, *Their Eyes Were Watching God*, appeared in 1937 and focuses particularly on the plight of black **women**. *Moses, Man of the Mountains* (1939) is a version of the book of Exodus written in black vernacular. *Dust Tracks on the Road* (1942) is an autobiographical work. Although Hurston continued to publish in newspapers and journals through the 1950s, her career declined from the 1940s onward, and she died in relative obscurity. Author Alice Walker, who did much to inspire a revival of Hurston's work in the 1970s, subsequently found and marked her grave. *See also* LITERATURE AND THEATER.

HYDROGEN BOMB. Known as the H-bomb or super bomb, the hydrogen bomb was a development in thermonuclear weaponry that relied on fusion rather than the fission used in the **atomic bomb** and was a thousand times more powerful than original nuclear bombs. Although a number of advisers, including **Albert Einstein** and J. Robert Oppenheimer, counseled against it, on 31 January 1950 President **Harry S. Truman** announced that he had ordered the development of the hydrogen bomb. The first full H-bomb test took place on Eniwetok Atoll in the Pacific Ocean on 1 November 1952 following earlier tests in May 1951. The **Soviet Union** successfully tested its own H-bomb on 12 August 1954, and **Great Britain** and France followed soon afterward.

– I –

ICKES, HAROLD LECLAIR (1874–1952). Born in Hollidaysburg, Pennsylvania, Harold Ickes was raised in Chicago, Illinois, following his mother's death. He graduated from the University of Chicago in 1897, began working as a newspaper reporter, and then gained his degree in law from the University of Chicago in 1904. He practiced law in Chicago and was active in **Republican Party** politics. During World War I, Ickes served in Europe with the Young Men's Christian Association. Despite the political climate, he remained active in Republican Party politics, and as a reformer, he supported Hiram Johnson's presidential nomination in 1924.

With the onset of the **Great Depression**, Ickes worked for **Franklin D. Roosevelt** and was appointed secretary of the interior in 1933, a post he held until 1946, becoming in the process one of the greatest public administrators of all time. Under his leadership the Department of the Interior expanded conservation policies and established several new national parks. Ickes helped to establish the **Civilian Conservation Corps** and was then appointed head of the **Public Works Administration** in 1933, but his cautious approach led to the creation of the **Civil Works Administration** under **Harry Hopkins**. A former secretary of the Chicago branch of the **National Association for the Advancement of Colored People**, Ickes worked assiduously to see the inclusion of **African Americans** in government agencies and ensure equal treatment under the **New Deal**. He desegregated the Department of the Interior and arranged for **Marian Anderson** to sing at the Lincoln Memorial in 1939 when she was denied the use of Constitution Hall. During **World War II**, Ickes was the petroleum and solid fuels administrator. He was critical of the internment of **Japanese Americans**. After the war, he retired from politics and spent most of his time writing his memoirs and columns for various newspapers.

IMMIGRATION AND NATIONALITY ACT, 1952. Known as the McCarran-Walter Act, the Immigration and Nationality Act was passed over President **Harry S. Truman**'s veto on 27 June 1952. The act was introduced by Senator **Pat McCarran**, a Democrat from Nevada, and Francis Walter, a Democrat from Pennsylvania. While it lifted the blanket exclusion on the immigration and naturalization of Asians, it expanded the quota system introduced in the 1920s and included clauses allowing the deportation or prevention of entry of any aliens linked to subversive organizations. In the climate of **Mc-Carthyism**, that meant communist or similar groups.

INCHON. Inchon was the port in North Korea where during the **Korean War** on 15 September 1950 General **Douglas MacArthur** made a daring amphibious landing with more than 70,000 troops more than 150 miles behind the North Korean army's lines. The attack was so successful that North Korean supply lines were cut and their strength halved. **United Nations** forces were then able to push back the North Koreans, only to be halted by the entry of communist **China** in November.

INDIAN REORGANIZATION ACT, 1934. Known as the Wheeler-Howard Act, the Indian Reorganization Act of 1934 was central to the "Indian New Deal" introduced by Commissioner of Indian Affairs **John Collier**. Intended to improve the situation of **Native Americans**, the act repealed the Dawes Severalty Act of 1887, restored surplus reservation lands to the tribes, and authorized the provision of funds to purchase additional lands. Loans were provided for existing Indian organizations and for those establishing tribal government and also to enable Native Americans to attend college and vocational training programs. However, while 180 tribes accepted the act, more than 70, including the Navajos, did not, and the measure was only a partial success.

INTERNAL SECURITY ACT, 1950. Also known as the McCarran Act or McCarran-Wood Act, the Internal Security Act passed on 23 September 1950 required communist organizations and their officials to register with the attorney general and excluded members of such organizations from the federal government. The act also provided for the exclusion, deportation, or denial of passports to members of communist organizations. The act was introduced by **Democrat Pat McCarran** and the chair of the **House Un-American Activities Committee**, Democratic representative John Stephen Wood, and it reflected the widespread fear of subversion during the period of

McCarthyism. It was passed over President **Harry S. Truman**'s veto. *See also* COMMUNIST PARTY OF THE UNITED STATES OF AMERICA (CPUSA).

INTERNATIONAL MONETARY FUND (IMF). The IMF was established by 44 countries at the **Bretton Woods Conference** in July 1944 and came into effect on 27 December 1945. It was intended to prevent a recurrence of the international economic instability of the 1930s by encouraging international monetary cooperation and the maintenance of exchange rates. The fund was established to provide aid to enable countries to maintain the value of their currencies in times of crisis. It commenced operations in 1946 with around $8 billion in funds from member nations. A weighted voting system that allocated votes according to the size of each country's contribution gave the United States the largest voting share.

The **Soviet Union** refused to join the IMF, but after Soviet collapse in the 1980s, the IMF played a major role in distributing Western aid to Russia and other former eastern bloc countries. The IMF was also instrumental in the post–**Cold War** era for the financial rescue of Mexico in 1994 and 1995 and handling of the Asian economic crisis of 1998. As of 2007 the IMF had 185 members.

IRON CURTAIN. Following the end of **World War II**, there was growing fear concerning the domination of Eastern European countries by the **Soviet Union (USSR)**. Speaking in Fulton, Missouri, on 5 March 1946, British prime minister **Winston Churchill** warned of the "expansive tendencies" of the USSR and declared that "From Stettin in the Baltic to Trieste in the Adriatic, an Iron Curtain has descended across the continent." In calling for a policy of strength, Churchill helped mobilize support for President **Harry S. Truman**'s **Truman Doctrine** and the policy of **containment** the following year. After 1947, the Iron Curtain increasingly became a reality with Europe divided between East and West in the developing **Cold War**. The curtain was finally pulled down in 1989 by populations of various East European countries rather than the West.

ISRAEL. Following the breakup of the Ottoman Empire after World War I, **Great Britain** established a mandate over Palestine backed by the League of Nations. However, the region was the scene of continuous conflict between the Arab and smaller Jewish population. The conflict escalated, inflamed by demands for partition and the creation of a separate Jewish state. The flight of Jewish refugees from **Germany** before and after **World War II** only served to increase tensions in the region, and when the British indicated they could no longer maintain their mandate, an alternative was sought. Calls for a temporary **United Nations** trusteeship were rejected in 1947 in favor of partition, a proposal initially supported by the United States. However, fighting between the two groups in Palestine erupted again, and on 14 May 1948 Israel, an independent Jewish state, was declared by the provisional Jewish government. It was recognized almost immediately by President **Harry S. Truman** despite the opposition of Secretary of State **George C. Marshall**. It seems that Truman responded both to criticism from **Republican** opponents and the powerful pro-Jewish lobby in the United States possibly with a view to the 1948 election. The immediate result was the outbreak of war between Israel and the Arab League, but support for Israel was also to have considerable long-term consequences for the United States.

IVES, CHARLES EDWARD (1874–1954). One of America's greatest composers, Charles Ives was born to a musical family in Danbury, Connecticut. He studied at Yale University from 1893 to 1997 and then entered the insurance business. His business was very successful, and he retired a wealthy man in 1930. Ives sold insurance by day and composed at night. Strongly influenced by his bandleader father and by church and folk **music**, he wrote complicated pieces combining hymns, gospel, folk, and other influences in a variety of pieces ranging from music for piano or organ, string quartets, and full symphonies. He published his "Concord Sonata" and a collection of 114 other pieces in 1922. Ives wrote little after that, and it was only in the later 1930s that he gained recognition for his "Second Piano Sonata." In 1947 his "Third Symphony" (1904) was awarded the Pulitzer Prize.

IWO JIMA. Iwo Jima was one of the famous battles in the U.S. "island hopping" campaign in the Pacific against **Japan** during **World War II**. More than 75,000 U.S. forces landed on the island of Iwo Jima

650 miles south of Tokyo from an armada of 880 vessels on 19 February 1945. They were faced by more than 22,000 Japanese troops who were dug in and hidden in a network of tunnels. The U.S. troops finally overcame their enemy on 16 March, by which time more than 18,000 Japanese and 7,000 U.S. Marines had been killed. The battle was recorded in a famous photograph of the marines raising a flag on the summit of Mount Suribachi. A statue commemorating that event forms the Marine Memorial in Arlington National Cemetery.

– J –

JACKSON, ROBERT HOUGHWOUT (1892–1954). Born in Pennsylvania, Robert Jackson left high school at 18 to work in a law office and attended Albany Law School for two years. He was admitted to the bar in 1913 and subsequently set up a law practice in Jamestown, New York. His success as a lawyer in the state led to his appointment as general counsel in the Treasury Department office, the Internal Revenue Service. He became U.S. solicitor general in 1938 and attorney general in 1940. In 1941, **Franklin D. Roosevelt** appointed Jackson to the **Supreme Court**, where he established a considerable reputation for the impressive style of his written arguments. His argument in *West Virginia State Board of Education v. Barnette* was widely quoted as a defense of individual liberty, and the formula he outlined in *Youngstown Sheet & Tube Co. v Sawyer* as a means of assessing the use of presidential power is still used. In 1945, Jackson was appointed chief prosecutor in the **Nuremberg War Crimes Trials**. While he was in **Germany**, President **Harry S. Truman** made **Fred Vinson** chief justice, and Jackson felt he had been passed over because of the influence of fellow justice **Hugo Black**. Their public animosity reflected badly on the court and tarnished an otherwise outstanding reputation.

JAPAN. Japan emerged as a world power toward the end of the 19th century and confirmed its position with the defeat of the Imperial Russian fleet in 1904. Theodore Roosevelt helped mediate the peace settlement in Portsmouth, New Hampshire, in 1905, and he also agreed to the Japanese imposition of a protectorate over Korea. A balance of power between the United States and Japan in the Pacific and the "Open Door" policy guaranteeing **China**'s territorial integrity was agreed in the Root-Takahira Agreement of 1907. However, by the 1930s a nationalistic and militaristic government had assumed power in Japan and it embarked on an expansionist policy in pursuit of raw materials and national aggrandizement, starting in 1931 with the invasion of Manchuria. In 1933, Japan left the League of Nations and in July 1937 invaded China.

The U.S. reaction to Japanese aggression was first to call for Japan to be "quarantined" and then to exert economic pressure, to which the Japanese responded with further expansion, occupying French Indochina (Vietnam, Laos, Cambodia) in 1940 and 1941 and announcing a New Order in Asia. The U.S. embargo on the export of scrap metal and aviation fuel in 1940 was followed by the freezing of Japanese assets in the United States in July 1941. Japan signed a Tripartite Pact with **Germany** and Italy on 27 September 1940 promising mutual support in the event of war with the United States, and in October 1941 the hard-line war minister, General Hideki Tojo, assumed power. Tojo was prepared to go to war if the United States did not resume trade relations, while the **Roosevelt** administration, through **Cordell Hull**, called first for an end to expansion in China and then in November 1941 insisted on withdrawal. Facing war, the Japanese launched a surprise air attack on the U.S. fleet in **Pearl Harbor** on Sunday morning, 7 December 1941. This attack brought the United States into **World War II**.

After initially seeming unstoppable, Japan was gradually overcome by a combination of naval defeats in the battles of the Coral Sea, **Midway**, and **Leyte Gulf**, combined with the fierce "island hopping" campaign culminating with the invasions of **Iwo Jima** and **Okinawa** in 1945. However Japan surrendered only after the dropping of the **atomic bombs** on **Hiroshima** and **Nagasaki** on 6 and 9 August 1945. Emperor Hirohito then insisted that the government accept the peace terms laid down by the **Allied powers** at the **Potsdam Conference**, and the formal surrender was signed aboard the USS *Missouri* on 2 September 1945. General **Douglas MacArthur** assumed control of the Allied occupation forces in Japan on 14 August 1945, and Japan was forced to accept political and economic reforms. On 8 September 1951, the United States and 48 other nations signed a final peace treaty with Japan in San Francisco, bringing the war to an end. The treaty was ratified by the U.S. Senate on 20 March 1952.

JAPANESE AMERICANS. Following the attack on **Pearl Harbor** in 1941 there were mounting fears among the population of the west coast states of subversion or "fifth column" among the resident Japanese American population of about 127,000. As a result President **Franklin D. Roosevelt** bowed to pressure from local politicians and military advisers and on 19 February 1942 issued Executive Order 9066 authorizing the compulsory relocation of Japanese Americans to 10 internment camps established mainly in Arizona and Utah by the **War Relocation Authority**. Some 112,000 people, two-thirds of whom were American-born (Nisei), were evacuated with only a few days to prepare or to dispose of their property. It was estimated that the total losses for the Japanese Americans were in excess of $400 million. The decision was upheld by the **Supreme Court** in *Hirabayashi v. United States* (1943) and *Korematsu v. United States* (1944). Despite this, some 12,000 Japanese Americans served in the U.S. Army, and the 442nd Infantry Combat Team of Nisei troops became the most decorated unit for its bravery in the Italian campaign.

Following the Supreme Court decision in *Endo v. United States* (1944) that citizens accepted as loyal could not be detained against their will, the camp inmates were gradually released, but only 58 percent returned to the west coast. The great majority quickly reintegrated back into society, but approximately 7,000 returned to **Japan**. Congress approved a mere $38 million in compensation in 1948, but in 1988 a full official and public apology was issued to the 60,000 survivors of those interned, each of whom was paid $20,000 in cash.

In addition to those held in the relocation camps, another 7,000 Japanese Americans and Japanese were held in camps run by the Immigration and Naturalization Service. Approximately 2,500 Japanese were interned in two camps in Hawaii. However, the majority of Japanese living in Hawaii were left at large in part because they were too sizeable a section of the population (35 percent), in part because martial law had been declared on the islands, and because of the greater degree of racial integration.

JEWISH REFUGEES. *See* EVIAN CONFERENCE; ISRAEL.

JOHNSON, HIRAM WARREN (1866–1945). Hiram Johnson qualified in law in 1888 and practiced in Sacramento and San Francisco,
California. He established himself in cases against political corruption in San Francisco and was elected as a **Republican** to the state
legislature in 1877, to the U.S. Congress in 1894, and as governor of
California in 1910. Johnson initiated a program of reform, including
railroad and public utility regulation; the initiative, referendum and
recall; workmen's compensation and child labor laws; the eight-hour
work day for women; and state commissions on industrial welfare,
industrial accidents, immigration, and housing. In 1912, he was
Theodore Roosevelt's running mate for the unsuccessful Progressive Party, and he returned as governor of California in 1914. He
was elected U.S. senator for the state in 1916 as a Republican and
progressive. Johnson supported the declaration of war on **Germany**
in 1917 but took a prominent part as one of the "irreconcilables" in
opposing the League of Nations in any form. In 1920, he became a
leading contender for the Republican presidential nomination but lost
to Warren Harding. He declined the vice presidential nomination,
failed to gain the Republican presidential nomination in 1924, and
continued to serve as a U.S. senator until his death.

Johnson's biggest achievement as senator was to see through the
approval for the construction of the Boulder Dam, later renamed the
Hoover Dam in 1928. In 1932, he declared his support for **Franklin
D. Roosevelt** and actively campaigned on his behalf. He subsequently declined the offer to become secretary of the interior but
continued to support most **New Deal** measures until 1937. In 1934,
Johnson won both the Republican and Democratic nominations for
reelection. He maintained his opposition to U.S. foreign involve-
ments and during the 1930s supported the neutrality acts. Johnson
was reelected again in 1940 but then supported Republican **Wendell
Willkie**'s presidential campaign. In 1941, he led the unsuccessful
opposition to Roosevelt's **Lend-Lease** measures. Ill health limited
his further participation in the Senate, but in 1945 Johnson voted
against the **United Nations Charter**. Johnson's long political character charted the path followed by many progressives in the first half
of the 20th century.

JOHNSON, HUGH SAMUEL (1882–1942). Hugh Johnson grew up in Oklahoma, graduated from West Point in 1903, and served with the First Cavalry in the Philippines and on national park duties. He wrote popular stories about military life for such magazines as *Colliers*, *Century*, and *Scribner's*. Johnson qualified in law in 1916 and served briefly as judge advocate with General John Pershing in the punitive expedition in Mexico. During World War I, he was involved in the development of the Selective Service System and became army representative to the War Industries Board. He rose to the rank of brigadier general.

Following his resignation from the army in 1919, Johnson became an executive with the Moline Plow Company. He also became an investigator for **Bernard Baruch** in 1927, and in 1933 he became part of **Franklin D. Roosevelt**'s team of advisers known as the "**Brain Trust.**" In this role, Johnson helped to draw up the **National Industrial Recovery Act** and was then appointed as administrator of the **National Recovery Administration (NRA)**. His energy and vitality did much to establish the NRA, and his wartime experience was evident in the **Blue Eagle** propaganda campaign associated with the agency. However, Johnson's rather volatile leadership of the NRA and his colorful language and private life attracted considerable criticism, and he was replaced in 1934. He then served briefly as head of the **Works Progress Administration** in New York City. After 1937, Johnson became increasingly critical of the **New Deal** and Roosevelt, whom he accused of being dictatorial in his syndicated newspaper columns and **radio** commentaries. In 1940 he supported **Republican** presidential candidate **Wendell Willkie** and also helped found the **America First Committee** to preserve U.S. neutrality. Johnson published his memoirs, *The Blue Eagle from Egg to Earth*, in 1935.

JOHNSON, LOUIS ARTHUR (1891–1966). Born in Roanoke, Virginia, Louis Johnson graduated with a law degree from the University of Virginia in 1912 and established a law practice in Clarksburg, West Virginia. A **Democrat**, he was elected to the West Virginia House of Delegates in 1916 and served until 1924 with a break while he was in the army during World War I. Johnson was in the infantry in France during the war and afterward was one of the founders of the American Legion. He was national commander of the organization from 1932 to 1933. During the interwar years, he continued his legal practice in West Virginia and Washington, D.C. He was chair of the Veterans Advisory Committee for the Democratic National Committee from 1936 to 1940 and also assistant secretary of war. During **World War II**, he was briefly President **Franklin D. Roosevelt**'s personal representative in India.

In 1948, Johnson was the Democratic Party's fundraiser, and it was widely assumed that his appointment as secretary of defense in 1949 was an acknowledgement of his contribution. His term in office was highly controversial, as it involved the unification and streamlining of the armed services. Johnson implemented President **Harry S. Truman**'s policies on tight budgets somewhat heavy-handedly, immediately cancelling the construction of a super aircraft carrier. His cuts seemed to target the navy and marines, and the secretary of the navy, **John L. Sullivan**, resigned. In June 1949, in what was known as the "revolt of the admirals," Johnson faced charges of malfeasance before the House Committee on Armed Services as a consequence of these policies. He was cleared but criticized for his methods.

In 1950, Johnson was also involved in a conflict with Secretary of State **Dean Acheson** over the **National Security Council** policy proposal **National Security Council Report 68** that recommended increased military expenditure. However, in the light of early military setbacks in the **Korean War**, he was criticized for leaving the armed forces ill-prepared. Furthermore, he seemed reluctant to control or discipline **Douglas MacArthur** when the general publicly flouted the president's orders. On 12 September 1950, Johnson was forced to resign and was replaced by General **George C. Marshall**. He resumed his legal practice in Washington.

JONES, J. (JOHN) MARVIN (1882–1976). Born in Texas, John Jones graduated from Southwestern University in 1905 and the University of Texas Law School in 1908. He practiced law in Amarillo, Texas, and was elected to the federal House of Representatives in 1917. He briefly served in the tanks corps during World War I but did not see service overseas. He served in Congress until his retirement in 1940, and he was of considerable influence in the House Committee on Agriculture from 1921 onward. He became chair of the committee in 1931 and was responsible for supporting and sponsoring much of the **New Deal**'s legislation relating to **agriculture**, including the **Agricultural Adjustment Act** and amendments to it in 1934 and the **Bankhead-Jones Farm Tenancy Act**. In 1940, Jones was appointed to the U.S. Court of Claims, and in 1943 he became head of the **War Food Administration** responsible for the production and distribution of foodstuffs. He returned to the Court of Claims in 1945 and became chief judge in 1947, a position he held until 1964.

JONES, JESSE HOLMAN (1874–1956). Jesse Jones was a successful Texas businessman who contributed to the development of Houston as a center of commerce and banking. In 1917, he was appointed director general of military relief for the Red Cross. Jones was a **Democratic Party** activist, and he accompanied Woodrow Wilson to the Versailles Peace Conference in 1918. In 1924, he acted as finance chairman for the Democratic presidential campaign. In 1932, **Herbert Hoover** appointed Jones to the **Reconstruction Finance Corporation (RFC)**. **Franklin D. Roosevelt** made him chairman of the RFC in 1933, a position he held until 1939 when he became federal loan administrator. In 1940, he became secretary of commerce and was able to continue his role as federal loan administrator following a special act of Congress. Jones was involved in a great deal of the war-planning after 1941, and at one point was head of 12 agencies, including the Department of Commerce, RFC, and Rubber Reserve Company. Jones had a long-running difference with **Henry A. Wallace**, and when Roosevelt asked him to step aside as secretary of commerce in favor of Wallace and to accommodate **Harry S. Truman** as vice president, he resigned all his political offices in 1945. He opposed Truman's election in 1948 and supported **Dwight D. Eisenhower** in 1952. Jones retired to Houston where he worked with a charitable organization, the Houston Endowment.

– K –

KAI-SHEK, CHIANG. *See* CHIANG KAI-SHEK.

KAISER, HENRY JOHN (1882–1967). Henry Kaiser began his career as a photographer in Lake Placid, New York, but moved to

Spokane, Washington, in 1906 where he worked first as a salesman and then in highway construction. In 1914, he established his own construction company in Vancouver, British Columbia. As his company expanded on the west coast, Kaiser moved his base to Oakland, California, in 1921. In 1931, he joined the consortium that won the bid to build the **Hoover Dam** and later the Bonneville Dam and **Grand Coulee Dam**.

In 1940, Kaiser won a contract to build cargo ships for **Great Britain**, and following America's entry into **World War II**, he established new yards to produce "**liberty ships**" for the United States. His company became famous for producing one-third of the nation's wartime cargo vessels. In 1945, Kaiser established the Kaiser-Frazer Automobile Company that was successful for a time in the immediate postwar period. However, faced with competition from **Ford**, General Motors, and Chrysler, the company ceased production in 1955. The Kaiser Steel Company and Kaiser Aluminum Company, however, continued to be successful. Equally successful was the Kaiser Health and Hospital Program that had began in 1938, with 1.5 million members by 1967. It was the country's largest health insurance program. Kaiser retired to Hawaii in 1954 and devoted his time to developing the island of Oahu and sponsoring **television** programs.

KARLOFF, BORIS (1887–1969). Born William Henry Pratt in England, the future actor immigrated to Canada in 1909, and after working in a variety of jobs, he turned to theater, acting in 1910 and taking the stage name Boris Karloff. He entered the United States in 1913 and found work as a film extra in Hollywood. His first known significant part was in *His Majesty, the American* in 1919. After taking a break from films, Karloff appeared in *The Forbidden Cargo* (1925), *Her Honor the Governor* (1926), and *The Bells* (1926). He successfully made the transition to sound and in 1931 appeared in 16 movies, most notably as the monster in *Frankenstein*. Karloff played in many horror films, including *The Old Dark House* (1932), *The Mask of Fu Man Chu* (1932), *The Mummy* (1932), *The Ghoul* (made in England in 1933), *The Black Cat* (1934), *The Raven* (1935), and he reprised his role as the monster in *Frankenstein's Bride* (1935). He last appeared as the monster in *Son of Frankenstein* (1939). Karloff also appeared in *The Body Snatcher* in 1945. However, he had returned to the stage and had some success on Broadway and on tour in *Arsenic and Old Lace* in 1941. He only played minor film roles after 1945 but continued his successful stage career in *The Linden Tree* (1948), *Peter Pan* (1950), and *The Lark* (1955). Karloff returned to England in 1959, but he did appear in a number of **television** series and films, as well as in the movies in *The Raven* (1963), *Targets* (1968), and several low-budget foreign horror films. *See also* CINEMA.

KEFAUVER, (CARY) ESTES (1903–1963). Born in Madisonville, Tennessee, Estes Kefauver graduated from the University of Tennessee in 1924 and qualified as a lawyer at Yale in 1927. He practiced law in Chattanooga, Tennessee, before being elected to Congress as a **Democrat** in 1939 following the death of the incumbent. He served five terms and generally supported the **New Deal**, particularly the **Tennessee Valley Authority**. Kefauver was elected to the Senate in 1948, and in 1950 he achieved national prominence as chair of the Senate investigation into organized crime, whose hearings were sometimes televised. Hearings were also held in major cities across the country in 1950 and 1951. The committee concluded that organized crime in the shape of the "Mafia" was dominated by two "families," one in Chicago and the other in New York City, both headed by Charles "Lucky" Luciano. Kefauver's book, *Crime in America* (1951), was a best seller.

Kefauver decided to run for the Democratic presidential nomination in 1952 but was defeated by **Adlai Stevenson**, who beat him again four years later. Stevenson chose Kefauver as his running mate in 1956, but they were defeated by the partnership of **Dwight D. Eisenhower** and **Richard M. Nixon**. Kefauver returned to the Senate, where although he was not a supporter of integration, he was regarded as the most liberal southern voice. He was reelected in 1960 and died half way through his term.

KELLY, EDWARD JOSEPH (1876–1950). Edward Kelly was born and raised in Chicago, Illinois. He left school early, studied civil engineering in night classes, and began working with the Metropolitan Sanitary District in 1894. In 1920, he became the chief engineer and in 1924 was made responsible for the redevelopment of the South Park, Illinois, lakefront area. Although he was not holding any elective office, Kelly, alongside wealthy businessman Patrick Nash, effectively ran the **Democratic Party** machine in Chicago. When Mayor Anton J. Cermak was killed during an assassination attempt on President **Franklin D. Roosevelt** in 1933, Kelly was selected to succeed. He was elected in 1935 and reelected in 1939 and again in 1943.

Kelly immediately tackled the problems brought to the city by the **Great Depression**, making payments to public teachers and municipal workers, collecting outstanding taxes and rent, and cutting city debt by $1 billion by the time he left office in 1947. He was a committed supporter of the **New Deal**, and he helped to ensure Roosevelt's unprecedented third nomination at the Democratic National Convention in 1940. In return, Chicago received generous federal funding through the **Works Progress Administration** and other agencies. By distributing this patronage, Kelly was able to build up an all-powerful party machine. He also attracted black voters by including **African Americans** in city government and supporting the election of **Arthur W. Mitchell** and later **William L. Dawson** to the U.S. House of Representatives. Kelly supported desegregated public schools and public housing. However, there was increasing criticism of such policies after the war and also of the corruption and association with organized crime within city government. In 1947, he chose not to seek reelection and instead headed an engineering and consulting firm until his death in 1950.

KELLY, EUGENE (GENE) CURRAN (1912–1996). Born in Pittsburgh, Pennsylvania, choreographer, dancer, singer, and film director Gene Kelly learned to dance at an early age, and after graduating from the University of Pittsburgh in 1933, he became an instructor at his family's dance studio. He moved to New York City and worked as a choreographer in 1937 and first appeared on Broadway in **Cole Porter**'s *Leave It to Me*. After working in a number of other productions, he got the leading role in the **Rodgers** and Hart musical *Pal Joey* in 1940. His Broadway success led him to Hollywood, where he starred with **Judy Garland** in *For Me and My Gal* in 1942 and **Rita Hayworth** in *Cover Girl* in 1944. After a brief stint in the Navy Air Service in 1944, he appeared in three films with **Frank Sinatra**, *Anchors Away!* (1945), *Take Me Out to the Ball Game* (1949), and

On the Town (1949), which was unusual for its use of both outside locations and studio shooting. This reflected Kelly's wish to distinguish himself from **Fred Astaire** and focus less on ballroom dancing. This was also evident in two films for which Kelly will always be remembered, *An American in Paris* (1951) and *Singin' in the Rain* (1952), which included the famous song and dance routine of the same name.

In 1951, Kelly was given a special Academy Award for his contribution to film in *An American in Paris*, marking the height of his career. Although he later received several lifetime achievement awards from various bodies, Kelly's subsequent films were not of the same quality, in part because of the decline in popularity of musical films with audiences. His last significant film as singer-dancer was *Brigadoon* (1954). Thereafter he gravitated toward production and direction, most notably directing *Hello Dolly!* in 1969. *See also* CINEMA; MUSIC.

KENNAN, GEORGE FROST (1904–). Diplomat and **foreign policy** specialist George F. Kennan was born in Milwaukee, Wisconsin. After graduating from Princeton University in 1925, he joined the Foreign Service and filled a number of State Department posts, most significantly as a member of the first U.S. mission to the **Soviet Union (USSR)** from 1933 to 1936. His experience there shaped his views of the Soviet Union, and those views influenced U.S. postwar foreign policy during the **Cold War**. From Russia, Kennan went to Prague and **Berlin**, and during **World War II** he was a counselor in Lisbon before returning to Moscow in 1944. In July 1946, he sent the famous "long telegram" back to the State Department outlining the postwar situation with regard to the USSR and the West. A version of this was subsequently published under the pseudonym "X" in *Foreign Affairs*. According to Kennan, the Soviet Union was committed to a policy of expansion, but if met at every point with firm "**containment**," the Communist state would collapse from its own inherent weaknesses. Although he stressed the use of economic power, the policy translated into the **Truman Doctrine**, and later the "domino theory" became one of military rivalry and confrontation known as the Cold War and spread from Europe across the rest of the globe.

After briefly serving as ambassador to the USSR in the 1950s, Kennan became professor of historical studies at the Princeton Institute for Advanced Studies where he authored a number of texts, including *American Diplomacy 1900–1950* (1951), *Soviet-American Relations, 1917–1941* (1956), and his own *Memoirs, 1925–1950* (1968). Kennan subsequently claimed that his theories had been wrongly applied, and he argued against U.S. involvement in Vietnam on the grounds that the issue there was nationalism not communism and that the outcome was not a matter of U.S. national security.

KENNEDY, JOSEPH PATRICK (1888–1969). The father of future president John F. Kennedy, Joseph Kennedy was educated at the Boston Latin School and Harvard University. In 1912, he began working as a state bank examiner and by 1914 had become president of a bank founded by his father. In 1914, he married Rose Fitzgerald, daughter of one of the first Irish Catholic Americans to be mayor of Boston. In 1917, Kennedy became assistant general manager of the Bethlehem Steel shipyards in Quincy, Massachusetts, and after the war he became manager of an investment banking company. From 1926 until 1930, he was part of a syndicate that bought a chain of movie theaters in the northeast and was also involved in the merger that created RKO Pictures. By the 1930s, he was a multimillionaire.

Kennedy made significant financial contributions to the election campaign of **Franklin D. Roosevelt** and held a number of positions under the **New Deal**. From 1934 to 1935, he was chair of the **Securities and Exchange Commission** and in 1937 chair of the U.S. Maritime Commission. In 1936, he published *I'm for Roosevelt*, spelling out why businessmen should support Roosevelt. Kennedy was appointed ambassador to **Great Britain** in 1938 but increasingly seemed to support appeasement and seemed openly anti-Semitic. He also suggested that democracy would disappear in Great Britain, and he returned home in 1940. In the 1950s, Kennedy was a supporter of Senator **Joseph McCarthy** and other conservatives. He transferred his political ambitions to his sons, and when Joseph Sr. was killed during **World War II**, the focus passed to John. While his great wealth helped secure the election of John F. Kennedy as president in 1960, his previous support for right-wingers was something of a handicap. Nonetheless, he will be remembered for creating a political dynasty.

KEYNES, JOHN MAYNARD (1883–1946). British economist John Maynard Keynes was one of the most influential figures in the history of economic theory and had a considerable impact on **Franklin D. Roosevelt's New Deal**. Educated at Eton College and Cambridge University, Keynes worked for the British Treasury, was editor of the prestigious *Economic Journal*, and was present at the Versailles Peace Conference in 1918. His highly critical study of the peace settlement, particularly the reparations imposed on **Germany**, was published as *The Economic Consequences of the Peace* in 1919. In the 1920s, he taught at Cambridge University and published several significant works, including *Treatise of Probability* (1921), *Tract of Monetary Reform* (1923), and *Treatise on Money* (1930). His major work, however, was *The General Theory of Employment, Interest, and Money* (1936), which offers a damning critique of laissez faire economics and calls for government intervention to regulate the economy, particularly through investment and spending. Keynes wrote to Roosevelt on several occasions and visited the United States in 1934, when he met the president. However, while some of the principles expounded by Keynes were evident in the New Deal, Roosevelt was by no means a total convert. It was only during **World War II** that Keynesian economics were finally accepted. Keynes worked for the British Treasury during the war, and in 1940 he wrote *How to Pay for the War*. He was also present at the **Bretton Woods Conference** in 1944 and 1945. His influence on modern-day economics is still heavily debated.

KEYSERLING, LEON H. (1908–1987). A key figure in shaping housing policy in the 1930s, Leon Keyserling was born in South Carolina. He graduated from Columbia University in 1928 and obtained his law degree from Harvard in 1931. He briefly taught economics at Columbia University before joining the legal staff of the **Agricultural Adjustment Administration (AAA)** in 1933. However, he left the AAA and became secretary and assistant to Senator **Robert F. Wagner** until 1937. Through Wagner, Keyserling had considerable input into the drafting of aspects of the **National Industrial**

Recovery Act, **National Housing Acts**, and **National Labor Relations Act**. Keyserling became counsel to the U.S. Housing Authority and then the Federal Public Housing Authority between 1937 and 1946. He also contributed to the writing of the **Democratic Party**'s platform in 1936, 1940, and 1944 and helped draft the **Employment Act** (1946) and **Housing Act** (1949). In 1946, he became a member and vice chair of the President's Council of Economic Advisers, and he was chair from 1950 until 1953, when he left public service. He founded the Conference on Economic Progress in 1953 and was its director until 1972.

KINSEY REPORT. Named after its author, the head of Indiana University's Institute of Sex Research, Alfred C. Kinsey, the Kinsey Report (*Sexual Behavior in the Human Male*) was published in 1948. It caused some controversy by showing that adultery, premarital sex, and homosexuality were much more prevalent than widely thought. Kinsey's second book, *Sexual Behavior in the Human Female* (1953), was equally controversial because of the evidence he produced showing that a high proportion of women also engaged in premarital sex and adultery. Critics, however, questioned Kinsey's methods and findings.

KNOX, FRANK (WILLIAM FRANKLIN) (1874–1944). Born in Boston, Massachusetts, Frank Knox attended Alma College in Michigan from 1893 until 1898, when he joined Theodore Roosevelt's Rough Riders in the Spanish-American War. After working as a reporter in Grand Rapids, Michigan, Knox established his own newspaper in 1902, which he sold in 1912 and took over the *Manchester Leader* in New Hampshire. During World War I, he served in the military and then resumed his newspaper career. In 1927, **William Randolph Hearst** hired him to run his newspapers in Boston, and the following year Knox became general manager of Hearst's newspapers. He left in 1930 to become the successful publisher/part owner of the *Chicago Daily News*.

As a **Republican**, albeit a progressive who had supported Theodore Roosevelt, Knox was a critic of **Franklin D. Roosevelt** and the **New Deal**. In 1936, he ran as **Alf Landon**'s vice presidential partner on the losing ticket. Knox was, however, in favor of supporting **Great Britain** after 1939, and in 1940 Roosevelt appointed him secretary of the navy. In that role he oversaw the wartime expansion of the force. He provided leadership after the disaster of **Pearl Harbor** and replaced Admiral Husband Kimmel with **Chester W. Nimitz**. Knox died following a series of heart attacks in 1944.

KNUDSEN, WILLIAM (1879–1948). Born in Copenhagen, Denmark, William Knudsen came to the United States in 1900. He worked for a time for a bicycle manufacturer in Buffalo, New York, and then switched to producing parts for the **Ford** Motor Company, where he eventually became production manager in 1918. He left Ford in 1921 and in 1923 joined General Motors (GM). From 1937 to 1940, he was president of GM. In 1940, Knudsen left GM to join the National Defense Advisory Commission to assist in war planning, and in 1941 with **Sidney Hillman**, he became codirector of the **Office of Production Management**. When the office was replaced by the **War Production Board** under **Donald Nelson**, Knudsen became director of war production in the War Department, and although he was a civilian, he received a commission. He remained in post until 1945 when he returned to GM.

KOREAN WAR. Formerly occupied by **Japan**, it was agreed at the **Potsdam Conference** in 1945 that Korea would be divided along the 38th parallel between North Korea, under the occupation of the **Soviet Union (USSR)**, and South, under U.S. control. In 1948, it was decided that Korea would be under the trusteeship of the USSR, the United States, and **Great Britain** for five years. However, in May 1948 a government in the South, the Republic of Korea, was established by Syngman Rhee, backed by the United States. Shortly afterward the People's Democratic Republic of Korea was established in the North under Kim Il Sung.

On 25 June 1950 the North Korean People's Army crossed the 38th parallel in an attempt to unify the country and quickly occupied most of the South including the capital, Seoul. On 27 June 1950, with the Soviet delegates absent, the **United Nations (UN)** Security Council approved police action in response to the North's aggression. Although ostensibly a UN force, the U.S. military constituted more than half of the combat troops, and President **Harry S. Truman** appointed General **Douglas MacArthur** as commander of the UN forces.

On 15 September 1950, MacArthur launched a remarkable counteroffensive with an amphibious landing behind the North Korean lines at Inchon. The UN forces quickly liberated Seoul and most of the territory up to the 38th parallel. Encouraged by MacArthur, President Truman announced that the goal was to unite Korea under a democratic government. The invasion of the North began in October 1950. When MacArthur's troops pushed toward the northern frontier with communist **China**, the Chinese responded by invading in turn and pushing UN forces back. When MacArthur publicly advocated all-out war with China and the use of **atomic** weapons in 1951, he was brought home and replaced with General **Matthew Ridgway**. By March 1951, the war had come to a stalemate, with the two armies facing one another just north of the 38th parallel. Peace talks began in July but dragged on until 1953 with disagreements about both the repatriation of Korean and Chinese prisoners of war and the location of the boundary between North and South. The final agreement was signed on 27 July 1953. More than 4 million people died in the conflict, including 36,940 Americans.

KOREMATSU V. UNITED STATES **(323 U.S. 214 1944).** The case of Fred Korematsu was one of the key cases relating to the internment of **Japanese Americans** during **World War II**. Korematsu was born in Oakland, California, and he was arrested and convicted for evading internment in 1942. He appealed against the conviction, and eventually his case was heard in the **Supreme Court**, which ruled on 18 December 1944 in a 6–3 majority decision that internment was justified during the war emergency. The dissenting justices were **Frank Murphy**, **Owen J. Roberts**, and **Robert Jackson**. Murphy argued that the internment was legalized racism. In 1983, a California court overturned Korematsu's convictions. He died in 2005. *See also ENDO V. UNITED STATES; HIRABAYASHI V. UNITED STATES.*

– L –

LA FOLLETTE, ROBERT MARION, JR. (1895–1953). The son of the famous progressive politician of the same name, Robert M. La Follette Jr. was born in Madison, Wisconsin, and attended the University of Wisconsin from 1913 to 1916 before leaving to become a clerk and then his father's secretary. When La Follette Sr. died in 1925, his son won the election to fill the vacant seat, and he held it as a **Republican** until 1947. Despite his party affiliation, after 1929 La Follette was highly critical of **Herbert Hoover** and supported many **New Deal** measures. In 1934, he joined his brother Philip in forming the Wisconsin Progressive Party and was reelected on that platform in 1934 and 1940. La Follette did not think **Franklin D. Roosevelt** went far enough and called for more radical measures. From 1936 on, he chaired the Senate Committee on Education and Labor and the La Follette Civil Liberties Committee, and he exposed the lengths large business corporations went to and the violence used against **trade union** organizations, like the **Memorial Day Massacre** in Chicago in 1937. He was an isolationist and a founding member of the **America First Committee** in 1940, but he did not vote against the war.

In 1946, La Follette was responsible for the introduction of the **Congressional Reorganization Act** that helped to streamline the legislative process. However, having rejoined the Republicans, he was defeated by **Joseph McCarthy** in the primary election of 1946, and in 1953 he committed suicide.

LA GUARDIA, FIORELLO HENRY (1882–1947). Fiorello La Guardia was born in New York City and raised in Arizona. His family went to Trieste, Italy, in 1898, and La Guardia worked for the United States consular service. From 1904 to 1906, he was acting consular agent in Fiume (now Croatia). He returned to the United States in 1907, graduated from New York University Law School in 1910, and practiced law in New York City. During World War I, he served as a major in the U.S. Air Force in Italy. He sat in the U.S. House of Representatives as a **Republican** from 1917 to 1921 and from 1923 to 1933 . He was president of the New York City Board of Aldermen from 1920 to 1921. While in Congress, La Guardia was cosponsor of the Norris-La Guardia Act. He lost his seat in Congress in the **Democratic** landslide of 1932, but in 1933 he was elected mayor of New York on a fusion ticket, supported by Republicans and reform groups.

As mayor, he was known as "the Little Flower," and he established a reputation for honesty and for reforming the city government. La Guardia's administration witnessed slum clearance and public housing development, the building of hospitals and childcare facilities, the construction of roads and bridges (including the Triborough Bridge and the airport that bears his name), and the unified the public transport system. He held the office until 1945 and was president of the United States Conference of Mayors from 1936 until 1945. La Guardia established a good relationship with President **Franklin D. Roosevelt** and during **World War II** was appointed head of the U.S. **Office of Civilian Defense (OCD)**. He found it impossible to do both jobs and was forced to drop the OCD in 1942. Weary of being mayor, he did not run again in 1945. In 1946, he became director of the United Nations Relief and Rehabilitation Administration, a position he held for a year.

LADD, ALAN WALBRIDGE (1913–1964). Actor Alan Ladd was born in Hot Springs, Arkansas, but moved to California at an early age. Although he was short, he was good at sport and a potential Olympic athlete in 1931. After graduating from school in 1933, he worked as a journalist and in a variety of minor jobs in and around film studios. In 1936, he found work in a number of roles in local **radio**, and from 1932 through the early 1940s, he played a number of often unaccredited minor parts in films. Ladd had a small part in *Citizen Kane* in 1941, but his breakthrough came in 1942 when he was cast opposite **Veronica Lake** in *This Gun for Hire*. Unable to serve in the military for medical reasons, Ladd made *China* in 1943 and appeared in several more successful movies with Lake, including *Duffy's Tavern* (1945), *The Blue Dahlia* (1946), and *Saigon* (1948). He also starred in *Two Years before the Mast* (1946) and *The Great Gatsby* (1949). Ladd's next major success was as the lone gunman in the western *Shane* (1953). He also starred in *The Red Beret* (1953) and *The Black Knight* (1954), but his career never reached the heights of his early successes. His last significant film appearance was in *The Carpetbaggers* (1964). *See also* CINEMA.

LABOR-MANAGEMENT RELATIONS ACT. *See* TAFT-HARTLEY ACT.

LAKE, VERONICA (1919–1973). One of the great movie stars of the 1940s, Veronica Lake was born Constance Ockleman in Brooklyn,

New York. Although her first acting role was at the age of eight, she did not begin performing seriously until her family moved to Hollywood in 1938. She got her first film role under the name of Constance Keane in 1939. Her first part as Veronica Lake was in *I Want Wings*, which was a success in 1941, followed by *Hold Back the Dawn* the same year. Lake was described as "one of the most beautiful" stars in Hollywood, and her blond hair covering one eye "peek-a-boo" style, became her trademark. She appeared in *Sullivan's Travels* and *This Gun for Hire* in 1942 and was a hit with Claudette Colbert in *So Proudly We Hail* in 1943. However, it was her pairing with **Alan Ladd** in *The Glass Key* in 1942 that established her most successful screen partnership. They also appeared together in *Duffy's Tavern* (1945), *The Blue Dahlia* (1946), and *Saigon* (1948). The latter did not do particularly well at the box office, and Paramount did not renew her contract after 1948. Lake appeared in a number of **television** shows between 1949 and 1951 and then worked on Broadway for about eight years. However, her string of broken marriages and alcoholism clearly affected her career, and she was forced to find employment in casual, low-paid work other than acting. She moved to Florida in 1965 and appeared in two low-budget films. In 1969, she moved to England but returned after two years and another divorce destitute and ill. She spent her last days in the hospital. *See also* CINEMA.

"LAME DUCK" AMENDMENT. *See* TWENTIETH AMENDMENT.

LAMOUR, DOROTHY (1914–1996). Born Mary Leta Dorothy Slaton in New Orleans, Louisiana, the famous pin-up girl and actress of the 1940s won a beauty contest in New Orleans in 1931 and then moved to Chicago to become a singer, using the name Lamour. She had some success, particularly on **radio**, and moved to Hollywood in 1936. She became a star in *The Jungle Princess* in 1936 and further established herself in a role as an exotic beauty in *The Hurricane* in 1937. Her popularity peaked between 1936 and 1952, and she was associated with **Bing Crosby** and **Bob Hope** in the Road series of movies, beginning with *The Road to Singapore* (1940). During **World War II**, Lamour was very popular in tours to raise money for **war**

bonds. Her film career was less successful in later years, although she appeared in *The Greatest Show on Earth* in 1952 and toured in the 1960s as a nightclub performer. *See also* CINEMA.

LANDON, ALFRED MOSSMAN (1887–1987). Alfred, better-known as "Alf," Landon was born in Pennsylvania, grew up in Ohio, and moved to Independence, Kansas. He obtained his law degree from the University of Kansas in 1908 and then worked in banking and the oil industry, a career he resumed after serving briefly in the army in 1918. Involved in politics as a progressive, Landon later returned to the **Republican Party** and was secretary to Governor Henry Allen in 1922 and organizer of the gubernatorial campaigns of William Allen White and Clyde M. Reed in 1924 and 1928. He was chosen as chair of the Kansas Republican Party that year but was pushed out by conservatives in 1930. Nonetheless, in 1932 he was elected governor in his own right defeating **Democratic** incumbent **Harry Woodring**. Landon implemented measures to counter the **Great Depression**, including a moratorium on farm mortgage foreclosures, restriction on bank withdrawals, regulation of utilities, and conservation of natural resources, while maintaining a balanced budget. He was the only Republican governor to be reelected in 1934.

In 1936, Landon was chosen as the Republican presidential candidate. While he was critical of **Franklin D. Roosevelt**'s deficit spending and advocated government efficiency and a balanced budget, his platform was a moderate reform one. He lost overwhelmingly and did not run for public office again. He served as vice chairman of the U.S. delegation to the Inter-American Conference in Lima, Peru, in 1938 and continued to speak on political matters right through the 1960s.

LANGE, DOROTHEA (1895–1965). Born Dorothea Margarette Nutzhorn in Hoboken, New Jersey, the photographer and photojournalist dropped her middle name and adopted her mother's maiden name after her father abandoned the family. A victim of polio at the age of seven, she was left with a permanently weakened leg. She studied photography in New York City and in 1918 moved to San Francisco, California, where she opened a portrait studio. In 1936, she joined the team of photographers in the federal **Resettlement Administration**, later called the **Farm Security Administration**, and began capturing the impact of the **Great Depression**. Many of her photographs of unemployed men and women became nationally and internationally known, but her best-known photo was of a migrant woman in Nipoma, California, that became known as *Migrant Madonna* (1936). In 1941, Lange gave up a Guggenheim Fellowship to photograph the relocation of **Japanese Americans**. Her photographs were consequently impounded by the army. She also photographed war workers and other individuals of the period, documenting the social impact of **World War II** for the **Office of War Information**, and the writing of the **United Nations Charter** for the State Department. In 1952, Lange was one of the founders of the magazine *Aperture*, but her declining health limited her work.

LATTIMORE, OWEN (1900–1989). Born in Washington, D.C., Owen Lattimore was raised, educated, and spent much of his early life in **China**, other than when he attended school in Switzerland and England. He returned to China in 1919 and worked in commercial insurance. He also traveled throughout Asia and wrote several accounts of his journey, including *Desert Road to Turkestan* (1929), *High Tartary* (1930), *Manchuria, Cradle of Conflict* (1932), and *Mongols of Manchuria* (1934). From 1928 to 1937, Lattimore held a fellowship at Harvard University and was editor of the journal *Pacific Affairs*. From 1938 to 1950, he was the director of the Walter Hines Page School of International Relations at Johns Hopkins University. In 1941, he was sent as the U.S. political adviser to Chinese nationalist leader **Chiang Kai-shek**. He returned to work in the Pacific Affairs Office of the **Office of War Information** in 1942.

In 1944, Lattimore traveled to the **Soviet Union** and China with **Henry A. Wallace**, and after the war he suggested delaying recognition of the nationalists in China and appeared sympathetic to the communists led by **Mao Zedong**. In 1950, **Joseph McCarthy** accused him of being "the top Russian spy," but he was cleared in the subsequent investigation. However, in 1952 Lattimore was indicted for perjury, having been accused of lying to a Senate subcommittee on internal affairs by denying that he had promoted communism. All charges were dropped by 1955, but his passport was withheld and he was unable to find work in the United States. Once he was allowed to travel again, he became professor of Chinese studies at the University of Leeds in England from 1963 to 1970. He authored several books on Chinese history and politics and an account of his experience of **McCarthyism** in *Ordeal by Slander* (1950).

LEE, RUSSELL WERNER (1903–1986). Born in Ottawa, Illinois, and orphaned at an early age, Russell Lee was educated at Culver Military Academy and Lehigh University, where he trained as a chemical engineer, graduating in 1925. After working as an engineer in 1929, Lee took up **art** and moved to California and then Woodstock, where he began working with photography. In 1936, he joined a team of photographers under **Roy Stryker** at the **Resettlement Administration**, which later became the **Farm Security Administration**, and was noted for several of his powerful images of migrant workers and rural communities.

Lee served as a photographer for Air Transport Command during **World War II** and then resumed work under Stryker and produced public relations photographs for Standard Oil and the coal industry. He moved to Austin, Texas, in 1947 and helped to document the housing condition of **Hispanic** workers and also those in mental institutions. In 1965, he became instructor of photography at the University of Texas, where he worked until his retirement in 1973.

LEHAND, MARGUERITE (1898–1944). Born in Potsdam, New York, Marguerite LeHand qualified as a secretary after leaving high school and worked at the **Democratic Party** National Headquarters in Washington, D.C., before becoming the private secretary to **Franklin D. Roosevelt** in 1920. She remained with Roosevelt through his political career until she suffered a stroke in 1941. Known as "Missy" in the Roosevelt family, LeHand had an extremely close relationship with the president and acted as hostess at official functions when **Eleanor Roosevelt** was absent. Although she predeceased him, the president had willed her half of his estate.

LEHMAN, HERBERT HENRY (1878–1963). Herbert Lehman, New York's longest-serving governor, began work in a textile company in 1899. By 1906, he had risen to vice president and treasurer of the company. In 1908, he joined his father's investment banking company,

Lehman Brothers. He worked for a number of charitable organizations, including the Joint Distribution Committee formed during World War I to aid Jews in Eastern Europe. During the war, Lehman served in the General Staff Corps in Washington, D.C., as a captain and was responsible for purchase and traffic.

After the war, Lehman entered **Democratic** politics as a friend and associate of **Alfred E. Smith** and had various roles in Smith's election campaigns in 1924 and 1928. Lehman became **Franklin D. Roosevelt**'s lieutenant governor in 1928, a position he held until 1932. In 1932, he was elected governor in his own right and was reelected in 1934 and 1936. In 1938, he was elected to the first four-year term in the same capacity. Under his direction, New York established a "little **New Deal**" of relief and recovery programs to alleviate the impact of the **Great Depression**, including unemployment insurance, minimum wages, and public housing. He resigned as governor in 1942 to become head of the Office of Foreign Relief and Rehabilitation Operations in the State Department. In 1943, the office became the **United Nations Relief and Rehabilitation Administration**, and Lehman was chosen as director general. He held the position until his resignation in 1946.

Unsuccessful in his bid for a seat in the U.S. Senate in 1946, Lehman was elected in 1950, where he fought for liberal causes and opposed Senator **Joseph McCarthy**. He retired from the Senate in 1956.

LEMKE, WILLIAM FREDERICK (1878–1950). Born in Albany, Minnesota, William Lemke moved with his family to North Dakota and studied at the University of North Dakota, Georgetown University, and Yale University. After gaining his law degree in 1905, he set up practice in Fargo, North Dakota, and also published the monthly *The Common Good*. Associated with farmers and farmers' movements, Lemke became attorney for the Nonpartisan League in 1916. The league captured control of the state's **Republican Party**, and Lemke became party chairman. In 1920, he was elected state attorney general. However, he was defeated in a recall election in 1921. He retired to his law practice for the remainder of the decade.

In 1932, Lemke was elected to the U.S. House of Representatives, where he sponsored legislation to ease bankruptcy proceedings against farmers and a proposal for the federal government to assist farmers in paying off their mortgages. When **Franklin D. Roosevelt**'s administration opposed this last measure, Lemke turned against the **New Deal** and joined **Charles Coughlin, Francis Townsend**, and **Gerald K. Smith** in the National Union. He was nominated as the union's presidential candidate in 1936 but secured less than 2 percent of the national vote. He failed to win election to the U.S. Senate in 1940 but remained in Congress as a representative from 1942 until his death.

LEND-LEASE ACT, 1941. Approved by Congress in March 1941, the Lend-Lease Act gave the president the power to transfer the title, lend, or lease any equipment to any nation whose defense was considered vital to the security of the United States. Initially intended to allow aid to **Great Britain**, during the course of **World War II** the United States provided $50 billion in aid to Great Britain, **China**, France, and the **Soviet Union (USSR)**. Almost 60 percent went to Great Britain. The Lend-Lease program was ended abruptly in September 1945.

The British finally completed repayment for Lend-Lease in December 2006, and not all loans were repaid by the USSR, which was an issue in the growing postwar confrontation that led to the **Cold War**.

LEROY, MERVYN (1900–1987). Born in San Francisco, California, film director and producer Mervyn LeRoy first appeared in vaudeville as an actor/singer in 1906. He began working in the film industry in 1919, and his first work as a director was *No Place to Go* in 1927. LeRoy's first big success was with the classic gangster film starring **Edward G. Robinson**, *Little Caesar* in 1931. In 1932, his critique of the southern convict labor system, *I Am a Fugitive from a Chain Gang*, starring **Paul Muni**, also won critical acclaim. In addition to gangster or social issues movies, LeRoy made a string of successful musicals, including *42nd Street* (1932), *Gold Diggers of 1933* (1933), and *Sweet Adeline* (1935). In 1939, he produced both the comedy *At the Circus*, starring the **Marx Brothers**, and *The Wizard of Oz*, the musical starring **Judy Garland**. During **World War II**, he made a number of educational films for the government, and in 1945 he won an Oscar for *The House We Live In*, a condemnation of racial prejudice starring **Frank Sinatra**. LeRoy continued to make films throughout the 1950s and 1960s but did not have the success of his earlier work. He codirected *The Green Berets*, the Vietnam war film starring **John Wayne**, in 1968. *See also* CINEMA.

LEVITT, WILLIAM JAIRD (1907–1994). Born in Brooklyn, New York, William Levitt became president of his father's building company in 1939 at the age of 22. After the war, he was responsible for building the mass-produced, identical, affordable single-family homes in **Levittowns** in several northeastern states. The rapid-assembly homes could be built at the rate of 36 a day. Levitt sold his company to International Telephone and Telegraph (ITT) in 1968 for $492 million. He attempted to develop similar schemes overseas but was unsuccessful and retired in 1982.

LEVITTOWN. Levittown was the name of the first town of mass-produced, affordable single-family homes built by **William J. Levitt** on Long Island, New York, with a population of more than 10,000 between 1947 and 1951. Similar towns were established outside Philadelphia, Pennsylvania, in 1951 through 1955 and in New Jersey in 1958. The New Jersey Levittown is now called Willingboro.

LEWIS, JOHN LLEWELLYN (1880–1969). The son of a Welsh immigrant, John L. Lewis was born in Iowa, where he began work in the coal mines in the 1890s. In 1907, he moved to Illinois, and he was elected president of the United Mine Workers of America (UMWA) local in 1910. In 1911, Lewis was appointed as a field representative for the **American Federation of Labor (AFL)**, and in 1917 he became vice president of the UMWA. He was elected president in 1920 and held the position until his retirement in 1960.

UMWA membership declined during the 1920s as the coal industry shrank in the face of foreign competition and the increased use of oil. The drop in membership increased with the onset of the **Great Depression** in the 1930s. Lewis, however, capitalized on the change in political climate with the advent of the **New Deal** and began to mobilize **trade union** membership. Lewis argued for the AFL to take a more militant approach and focus on organizing workers on an industrywide basis rather than by craft. As differences within the AFL exploded into physical conflict in 1935, he joined with **Sidney Hillman** and **David Dubinsky** to establish a Committee for Industrial Organization. The committee became the leading force in increasing union membership during the 1930s, and Lewis played an active role in these developments. In 1938, the Committee for Industrial Organizations became an autonomous labor organization, the **Congress of Industrial Organizations (CIO)**.

Lewis became increasingly critical of the administration of **Franklin D. Roosevelt** and in 1940 openly supported the **Republican** candidate, **Wendell Willkie**. In 1940, he also stepped down as president of the CIO. Lewis's growing opposition to Roosevelt's war administration caused differences within the CIO leadership, and in 1942 Lewis took the UMWA out of the organization. His conflict with Roosevelt heightened when he led the miners in a series of strikes at the height of **World War II** in 1943. He continued his confrontational methods after the war, and strikes in the face of a federal injunction in 1946 resulted in massive fines for the union. In the 1950s, Lewis collaborated more with mine owners in return for pension and health care programs for the miners. After his retirement in 1960, he was director of the union retirement and welfare funds and some of his decisions with regard to investments were detrimental to the funds' viability

LEYTE GULF. Between 22 and 27 October 1944, the U.S. Navy and the Japanese navy fought one of the greatest naval battles in history when they met in four confrontations in Leyte Gulf in the Philippine Sea during **World War II**. The outnumbered Japanese fleet suffered such huge losses that it was no longer a force in the war. The U.S. Navy, under Admiral **Chester W. Nimitz**, lost 27 ships, and the Japanese lost more than 60 vessels, including five aircraft carriers.

LIBERTY SHIPS. "Liberty ships" were mass-produced cargo ships made as part of the emergency construction program to supply **Great Britain** and the U.S. Merchant Marine during **World War II**. The ships were quick and easy to build using prefabricated parts put together in an assembly-line method in 18 different shipyards, mainly the **Kaiser** yards. Construction initially took 230 days, but eventually a ship was produced in 42 days, and one was constructed in just under five days. A total of 2,751 "liberty ships" were built. They were given the name "liberty ships" when **Franklin D. Roosevelt** quoted Patrick Henry's words, "Give me liberty or give me death" in launching them. A faster, stronger version appeared in the later years of the war known as "victory ships."

LILIENTHAL, DAVID ELI (1899–1981). The son of Czech immigrants, David Lilienthal was born in Morton, Illinois. He attended DePauw University and Harvard Law School. After graduating in 1923, he practiced law in Chicago. His expertise in utility law led to his appointment to the Wisconsin State Utility Commission in 1931, and President **Franklin D. Roosevelt** appointed him head of the **Tennessee Valley Authority (TVA)** in 1933 with responsibility for the power program. Lilienthal clashed with one of the codirectors, Harcourt Morgan, over charging lower rates than existing power companies. Although Roosevelt removed Morgan from office, Lilienthal was also publicly attacked by **Wendell Willkie**, who headed a major utility company in the Tennessee Valley. Lilienthal survived, and the TVA eventually purchased Willkie's company. In 1941, Lilienthal became chair of the TVA. His outspoken defense of the authority often led to clashes with members of Congress. Lilienthal's position is summed up in his book, *TVA: Democracy on the March* (1944).

Reappointed chair by President **Harry S. Truman** in 1945, in January 1946 Lilienthal moved to become chair of an advisory committee on atomic energy and then head of the new **Atomic Energy Commission (AEC)**. Despite some congressional opposition, he was confirmed in the post in April 1947. He expanded the production of atomic weapons and the use of atomic energy in private industry. His term was extended for another two years in 1948. After resigning in 1950, Lilienthal became an industrial consultant and then head of an industrial minerals producing company. In 1955, he was appointed chief executive of an international resource development organization.

Although a controversial figure, Lilienthal received many public awards, including the Public Welfare Medal of the National Academy of Sciences and commendations from the governments of Brazil and Peru. *See also* ATOMIC BOMB.

LINDBERGH, CHARLES AUGUSTUS (1902–1974). Charles A. Lindbergh became a national hero after making the first single-handed, nonstop transatlantic flight from New York to Paris in his airplane, *The Spirit of St Louis*, on 20 May 1927. He had previously flown in the Army Air Service and as an airmail pilot between Chicago and St. Louis. He was awarded the Congressional Medal of Honor for his flight, and *Time* magazine made him its first "Man of the Year." He subsequently worked to promote aviation and was employed by various airline companies. Lindbergh was in the headlines again in 1932 when his 20-month-old son was abducted and found dead two months later. A German-born carpenter, **Bruno Hauptmann**, was tried and executed for the murder in April 1936.

The Lindbergh's left the United States in 1935 to live first in England and then France. Lindbergh visited **Germany** in 1936, 1937, and 1938 on behalf of the U.S. Army to inspect the air forces in that country, Poland, and Czechoslovakia. He became convinced that Germany had a superior air force and that any war could destroy Western civilization. He had a number of meetings with the German air minister, Hermann Goering, and in 1938 was awarded the Service Cross of the German Eagle at a state dinner. He returned to the United States in 1939 and became a leading noninterventionist and a member of the **America First Committee**. He was highly criticized for comments that appeared anti-Semitic and pro-Nazi, particularly in a speech in September 1941 accusing the Jews of controlling the media.

Upon U.S. entry into **World War II** in 1941, Lindbergh tested aircraft as a civilian. Nonetheless he flew combat missions in the Pacific in 1944. After the war, he continued to work for the U.S. air force and the Defense Department, and in 1954 President **Dwight D. Eisenhower** promoted him to brigadier general. His autobiography, *The Spirit of St. Louis* (1953), was awarded a Pulitzer Prize in 1954.

LIPPMANN, WALTER (1889–1974). Born to wealthy German Jewish parents in New York City, Walter Lippmann made a name as a brilliant student at Harvard. He left the university in 1910 to become a journalist at the socialist newspaper *Boston Common*. Part of the radical Greenwich Village set, Lippmann produced a call for reform in his *Preface to Politics* in 1912. In 1914, he published *Drift and*

Mastery, which captured much of the progressive ethos in advocating government run scientifically by a public-minded elite. The same year, Lippmann joined the staff of the *New Republic* magazine. He supported U.S. entry into World War I and joined a team of planners to draw up plans for the postwar world. He was one of the U.S. advisers at the Versailles Peace Conference but was disillusioned by the terms of the peace treaty and became a critic of it and the League of Nations. His wartime experience also made him skeptical of the democratic process, and his *Liberty and the News* (1920) and *Public Opinion* (1922) suggested that government was best left to the experts.

In 1922, Lippmann joined the newspaper *New York World*, where he established a reputation as one of the leading journalists of his day. His book examining the "lost generation," *A Preface to Morals* (1929), had a wide readership. Lippmann became a contributor to the conservative newspaper *New York Herald Tribune* in 1931, and his columns were nationally and internationally syndicated. While he was initially enthusiastic about the **New Deal**, Lippmann became increasingly critical. In criticizing what he saw as excessive collectivism and centralization, it appeared that he was defending laissez faire, but in fact he owed a great deal to the influence of **John Maynard Keynes**.

In the late 1930s, Lippmann advocated U.S. support for **Great Britain** against Nazi **Germany**, and during the war he wrote a best seller entitled *United States Foreign Policy: Shield of the Republic* (1943), advocating a continuation of the Grand Alliance with Great Britain and the **Soviet Union (USSR)**. When the alliance broke up after the war, Lippmann wrote a critical study of containment, *The Cold War* (1947), and he was probably the originator of the phrase used to describe postwar relations with the USSR.

Lippmann was awarded the Presidential Medal of Freedom in 1964 and worked for the CBS television network for a number of years. However, he became increasingly critical of Lyndon Johnson's policies in Vietnam, and he retired from journalism in 1967.

LITERATURE AND THEATER. While the literature of the 1920s is mostly remembered for the "lost generation" of writers who were disaffected, alienated, and often out of the country, the 1930s in particular are remembered for the novels of social protest and social realism, some often having a "proletarian" emphasis. Chief among these is **John Steinbeck**'s depiction of the rural poor in *Grapes of Wrath* (1939), but also significant was James T. Farrell's *Studs Lonigan* trilogy (1932–1935) and **Erskine Caldwell**'s depiction of southern poverty in *Tobacco Road* (1932). The southern emphasis was also evident in the body of writing by **William Faulkner**. Politics too seemed important, as indicated in Sinclair Lewis's *It Can't Happen Here* (1933) or **Ernest Hemingway**'s novel of the **Spanish Civil War**, *For Whom the Bell Tolls* (1940). One of the most powerful books of racial protest, *Native Son* by **African American** author **Richard Wright**, also appeared in 1940. But not all writing was intent on grim realism. Children's author Laura Ingalls Wilder had enormous success with her Little House novels, especially *Little House on the Prairie* (1935), looking back on pioneer days, and **Margaret Mitchell**'s Civil War romance *Gone with the Wind* (1936) was a great hit both as a book and film.

Some of the social themes examined by novelists were also explored by established playwright Eugene O'Neill in *Ah, Wilderness!* in 1933 and *The Iceman Cometh*, written in 1939 but staged in 1946. In 1936, O'Neill received the Nobel Prize for Literature for his work during the 1920s. Political comments can be found in Clifford Odets's *Waiting for Lefty* (1935). Also significant is Lillian Hellman's *Children's Hour* (1934) and *The Little Foxes* (1939). The latter was made into a film in 1941 starring **Bette Davis**. Hellman was among those **blacklisted** during the period of **McCarthyism** in the 1950s, a theme that itself lay behind **Arthur Miller**'s postwar masterpiece *The Crucible* (1953). Miller had already established himself with earlier plays, especially *Death of a Salesman* (1949). The other major playwright of the period was **Tennessee Williams**, whose depiction of southern society in *The Glass Menagerie* (1944) and *A Street Car Named Desire* (1947) reflected similar concerns of Faulkner, of Eudora Welty in *Delta Wedding* (1946), and of Carson McCullers in *The Heart Is a Lonely Hunter* (1940), *Reflections in a Golden Eye* (1941), and *The Member of the Wedding* (1946).

A number of new literary figures emerged during **World War II**. War poets Randall Jarrell and Karl Shapiro, novelist John Hersey with the Pulitzer Prize-winning *A Bell for Adano* (1944), Irwin Shaw with *The Young Lions* (1948), **Norman Mailer** with *The Naked and the Dead* (1948), and James Jones with *From Here to Eternity* (1951) all dealt with the subject of war, while issues of Jewishness and general alienation were central concerns of Saul Bellow first in *Dangling Man* (1944) and then in *The Victim* (1947). Bellow became a major writer from the 1950s through the 1970s. Alienated youth began to appear in novels such as J. D. Salinger's *Catcher in the Rye* (1951), while *Invisible Man*, Ralph Ellison's literary masterpiece dealing with the alienation of African Americans, was published in 1952. More popular literature included the religious novels of Lloyd C. Douglas, like *The Robe* (1943), and the historical romance by Kathryn Winsor, *Forever Amber* (1944). Both of these were made into films. *See also* BUCK, PEARL SYDENSTRICKER; FEDERAL THEATER PROJECT; FEDERAL WRITERS' PROJECT; FROST, ROBERT LEE; HURSTON, ZORA NEALE; POUND, EZRA (WESTON) LOOMIS; WILDER, THORNTON NIVEN.

"LITTLE STEEL" FORMULA. The "Little Steel" formula was a method worked out by the **National War Labor Board** in July 1942 to control wage increases. In response to a demand by the steel workers in the Bethlehem, Republic, Youngstown, and Inland steel companies, for a dollar-a-day increase, the board agreed on a 15 percent increase to cover the period beginning in January 1941 until May 1942. This formula became the general principle applied after the passage of the **Economic Stabilization Act** in October 1942.

LOMBARD, CAROLE (1908–1942). Born Jane Alice Peters in Fort Wayne, Indiana, Carole Lombard had her first role in motion pictures in 1920. Fox Studios employed her when she was 16 years old. Despite facial scarring from an automobile accident, she was able to sign a contract with Mack Sennett in 1927 and appeared in a number of comic roles before leaving the company in 1928. In 1930, Lombard joined Paramount Pictures and made several minor movies prior to making a name for herself in *20th Century* (1934), *Hands across the Table* (1935), *My Man Godfrey* (1936), *True Confession* (1937), and *Nothing Sacred* (1937). Her "screwball" comic roles reflected the mood of the 1930s. During **World War II**, Lombard campaigned across the country to help sell **war bonds**. She died when her flight back from one of these appearances crashed near Las Vegas. *See also* CINEMA.

LONDON ECONOMIC CONFERENCE, 1933. The World Monetary and Economic Conference, better known as the London Economic Conference, met in June and July 1933 in response to the growing crisis of the **Great Depression**. Attempts to reach an agreement on tariff reduction and currency stabilization failed, and the United States refused to discuss war debt. Before the conference ended, President **Franklin D. Roosevelt** called the U.S. delegation home, effectively undermining the conference.

LONDON NAVAL CONFERENCE, 1935–1936. The London Naval Conference was a conference held in London, England, between the United States, **Great Britain**, and **Japan** that met between December 1935 and March 1936 to consider Japanese protests against the earlier Washington Naval Treaty of 1922 that limited the building of battleships by each nation to a ratio of 5:5:3, respectively. When the Japanese demand for parity was rejected, they withdrew, and Great Britain and the United States cemented an agreement to exchange information on naval construction programs and limit the building of certain warships in peacetime.

LONG, HUEY PIERCE (1893–1935). Huey Long was born in Winnfield, Louisiana. Despite winning a scholarship to Louisiana State University, he was unable to afford student life and worked in a variety of jobs while studying law in his own time. Long entered Louisiana politics as a member of the Railroad Commission that existed from 1918 to 1921, which then became the Public Service Commission, which stayed in place from 1921 to 1928. After failing to win election in 1924, he was elected governor of Louisiana for the **Democratic Party** in 1928 and built a reputation as a populist reformer. He raised taxes to pay for school books, started a program for bridge and road construction, and improved the University of Louisiana at Baton Rouge. He largely ran the state as a one-party state using patronage and intimidation to maintain control.

Having survived an impeachment trial because of his taxation policies, Long was elected to the U.S. Senate in 1930 and adopted the nickname "Kingfish." He continued as governor until one of his supporters could replace him in 1932. Initially sympathetic, he became increasingly critical of **Franklin D. Roosevelt**'s **New Deal**. In 1934, Long outlined his "Share Our Wealth" program in a manifesto entitled *Every Man a King*, which promised each family a guaranteed cash income, old-age pensions, and reduced work hours financed by placing a ceiling on incomes and property ownership. In 1935, he announced his candidacy for the Democratic presidential nomination, and it appeared likely that he could attract as much as 10 percent of the vote. Roosevelt, who described him as one of the "two most dangerous men in America," regarded him as a serious threat, and the revenue bill he submitted to Congress was in part a response to Long's challenge. However, Long died on 10 September 1935 after being gunned down on the steps of the state capitol in Baton Rouge by Dr. Carl Weiss, the son-in-law of a political opponent.

LORENTZ, PARE (1905–1992). Born Leonard McTaggart Lorentz in West Virginia and educated at West Virginia Wesleyan College and the University of West Virginia, Lorentz moved to New York City in 1924. After working as an editor for General Electric, he became a film reviewer and critic and adopted his father's name, Pare. In addition to reviewing for the *New York Evening Journal*, *Vanity Fair*, *Town & Country*, and *McCall's*, Lorentz wrote two books, *Censored: The Private Life of the Movies* (1930) and *The Roosevelt Years* (1934). A supporter of **Franklin D. Roosevelt** and the **New Deal**, he joined the **Resettlement Administration** in 1935 to produce "films of merit." His first film, *The Plow That Broke the Plains*, a study of soil erosion and the **Dust Bowl**, was well-received by critics and the public. He then made *The River* (1938), a study of the Mississippi River and Ohio River and the problems of flooding for the **Farm Security Administration**. Impressed by the film, Roosevelt created the U.S. Film Service with Lorentz as its head in 1938. His study on the impact of poverty on infant mortality, *The Fight for Life*, was made in 1940. However, congressional opposition to such work, viewed by some as New Deal propaganda, led to the cessation of funding.

After briefly but unsuccessfully working in Hollywood, during the war Lorentz served as a major in the Army Air Corps and made 200 briefing films. He was awarded the Legion of Merit in 1944. In 1946, he became head of the Film Section of the War Department's Civil Affairs Division and in 1946 made *The Nuremberg Trials*. He resigned his position in 1947 and established his own production company but mainly worked as a consultant and film reviewer. Lorentz's documentaries from the 1930s received several awards from the film industry, and in 1963 he was awarded a gold medal for *The River* by the secretary of agriculture. *See also* CINEMA.

LOS ANGELES RIOT, 1943. Like many cities during **World War II**, Los Angeles, California, experienced an enormous increase in population as workers flocked to the wartime aircraft industry and shipyards. The city saw a massive influx of **Hispanic Americans** and **African Americans**. Of the 2.8 million inhabitants in Los Angeles County in 1945, 250,000 were Mexican American, many recent arrivals. A total of 60,000 African Americans also entered the city in search of work. Some 50,000 service personnel from nearby bases and ports also entered the city on weekends. Tensions over jobs, housing, and recreational areas were inflamed by racial prejudices, and Mexican youths (*pachucos*), who demonstrated their rebellion by wearing "zoot suits" (baggy trousers tight at the ankle and long loose draped jackets), were often the target of attacks by white servicemen. In June, the conflict led to a series of violent clashes that turned into four days of rioting between 3 and 7 June, primarily white soldiers and sailors attacking Mexican Americans and some African Americans. Most of the 600 people arrested were, however, Mexican Americans. The fighting ended when the city was declared off-limits to servicemen. The Los Angeles City Council passed an ordinance banning "zoot suits." *See also* DETROIT RACE RIOT; HARLEM RACE RIOT, 1943.

LOUIS, JOE (1914–1981). Born Joe Louis Barrow, the son of sharecroppers and grandson of slaves in Alabama in 1914, the future heavyweight boxing champion Joe Louis was one of eight children. When Louis was about two, his father, Monroe Barrow, was committed to a state mental institution suffering from schizophrenia and his mother later re-married and the family moved to Detroit in 1926. Having dropped out of school Louis worked in a number of laboring jobs and began boxing in his early teens. He fought his first amateur fight in 1932. Having mistakenly omitted the name "Barrow" from his registration forms, he became known thereafter as Joe Louis. After winning 50 of his 54 contests, in 1933 he won the National American Athletic Union light heavyweight title. Before turning professional in 1934, Louis fought 58 amateur bouts, lost four, won 54, 43 of which were by knock out.

Carefully coached by his manager and trainer on how to behave as an **African American** competing in a sport dominated by whites, Louis successfully fought 18 opponents before meeting the former heavyweight champion, **Primo Carnera**, in 1935. Louis knocked the giant Italian out in the sixth round. He went on to fight and knock out three other contenders for the heavyweight title: King Levinsky, Paulino Uzcudun, and then another former heavyweight champion, **Max Baer**. His ferocious punches won Louis the nickname of "Brown Bomber."

On 19 June 1936, Louis faced another former heavyweight champion, the German Max Schmeling. Perhaps underestimating his opponent, Louis did not train properly for the bout and was knocked out in the twelfth round. He made his comeback on August 18 when he knocked out Jack Starkey in the third round. After a number of relatively easy fights, he was matched against **James Braddock** (known as the "Cinderella Man" due to his come back) for the world heavyweight championship ahead of Schmeling in 1937 and on June 22, 1937 in front of a crowd of 45,000 at Comiskey Park, Chicago, he came back from an early knock down to k.o. Braddock in the eighth round and win the heavyweight title. At the age of 22, Louis became the youngest heavyweight champion in history. After fighting several defenses of his title, Louis finally got his rematch with Max Schmeling in 1938. The fight on 22 June 1938 assumed enormous significance as it was presented in terms of competing nations, ideologies, and races. Schmeling was portrayed as the representative of Nazi **Germany** while and Louis now symbolized liberal democracy and racial equality. Louis knocked out Schmeling within the first three minutes of round one.

Louis successfully defended his title in 14 fights—often against insignificant challengers—before he faced Billy Conn on June 18 1941. In what is regarded as one of the greatest fights of the twentieth century Louis knocked out Conn in the thirteenth round. The champion went on to defeat Buddy Baer in January 1942 and then gave most of his purse to the Navy Relief fund. Shortly afterward, he enlisted in the U.S. Army as a private. He fought several bouts while in the army, and again in 1942 donated his winnings to the Army Emergency Relief Fund as well as paying to provide seats for servicemen. Made sergeant in August 1942 and staff sergeant 1944, Louis's role in the army was largely public relations, boosting morale by fighting exhibition bouts for service personnel. He also featured in war posters, army publications, and in a film *This Is the Army*, with future-president Ronald Reagan in 1943. In recognition of his patriotic work, Louis was awarded the Legion of Merit by the army in 1945.

Louis returned to the ring for an eagerly awaited rematch against Billy Conn on 19 June 1946. Before the fight, Conn indicated that he would outrun the champion, to which Louis replied with the famous remark, "He can run but he can't hide." Louis won with a knockout in the eighth. Faced with huge tax demands from the IRS, Louis continued to fight beyond his prime, but after successfully knocking out "Jersey" Joe Walcott in a rematch in 1948, he retired from the ring in 1949. His debts forced him to make a comeback in 1951, but after being beaten by Rocky Marciano in 1951, he retired once more. In defending his title over a 12-year period and winning 23 of the 27 contests with knockouts, Louis had secured his place as one of the greatest fighters of all time.

However, his career after retiring was to be one of slow decline. He found employment for a while in advertising, but as his tax liabilities increased Louis became a professional wrestler to earn more. He also performed briefly in a circus. He stopped wrestling due to injury in 1957 and subsequently became a "greeter" in Caesar's Palace, Las Vegas. In later years, he became addicted to alcohol and drugs and was briefly hospitalized in 1970. In 1977, he suffered a massive heart attack and was subsequently confined to a wheelchair. He was supported through illness and declining years by show business friends, including **Frank Sinatra**. Following his death in 1981 Louis was buried in Arlington National Cemetery in Washington, D.C., on the special instructions of President Ronald Reagan. Louis was awarded the Congressional Medal of Honor in 1982.

LOVETT, ROBERT ABERCROMBIE (1895–1986). Born in Texas, Robert Lovett was a graduate of Yale in 1918 and Harvard University in 1921. He began a career in banking as a clerk and eventually became a partner in Brown Brothers Harriman & Co., working with **Averell Harriman**. In 1940, Lovett became special assistant to secretary of war **Henry L. Stimson** and then was appointed assistant secretary of war. He was awarded the Distinguished Service Medal for his work by President **Harry S. Truman** in 1945. From 1946 to 1949, he became assistant secretary of state to General **George C. Marshall** and then turned deputy when Marshall became secretary of defense in 1950. In 1951, Lovett became secretary of defense and oversaw the mobilization during the **Korean War** until he left office in 1953. He declined a cabinet appointment in John F. Kennedy's administration in 1961 but did act as a policy adviser. In 1963, Lovett was awarded the Presidential Medal of Freedom for his work in government.

LUCE, CLARE BOOTHE (1903–1987). Born to a poor family, Clare Boothe Luce rose to be a successful journalist, editor, playwright, socialite, politician, and, after her first marriage failed, wife to the media magnate **Henry R. Luce**. After briefly working as an actor, from 1930 to 1934 she worked as an editor at the fashion magazines *Vogue* and *Vanity Fair*. She wrote a number of plays that became even more successful as films, including *The Woman* (1936), *Kiss the Boys Goodbye* (1938), and *Margin of Error* (1939). A later screenplay, *Come to the Stable* (1949), was nominated for an Academy Award.

From 1939 to 1940, Luce was a war correspondent in Europe for *Life* magazine. A **Republican**, she served in the U.S. House of Representatives from 1943 to 1947. During **Dwight D. Eisenhower**'s administration, she was the U.S. ambassador to Italy from 1953 to 1956 and to Brazil in 1959. Having failed to win party support for her candidacy for the U.S. Senate in 1964, Luce joined her husband in retirement. However, she sat on Ronald Reagan's Foreign Intelligence Advisory Board from 1981 until 1983. She was awarded the Presidential Medal of Freedom in 1983 in recognition of her achievements. *See also* CINEMA; LITERATURE AND THEATER.

LUCE, HENRY ROBINSON (1898–1967). The son of a missionary, Henry Luce was born in **China**. He was a student at Yale University and became a commissioned officer in the U.S. Army in 1918. He returned to college in 1919 and graduated in 1920. After a brief period of study at Oxford University, Luce returned to the United States where, with Briton Hadden, he established *Time* magazine in 1923. In 1930, Luce founded *Fortune*, a journal aimed at businessmen. Time, Inc. expanded and in 1935 began a documentary newsreel series, The March of Time. In 1936, Luce began production of *Life*, a magazine of photojournalism. *Time* and *Life* were enormously influential journals and had a huge circulation until they were undermined by the advent of **television**.

In an editorial entitled "The American Century" in *Life* in 1941, Luce argued that the United States should abandon isolationism and take a lead in rebuilding a peaceful world after an **Allied** victory. Luce supported the presidential campaign of **Republican Wendell Willkie** in 1940 and **Dwight D. Eisenhower** in 1952. After the war, Luce became increasingly conservative and was an advocate of strong resistance to perceived **Soviet** expansion. A major figure in the **"China Lobby"** in 1949, he blamed **Harry S. Truman**'s administration for the loss of China to the communists. He became an ardent supporter of Nationalist China (*see* TAIWAN). Luce later supported groups involved in attacks on Fidel Castro's Cuba, and he approved of U.S. involvement in the war in Vietnam. In the 1950s, he launched *House & Home* and *Sports Illustrated* magazines. He retired in 1964.

LUDLOW AMENDMENT. First proposed by the **Democratic** congressman from Indiana, Louis Ludlow, in 1935, the Ludlow Amendment was reintroduced following the *Panay* **incident** in December 1937. The amendment called for a popular referendum before any declaration of war unless there was an attack on the United States or its possessions. The resolution was narrowly rejected by a vote of 209 to 188 on 10 January 1938.

– M –

MACARTHUR, DOUGLAS (1880–1964). Douglas MacArthur graduated first in his class from West Point in 1903. He was a member of the General Staff in France during World War I and successfully commanded the 42nd Rainbow Division. After the war, MacArthur became superintendent at West Point from 1919 to 1922. He became a major general in 1928 and commander of the Philippines Department in 1928. From 1930 to 1935, he was general and chief of staff of the U.S. Army. In 1932, he led the troops who forcibly ejected the **Bonus Army** from Washington, D.C. MacArthur was director of organization of national defense for the Philippines from 1935 until 1937, when he retired. Recalled to active service in 1941 as a lieutenant general, he was placed in command of the U.S. Forces in the Far East. He was forced to flee the Philippines following the Japanese invasion in 1941 but announced "I shall return."

MacArthur was made supreme commander of the **Allied** forces in the southwest Pacific in 1942. As promised, he led the forces in the "island hopping" campaign, bypassing major Japanese strongholds to retake the Philippines in 1944. MacArthur was made a general of the army in December 1944. He received the Japanese surrender in Tokyo in September 1945 and became supreme commander for the Allied powers in **Japan** and was effectively ruler of the country until 1951. In 1950, MacArthur became commander of the United Nations forces that responded to the attack of North Korea upon the South in what became the **Korean War**. When Chinese forces became involved, MacArthur called for all-out war and the use of **atomic** weapons. He was dismissed in 1951 because of his differences with President **Harry S. Truman** about atomic weapons and other issues but returned to the United States as a public hero. He made an emotional address to Congress on April 19, 1951, in which he said "Old soldiers never die. They just fade away." He clearly had presidential ambitions, but after playing a key role at the **Republican** National Convention in 1952, he failed to get the nomination and faded from the political scene. His book, *Reminiscences*, was published in 1964.

MACLEISH, ARCHIBALD (1892–1982). Born to a wealthy family in Glencoe, Illinois, poet Archibald MacLeish was educated at Hotchkiss Preparatory School. He graduated from Yale University in 1915 and entered Harvard Law School. His first poetry was published as *Tower of Ivory* in 1917. His studies were interrupted by the war, and he served in the artillery, seeing action on the Marne. After World War I, MacLeish returned to Harvard and graduated in 1919. After working as a lawyer in Boston, Massachusetts, in 1923 he left for France and did not return to the United States until 1929. He published a number of poems, including "Ars Poetica" (1926) and the collections *Pot of Earth* (1925) and *The Hamlet of A. MacLeish* (1928). From 1929 to 1938, MacLeish wrote for **Henry R. Luce**'s *Fortune* magazine. He wrote a number of successful plays, including *Panic* (1935), *Fall of the City* (1937), and *Air Raid* (1938), and produced a collection of photographs, *Land of the Free* (1938). His major achievements were the long poems, "Conquistador" (1932), for which he won the Pulitzer Prize in 1933, and his defense of democracy in "America Was Promises" (1939).

A strong supporter of **Franklin D. Roosevelt** and the **New Deal**, MacLeish was appointed to head the Library of Congress in 1939. He held the position for five years, and while also writing speeches for Roosevelt, he became head of the **Office of Facts and Figures** in 1941 and then assistant director of the **Office of War Information** from 1942 to 1943. In 1945, MacLeish was a delegate to the first meetings of the **United Nations Educational, Scientific, and Cultural Organization**.

After the war, MacLeish returned to poetry with *Act Five and Other Poems* (1948). He became professor of rhetoric at Harvard in 1949, a position he held until 1962, and in 1952 he won his second Pulitzer Prize for Poetry for *Collected Poems, 1917–1952*. He became president of the American Academy of Arts and Letters in 1953. His play, *J. B.*, won a third Pulitzer Prize in 1955. He continued to write poetry until his death, but he is remembered primarily as a writer of the 1930s. *See also* LITERATURE AND THEATER.

MAILER, NORMAN KINGSLEY (1923–2007). Born in Long Branch, New Jersey, and brought up in Brooklyn, New York, Norman Mailer graduated with a B.S. from Harvard in 1943 and was drafted into the army during **World War II**. The experience he gained during the war in the Philippines provided the basis for his best-selling novel *The Naked and the Dead* (1948), which established him as one of the leading postwar literary figures. He also developed a reputation for his outspoken and often outrageous celebration of pugnacious masculinity, reminiscent in some respects of **Ernest Hemingway**. Having failed to have his best seller made into a movie, Mailer next produced *Barbary Shore* (1951), a novel of **Cold War** politics and the film world.

He was a cofounder of the journal *The Village Voice* in 1955 and became one of the proponents of the "new journalism." Among his work is a collection of essays, *Advertisements for Myself* (1959); a nonfiction study of the 1967 antiwar march on the Pentagon, *Armies of the Night* (1968), which won him the Pulitzer Prize; and another nonfiction work, *The Executioner's Song* (1979), which also won a Pulitzer. Mailer wrote a total of 39 books, including 11 novels. His last novel, *The Castle in the Forest* (2007), is a fictional account of **Adolf Hitler**'s childhood. *See also* LITERATURE AND THEATER.

MANHATTAN PROJECT. The Manhattan Project was the name given to the scheme to develop the **atomic bomb** in the United States during **World War II**. Initiated under the **Office of Scientific Research and Development** in 1942, direction was placed in the hands of General **Leslie R. Groves**, and the project got its name from the location of the headquarters of the U.S. Army Corps of Engineers in New York, where the top-secret endeavor was based. The development of the bomb cost more than $2 billion, and research was carried out by more than 600,000 scientists and technicians working in different locations, including Hanford, Washington; Stagg Field, Chicago; and Oak Ridge, Tennessee. However, the main development of the bomb, under the leadership of **J. Robert Oppenheimer**, centered in Los Alamos, New Mexico. The first successful test was conducted at Alamogordo, New Mexico, on 16 July 1945, and the first bomb was dropped on **Hiroshima**, Japan, on 6 August 1945.

MAO ZEDONG (MAO TSE-TUNG) (1893–1976). Chinese communist leader Mao Zedong was born into a peasant background and trained as a teacher. He helped establish the Chinese Communist Party in 1921 and led an uprising against the national government led by **Chiang Kai-shek** in 1927 and established the Soviet Republic of **China**. When his forces were surrounded in 1934, he led them on the "Long March" more than 6,000 miles from southeast China to the north, where they were able to regroup. When war began with **Japan** in 1937, the communists united with the national government against their common enemy in an uneasy alliance. After the Japanese were defeated, fighting with the nationalists resumed, and Mao was victorious in 1949, establishing the People's Republic of China. Mao, known as Chairman Mao, was ruler of China until his death, taking the country through both the "Great Leap Forward" from 1958 to 1962 and the Cultural Revolution in 1966. Although a long-term opponent of the United States, in 1971 Mao invited President **Richard M. Nixon** to visit the following year and paved the way toward opening relations between the two nations.

MARCH ON WASHINGTON MOVEMENT (MOWM). In January 1941, black **trade union** leader **A. Philip Randolph** called upon **African Americans** to march on Washington on 1 July in protest against the continued discrimination against them in the armed forces and defense industries. When President **Franklin D. Roosevelt**'s administration failed to respond, other **civil rights** organizations, including the **National Association for Advancement of Colored People**, joined with Randolph to form MOWM. Faced with the threat of a protest numbering 10,000 or more, Roosevelt issued Executive Order 8802 on 27 June 1941 ordering an end to discrimination in defense industries and establishing a **Fair Employment Practices Committee** to investigate breaches of the order. MOWM held a series of rallies in New York City, Chicago, and St. Louis in 1942 but gradually declined in influence during **World War II**. It had, however, established an important precedent that was to be replicated in 1963.

MARSHALL, GEORGE CATLETT (1880–1959). Born in Uniontown, Pennsylvania, George Marshall was a graduate of Virginia Military Institute. He was commissioned in 1902 and served in the **Philippines** and then in the American Expeditionary Force during World War I helping plan several major offensives. After the war, he was aide-de-camp to General John J. Pershing, served in **China**, and was head of Fort Benning Infantry School in Georgia. Marshall was appointed army chief of staff in 1929 and served throughout **World War II** as President **Franklin D. Roosevelt**'s chief advisor. He was made a general of the army in December 1944 and oversaw the wartime expansion of the army before retiring in 1945. In November 1945, he was sent to China as ambassador in an unsuccessful attempt to resolve the conflict between **Chiang Kai-shek** and **Mao Zedong**.

In 1947, President **Harry S. Truman** appointed Marshall secretary of state, and he played a major role in the early **Cold War**, initiating the **European Recovery Program**, or Marshall Plan, to encourage economic recovery as a way of combating communism. He was secretary of defense from 1950 to 1951 and was involved in the dismissal of General **Douglas MacArthur** during the **Korean War**. Marshall retired in 1951 and was awarded the Nobel Peace Prize in 1953.

MARSHALL, THURGOOD (1908–1993). The first **African American** to serve as a **Supreme Court** justice, Thurgood Marshall was born Thoroughgood in Baltimore, Maryland. He shortened his name at an early age. He graduated from Lincoln University in 1930. Denied entrance to the University of Maryland Law School because he was African American, Marshall went instead to Howard University Law School in Washington, D.C., where he graduated in 1933. At Howard, he was to be strongly influenced by **Charles H. Houston**, who he succeeded as chief counsel to the **National Association for the Advancement of Colored People (NAACP)** in 1939. Marshall had already won a case in Baltimore (*Murray v. Pearson*) in 1936 that challenged segregation in the university system in Maryland. As NAACP counsel, he successfully led a long-term attack on segregation devised by Hamilton when he argued the cases *Smith v. Allwright* (1944), *Shelley v. Kraemer* (1948), *Sweatt v. Painter* (1950), and *McLaurin v. Oklahoma State Regents* (1950), culminating with *Brown v. Board of Education of Topeka* (1954). Marshall also helped draft the constitutions of the newly independent states of Ghana and Tanzania.

In 1961, President John F. Kennedy appointed Marshall to the U.S. Court of Appeals, and in 1965 President Lyndon Johnson made him the first African American solicitor general. Two years later he was appointed to the Supreme Court, where he took a firm liberal position supporting abortion rights, opposing the death penalty, and supporting individual civil liberties. He retired in 1991.

MARSHALL PLAN. *See* EUROPEAN RECOVERY PROGRAM (ERP).

MARTIN, JOSEPH WILLIAM (1884–1968). Born in Massachusetts, Joseph Martin began working as a newspaper reporter after leaving high school. He became the owner of a small-town paper in 1908 and an insurance agency in 1918. A **Republican**, Martin served in the Massachusetts house of representatives from 1911 to 1914 and in the senate from 1915 to 1917. He was executive secretary of the State Republican Committee from 1922 to 1925 and was elected to the federal House of Representatives in 1924, serving from 1925 until 1967. By 1939, Martin was house minority leader, and as an opponent of President **Franklin D. Roosevelt**'s **New Deal**, he helped establish the coalition with conservative **Democrats**. Roosevelt included him with **Bruce Barton** and **Hamilton Fish** in the critical mantra "Barton, Martin, and Fish" during the 1940 election campaign. Following the Republican victories in 1946, Martin became speaker of the house in 1947. He supported the **Taft-Hartley Act**, the **National Security Act**, and the **Marshall Plan**. He continued as minority leader in 1949 and became speaker once more from 1953 to 1955. He lost his place as minority leader in 1959 and failed to regain the nomination in the 1966 election.

MARX BROTHERS. The comedy team the Marx brothers, born to German Jewish immigrants in New York City, consisted of Chico (Leonard, 1887–1961), Harpo (Adolph/Arthur, 1888–1964), Groucho (Julius Henry, 1890–1977), Gummo (Milton, 1892–1977), and Zeppo (Herbert, 1901–1979). They began appearing in vaudeville from 1905 onward, originally as the musical act "The Three (or Four) Nightingales," but in 1912 they switched to comedy with a peculiar brand of slapstick and verbal humor. During World War I, they became "The Four Marx Brothers," and by the mid-1920s had established themselves as one of the country's funniest routines. Their Broadway shows, *Cocoanuts* and *Animal Crackers*, were made into films by Paramount Studios in 1929 and 1930. The shows followed by *Monkey Business* (1931), *Horse Feathers* (1932), and *Duck Soup* (1933), when they left Paramount and made *A Night at the Opera* (1935) and *A Day at the Races* (1937) with Metro-Goldwyn-Mayer (MGM). By this time, Gummo and Zeppo left to take up management. After *Room Service*, made for RKO in 1938, the Marx Brothers returned to MGM to make *At the Circus* (1939) and *The Big Store* (1941). They retired briefly but returned to show business to make *A Night in Casablanca* (1946) and *Love Happy* (1949) with United Artists. Afterward, the brothers went their separate ways and entered **radio** and theatrical management. Groucho had a very successful career hosting a quiz show on **radio**, *You Bet Your Life*, and then on **television** from 1947 to 1961. Several of the Marx Brothers' films are now regarded as classics of zany humor, rich with puns and ad-libs drawing upon the American immigrant background. *See also* CINEMA.

MCCARRAN, PATRICK (PAT) ANTHONY (1876–1954). Born the son of Irish immigrants in Reno, Nevada, Patrick ("Pat") McCarran attended the University of Nevada but did not complete his studies. He subsequently studied law part-time while farming and was admitted to the bar 1905. McCarran was elected to the Nevada state legislature as a **Democrat** in 1902 and was elected to the Nevada **Supreme Court** in 1913, where he served until 1918. He failed to win election to the U.S. Senate in 1916 and 1926 but was successful in 1932. He became increasingly conservative and opposed the **National Recovery Administration**, **Tennessee Valley Authority**, and **National Youth Administration** and the attempted "**court packing**" in 1937. Nonetheless, he was reelected three times and served until his death.

After **World War II**, McCarran was an outspoken critic of **Harry S. Truman**'s administration, and as a member of the "**China lobby**" he accused the president of selling out to the communists. In 1950, he cosponsored the **Internal Security Act** that contributed to the repressive atmosphere generated by **Joseph McCarthy**, and as chair of the Senate Internal Security Subcommittee, he was responsible for the attack on **Owen Lattimore**. He also supported the **Immigration and Nationality Act** of 1952 that maintained ethnic and racial quotas and incorporated stronger clauses for the exclusion and deportation of "dangerous aliens."

MCCARRAN-WALTER ACT. *See* IMMIGRATION AND NATIONALITY ACT.

MCCARRAN-WOOD ACT. *See* INTERNAL SECURITY ACT.

MCCARTHY, JOSEPH RAYMOND (1908–1957). Born on a farm near Appleton, Wisconsin, McCarthy left school at the age of 14 to raise poultry. When the business failed, he returned to high school, crammed four years of work into two terms, and entered Marquette University in Milwaukee. He gained a law degree in 1935 and established a legal practice in Wisconsin, but in 1937 he won election as a circuit judge. His victory was achieved partially by questioning the incumbent's good name, a tactic that was to become a hallmark of his later political career.

The youngest judge in Wisconsin, McCarthy gained a reputation for efficiency by dealing with business speedily and providing "quickie divorces." Although exempt from the draft as a judge, McCarthy enlisted in the marines in 1942 and spent **World War II** as an intelligence officer in the Pacific. He claimed to have suffered wounds as a "tail gunner" when his plane crash-landed under Japanese fire, but his only injury was a broken leg from falling onboard a ship. McCarthy also exaggerated the number of bombing missions he flew in. In 1946, he defeated incumbent **Robert M. La Follette Jr.** in the **Republican** senatorial primary election and then won the election.

McCarthy's early career in the U.S. Senate was undistinguished. He was nicknamed "Pepsi Cola Kid" for efforts on behalf of the soft drink company. In need of an issue with which to gain attention, he decided on the threat posed by communists. On 7 February 1950, in a speech to a Republican women's group in Wheeling, West Virginia, McCarthy announced that he had a list of names of known communists working in the State Department. The original number he gave was 205, but it later became 87. Elements of his speech came from an earlier speech by **Richard M. Nixon**, and the figures were based on government figures following the implementation of the **Federal Loyalty Program**. McCarthy was also given information by **J. Edgar Hoover**. He subsequently named Asian scholar **Owen Lattimore** as a "top Russian agent" but failed to produce a shred of evidence. McCarthy's charges were dismissed by a Senate investigation headed by **Millard Tydings** as a "fraud and a hoax," but it made little difference. The revelations in the **Alger Hiss** case gave McCarthy's claims substance, while both the **Soviet atomic bomb** test and the "loss" of **China** to communism in 1949 smacked to many people of betrayal. The outbreak of the **Korean War** in June 1950 also added weight to his views. Fellow Republicans were also happy to benefit from his attacks on the **Truman** administration as he denounced **Dean Acheson** for complicity in communist victories and accused General **George C. Marshall** of being "soft on communism."

Reelected in 1952, McCarthy became chair of the Senate Committee on Government Operations, and aided by his chief counsel, **Roy Cohn**, he held hearings in 1953 investigating several branches of government ranging from the Printing Office to the Foreign Service. However, in the fall of 1953, he began investigating the army, and his charges led to televised Senate hearings in 1954. In front of millions of viewers, McCarthy was revealed as a blustering bully by army counsel Joseph Welch. A documentary by respected **television** commentator **Edward R. Murrow** further discredited McCarthy. On 2 December 1954, the Senate passed a vote of censure against him for bringing the chamber "into dishonor and disrepute." McCarthy quickly faded from the public eye and died an alcoholic. **McCarthyism**, however, had had an enormous impact, and its effects lingered for some time. *See also* FEDERAL BUREAU OF INVESTIGATION (FBI); HOUSE UN-AMERICAN ACTIVITIES COMMITTEE (HUAC).

"MCCARTHYISM." "McCarthyism" was the name given to campaigns led by the **Republican** Senator **Joseph McCarthy** to root out communist sympathizers and agents in government, particularly the State Department. Although McCarthyism proper began with his infamous speech in Wheeling, West Virginia, in February 1950, in which he declared he had a list of names of known communist agents working in the State Department, the anticommunist hysteria had already begun in 1947 with the hearings held by the **House Un-American Activities Committee** in Hollywood, California, and in the case of **Alger Hiss**. McCarthyism provided easy answers to such questions as why America "lost" **China** to the communists and how the **Soviet Union** was able to develop its own **atomic bomb**. The mood was sustained by the outbreak of the **Korean War** and

McCarthy's own adept use of the media. The **McCarran Internal Security Act** in 1950 was intended to identify subversives, and McCarran's investigation of people like **John Stewart Service** in 1951 also was aimed at identifying "loyalty risks." The publication of *Red Channels* (1950) and the **blacklisting** of people named as communist sympathizers, ranging from **Charlie Chaplin** to **Aaron Copland** to **Edward G. Robinson** to **Orson Welles** merely added to the hysteria. However, the army hearings in which McCarthy was exposed before huge **television** audiences and the conclusion of the Korean War brought an end to the more extreme aspects of what many described as a "witch hunt"—the inspiration for **Arthur Miller**'s play about the Salem witch hunts, *The Crucible* in 1953. *See also* BLACKLIST; CINEMA; FEDERAL LOYALTY PROGRAM; HOLLYWOOD TEN; LATTIMORE, OWEN.

MCCLOY, JOHN JAY (1895–1989). Born in Philadelphia, Pennsylvania, John McCloy graduated from Amherst College in 1919 and Harvard Law School in 1921. He became a successful corporation lawyer and was counsel for Schechter Poultry Corp. in *Schechter Poultry Corp. v. United States* in 1935. He also traveled widely in Europe and acted as legal counsel for the German company I. G. Farben in the 1930s. He shared a box with **Adolf Hitler** and Herman Goering at the 1936 **Berlin** Olympics. From 1941 to 1945, McCloy was assistant secretary of war, where he worked with **Robert Lovett**. He was involved in a number of controversial decisions, supporting the internment of **Japanese Americans** and ruling out the bombing of railway lines and gas chambers in and around concentration camps. After the war, he became president of the World Bank from 1947 to 1949 and from 1949 to 1952 was the U.S. commissioner for Germany. He was implicated in protecting wanted Nazi war criminal Klaus Barbie and then criticized for reducing the sentences of jailed Nazis, including the arms manufacturer Alfred Krupp. McCloy was chair of Chase Manhattan Bank from 1953 to 1960, the Ford Foundation from 1958 to 1965, and the Council for Foreign Relations from 1954 to 1970. He acted as an adviser to presidents John F. Kennedy, Lyndon Johnson, **Richard M. Nixon**, Jimmy Carter, and Ronald Reagan.

MCGRANERY, JAMES PATRICK (1895-1962). Born in Philadelphia, Pennsylvania, James McGranery left school early and worked in the printing business before serving in the army during World War I. After the war, he went to Temple University Law School and graduated in 1928. After practicing law, McGranery, a **Democrat**, was elected to the U.S. House of Representatives in 1936 and held his seat for Pennsylvania until 1943, when he became assistant U.S. attorney general. In 1946, he was appointed federal judge in the Eastern Division of Pennsylvania. In 1952, McGranery was appointed to succeed **J. Howard McGrath** as attorney general, and he began the process of reviving the Justice Department before being replaced following the **Republican** election victory. He practiced law in Philadelphia and Washington, D.C., until his death.

MCGRATH, J. (JAMES) HOWARD (1903–1966). Born in Rhode Island and a graduate of Providence College in 1926 and Boston University in 1929, J. Howard McGrath passed the bar and practiced law in Rhode Island, where he became city solicitor in Central Falls. A **Democrat**, McGrath was U.S. attorney general for Rhode Island from 1935 to 1940 and was elected governor in 1940. He was re-elected in 1942 and 1944, was U.S. solicitor general from 1945 to 1946, and was elected to the U.S. Senate for Rhode Island in 1946. From 1947 to 1949, he was chair of the Democratic National Committee. In 1949, President **Harry S. Truman** appointed him U.S. attorney general, but his undistinguished leadership and failure to deal with issues of corruption and general incompetence led to his forced resignation in 1952. He subsequently practiced law and made an unsuccessful attempt to be reelected to the Senate in 1960.

MCLAURIN V. OKLAHOMA STATE REGENTS **(339 U.S. 637 1950).** George W. McLaurin was an **African American** student initially denied admission to the all-white University of Oklahoma but later admitted to study for his Ph.D. in education after suing to gain admission in 1948. He was kept segregated in classrooms, the library, and the cafeteria and filed another lawsuit claiming that he was denied his rights under the Fourteenth Amendment. His case was upheld by the **Supreme Court** on 5 June 1950. *See also MISSOURI*

EX REL. GAINES V. CANADA; SIPUEL V. OKLAHOMA BOARD OF REGENTS; SWEATT V. PAINTER.

MCNUTT, PAUL VORIES (1891–1955). Paul McNutt was born in Franklin, Indiana, and studied at Indian University and later Harvard Law School in 1913. He gained his law degree in 1916. During World War I, McNutt entered the army and served in the artillery in the United States. After the war, he became a member of the Indiana University Law School. A **Democrat**, McNutt was elected state governor in 1932. He introduced a series of reforms, including income tax, welfare reform, and state pensions. However, he was criticized because state employees were required to donate 2 percent of their wages to the Democratic Club, and hc also sanctioned the use of state troops during labor disputes.

President **Franklin D. Roosevelt** appointed McNutt high commissioner to the Philippines in 1937. He resigned in 1939 and became director of the **Federal Security Agency**. McNutt considered running for the presidential and then vice presidential nomination in 1940 but decided to remain at the agency and then became chair of the **War Manpower Commission**. After the war, he returned to the Philippines as high commissioner, where he helped see through the transition to independence. He then became ambassador to the country until 1947, when he returned to legal practice for eight years.

MCREYNOLDS, JAMES CLARK (1862–1946). James McReynolds graduated from Vanderbilt University in 1882 and the University of Virginia Law School in 1884. He established a law practice in Nashville, Tennessee, where he became a leading member of the legal, political, and social establishment. In 1903, McReynolds was hired by the Justice Department and was the chief prosecutor of the American Tobacco Trust. He resigned in 1911 but in 1913 was appointed attorney general by President Woodrow Wilson. He was again responsible for filing several major antitrust suits. In 1914, Wilson nominated McReynolds to serve on the **Supreme Court**. McReynolds did not play a particularly significant role on the court until the 1930s when he became a persistent critic of **Franklin D. Roosevelt** and an opponent of the extension of federal power under the **New Deal**. He spoke out angrily against the president following the attempted "**court packing**" in 1937 but increasingly found himself in a minority as the nature of the court changed. Critics regarded McReynolds as one of the worst and most conservative justices to serve on the court. In 1941, he retired in despair following Roosevelt's third election victory.

MEMORIAL DAY MASSACRE, 1937. During the steel strike of 1937 organized by the **Steel Workers' Organizing Committee**, some 300 pickets outside Republic Steel Corporation in South Chicago, Indiana, were fired on by police and company guards. A total of 10 strikers were killed and more than 100 were injured, and 22 policemen were also hurt. Many of those killed were shot in the back as they attempted to flee the violence. The incident did much to win public sympathy for the strikers and further added to the discreditability of businessmen. *See also* CONGRESS OF INDUSTRIAL ORGANIZATIONS (CIO); TRADE UNIONS.

MERCER, LUCY PAGE (1891–1948). Lucy Mercer was born in Washington, D.C., and had returned from a convent school in Austria when she became **Eleanor Roosevelt**'s personal secretary in 1914. In 1918, Eleanor discovered that **Franklin D. Roosevelt** was having an affair with Mercer. They agreed to maintain their marriage rather than divorce, and FDR agreed not see Mercer again. Mercer married Winthrop Rutherford in 1920. However, it seems likely that the relationship with FDR did continue, and after Rutherford's death in 1944, the president began to see Mercer once more. She was with him when he died.

MERCHANT MARINE ACT, 1936. The Merchant Marine Act of 29 June 1936 was intended to further national defense by providing for the development of an adequate and well-balanced merchant marine and granting federal funding to enable the building or chartering of vessels, provide subsidies for ship owners, and establish a training program for merchant seamen. A U.S. Merchant Marine Cadet Corps, which led to the Merchant Marine Academy in 1938, was established.

MERRIAM, CHARLES EDWARD (1874–1953). Political scientist Charles Merriam was born in Iowa. He earned his first degree from Lenox College in Hopkinton, Iowa, and then taught for a year, studied law at the State University of Iowa, and went to Columbia University, where he completed his M.A. in 1897 and his Ph.D. in 1900. Beginning in 1900 Merriam taught at the University of Chicago. He was active in Chicago's reform politics and was elected as **Republican** alderman to the city council in 1909 and served until 1917. Merriam ran for mayor in 1911 as a progressive Republican but was narrowly defeated. With **Harold Ickes**, he established the Illinois Progressive Party and backed first **Robert M. La Follette Sr.** and then Theodore Roosevelt.

Merriam worked as an examiner for the Chicago Aviation Board and later the Committee of Public Information during World War I. In 1918, he acted as a high commissioner of information in Rome. In the 1920s, Merriam built the Political Science Department at the University of Chicago into one of the leading schools of its kind. In 1923, he was one of the founders of the Social Science Research Council, and in 1925 he was elected president of the American Political Science Association. From 1929 to 1933, Merriam served on President **Herbert Hoover**'s Research Committee on Social Trends, which issued its report in 1933.

In 1933, President **Franklin D. Roosevelt** appointed Merriam to the National Planning Board (later the **National Resources Planning Board**) established under the **National Industrial Recovery Act**, and he remained one of the team of planners throughout the **New Deal**. He argued for reorganization of the executive branch and from 1936 to 1937 served on the President's Committee on Administrative Management that brought about restructuring in the **Reorganization Act** of 1939. Merriam continued to serve on the National Planning Board until it was abolished in 1943. His many publications include *American Political Ideas* (1920), *The American Political System* (1922), and *New Aspects of Politics* (1925), and in his roles in government he provided an important link between academia and public policy.

MIDWAY ISLANDS. The Midway Islands, in the north Pacific northwest of Hawaii, were the scene of the crucial naval battle between the United States and **Japan** during **World War II**. Lasting from 4 June to 7 June 1942 and coming a month after the Battle of the Coral Sea, the battle was a major victory for the U.S. Navy, as the Japanese lost four aircraft carriers and a heavy cruiser in addition to countless aircraft, while the United States lost only one carrier. From this point onward, the U.S. fleet was at least equal in strength to the Japanese and after the battle could take the offensive.

MILLER, (ALTON) GLENN (1904–1944). Born in Clarinda, Iowa, Glenn Miller learned to play the trombone at school, and after two years at the University of Colorado, he left in 1924 to join a band. After playing with a variety of different bands, he organized his own band in 1937. When this failed, Miller formed a second band in 1938 that began to achieve national success with weekly **radio** broadcasts and appearances in films. Their hit songs include "In the Mood," "Tuxedo Junction," "Pennsylvania 6-500," "Little Brown Jug," "Moonlight Serenade," and "Chattanooga Choo Choo." In 1942 the band broke up to contribute to the war effort, and Miller joined the Army Air Corps, where he formed a band to entertain the troops. In June 1944, the band went to England, where they performed and were broadcast on the Armed Forces Network. In December 1944, a plane carrying Miller to France disappeared without trace in bad weather and was assumed to have crashed at sea. The film *The Glenn Miller Story*, starring **James Stewart**, was a popular success in 1953. *See also* MUSIC.

MILLER, ARTHUR ASHER (1915–2005). Playwright Arthur Miller was born to German Jewish parents in New York City. He graduated from high school in 1933 and attended University of Michigan at Ann Arbor, where he abandoned the study of journalism for English **literature**. He wrote his first play, *No Villain*, in 1936, and his second, *Honors at Dawn*, in 1937 while still a student. Both were awarded prizes. Miller graduated in 1938 and joined the **Federal Theater Project**. When the project was halted by Congress, Miller found work in the Brooklyn Navy Yard and continued writing plays. His first Broadway play was *The Man Who Had All the Luck* in 1944, but it soon closed. In 1947, he produced the award-winning *All My Sons*, which was very successful. He built his own studio in

Roxbury, Connecticut, and it was there that *Death of a Salesman* was first performed in 1949. With Lee J. Cobb playing the role of Willie Loman, the play became an instant classic and was awarded the Pulitzer Prize.

In 1953, Miller wrote *The Crucible*, a play about the Salem witchcraft trials in the 17th century but that was clearly relevant to the United States during the period of **McCarthyism**. Miller was himself denied a passport in 1954, and following his marriage to Marilyn Monroe in 1956, he was called to appear before the **House Un-American Activities Committee**. Miller refused to name names and was fined and jailed for contempt of Congress. The conviction was overturned in 1958. In 1964, Miller produced *After the Fall*, based on the life of Monroe. They were divorced in 1961, and Monroe committed suicide in 1962. His most successful play after *Death of a Salesman* was *The Price* in 1968. His autobiography, *Time Bends*, was also well-received. *See also* LITERATURE AND THEATER.

MILLER, DORIE (1919–1943). Born in Waco, Texas, the son of black sharecroppers, Dorie Miller joined the navy as a mess attendant—one of the few positions in the navy open to **African Americans** at the time—in 1939. He was aboard the battleship USS *West Virginia* at **Pearl Harbor** when the Japanese attacked on 7 December 1941. Miller carried his wounded captain to safety and then, although not trained, manned a gun, which he kept firing until ordered to stop. When the black newspaper, the *Pittsburgh Courier*, heard the story in March 1942, it began to press for Miller to be awarded the Medal of Honor. Despite public and congressional support, the request was denied by Secretary of the Navy **Frank Knox**. However, President **Franklin D. Roosevelt** intervened, and he was awarded the Navy Cross. After spending some time in public relations for the navy, Miller returned to active service at sea. He was among the crew of the escort carrier *Liscombe Bay* lost when the ship was sunk in the Battle of Makin on 24 November 1943.

MILLER-TYDINGS ACT, 1937. Passed after the **National Recovery Administration** was been declared unconstitutional, the Miller-Tydings Act legalized price-maintenance agreements between manufacturers and retailers as a way of curbing competition and stabilizing prices where state fair trade laws existed. In 1951, the **Supreme Court** declared all such state laws unconstitutional.

MINTON, SHERMAN (1890–1965). Born in Georgetown, Indiana, Sherman Minton graduated from Indiana University in 1915 and Yale Law School in 1916 and established a law practice in Albany, Indiana. He served in the infantry in France during World War I and afterward returned to Albany. In 1933, he joined the Indiana Public Service Commission and in 1934 was elected as a **Democrat** to the U.S. Senate. A supporter of **Franklin D. Roosevelt**, Minton backed the president during the "**court packing**" controversy. He also supported Roosevelt's **foreign policy** initiatives. As a result he was defeated in the elections of 1940 and in 1941 was appointed to the Court of Appeals, Seventh Circuit. In 1949, President **Harry S. Truman** appointed Minton to the **Supreme Court** following the death of Justice **Wiley B. Rutledge**. Minton did not prove as liberal a justice as had been anticipated. He generally voted to uphold federal initiatives like the **Federal Loyalty Program** and elected to sustain the convictions in *Dennis v. United States* in 1951. He also supported the administration in *Youngstown Sheet & Tube Co. v. Sawyer* in 1952. Minton did, however, back measures against racial discrimination in *Shelley v. Kraemer* in 1948, *Sweatt v. Painter* in 1950, and the landmark *Brown v. Board of Education of Topeka* declaring segregation in schools unconstitutional in 1954. He retired due to ill-health in 1956.

***MISSOURI EX REL. GAINES V. CANADA* (305 U.S. 337, 1938).** The state of Missouri provided separate educational facilities for white and black Americans. However, it did not have a separate law school. When an **African American** Lloyd Gaines applied for entry to the Missouri Law School in 1936, he was denied. Gaines sued the school (Canada was the name of the registrar), and on 12 December 1938 the **Supreme Court** ruled six to two that he had been denied his rights under the Fourteenth Amendment and that the state had to provide equal in-state education. *See also MCLAURIN V. OKLAHOMA STATE REGENTS; MORGAN V. COMMONWEALTH OF VIRGINIA; SIPUEL V. OKLAHOMA BOARD OF REGENTS; SWEATT V. PAINTER.*

MITCHELL, ARTHUR WERGS (1883–1968). Born in Lafayette, Alabama, Arthur Mitchell worked his way through Tuskegee Institute and qualified as a teacher. He established Armstrong Agricultural School in West Butler, Alabama, in 1908 and served in the infantry during World War I. He studied briefly at Columbia University and was admitted to the bar. He began to practice law in Washington, D.C., in 1927 but moved to Chicago in 1929. A lifelong **Republican,** Mitchell switched to the **Democratic Party** and in 1935 became the first **African American** Democratic congressman when, supported by Mayor **Edward Kelly**, he defeated Oscar De Priest. His most notable action came in 1937 after he was forced to give up a first-class seat in a train crossing into Arkansas and move to the segregated "Jim Crow" car. In 1941, Mitchell took the case all the way to the **Supreme Court**, which ruled that he had been denied equal treatment. A number of rail companies abandoned segregation for first-class customers, but segregated coaches remained for other passengers until 1956. After he chose not to stand for reelection in 1942, Mitchell was succeeded by **William L. Dawson**.

MITCHELL, MARGARET MUNNERLY (1900–1949). Author Margaret Mitchell was born and raised in Atlanta, Georgia. She attended Smith College in 1918 but left the following year after the death of her mother. From 1922 to 1926, Mitchell wrote for the *Atlanta Journal* Sunday magazine. In 1936, she wrote the romantic epic novel of the American Civil War and Reconstruction, *Gone with the Wind*. An enormous best seller, the book won her the Pulitzer Prize in 1937. The 1939 film based on the book produced by David O. Selznick and starring English actress Vivien Leigh as Scarlett O'Hara and **Clark Gable** as Rhett Butler won eight Oscars. Before she had the opportunity to publish more, Mitchell was struck and killed by an automobile in Atlanta. *See also* CINEMA; LITERATURE AND THEATER.

MITCHELL, WESLEY CLAIR (1874–1948). After obtaining his Ph.D. at the University of Chicago in 1899, Wesley Mitchell taught at the University of California, Columbia University, and the New School for Social Research. During World War I, he served as head of the Price Section of the War Industries Board. Mitchell founded the National Bureau of Economic Research in 1920 to undertake quantitative studies of the U.S. business cycle. He published a number of key texts, including two works entitled *Business Cycles* (1913, 1927). In 1921, he took part in the President's Unemployment Conference. He succeeded **Charles Merriam** as chair of the Social Science Research Council in 1927, led the group that produced the president's *Report on Recent Economic Changes* (1929), and chaired President **Herbert Hoover**'s Research Committee on Social Trends, which reported in 1933. That year Mitchell was appointed to the National Planning Board created to serve the **Public Works Administration**. He resigned in 1935 to concentrate on his work with the National Bureau of Economic Research. He was the author of several books, including *Business Cycles* (1913); *The Art of Spending Money* (1927); and with Arthur Burns, *Reassessing Business Cycles* (1946). Mitchell was president of the American Association for the Advancement of Science in 1938 and the Academy of Political Science from 1940 to 1941. Alongside Merriam, he showed the element of continuity in thinking about planning between World War I and the **New Deal**.

MOLEY, RAYMOND (1886–1975). Raymond Moley was born in Ohio, and after graduating from Baldwin-Wallace College in 1906, he became superintendent of schools in Olmstead Falls, Ohio. After gaining a master's degree from Oberlin College in 1913, Moley taught at Western Reserve University from 1916 to 1919. He was awarded a Ph.D. from Columbia University in 1918, and he taught government there beginning in 1923 and then public law from 1928 to 1954. He wrote a number of books, including *Lessons in American Citizenship* (1917), *The State Movement for Efficiency and Economy* (1918), and *Parties, Politics, and People* (1921). His work as research director of the New York State Crime Commission in 1926 and 1927 and for the New York State Commission on the Administration of Justice from 1931 to 1933 brought him to the attention of **Samuel I. Rosenman**, who asked him to form the group of advisers in 1932 that became known as the "**Brain Trust**" in President **Franklin D. Roosevelt**'s **New Deal**. Moley was made assistant secretary of state in 1933.

Moley made a significant contribution to the New Deal as a presidential speechwriter, shaping early legislation, bringing talented individuals into the administration, and acting as a publicist for the New

Deal through his role as editor of the magazine *Today*. However, Moley's relationship with the president deteriorated after Roosevelt undermined the commitments he made at the **London Economic Conference** on currency stabilization. Furthermore, he disagreed with the **Wealth Tax Act** of 1935 and the apparent shift to the left in the "**Second New Deal**." Critical of the attempt at "**court packing**" in 1937, Moley joined the **Republican Party** and campaigned on behalf of **Wendell Willkie** in 1940. He then returned to Columbia University and wrote several more books on government and politics.

MORGAN, ARTHUR ERNEST (1878–1975). Born in Cincinnati, Ohio, Arthur Morgan was raised in Minnesota. After leaving high school, he learned engineering from his father and became head of a successful engineering company by 1915. He became a specialist in flood control and advised state governments on drainage and irrigation projects. From 1920 to 1936, Morgan was president of Antioch College, although he was on leave for the last three years there after being appointed chair of the **Tennessee Valley Authority (TVA)** by President **Franklin D. Roosevelt**. However, conflicts with other directors of the TVA, particularly Harcourt Morgan and **David E. Lilienthal**, led Morgan to publicly criticize the TVA for not doing enough in terms of regional planning. In 1938, he was fired and replaced by Harcourt Morgan. Arthur Morgan subsequently became president of Community Service, Inc., and of a housing corporation in Ohio. In 1950, he served as temporary chair of the Conciliation and Arbitration Board for U.S. Steel and the **Congress of Industrial Organizations**. Morgan also wrote several books, including *The Small Community* (1942), *Small Community Economics* (1945), *Edward Bellamy* (1945), *The Community of the Future* (1956), and *The Making of the TVA* (1974).

MORGAN V. COMMONWEALTH OF VIRGINIA (328 U.S. 373 1946). In 1946, an **African American** woman, Irene Morgan, was arrested for refusing to give up her seat and move to the segregated area on a bus traveling from Virginia to Baltimore, Maryland. She was fined for failing to obey the segregation laws, which she denied, and for resisting arrest, to which she pleaded guilty. Backed by the **National Association for the Advancement of Colored People** and the association's lawyer, **Thurgood Marshall**, Morgan appealed the issue of segregation on the grounds that her journey involved interstate travel. The **Supreme Court** ruled by 7–1 in her favor on the grounds that no state law "can reach beyond its border" and therefore that segregation in interstate transportation was unconstitutional. In 1947, 16 members of the Congress of Racial Equality (CORE) rode into the South on buses on a "journey of reconciliation" to test the law. Twelve of them were arrested, although in most cases no charges were brought against them and little attention was given to the events. However, in 1961 CORE launched "Freedom Rides" into the South that received national and international coverage and challenged the persistence of segregation in interstate transportation. *See also MCLAURIN V. OKLAHOMA STATE REGENTS; MISSOURI EX REL. GAINES V. CANADA; SIPUEL V. OKLAHOMA BOARD OF REGENTS; SWEATT V. PAINTER.*

MORGENTHAU, HENRY, JR. (1891–1967). Henry Morgenthau was born into a wealthy Jewish family in New York City and educated at Phillips Exeter Academy, Sachs Collegiate Institute, and Cornell University, but he left the university after three years in 1913 without graduating. During World War I, Morgenthau worked in the Food Administration. Having studied **agriculture** and purchased farmland in New York, from 1922 onward he published the farm journal *American Agriculturalist*. A personal friend of **Franklin D. Roosevelt**, Morgenthau was appointed chair of the New York Agricultural Advisory Commission in 1928 and commissioner on conservation in 1930. When Roosevelt became president, Morgenthau became chair of the Federal Farm Board (which had been created in 1929) and helped create the **Farm Credit Administration**. At the start of 1934 he became secretary of the treasury, a post he held until 1945.

As secretary of the treasury, Morgenthau defended the dollar by buying and selling foreign currencies, gold, and dollars. In this way, he helped establish the dollar as the strongest currency by 1938. Although a fiscal conservative, he accepted deficit spending and managed by a double-budget system, a normal budget and emergency budget that provided for various **New Deal** agencies. During **World War II**, he worked to finance the war effort through the sale of **war bonds** that raised more than $200 billion. Morgenthau was also involved in planning for the postwar settlement. He proposed, in what became known as the "Morgenthau Plan," that **Germany** be stripped of industrial resources and turned solely into an agricultural producer, a plan that was never adopted. Morgenthau resigned shortly after Roosevelt's death and devoted himself to fundraising for Jewish causes. He became chair of the United Jewish Appeal from 1947 to 1950 and chair of the American Financial and Development Corporation for **Israel** from 1951 to 1954.

MOSCOW CONFERENCE, 1943. The Moscow Conference was a meeting of the foreign ministers of **Great Britain**, the United States, and the **Soviet Union** in 1943 where it was agreed that an international organization should be established to maintain peace in the postwar world. Attended by **Cordell Hull**, the conference also secured **Joseph Stalin**'s agreement to enter the war against **Japan** once the Nazis were defeated in Europe.

MUNDT, KARL EARL (1900–1974). Karl Mundt was born in South Dakota. He obtained a B.A. from Carleton College in 1923 and an M.A. from Columbia University in 1927. After several years as a teacher, he joined his father in the family loan and investment company from 1927 to 1936. A **Republican**, he was elected to the U.S. House of Representatives for South Dakota in 1938. A firm isolationist, Mundt opposed **Selective Service** and **Lend-Lease**. In 1948, he was appointed to fill the vacant U.S. Senate seat left by the resignation of Vera Bushfield. He was elected in his own right and held the seat until shortly before his death. As a member of the **House Un-American Activities Committee (HUAC)**, Mundt played a leading role in the case of **Alger Hiss**. He also tried, unsuccessfully, to get HUAC to investigate the Ku Klux Klan. With **Richard M. Nixon**, Mundt drafted a version of what was to become the McCarran Act, or the **Internal Security Act** of 1950. In 1954, he chaired the Army-McCarthy hearings that eventually led to **Joseph McCarthy**'s downfall. *See also* MCCARTHY, JOSEPH RAYMOND.

MUNI, PAUL (1895–1967). Actor Paul Muni was born Meshilem Meier Weisenfreund in Galicia (now Ukraine). His family immigrated to the United States in 1902, and Muni first appeared on stage in Yiddish **theater** in 1907. His first Broadway appearance was in *We Americans* in 1924. He received an Oscar nomination for his role in *The Valiant* (1929) and returned to Broadway before starring in the role of the gangster *Scarface* in 1932. That same year, he appeared in **Mervyn Leroy**'s powerful study of the southern convict system set against the harsh backdrop of the **Great Depression**, *I Am a Fugitive from a Chain Gang*, for which he received an Academy Award nomination. Muni made several biographical films, including *The Story of Louis Pasteur* (1936), *The Life of Emile Zola* (1937), and *Juarez* (1939). His portrayal of Pasteur won him an Oscar. In 1937, Muni played a Chinese farmer in the film version of **Pearl S. Buck**'s *The Good Earth*. Muni only made six more films, his final one being *The Last Angry Man* in 1959. He did, however, continue to work on the stage and won a Tony Award in 1955 for his role in *Inherit the Wind*. *See also* CINEMA.

MURPHY, FRANK (FRANCIS) WILLIAM (1890–1949). Born in Harbor Beach, Michigan, Frank Murphy was a graduate of the University of Michigan in 1912 and the University of Michigan Law School in1914. He served in the army in France during World War I and after the war was appointed U.S. attorney for the Eastern District of Michigan. He returned to private practice in 1920, taught law at the University of Detroit, and became a judge in the recorder's court in Detroit in 1923. A member of the **Democratic Party**, in 1930 Murphy was elected mayor of Detroit. He introduced work relief programs to combat the high unemployment rate in the city and was reelected in 1932. In 1933, he was appointed governor-general of the Philippines, where he supported moves toward independence but left the post to become governor of Michigan in 1936.

A supporter of President **Franklin D. Roosevelt** and the **New Deal**, Murphy introduced a "Little New Deal" in Michigan, reforming the civil service, improving workmen's compensation, and increasing spending on education. He refused to use state troops to intervene in the **"sit-down strikes"** in the automobile industry in 1937. Murphy was defeated in the 1938 election. In 1939, he was appointed U.S. attorney general, and he led the investigation that destroyed the Pendergast machine in Kansas City. In 1940, Roosevelt appointed Murphy to the **Supreme Court**, where he became one of the more liberal justices, particularly on **civil rights** issues. He was critical of the internment of **Japanese Americans** and dissented in the cases of *Hirabayashi v. United States* and *Korematsu v. United States*. Murphy's career was cut short by heart disease, and he died of a coronary thrombosis.

MURRAY, PHILIP (1886–1952). Philip Murray was born the son of a miner in Scotland and came to the United States with his family in 1902. He became a naturalized citizen in 1911. He worked as a miner near Pittsburgh, Pennsylvania, and became president of the local district of the United Mine Workers Union (UMW) in 1916. By 1920 he was vice president of the union under **John L. Lewis.** Murray sat on the National War Labor Board and National Coal Production Committee during World War I. In the 1930s, he supported President **Franklin D. Roosevelt** and the **New Deal** and was a member of the board of the **National Recovery Administration (NRA)**. In 1935, Murray, Lewis, and **Sidney Hillman** were the leading forces in the formation of the Committee for Industrial Organizations within the **American Federation of Labor**. Murray became president of the **Congress of Industrial Organizations** in 1940.

In 1936, Murray took charge of leading the **Steel Workers' Organizing Committee** that secured recognition from "Big Steel," including the U.S. Steel Corporation, in 1937. "**Little Steel**" held out until 1941. From 1942 to 1952, Murray was president of United Steel Workers of America (USWA). By then, differences with Lewis, particularly with regard to the "no-strike pledge" during **World War II**, had led to his expulsion from the UMW. During the war, Murray supported the **Fair Employment Practices Committee** and called for the integration of black workers in **trade unions** and employment. After the war, he opposed the **Taft-Hartley Act** and worked to redefine some of its applications. Although a close adviser to **Harry S. Truman**, Murray was involved in a confrontation with the president in 1952 when Truman threatened to nationalize the steel industry to prevent a strike. When the **Supreme Court** ruled against the president in *Youngstown Sheet & Tube Co. v. Sawyer*, Murray led the USWA on strike. Although he was forced to end the strike after 51 days, agreement was reached in 1952 recognizing some of the union's demands. It was the last major event in Murray's life.

MURROW, EDWARD ROSCOE (R.) (1908–1965). Famous **radio** and **television** broadcast journalist Edward R. Murrow was born Egbert Roscoe Murrow in Greensboro, North Carolina. Murrow's family later moved to Washington, where he attended the Washington State University. He joined the CBS network as director of talks and education in 1935 and in 1937 became director of the CBS European Bureau. It was at the bureau that Murrow began to establish his reputation for clear, accurate, on-the-spot reporting marked by a sense of integrity and social responsibility. He appointed **William L. Shirer** to join the bureau, and together they broadcast radio reports on events in Europe leading up to the outbreak of **World War II**, including the Anschluss of 1938, the Sudeten crisis, and the invasion of Poland. Murrow became famous for his reports from London during the Blitz, which began "This is London" and ended with the catch-phrase "Goodnight and good luck" that became his hallmark.

After the war, Murrow returned to the United States, where he briefly served as vice president of CBS and director of public affairs. However, he returned to broadcasting on radio and television in 1947, and from 1950 to 1951 he hosted *Hear It Now* and from 1952 to 1958 the award-winning television program *See It Now*. In March and April 1954, Murrow was responsible for a series of programs exposing Senator **Joseph McCarthy**'s methods to the viewing public. Although it is not clear what effect the programs had, coupled with the televised Army-McCarthy hearings, they contributed to McCarthy's downfall. The programs later became the subject of the Hollywood movie *Good Night and Good Luck* (2006). *See It Now* lost its advertising sponsorship and was taken off the air in 1958.

In addition to programs with political content, Murrow also hosted the lighter Person to Person series of conversations with celebrities from 1953 to 1959. In 1961, President John F. Kennedy appointed him director of the U.S. Information Agency, a position he held until 1964. Murrow was awarded the presidential Medal of Freedom in 1964 and given a posthumous knighthood by the British government in 1965.

MUSIC. Music of the 1930s often directly reflected the impact of the **Great Depression**, as best summed up by **Yip Harburg**'s song "Brother Can You Spare a Dime?" (1932) and recorded by a number of singers, including **Bing Crosby**. Folk singer **Woody Guthrie**

captured the experience of the "**Okies**" in his many "**Dust Bowl** ballads" but also provided reaffirmation with "This Land Is Our Land" (1940). Songs from film and Broadway musicals were also successful and provided a vehicle for several of **Irving Berlin, George** and **Ira Gershwin**, and **Cole Porter**'s compositions. Musicals continued to be successful during **World War II**, and in *Oklahoma* and *Carousel*, popular songwriters **Rodgers** and **Hammerstein** captured the joyful aspects of America's rural experience in the same way that serious composer **Aaron Copland** looked to the past for inspiration in his celebration of American values. The 1944 hit musical *Meet Me in St. Louis*, starring **Judy Garland**, also presented a nostalgic image of bygone America.

The big band sound continued with Tommy Dorsey, **Duke Ellington, Benny Goodman**, and **Glenn Miller**, who's "Don't Sit under the Apple Tree (with Anyone Else but Me)" captured the hopes of many departing servicemen during **World War II**. The big hit of the war years was Berlin's nostalgic "White Christmas" from the movie *Holiday Inn* (1942), sung by Crosby. Berlin's "God Bless America" also became widely known during the war years. The precursors of the screaming fans of later years were the "bobby-soxers," who mobbed **Frank Sinatra** during his performances in the early 1940s. The Andrews Sisters (Patty, Maxene, and Laverne) attracted a more sedate audience, but like many other stars, they entertained troops on **United Service Organizations** tours during the war and had huge hits with "I'll Be With You in Apple Blossom Time" (1940) and "I Can Dream Can't I?" (1945).

Other forms of music, particularly jazz, were developing in new directions. Led by **African American** musicians like **Louis Armstrong**, in the late 1930s there was a revival of the "Dixieland" jazz of the 1920s, while during the 1940s more avant-garde black musicians, most notably Charlie Parker, Thelonius Monk, Dizzie Gillespie, and Miles Davis, were developing bepop and "cool" jazz. Blues was emerging as the urban, electrified rhythm 'n' blues and establishing the foundations on which rock 'n' roll would be built in the 1950s. *See also* ANDERSON, MARIAN; CANTOR, EDDIE; CINEMA; FEDERAL MUSIC PROJECT; HART, LORENZ MILTON; HAYES, ROLAND; IVES, CHARLES EDWARD; ROBESON, PAUL LEROY BUSTILL; VALLEE, RUDY.

– N –

NAGASAKI. Nagasaki was the large seaport and center of war production on the west coast of Kyushu, **Japan**, where the second **atomic bomb** was dropped from a U.S. Air Force B-29 bomber on 9 August 1945. The original choice of target, Kokura, had been obscured by clouds forcing the aircrew to turn to Nagasaki as the alternative. The bomb, named "Fat Man," was bigger than the one dropped on **Hiroshima**, but damage was limited by the proximity of the sea and a mountain range. Nonetheless, 2.6 square miles of city were totally destroyed and 80,000 people were killed. The following day, the Japanese government announced that it would accept the terms for surrender outlined at the **Potsdam conference**.

NATIONAL ASSOCIATION FOR THE ADVANCEMENT OF COLORED PEOPLE (NAACP). Formed in 1910 as an outgrowth of the 1909 National Negro Congress called by white reformers and journalists Oswald Garrison Villard, Mary White Ovington, and William Walling following the race riot in Springfield, Illinois, the NAACP became the leading **civil rights** organization in the United States until the 1950s. With its monthly journal *The Crisis*, edited by **African American** W. E. B. Du Bois, the NAACP quickly grew in size and by 1919 had a membership of 90,000. Although many of the leading officers were white, after World War I the organization was increasingly influenced by its African American national secretary, James Weldon Johnson, and field secretary, **Walter White**. The association organized a silent protest following the East St. Louis Riot in 1917, led the campaign against lynching in the 1920s, and in the 1930s took part in the defense of the **Scottsboro Boys**. It also had some success influencing President **Franklin D. Roosevelt**'s **New Deal**, particularly through **Eleanor Roosevelt**.

In 1939, the NAACP established a legal defense and educational fund that began the legal challenges to segregation that culminated in the *Brown v. Board of Education of Topeka* decision in 1954. That year, the association also began to work with other groups to challenge segregation and discrimination in national defense, and in 1941 it supported **A. Philip Randolph**'s call for a **March on Washington** that led to the creation of the **Fair Employment Practices Commit-**

tee. After **Pearl Harbor**, the NAACP supported the war effort but maintained the pressure for full inclusion of African Americans. During the war, **Walter White** toured U.S. Army bases in Europe and reported on discrimination. The membership of the NAACP grew from about 21,000 in 1930 to 54,000 by 1940. By the end of **World War II**, it had reached more than 500,000.

After the war, the organization continued to support cases testing segregation in education, support voter registration movements in the South, and encourage President **Harry S. Truman** to speak out against racial violence. However, the NAACP suffered to some extent during the **Cold War** in that it was often accused by its opponents of being influenced by communism. In attempting to answer such charges, the organization tended to avoid association with radical ideas or individuals. By the mid-1950s, it was seen by the younger generation of African Americans as established and rather conservative. It was supplanted to some extent by new groups like the Southern Christian Leadership Conference, Student Nonviolent Coordinating Committee, and Congress of Racial Equality (CORE). However, it provided much needed legal and financial support to these groups during the 1960s, and while they tended to disappear after 1973, the NAACP remained as an influential voice for black Americans.

NATIONAL ASSOCIATION OF MANUFACTURERS (NAM). Formed in 1895 in Cincinnati, Ohio, originally with 583 companies involved, NAM became one of the most influential business organizations in the United States. During World War I and immediately afterward, it pressed for the "open shop" and supported the "American Plan" as a way of resisting **trade union** growth. Membership in the mid-1920s was 5,350, but it fell during the **Great Depression** to less than 1,500. Led by Robert L. Lund, NAM opposed much of the **New Deal** and spent more than $15 million between 1934 and 1947 on a media campaign against what it saw as antibusiness policies. From the mid-1930s, it grew in strength again to about 3,000 members. NAM consistently campaigned against **Franklin D. Roosevelt**. After **World War II**, the association lobbied strongly in support of the **Taft-Hartley Act** and helped ensure that it passed over **Harry S. Truman**'s veto. By 1952, its membership was approximately 16,000 companies. It continues to be a significant voice for business.

NATIONAL DEFENSE ADVISORY COMMISSION (NDAC). As entry into **World War II** seemed ever more likely President **Franklin D. Roosevelt** took preliminary steps in war mobilization, appointing a National Defense Advisory Commission of experts to advise the Council of National Defense—the secretaries of agriculture, commerce, labor, interior, navy, and war—on matters of industrial production, raw materials, employment, farm products, transportation, consumer protection, and price controls. However, the body lacked central control and coordination and gave way in January 1941 to the **Office of Production Management** under the joint direction of **Sidney Hillman** and **William Knudsen**.

NATIONAL FARMERS' UNION (NFU). First organized in 1902 in Texas to further cooperative action and nonpartisan political action on behalf of farmers, the NFU grew rapidly in the South. It flourished in the 1920s and together with the **American Farm Bureau Federation** was one of the most important farm bodies. The NFU called for protection to guarantee farmers their costs of production and a fair profit. Although the **Agricultural Adjustment Act** did not deliver this but provided instead for parity, the NFU largely supported Roosevelt's **New Deal** program, though some more militant elements within the organization supported the Farm Holiday movement. As the NFU focused on the needs of smaller farmers, sharecroppers, and tenant farmers, it was generally happy with such New Deal agencies as the **Resettlement Administration** and later the **Farm Security Administration**. Its relations with both the Roosevelt and **Truman** administrations were generally good. *See also* AGRICULTURE.

NATIONAL HOUSING ACT, 1934. The National Housing Act of 1934 established the **Federal Housing Administration** to insure banks, mortgage providers, and building and loan associations to enable them to make loans for home and farm building or improvement. *See also* NATIONAL HOUSING ACT, 1937; NATIONAL HOUSING ACT, 1949.

NATIONAL HOUSING ACT, 1937. Passed in 1937 and also known as the Wagner-Steagall Act, the National Housing Act of 1937 was intended to deal with the issue of poor housing and provide for slum clearance. It established the **United States Housing Authority (USHA)** to provide loans to states, local communities, and municipal housing authorities. By 1941, USHA had assisted in the construction of some 120,000 low-income family housing units. In 1942, the authority became the Federal Public Housing Authority within a newly created **National Housing Agency**. *See also* NATIONAL HOUSING ACT, 1934; NATIONAL HOUSING ACT, 1949.

NATIONAL HOUSING ACT, 1949. Passed on 15 July 1949, the National Housing Act of 1949 provided $1.5 billion for slum clearance and proposed a public housing development of 810,000 new homes. Only about 300,000 were built. *See also* NATIONAL HOUSING ACT, 1934; NATIONAL HOUSING ACT, 1937.

NATIONAL HOUSING AGENCY (NHA). The NHA was established in 1942 to bring together the various federal housing bodies, principally the Federal Housing Authority, **Federal Housing Administration (FHA)**, and Federal Home Loan Bank Administration. It was also intended to provide housing for defense workers during **World War II**. The agency spent $2.3 billion for this purpose and built 2 million units, albeit many of them of a temporary nature. In 1949, the NHA was abolished and its functions were assumed by the National Housing and Home Finance Agency. *See also* NATIONAL HOUSING ACT, 1934; NATIONAL HOUSING ACT, 1937.

NATIONAL INDUSTRIAL RECOVERY ACT (NIRA), 1933. One of the cornerstones of the **New Deal** in its "**First Hundred Days**," NIRA was intended to bring about industrial recovery by establishing codes of fair competition that would provide manufacturers with a decent price for their goods and provide workers with a fair wage. The act suspended antitrust legislation to allow industries within the same area to agree on voluntary codes, setting prices and wages. Section 7 guaranteed workers the right to organize. Some 2 million employers agreed on approximately 500 codes. Almost 22 million workers came under these agreements.

Title II of the act established an emergency **Public Works Administration** with $3.3 billion to provide work relief through the construction of dams, public buildings, roads, airports, and other projects. This was to be partially funded by excess profits taxes authorized under Title III. A **National Recovery Administration (NRA)**, under **Hugh Johnson**, was established to oversee the operation of the act. The codes were approved by the NRA with the famous **Blue Eagle** symbol. In 1935, the **Supreme Court** ruled NIRA unconstitutional in *Schechter Poultry Corp. v. United States*. It was not replaced and has largely been judged a failure by historians.

NATIONAL LABOR BOARD (NLB). Established in 1933 to ensure that the labor-related aspects of the **National Industrial Recovery Act (NIRA)** were applied, the NLB was chaired by Senator **Robert F. Wagner** and included labor and business representatives. It helped settle several industrial strikes but increasingly faced criticism from employers and organizations like the **National Association of Manufacturers**. When companies decided to ignore clause 7(a) of NIRA, the board had no power. When General Motors made clear that it would not cooperate when faced with a dispute, President **Franklin D. Roosevelt** bypassed the board. The NLB was abolished in 1934 by executive order. It was replaced by the **National Labor Relations Board**.

NATIONAL LABOR RELATIONS ACT, 1935. Also known as the Wagner Act after its sponsor Senator **Robert F. Wagner**, the National Labor Relations Act was signed by President **Franklin D. Roosevelt** on 5 July 1935. It was intended as an alternative to the labor clauses in Section 7(a) of the **National Industrial Recovery Act**, which the **Supreme Court** declared unconstitutional in 1935, and it provided for free collective bargaining and recognition of **trade unions**. It prohibited strike breaking, "yellow dog" contracts, **blacklisting**, and other antiunion measures. The act established a three-man **National Labor Relations Board** to investigate and prevent unfair labor practices, determine employees' representatives in collective bargaining, and mediate in labor disputes. The act served as an enormous encouragement to trade unions, whose strength increased almost three-fold in the 1930s.

NATIONAL LABOR RELATIONS BOARD (NLRB). The NLRB was a three-man board established by the **National Labor Relations**

Act in 1935. It was responsible for overseeing secret ballots of employees to decide whether they wanted union representation and also to prevent and remedy unfair labor practices. It replaced the defunct **National Labor Board (NLB)**. President **Franklin D. Roosevelt** appointed J. Warren Madden of the University of Pittsburgh; Edwin S. Smith, a former commissioner of labor for Massachusetts and previous member of the NLB; and John M. Carmody, an expert in labor relations and former chief engineer in the **Civil Works Administration**. Increasingly attacked by political opponents and by such groups as the **National Association of Manufacturers** and conservative **trade unions** in the **American Federation of Labor**, the NLRB's powers were reduced by the **Taft-Hartley Act** in 1947. However, it continues to work as an important intermediary in employer-labor relations.

NATIONAL LABOR RELATIONS BOARD V. JONES & LAUGHLIN STEEL CORP. (301 U.S. 1 1937). In the case *National Labor Relations Board v. Jones & Laughlin Steel Corp.* on 12 April 1937, the **Supreme Court** upheld the constitutionality of the **National Labor Relations Act**. The **National Labor Relations Board (NLRB)** had found the Jones & Laughlin Steel Corp. guilty of unfair labor practices in firing union members and had ordered it to cease and desist. When the company refused to comply, the NLRB took them to court, and the case eventually reached the Supreme Court. The court upheld the right of Congress to legislate on labor relations and extended the meaning of interstate commerce in arguing that some intrastate commerce could be within a "stream" or "flow" of interstate commerce and therefore crucial to it. *See also* TRADE UNIONS.

NATIONAL NEGRO CONGRESS (NNC). Concern about the situation of **African Americans** during the **Great Depression** led to a conference on "the economic status of the Negro" in 1935. Among those involved were **Ralph Bunche, A. Philip Randolph,** Alain Locke, and James Ford of the **Communist Party of the United States of America**. Following the meeting, some 800 delegates gathered in Chicago in 1936 to establish the NNC, a body representing approximately 600 separate organizations committed to campaigning nationally for African Americans primarily on economic issues, with

Randolph as president. While the NNC lobbied in Washington, D.C., against racial discrimination in the **New Deal**, it campaigned at the local level in support of voter registration in Baltimore and in efforts to secure greater employment in Harlem and Chicago. It also fought to increase unionization of black workers. However, it collapsed in 1940 with the withdrawal of communist support, although the movement officially existed until 1948. Experience with the NNC shaped Randolph's thinking when planning the **March on Washington** in 1941 and the decision to exclude white participants.

NATIONAL RECOVERY ADMINISTRATION (NRA). Established under the **National Industrial Recovery Act (NIRA)** in 1933 to administer the act and establish industrial codes to establish fair prices and fair labor practices and limit "destructive" competition, the NRA was headed by General **Hugh S. Johnson** and was a central element in the **"First New Deal."** It used the **Blue Eagle** system to endorse products manufactured under the codes. The NRA approved more than 541 codes. However, the **Supreme Court** ruled the NIRA unconstitutional in *Schechter Poultry Corp. v. United States* in 1935.

NATIONAL RESOURCES PLANNING BOARD (NRPB). The NRPB was created in September 1939 and abolished in July 1943. It succeeded the National Planning Board established under the **National Industrial Recovery Act** in 1933. The board's function was to develop planned proposals for the exploitation, development, and use of national resources. They established committees to look at industrial resources, transportation, energy, water use, land use, and the structure and workings of the economy. From 1939 to 1943, the NRPB was involved in planning for war and also for the postwar. Its report on postwar planning in 1943 called for a widespread program for social reform, and it came under increasing congressional criticism, which led to its demise in 1943. Some of its proposals found fruit in the **G.I. Bill of Rights** and the **Employment Act** of 1946.

NATIONAL SCIENCE FOUNDATION. Created in 1950 by Congress as an independent body "to promote the progress of science; to advance national health, prosperity, and welfare; to secure the national defense," the National Science Foundation provided funding for basic scientific research, much of it related to military uses, to maintain the U.S. scientific leadership.

NATIONAL SECURITY ACT, 1947. Passed by Congress on 26 July1947 as part of President **Harry S. Truman**'s **Cold War** program, the National Security Act reorganized the U.S. armed forces, merging the Department of War and Department of Navy into one national military establishment, which became the U.S. Department of Defense in 1949. A separate Department of the Air Force was also created. Furthermore, the act established the **National Security Council** and the **Central Intelligence Agency**.

NATIONAL SECURITY COUNCIL (NSC). Established as part of the reorganization of military and **foreign policy**-shaping agencies under the **National Security Act** of 1947 in response to the developing **Cold War**, the NSC consisted of the president, vice president, chief of the **National Security Resources Board**, secretary of defense, and secretary of state. The NSC advises the president on domestic, foreign policy, and national security issues and helps formulate U.S. defense and foreign policy. From 1949, the NSC included the secretary of treasury and the Joint Chiefs of Staff. It was located in the Office of the President, and President **Dwight D. Eisenhower** extended it to include a Planning Board and Coordinating Board. Under President John F. Kennedy, the role of national security adviser developed as the leading voice of the NSC. *See also* NATIONAL SECURITY COUNCIL REPORT 68 (NSC-68).

NATIONAL SECURITY COUNCIL REPORT 68 (NSC-68). Following the fall of **China** to the communists and the end of the U.S. atomic monopoly with the testing of an **atomic bomb** by the **Soviet Union** in 1949, the **National Security Council (NSC)** reassessed U.S. **foreign policy**. Their report in April 1950, National Security Council Report 68, predicted an "indefinite period of tension and danger" requiring determined action to resist attempted Soviet world domination. The report, primarily authored by **Paul Nitze**, called for a huge increase in defense spending to ensure greater military preparedness and a strengthening of the West's defensive capabilities.

Following the outbreak of the **Korean War** in June 1950, military spending was increased, rising from $13.5 billion in 1950 to nearly $50 billion a year later. In providing a blueprint for military rather than economic and political action, NSC-68 was seen as marking an escalation in the **Cold War**.

NATIONAL SECURITY RESOURCES BOARD. The National Security Resources Board was established under the **National Security Act** of 1947 to coordinate the strategic needs of the nation at any given time. The board was responsible for surveying the nation's industrial, material, and other resources in relation to military and defense requirements.

NATIONAL WAR LABOR BOARD (NWLB). The NWLB was created on 12 January 1942 within the Office of Emergency Management to resolve disputes between labor and management in defense industries through conciliation, mediation, and arbitration. The board consisted of 12 members equally representing **trade unions**, management, and public interest groups. Its responsibilities were extended to include wage stabilization. In total, it was involved in 17,650 disputes affecting 12 million workers. In July 1942, the NWLB adopted the **"Little Steel" formula** to control wage rises by limiting wage increases to 15 percent over levels of January 1941 to cover the rise in the cost of living. Rises were further restricted from 1943 onward. The NWLB also introduced a "maintenance of membership" policy in 1942, which committed workers to union membership after an initial 15-day opting-out period at the start of defense contracts. When **Sewell Avery** of Montgomery Ward refused to accept the policy, he was physically removed from his office, and the company was twice taken over by the military. The board was transferred to the Department of Labor in 1945 and abolished in 1946.

NATIONAL YOUTH ADMINISTRATION (NYA). Established by President **Franklin D. Roosevelt** by executive order in 1935, the NYA was created to provide part-time work for college and high school students. More than 4 million young people were employed by the administration during its existence. Among them were many **African Americans**, and the NYA included a Division of Negro

Affairs headed by **Mary McLeod Bethune**. The administration was absorbed into the **Federal Works Agency** in 1943.

NATIVE AMERICANS. From the late 19th century to the late 20th century, Native Americans constituted the poorest and most overlooked minority in the United States. They numbered 250,000 in 1900, and the majority of them were located on reservations in the West and Southwest. By 1930, almost half of their territory, more than 86 million acres, had gone to white Americans. Full citizenship was only granted in 1924. In 1928, a federal government report, *The Problem of Indian Administration*, declared categorically that "an overwhelming majority of Indians are poor, even extremely poor." The **Great Depression**, coupled with the effects of drought in the 1930s, exacerbated the already dire conditions. It was not until the **New Deal** and the appointment of **John Collier** as Indian Commissioner that the problems of Native Americans began to be seriously considered.

Collier was appointed commissioner of Indian affairs in 1933. Using funds from the **Civilian Conservation Corps**, **Public Works Administration**, and **Works Progress Administration**, he provided for the construction of schools and hospitals on Indian land. He also introduced the **Indian Reorganization Act** of 1934, which halted the sale of land to individuals and enabled tribes to recover unallocated lands. However, not all Native Americans supported the legislation, and Collier resigned in 1945.

During **World War II**, 25,000 Native Americans served in the military, with the largest number of 22,000 serving in the army. They were not segregated, and many served with distinction. Several Navajo Indians served in communications as "code talkers," as their language was unknown to the enemy. One of the most famous Native Americans during the war was a Pima Indian, Ira Hayes, who was one of the men who took part in the famous flag raising on Mount Suribachi on **Iwo Jima**. Some 40,000 Native Americans also left reservations to work in defense programs during the war. They continued to leave the reservations during the 1950s.

NELSON, DONALD MARR (1888–1959). Born in Hannibal, Missouri, Donald Nelson graduated from the University of Missouri in

1911 and in 1912 began working as a chemist with the Sears, Roebuck and Company. He remained with the company for 30 years, eventually becoming executive vice president and chairman of the executive committee in 1939. Seen as sympathetic to the **New Deal** in 1940, he was appointed to head the National Defense Advisory Committee and then the Division of Purchases of the **Office of Production Management**. After the United Stares entered **World War II**, in January 1942 Nelson became head of the **War Production Board (WPB)** to govern all aspects of war production. He was able but indecisive and allowed his authority, extended under the second **War Powers Act** of 1942, to be diluted with the appointment of "czars" responsible to President **Franklin D. Roosevelt** for petroleum, rubber, and even manpower. Even more problematic was the independence of the military procurement agencies. Nonetheless, the WPB was able to limit nonessential production and prioritize production, but when the board proposed that companies that did not have war contracts could prepare for postwar reconversion, the military objected. Nelson was relieved of his job in August 1944 and sent on a fact-finding mission to **China** and the **Soviet Union**. After the war, he retired from government service and became president of the Society of Independent Motion Picture Producers until 1947. He later became chair of Electronized Chemicals and president of Consolidated Caribou Silver Mines.

NEUTRALITY ACTS, 1935, 1936, 1937, 1939. Determined to avoid the mistakes that led to U.S. involvement in World War I, isolationists in Congress enacted a series of Neutrality Acts in the 1930s, beginning with a ban on the export of implements to belligerents and forbidding U.S. vessels from carrying munitions to warring nations. In 1936, this first measure also included limits to extending loans to belligerents. In 1937, the president was given the power to prohibit even the carrying of nonmilitary materials on U.S. ships and allow trade only on a cash-and-carry basis—the purchasers had to pay for goods and ship them themselves. The 1939 act codified the existing legislation, maintaining the cash-and-carry principle but prohibiting U.S. citizens from traveling on the ships of belligerent nations and banning U.S. ships from sailing to belligerent ports and even into war zones.

NEW DEAL. Accepting the **Democratic Party**'s nomination in June 1932 President **Franklin D. Roosevelt** promised the American people "a new deal" to tackle the problems of the **Great Depression**. The phrase was used by the press to describe the legislative program he enacted following his successful election. The New Deal represented an unprecedented period of federal reform. It promised relief, recovery, and reform, and has traditionally been seen in terms of a "**First New Deal**" and a more radical "**Second New Deal**." In the "**First Hundred Days**" the Roosevelt administration secured the passage of 15 major bills, reforming **banking** and investment, establishing relief agencies, and initiating programs of industrial and **agricultural** recovery. This was achieved through the **Emergency Banking Act**, Glass-Steagall Act, **Securities and Exchange Act**, **Federal Emergency Relief Administration**, **National Industrial Recovery Act**, and **Agricultural Adjustment Act**. Relief was also provided through the **Public Works Administration**, **Civilian Works Administration**, **Civilian Conservation Corps**, and **Tennessee Valley Authority**. The First New Deal ended in 1934.

In the face of growing opposition from groups like the **American Liberty League** and such individuals as **Huey Long**, Father **Charles Coughlin**, **Upton Sinclair**, and **Francis Townsend**, some of whom appeared to offer more radical programs and growing labor militancy, the New Deal embarked upon a further wave of reform. Additional legislation was also needed as a consequence of the **Supreme Court**'s decision in *Schechter Poultry Corp. v. United States* declaring the **National Recovery Administration** unconstitutional. From 1935, a Second New Deal, including further legislation to tackle the continuing problem of unemployment and introduce several major reforms, began. The **Works Progress Administration** established a massive series of public works that eventually employed almost one-third of the unemployed. Reform came in the shape of the **Social Security Act** and the **National Labor Relations Act** or Wagner Act. The Social Security Act established a basic pension system and unemployment insurance, while the National Labor Relations Act guaranteed workers the right to organize and prohibit unfair labor practices on the part of employers. The **Fair Labor Standards Act** set minimum wage levels and maximum works hours in interstate commerce. Further housing reform was also initiated with the **National Housing Act** of 1937. At the same time, some attempt at wealth redistribution was evident in the **Wealth Tax Act** of 1935.

The Second New Deal ran out of steam due to a further economic downturn, known as the "Roosevelt recession," in 1937, and because of the political controversy occasioned by Roosevelt's attempt at "**court packing**" to change the make up of the **Supreme Court**. Increasingly, too, foreign affairs began to dominate political concerns, and once the United States entered **World War II**, "Dr. Win the War" replaced "Dr. New Deal."

NIEBUHR, REINHOLD (1892–1971). This influential theologian was born Karl Paul Reinhold Niebuhr in Wright City, Wisconsin. Raised in a religious family, Niebuhr graduated from the German Evangelical Synod's Eden Theological Seminary in St. Louis in 1913 and gained an M.A. from Yale Divinity School in 1915. From 1915 to 1928, he was pastor at the Bethel Evangelical Church in Detroit, where his powerful sermons helped swell the congregation from 65 to 600 members. During World War I, he supported the dropping of "German" from the Synod's title and abandoning the use of the German language. After the war, he became a pacifist and, as a result of his knowledge of Detroit's car factories, increasingly socialist. From 1928 until his retirement in 1960, Niebuhr was professor at the Union Theological Seminary in New York City. In 1929, he became editor of the socialist *World Tomorrow*, and he stood as a socialist candidate for election to the New York state senate in 1930 and to Congress in 1932. He was unsuccessful on both occasions.

Niebuhr authored a number of influential books, including *Moral Man and Immoral Society* (1932), *An Interpretation of Christian Ethics* (1935), *Beyond Tragedy* (1937), *The Nature and Destiny of Man* (two volumes, 1941, 1943), *The Children of Darkness* (1944), and *The Irony of American History* (1952). He was chair of the Union for Democratic Action, a left-wing but anticommunist group, and he also campaigned in support of aid to **Great Britain** prior to 1941. After the war, he was a founding member of **Americans for Democratic Action** and a critic of **Joseph McCarthy**. In 1949, he was an official U.S. delegate to the **United Nations Educational, Scientific, and Cultural Organization** General Conference in Paris. He continued to lecture widely, and in 1964 he was awarded the Medal of Freedom by President Lyndon Johnson. Nonetheless Niebuhr was a critic of U.S. involvement in the war in Vietnam. His message of Christian realism and opposition to injustice was an inspiration for civil rights leaders like Martin Luther King Jr. and made him a major influence in postwar America.

NIMITZ, CHESTER WILLIAM (1885–1966). Chester Nimitz was born in Fredericksburg, Texas. He graduated from the U.S. Naval Academy in 1905 and served in the navy in the Far East until 1908 when he began working in submarines. During World War I, Nimitz was an engineering aide and chief of staff to the commander of the U.S. submarine force. He held various posts between 1918 and 1922 and was director of the Naval Reserve Officer Training Corps at the University of California at Berkeley, in 1926. He was made captain in 1927 and served in San Diego, California, from 1929 to 1933. Nimitz became a rear admiral in 1938 and after **Pearl Harbor** in 1941 was appointed to replace Admiral Husband Kimmel by Secretary of the Navy **Frank Knox**. Nimitz became commander in chief of the Pacific Fleet, and when it was divided, he led the Pacific Ocean Fleet though the battles in the Coral Sea in 1942, **Midway** in 1942, and **Leyte Gulf** in 1944 and oversaw the invasions of **Iwo Jima** and **Okinawa**. He was made admiral of the fleet in 1944. From 1944 to 1946, he was chief of naval operations, and he signed the Japanese surrender on 2 September 1945 on behalf of the U.S. government. He retired in 1947.

NITZE, PAUL (1907–2004). Born in Amherst, Massachusetts, Paul Nitze graduated from Harvard University in 1928 and began a successful career in investment banking. In 1940, he joined the War Department as assistant to **James V. Forrestal** and then from 1942 headed various war agencies involved in defense production during **World War II**. Nitze also was a cofounder of the School of Advanced International Studies in Washington, D.C., in 1943. From 1944 to 1946, he was part of the team that worked on the Strategic Bombing Survey to determine the effectiveness of **Allied** bombing raids in Europe and Asia. After the war, Nitze worked first as an assistant to **William Clayton** in the State Department and assisted with the drafting of the **European Recovery Program** in 1947 and then joined the State Department's Policy Planning Staff. He became director of this body in 1950 and was principal author of the **National Security Council Report 68**.

Nitze left office in 1953 but was **foreign policy** advisor to John F. Kennedy during his presidential campaign in 1960. In 1961, he was appointed assistant secretary of defense and from 1963 to 1967 was secretary of the navy and then deputy secretary of defense from 1967 to 1969. He led the U.S. Delegation to the Strategic Arms Limitation Talks (SALT) in 1969. As an advisor to President Ronald Reagan, Nitze helped negotiate the resumption of the Strategic Arms Reduction Talks (START) in 1981 and bring about the Intermediate Range Nuclear Forces Treaty, 1981–1984. He was awarded the Presidential Medal of Freedom by Reagan in 1985.

NIXON, RICHARD MILHOUS (1913–1994). 36th vice president and 37th president of the United States. Richard M. Nixon was born in Yorba Linda, California. He attended Whittier College and then Duke Law School, where he graduated in 1937. He practiced law in Whittier, California, from 1937 until 1942, when he moved to Washington, D.C., to work in the **Office of Price Administration**. From 1942 to 1946, he served in the navy in the Pacific and rose to the rank of lieutenant commander.

A **Republican**, in 1946 Nixon defeated the five-term **Democratic** congressman, Jerry Voorhis. He came to public prominence as the member of the **House Un-American Activities Committee**, which helped expose **Alger Hiss** and secure his subsequent conviction for perjury. In 1950, Nixon won election to the U.S. Senate when he beat **Helen Gahagan Douglas**, whom he identified as a communist sympathizer. She in turn labeled him "Tricky Dicky," a nickname often used by his opponents in later years. In 1952, he secured the nomination as **Dwight D. Eisenhower**'s vice presidential candidate. However, he was accused of receiving illegal campaign contributions but answered the charges in a now famous television speech in which he claimed he had only accepted one gift—a dog named Checkers—whom he would keep.

As vice president Nixon campaigned actively for other Republican candidates and was used to attack **Adlai Stevenson**. He also attracted publicity when he was attacked by an anti-American crowd while touring Latin America in 1958 and again in 1959 when he publicly engaged in a "kitchen debate" with the **Soviet** premier Nikita Khrushchev at the U.S. exhibition in Moscow. Chosen as the Republican presidential candidate in 1960, Nixon was only narrowly defeated by Democrat John F. Kennedy but chose not to contest the election results. Defeated again in the gubernatorial contest in California in 1962, it appeared that his political career was over when he announced to the press that they would not have him "to kick around anymore."

Taking up a law practice in New York City, Nixon restored his position in the Republican Party by working hard behind the scenes. Having reestablished himself once more, he won the presidential nomination in 1968 and easily defeated **Hubert Humphrey**. As president, Nixon promised to "bring the nation together." However, his presidency saw the escalation of the war in Vietnam with further bombing of the North and invasions into Cambodia and Laos that brought massive demonstrations at home. Although he secured the peaceful withdrawal of U.S. troops in 1973, South Vietnam was overrun by northern forces in 1975. Elsewhere in foreign affairs, Nixon began the process of détente with communist **China** and the Soviet Union, visiting both countries in 1972 and initiating arms limitation agreements.

At home, Nixon was successful in extending social security and introducing environmental reform. His attempts at welfare and healthcare reform were less successful. He reluctantly accepted busing to bring about school desegregation and called for a period of "benign neglect" in **civil rights**. This approach helped further strengthen Republican support in the traditionally Democratic South. In 1972, Nixon won reelection with a massive majority. However, when it was revealed that individuals associated with the Republican Party and linked to the White House had been involved in the break-in at the Democratic Party office in the Watergate Complex in Washington, the Nixon administration became involved in a cover-up. Congressional investigations revealed a history of "dirty tricks" that led back to the Oval Office. Faced with the possibility of impeachment, on 9 August 1974 Nixon became the only president to resign from office. He retired to California and subsequently received a full pardon for any possible wrongdoing from his successor, Gerald Ford.

NORMANDY LANDINGS. Normandy, a region in northern France, was the location of **"Operation Overlord,"** the **Allied D-Day** landings that began the invasion of Europe on 6 June 1944. More than 150,000 troops (57,000 of them U.S. troops) landed in several locations, code-named Gold Beach (British), Juno Beach (British), **Omaha Beach** (U.S.), Sword Beach (Canadian), **Utah Beach** (U.S.), and Pointe du Hoc west of Omaha Beach (U.S.). Despite heavy casualties, the landings were successful.

NORRIS, GEORGE WILLIAM (1861–1944). Born in Ohio, George Norris qualified in law at Valparaiso University in Indiana in 1883. He moved to Nebraska in 1885 and established a law practice. A **Republican**, Norris won election as a county prosecuting attorney in 1892, a judge in 1895, and a congressman to the U.S. House of Representatives in 1902. He held that position until 1912, when he was elected to the U.S. Senate, a seat he held almost until his death. An independently minded progressive, Norris opposed U.S. intervention in the affairs of Latin American nations, and he supported neutrality in the war in Europe. He was one of the six senators, alongside **Robert M. La Follette Sr.**, James K. Vardaman, William Stone, Asle J. Gronna, and Harry Lane, who voted against the declaration of war in 1917. He also voted against the Versailles peace treaty and entry into the League of Nations in 1919.

Throughout the 1920s Norris increasingly sided with Republican insurgents in favor of policies to aid farmers, and he supported the McNary-Haugen bills. He was particularly conspicuous in calling for public ownership and development of the Muscle Shoals facilities in Alabama. Norris was cosponsor of the Norris-La Guardia Antiinjunction Act of 1932 that extended some protection to organized labor in the event of strikes. He also sponsored the **Twentieth Amendment** to the Constitution, ending the "lame duck" sessions of Congress from December to March following the election.

Although a Republican, Norris was highly critical of **Herbert Hoover**, and supported **Franklin D. Roosevelt** and the **New Deal** during the 1930s, and led the fight in favor of the **Tennessee Valley Authority** in 1933. He sponsored the Rural Electrification Act of 1936 providing funding for the **Rural Electrification Administration** and the Farm Forestry Act of 1937. He increasingly supported

Roosevelt in foreign affairs, moving away from his earlier isolationist stance. In 1936, he was reelected as an independent progressive but was defeated in 1942 and retired from public life.

NORTH ATLANTIC TREATY, 1949. Signed in Washington, D.C., on 4 April 1949, the North Atlantic Treaty was a treaty of mutual defense between the United States, Canada, and 10 Western European nations, including France, **Great Britain**, Belgium, Luxembourg, the Netherlands, Denmark, Norway, Iceland, Italy, and Portugal. The agreement stated that any attack on one of signatories would be regarded as an attack on them all, and it was a response to what was seen as the threat of attack by the **Soviet Union** following the communist takeover in Czechoslovakia in February 1948 and the **Berlin Airlift** from June 1948 to May 1949. The European nations had already established the basis of the agreement with the Brussels Treaty in March 1948, and approval of U.S. participation had been signaled by **Republicans** in Congress with the **Vandenberg Resolution** in June 1948. In January 1950, an administrative body, the **North Atlantic Treaty Organization**, was established as the command structure. Greece and Turkey joined the alliance in 1952, the **Federal Republic of Germany** in 1955, and Spain in 1982. The Soviet Union responded to the inclusion of West **Germany** by creating its own alliance, the Warsaw Pact, in 1955. *See also* CONTAINMENT; MARSHALL PLAN.

NORTH ATLANTIC TREATY ORGANIZATION (NATO). Established in January 1950 to implement the provisions of the **North Atlantic Treaty**, NATO established a center in Brussels, Belgium, and in 1951 the Supreme Headquarters Allied Powers Europe (SHAPE) was created in France with General **Dwight D. Eisenhower** as its first commander. Following the incorporation of the **Federal Republic of Germany** into NATO in 1955, the **Soviet Union** responded by creating the Warsaw Pact, a military alliance of communist-dominated Eastern Europe. In 1966, France left NATO because of what it perceived as U.S. domination. Nonetheless, NATO continued in existence, although its role was increasingly questioned with the end of the **Cold War** in 1990. However, it was recently enrolled in the "war against terror," and its membership expanded with the inclusion of a number of former Soviet satellites in Eastern Europe.

NUREMBERG WAR CRIMES TRIALS. The trial of Nazi war criminals, as agreed by the **Allied powers** at the **Yalta Conference**, was held in Nuremburg, Germany, and lasted from 1945 to 1949. The first and main trial of 21 surviving (**Adolf Hitler** and several others committed suicide before the war's end) leading figures in the Nazi government lasted from November 1945 to October 1946. It resulted in the conviction and execution of 10 men, including Air Marshal Hermann Goering, but he escaped the penalty by committing suicide the night before he was to be hanged. Eight of the remaining individuals, including Hitler's deputy Rudolph Hess and his architect Rudolph Speer, were convicted and sentenced to prison terms.

NYE, GERALD PRENTICE (1892–1971). Born in Wisconsin, Gerald Nye became a journalist in Iowa and then North Dakota, where he acquired two papers, the *Fryburg Pioneer* in 1919 and the *Griggs County Sentinel-Courier* in 1920. He was appointed to the U.S. Senate in 1925 when the incumbent died and was then elected in his own right in 1926. A **Republican** in the progressive mold, Nye was involved in the investigations into the Teapot Dome Scandals and critical of the probusiness policies of the administration of Calvin Coolidge. He was also a strong advocate of aid programs for farmers. However, he was equally critical of some aspects of the **New Deal**, particularly the **National Recovery Administration**, which he saw as aiding monopoly, and the **National Labor Relations Board**, which he saw as too sympathetic toward the **Congress of Industrial Organizations**.

From 1934 through 1936, Nye headed a Special Senate Committee investigating the role of munitions manufacturers—labeled "merchants of death"—in initiating U.S. involvement in World War I. The committee encouraged concerns that the United States would once again be dragged into a war that helped secure the passage of the **Neutrality Acts** of 1935, 1936, and 1937. As the threat of war approached, Nye was an outspoken isolationist and a founding member of the **America First Committee** in 1940. In 1944, he was defeated in the election and retired from politics. He set up a consulting business in Washington, D.C. From 1960 to 1964, he worked for the **Federal Housing Administration** on housing for the elderly, and from 1964 to 1968 he assisted the Senate Committee on Aging, after which he practiced law.

– O –

OFFICE OF CIVILIAN DEFENSE (OCD). Established by executive order in May 1941, the OCD was authorized to coordinate national civilian defense and promote civilian morale. Headed by **Fiorello La Guardia**, it established local civilian defense units to provide air raid precautions, first aid, and fire protection in the event of enemy attack. In some towns, the local OCD planted "victory" gardens to provide extra foodstuff. In other areas, it led drives to collect scrap metal, paper, and rubber. **Eleanor Roosevelt** directed the OCD's Volunteer Participation Committee, but when some of her appointments provoked criticism from Congress in 1942, she resigned. Approximately 10 million people played a part in the OCD during the war.

OFFICE OF ECONOMIC STABILIZATION (OES). Established by President **Franklin D. Roosevelt** in October 1942 and headed by **James F. Byrnes**, the OES was intended to resolve disputes between various war agencies and establish policies on wages, salaries, prices, rents, and profits to control rises in the cost of living. The OES did not intervene directly in the economy but instead coordinated the work of the **Office of Price Administration** and the **National War Labor Board**. It was replaced in 1943 by the **Office of War Mobilization**, which later became the Office of War Mobilization and Reconversion.

OFFICE OF FACTS AND FIGURES (OFF). Established in 1941 under the leadership of **Archibald MacLeish** and intended to provide the truth rather than propaganda during **World War II**, the OFF was replaced in June 1942 by the **Office of War Information**.

OFFICE OF PRICE ADMINISTRATION (OPA). Initially created as the Office of Price Administration and Civilian Supply in April 1941, the OPA was established on 28 August 1941. The OPA was authorized to issue price schedules on vital commodities but had limited powers. On 30 January 1942, Congress passed the **Emergency Price Control Act** giving the OPA greater power to impose price ceilings on goods, services, and rents. In October, the administration was granted power under the **Economic Stabilization Act** to introduce rationing. Almost 90 percent of food prices were frozen, and rationing was introduced on sugar, gasoline, oil, cars, tires, and meat. The OPA was headed first by **Leon Henderson** and from 1943 onward by **Chester B. Bowles**. After the war, rationing came to an end, and price controls gradually ended. The OPA was finally disbanded in 1947.

OFFICE OF PRICE STABILIZATION (OPS). Created on 9 September 1950 to control inflation during the **Korean War**, the OPS was able to introduce mandatory price controls but appealed to business and industry to observe "voluntary pricing standards." However, on 26 January 1951 it ordered a general price freeze, but it proved difficult to enforce. The office was abolished in 1953.

OFFICE OF PRODUCTION MANAGEMENT (OPM). The OPM was established in January 1941 to supervise the production and allocation of raw materials for national defense production. It had two codirectors, **Sidney Hillman** and **William Knudsen**. Largely an advisory body, the OPM was replaced in 1942 after the United States entered **World War II** by the **War Production Board** under **Donald M. Nelson**.

OFFICE OF SCIENTIFIC RESEARCH AND DEVELOPMENT (OSRD). Established in June 1941 to recruit scientists to work on defense-related projects, the OSRD also compiled a roster of the nation's scientific experts. Headed by **Vannevar Bush**, the office led developments in sonar, radar, fuses, bomb sights, penicillin, and sulfa drugs. It played a major role in directing the development of the **atomic bomb**, and in 1946 it was absorbed into the **Atomic Energy Commission**.

OFFICE OF STRATEGIC SERVICES (OSS). The OSS was established by executive order in July 1942 to coordinate military intelligence during **World War II**. Headed by **William J. Donovan**, the OSS was responsible for gathering intelligence and espionage activities behind enemy lines. Allen Dulles was in charge of the office in Switzerland that used its location in a neutral country to gather information about the Nazi war effort. The OSS had more than 16,000 agents involved in espionage, sabotage, or guerrilla activities in Europe and Asia. The office was regarded with suspicion by military figures and the **Federal Bureau of Investigation** and was judged to be unsuccessful in some quarters. It was abolished by President **Harry S. Truman** in 1945. However, the OSS paved the way for the **Central Intelligence Agency**, established in 1947.

OFFICE OF WAR INFORMATION (OWI). Established on 13 June 1942, the OWI replaced the **Office of Facts and Figures** as the agency responsible for the domestic dissemination of news and information relating to the war through the various forms of media—newspapers, **radio**, and film. The OWI produced posters intended to encourage war mobilization and support for the war effort, including the famous **Four Freedoms** series by **Norman Rockwell**. In addition, a photographic unit headed by **Roy Stryker** recorded aspects of war mobilization for publication. The OWI provided guidelines for filmmakers explaining what was appropriate to show in **cinema**. It was also involved in international activities intended to demoralize and undermine the enemy and encourage support from neutrals through the dissemination of information about **Allied** war aims and the progress of the war. The Voice of America radio broadcasts were established in 1942 under the OWI.

Led by **Elmer Davis**, the OWI tried to avoid being seen as a propaganda agency by concentrating on factual information, but it was viewed by critics as acting on behalf of particular interests. **Republicans** saw the OWI as a propaganda agency for **Franklin D. Roosevelt** and the **Democratic Party**, and in 1943 Congress reduced its funding and its domestic activities were limited. It was abolished completely in 1945. *See also* WORLD WAR II.

OFFICE OF WAR MOBILIZATION (OWM). Headed by **James F. Byrnes**, the OWM was established on 27 May 1943 to replace the **Office of Economic Stabilization** to coordinate the various war agencies. It was renamed Office of War Mobilization and Reconversion in October 1944. Byrnes was named as director of war mobilization with responsibility for overseeing the activities of all federal agencies involved in civilian aspects of the war effort. Byrnes had authority to settle disputes between federal agencies involved in war production. At the end of **World War II**, the agency took on the task of directing the reconversion from military to civilian production. The OWM was abolished on 19 July 1945.

"OKIES." The term *Okie* was an abbreviation of Oklahoman but was applied to the thousands of migrant workers and others who left the Midwestern states of Oklahoma, Arkansas, and Missouri, driven out by the economic collapse in the **Great Depression** and the **Dust Bowl**. It became a pejorative term: As a character in **John Steinbeck**'s novel *The Grapes of Wrath* said, it used to mean you were from Oklahoma, "Now it means you're a dirty son of a bitch. Okie means you're scum." The majority of migrants headed West to California, Oregon, and Washington, where they were often met with resentment and discrimination. They did not assimilate into the local population until well into **World War II**.

OKINAWA. The Japanese-held island of Okinawa, located 300 miles south of mainland **Japan**, was the site of one of the fiercest battles of **World War II** in the Pacific. The U.S. invasion began from 1,300 ships on 1 April 1945 and involved more than 250,000 soldiers, marines, and seamen. More than 2,000 Americans and 110,000 Japanese lost their lives before the battle ended on 30 June 1945. A total of 36 U.S. ships were destroyed in the conflict, some by the kamikaze pilots who flew their planes into the ships, and 16 Japanese vessels were lost. The capture of Okinawa and **Iwo Jima** provided additional locations from which the United States could launch air raids against Japan.

OMAHA BEACH. Omaha Beach was the code name given to one of the U.S. locations in the **Normandy landing** on **D-Day** 6 June 1944. Situated between Sainte-Honorine-de-Pertes and Vierville-sur-Mer in northern France, the beach is five miles long and was heavily defended by German forces. The U.S. forces, many of them blown off course, suffered their heaviest casualties of the invasion, losing almost 3,000 out of the 34,000 troops who landed. The landing was ultimately successful only because of resourceful leadership on the beach and naval bombardment that gradually destroyed the enemy emplacements.

OPERATION HUSKY. Operation Husky was the code name given to the invasion of Sicily by more than 160,000 **Allied** troops on 9 and 10 July 1943 during **World War II**. It ultimately led to the fall of Sicily in August 1943 and the invasion of Italy. At the time, it was the largest amphibious landing in history, and it provided invaluable lessons for the **Normandy landings** on **D-Day** in 1944. *See also* OPERATION OVERLORD; OPERATION TORCH.

OPERATION OVERLORD. Operation Overlord was the code name given to the **Normandy landings** by **Allied** forces. Originally planned for 1 May 1944 but delayed due to bad weather, the invasion on **D-Day** 6 June 1944 eventually led to the defeat of **Germany** during **World War II**. *See also* OPERATION HUSKY; OPERATION TORCH.

OPERATION TORCH. Operation Torch was the code name given to the invasion of North Africa by more than 73,000 **Allied** troops at Casablanca, Oran, and Algiers in Morocco and Algeria on 8 November 1942. The successful landings enabled the Allies to push into Tunisia, where they eventually overwhelmed the German army in April 1943. These victories paved the way for the invasion of Sicily in July. *See also* OPERATION HUSKY; OPERATION OVERLORD.

OPPENHEIMER, (JULIUS) ROBERT (1904–1967). Born to German immigrant parents in New York City, J. Robert Oppenheimer obtained a degree in chemistry from Harvard University in 1925 and a Ph.D. in physics from the University of Göttingen, **Germany**, in 1927. After further research at different institutions, he joined the physics department at the University of California at Berkeley, where he became a full professor in 1936. He joined the **Manhattan Project** in 1942 and was involved in the development of the first **atomic bomb** in Los Alamos, New Mexico. He resigned from the project after the first successful test explosion in July 1945 and returned to Berkeley. From 1947 until 1966, Oppenheimer worked at the Institute for Advanced Study at the University of Princeton. He was a member of the General Advisory Committee to the U.S. **Atomic Energy Commission (AEC)** from 1947 to 1953 and was appointed president of the American Physical Society in 1948.

In 1953, Oppenheimer, whose doubts about the development of the **hydrogen bomb** were well-known, was accused of being a security risk by Senator **Joseph McCarthy**, and the AEC revoked his security clearance. Despite protests from the scientific community, the order was not overturned. Oppenheimer continued his work at Princeton and as a speaker and lecturer. In 1963, he was awarded the Enrico Fermi Prize for his contributions to science by President John F. Kennedy, and the award was presented by President Lyndon Johnson after Kennedy's death.

ORGANIZATION OF AMERICAN STATES (OAS). The OAS was established at the Inter-American Conference in Bogota, Colombia, on 30 April 1948. It expanded on the **Rio Pact**. The OAS confirmed inter-American cooperation and hemispheric solidarity; prohibited military, political, or economic intervention in the affairs of one state by another; and promised cooperation with the **United Nations** and its goals. However, in allowing united military action between the United States and Latin American countries, it was also an extension of **containment**.

OWENS, JESSE (JAMES) (1913–1980). The **African American** champion athlete was born James Owens in Alabama, but his family moved to Cleveland, Ohio, when he was young. After studying at a local high school, he went to Ohio State University, where he quickly excelled in track and field. Having just missed qualifying for the 1932 Olympics, he set three new world records and equaled another in Ann Arbor, Michigan, before competing in the 1936 **Berlin** Olympics. There, in front of the German leader **Adolf Hitler**, Owens shattered the Nazi myth of Aryan supremacy when he won four gold medals, breaking Olympic records in the 100-meter race, 200-meter race, long jump, and the 400-meter relay. Hitler left the stadium before the presentations took place. African Americans also won gold medals in the 800-meter race (John Woodruff), 400-meter race (Archie Williams), and high jump (Cornelius Johnson).

After Berlin, Owens decided to return to the United States to take up commercial offers rather than tour Europe with the rest of the American team, and as a result he was banned from competing in amateur athletics by the American Athletics Union. The commercial opportunities involved competing against other sportspeople, like **Joe Louis**, or racing horses or motor bikes. Owens's venture into the dry cleaning business ended in bankruptcy, and he was employed for some time in limited public relations roles. In the mid-1950s, he was employed by the State Department and sent as a goodwill ambassador to a number of countries in Asia, but in the 1960s he was prosecuted and fined for tax evasion. Owens did not take any part in the **civil rights** protests of the period and was highly critical of the athletes who adopted the black power pose at the 1968 Mexico Olympics. In the 1970s, Owens's career improved, and he became a successful spokesman for the Ford Motor Company and American Express. In 1976, he was awarded the Medal of Freedom by President Gerald Ford; after his death, he was awarded the Congressional Gold Medal.

– P –

PALESTINE. *See* ISRAEL.

PANAY **INCIDENT.** The USS *Panay* was a gunboat used by the U.S. Navy to patrol the Yangtze River in **China** to protect American lives and commerce. On 12 December 1937, it had been picking up American consular staff from Nanking when it came under attack by Japanese aircraft and was sunk. Three lives were lost and 48 were wounded. Following protests, the Japanese government apologized for the attack and paid an indemnity of $2.2.million. The incident did much to increase public antipathy toward **Japan**.

PATTERSON, ROBERT PORTER (1891–1952). Born in Glen Falls, New York, Robert Patterson was a graduate of Union College in 1912 and Harvard Law School in 1915. After working in a law firm headed by Elihu Root, he served in the National Guard in the expeditionary force that went to Mexico in 1916. During World War I, he served with distinction in the army and was wounded and awarded the Silver Star and Distinguished Service Cross. After the war, he established a law firm in New York City. In 1930, he was chosen as a judge on the U.S. District Court for southern New York, and in 1939 he was appointed to the U.S. Court of Appeals, Second Circuit. In 1940, Patterson became an assistant to Secretary of War **Henry L. Stimson** and in 1941 was appointed as undersecretary. Patterson played a major part in organizing the mobilization for war, and in 1945 he was made secretary of war by President **Harry S. Truman**. He left in 1947 to resume his private law practice. Patterson died in a plane crash in 1952.

PATTON, GEORGE SMITH (1885–1945). George S. Patton was born in California and educated at Virginia Military Institute and West Point Military Academy, where he graduated in 1909 and joined the cavalry. In 1912, he competed in the pentathlon in the Olympic Games. Patton took part in the punitive expedition against Mexico in 1916 and 1917 and then in France during World War I. He was aide to General Jack Pershing before being assigned to the new tank corps. He led a tank brigade at the Battle of St. Mihiel in 1918 and was awarded the Distinguished Service Cross for his bravery.

After the war, Patton attended cavalry school and later the army war college. In 1932, he was one of the officers who led troops against the **Bonus Army** in Washington, D.C. After the United States joined **World War II**, Patton commanded the First Armored Corps in Africa. In July 1943, he took command of the 7th Army during the invasion and campaign in Sicily and was responsible for the seizure of Palermo, Italy. Known for his intemperate language and aggressive manner, Patton caused a public outcry when he called two soldiers in a field hospital cowards and struck one of them. General **Dwight D. Eisenhower** made him issue a public apology but refused to court-martial him. Patton led the 3rd Army following the **D-Day** invasions of Europe, and he helped turn the tide during the **Battle of the Bulge** in 1944, when he led his forces more than 100 miles in bad weather to relieve the army in **Bastogne**, Belgium. After the war, Patton was placed in command in Bavaria, **Germany**, but he was removed for failing to impose the policies of denazification as rigorously as required. He also urged that a firm stand be taken against the **Soviet Union**. Patton died following a road accident.

PEALE, NORMAN VINCENT (1898–1993). An influential preacher and minister, Norman Vincent Peale was born in Bowersville, Ohio, to a religious family. He graduated from Ohio Wesleyan College in 1920 and worked as a journalist before entering Boston University in 1921 to study for the ministry. In 1924, Peale became minister to a church in Brooklyn, New York, and immediately began to attract large congregations to hear his sermons. In 1927, he moved to a Methodist church in Syracuse, New York, but in 1932 took over the Marble Collegiate Church in New York City and joined the Reformed Church of America. The following year he also began to preach via the **radio**, and his new radio program, *The Art of Living*, began to attract large audiences. Peale also distributed his sermons by mail as *Guideposts* magazine. His books, *A Guide to Confident Living* (1948) and *The Power of Positive Thinking* (1952), were both best sellers. With Billy Graham, Peale was one of the two most influential religious figures in postwar America. A film of his life, *One Man's Way*, was made in 1963. He opposed the election of John F. Kennedy because of his Catholicism and subsequently became closely associated with **Richard M. Nixon** and his family. President Ronald Reagan awarded Peale the Presidential Medal of Freedom in 1984.

PEARL HARBOR. Located on the island of Oahu in Hawaii, Pearl Harbor became the base for the U.S. Pacific Fleet in April 1940 in response to growing tensions between the United States and **Japan**. As relations further deteriorated and war seemed likely, in January 1941 the Japanese admiral, Isoruku Yamamoto, began to plan a surprise preemptive attack on the harbor. When this was approved by the government of Hideki Tojo, Yamamoto moved his fleet to the Kurile Islands in November and early in the morning of 7 December launched an air attack from 275 miles north of Pearl Harbor.

Although U.S. intelligence knew an attack was imminent, they had no idea of where or when. At the time of the bombing, negotiations between Japan and the **Roosevelt** administration were still ongoing in Washington, D.C. In two hours, on a day Roosevelt said would "live in infamy," the Japanese sank 18 warships, destroyed almost 200 aircraft, and killed 2,403 U.S. service personnel. The U.S. aircraft carriers were at sea and escaped damage. Other vital resources remained undamaged, and the attack did not prove to be the devastating setback the Japanese had wanted. Rather, it provided the rally cry, "Remember Pearl Harbor" and helped bring about the rapid mobilization of the U.S. war effort. The Pearl Harbor site is now a national historic site, and the sunken USS *Arizona* remains a memorial to those who died.

PEEK, GEORGE NELSON (1873–1943). George N. Peek was born in Polo, Illinois, and studied briefly at Northwestern University in 1891. He worked first as an office assistant and subsequently found employment with Deere and Webber, a branch of the John Deere Plow Company. In 1901, Peek became general manager of the Deere Company in Omaha, Nebraska, and in 1914 vice president in charge of sales in Deere's main office in Moline, Illinois. During World War I, he was an industrial representative on the War Industries Board and in 1918 became commissioner of finished products. In 1919, Secretary of Commerce William C. Redfield appointed Peek to chair the Industrial Board of the Department of Commerce, but Peek resigned after only a few months due to conflict over price issues with the railroad director, Walker D. Hines.

From 1919 to 1923 Peek was president and general manager of the Moline Plow Company. He resigned over differences with the company's vice president, **Hugh S. Johnson.** As president of the American Council of **Agriculture**, Peek supported the government farm support initiatives proposed in the McNary-Haugen bills between 1924 and 1928. He was an active supporter of **Franklin D. Roosevelt** in 1932 and was appointed to head the **Agricultural Adjustment Administration (AAA)** in 1933. However, Peek did not accept that there was a farm surplus and opposed the AAA program to reduce production, and Roosevelt was forced to ask for his resignation after only a few months. He was appointed instead as adviser on foreign trade and president of the Export-Import Bank, but again differences over policy led to his resignation in 1935. Peek became a critic of **New Deal** farm policies and Roosevelt's interventionist policies. In 1936, he supported **Republican Alf Landon**, and he was also a member of the National Committee of the **America First Committee** established in 1940 to keep the United States out of the European wars.

PELLEY, WILLIAM DUDLEY (1890–1965). Born in Lynn, Massachusetts, William Pelley became a journalist after leaving school and wrote for such magazines as *Collier's* and the *Saturday Evening Post*. He traveled widely in Europe, served with the YMCA during World War I, and was in Siberia with the U.S. Army in 1919. He subsequently spent time in Russia and became anticommunist and anti-Semitic. Returning to the United States in 1920, he was a successful author and scriptwriter in Hollywood until 1929. In 1928, he claimed to have had an out-of-body experience, and he began to write about spiritual matters and politics. He established Galahad College in Asheville, North Carolina, in 1932, and after **Adolf Hitler**'s rise to power in **Germany**, he formed the right-wing Silver Legion with its uniformed Silver Shirts group in 1933. The Silver Legion, which had a membership of about 15,000, was briefly associated with the followers of **Huey Long** and Father **Charles Coughlin**, but in 1936 Pelley ran as the presidential candidate for the Christian Party. He received less than 1,600 votes. In 1941, after suggesting that the government had lied about the extent of the losses at **Pearl Harbor**, he was arrested and charged with sedition and treason. Pelley was sentenced to 15 years in prison in 1942 and was not released until 1950, at which time he resumed his career as a publisher.

PERKINS, FRANCES (1882–1965). Born Fannie Coralie Perkins, Frances Perkins was a graduate in chemistry and physics of Mount Holyoke College and Columbia University. She taught from 1904 to 1907 and also worked in the Chicago Commons and Hull House settlements. Perkins became executive secretary of the New York Consumer's League from 1910 to 1912 and worked as an authority on industrial safety with the New York Committee of Safety from 1912 to 1917. She served on the Industrial Commission of New York State in 1921 and was appointed by **Alfred E. Smith** to chair the New York State Industrial Board in 1926. She held the position until 1929, when she became secretary of labor for New York under Governor **Franklin D. Roosevelt**. She worked to improve workmen's compensation, conditions and hours of work, and factory inspection, and she called for unemployment insurance at the national level. Following his election to the presidency, Roosevelt made Perkins the first **woman** cabinet officer when he appointed her secretary of labor in 1933.

Perkins was involved in shaping several pieces of **New Deal** legislation, including the **Social Security Act** and **Fair Labor Standards Act**. She also tried to persuade the **American Federation of Labor** and **Congress of Industrial Organizations** to come to some agreement but was not successful. Employers often attacked her for being too soft on **trade unions**, and in 1938 there was an attempt to impeach her for failing to deport the Australian-born leader of the Californian longshoreman, **Harry Bridges**.

During **World War II**, many of the functions of the Labor Department were handled by war agencies. Perkins remained at her post until July 1945, when President **Harry S. Truman** appointed her to the Civil Service Commission. She held the position until 1952. Afterward Perkins became a lecturer at a number of universities and in the late 1950s held a visiting professorship at Cornell.

PHILIPPINE INDEPENDENCE ACT, 1934. Also known as the Tydings-McDuffie Act, the Philippine Independence Act was approved on 24 March 1934 and provided for the Philippine Islands to achieve independence after a 10-year transitional period of constitutional development. The Philippines gained their independence under the act on 4 July 1946.

POINT FOUR PROGRAM. The fourth point of President **Harry S. Truman**'s inaugural address on 20 January 1949 called for a "bold new program" of scientific and technical assistance for the "underdeveloped areas" of the world. Intended as part of the policy of **containment** in the **Cold War**, the program was approved by Congress in May 1950 with an appropriation of $35 million. Some of this was to support the **United Nations Educational, Scientific, and Cultural Organization** programs of aid, and further appropriations were recommended in 1951 and 1952. Although assistance was given to more than 30 countries, in reality the amount of aid provided was a mere fraction of the appropriation.

POLITICAL ACTION COMMITTEE (PAC). The PAC was first established by the **Congress of Industrial Organizations** in 1944 to circumvent controls placed on direct political contributions by **trade unions** under the **War Labor Disputes Act**. The PAC enabled funds to be raised to support candidates. Generally this meant support for **Democratic** candidates. In the 1960s, other groups, businesses, and organizations adopted PACs.

POLLOCK, JACKSON (1912–1956). Hailed as America's "greatest living painter" in 1949, artist Jackson Pollock was born in Cody, Wyoming. He studied under Thomas Hart Benton in New York City in the 1930s and for a time was employed by the **Works Progress Administration**. In 1946, he began the distinctive style of painting by dripping paint onto the canvas to create abstract patterns. He achieved national prominence through an article in *Life* magazine in 1949 and became a best-selling artist in the early 1950s. He died in an automobile crash. *See also* ART.

PORTER, COLE (1891–1964). Prolific songwriter Cole Porter was educated at Worcester Academy, Yale, and Harvard's law and music schools. Having already written several musical comedies and hundreds of songs while at Yale, in 1916 he and T. Lawrason Riggs wrote a musical comedy, *See America First*, produced on Broadway in 1916. Porter went to France in 1917. A number of his songs were included in English musical shows from 1918 to 1922. Porter's music was part of *Within the Quota*, performed in Paris and New York in 1923, the *Greenwich Village Follies* in New York in 1924, *Paris* in 1928 also in New York, *La Revue des Ambassadeurs* performed in Paris in 1928, and *Wake Up and Dream* performed in London in 1929. Porter rose to even greater prominence in the 1930s with songs for shows and movies, the most famous being "Night and Day" from *The Gay Divorcee* (1932), "I Get a Kick out of You" from *Anything Goes* (1934), "Begin the Beguine" from *Jubilee* (1935), "I've Got You under My Skin" from the movie *Born to Dance* (1936), and "In the Still of the Night" from the film *Rosalie* (1937). He continued to write throughout the 1940s and 1950s, most notably for *Kiss Me, Kate* (1948), *Can-Can* (1953), and the film *High Society* (1956), for which his song "True Love" won an Academy Award. However, Porter's sophisticated, languid, and often sensual music seemed to belong more appropriately in the interwar period. *See also* CINEMA; LITERATURE AND THEATER.

POTSDAM CONFERENCE, 1945. Following the defeat of Nazi **Germany**, the leaders of the victorious **Allied powers** met at Potsdam, near **Berlin**, for a conference from 17 July to 2 August 1945. It was the first opportunity for the new U.S. president, **Harry S. Truman**, to meet his British and **Soviet** counterparts, **Winston Churchill** and **Joseph Stalin**. Churchill was replaced on 27 July by Clement Attlee, who became prime minister following his election victory. Although no substantive agreements were reached, those made at the **Yalta Conference** on the division of Germany into zones were confirmed, but there was some indication that the Russians would oppose moves toward economic reunification. The Eastern Frontier between Germany and Poland was also agreed on, but the amount of reparations to be paid to the Soviet Union was scaled down considerably. Truman indicated that he expected elections and a new government to be established in Poland. He also informed Stalin that the United States had developed a new and powerful weapon but made no direct reference to the **atomic bomb**. Stalin confirmed his intention to enter the war against **Japan**. Code-named "Terminal," the Potsdam meeting was the last meeting of the respective heads of state for 10 years as relations quickly deteriorated with the onset of the **Cold War**.

POUND, EZRA (WESTON) LOOMIS (1885–1972). Ezra Pound studied at the University of Pennsylvania and Hamilton College and graduated with an M.A. from the University of Pennsylvania in 1906. After being dismissed from a teaching position in 1907 for "bohemian" behavior, Pound traveled in Europe before settling in London, England, where he became part of the literary avant-garde from 1908 until 1920. He remained an expatriate for the rest of his life. Pound's first volume of poetry, *A Lume Spento*, was published in 1908. This was followed by *Personae* (1909), *Canzoni* (1911), and *Ripostes*

(1912). During this period, he established the Imagist movement and later joined the Vorticists, with whom he published two volumes of *BLAST: A Review of the Great English Vortex* between 1914 and 1915. After World War I, Pound published *Hugh Selwyn Mauberley* (1920) and worked with T. S. Eliot on *Waste Land* (1922). In 1921, Pound joined the expatriate set, including Gertrude Stein and **Ernest Hemingway** in Paris, but in 1924 he moved to Rapallo, Italy, where he remained until the end of the war.

During the interwar period, Pound produced his *Cantos* series of poems, published from 1925 to 1940. He increasingly identified with Italy and Benito Mussolini, was critical of **Franklin D. Roosevelt** and the **New Deal**, and wrote *Jefferson and/or Mussolini* in 1937. Cantos XXXI to LXXI appeared in the 1930s. Between 1941 and 1943 Pound made several broadcasts for **Radio** Rome attacking U.S. policies. Accused of treason, he was arrested in 1945 and after an imprisonment in Pisa, Italy, was transferred to Washington, D.C., where he was found unfit to stand trial. From 1945 until 1958, Pound was held in an insane asylum. His work the *Pisan Cantos* appeared in 1948 and was controversially awarded the Bollingen Prize in Poetry in 1949. He was awarded the Pulitzer Prize for Poetry in 1950. Those who felt that he had been a traitor during the war criticized both awards. Pound published several other works before his death, but none reached the level of his earlier poetry. *See also* LITERATURE AND THEATER.

POWELL, ADAM CLAYTON, JR. (1908–1972). Born in New Haven, Connecticut, Adam Clayton Powell Jr. moved to New York City with his family in 1909. After briefly attending City College, he graduated from Colgate College in 1930 and completed a master's degree in religious education at Columbia University in 1932. Powell accepted a position as business manager at his father's church in Harlem and then succeeded his father as pastor in 1937. Using the pulpit and a regular column in the black newspaper, *Amsterdam News*, Powell was active in mobilizing black protests against discrimination in New York. He was involved in the **National Negro Congress**, encouraged "Don't buy where you can't work" boycotts of white-owned stores, and in 1938 helped found the Greater New York Coordinating Committee on Employment.

In 1941, Powell became the first black person elected to the New York City Council, and in 1944 he won election as a **Democrat**—although also with support of the **Republicans**—to the U.S. House of Representatives to become, with **William L. Dawson**, only the second black congressman at the time. During **World War II**, he published the militant paper, *People's Voice*, and worked for the **Office of Price Administration**. A flamboyant and independent man, Powell supported **Dwight D. Eisenhower** in 1956 because he felt he had done more for **civil rights**. In 1960, Powell forced Bayard Rustin to resign from the Southern Christian Leadership Conference because of his homosexuality. However, in 1967 Powell himself was accused of having misused public money for personal gain and was excluded from the House. In 1969, the **Supreme Court** ruled in his favor, and he returned to Congress, but in 1970 be failed to be renominated.

PRESIDENTIAL SUCCESSION ACT, 1947. Under the terms of the law of 1886 providing for the order of succession to the presidency in the event of removal, resignation, death, or incapacity of the president, the next in line after the vice president was the senior cabinet officer, that is, the secretary of state. **Harry S. Truman**, who had assumed the presidency following **Franklin D. Roosevelt**'s death, did not think this was democratic since cabinet officers are appointed rather than elected. He therefore recommended making the next in line of succession after the vice president the speaker of the House of Representatives, followed by the President pro tempore of the Senate, and then the cabinet officers in order (State, Treasury, Defense, and so forth). The act was passed and the changes went into force on 18 July 1947.

PROGRESSIVE PARTY. Following **Henry A. Wallace**'s announcement of his candidacy for the presidency in December 1947, a Progressive Party was formed in July 1948 to support Wallace and Senator Glen Taylor of Idaho as his running mate. The party opposed the **Truman Doctrine** and **Marshall Plan**, called for better relations with the **Soviet Union**, and was against the peacetime draft. It was endorsed by the **Communist Party of the United States of America** and American Labor Party. In the election, it received just over 1 million votes, less than 3 percent of the popular vote.

PUBLIC HOUSING ADMINISTRATION (PHA). Created in July 1947 as part of the reorganization and rationalization of government agencies, the Public Housing Administration took over the functions of the **United States Housing Authority** and **Federal Public Housing Authority**.

PUBLIC WORKS ADMINISTRATION (PWA). Established under Title II of the **National Industrial Recovery Act** in 1933 as the Federal Emergency Administration of Public Works to combat unemployment and to "prime the pump" of the economy, the PWA was funded with $3.3 billion to be granted to support state and municipal public works projects. The act provided 30 percent of the cost of projects with the rest in the form of loans. **Harold Ickes** was appointed to head the administration. Although the PWA ultimately spent almost $6 billion and provided jobs for 2 million workers on numerous projects, including the **Grand Coulee Dam**, it was regarded as too slow and ineffective. In 1933, the **Civil Works Administration** was created under **Harry Hopkins** to provide immediate short-term work relief, and in 1935 the **Works Progress Administration** was set up as a more effective alternative. The PWA was incorporated into the **Federal Works Agency** in 1939.

PURGE OF 1938. Angered by conservative members of the **Democratic Party** who were forming a conservative bloc with **Republicans** in Congress, President **Franklin D. Roosevelt** actively intervened in the elections of 1938 to try to block the nomination of several incumbent Democrats. Such an action was unprecedented and was referred to as the "purge," echoing the actions of totalitarian leaders in Nazi **Germany** and the **Soviet Union**. In the event, the attempt failed, and only one of the conservatives was defeated. It also increased the impression that the president was assuming dictatorial powers and increased opposition rather than reducing it.

PYLE, ERNEST (ERNIE) TAYLOR (1900–1945). Famous war correspondent Ernie Pyle was born in Indiana. He did not complete his studies at the University of Indiana, but after brief service in the navy in 1918, he began work in newspapers. After working with the *Washington Daily News*, Pyle moved to New York City to write for the *New York Evening World* and *Evening Post*. He returned to Washington, D. C., to become editor of the *Daily News* from 1932 to 1935, before becoming a roving reporter for the Scripps Howard newspaper chain. In 1940, Pyle went to **Great Britain** to cover the "Blitz," and after 1941 he was a war correspondent with the U.S. Army in Europe, Africa, and Asia during **World War II**. His reports of the life of ordinary soldiers captured the imagination of the public, and he was dubbed "the most widely read correspondent." His collected reports were published as *Ernie Pyle in England* (1941), *Here Is Your War: The Story of G.I. Joe* (1943), and *Brave Men* (1944). Pyle was awarded the Pulitzer Prize for his writing in 1944 but was killed in the fighting in **Okinawa** in 1945.

– R –

RADIO. During the 1930s and 1940s, radio increasingly became a chief source of news and entertainment. Already well-established in the 1920s, radio had two national networks, the National Broadcasting Corporation (NBC) and Columbia Broadcasting System (CBS). By 1930, approximately 12 million homes had radio, and by the end of the decade, that number had risen to 28 million, or 80 percent of the population. By 1945, the number was about 33 million. With the development of Bakelite, radios became stylish pieces of furniture around which the family would gather to listen to the comedy of **Amos 'n' Andy**, **Jack Benny**, **George Burns**, **Gracie Allen**, **Will Rogers**, and **Bob Hope**. Audiences were entertained by such characters as Dick Tracy, The Green Hornet (originally The Hornet), and The Shadow. So convincing was **Orson Welles**'s 1938 reading of the H. G. Welles novel *War of the Worlds* as a newscast that audiences believed Martians really were invading, while other listeners were shocked by the sexual references of **Mae West** in a 1937 skit about the Garden of Eden. **Music** programs and **sporting** events were also major attractions, but audiences could also be reached directly by such politicians as Father **Charles Coughlin**, the "radio priest," or by the president, **Franklin D. Roosevelt**, through his influential "**fireside chats**." During **World War II**, Americans listened to the radio reports of **Edward R. Murrow** and others, and it was through radio that many first heard of Roosevelt's death. Commercial advertising on radio was suspended for several days as the nation mourned. Radio broadcasts covered many of the events of the **Cold War** era, ranging from presidential addresses to congressional hearings featuring Senator **Joseph McCarthy**. *See also* CANTOR, EDDIE; CROSBY, BING; FIELDS, WILLIAM CLAUDE (W. C.); GOODMAN, BENNY; GUTHRIE, WOODOW WILSON ("WOODY"); MILLER, (ALTON) GLENN; PEALE, NORMAN VINCENT; SINATRA, FRANCIS (FRANK) ALBERT; TELEVISION; VALLEE, RUDY; VOICE OF AMERICA.

RAFT, GEORGE (1895–1980). Actor George Raft was born George Ranft in New York City. He changed his name in 1917. Raft's stage career began as a professional dancer and actor, but in 1929 he went to Hollywood and appeared in his first film, *Queen of Night Clubs*. Other early films included *If I Had a Million* (1932) and *Night after Night* (1932) with **Mae West**. However, Raft's big breakthrough came with the lead in *Scarface* (1932), which established him, alongside **Humphrey Bogart** and **James Cagney**, as one of the leading movie gangster characters. Among his other successes were *The Glass Key* (1935), *Souls at Sea* (1937), *Invisible Stripes* (with Bogart in 1939), *They Drive by Night* (also with Bogart in 1940), and *Each Dawn I Die* (with Cagney in 1939). After *Manpower* (1941), *Backgound to Danger* (1943), and *Follow the Boys* (1944), Raft's career declined. The 1950s **television** series *I Am the Law*, in which he starred, was a flop, and Raft faced financial and tax problems. He was also denied entry into **Great Britain** because of his underworld connections. Raft appeared in *Some Like It Hot* (1959), the original film version of *Ocean's 11* (1960) and *Casino Royale* (1967). His last film appearance, also with West, was in *Sextette* (1978). *See also* CINEMA.

RAILROAD RETIREMENT ACTS, 1934, 1937. The Railroad Retirement Acts were federal laws providing annuity payments for railroad workers, with two-thirds paid for by the companies and one-third by the workers, with retirement at age 65. The first act was declared unconstitutional by the Supreme Court in 1935. It was replaced by the Railroad Retirement Act of 1937, which incorporated similar provision but was financed through a tax levied on carriers and employees.

RAILROADS. The railroad industry, which began in the early 19th century and grew with increasing rapidity from the 1830s onward, was central to U.S. economic growth. By 1860, there were more than 30,000 miles of railroad track in the United States. The greatest wave of railroad construction came after the Civil War in conjunction with westward expansion and settlement and massive industrialization in the East. The first transcontinental railroad was completed in 1869, and by the start of the 20th century more than 200,000 miles of track had been laid.

The railroad industry also witnessed the development of huge corporations headed by entrepreneurs. Despite the beginning of regulation with the creation of the Interstate Commerce Commission in 1886, the ruthless profiteering and shady business practices of such men led to calls for reform. Legislation aimed at curbing railroad monopolies and controlling the rates charged by companies was passed under both Theodore Roosevelt and Woodrow Wilson. During World War I, the government took over operation of railroads and, although there were calls for the practice to continue, they were returned to private ownership under the Railroad Transportation Act of 1920.

Postwar readjustments led to labor conflict in the industry and a major railroad strike in 1922. The development of the automobile and air transportation and the earlier overexpansion of uneconomic lines placed the industry in an increasingly unfavorable position from the 1920s onward. By 1929, interstate rail travel had fallen by 18 percent. Railroad mileage, which peaked at 254,000 miles in 1916, had fallen to 249,619 miles by 1930. Many railroad companies were heavily in debt and in 1932 were provided with loans by the **Reconstruction Finance Corporation**. In 1933, the Emergency Railroad Transportation Act consolidated the railroads into three regional groups and established a coordinator to prevent duplication of services and bring about greater cooperation. The development of diesel and some new lines contributed to some increase in rail travel in the late 1930s. Reforms were also introduced to benefit rail workers. Two **Railroad Retirement Acts** providing retirement payments to railroad workers were introduced under the **New Deal**, the first in 1934. When it was declared unconstitutional in 1935, a second was passed in 1937. Benefits were increased in 1951.

Railroads faced a considerable demand during **World War II**, and they avoided falling under government control by pooling resources and adopting centralized traffic control. Timetabling was managed through the federal Office of Defense Transportation. The war provided railroads with a new lease on life as they were the major form of freight transportation during the war and experienced a huge increase in passenger travel. However, after the war the railway system again faced competition from road and air transport, particularly after the development of the federal highway system in the mid to late 1950s, and they declined in importance.

RAILWAY LABOR ACT, 1934. An amendment to the Railway Labor Act of 1926 passed to give railway workers the same rights to collective bargaining provided to other workers under the **National Industrial Recovery Act**, the Railway Labor Act passed on 21 June 1933 established a National Railway Adjustment Board with both employee members and members from **trade unions**. The act protected workers' organizations from interference and prohibited "yellow dog contracts" requiring workers to join company unions.

RANDOLPH, A. PHILIP (1889–1979). A. Philip Randolph was born in Florida and attended the Cookman Institute. In 1911, he moved to New York City and took courses at City College. Together with Chandler Owen, Randolph opened an employment office in Harlem to try to unionize fellow **African American** migrants and enlist black recruits for the Socialist Party. In 1917, Randolph and Owen began to produce *The Messenger*, a left-wing journal aimed at black audiences. Their opposition to African American participation in the war effort during World War I led to them being charged under the Sedition Act, but the charge was dismissed because the judge believed they were the dupes of white radicals. During the Red Scare, *The Messenger* was described as the "most able and most dangerous" of all black publications.

After World War I, Randolph voiced opposition to Marcus Garvey's call for racial separatism and from 1925 onward was involved in trying to organize the Pullman car porters into a **trade union**. He established the Brotherhood of Sleeping Car Porters (BSCP) with *The Messenger* as its official publication. In 1935, the BSCP was finally given a charter by the **American Federation of Labor** and recognized by the Pullman Company in 1937. Randolph was the BSCP president until his retirement in 1968. He was appointed to the New York City Commission on Race in 1935 and also became president of the **National Negro Congress** concerned with the economic situation of African Americans. Faced with continued discrimination in the developing defense industries, in 1940 Randolph called for a **March on Washington** to protest in July 1941. Threatened by a potentially embarrassing demonstration, President **Franklin D. Roosevelt** issued an executive order outlawing discrimination and establishing a **Fair Employment Practices Committee** to investigate complaints, and the march was called off. Randolph unsuccessfully campaigned for the establishment of a permanent fair employment practices act. With the reintroduction of selective service after **World War II**, Randolph again mobilized black opinion to protest against segregation in the armed forces, and in 1948 President **Harry S. Truman** issued Executive Order 9981 initiating the integration of the military.

Randolph organized a Prayer Pilgrimage in Washington, D.C., in 1957 and supported Youth Marches for Integrated Schools in 1958 and 1959. In 1955, he was appointed as one of the vice presidents of the newly merged AFL-CIO. It was Randolph who in 1963 suggested a March on Washington for Jobs and Freedom. The march was one of the highpoints of the **civil rights** demonstrations of the 1960s. However, Randolph subsequently agreed to a moratorium on demonstrations to support Lyndon Johnson in the presidential election. The same year, Randolph established the Randolph Institute to encourage links between labor organizations and the civil rights movement. Although such actions separated him from the increasingly militant and separatist black power groups, he remained an influential figure in civil rights until his death. *See also* NATIONAL ASSOCIATION FOR THE ADVANCEMENT OF COLORED PEOPLE (NAACP).

RANKIN, JEANNETTE (1880–1973). Born in Missoula, Montana, Jeannette Rankin was a graduate of the University of Montana in 1902 and the New York School of Philanthropy in 1909. She was a social worker in Seattle in 1909 and became involved in the **women's** suffrage campaign. Following Montana's acceptance of female suffrage in 1914, Rankin was the first woman to serve in the U.S. Congress when she was elected on a progressive **Republican** platform in 1916. She voted against U.S. entry into World War I. Having failed to be elected to the U.S. Senate in 1918, Rankin returned to social work and became active in a number of women's causes and was particularly active in peace organizations, notably the Women's International League for Peace and Freedom. She returned to the U.S. House of Representatives in 1940 on an antiwar platform and became a supporter of the **America First Committee**. Rankin's vote was the sole vote cast against war in 1941, and she did not seek reelection in 1942 but turned instead to lecturing and working for the National Consumers' League and Women's International League for Peace and Freedom. After **World War II**, she became interested in nonviolent campaigns for **civil rights** and visited India several times. She later protested against the war in Vietnam and in 1968 led several thousand women in an antiwar demonstration in Washington, D.C.

RASKOB, JOHN JAKOB (1879–1950). Born in Lockport, New York, after leaving college John Raskob became a business secretary. He held a number of different posts in business before he became bookkeeper and then personal secretary to Pierre S. du Pont in 1900. While with du Pont, Raskob was involved in the absorption of General Motors. He became finance director and then vice president of General Motors from 1918 to 1928 but continued to work for du Pont until 1946. A multimillionaire, Raskob wrote an article in the *Ladies Home Journal* in 1929 entitled "Everybody Ought to Be Rich" that seemed to sum-up the 1920s. However, Raskob was a friend and supporter of **Alfred E. Smith**, and he became chair of the Democratic National Committee in 1928 and supported Smith's unsuccessful presidential campaign. Raskob resigned his position and returned to General Motors in 1932, when **Franklin D. Roosevelt** won the nomination. He subsequently was active in the anti-**New Deal American Liberty League**, and after he retired in 1946 he was involved in a number of charitable organizations and the Catholic Church. The Empire State Building, which he financed in competition with the Chrysler Building (completed in October 1928 at 1,045 feet tall), is a lasting memorial to him. The Empire State Building was completed in 1931 and stood 1,453 feet tall.

RATIONING. Rationing of raw materials, foodstuff, and consumer goods went into effect during **World War II** starting with rubber and tire rationing in spring 1942. This was followed with some controls on gasoline in May 1942—primarily to save on rubber—and it was extended to nationwide gasoline rationing in December 1942. As shortages began to effect supplies of meat, sugar, butter, and canned goods, the **Office of Price Administration** introduced coupons that could be used when purchasing scarce items, beginning with sugar and then coffee. By the end of 1943, many items were rationed in this manner. Neither rationing nor shortages were as severe as those experienced in other nations during the war, and most of the controls were lifted in August 1945. A few continued into 1956.

RAYBURN, SAMUEL (1882–1961). Born in Tennessee, Samuel Rayburn's family moved to Texas in 1887. Rayburn graduated from East Texas Normal College in 1903 and then taught for two years. In 1906, he was elected as a **Democrat** to the state legislature, where he became speaker of the house. He also studied law and was admitted to the bar in 1908. In 1912, Rayburn was elected to Congress, where he became a close associate of **John Nance Garner**. Rayburn rose to importance in the House, and as Chair of the House Interstate Commerce Committee, he had considerable influence on **New Deal** legislation, particularly the **Securities Act** of 1933, **Securities and Exchange Act** of 1934, and the Rural Electrification Act of 1936. Rayburn became speaker of the house in 1940 and held the post until 1957, other than when the **Republicans** were in the majority from 1947 to 1948 and 1953 to 1954. Rayburn worked closely with **Harry S. Truman**, remained loyal when the **Dixiecrats** bolted the party in 1948, worked to enable the passage of **civil rights** legislation in 1957 and 1960, and helped to nurture the career of Lyndon B. Johnson. Known for his honesty, integrity, and political know-how, the Rayburn House Office Building built in 1965 adjacent to the U.S. Capitol is a memorial to his name.

RECESSION OF 1937–1938. Known as the "Roosevelt Recession," the downturn in the economy of almost 30 percent between September 1937 and June 1938 was a major setback for the **New Deal**. It was prompted in part by cuts in federal spending and the impact of the new **Social Security** taxes. Although the economy improved from mid-1938 onward, full recovery did not come until government spending increased with defense preparations from 1940 forward. *See also* ROOSEVELT, FRANKLIN DELANO.

RECONSTRUCTION FINANCE CORPORATION (RFC). The RFC was established by Congress in 1932 after the recommendation of **Herbert Hoover** to "provide emergency financing facilities for financial institutions," and to "aid in financing agriculture, commerce, and industry" to counter the effects of the **Great Depression**. Its primary concern was to halt the run on banks and restore faith in the financial system to encourage a revival of industry. It was initially headed by Charles Dawes and was described by some as a "rich man's dole." Before the end of the Hoover administration, the RFC had lent $1.5 billion to **banks**, mortgage loan companies, railroads, insurance companies, and agricultural credit organizations. President **Franklin D. Roosevelt** expanded the RFC's role as a major funding agency supporting other **New Deal** agencies, and it was grouped with other agencies as the **Federal Loan Agency** in 1939. It survived in various forms and was involved in financing a number of war-related activities involving the purchase and sale of vital war materials. Its capital stock, originally $500 million, was reduced in 1948 to $100 million. Revelations of various financial irregularities and misuse of funds involving members of the **Democratic Party** in the 1950s led to its dissolution in 1954.

RED BALL EXPRESS. The Red Ball Express was the code name given to the supply route than ran from Cherbourg on the French coast to frontline U.S. troops between 25 August and 16 November 1944 following the breakout from **Normandy** after **D-Day**. Approximately 6,000 trucks were used to move more than 12,000 tons of supplies daily to enable the **Allied** advance to continue. Many of the truck drivers were **African American** servicemen.

RED CHANNELS. Subtitled "A Report of Communist Influence in Radio and Television," *Red Channels* was a booklet produced in

1950, written by a former **Federal Bureau of Investigation** agent, Theodore Kirkpatrick, and a right-wing television producer, Vincent Harnett, and published by the right-wing journal *Counterattack*. It listed 151 individuals in **theater**, film, and **radio** broadcasting with links to left-wing organizations. Among those named were harmonica player Larry Adler, musical director and conductor Leonard Bernstein, actor Lee J. Cobb, composer **Aaron Copland**, writer **Dashiell Hammett**, folksinger Pete Seeger, and playwright **Arthur Miller**. All were **blacklisted** by Hollywood until they cleared their names before the **House Un-American Activities Committee**. Some chose not to do so.

REED, STANLEY FORMAN (1884–1980). Born in Kentucky, Stanley Reed studied for his B.A. at Kentucky Wesleyan College in 1902 and Yale University in 1906, where he graduated in 1908. He studied law at the University of Virginia and Columbia Law School but did not complete his program. He spent a year at the Sorbonne in Paris in 1908. Reed was admitted to the bar in Kentucky in 1910 and established a practice in Maysville that year. He served in the Kentucky General Assembly from 1912 to 1916, leaving to serve in the army in World War I. After the war, Reed worked for a law firm and was appointed general counsel to the Federal Farm Board by **Herbert Hoover** in 1929. In 1932, he became counsel to the **Reconstruction Finance Corporation** and in 1935 was appointed solicitor general.

In 1938 President **Franklin D. Roosevelt** appointed Reed to the **Supreme Court**, where he consistently upheld **New Deal** measures involving federal regulation of the economy. Generally regarded as a moderate, Reed wrote the majority argument in *Smith v. Allwright* and later supported the decision in *Brown v. Board of Education of Topeka* against segregation in schools. He retired in 1957 and became a judge in the lower courts. He was appointed by President **Dwight D. Eisenhower** to chair the U.S. Civil Rights Commission but declined the appointment to maintain the impartiality of the judiciary.

REGIONALISTS. The regionalists were a group of artists who focused on rural scenes, mainly in the Midwest, and celebrated the American landscape and history. Chief among them were **John Steuart Curry**,

Thomas Hart Benton, and **Grant Wood**. Wood perhaps summed up the underlying themes of the movement best when he said he depicted "a country rich in the arts of peace, a homely, loveable nation, infinitely worth any sacrifice necessary to its preservation." The artists shared many of the attributes of those producing work in the "**American Scene**" in that they reflected American themes and styles rather than those of European modernists. *See also* ART.

REORGANIZATION ACT, 1939. The need to improve the efficiency and management of the federal government was an increasing concern in the 1930s with the growth of government agencies in the **New Deal** and regular charges of waste and inefficiency. In 1936 President **Franklin D. Roosevelt** appointed a Committee on Administrative Management to examine the issue, and it reported in 1937. The report called for the creation of six executive assistants and a permanent National Resources Planning Board to assist the president; executive control of accounts and budget proposals; and additional cabinet posts, together with civil service reform. Linked by many people to the president's attempt at "**court packing**," critics viewed the measure as another step toward excessive presidential authority. In 1938 the Executive Reorganization Bill was defeated in both houses of Congress. An amended bill, excluding civil service reform and the creation of new departments, was passed in 1939. Following the passage of this legislation, Roosevelt was able to establish a **Federal Security Agency**, **Federal Works Agency**, **Federal Loan Agency**, and Executive Office of the President to consolidate management of government.

REPEAL AMENDMENT. *See* TWENTY-FIRST AMENDMENT.

REPUBLICAN PARTY. For much of the latter half of the 19th century and early years of the 20th century, the party of Abraham Lincoln—the **Republican Party**—dominated politics, controlling both the White House and Congress. However, from the turn of the century onward, the conservative element in the party was increasingly challenged by progressive insurgents demanding reform. Those divisions enabled Woodrow Wilson to win the presidential election in 1912, and the **Democrats** also gained control of both the House and the Senate. The demise of the reform impulse and the reaction to the Versailles peace settlement and League of Nations at the end of World War I restored some unity to the Republican Party and enabled them to regain control of the White House under Presidents Warren Harding, Calvin Coolidge, and **Herbert Hoover**. Nonetheless, a number of progressive Republicans like **William Borah**, **Hiram Johnson**, and **George Norris** followed an independent line. The Republicans had majorities in the House and Senate from 1919, until the **Great Depression** destroyed their credibility and led to a Democratic landslide in the election of 1932 that saw **Franklin D. Roosevelt** triumph with the promise of a **New Deal**.

The Democratic domination of Congress tightened in 1934, and the ineffectual **Alf Landon** was easily beaten by Roosevelt in 1936. In the 75th Congress from 1937 to 1939, the Republicans only held 16 Senate seats to the Democrats' 76 and 88 seats in the House to the Democrats' 334. However, following Roosevelt's attempted "**court packing**," a further downturn in the economy, and a wave of industrial disputes, the Republicans began to regain some ground and, led by **Robert A. Taft**, were able to form a "conservative coalition" with southern Democrats in Congress. Divisions within the party resurfaced in response to the growing conflict in Europe. Taft and **Arthur H. Vandenberg** were both staunchly isolationist, while others led by **Henry L. Stimson** and **Frank Knox** argued for support for **Great Britain** and France. In 1940, with the campaign for nomination divided between Taft, Vandenberg, and **Thomas E. Dewey**, the party united behind the dark horse, **Wendell Willkie**, who won on the sixth ballot. He was defeated convincingly by Roosevelt in the election.

During **World War II**, the Republicans continued to gain ground in Congress, and in 1942 the "conservative coalition" was strengthened by Democratic losses outside the South. Although they increased their numbers in Congress, the Republicans could still not win the wartime presidential election, and Dewey was defeated in 1944. However, a massive swing in their favor enabled the party to capture both houses in the 80th Congress from 1947 to 1949 and promised victory in the presidential campaign against **Harry S. Truman** in 1948. However, when Truman presented Congress with a series of reform measures, which the conservatives overwhelming rejected, he labeled it "the do-nothing Congress," and his whirlwind cross-country campaign produced an upset victory against Dewey. The Democrats regained control of Congress in 1949, but the Republicans recovered and won the presidency with **Dwight D. Eisenhower** in 1952. By this time the party was aggressively anticommunist in **foreign policy**, probusiness in economic policy, and against waste and inefficiency in government. It was but inclined to accept basic social welfare provision.

RESETTLEMENT ADMINISTRATION (RA). The RA was created in 1935 to coordinate several agricultural policies under the **New Deal** and provide assistance for displaced farmers under the leadership of **Rexford Tugwell**. The RA was also empowered to assist farm tenants become homeowners. It was intended that some 500,000 families would be resettled, but only 4,441 were, and most attention was given to providing camps for migrant workers and the building of three towns under the Suburban Resettlement scheme. Because of continued problems in rural areas, the RA was replaced by the **Farm Security Administration** in 1937.

REUTHER, WALTER (1907–1970). Future labor leader Walter Reuther was born in West Virginia and left school at the age of 16 to work. In 1927, he went to Detroit, Michigan, to work for Ford Motor Company. In 1932, he went to Europe and spent two years working in the automobile industry in the **Soviet Union**. He returned to the United States in 1935 and in 1936 became a labor organizer for the **Congress of Industrial Organizations (CIO)** and the United Auto Workers (UAW). He led a successful **sit-down strike** in 1936 and took part in the Flint Strike in 1937. He was badly beaten by men working for Ford Motor Company outside the River Rouge plant in Detroit. During **World War II**, Reuther became the UAW vice president and in 1946 president. In 1946, he called upon General Motors (GM) to give a 30 percent increase in wages without raising the price of their automobiles, arguing that it would boost consumption and help avoid a return to the conditions of the **Great Depression**. In 1948, he won an automatic cost of living agreement from GM and subsequently linked wage rises to productivity.

Reelected to the UAW presidency in 1947, Reuther took a strong anticommunist position and was a founding member of **Americans for Democratic Action**. He also worked to establish procedures that would avoid strikes and helped win pensions and health benefits as part of the auto workers' contracts. In 1952, Reuther became president of the CIO and helped secure the merger with the **American Federation of Labor (AFL)** in 1955. However, he withdrew the UAW from the AFL-CIO in 1968 because of what he saw as the organization's complacency. He was killed in an air crash in 1970.

REVENUE ACT, 1942. One of the most important revenue acts introduced during **World War II**, the Revenue Act of 1942 for the first time extended federal income tax to the majority of the working population. Personal exemptions were lowered to $500 for single individuals and $1,200 for married couples. In 1939, only 4 million Americans paid income tax. In 1943 this number rose to 43 million, and by the end of the war it was 50 million. Surtaxes, corporation taxes, and inheritance taxes were also raised. In 1943, the system of payroll tax deductions on a "pay-as-you-go" system was introduced.

REVENUE ACTS, 1935, 1936, 1938. Reversing the trend of the previous Republican administrations and indicative of the more radical approach of the "**Second New Deal**," the Revenue Acts increased general taxes, estate and gift taxes, and excess profits taxes and introduced an undistributed profits tax on corporate income. The Revenue Act of 1935, dubbed the Wealth Tax, increased the tax on incomes more than $50,000 from 59 percent to 75 percent and more than $5 million to 79 percent, and it also increased estate taxes and corporation taxes. These measures prompted an angry response from business interests and also attracted criticism from those who believed the increased taxes triggered the **Recession of 1937–1938**. In 1938, Congress repealed the undistributed profits tax and increases in normal taxes introduced in 1936, but they were forced to restore some of these when President **Franklin D. Roosevelt** threatened to veto the bill. Eventually a compromise bill retaining certain elements passed without the president's signature.

RHEE, SYNGMAN (1875–1965). South Korean leader Syngman Rhee spent most of the time between 1905 and 1945 in exile. He spent several years in the United States and studied at George Washington University and Princeton, where he obtained a Ph.D. He was elected president of the Republic of Korea (South Korea) in 1948 and maintained power throughout the **Korean War**. He was reelected in 1952, 1956, and 1960. However, his increasingly authoritarian rule provoked a popular uprising, and he fled to Hawaii in 1960.

RIDGWAY, MATTHEW BUNKER (1895–1993). Born to a military family in Fort Monroe, Virginia, Matthew Ridgway graduated from West Point in 1917. During World War I, he served in the United States. After the war, he held a number of peacetime positions, including postings in **China**, Nicaragua, Panama, Brazil, and the Philippines. In 1942, Ridgway took command of the 82nd Division, the first airborne division in the U.S. Army. He led them in action in North Africa, Sicily, and **Normandy**. In 1950, he successfully took command of the demoralized U.S. Eighth Army, which had been pushed back by the Chinese in the **Korean War**, and in April 1951 he replaced the disgraced General **Douglas MacArthur** as commander of the **United Nations (UN)** forces. Under his leadership, UN forces maintained the stalemate with their Chinese and North Korean opponents rather than seek territorial gains. In May 1952, Ridgway replaced General **Dwight D. Eisenhower** as the supreme **allied** commander in Europe for the **North Atlantic Treaty Organization**. The following year he became the U.S. Army chief of staff. However, Ridgway was opposed to the "New Look" policy of reliance on air power and nuclear weaponry and the principle of "massive retaliation," and he retired in 1955. He became an executive at the Mellon Foundation, but as an advisor to President Lyndon B. Johnson in the 1960s, he spoke out against escalation of U.S. involvement in the war in Vietnam.

RIO PACT. The Rio Pact, formally known as the Inter-American Treaty of Reciprocal Assistance, was agreed upon at the meeting of American nations in Rio de Janeiro, Brazil, between 15 August and 2 September 1947. While it represented a continuation of the **"Good Neighbor" Policy** and was a formulation of the agreement at **Chapultepec**, the pact established a regional defense alliance that was further developed in the creation of the **Organization of American States** as part of the policy of **containment**. The importance of the agreement was highlighted by President **Harry S. Truman**'s attendance at the final sessions of the meeting. *See also* FOREIGN POLICY.

ROBERTS, OWEN JOSEPHUS (1875–1955). Supreme Court Justice Owen Roberts was educated at the University of Pennsylvania and the University of Pennsylvania Law School, where he graduated in 1898. He practiced law in Philadelphia, Pennsylvania, and for 22 years taught at the University of Pennsylvania Law School. In 1918, Roberts became a special deputy U.S. attorney. In 1924, President Calvin Coolidge appointed him, together with Atlee Pomerene, to prosecute those involved in the Teapot Dome scandal.

In 1930, President **Herbert Hoover** nominated Roberts to fill the empty seat on the Supreme Court following the death of Edward Sanford. With the new chief justice **Charles Evans Hughes**, Roberts held the balance between the conservatives and liberals in the court. The court became increasingly liberal on issues of freedom of speech and, in the case of the **Scottsboro Boys**, on the right of defendants to have counsel appointed for their defense. However, Roberts tended to side with the conservatives in cases concerning the extension of government authority under the **New Deal**. But following Franklin D. Roosevelt's attempt to alter the composition of the court, Roberts made "a switch in time that saved nine" and sided with the liberal group to uphold minimum wage laws, the **National Labor Relations Act**, and the **Social Security Act**. Roberts tended to be more conservative on **civil rights** and civil liberties and supported white primaries in 1935, compulsory flag salutes, and the pledge of allegiance in public schools in 1940. However, he dissented against the decision to uphold the evacuation of **Japanese Americans** during **World War II**.

Following his retirement in 1945, Roberts was dean of the University of Pennsylvania Law School from 1948 to 1951. He was also chair of the security board of the **Atomic Energy Commission**. His Holmes lectures at Harvard Law School in 1951 were published as *The Court and the Constitution* (1951).

ROBESON, PAUL LEROY BUSTILL (1898–1976). American singer, actor, athlete, and **civil rights** activist Paul Robeson was born the son of a former slave in Princeton, New Jersey. He attended

Rutgers College. An outstanding scholar and athlete, he became the first **African American** all-American in football in 1917 and again in 1918. Following his graduation in 1919, Robeson went to Columbia University Law School, where he obtained his degree in 1923 and began working in a New York City law firm. Following a racial slight, he gave up law and joined Eugene O'Neill's Provincetown Players and starred in *All God's Chillun Got Wings* and *The Emperor Jones* in 1924. Robeson began his solo singing career with a performance of gospel songs at Carnegie Hall in 1925 and was celebrated for singing and acting in various musicals, most famously for his performance of "Ol' Man River" in *Showboat* (1928). In 1930, he achieved critical acclaim for his portrayal of *Othello* in London, and he went on to appear in 11 movies, including *Song of Freedom* (1936), *King Solomon's Mines* (1937), and *Proud Valley* (1940), in addition to film versions of his stage successes. He was the best-known black entertainer of his day.

Embittered by racial prejudice in the United States, Robeson spent more time performing in Europe after 1928. In the 1930s, he visited the **Soviet Union** and became an advocate of communism. He went to Spain in 1938 to support the **Republican** forces in the **Spanish Civil War**. He returned to the United States at the outbreak of **World War II** and achieved great success when he became the first African American to play the lead in *Othello* in the United States in 1943. After the war, Robeson continued to support left-wing causes and was a founder and chair of the **Progressive Party**. His political sympathies and outspoken remarks led to his being investigated by congressional committees, which labeled him a communist and led to his being **blacklisted** as an entertainer. His passport was revoked from 1950 to 1958, effectively destroying his career. The Soviet Union awarded Robeson the Stalin Peace Prize in 1952, and he left the United States in 1958 and did not return until 1963. He lived out his remaining years in virtual seclusion but was remembered with several awards for his contributions to the arts and civil rights. *See also* CINEMA; LITERATURE AND THEATER.

ROBIN MOOR. The *Robin Moor* was an unarmed U.S. merchant ship sunk by a German submarine in the south Atlantic Ocean 700 miles off the coast of Africa on 21 May 1941. The crew was cast adrift in lifeboats with limited supplies. In a message to Congress, President **Franklin D. Roosevelt** deemed it "an act of piracy" and called for action to resist the spread of German naval power.

ROBINSON, EDWARD GOLDENBERG (1893–1973). Born Emanuel Goldenberg to a Jewish family in Bucharest, Romania, Edward G. Robinson, as he was later known, came to the United States with his family in 1903. After attending high school in New York City, he enrolled in City College of New York but won an acting scholarship and began his stage career under his new name in 1913. He served in the navy during World War I. Robinson appeared in more than 30 New York stage plays between 1913 and 1929 and in his first named film role in 1923. His career took off after his role as the gangster Rico in *Little Caesar* in 1931. He was cast in similar roles in several B movies, including *Five Star Final* (1931), *Smart Money* (1931), *Tiger Shark* (1932), and *Kid Galahad* (1937) with **Humphrey Bogart**. In the 1940s, he starred in *The Sea Wolf* (1941) and two biographical studies, *Dr. Ehrlich's Magic Bullet* (1940) and *A Dispatch from Reuters* (1940) and played successful roles in such thrillers as *Double Indemnity* (1944), *The Woman in the Window* (1945), and *Scarlet Street* (1945), before returning to a gangster role to critical acclaim in *Key Largo* (1948), again with Bogart.

Robinson was called to testify before the **House Un-American Activities Committee** on more than one occasion between 1950 and 1952, and under pressure he named several communist sympathizers in the film community. His film career declined afterward, but he had some success in *A Hole in the Head* (1959) with **Frank Sinatra**, *The Prize* (1963), and *The Cincinnati Kid* (1965) with Steve McQueen. Among his last films were *Mackenna's Gold* (1969) and *Song of Norway* (1970). Robinson was given an honorary Oscar in 1973 shortly after his death. *See also* CINEMA.

ROBINSON, JACK ("JACKIE") ROOSEVELT (1919–1972). Born in Georgia, Jackie Robinson grew up in Pasadena, California, and was a student at the University of California in Los Angeles, where he became the first student to letter in four sports—football, basketball, baseball, and track. He played professional football for the Los Angeles Bulldogs in 1941 and joined the army in 1942. He successfully fought to be admitted to integrated officer training but was court-martialed for refusing to accept segregation in public transport in 1944. He was given an honorable discharge. He joined the all-black Kansas City Monarchs baseball team in 1944 but was signed by Branch Rickey for the minor league team for the Brooklyn Dodgers, the Montreal Royals, in 1946. On 15 April 1947, Robinson became the first **African American** to play major league baseball when he appeared for the Dodgers. Despite considerable abuse and provocation from some players and crowds, he was a great success, becoming rookie of the year in 1947 and the National League's most valuable player in 1949, and he helped the Dodgers win six National League pennants between 1947 and 1956. He became the first African American to be inducted into the Baseball Hall of Fame in 1962.

Following his retirement from baseball in 1957, Robinson became vice president of Chock Full o'Nuts, a coffee house chain. He retired from that position in 1964 to campaign in the political arena. He was also active in **civil rights** as a member and fundraiser for the **National Association for the Advancement of Colored People**, and he campaigned for the appointment of a black baseball manager. In 2005, Robinson was posthumously awarded the Congressional Gold Medal.

ROCKWELL, NORMAN (1894–1978). Norman Rockwell was born in New York City and attended the Chase Art School in 1910. He quickly found work as a book and magazine illustrator and in 1913 became an editor and an illustrator for *Boy's Life* magazine. He provided illustrations for many magazines and journals. However, he is best known for his covers for the *Saturday Evening Post*—he produced more than 320 between 1916 and 1963. Rockwell's paintings focused on scenes from U.S. history and everyday life and always depicted warmth and humor. In 1943, he produced four paintings for the *Saturday Evening Post* representing the **Four Freedoms**. They had such an impact that they were used as war posters by the **Office of War Information** in support of **war bonds**, and it was estimated that they helped raise $130 million. Equally famous was Rockwell's painting of **Rosie the Riveter** that appeared on the *Saturday Evening Post* cover on 29 May 1943. Beginning in 1963 Rockwell produced illustrations for *Look* magazine and portraits of such presidents as

Dwight D. Eisenhower, John F. Kennedy, and Ronald Reagan. His work featured space flight, **civil rights**, and the war on poverty. Rockwell died on 8 November 1978 in his home with an unfinished painting on his easel. *See also* ART.

RODGERS, RICHARD (1902–1979). Songwriter Richard Rodgers was born in Arverne, New York, and studied at Columbia College, where he met lyricist **Lorenz Hart** and formed a successful partnership that lasted until 1942. After leaving Columbia College in 1921, Rodgers studied at the Institute of Musical Art in New York City. In 1935, he and Hart had their first success with *The Garrick Gaieties* and then produced a string of hits, including *The Girl Friend* (1926), *A Connecticut Yankee* (1927), and *Evergreen* (1930). From 1930 until 1934, Rodgers and Hart worked in Hollywood but were not enormously successful. In 1935, they returned to Broadway and for five years had a string of hits, but in 1941 Rodgers began writing with **Oscar Hammerstein** as Hart's physical and mental health deteriorated. In 1943, the new partnership had its first success with *Oklahoma!*, which had a record-breaking run of more than 2,248 performances. This was followed by other great productions, including *Carousel* (1945), *South Pacific* (1949), *The King and I* (1951), and *The Sound of Music* (1959), all of which eventually appeared in film form. Their partnership ended with Hammerstein's death in 1960.

Rodgers was awarded two Pulitzer Prizes, seven Tony Awards, and an Oscar, among several other prizes in recognition of his contribution to **music**. *See also* CINEMA.

ROGERS, GINGER (1911–1995). Born Virginia Katherine McMath in Independence, Missouri, dancer and actress Ginger Rogers began performing in vaudeville in 1925 and by 1930 had appeared in a few short films and on Broadway, most notably in *Top Speed* from 1929 to 1930 and *Girl Crazy* from 1930 to 1931. In 1933, she appeared in a number of films, including *42nd Street*, *Gold Diggers of 1933*, and *Flying Down to Rio*, with **Fred Astaire**. Thus began a successful partnership that continued with *The Gay Divorcee* (1934), *Roberta* (1935), *Top Hat* (1935), *Follow the Fleet* (1936), *Swing Time* (1936), and *Shall We Dance* (1937). Rogers also made several films without Astaire, including *Stage Door* (1937) with **Katherine Hepburn**, and

Vivacious Lady (1938) with **James Stewart**. She received an Academy Award for Best Actress in *Kitty Foyle* in 1940 and appeared in a number of films in the 1940s, including *Tales of Manhattan* (1942), *I'll Be Seeing You* (1944), and *It Had to Be You* (1947). She was reunited with Astaire in *The Barkleys of Broadway* (1949) and made several other successful films in the 1950s. Rogers returned to the stage and toured in both musicals and nonmusicals between 1951 and 1984, including *Annie Get Your Gun*, *The Unsinkable Molly Brown*, *Mame*, *Anything Goes*, and *Hello, Dolly!* From 1954 onward, she also made a number of **television** appearances. Her last film role was in *Harlow* in 1965, and her last stage performance was in *Charley's Aunt* in 1984. *See also* CINEMA; LITERATURE AND THEATER.

ROGERS, WILL (WILLIAM PENN ADAIR) (1879–1935). A Cherokee born in the Indian Territory of Oklahoma, Will Rogers began his career as a cowboy in Texas in 1898. In 1902, he traveled to Argentina as a cowhand and then onto South Africa. It was in South Africa that he found work in a Wild West show riding and roping. He toured in New Zealand and Australia before returning to the United States. During performances with the *Ziegfeld Follies* in 1916, Rogers developed his style of humorous social commentary. In 1920, he began to write columns for the press, particularly for the *Saturday Evening Post*. In 1918, Rogers also began appearing in motion pictures. He made 48 silent comedies before turning to sound film in 1929. A series of movies in which he played different western personas appeared in the 1930s, including *State Fair* (1933), *David Harum* (1934), and *Steamboat 'Round the Bend* (1935). Rogers became a well-known radio personality during the 1930s, and his folksy wit and humorous observations on political and other matters seemed to capture a popular mood for nostalgia. When he died in an airplane crash in Alaska in 1935, he was heavily mourned. *See also* CINEMA.

ROONEY, MICKEY (1920–). Born Joe Yule to a vaudeville family, Mickey Rooney took his stage name in 1932 after starring in a series of silent movies from 1927 to 1936 in a role as Mickey McGuire. He went on to be a child star in the 1930s, particularly as Andy Hardy, a character he played in 15 films starting with *A Family Affair* in 1937.

Rooney also played Puck in *A Midsummer Night's Dream* in 1935 and starred in *Boy's Town* in 1938. He made several musicals with another child star, **Judy Garland**, including *Babes in Arms* (1935), *Strike Up the Band* (1940), *Babes on Broadway* (1941), and their last film together, *Words and Music* (1948). Rooney starred in non-musical roles in such successes as *The Human Comedy* (1943) and *National Velvet* (1944), where he played opposite a young Elizabeth Taylor. He entered the military in 1944, and after **World War II** his **cinema** career was less successful, although still extensive. Among his most memorable films were *The Bridge of Toko-Ri* (1954), *Requiem for a Heavyweight* (1962), and *The Black Stallion* (1979). Rooney appeared in 200 movies and in 1983 was given a Lifetime Achievement Award by the Academy of Motion Pictures.

ROOSEVELT, (ANNA) ELEANOR (1884–1962). Eleanor Roosevelt was born in New York City into America's social elite. Her uncle was President Theodore Roosevelt, and Eleanor benefited from the best education available, despite the death of her parents at an early age. When she returned from her schooling in London, England, Eleanor joined the National Consumers' League and worked with immigrant children. In 1905, she married **Franklin D. Roosevelt**, a sixth cousin once removed. The couple had six children between 1906 and 1916, one of whom died as an infant. She was for a long time dominated by her husband's mother, but during World War I, Eleanor began to develop an independent public role when she worked for the Red Cross and Navy League. She came to an accommodation with FDR after discovering his affair with her own social secretary, **Lucy Mercer**, and became more involved in activities with **women**'s suffrage groups and **trade unions**, particularly the League of Women Voters, Women's Trade Union League, and Women's Division of the Democratic National Committee. Her independence further developed in 1921 following FDR's affliction with poliomyelitis, a crippling viral infection that left him permanently disabled. Eleanor helped him overcome the disability and continue his political career. Eleanor herself later developed a relationship with reporter Lorena Hickok that was clearly extremely close, possibly even physical.

By 1928, Eleanor headed the Women's Division of the **Democratic Party**, and when FDR became governor of New York, she often performed inspections of state facilities on his behalf. Once FDR became president, Eleanor acquired the role of an active first lady, transforming the position as much as her husband did the presidency. She was often attacked for her actions on behalf of women and **African Americans** and for the views she expressed in speeches, radio broadcasts, and her daily newspaper column, "My Day," that began in 1935. In 1939, Eleanor publicly announced her resignation from the Daughters of the American Revolution after the organization refused to allow black opera singer **Marian Anderson** to perform in Constitution Hall. Roosevelt helped arrange an alternative performance at the Lincoln Memorial. She continued to campaign on behalf of African Americans during **World War II**.

During the war, Eleanor served briefly as assistant director of the **Office of Civilian Defense**, but her service ended following congressional criticism. She worked energetically throughout the war on morale-raising activities, visiting many parts of the United States, the Caribbean, the Pacific, and **Great Britain**. Following FDR's death in 1945, Eleanor was appointed U.S. representative to the **United Nations (UN)**, a position she held until 1953. She chaired the Human Rights Commission from 1946 to 1951 and was instrumental in the adoption of the Universal Declaration of Human Rights in 1948. Eleanor twice visited the **Soviet Union** in the 1950s. She also campaigned on behalf of birth control and continued to have some influence on the Democratic Party. John F. Kennedy appointed her as representative to the UN once more in 1961 and as chair of the National Commission on the Status of Women. *See also* HICKOK, LORENA ALICE ("HICK").

ROOSEVELT, FRANKLIN DELANO (1882–1945). 32nd president of the United States. Born in Hyde Park, New York, into a wealthy family, Franklin D. Roosevelt was educated at Groton School, Harvard, and Columbia University Law School. He briefly practiced law in New York City before entering the state senate as a **Democrat** in 1910. In 1913, he was appointed assistant secretary of the navy, a post previously held by his uncle, Theodore Roosevelt. His role in the navy enhanced his reputation, and after the war he was nominated as the Democratic Party's vice presidential candidate to run alongside James M. Cox in the unsuccessful campaign of 1920.

In 1921, Roosevelt developed polio, which left him severely paralyzed and threatened to destroy his political career. However, aided by his wife, **Eleanor Roosevelt**, he fought to overcome the disability and in 1928 succeeded **Alfred E. Smith** as governor of New York. As the effects of the **Great Depression** began to tell, Roosevelt introduced measures to develop public electric power, reduce utility rates, and provide relief for the unemployed. He was reelected in 1930 and then defeated Smith and **John Nance Garner** to win the Democratic presidential nomination in 1932. He broke with tradition and flew to Chicago, Illinois, to accept the nomination. In his speech on 2 July, he promised "a **New Deal** for the American people," and this quickly became the label applied to his New Deal program. His election campaign was impressively vague, but he projected a positive air and promised an "enlightened administration." He was critical of **Herbert Hoover** for failing to balance the budget and increasing government bureaucracy.

Roosevelt won a convincing victory with 57 percent of the popular vote to Hoover's 40 percent and 472 Electoral College votes to 59. He did little between his victory and his inauguration but did survive **Guiseppe Zangara**'s assassination attempt in February 1933. However, declaring there was "nothing to fear but fear itself," in his inaugural address in March 1933, he promised a wide-ranging program of measures to combat the deepening Depression. He followed up with a remarkable wave of action in what became known as the **"First Hundred Days,"** establishing the New Deal as a reforming administration of unheard-of proportions. The New Deal formed the basis of the modern welfare state and the framework of U.S. politics for the next half century, and Roosevelt served an unprecedented four terms, being reelected in 1936, 1940, and 1944.

Roosevelt outlined the approach of the New Deal in a **"fireside chat"** on 28 June 1934, when he called for relief, recovery, and reform. In the **"First New Deal,"** the emphasis was on relief and recovery, and the deal witnessed a flood of legislation to halt the financial collapse (**Emergency Banking Act**), restore faith in financial institutions (**Securities Act, Securities and Exchange Act**), provide work for the unemployed (**Public Works Administration, Civil Works Administration, Civilian Conservation Corps**), encourage industrial and agricultural recovery (**National Industrial**

Recovery Act, Agricultural Adjustment Act), and tackle problems of soil erosion, flood control, and regional poverty (**Tennessee Valley Authority**).

This plethora of alphabet agencies marked a massive departure in the role of the federal government and established Roosevelt as one of those most significant figures in modern U.S. history. A "**Second New Deal**" from 1935 to 1937 had more emphasis on reform and is often seen as a move to the "left" in response to radical criticisms and the persistence of high unemployment and poverty. In addition to increasing taxes on wealth and business (**Revenue Acts, Wealth Tax Act**), relief was further extended in 1935 with the **Works Progress Administration** and **National Youth Administration**. Agricultural problems were further addressed by the **Resettlement Administration** in 1935, which was later replaced by the **Farm Security Administration**. Problems of poverty in old age and the issue of unemployment insurance were tackled with the **Social Security Act** of 1935, while conditions at work and the right to **trade union** membership were dealt with for the first time by federal government in the **National Labor Relations Act** of 1935 and **Fair Labor Standards Act** of 1938. This reform came to an end due to increasing congressional opposition, particularly following Roosevelt's attempt at "**court packing**" to alter the balance of the **Supreme Court** to protect the new legislation. Politics also became increasingly dominated by foreign affairs and the approach of war with Europe.

Roosevelt moved the United States to support **Great Britain** in the conflict with **Germany**, through the **Destroyers-for-Bases Agreement**, the **Lend–Lease Act**, and the joint statement with **Winston Churchill** in the **Atlantic Charter** in 1941. Following the attack by **Japan** on **Pearl Harbor** on 7 December 1941, described by Roosevelt as a "date which will live in infamy," the president asked Congress for and received a declaration of war. As commander in chief Roosevelt headed the enormous mobilization of U.S. manpower and industrial might. "Dr. New Deal" was replaced by "Dr. Win the War," and a wave of war agencies displaced many of the New Deal bodies. The war also effectively ended the Depression and brought full employment and job opportunities for **women** and **African Americans**. During the course of the war, Roosevelt headed discussions with the **Allied powers**—Great Britain, the **Soviet Union**, and **China**—and met with other leaders at the **Moscow, Tehran,** and **Yalta conferences**. He established good relations with both Churchill and **Joseph Stalin**, but critics later suggested that he failed to take a tough enough stand against the Soviet leader and created problems for his successors.

Having defeated **Republican** candidate **Wendell Willkie** in 1940, the American people reelected Roosevelt in 1944 when he defeated **Thomas E. Dewey**. He died in office on 12 April 1945, leaving his vice president, **Harry S. Truman**, the unenviable task of following one of the greatest leaders in U.S. history.

"ROOSEVELT RECESSION." *See* RECESSION OF 1937–1938; ROOSEVELT, FRANKLIN DELANO.

ROSENBERG, ETHEL GREENGLASS (1915–1953) and ROSEN-BERG, JULIUS (1918–1953). Both Ethel Greenglass and Julius Rosenberg were born to Jewish families in New York City. They met as members of the Young Communist League in the 1930s and married in 1939. Julius graduated from City College of New York in 1939 in electrical engineering. Ethel worked as a secretary. In 1940, Julius Rosenberg joined the Army Signal Corps and worked on radar equipment. He was dismissed in 1945 after being accused of being a communist, and together with Ethel and her brother, David Greenglass, they established a machine shop in Manhattan. When David Greenglass, who had worked in Los Alamos, New Mexico, on the **atomic bomb**, was charged with spying in 1950, he named his sister and brother-in-law as spies who had passed secrets to the **Soviet Union**. Greenglass was the chief witness against the Rosenberg's in their trial, which began on 6 March 1951 and which was aggressively prosecuted by the assistant U.S. attorney, **Roy Cohn**. Neither of the Rosenbergs would answer questions about their links with the **Communist Party of the United States of America**. They were convicted on 29 March 1951 and executed by electrocution on 19 June 1951, despite international appeals on their behalf. The Rosenbergs were the only U.S. spies executed. In the 1990s, material from the **Soviet** archives suggested that Julius Rosenberg was guilty but cast doubt on the conviction of Ethel.

ROSENMAN, SAMUEL IRVING (1896–1973). One of **Franklin D. Roosevelt**'s closest advisers and speechwriter and editor of the president's public papers and addresses, Samuel I. Rosenman was born of Ukrainian Jewish parents in San Antonio, Texas. He moved to New York City with his family in 1905. Rosenman served in the army during World War I and then attended Columbia University and Columbia University Law School, graduating in 1919. A **Democrat**, he was elected to the New York State Assembly in 1921 and retired in 1926 to work with the state Legislative Drafting Commission. Rosenman began writing speeches for Roosevelt during his gubernatorial campaign in 1928 and subsequently became the governor's chief of staff. It was Rosenman who coined the phrase "**New Deal**" in Roosevelt's speech accepting the Democratic presidential nomination in 1932. In 1933, he won election to the New York State **Supreme Court** and also continued his speechwriting and advisory role in the White House. In 1943, he resigned from the court to act as special counsel to the president during **World War II** and was involved in the creation of the **Office of Production Management** and the **National Housing Agency**. After Roosevelt's death, Rosenman continued as an adviser to **Harry S. Truman** until 1946, when he retired to take up private practice. He served on a number of public bodies before his death and was actively involved in Jewish causes.

ROSIE THE RIVETER. Rosie the Riveter was the iconographic figure who appeared on several war posters and in a propaganda film during **World War II** to encourage **women** to enter war industries. In 1942, using Michigan factory worker Geraldine Doyle as a model, graphic artist J. Howard Miller produced a poster of a woman war worker with her sleeve rolled up, flexing her muscle under the slogan "We Can Do It!" for the Westinghouse company that became widely distributed. A song titled "Rosie the Riveter" was released in 1942; in 1943, Mrs. Rose Will Monroe, a worker in Willow Run, Detroit, and mother of two, appeared in two films about war workers. **Norman Rockwell** then produced a cover painting for the *Saturday Evening Post* on 29 May 1943 featuring a muscular woman in dungarees with a riveting gun across her lap, in which he used 19-year-old Mary Doyle Keefe as his model. Numerous photographs of women workers in the shipyards and aircraft industry were also used. Miller's poster was used on a postage stamp in 1999, and a Rosie the Riveter Memorial Park was opened on the site of a wartime shipyard in Richmond, Virginia, in 2000.

ROTHSTEIN, ARTHUR (1915–1985). Born in New York City, Authur Rothstein studied science and became interested in photography at Columbia University, where he met **Roy Stryker**. In 1936, he joined Stryker's team of photographers at the **Resettlement Administration**, later replaced by the **Farm Security Administration**. Rothstein's work included powerful images of the **Dustbowl** and the poverty of rural life, most famously perhaps in his images of Gee's Bend, Alabama, in 1937. In 1940, he went to work at *Look* magazine. From 1943 to 1946, he worked with the Army Signal Corps before returning to *Look*, where he worked until 1972 when he joined *Parade*. Rothstein also taught at Columbia University and other universities through the 1960s and authored a number of books on photography and photojournalism. *See also* ART.

ROYALL, KENNETH CLAIRBORNE (1894–1999). Born in North Carolina, Kenneth Royall graduated from the University of North Carolina in 1914 and Harvard Law School in 1917. He served in the army during World War I and began a private law practice in 1919. Royall was president of the North Carolina Bar Association from 1929 to 1930. In 1942, he became legal secretary in the Army Service Forces and unsuccessfully defended eight German saboteurs who were tried in secret by military commission. Six were executed. In 1945, he became special assistant and then undersecretary to Secretary of War **Henry L. Stimson**. Royall carried out the reform of the court-martial system. In 1947, President **Harry S. Truman** appointed him secretary of war, and when that office was replaced by secretary of defense, Royall became secretary of the army. He retired in 1949 to practice law in New York City until 1968. He also served on the Presidential Racial Commission in 1963.

RURAL ELECTRIFICATION ADMINISTRATION (REA). Created within the Department of the Interior by executive order on 11

May 1935, the REA was funded with $40 million a year for 10 years to assist states and farm cooperatives in bringing electric power to rural areas. By 1939, 417 cooperatives and almost 300,000 farms had received electric power. In 1939, the REA was transferred to the Department of Agriculture. By 1951, more than $2.35 billion had been loaned, and electric lines had been laid to supply 3.5 million consumers. *See also* AGRICULTURE.

RUTLEDGE, WILEY BLOUNT (1894–1949). Born in Kentucky, Wiley Rutledge attended the University of Wisconsin and graduated in 1914. From 1915 until 1920, he taught in schools in Indiana, New Mexico, and Colorado. He obtained his law degree from the University of Colorado in 1922 and practiced law in Boulder, Colorado, from 1922 to 1924. After teaching at a number of law schools, he became dean of the law school first at Washington University in 1930 and then at the University of Iowa College of Law in 1935. He was appointed to the U.S. Court of Appeals in the District of Columbia in 1939 and the **Supreme Court** in 1943. A staunch supporter of the **New Deal**, he was also a civil libertarian, supporting the right to jury trial and religious freedom.

– S –

SAN FRANCISCO CONFERENCE, 1945. Convened on 25 April 1945 the conference at San Francisco was attended by representatives of 50 nations and was the location where the **United Nations Charter** was completed. The charter was signed on 26 June and went into effect on 24 October 1945.

SAN FRANCISCO LONGSHOREMEN'S STRIKE. In the summer of 1934, a strike of stevedores on the West Coast escalated following the shooting of two strikers in San Francisco on 5 July. Led by **Harry Bridges**, other **trade unions** instigated a general strike involving 12,000 workers in San Francisco on 16 July 1934. The strike lasted four days before being settled on the dock workers' terms by arbitration.

SANDBURG, CARL (1878–1967). After a time as an itinerant worker and serving in the Spanish-American War, poet and writer Carl Sandburg became a reporter in Milwaukee, Wisconsin, and then worked for the *Chicago Daily News*. His poetry celebrating the city and working people, *Chicago Poems* (1915), *Cornhuskers* (1918), and *Smoke and Steel* (1920), won him prizes and national and international recognition as a "poet of the people." He was awarded a Pulitzer Prize in 1940 for his four-volume biography of Abraham Lincoln, *The War Years* (1939), and for his *Complete Poems* in 1951. He was awarded the gold medal of the American Academy of Arts and Letters in 1952 for his work in history and biography. He published *Harvest Poems* in 1960 and *Honey and Salt* in 1963. *See also* LITERATURE AND THEATER.

SCHECHTER POULTRY CORP. V. UNITED STATES (295 U.S. 495 1935). In *Schechter Poultry Corp. v. United States*, the Schechter Poultry Corporation and Schechter Live Poultry Market were charged with violating the codes agreed upon in the poultry business in New York City under the **National Industrial Recovery Act (NIRA)**. The Schechters were convicted and appealed, and when the circuit court ruled that it had no power to examine the maximum hours and minimum-wage aspects of the case, it went to the **Supreme Court**. On 27 May 1935, the court ruled unanimously that the NIRA was unconstitutional in delegating legislative powers to the president and regulating business that was not interstate. The decision dealt a death blow to the NIRA and the **National Recovery Administration**.

SCHLESINGER, ARTHUR MEIER, JR. (1917–2007). Born Arthur Bancroft Schlesinger Jr., the future historian later changed his name to that of his father, Arthur Meier Schlesinger Sr., himself a distinguished historian. Schlesinger Jr. attended the Collegiate School and Phillips Exeter Academy. He went to Harvard in 1938 but did not complete his Ph.D. During **World War II**, he served in the **Office of War Information** and from 1943 to 1945 in the **Office of Strategic Services**. He continued his historical research and in 1945 was awarded the Pulitzer Prize for his book *The Age of Jackson*. His three-volume study, *The Age of Roosevelt*, came out in 1957, 1958, and 1960, respectively. From 1946 to 1961, Schlesinger was professor of history at Harvard and from 1966 professor of humanities at the City University of New York.

However, Schlesinger's significance was as much for his influence on politics as for his historical writing. A supporter of liberal politics, he was an influential member of **Americans for Democratic Action**; in 1949, he wrote *The Vital Center*, calling for a reformist alternative to what he perceived as the totalitarianism of the communist left and fascist right. Schlesinger was a speechwriter for **Adlai Stevenson**, John F. Kennedy, Robert F. Kennedy, and George McGovern. His study of the Kennedy presidency, *A Thousand Days* (1966), won another Pulitzer Prize. He also wrote the study *Robert F. Kennedy and His Times* (1978). Among his other works were *Bitter Heritage* (1967), *Violence: America in the Sixties* (1968), and the influential study *The Imperial Presidency* (1973).

SCOTTSBORO BOYS. Scottsboro, Alabama, was the location of a trial that became an international cause célèbre in the 1930s. In March 1931, nine black youths ranging in ages from 12 to 21 were accused of raping two white **women** while riding a freight train traveling from Chattanooga, Tennessee, to Memphis, Tennessee. The nine boys were Roy and Andy Wright, Eugene Williams, Haywood Patterson, Ozie Powell, Clarence Norris, Olen Montgomery, Charlie Weems, and Willie Roberson. They were arrested in Paint Rock, Alabama, and sent to Scottsboro to face trial. Twelve-year-old Roy Wright was released when the judge declared a mistrial, but an all-white male jury found the other eight youths guilty, and they were all sentenced to death, despite a lack of strong evidence against them and the unreliable nature of the two main witnesses. The **Communist Party of the United States of America** immediately mobilized an appeal for the black teenagers through their legal department, the International Labor Defense (ILD). The **National Association for the Advancement of Colored People (NAACP)** mobilized separately on the boys' behalf and called on the famous labor lawyer, Clarence Darrow, to defend the case, but it was the ILD that initially acted for the boys.

In 1932, in *Powell v. Alabama*, the **Supreme Court** ruled that the **African Americans** had not had an adequate defense and ordered a retrial. In a second trial, the jury once again convicted and called for the death penalty, but the presiding judge overturned the conviction on the grounds that the evidence of the two women in the case was unreliable. A third trial was held with the same result as the previous two, and once again the case was taken to the Supreme Court. In *Norris v. Alabama* (1935), the court overturned the convictions on grounds of discrimination due to the exclusion of blacks from the juries. The Alabama state prosecutors dropped the charges against four of the youths but brought five back to trial and once again secured guilty convictions. One of the accused, Clarence Norris, was sentenced to death; three were given sentences ranging from 75 to 99 years; and one, Ozzie Powell, was sentenced to 25 years for assaulting a police officer. The Scottsboro Defense Committee, coordinated by the NAACP, was able to secure the reduction of the death penalty for Norris to life imprisonment. By 1950, all of the boys had been freed on parole or appeal, or in one case, as with Patterson, escaped.

"SECOND NEW DEAL." The **New Deal** has traditionally been divided into two parts with a **"First New Deal"** covering 1933 and 1934 and the "Second New Deal" lasting from about 1935 through 1937. The emphasis in the "Second New Deal" was more on reform measures to tackle the long-term problems identified as a result of the **Great Depression**. Consequently, it has often been seen as a move to the "left" because of the emphasis on social welfare like the **Social Security Act** and prolabor legislation like the **National Labor Relations Act**. The "Second New Deal" came to an end with the attempt at **"court-packing"** and the so-called **"Roosevelt recession"** in 1937. The last major piece of legislation of the Second New Deal was the **Fair Labor Standards Act** in 1938. Foreign affairs also began to dominate politics as the crisis in Europe developed with the approach of **World War II**.

SECURITIES ACT (FEDERAL SECURITIES ACT), 1933. Intended to provide protection for investors, the Securities Act of 27 May 1933 required the sellers of securities to provide detailed information to the Federal Trade Commission and provide the potential investor with a detailed prospectus outlining details of the securities and the company concerned.

SECURITIES AND EXCHANGE ACT, 1934. The Securities and Exchange Act was a supplement to the **Securities Act** that required all stock exchanges to register and provide details of securities, dealers, and brokers. It created a **Securities and Exchange Commission** to administer the act.

SECURITIES AND EXCHANGE COMMISSION (SEC). Established under the **Securities and Exchange Act** of 1934 as part of the **New Deal** program to stabilize financial institutions, the SEC was an independent regulatory agency created to enforce the federal securities laws and license and regulate stock exchanges. The SEC consisted of five members. The first chair appointed by President **Franklin D. Roosevelt** was **Joseph P. Kennedy**.

SECURITY COUNCIL. The Security Council is the senior body of the **United Nations (UN)**. The **Allied** leaders agreed at the **Yalta Conference** that it would consist of five permanent members—the United States, **Great Britain**, **China**, France, and the **Soviet Union**—and six elected nations chosen on a rotating basis for a two-year period. The permanent members were given veto powers over decisions of the UN General Assembly. The council sits in continuous session and considers any peace-threatening situations.

SELECTIVE SERVICE ACTS, 1940, 1948. The Selective Training and Service Act introduced on 6 September 1940 was the first-ever peacetime draft in the United States. It initially required all males between the ages of 21 and 36 to register. Men were selected by a lottery at the state level through 40,000 local boards. More than 16 million males registered immediately, and 1 million were inducted between 1940 and 1941. In 1942, the draft age was lowered to 18, and the upper limit was raised to 37, but all men between 18 and 65 were required to register. Between 1941 and 1945, 10 million men were drafted.

The original act came to an end in March 1947 and was replaced by a second act on 22 April 1948, which required all men between the ages of 18 and 26 to register. With the outbreak of the **Korean War,** the act was further amended by the Universal Military Service and Training Act in 1951 that extended the period of service from 18 to 24 months. Proposals to introduce six months compulsory military training for all able-bodied 18-year-old males were defeated in 1952. *See also* CONSCIENTIOUS OBJECTORS.

SELECTIVE SERVICEMEN'S READJUSTMENT ACT, 1944. Often known as the "G.I. Bill of Rights," the Selective Servicemen's Readjustment Act of 1944 provided financial support to enable those who had served in the military to return to school or college, get guaranteed loans for home or business purchase or improvement, or qualify for 52 weeks of unemployment compensation at $20 per week. By 1951, 8 million veterans—more than 50 percent—had befitted from the educational provisions of the act, and 4.3 million had used the support to purchase homes. In 1952, the act was extended to veterans of the **Korean War** in the Veterans' Readjustment Act. It was subsequently extended again to provide support for veterans of the Vietnam War.

SELZNICK, DAVID O. (1902–1965). David Selznick took over his father's filmmaking business in 1923 and after some success moved to Metro-Goldwyn-Mayer (MGM) and became a producer. He moved to Paramount in 1928 and produced a number of successful movies. He established his own production unit in 1931 and then worked for RKO, for whom he made *King Kong* in 1933. Selznick returned to MGM in 1933 and produced some famous films, particularly versions of such literary works as *David Copperfield* (1935) and *Anna Karenina* (1935). His later productions included *Little Lord Fauntleroy* (1936), *The Prisoner of Zenda* (1937), and *Gone with the Wind* (1939). Selznick later made a number of major movies with director Alfred Hitchcock, including *Rebecca* (1940) and *Spellbound* (1945). Following the success of *Gone with the Wind*, he was awarded the Irving G. Thalberg Memorial Award by the Academy of Arts for his outstanding contribution to the movie industry. Selznick continued to produce films into the 1950s despite declining success and failing health. *See also* CINEMA.

SERVICE, JOHN STEWART (1909–1999). John Stewart Service was born the son of missionaries in **China**. He completed his high school education in California and graduated from Oberlin College in

1931. After taking the Foreign Service entrance examination in 1933, he was posted to China. During **World War II**, Service was critical of **Chiang Kai-shek**. He also spent some time liaising with **Mao Zedong** and wrote positively about the communist leader. In 1945, Service returned home and was indicted but cleared by a grand jury in the *Amerasia* affair. However, in March 1950 he was accused of working with the communists by Senator **Joseph McCarthy**. Service was twice cleared by internal investigations but subsequently dismissed on grounds of "reasonable" doubt. He appealed the decision, and it eventually reached the **Supreme Court**, which ruled in his favor. Service returned to the State Department in 1957 but was given limited responsibility and retired in 1962. He completed an M.A. at the University of California, Berkeley, and became a librarian in the Center of Chinese Studies. In 1971, he was invited back to China in advance of the visit by President **Richard M. Nixon**.

SHAEF. *See* SUPREME HEADQUARTERS OF THE ALLIED EXPEDITIONARY FORCES (SHAEF).

SHAHN, BEN (1898–1969). Born in Lithuania, Ben Shahn immigrated to the United States with his family in 1906 and settled in Brooklyn, New York. He trained as a typographer and studied at New York University from 1919 to 1921, City College of New York in 1922, and the National Academy of Design in 1922. His paintings of Italian anarchists Ferdinando Nicola Sacco and Bartolomeo Vanzetti, executed after being convicted for murder, and of labor activist Tom Mooney, attracted public attention, and Shahn worked as an assistant to Diego Rivera on a controversial mural in Rockefeller Center in New York City in 1933. He also worked on a mural for the New York **Public Works Administration**. He was recommended to **Roy Stryker**, the head of the **Resettlement Administration (RA)**, by **Walker Evans** and joined the team of photographers documenting the United States during the **Great Depression**. Shahn left the RA, then the **Farm Security Administration**, in 1938. He worked on a number of government commissions as a muralist and from 1942 to 1943 produced graphic designs for the **Office of War Information**, creating several powerful antifascist posters. Shahn also did work for the **Congress of Industrial Organizations** and **Political Action**

Committee. In 1947, he worked for **Henry A. Wallace** producing campaign materials and posters. Notable among his later work is *The Saga of the Lucky Dragon* (1960–1962), depicting the experience of Japanese fishermen exposed to radiation due to U.S. nuclear tests in the Pacific.

SHAPE. *See* SUPREME HEADQUARTERS ALLIED POWERS EUROPE (SHAPE).

SHELLEY V. KRAEMER **(334 U.S. 1 1948).** When an **African American** family by the name of Shelley bought a house in St. Louis, Missouri, in 1945, neighbors sued to prevent them from taking ownership citing a restrictive covenant in the deeds prohibiting the sale of the property to nonwhites. The case reached the **Supreme Court**, and in 1948 the court ruled that such covenants were unconstitutional.

SHIRER, WILLIAM LAWRENCE (1904–1993). Journalist and historian William L. Shirer was born in Chicago, Illinois, and educated at Coe College in Cedar Rapids, Iowa. He was the European correspondent for the *Chicago Tribune* from 1925 to 1932 and then joined the **Berlin** office of the Universal News Service. In 1937, **Edward R. Murrow** recruited him for CBS's European Bureau, and working from Vienna, and then Berlin, he reported on the Anschluss with Austria, the German march into the Sudetenland, and the invasion of Poland. He also provided the American audience with an insight into Nazi **Germany**. He was with the German troops when they invaded France and provided first-hand reports of the signing of the armistice between France and Germany on 22 June 1940. Rather than submit to Nazi controls, Shirer fled from Germany in December 1940. He published his *Berlin Diary* in 1941. At the end of the war, he reported on the **Nuremburg War Crimes Trials**.

In 1947, after a difference with Murrow, Shirer left CBS. He worked as a columnist for the *New York Herald Tribune* and gave public lectures and broadcasts. In 1960, he published his best-selling volume, *The Rise and Fall of the Third Reich*, establishing his reputation as one of the foremost historians of Nazi Germany. He subsequently published a number of other historical studies, including *The Rise and Fall of Adolf Hitler* (1961), *Sinking the Bismarck* (1962), and several works of fiction.

SHOUSE, JOUETT (1879–1968). Born in Kentucky, Jouett Shouse moved with his family to Missouri, where he attended school and the University of Missouri at Columbia. He was editor of the *Lexington Herald*, from 1898 to 1904, practiced law, and served as a state senator from 1913 to 1915 and then U.S. congressman from 1915 to 1918. He was assistant secretary of the treasury at the end of Woodrow Wilson's administration from 1919 to 1920. In the 1920s, Shouse was president of the Association against the Prohibition Amendment and, active in the **Democratic Party**, he served as chair of the Democratic National Committee from 1929 until 1932. Increasingly disenchanted with the **New Deal**, he was active in the **American Liberty League**. He subsequently worked for different business interests and continued his own law practice until his retirement in 1965.

SILVER PURCHASE ACT, 1934. Intended as an inflationary measure to increase money supply, the Silver Purchase Act of 1934 empowered the Treasury Department to purchase all domestic silver until either the price of silver reached $1.29 an ounce or the amount held by the Treasury equaled one-third of the value of federal gold stocks. The Treasury also purchased $1 billion worth of silver abroad. The measure had little effect at home but did adversely affect foreign nations with a silver monetary system.

SINATRA, FRANCIS (FRANK) ALBERT (1915–1998). Singer Frank Sinatra was born of Italian immigrant parents in Hoboken, New Jersey. He did not finish high school, and after working in a variety of casual jobs, he took up singing in 1932. After some success performing with a group, he earned a living as a singing waiter until he was discovered by Harry James, who hired him to sing with his band in 1939. He joined Tommy Dorsey's band later that year. He had his first hit with Dorsey, "I'll Never Smile Again" in 1940, and appeared in two films, *Las Vegas Nights* (1941) and *Ship Ahoy* (1942). Deferred from military service because of a punctured eardrum, Sinatra left the Dorsey band in 1942 to pursue a solo career.

Appearing with the **Benny Goodman** band in December that year, he was met with screaming fans and became a teenage idol. His earlier recording of "All or Nothing at All" became a hit in 1943, and Sinatra not only hosted a regular **radio** program for two years but also appeared in a string of films, including *Anchors Aweigh* (1945), *On the Town* (1949), and *Take Me to the Ball Game* (1949). He also starred in his own **television** series from 1950 to 1952.

After a lull in which it seemed that his career might come to an end, Sinatra achieved renewed success as an actor and a singer, starting with his appearance in the film *From Here to Eternity* in 1953, which won him an Oscar for Best Supporting Actor. He was nominated as best actor for his role in *The Man with the Golden Arm* (1955). Sinatra signed with a new record company, Columbia Records, and began working with arranger Nelson Riddle. He recorded more than 300 songs between 1953 and 1962, many of them becoming classics. In 1960, he established his own Reprise Records and by the late 1980s had recorded more than 400 songs, including the major hits "Strangers in the Night" (1966), "That's Life" (1966), "Something Stupid" (1967), and "My Way" (1969). He continued to make films, including the highly-acclaimed *Manchurian Candidate* in 1962. He retired in 1971, made a comeback in 1973, made several new records, and performed live before huge crowds before finally retiring for good in 1994. In 1997, he was awarded the Congressional Gold Medal to add to his many film and record awards. *See also* CINEMA; MUSIC.

SINCLAIR, UPTON BEALL (1878–1968). Born in Baltimore, Maryland, writer Upton Sinclair graduated from the City College of New York in 1897, briefly attended graduate school at Columbia University, and joined the **Socialist Party of America** in 1902. Challenged to write a novel about capitalism, Sinclair produced *The Jungle* in 1906, a study of immigrant life and work in Chicago, Illinois. The descriptions of meatpacking in the book helped secure the passage of the Pure Food and Drug Act. Sinclair wrote more than 90 books, mostly works of social protest, including *Cry for Justice* (1915), *King Coal* (1917), *Oil*, (1927), and *Boston* (1928), dealing with the Ferdinando Nicola Sacco and Bartolomeo Vanzetti murder case.

Sinclair moved to California after World War I and ran for office as a socialist candidate several times. His greatest achievement in politics came in 1934 when his End Poverty in California movement and his book, *I, Governor of California, and How I Ended Poverty* (1933), won him the **Democratic Party**'s gubernatorial nomination. Sinclair's proposed program of production for use not profit had great appeal. However, a well-financed opposition orchestrated by the largely **Republican**-owned press led to his defeat, although his campaign helped push the **New Deal** to the left. Sinclair retired from politics but continued to write, producing such political novels dealing with the rise of **Adolf Hitler** and fascism as *It Can't Happen Here* (1935), which was turned into a dramatic production by the **Federal Theater Project**; the 1943 Pulitzer Prize-winning *Dragon's Teeth* (1942) and the 11-volume Lanny Budd series. The last book in the series, *The Return of Lanny Budd* (1953), dealt with America's anti-Soviet position during the **Cold War**. He published *The Autobiography of Upton Sinclair* in 1962. *See also* LITERATURE.

SIPUEL V. OKLAHOMA BOARD OF REGENTS (332 U.S. 631 1948). Ada Sipuel became the first **African American** woman admitted to the University of Oklahoma School of Law in 1949. She first applied in 1946 but was denied entry on grounds of her race. When ordered to provide facilities for her, the university established a separate building with separate staff. In *Sipuel v. Oklahoma Board of Regents*, Sipuel sued the university, and on 12 January 1948 the **Supreme Court** ruled that as the separate provision provided was inadequate, she must be admitted under the equal rights provision of the Fourteenth Amendment. Sipuel was, however, forced to sit separately in classes, the library, and the cafeteria. Such action was subsequently prohibited by the Supreme Court in *McLaurin v. Oklahoma State Regents* in 1950. *See also* SWEATT V. PAINTER.

SIT-DOWN STRIKES. During the 1930s, various groups of workers adopted a new method of striking. Rather than simply withdraw their labor by walking out, they brought about the closure of factories by sitting down and occupying the plant. The first such strike occurred in 1936 among members of the United Automobile Workers union at the Fisher Body plant of General Motors (GM) in Flint, Michigan. The strike lasted 40 days, and Governor **Frank Murphy** mobilized the National Guard to prevent violence. GM eventually signed an agreement recognizing the union. In 1936, there were 48 sit-down strikes, and in 1937 there were more than 450 in different industries, but in 1939 in *National Labor Relations Board v. Fansteel Metallurgical Corp.*, the **Supreme Court** ruled that sit-down strikes were illegal. Nonetheless, the sit-down was inspirational during the **civil rights** protests of the 1960s. *See also* AMERICAN FEDERATION OF LABOR (AFL); CONGRESS OF INDUSTRIAL ORGANIZATIONS (CIO); REUTHER, WALTER; TRADE UNIONS.

SKELTON, ("RED") RICHARD BERNARD (1913–1997). Born in Vincennes, Indiana, Red Skelton began working as a boy delivering papers and singing. He left school at the age of 14 to work on river showboats and later toured with a circus and appeared in burlesque shows. In 1938, Skelton gave a performance before President **Franklin D. Roosevelt** in the White House, and it led to a role in the movie *Having a Wonderful Time* in 1938. He went on to appear in 24 movies in the 1940s, like *Whistling in the Dark* (1941), which led to a successful **radio** series, *Scrapbook of Satire*, which ran from 1941 to 1944 and introduced such characters as the Mean Widdle Kid and Clem Kadiddlehopper. Drafted into the army in 1944, Skelton frequently performed for the troops, but he was released on a medical discharge in 1945.

After the war, Skelton resumed his film and radio career. Among his film successes were *The Fuller Brush Man* (1948), *A Southern Yankee* (1948), and *Neptune's Daughter* (1949). In the 1950s, he achieved great success on **television** with the *Red Skelton Show*, which began on NBC in 1951 and moved to CBS in 1953. It ran until 1970 and won Emmy Awards in 1951 and 1961. Skelton was inducted into the Academy of Television Arts and Sciences Hall of Fame in 1986.

Judged by some to be the greatest clown in show business, Skelton's own personal life was marked by tragedy. He was married several times, his eight-year-old son died of leukemia, and a former wife committed suicide. *See also* CINEMA.

SMITH, ALFRED (AL) EMANUEL (1873–1944). Al Smith, as he came to be known, was born and raised in New York City, where he worked a variety of jobs, including the fish market, having left school at the age of 14. He was involved in local politics at an early age and elected to the New York State legislature in 1903, where he served until 1915. He became **Democratic Party** leader in 1911 and speaker in 1913. Smith took part in the state factory commission established after the Triangle Shirtwaist Factory fire that killed 146 people in 1911, and he sponsored a number of bills to protect the health and safety of workers, particularly **women** and children. He was sheriff of New York County from 1915 to 1917 and president of the New York Board of Aldermen in 1917. In 1918, he was elected governor of New York and served for four terms from 1919 to 1920 1923 to 1928. Following his failure to win reelection in 1920, Smith served on the National Board of Indian Commissioners and Port of New York Authority. He also acted as chairman of the United States Trucking Corporation.

Smith's time as governor was associated with the continuation of a reform program: limiting the working hours of women and children, improving **railroad** safety, expanding public education, and reforming state government. He also supported measures to repeal prohibition. In 1924, he failed to win the Democratic Party's presidential nomination for the presidency. He won the nomination in 1928, but lost the election in part because of his Catholic-Irish background and his opposition to prohibition. However, given the apparent prosperity at the time, **Herbert Hoover**'s election victory for the **Republicans** was fairly inevitable.

Following his defeat, Smith became president of the company that managed the Empire State Building in New York City. Having failed to win the party's nomination himself, he reluctantly supported **Franklin D. Roosevelt**'s nomination in 1932 and became increasingly critical of the **New Deal** for creating what he saw as a class conflict. In 1936, he joined the **American Liberty League** and campaigned against Roosevelt and in favor of Republican **Alf Landon**. In 1940, Smith supported **Wendell Willkie**. Although he supported U.S. involvement in **World War II**, Smith was given no role in the war administration.

SMITH, GERALD LYMAN KENNETH (1898–1976). Gerald Smith was born in Wisconsin and graduated from Valparaiso University in 1917. He attended Butler University in Indiana, where he became active in the Ku Klux Klan. In 1928, he moved to Shreveport, Louisiana, and in 1928 became a church minister. In 1930, he was appointed as assistant to **Huey Long** and was the organizer of the national Share Our Wealth clubs. Smith assumed leadership of the clubs following Long's assassination in 1935. In 1936, he joined with **Francis Townsend** and Father **Charles Coughlin** to form the **Union Party**. In 1936, Smith also began to echo the German Nazi movement and called on young American men to seize the government. He was expelled from the Union Party in 1936 because of his extreme views. He campaigned against U.S. entry into **World War II** and organized the America First Party in 1942, publishing a right-wing journal, *The Cross and the Flag*. He ran as presidential candidate for the America First Party in 1944 and attracted a mere 1,781 votes. In 1947, he called for a Christian Nationalist Crusade and attacked Jews, denying the Holocaust and calling for the deportation of **African Americans** to Africa and the dissolution of **United Nations**. In the 1948 election, he received 48 votes. Smith established a center in Los Angeles, California, in 1953 but in 1964 moved to Eureka Springs, Arkansas. In 1966 he erected a huge statue of Jesus, *Christ of the Ozarks*, on a nearby mountain and organized a regular passion play and established a Bible museum.

SMITH, HOWARD WORTH (1883–1976). Born in Virginia, Howard Smith graduated from Bethel Military Academy in 1901 and Virginia Law School in 1903. He had his own legal practice from 1904 to 1917 and during World War I was an assistant general counsel to the Alien Property Custodian. After the war, he served as commonwealth attorney of Alexandria, Virginia; judge on the corporation court of Alexandria until 1928; and judge on the judicial circuit of Virginia from 1928 to 1930. In 1930, Smith was elected as a **Democratic** congressman to the U.S. House of Representatives. He became a member of the House Rules Committee in 1933. A typical states' rights Democrat, Smith was one of the conservative bloc in Congress that opposed much of the **New Deal**. President **Franklin D. Roosevelt** attempted to have him unseated in the **"purge of 1938"** but failed. In 1939, he was one of the leaders of the investigation that attacked the **National Labor**

Relations Board and in 1940 was the sponsor of the **Smith Act**—also known as the Alien Registration Act—aimed at radical groups. During the war, he cosponsored the Smith-Connally Act—also known as the **War Labor Disputes Act**. From 1955 onward, Smith was a powerful influence as chair of the House Committee on Rules and worked to block increases in **social security**, housing reform, and **civil rights** legislation. He inserted a clause requiring equal opportunity for **women** in the 1965 Civil Rights Act. Some historians have claimed that it was a deliberate attempt to jeopardize the act, while others have pointed to Smith's history of support for women's rights and see it as a genuine move on his part. In 1966, he was defeated for renomination and resumed his private legal practice in Alexandria.

SMITH ACT, 1940. The Alien Registration Act of 1940, known as the Smith Act, made it illegal to advocate, teach, or organize the overthrow of any government in the United States by force or violence or to disseminate material calling for such action. It also required all noncitizens to register with the government. The legislation was used in 1949 to prosecute a number of the leaders of the **Communist Party of the United States of America**. However the **Supreme Court** increasingly found such convictions unconstitutional, and by the late 1950s the act was more or less inoperative, although it remains on the statute books.

***SMITH V. ALLWRIGHT* (321 U.S. 649 1944).** In *Smith v. Allwight*, the **Supreme Court** ruled in favor of Lonnie E. Smith, an **African American** from Houston, Texas, who had sued the state **Democratic Party** for excluding black voters from participating in the state primary. The court accepted the argument that as Texas was virtually a one-party state, exclusion from the primary effectively denied black voters of their franchise. In arriving at this decision, the court overturned its previous ruling in the 1935 case *Grovey v. Townsend*, when it had accepted exclusion of African Americans on the grounds that the Democratic Party was a private organization. *See also* CIVIL RIGHTS.

SMITH-CONNALLY ACT. *See* WAR LABOR DISPUTES ACT.

SOCIAL DEMOCRATIC FEDERATION (SDF). The SDF was formed in 1936 by individuals disgruntled with the leadership of the **Socialist Party of America**. Led by Jasper McLevy, the socialist mayor of Bridgeport, Connecticut, from 1933 to 1957, and Algernon Lee, president of the Rand School of Social Science in New York City, the SDF called for a broad liberal-left third party but with little success. The SDF eventually merged back into the Socialist Party in 1956.

SOCIAL SECURITY ACT, 1935. The central pillar of the U.S. welfare system, the Social Security Act was passed in 1935 and amended and extended successively thereafter. The act established a Social Security Board—later the Social Security Administration within the **Federal Security Agency**—to administer the terms of the act and provide for unemployment compensation; old-age insurance; assistance for the destitute blind; and assistance for homeless, disabled, dependent, and delinquent children. Unemployment compensation was financed by a federal tax on employer payrolls—initially 1 percent and rising to 3 percent by 1938—to be administered at the state level. Old-age insurance was a federal program financed by equal taxes on employers and employees starting at 1 percent in 1937 and rising to 3 percent by 1949. Pension payments started for those over the age of 65 in January 1942. In 1939, this payment was brought forward to 1940 and survivors' insurance was also added. Southern congressmen amended the original bill to exclude agricultural and domestic workers, thus eliminating the majority of **African Americans**. These restrictions were gradually lifted through amendments in 1950, 1954, and 1956, and single parents were given benefits from 1950 onward. Medicare and Medicaid were added in 1965.

SOCIALIST LABOR PARTY (SLP). Originally formed in 1877 and led by Daniel De Leon, the SLP was the first national Marxist party in the United States. The SLP had some success in attracting support in the 1890s, but expectation that it would be even more successful during the **Great Depression** turned out to be misplaced. In 1932, its presidential candidate, Verne L. Reynolds, received only 34,028 votes. In 1936, with John W. Aiken as the candidate, the vote fell to 12,790. Support for the party appeared to rise in 1944 with 45,226 votes, probably a reflection of wartime sympathy with the **Soviet Union**, but this did not continue. Under the leadership of Eric Hass, there was another revival in fortunes in the late 1950s and 1960s, but the SLP was always a minority party. It did not put forward a presidential candidate after 1976.

SOCIALIST PARTY OF AMERICA (SPA). In 1901, the Social Democratic Party, led by Eugene V. Debs, joined with reformist elements of the **Socialist Labor Party**, led by Morris Hillquit, to establish the SPA. The SPA was committed to state ownership of the means of production and the equitable distribution of wealth among the working classes. It sought to achieve these ends through evolutionary rather than revolutionary means and supported social and economic reform through the political process. Support for the SPA was particularly strong in working-class immigrant communities, but it began to attract such middle class intellectuals as **Upton Sinclair**, **Walter Lippmann**, and John Reed in the years before 1914. However, when the party opposed U.S. entry into World War I, many people deserted, and the majority of its leaders were jailed under the wartime Espionage Act and Sedition Act. At the end of the war, the party divided between those who wished to follow a revolutionary path along **Soviet** lines and those who continued to espouse a reformist path. The Red Scare of 1919 and 1920 further weakened the party, and membership fell from 24,661 in 1921 to a mere 8,477 by 1926.

In the 1930s and 1940s, the leader of the party was **Norman Thomas**, but even at the height of the **Great Depression**, he attracted less than 900,000 votes, about 2 percent of the vote (the total number of voters having increased considerably since 1912 with the enfranchisement of **women**.) After 1932 the SPA was increasingly undermined by the reforms introduced by the **New Deal** and was divided by factional differences. The vote for Thomas in 1936 was 187, 720, and in 1940 it fell to 99, 557. During the **Cold War** years, and with the effects of **McCarthyism**, membership in the SPA fell to below 2,000. The party was increasingly more of a radical wing of the **Democratic Party**, and in 1968 it supported Democratic presidential candidate Hubert Humphrey. After 1956, it did not run its own candidate again until 1976. *See also* TRADE UNIONS.

SOIL CONSERVATION ACT AND DOMESTIC ALLOTMENT ACT, 1935, 1936. In 1933, Congress made the Soil Conservation Service part of the Department of the Interior on a permanent basis, then relocated it within the Department of **Agriculture** in 1935, and established soil conservation districts throughout the country as a way of tackling the problems of flooding and erosion. The Soil Conservation and Domestic Allotment Act of 1936 was passed after the **Supreme Court** declared the **Agricultural Adjustment Administration** unconstitutional. It provided for payments of up to $10 per acre for farmers who substituted such soil-conserving crops as peas, beans, clover, rye, and alfalfa for such soil-depleting crops as cotton, corn, tobacco, and wheat. Money was also provided to assist farmers using fertilizers, lime, potash, and phosphates.

SOUTHERN TENANT FARMERS' UNION (STFU). Formed in July 1934 in Arkansas, the STFU was an organization of sharecroppers, tenant farmers, and small landowners formed by socialists to protest against the impact of the **Great Depression** in rural areas and the discrimination in payments between landowners and tenants made under the **Agricultural Adjustment Act**. The STFU spread to Missouri, Oklahoma, Texas, Mississippi, and Alabama, and in 1935, with a membership of about 25,000, the organization struck for higher wages for picking cotton. The violent reaction of landowners to the SFTU brought the plight of tenant farmers to the national attention and led to the passage of the **Bankhead-Jones Farm Tenancy Act** of 1937. However, division within the STFU between socialist and communist sympathizers weakened the organization, and by 1943 it had effectively disappeared.

SOVIET UNION (USSR). The Union of Soviet Socialist Republics (USSR) was established in 1922 following the success of the Bolsheviks after the Russian Revolution of October 1917 and the Civil War in the former Imperial Russia. A one-party state committed to the principle of communism, beginning in 1924 the USSR was led by **Joseph Stalin**, who increasingly exerted dictatorial control. Until his death in 1953, Stalin led the USSR through rapid industrial development brutally imposed under Five-Year Plans. He enforced his views through a series of "purges" and show trials that resulted in the removal of any political opponents.

The United States did not recognize the USSR until 1933, but relations were distant until both countries became **allies** in response to **Adolf Hitler**'s expansionist policies in 1941. Meetings between Stalin, **Winston Churchill**, and President **Franklin D. Roosevelt** at **Tehran**, **Yalta**, and **Potsdam** were reasonably successful, but once the war was over, old suspicions and rivalries based on fundamental ideological differences resurfaced. The presence of Soviet armies in Eastern Europe and the imposition of communist-backed governments in Poland, Czechoslovakia, and elsewhere led to a **Cold War** that dominated world affairs until the collapse of the USSR in 1991.

In the immediate aftermath of the war, the new U.S. president, **Harry S. Truman**, was much less inclined than Roosevelt to be conciliatory, and he immediately stopped **lend-lease** aid to Russia and demanded that the USSR honor wartime agreements, even though they were sometimes rather ambiguous in meaning. In a speech in February 1946, Stalin reaffirmed the prewar view of irreconcilable differences between socialism and capitalism and the inevitability of conflict between the two. Soviet control in Eastern Europe was tightened and reinforced in 1947 with the establishment of the Communist Information Bureau (COMINFORM). In face of the perceived Soviet threat, Truman announced the **Truman Doctrine** and a policy of **containment** in March 1947, and a program of economic aid to Europe under the **Marshall Plan** was announced in June that year. Although the USSR was invited to participate in the plan, it rejected the notion of external inspections and withdrew, taking its eastern satellites with it. It instead established an equivalent Molotov Plan.

The economic recovery of Western Europe sharpened differences over the future of **Germany** and demands for the payment of reparations to the USSR, which came to a head when the Western Allies— **Great Britain**, France, and the United States—established a common currency and began the economic unification of the West German sectors. The USSR responded by imposing a blockade on **Berlin** in June 1948, resulting in the **Berlin Airlift** which lasted until May 1949. The Western powers responded to the threatening Soviet action with the formation of the **North Atlantic Treaty Organization (NATO)** in April 1949. When West Germany was included in NATO in 1955, the USSR established the Warsaw Pact among the communist states of Europe. The growing military confrontation was made more dangerous by the successful testing of an **atomic bomb** by the USSR in 1949 and by the support given to **Mao Zedong**'s communist **China** that year. While direct conflict was avoided, Stalin, perhaps reluctantly, supported the North in the **Korean War**.

Although Cold War tensions eased to some extent following Stalin's death, the confrontation between the USSR and the United States dominated international affairs until the 1990s, at times, as with the Cuban Missile Crisis of 1962, coming close to open conflict. Ultimately, however, the costs of this global struggle proved too much for the USSR, and despite attempted reform in the 1980s, it disintegrated with the withdrawal of separate states in 1991.

SPANISH CIVIL WAR, 1936–1939. The Civil War in Spain began when military leaders led by General Francisco Franco rose in revolt against the left-wing Republican government. Spain became an ideological battleground between left and right as the **Soviet Union** backed the Republicans, while **Adolf Hitler**'s Nazi **Germany** and Mussolini's fascist Italy supported Franco. Opinion in the United States was divided about the war, and the government of **Franklin D. Roosevelt** supported the nonintervention policy urged by **Great Britain** and France and adopted a policy of impartial neutrality. As support for the Republicans grew, Roosevelt asked for and in January 1937 obtained a congressional resolution imposing an embargo on war materials going to Spain. This did not, however, prevent American volunteers from taking part, and several thousand joined the Abraham Lincoln Brigade and George Washington Brigade to fight for the Republican cause. Among those who supported the cause was **Ernest Hemingway** and members of the League of American Writers.

SPORT. Sport was affected by the **Great Depression** and **World War II** in terms of reduced audiences at live events, but it continued to attract huge audiences on the **radio**. Stars from the 1920s like the baseball player Babe Ruth continued to play, although with a 10 percent pay cut, but new figures also emerged. The rise of **African**

American athletes was a significant development with the domination of boxing by **Joe Louis** from 1937, the success of **Jesse Owens** and other black athletes at the 1936 **Berlin** Olympics, and the breakthrough of black baseball players on previously all-white teams, starting with **Jackie Robinson** in 1947.

Radio audiences listened to Louis's fights in huge numbers and were also thrilled by the achievements of **Joe DiMaggio**, who led the New York Yankees to nine World Series victories between 1936 and 1951. Louis and DiMaggio, like many sportsmen, entered the U.S. armed forces during **World War II**. Of the 5,700 baseball players in the Major League and Minor League, 4,000 donned military uniforms. As a result, many of the games were of a lower level of play than normal. The St. Louis Cardinals and New York Yankees dominated baseball, winning four of the wartime World Series between them. The fifth, in 1945, was won by the Detroit Tigers. After the war, the Yankees resumed their monopoly, winning the World Series in 1947 and from 1949 through 1953. American football was affected in a similar way, and many teams relied on older players or those who were regarded as unfit for military service. Many colleges did not have football teams during the war, and instead service teams were the main attraction, with the army's team being outstanding.

STALIN, JOSEPH VISSARIONOVICH (1879–1953). Born Joseph Dzhugashvili in Georgia, Russia, the future leader of the **Soviet Union** assumed the name Stalin, meaning "man of steel," in 1913. By then, he had become a communist and member of the Bolshevik movement. He was jailed and exiled several times between 1902 and 1917, but following the Bolshevik Revolution in 1917, he increased his influence and was appointed general secretary of the Central Committee of the Communist Party of the Soviet Union in 1922. He assumed power after Vladimir Lenin's death in 1924 and gradually displaced his enemies, most notably Leon Trotsky in 1928. He consolidated his dictatorial rule with the "Great Purge" during the 1930s. Under Stalin's Five-Year Plans launched in 1928, the Soviet Union went through rapid, enforced industrialization that cost some 10 million lives by execution or through famine.

Isolated from the West, Stalin hoped to prevent an attack by Nazi **Germany** when he signed a Nonaggression Pact in August 1939.

However, the Soviet Union was attacked in June 1941, and the USSR and **Great Britain** suddenly became unlikely **Allies** and were joined in December 1941 by the United States in **World War II**. Although German forces almost took Moscow, Stalin mobilized the Russian people in defense of "Mother Russia," and the tide of battle turned at Stalingrad between August 1942 and February 1943. Soviet armies pushed into Poland and eventually Germany itself.

Although Stalin was angered by apparent delays in opening a Second Front, agreement about the shape of the postwar world appeared to be reached in conferences where he met his counterparts, **Winston Churchill** and **Franklin D. Roosevelt** at **Tehran** and **Yalta**, and **Harry S. Truman** at **Potsdam**. However, after the war, Stalin announced in a speech launching another Five-Year Plan on 9 February 1946 that there were irreconcilable differences between communism and capitalism that would lead to war. Disagreements about the future of Germany and about governments in Eastern Europe, particularly Poland, led to growing hostility culminating in the onset of the **Cold War** in 1947. Stalin gradually increased communist control in Poland, East Germany (later the **German Democratic Republic**), Czechoslovakia, Hungary, Rumania, and Bulgaria. For many people in the West, he became a second **Hitler**, an example of totalitarianism and the personification of communist dictatorship. Soviet policy gradually became more flexible after his death in 1953, and there were denunciations of the "cult of personality" he had fostered.

STATES' RIGHTS PARTY. In 1948, many southerners bolted the **Democratic** National Convention in 1948 to form the States' Rights Party due to the adoption of a strong **civil rights** plank and **Harry S. Truman**'s call for the beginning of desegregation in the U.S. armed forces. Known as **Dixiecrats** and with the slogan "Segregation Forever," they nominated **Strom Thurmond**, governor of South Carolina, as their presidential candidate. In the election, they carried Louisiana, Mississippi, Alabama, and South Carolina and won 39 Electoral College votes. Despite this and defections to the liberal **Progressive Party**, Truman won the election. The Dixiecrats reappeared as the American Independent Party behind the candidacy of Governor George Wallace of Alabama in 1968 in what eventually led to a realignment of political party structures in the United States.

STEAGALL, HENRY BASCOM (1873–1943). Born in Clopton, Alabama, Henry Steagall attended Southeast Alabama Agricultural School and then the University of Alabama, Tuscaloosa. He graduated with a degree in law in 1893 and practiced in Ozark. In 1898, he was appointed county solicitor, and in 1906 he served one term in the state legislature. In 1914, he was elected as a **Democratic** representative to Congress and served until his death. Steagall became chair of the House Committee on Banking and Currency in 1930 and helped establish the **Reconstruction Finance Corporation**. He was cosponsor of the 1933 Glass-Steagall Act that separated investment **banking** from commercial banking. Steagall supported President **Franklin D. Roosevelt** and the **New Deal** and helped push through the **Banking Acts** of the "**First Hundred Days**." During the war, he maintained a watching brief on the impact of wartime controls on **agriculture**.

STEEL WORKERS' ORGANIZING COMMITTEE (SWOC). In June 1936, the newly formed **Committee of Industrial Organization** targeted a bastion of antiunionism since the late 19th century—the steel industry—as their focus for **trade union** membership drives. They established the SWOC, led by **Philip Murray**, and on 2 March 1937 the "Big Steel" companies agreed to recognize the unions rather than face strikes. Smaller companies led by Republic Steel, Bethlehem Steel, and Youngstown Sheet & Tube, however, refused to such an agreement, and a bitter strike ensued. One of the worst episodes in U.S. labor history occurred in the **Memorial Day Massacre** outside the Republic Steel plant in South Chicago, Indiana, when 10 people were killed. Despite a wave of public sympathy for the strikers, the "**Little Steel**" companies did not recognize the unions until 1941.

STEINBECK, JOHN ERNST (1902–1968). Writer John Steinbeck was born in Salinas, California. He enrolled at Stanford University in 1919 but studied only erratically and left without graduating in 1925. After failing to establish himself as a freelance writer in New York City, Steinbeck took a number of casual jobs and concentrated on writing. His first novel, *Cup of Gold*, was published in 1929. It was in the 1930s that Steinbeck emerged as a major literary figure with his novels of social commentary, including *To a God*

Unknown (1933), *Tortilla Flat* (1935), *In Dubious Battle* (1936), *Of Mice and Men* (1937), and the classic that helped define the **Great Depression** years, *Grapes of Wrath* (1939). A best seller, *The Grapes of Wrath* charted the experience of the Joad family, displaced tenant farmers from Oklahoma who made the migration westward to California in hopes of finding a better life. It incorporated documentary passages with fictional narrative and captured the suffering of thousands of similar "**Okies**." Although criticized by farmers' and growers' associations and some migrant groups, it was awarded the Pulitzer Prize in 1940. The film of the same name, starring **Henry Fonda**, was also a huge success that year. Seventeen of Steinbeck's books were made into films, and he also had some success as a screenwriter. His screenplay for *Lifeboat* (1944) won an Academy Award in 1945.

In 1942, Steinbeck published a fictional account of European resistance to the Nazis in *The Moon Is Down*, but he struggled to match his earlier success. After a period as a war correspondent, he produced the humorous *Cannery Row* (1945) and a string of much less significant works. With *East of Eden* (1952), a modern tale of Cain and Abel, Steinbeck once again recaptured his previous form, and in 1962 he was awarded the Nobel Prize for **Literature**. However, stung by critical reviews of his *The Winter of Our Discontent* (1961), he abandoned fiction and concentrated on journalism and more famously a travelogue, *Travels with Charley: In Search of America* (1962). His last published work, *America and Americans* (1966), reflected his disillusionment with the hypocrisy, greed, and racial division he witnessed in the country. He was awarded the Medal of Freedom by President Lyndon Johnson.

STETTINIUS, EDWARD REILLY, JR. (1900–1949). Born in Chicago, Edward Stettinius Jr. attended school in Connecticut and then enrolled in the University of Virginia. He left the university in 1924 without graduating and took a job in the Hyatt Roller Bearing company of General Motors (GM). In 1931, he became vice president of GM. Because of his long-time involvement in social work, Stettinius also worked as a liaison officer between the **National Industrial Recovery Administration** and the Industrial Advisory Board. In 1934, he became vice chairman in the Finance Department of U.S. Steel and implemented a new welfare program for employees. In 1938, he took over as chair of U.S. Steel, a position he held until 1940 when he was appointed chair of the War Resources Board, a short-lived body created by President **Franklin D. Roosevelt** in 1939 to plan industrial mobilization. In 1941, he became a director in the **Office of Production Management** and in 1942 was put in charge of the **Lend-Lease** administration. In 1943, he succeeded **Sumner Welles** as undersecretary of state, and he was involved in the reorganization of the department. In 1944, Stettinius visited **Great Britain** to discuss postwar economic issues, and in 1944 he headed the U.S. Delegation at the **Dumbarton Oaks Conference**, where he helped draft the plans for the **United Nations (UN)**.

In 1944, President Roosevelt appointed Stettinius to succeed **Cordell Hull** as secretary of state. He accompanied the president to the **Yalta Conference**, where he played a leading role in policymaking. He also went to the conference in Mexico City, Mexico, that produced the **Chapultepec Agreement**. Afterward, Stettinius led the U.S. Delegation to the **San Francisco Conference**, which established the UN and worked to overcome conflict with the delegates from the **Soviet Union** to secure the final agreement in June 1945. Stettinius became the first U.S. representative to the UN General Assembly after **Harry S. Truman** replaced him as secretary of state with **James F. Byrnes**. Frustrated at his lack of involvement in shaping postwar **foreign policy**, Stettinius resigned his position in 1946 and became rector of the University of Virginia. He also became involved in promoting U.S. investment in Liberia. In 1949, *Roosevelt and the Russians*, his account of the Yalta Conference justifying Roosevelt's decisions was published.

STEVENSON, ADLAI EWING, II (1900–1965). Born in Los Angeles, California, Adlai Stevenson moved to Bloomington, Illinois, as a child, where he attended a number of schools before going to Choate and Princeton University. After briefly working as a journalist, he went to Northwestern Law School in 1925. Once he was qualified, he worked in a legal practice in Chicago, Illinois, until 1933, when he went to Washington, D.C. He returned to Chicago after two years. His speeches and writing on behalf of the Committee to Defend America by Aiding the Allies brought him to the attention of **Frank**

Knox. When Knox became secretary of the navy in 1940, he appointed Stevenson as his special assistant.

During the war, Stevenson led the Foreign Economic Mission to determine the economic needs of Italy following the country's liberation and later went to Europe on behalf of the U.S. Strategic Bombing Survey. In 1945, he worked for the State Department to mobilize public support for the **United Nations (UN)**, and he became senior adviser to the U.S. Delegation and a delegate in the New York sessions in 1946 and 1947.

In 1948, Stevenson was elected **Democratic** governor of Illinois and did much to tackle corruption in public service. He gained national prominence for his refusal to implement a loyalty oath. In 1952, he was nominated on the fourth ballot as the presidential candidate for the Democratic Party. Although an inspirational and intelligent speaker, Stevenson was easily defeated by the Republican candidate, **Dwight D. Eisenhower**. Nonetheless, he was chosen again in 1956 but was defeated once more by Eisenhower. In 1960, he lost the nomination to John F. Kennedy, who appointed him ambassador to the UN. He was very involved during the Cuban Missile Crisis in October 1962, when he advocated concessions to reach a settlement. Under President Lyndon Johnson, Stevenson opposed the escalation of the war in Vietnam and the unilateral intervention in the Dominican Republic. He died of a heart attack while on a visit to London, England.

STEWART, JAMES MAITLAND (1908–1997). The actor, James Stewart (better known as "Jimmy"), was born in Indiana, Pennsylvania. After attending Mercersburg Academy, he went to Princeton University in 1928 and graduated with a degree in architecture in 1932. However, he had already begun acting while a student. Soon after leaving Princeton, he found work with a theater group, making his first appearance on Broadway that year. After several successful stage roles, he signed with Metro-Goldwyn-Mayer in 1934 and appeared in his first film in 1936. Stewart acted in a number of movies including *You Can't Take It with You* (1938) and *It's a Wonderful World* (1939) and also did **radio** work before his major breakthrough as a star in the western, *Destry Rides Again* and **Frank Capra**'s *Mr. Smith Goes to Washington*, both in 1939. In 1940, he won an Oscar for his role in *The Philadelphia Story* in which he starred with **Cary Grant** and **Katherine Hepburn**.

Stewart was initially rejected for the draft as underweight, but after fattening himself up was accepted for the Army Air Corps in 1941. He rose to the rank of colonel and was awarded the Air Medal and Distinguished Flying Cross and the French Croix de Guerre for his service during **World War II**. After the war, Stewart starred in the lead role in Capra's *It's a Wonderful Life*. Although not an enormous success at the time, the film was to become a perennial Christmas classic in later years. However, his career was really re-established with his performances in the western *Winchester '73* and the comedy *Harvey*, both in 1950. He also played the lead in *Broken Arrow* (1950), *The Greatest Show on Earth* (1952), *The Glenn Miller Story* **(1953)**, and in two films by Alfred Hitchcock, *Rear Window* (1954) and *Vertigo* (1958), and as **Charles Lindbergh** in *The Spirit of St. Louis* (1957). Stewart's career in **cinema** spanned through to the 1970s; in addition, he often appeared in roles on **television**. He was given a Life Achievement Award by the American Film Institute in 1980 and an Honorary Academy Award in 1985.

STILWELL, JOSEPH WARREN (1883–1946). Born in Florida, Joseph Stilwell graduated from West Point Military Academy in 1904. He served two tours of duty in the Philippines and also taught at West Point before serving as an intelligence officer during World War I. He was awarded the Distinguished Service Medal for his achievements. After the war, Stilwell held a number of commands, including Fort Benning and Fort Leavenworth. He also served on three separate occasions in **China**, where he became familiar with **Chiang Kai-shek**.

During **World War II**, Stilwell commanded forces in the China-Burma Campaign and also served as chief of staff to Chiang. Reliant on poorly led Chinese troops, Stilwell was forced out of Burma, leading a group on foot into India. In 1943, he was appointed deputy supreme allied commander under British Vice Admiral Lord Louis Mountbatten, and despite differences with the British, he was successful in leading the forces in retaking northern Burma and establishing the Ledo Road—later renamed the Stilwell Road—as an alternative supply route into China. However, Stilwell was increasingly critical of Chiang's corruption, the misuse of **Lend-Lease** funds, and the failure to engage with the Japanese forces. At Chiang's insistence, he returned to the United States in 1944. Stilwell saw further action in **Okinawa** in 1945 and then was made head of the War Department Equipment Board. He died of cancer in 1946.

STIMSON, HENRY LEWIS (1867–1950). One of America's longest-serving statesmen, Henry L. Stimson was born in New York City; attended Phillips Academy, Andover; and graduated from Yale University in 1888. He went to Harvard Law School, qualified in law in 1890, and practiced in New York City. Stimson was U.S. attorney for southern New York and in 1910 ran unsuccessfully as the **Republican** candidate for governor. In 1911, President William Howard Taft appointed him secretary of war. He resumed his legal practice in 1916.

During World War I, Stimson served as a colonel with the artillery in France and then resumed his career as a Wall Street lawyer. In 1927, President Calvin Coolidge appointed him to mediate between warring factions in Nicaragua. From 1927 to 1929, he served as governor general of the Philippines and resisted early moves toward independence.

In 1928, President **Herbert Hoover** appointed Stimson as secretary of state, and in that capacity he chaired the U.S. Delegation to the London Naval Conference from 1930 to 1931. In 1931, he issued a statement that became known as the Stimson Doctrine, expressing the opposition of the United States to the Japanese conquest of Manchuria and refusing to accept any change in territorial possession as a consequence of the invasion. Stimson tried to mobilize European opposition to Japanese aggression and would have preferred to take stronger action, but he bowed to Hoover's wishes to maintain a purely limited diplomatic response.

In 1940, Stimson was one of two Republicans appointed to the cabinet when President **Franklin D. Roosevelt** made him secretary of war (the other was **Frank Knox**). He supported the introduction of **Selective Service** in 1940 and advocated support for **Great Britain** before the attack on **Pearl Harbor**. Once the United States became involved in the war, he called for a speedy invasion of Europe. He expressed opposition about the massive bombing of **Germany** and the later firebombing of Tokyo, and he recommended offering the

Japanese terms for surrender that would allow them to keep the emperor. Stimson also opposed the plan proposed by **Henry Morgenthau** with regard to postwar Germany, arguing that the economic destruction of the country would simply repeat the mistakes that had followed World War I. However, he was also the president's senior adviser on atomic weapons and accepted the dropping of the **atomic bombs** in 1945 and was responsible for the choice of targets. Nonetheless, at the war's end, he seemed to suggest a policy of cooperation with the **Soviet Union** rather than confrontation based on atomic superiority. Stimson published his memoirs, *On Active Service in Peace and War*, in 1948.

STOCK MARKET CRASH. *See* WALL STREET CRASH.

STONE, HARLAN FISKE (1872–1946). Born in Chesterfield, New Hampshire, and a graduate of Amherst College in 1894 and Columbia University Law School in 1898, Harlan Fiske Stone became the eleventh chief justice of the **Supreme Court**. After beginning his own private law practice, he joined the faculty of Columbia University Law School in 1899, where he became dean in 1910. In 1924, President Calvin Coolidge appointed him as attorney general, where he helped reform the federal prison service and the Alien Property Custodian's Office, an area of corruption during the previous administration. He was appointed to the Supreme Court in 1925. With **Louis D. Brandeis** and **Benjamin Cardozo**, who replaced Oliver Wendell Holmes in 1932, Stone was part of the "liberal" group on the Supreme Court and an upholder of judicial restraint.

A defender of civil liberties, Stone dissented in *Minersville School District v. Gobitis* in 1940 against the decision approving mandatory saluting of the flag in public schools. The court accepted his view when it reversed their original ruling in 1943 in **West Virginia State Board of Education v. Barnette**. President **Franklin D. Roosevelt** appointed Stone as chief justice to succeed **Charles Evans Hughes** in 1941. However, he did not seem able to impose his personality or a consistent view on the court. His own position was often difficult to characterize as he supported the decisions upholding the internment of **Japanese Americans** but dissented when the court ruled to uphold the right to deny citizenship to conscientious objectors in *Girouard v. United States* in 1946. He died shortly after reading that decision.

STRYKER, ROY EMERSON (1893–1975). Born in Great Bend, Kansas, Roy Stryker graduated from high school in 1912 and entered the Colorado School of Mines. He failed to complete his studies and served in the infantry during World War I. After the war, Stryker went to Columbia University to study economics. There he met **Rexford Tugwell**, and after graduating he taught economics with him. When Tugwell was appointed to head the **Resettlement Administration (RA)** in 1935, he made Stryker chief of the Historical Division of Information with responsibility for documenting the impact of the **Great Depression** on rural America. Stryker gathered a team of photographers, including **Walker Evans, Dorothea Lange, Russell Lee, Arthur Rothstein**, and **Ben Shahn**. The project continued after 1937 when the RA became the **Farm Security Administration**, and together the group compiled some of the most iconic images of the 1930s. Of 250,000 photographs, some 77,000 were used in such magazines as *Life* and *Fortune* by the press and in exhibitions across the country to publicize the plight of the rural poor and the work of the **New Deal**.

In 1942, the photographic unit was reassigned to the **Office of War Information** and then disbanded. Stryker resigned his position and worked for Standard Oil from 1943 to 1950, again choosing photographers to record the company's work. Some of the team of photographers followed Stryker when he established the Pittsburgh Photographic Library at the University of Pittsburgh from 1950 to 1952. From there, Stryker documented the work at Jones & Laughlin Steel before returning to Colorado, where he did freelance work and acted as a consultant.

SULLIVAN, JOHN LAWRENCE (1899–1982). Born in New Hampshire, John L. Sullivan was a graduate of Dartmouth College in 1921 and Harvard Law School in 1924, and he practiced law in New Hampshire. A **Democrat**, he failed twice to win the gubernatorial elections in the 1930s but in 1939 became first assistant to the commissioner of the Internal Revenue Service and then was chosen as assistant secretary in the Treasury. In 1947, he was awarded a Distinguished Service Award and Silver Medal for his work on wartime finances. In 1945, he was appointed assistant secretary of the navy for air and then undersecretary of the navy before finally becoming secretary of the navy in 1947. However, Sullivan resigned in protest at the policies of the defense secretary, **Louis Johnson**, in 1949 and returned to his legal practice.

SUPREME COURT. The Supreme Court is the highest federal court in the land consisting of nine justices, each appointed for life by the president. During the progressive period prior to World War I, the court moved from its predominantly conservative and probusiness position upholding principles of laissez faire to a more reformist stance that recognized that law should respond to social change. The court upheld limitations on working hours where the health and safety of workers—both men and **women**—were affected but not where it violated workers' rights to accept whatever working conditions they chose. Regulation of trusts was upheld but increasingly narrowed to apply only to "unreasonable" restraint of trade.

In the 1920s, the court once more tended to protect business and private property. Warren Harding's conservative appointments resulted in decisions against child labor laws and a minimum wage law for women but upheld restrictions on **trade unions**. When **Franklin D. Roosevelt** became president in 1933, the court had a solid bloc of four conservatives—**Pierce Butler, James McReynolds, George Sutherland**, and **Willis Van Devanter**. They were often supported by **Owen J. Roberts**. The liberals on the court were **Louis Brandeis, Benjamin Cardozo**, and **Harlan Fiske Stone**. Chief Justice **Charles Evans Hughes** tended to take a middle position.

In 1935, the court declared by a five-to-four margin three **New Deal** measures unconstitutional, including the **National Industrial Recovery Act**. They also ruled against a number of social reform measures at the state level and in 1936 declared the **Agricultural Adjustment Administration** unconstitutional. Faced with the possibility that the court would effectively undermine the rest of the New Deal, President Roosevelt attempted to alter the court's composition. In 1937, he proposed a measure that would allow the appointment of up to six new justices on the basis of one for every sitting justice over the age of 70 who failed to retire. The proposed court reorganization act was seen as "**court packing**" and was met with considerable congressional and public opposition. However, on 29 March 1937 in the "switch in time that saved nine," the court reversed itself and ruled in favor of a state minimum wage law in *West Coast Hotel Co. v. Parrish*. One of the conservatives on the court, Van Devanter also indicated that he would retire. Subsequent retirements allowed Roosevelt to make further sympathetic appointments, and the court increasingly adopted a more liberal position and approved the later reform measures. The court reorganization act was defeated in Congress in July 1937. *See also* BLACK, HUGO LAFAYETTE; BYRNES, JAMES FRANCIS; DOUGLAS, WILLIAM ORVILLE; FRANKFURTER, FELIX; JACKSON, ROBERT HOUGHWOUT; MURPHY, FRANK (FRANCIS) WILLIAM; REED, STANLEY FORMAN.

SUPREME HEADQUARTERS ALLIED POWERS EUROPE (SHAPE). SHAPE was established in April 1951 as part of the **North Atlantic Treaty Organization** under the command of General **Dwight D. Eisenhower**.

SUPREME HEADQUARTERS OF THE ALLIED EXPEDITIONARY FORCES (SHAEF). SHAEF was initially established in London, England, during **World War II** under the command of General **Dwight D. Eisenhower**. Once the **Allied** forces were established in Europe, it moved to Versailles, France.

SUTHERLAND, (ALEXANDER) GEORGE (1862–1942). Born in England, George Sutherland moved to the United States with his family in 1864 and settled in Utah. Sutherland was educated at Brigham Young Academy and graduated in 1881. In 1896, he was elected as a **Republican** senator in Utah's first state legislature and became chair of the judiciary committee. In 1900, he was elected to the U.S. House of Representatives and 1905 was appointed to the U.S. Senate, where he established a national reputation as a legal expert and leading opponent of Woodrow Wilson. He was defeated in the election of 1916.

In 1922, Sutherland was appointed to the **Supreme Court** by President Warren Harding. He wrote the majority opinion in *Adkins* *v. Children's Hospital*, ruling against minimum wage legislation for **women**, a decision that was overturned against his dissent in *West Coast Hotel Co. v. Parrish* in 1937. While he voted with the other conservative justices—**Willis Van Devanter**, **James McReynolds**, and **Pierce Butler**—against most of the **New Deal** measures, Sutherland also wrote the majority decision in 1936 recognizing that the president had substantial powers in **foreign policy** matters deriving from needs of international relations. He also wrote the majority opinion overturning the conviction of the **Scottsboro Boys** in *Powell v. Alabama* in 1932 and concurred with the ruling that a tax on newspaper advertising was an unconstitutional restraint of the press. Although suffering ill-health, he refused to retire until after President **Franklin D. Roosevelt**'s attempt at "**court packing**" had been defeated. He finally retired in 1938.

SWEATT V. PAINTER **(339 U.S. 629 1950).** Herman Sweatt was an **African American** who was rejected by the University of Texas when he applied for admission to the Law School in 1946. When Sweatt filed a lawsuit claiming that he was being denied the rights guaranteed under the Fourteenth Amendment, the university established a separate law school for African Americans, as approved by the **Supreme Court** in *Missouri ex rel. Gaines v. Canada* in 1938. Sweatt refused to accept this, and in *Sweatt v. Painter* in June 1950, the court found in his favor, recognizing that the university could not make a separate provision that was equal in quality to its main law school. This decision, along with *McLaurin v. Oklahoma State Regents*, was an important step toward the landmark ruling against segregation in pubic schools in *Brown v. Board of Education of Topeka* in 1954. *See also* CIVIL RIGHTS.

SWOPE, GERARD (1872–1957). Gerard Swope was an engineer with the Western Electric Company in Chicago, Illinois, who served as an assistant to George W. Goethals during World War I. In 1919, he joined General Electric as president of its international operations and became chairman of General Electric itself in 1922. With **Owen Young** as chairman, Swope took control of day-to-day running of the company and with great attention to detail helped increase sales and production through increased efficiency and a reduced workforce.

Swope, who had lived and worked at the Hull House settlement in the 1890s, was instrumental in the introduction of policies of "welfare capitalism" but was unsuccessful in gaining employee approval for an unemployment insurance plan.

In response to the **Wall Street Crash**, Swope proposed the "Swope Plan" in 1931, which called upon companies to organize by industry and agree on codes of fair competition with agreed working hours and conditions in return for the suspension of the Sherman Antitrust Act. Elements of the plan were discernable in the **New Deal**'s **National Recovery Administration (NRA)**. Swope chaired the Department of Commerce's Business Advisory and Planning Council formed to advise the NRA in 1933. He later worked toward the implementation of **social security** and labor relations legislation and was a member of the **National Labor Relations Board**. He accepted union recognition within General Electric between 1936 and 1939, and after his retirement in 1939 he served as chair of the New York City Housing Authority. He briefly returned to General Electric during **World War II**. After the war, he chaired the Institute of Pacific Relations looking at U.S. **foreign policy** in the Far East. *See also* TRADE UNIONS.

SYMINGTON, (WILLIAM) STUART (1901–1988). Stuart Symington was born in Amherst, Massachusetts, but his family moved to Baltimore, Maryland, where he went to school. He enlisted in the military at the age of 17 and after the war went to Yale but left in 1923 without graduating. He became an iron molder, studied at night, and by 1925 was president of the Eastern Clay Company. After holding several other executive posts, Symington became chair of the Surplus Property Board in 1945 and then assistant secretary of war for air in 1946. In 1947, he was appointed first secretary of the air force, and he helped establish the new service. In 1950, he chaired the **National Security Resources Board** and in 1951 the **Reconstruction Finance Corporation**.

In 1952, Symington was elected **Democratic** state senator for Missouri. He stood unsuccessfully for the Democratic Party's presidential nomination in 1960. The successful candidate, John F. Kennedy, considered Symington as his vice presidential running mate but finally opted for Lyndon Johnson. Instead, Symington served four terms as senator, in which time he was a critic of **Joseph McCarthy**, a supporter of defense spending, and initially a supporter of U.S. involvement in Vietnam. He changed his position after 1967. Critical of the administration of **Richard M. Nixon**, Symington opposed the antiballistic missile system. He retired in 1976.

– T –

TAFT, ROBERT ALPHONSO (1889–1953). Born in Cincinnati, Ohio, Robert A. Taft was the son of William Howard Taft, president of the United States from 1908 to 1912 and chief justice on the **Supreme Court** from 1921 to 1930. Taft graduated from Yale University in 1910 and Harvard Law School in 1913. He practiced law in Cincinnati and during World War I worked with **Herbert Hoover** at the U.S. Food and Drug Administration. He returned to his law practice after the war but was elected as a **Republican** to the Ohio state legislature in 1921, where he served until 1930 when he was elected to the state senate. Taft was elected to the U.S. Senate in 1938 and was an outspoken critic of the **New Deal** and a defender of what was seen as traditional values of individualism. He was also an isolationist and opposed the revisions to the **neutrality** legislation in the late 1930s, the **Lend-Lease Act**, and the **Destroyers-for-Bases Agreement**. Although once in the war Taft supported the effort, he nonetheless appeared to be in favor of a negotiated peace with **Germany**.

Taft was reelected in 1944, and after the war he continued to oppose big government but accepted federal aid to education, federal housing programs, and even national health provision. He maintained his isolationist position and did not see the **Soviet Union** as a threat. While he accepted the **United Nations (UN)**, he opposed the **North Atlantic Treaty Organization** and involvement in the **Korean War**. He also criticized President **Harry S. Truman**'s policy toward **China** and as part of the **China lobby** accused the president of being "soft on communism." He also supported **Joseph McCarthy**'s attacks on the administration. However, Taft's most significant contribution to postwar politics was the **Taft-Hartley Act** of 1947, aimed to curb the power of **trade unions**. Although he was seen as "Mr. Republican,"

Taft failed to win his party's nomination for the presidency in 1940 and again in 1948 and 1952. He died of cancer in 1953.

TAFT-HARTLEY ACT, 1947. Named after the respective chairmen of the two congressional labor committees, Senator **Robert A. Taft** and representative Fred L. Hartley Jr., the Taft-Hartley Act, also known as the Labor-Management Relations Act, was passed over President **Harry S. Truman**'s veto on 23 June 1947. The measure was introduced following a wave of strikes in 1946 and increasing criticism of **trade unions**. The **Republican Party**'s victories in the congressional elections that year gave conservatives the majorities to enact legislation to curb labor. The act increased the membership of the **National Labor Relations Board (NLRB)** from three to five, made it illegal for workers to impose a closed shop, only allowed a union shop after a majority vote of all employees. The act required workers to agree in writing for union dues to be deducted from paychecks, prohibited secondary strikes, and banned strikes among federal employees. To prevent "wildcat" strikes, the act required an 80-day cooling-off period. Unions and employers were both prohibited from using coercive measures. The act also prevented unions from contributing directly to political campaigns, and it required union leaders to file affidavits confirming that they were not members of the **Communist Party of the United States of America** before they could apply to the NLRB.

The Taft-Hartley Act became the focus of trade union opposition and in 1948 threw support behind Truman in the election campaign. While the act remains on the statute books, it has not had the limiting force that many anticipated.

TAIWAN. Formerly known by Europeans as Formosa, the island off the coast of **China** was ceded to **Japan** in 1895 but restored to China in 1945. When **Chiang Kai-shek** was defeated by **Mao Zedong**'s communist forces in 1949, Chiang occupied Formosa, imposed control, and established the capital, Taipei, as the center of the Republic of China. Taiwan was not recognized by the People's Republic, and in 1950 President **Harry S. Truman** dispatched the U.S. Seventh Fleet to defend the island against a possible invasion. The U.S. commitment was reaffirmed in 1958 when communist China again threatened military action. The refusal of the People's Republic to recognize Taiwan as an independent state led to its exclusion from the **United Nations** until 1971, when it replaced the Republic of China in the chamber. The United States ended their defense ties with Taiwan after recognizing communist China in 1979.

TAYLOR, MAXWELL DAVENPORT (1901–1987). Born in Missouri, Maxwell Taylor graduated from West Point in 1922 and joined the Army Corps of Engineers. He held several minor positions during the interwar years and attended the Army War College in 1939. As commander of the 101st Airborne Division during **World War II**, Taylor took part in the campaign in Sicily and, operating behind the lines in Rome, successfully prevented a parachute drop into areas covered by German troops. He was the first general to land in France when he parachuted into **Normandy** on **D-Day** on 6 June 1944. After the war, he was superintendent of West Point until 1949, when he took command of the **Allied** forces in **Berlin**, a position he held until 1951. In 1953, he took command of the Eight Army in the **Korean War** and was involved in the last major battle of the war.

From 1955 to 1959, Taylor was army chief of staff. However, he disagreed with President **Dwight D. Eisenhower**'s "New Look" defense policy with its reliance on nuclear power and massive retaliation and retired in 1959. He outlined his views in *The Uncertain Trumpet* published in 1960. In 1961, Taylor became President John F. Kennedy's personal military adviser and from 1962 to 1964 chair of the Joint Chiefs of Staff. Having gone to Vietnam on a fact-finding tour, Taylor initially recommended the use of U.S. ground troops in Vietnam but later argued in favor of bombing the North and key targets rather than a further escalation of the war. He became a special consultant to the president and chair of the Foreign Intelligence Advisory Board and later president of the Institute for Defense Analyses. His autobiography, *Swords and Plowshares*, was published in 1972.

TECHNOCRACY. Led by engineer Howard Scott, the technocracy movement appeared in the early 1930s and proposed that only trained and qualified engineers could ensure the full and efficient use of the nation's industrial power and natural resources. They argued that machinery could replace manual labor. They proposed that the natural resources of the country be divided equally through "energy certificates" that would replace money. Scott established Technocracy, Inc., but exposés about his lack of qualifications and shady past undermined his credibility. Moreover, once the **New Deal** began to take effect, faith in political action was to some extent restored.

TEHRAN CONFERENCE, 1943. The first wartime meeting of leaders of the "big three"—the United States, **Great Britain**, and the **Soviet Union**—took place in Tehran, Iran, from 28 November to 1 December 1943. While the two Western leaders, **Franklin D. Roosevelt** and **Winston Churchill**, confirmed to **Joseph Stalin** that a second front would open with an invasion of Europe in May 1944, Churchill and Stalin made agreements about divisions of influence in Eastern Europe. While they agreed that power would be shared equally in Yugoslavia and Hungary, Churchill conceded total control of Rumania and Bulgaria to the Soviet Union. Stalin also indicated that he would join the war against **Japan** when the war in Europe ended.

TELEVISION. Television (TV) was only just developing at the end of the 1930s, with only one station in New York City and about 1,000 sets in operation by 1939. By 1941, there were 13 stations and the 521 lines of signal had become standard, but **World War II** diverted attention and resources, and development slowed until after 1945. In 1946, the three TV networks were the American Broadcasting Company (ABC), Columbia Broadcasting System (CBS), and National Broadcasting Company (NBC), and from the late 1940s onward television sales began to steadily increase. Although primarily black and white, color TV was already available from about 1950. By October 1950, there were 8 million TV sets in operation. By 1955, almost half of U.S. homes, more than 25 million, already had TV.

The first drama series, the *Kraft Television Theater*, began in1947; Gillette paid $100,000 to sponsor the return boxing match between **Joe Louis** and Jersey Joe Walcott; the comedy series *I Love Lucy* began in 1951 and was watched in more than 10 million homes a year later; and *The Today Show* began in 1952. The growing significance of the new medium was apparent in September 1952 when **Repub-**

lican vice presidential candidate **Richard M. Nixon** made the first televised public appeal directly to voters in his "Checkers" Speech. Equally significant were the televised Army–McCarthy hearings that were broadcast between April and June 1954 and at times watched by 20 million people, when the true character of **Joseph McCarthy** was exposed.

TEMPORARY NATIONAL ECONOMIC COMMITTEE. Following a message from President **Franklin D. Roosevelt** in April 1938 concerning issues of business monopoly, Congress established a Temporary National Economic Committee between 1938 and 1941 to perform a detailed study of the economy. The committee was chaired by Joseph C. O'Mahoney and consisted of senators, congressmen, and representatives from various government departments and agencies. It held 15 hearings and compiled 37 volumes of testimony. A number of monographs of a technical nature were also produced, along with the committee's final report. Its recommendations were of a rather general nature: more antimonopoly regulation, a return to freer competition, and support for small businesses. They were largely ignored, particularly once the United States entered **World War II**.

TENNESSEE VALLEY AUTHORITY (TVA). The TVA was established by an act of Congress on 18 May 1933 during the "**First Hundred Days**" of the **New Deal**. The TVA was to utilize and control the Tennessee River through the creation of hydroelectric schemes and irrigation systems. The authority was also to incorporate the government-owned nitrate facilities at Muscle Shoals that had been an issue of concern in the 1920s. These developments impacted seven states and more than 3 million people. It brought work, opened up areas to roads, and provided power for domestic consumers and industry. Although often criticized by private power companies and defenders of private enterprise, the TVA was largely judged as a success. It built 16 dams and during **World War II** produced vital nitrates for munitions and powered manufacturing in the area, and it was the largest producer of electricity in the United States. It also helped eradicate malaria in the region by 1952.

THOMAS, NORMAN MATTOON (1884–1968). Socialist Party of America leader Norman Thomas studied politics under Woodrow Wilson at Princeton University and then turned to theology. He was a Presbyterian pastor and worked in the New York settlement houses until 1918. A pacifist, Thomas opposed entry into World War I and was one of the founders of the Fellowship of Reconciliation, a group of pacifist clergymen. He was also one of the founders of the **American Civil Liberties Union**. He was an associate editor of *The Nation* from 1921 to 1922 and codirector of the League of Industrial Democracy from 1922 to 1937. He ran unsuccessfully as the socialist candidate in the New York gubernatorial campaign in 1924 and as the party's presidential candidate in 1928, 1932, and 1936, offering a moderate, non-Marxist brand of socialism critical of Soviet-style communism. Thomas initially worked to keep the United States out of the war in Europe and was a founding member of the **America First Committee**, but after 1941 he supported the war effort, although he opposed certain government policies, like the internment of **Japanese Americans**. He was the socialist presidential candidate again in 1940, 1944, and 1948 but later suggested that the party should abandon such campaigns and support progressive **Democrats**. Thomas resigned his official positions in the party in 1955, while continuing as its leading spokesman. In his later years, he spoke out against U.S. military involvement in Vietnam.

THURMOND, (JAMES) STROM (1902–2003). Born in Edgefield, South Carolina, Strom Thurmond graduated with a degree in horticulture from Clemson College in 1923. After working as a farmer, teacher, and athletics coach, he became education superintendent in Edgefield in 1929. Having been admitted to the bar in 1930, he became the Edgefield town and country attorney that year until 1938. He also served in the state senate from 1933 to 1938, when he became a circuit court judge. Thurmond resigned to join the army in 1941 and won a number of awards for his military service.

After **World War II**, Thurmond was elected as the **Democratic** governor of South Carolina, but in 1948 he ran as presidential candidate for the **States' Rights Party** against **Harry S. Truman** because of the president's racial policies. Committed to segregation,

Thurmond carried four states and won 39 Electoral College votes with more than 1 million votes. He was defeated in the campaign for the U.S. Senate in 1950 but in 1954 became the first candidate to be elected to the Senate in a write-in vote. He stood for reelection in 1956 and won. He served until his retirement in 2003 as the oldest person to have sat in the Senate. In 1957, Thurmond broke the record for the longest filibuster when he spoke for over 24 hours against the 1957 Civil Rights Act. In 1964, he switched allegiance to the **Republican Party**. In the 1970s, Thurmond accepted integration, and after his death a black woman was acknowledged by his family as his illegitimate daughter. *See also* CIVIL RIGHTS.

TOWNSEND, FRANCIS EVERETT (1867–1960). Born in Fairbury, Illinois, Francis Townsend grew up in Nebraska. After failing as a farmer in Kansas, he attended Nebraska Medical School in Omaha and graduated in 1903. He established a medical practice in South Dakota, and after serving as a doctor in the army during World War I, he moved to Long Beach, California in 1920. However, his practice was insufficient to support him, and he had to find other part-time work or risk facing old-age in poverty. In 1934, Townsend and the realtor for whom he had been working established the Old-Age Revolving Pensions, Ltd. and began to publicize his idea for a government-run pension scheme that would provide $200 per month for everyone over the age of 60 not in employment financed by a business tax. By 1935, there were more than 3,000 "Townsend Clubs" across the country with a membership of more than 500,000. When the plan was introduced to Congress in January 1935, it attracted more than 20 million signatures in support of legislation. The movement posed a political challenge to President **Franklin D. Roosevelt** and the **New Deal** and contributed to the move "left" in the "**Second New Deal**." It provided additional impetus for the **Social Security Act**. Once that measure was enacted, the Townsend movement lost its drive, and it was also economically unsound. Townsend then joined Father **Charles Coughlin** in the **Union Party** in 1936 but left before the election to support **Alf Landon**. He continued to support the **Republican Party** and spoke on behalf of the elderly for the remainder of his life.

TRADE AGREEMENTS ACT, 1934. Passed in 1934, the Trade Agreements Act enabled the president to negotiate tariff agreements with foreign governments and increase or reduce rates by up to 50 percent to stimulate trade and promote economic recovery. By 1937, some 30 agreements had been negotiated by Secretary of State **Cordell Hull**.

TRADE UNIONS. Although the organization of working people in a particular craft or industry in response to industrialization and the rise of the factory system began in the early 19th century, it was not until the **American Federation of Labor (AFL)** emerged under the leadership of Samuel Gompers in the 1880s as an organization of skilled workers using collective bargaining to achieve better wages and conditions in the workplace that they achieved lasting prominence. However, while the AFL concentrated on skilled workers, unskilled immigrant and **African American** employees were largely ignored. The AFL was briefly challenged in its role as mouthpiece of the working classes in the 1890s by the **Socialist Party of America** and the Industrial Workers of the World. These radical challenges did much to prompt progressive reformers into action, but in the long run they had only a limited appeal to U.S. workers.

During World War I, unions gained strength and recognition as a consequence of labor shortages and their participation in the mobilization of manpower. In 1919 there were 5 million members. However, a concerted counterattack by employers, aided by the conservative **Republican** administrations and the antipathy of the **Supreme Court** in the 1920s, led to a drop in membership to only 3 million. The reluctance of AFL leaders, especially Gompers's successor in 1924, **William Green**, to organize industrial workers or engage in militant action left the organization even weaker and facing terminal decline. Faced with further losses during the **Great Depression**, some union leaders, particularly **John L. Lewis**, called for a revitalized effort to organize workers on an industrial basis, including the unskilled. This caused a rift with the AFL and eventually led to the emergence of the **Congress of Industrial Organizations (CIO)** in 1938. Although this schism appeared to be the final straw, paradoxically, the 1930s turned out to be one of the greatest periods of union growth and militancy.

With the election of **Franklin D. Roosevelt** and the start of the **New Deal**, government now supported union activity. The first step toward recognition came with Section 7(a) of the **National Industrial Recovery Act**, which recognized the right to organize, recognized the right to collective bargaining, and prohibited company unions. When the act was declared unconstitutional, new legislation like the **National Labor Relations Act**, introduced by Senator **Robert F. Wagner** in 1935, specifically provided union recognition and banned obstruction by employers. The **Fair Labor Standards Act** of 1938 established minimum wages and maximum work hours. This sympathetic government attitude spurred on organizers in both the AFL and CIO, and their determination often led to industrial action. In 1937, almost 2 million workers took part in 4,720 strikes, the most significant being those led by the **Steel Workers' Organizing Committee** and also those in the car industry, starting in Flint, Michigan. The violence experienced in incidents like the **Memorial Day Massacre** in Chicago in 1937 and the revelations of the Senate committee chaired by **Robert M. La Follette Jr.** that some employers literally had small armies of spies and strikebreakers armed with an arsenal of weapons did much to win public sympathy for the unions. By 1940, more than 8 million workers were union members.

The unions played an important role during **World War II**, and the war helped consolidate some of the earlier gains. In December 1941, the unions issued a "no-strike pledge" and indicated their willingness to cooperate with government and business. In January 1942, President Roosevelt established a **National War Labor Board (NWLB)** to resolve disputes that could jeopardize the war effort. In 1942, the NWLB adopted the "maintenance of membership" clause that ensured that members of unions remained so for the duration of war contracts. Coupled with full employment, this resulted in the addition of almost 5 million new union members and a total membership of more than 14 million by 1945. However, as unions grew in size, it often became harder for union officials to manage them. As wartime inflation pushed up prices, union members began to revolt against the restrictions imposed on wage increases under the **"Little Steel" formula** and the no-strike pledge. In 1943, almost 2 million workers took part in 3,700 strikes, and in 1944 more than 2 million were involved in 5,000 stoppages. Congress responded in 1943 by passing the **War Labor Disputes Act** in an attempt to curb would-be strikers.

When a wave of strikes involving 5 million workers broke out during the period of postwar reconversion from 1946 to 1947, major elements of this legislation became permanent in the **Taft-Hartley Act**. Despite this, there was not the postwar reaction against unions that there had been in 1919, and although President **Harry S. Truman** alienated some workers with his response to the miners' and railway workers' strikes in 1946, organized labor was increasingly wedded to the **Democratic Party** both in terms of domestic policies and in support of the anticommunist strategies abroad. While support for the Democratic Party was channeled through **Political Action Committees**, unions that supported **Henry A. Wallace** in 1948 were expelled from the CIO, and both **Philip Murray** and **Walter Reuther** orchestrated campaigns against communist sympathizers in their organization. Thus, although by 1955 union membership stood at 17.5 million or 36 percent of the labor force, by the time the AFL and CIO merged later that year, much of the militant reforming zeal evident in the 1930s had disappeared. *See also* COMMUNIST PARTY OF THE UNITED STATES OF AMERICA (CPUSA); DUBINSKY, DAVID; GREEN, WILLIAM; HILLMAN, SIDNEY; SIT-DOWN STRIKES; WAR LABOR DISPUTES ACT; *YOUNGSTOWN SHEET & TUBE CO. V. SAWYER*.

TREATY OF SAN FRANCISCO, 1951. Signed on 8 September 1951 by the United States and 48 nations representing the **Allied powers**—save the **Soviet Union**, which declined to attend—the Treaty of San Francisco officially brought a cessation of hostilities in **World War II**'s Pacific theater and restored **Japan**'s sovereignty. The treaty went into effect on 28 April 1952. It was controversial from the start in that while Japan renounced its various territorial claims over neighboring nations and territories and agreed to pay compensation to Allied civilians and prisoners of war, it did not provide reparation payments for Asian nations overrun by Japanese armies during the war. Neither communist nor nationalist, **China** was represented at the signing. Some of the clauses of the treaty have subsequently been challenged in U.S. courts. A separate agreement with Japan, signed on the same day, allowed U.S. troops to remain in the country. *See also* UNITED STATES-JAPANESE SECURITY TREATY.

TRUMAN, BESS (ELIZABETH VIRGINIA) (1885–1982). The future first lady was born Elizabeth Wallace in Independence, Missouri. She first met **Harry S. Truman** at the age of five, and they met again 16 years later. They got engaged in 1917 and married in 1919. After two still births and several miscarriages, Bess gave birth to a daughter, Mary Margaret, who was her only child.

Bess was not particularly active in her husband's political life, but during **World War II** she worked in the Red Cross and the **United Service Organizations** and also as a secretary in her husband's office. When Harry became president in 1945, Bess assumed the role of first lady. She has been described as "the least active first lady in the 20th century," but she did reinstitute the White House social season after the war and was a hard-working hostess at numerous official functions. She also took on formal roles as president of the Girl Scouts, Red Cross, and other organizations. However, unlike her predecessor, **Eleanor Roosevelt**, Bess avoided publicity and only gave one press conference. She was unassuming and unpretentious, and she continued to visit the same beauty parlor while in the White House. As President Truman's published correspondence later made clear, Bess was also his trusted presidential adviser and confidante. After leaving the White House, she achieved her ambition and retired with her husband to an ordinary house in Independence.

TRUMAN, HARRY S. (1884–1972). 34th vice president and 30th president of the United States. Harry S. Truman was born in Lamar, Missouri. The "S" was added to his name to appease both paternal and maternal grandfathers, Anderson Shippe Truman and Solomon Young. The family moved to Independence, Missouri, in 1890. Truman finished high school in 1901 and had a number of jobs, including timekeeper and bank clerk. He served in a National Guard artillery unit in Kansas City, Missouri, and when the United States entered World War I, he rose from lieutenant to captain in charge of a battery in the 129th Artillery Regiment. He saw action in France during the Argonne offensive.

After the war, Truman married Bess Wallace and opened a haberdashery store in Kansas City. He lost this business and a farm in the recession of 1920 through 1922. A member of the **Democratic Party**, in 1922 he was elected district court judge with the support of Kansas City "Boss" Tom Pendergast. Truman advocated economy and efficiency and improved rural roads, and he also looked after the interests of his political backers. Nonetheless, he was defeated in 1924 but elected presiding judge of the county court in 1926 and again in 1930. In 1934, he was elected to the U.S. Senate.

As senator, Truman supported **Franklin D. Roosevelt** and served on the Interstate Commerce Committee, where he built strong relations with the railway unions. He was reelected in 1940 and in 1941 was appointed chair of a select committee investigating defense production. The committee was critical of waste and inefficiency in war contracts, and Truman made a reputation as a defender of small businesses.

In 1944, Truman was chosen as a compromise candidate for the vice presidency over **Henry A. Wallace**. Successfully elected, he had little personal contact with the president before Roosevelt's death on 12 April 1945 propelled him into the White House. As president, Truman had to provide the leadership in bringing **World War II** to a successful conclusion and ensure a lasting peace settlement. While the German armies were already beaten and surrendered on 7 May, it was Truman who made the decision to drop the **atomic bombs** on **Hiroshima** and **Nagasaki**, a move that finally ensured **Japan**'s agreement to surrender on 14 August 1945.

Truman set a new tone in relations with the **Soviet Union** in his first meeting with Soviet Foreign Minister Vyacheslav Molotov in April when the president addressed him in very strong terms about the Soviet failure to honor agreements in Eastern Europe. Truman met with the other **Allied** leaders, British prime minister **Winston Churchill** (replaced following his defeat by Clement Attlee) and Soviet leader **Joseph Stalin**, at the last major wartime conference in **Potsdam** in **Germany** in July 1945. Although agreement was reached on a number of issues, including Soviet entry into the war against Japan, relations were less cordial than had previously been the case. As relations with the Soviet Union deteriorated, Truman endorsed the policy of **containment** when he announced the **Truman**

Doctrine in his speech on 12 March 1947 asking Congress to approve aid to Greece and Turkey. This was followed on 3 April 1948 by the creation of the **Marshall Plan** to provide aid to Europe. As the **Cold War** between East and West developed, Truman approved the **National Defense Act** in 1947 reorganizing the armed forces and creating the **Central Intelligence Agency** and **National Security Council.** When faced with the **Berlin** blockade in June 1948, Truman opted against the use of military force and instead ordered the airlift of supplies that continued until May 1949 when the blockade was lifted. However, Truman approved U.S. involvement in **North Atlantic Treaty Organization** in April 1949 as a further defensive measure against the perceived threat of communism in Europe.

At home, Truman had to see the country through reconversion from wartime to peacetime production. The ending of wartime controls with the demise of the **Office of Price Administration** in November 1946 was followed by inflation and a wave of industrial unrest. In 1946, more than 4.6 million workers were involved in almost 5,000 strikes, including a coal strike in March and a rail strike in May. Truman, whose desktop motto was "The Buck Stops Here," responded on 17 May by seizing the **railroads** and mines on 21 May. He followed the act on 25 May with a speech to Congress that was highly critical of **trade unions** and included a threat to draft strikers, if necessary. When the miners, led by **John L. Lewis,** ignored a court order and again began a strike in 1946, Truman's public opinion ratings fell from 87 percent in June 1945 to 32 percent. Although he took the mine union to court and forced them back to work, the damage was done, and in the congressional elections the **Republicans** captured both houses of Congress for the first time since 1930. Truman regained some of his standing with the unions when he vetoed the **Taft-Hartley Act** in 1947, but it was still passed over his veto.

Truman won support from one section of the population while losing it from another. Appalled by the violence suffered by returning **African American** G.I.s, Truman became the first president to publicly speak out against such acts when he addressed the annual meeting of the **National Association for the Advancement of Colored People** in a national broadcast from the steps of the Lincoln Memorial on 29 June 1947. Having failed to establish a permanent **Fair Employment Practices Committee**, the president established a Committee on Civil Rights in 1946. Its report, *To Secure These Rights*, published in 1947, called for an end to discrimination in employment, housing, transportation, and public accommodation and also called for an end to discrimination in the federal civil service and armed forces, as well as **antilynching** legislation and protection for voting rights. On 26 July 1948, Truman issued Executive Order 9981 directing the beginning of desegregation in the armed forces. Another order called for an end to discrimination in the federal civil service.

Truman's stand on race alienated large numbers of southern Democrats, many of whom bolted the party to support **Strom Thurmond**'s **Dixiecrats** in the 1948 elections. Some liberals also left the party to support Wallace's **Progressive Party**. To many observers it seemed that Truman's defeat was inevitable. However, faced by a lackluster campaign from the Republican candidate, **Thomas E. Dewey**, and a barnstorming performance from Truman in a "whistle-stop" tour across the country, the result was an upset victory for the president and a return to Democratic control in Congress. In his inaugural address on 5 January 1949, Truman promised a "**Fair Deal**" for "every segment of our population and every individual." However his program of reform was largely blocked by an alliance of conservative Democrats and Republicans and because of the impact of the Cold War on domestic politics.

In the area of **foreign policy**, the United States faced major setbacks when the **Soviet Union** exploded its first atomic bomb on 29 August 1949, ending the U.S. monopoly. On 21 December 1949, **Chiang Kai-shek** was forced to leave mainland **China** for **Taiwan** by the communist forces led by **Mao Zedong**. These developments were seen as defeats by Republican critics who blamed communist sympathizers within the government, particularly the State Department. Truman responded to such charges by establishing the **Federal Loyalty Program** in 1947, but this merely provided ammunition for his critics. Their suspicions appeared to be confirmed by the revelations made by **Whittaker Chambers** before the **House Un-American Activities Committee** in August 1948 and the subsequent trial of **Alger Hiss** and his conviction for perjury in 1950. This provided the backdrop for Senator **Joseph McCarthy**'s speech in Wheeling, West Virginia, that unleashed the further accusations and investigations, or "witch hunt," known as **McCarthyism**. The **Internal Security Act** of 1950, also known as the McCarran Act or McCarran-Wood Act, intended to deal with suspected communist infiltration, was passed over Truman's veto.

Events overseas strengthened McCarthy's position. Truman responded to the invasion of South Korea by the North on 25 June 1950 by calling for a **United Nations' (UN)** police action and announcing that U.S. military forces would be led by General **Douglas MacArthur** on behalf of the UN. When communist China sided with North Korea in October 1950, MacArthur recommended attacking China and using atomic bombs. Truman refused, and after MacArthur's forces were pushed back, the general openly criticized the president's decision and was called home. The war, now a stalemate, ended on 27 July 1953. Elsewhere in Asia, Truman made what turned out to be a fateful decision in 1950 when he recognized French rule in Vietnam and approved a substantial aid package to assist the French in their war against the procommunist nationalist forces led by Ho Chi Minh.

The **Korean War**, the president's public differences with MacArthur, and several scandals involving minor members of the administration—particularly in the Internal Revenue Service—led to a drop in Truman's popularity to the lowest levels ever recorded. This was exacerbated by his seizure of the steel mills on 8 April 1952 in an industrial dispute in which the employers rejected a raise approved by the **Wage Stabilization Board**. The president was viewed as being too sympathetic to the labor unions for not using the Taft-Hartley Act to delay the strike. The **Supreme Court** ruled the seizure unconstitutional in *Youngstown Sheet & Tube Co. v. Sawyer* on 2 June 1952.

After losing in the New Hampshire primary to **Estes Kefauver** in March, Truman announced his decision not to stand for reelection. He and **Bess Truman** returned to their home in Independence, Missouri, where he worked on his *Memoirs*, published in 1955 and 1956, and established the Truman Library. He toured Europe in 1956 and was given an honorary degree by the University of Oxford. In 1964, he was honored by Congress, and in 1965 he was present at the White House for the signing of the Medicare bill. Truman's reputation has improved since his death because of his lack of pretension, forthright manner, and honesty. *See also* BERLIN AIRLIFT; HOUSING ACT, 1949.

TRUMAN DOCTRINE. On 12 March 1947, President **Harry S. Truman** asked Congress for $400 million in economic and military aid to Greece and Turkey. His message was a response to **Great Britain**'s warning that it could no longer underwrite the Greek monarchy, which was embroiled in a civil war against communist rebels supported by Yugoslavia's communist leader, Josip Broz Tito. Oversimplifying and also overstating the situation, Truman declared that the **Soviet Union** intended to use the civil war to dominate Greece and then Europe, the Middle East, and Asia. Every nation, he insisted, had to choose between "alternative ways of life"—democratic rule or communist terror. Named the Truman Doctrine, this speech was hailed by the press and public. Former isolationists like **Republican** senator **Arthur H. Vandenberg** were persuaded by Truman's argument, and Congress passed the proposed legislation in May 1947.

The Truman Doctrine marked the acceptance of a worldwide policy of resistance to real or perceived Soviet expansion along the lines of **George F. Kennan**'s principle of **containment** and indicated the start of the **Cold War**. The aid to Greece and Turkey was followed with the **Marshall Plan** and the later establishment of **North Atlantic Treaty Organization**.

TUGWELL, REXFORD GUY (1891–1979). Rexford Tugwell, who was born in Sinclairville, New York, was a graduate of Pennsylvania's Wharton School of Finance and Commerce. He was briefly a professor at Washington University and the American University in Paris, before taking the post of professor of economics at Columbia University, which he held from 1920 until 1937. In 1932, he joined President Roosevelt's **"Brain Trust"** and became undersecretary of **agriculture**. In 1935, he became head of the **Resettlement Administration** but resigned in 1937 because of the criticism the agency received. After a year in business, he became a member of the New York Planning Commission. In 1942, he was appointed governor of Puerto Rico and served until 1946. From 1946 until 1957, Tugwell was professor at the University of Chicago and then a member of the Center for the Study of Democratic Institutions in Santa Barbara, California. He retired in 1964. Tugwell authored 20 books, including *The Democratic Roosevelt* (1957) and *The Brains Trust* (1968).

TWENTIETH AMENDMENT. Passed on 3 March 1932 and ratified on 23 January 1933, the Twentieth Amendment reduced the gap between the election of a new president and a new Congress from November to January rather than March. It also ended "lame duck" Congresses that had met from December to March and had included congressmen defeated in the November elections. *See also* APPENDIX B.

TWENTY-FIRST AMENDMENT. Passed on 20 February 1933 and ratified on 5 December 1933, the Twenty-First Amendment repealed the Eighteenth Amendment and so ended prohibition in the United States. The amendment was ratified directly by state conventions, the first time such a device had been used since the approval of the Constitution itself. The vote for delegates in favor of repeal was approximately 73 percent of votes cast. Control of alcohol after 1933 became a state issue rather than a federal one. *See also* APPENDIX B.

TWENTY-SECOND AMENDMENT. Passed on 24 March 1947 and ratified on 26 February 1951, the Twenty-Second Amendment was passed to prevent an individual from being elected president more than twice and to establish that no president who had served more than two years of a term could be elected more than once. The amendment did not to apply to President **Harry S. Truman**, but he did not stand for reelection in 1952. *See also* APPENDIX B.

TYDINGS, MILLARD EVELYN (1890–1961). Born in Maryland, Millard Tydings graduated from Maryland Agricultural College in 1910 and the University of Maryland Law School in 1913. He briefly practiced law before entering the Maryland House of Delegates as a **Democrat** in 1915. During World War I, Tydings served in the army and rose from private to lieutenant colonel in command of a machine gun brigade. He was awarded the Distinguished Service Cross and Distinguished Service Medal for his bravery and afterward wrote a book *The Machine Gunners of the Blue and the Gray* (1920) based on his war experiences. Tydings returned to the Maryland House of Delegates in 1919 and was elected to the Maryland Senate in 1921 and then to the U.S. House of Representatives in 1922. In 1926, he was elected to the U.S. Senate, where he made a name for himself as an opponent of prohibition and a campaigner for Philippine independence.

Tydings was an advocate of states rights and increasingly critical of the **New Deal** and attacked the **National Recovery Administration**, **Agricultural Adjustment Administration**, and **Tennessee Valley Authority**. He was one of the leaders of the opposition to **Franklin D. Roosevelt**'s attempted "**court packing**" in 1937. Having survived Roosevelt's attempted "**purge**" of his opponents in 1938, Tydings allowed his name to be put forward as a potential candidate against the president for the Democratic nomination in 1940. He continued to be critical of government waste and bureaucracy throughout **World War II**. After the war, he called for the elimination rather than simply the control of **atomic bombs**.

In 1950, Tydings headed the Senate committee investigating the charges of communist infiltration made by **Joseph McCarthy** in his speech in Wheeling, West Virginia. The committee found the accusations to be a "hoax and a fraud." However, their findings had little effect, and McCarthy attacked Tydings when he stood for reelection in 1950 and contributed to his defeat in a particularly dirty campaign. After practicing law in Washington, D.C., Tydings attempted to return to the Senate in 1956 but was too ill.

TYDINGS-MCDUFFIE ACT, 1934. *See* PHILIPPINE INDEPENDENCE ACT.

– U –

UNION OF SOCIALIST SOVIET REPUBLICS (USSR). *See* SOVIET UNION (USSR).

UNION PARTY. In 1936, various groups critical of **Franklin D. Roosevelt** and the **New Deal** gathered to oppose his reelection. They included Father **Charles Coughlin** and the National Union for Social Justice, **William Lemke** and the Nonpartisan League, **Francis Townsend**, and **Gerald K. Smith** of the "Share Our Wealth" Plan. Their candidate for the presidency was Lemke, and they called for economic protectionism, isolationism, inflation of the currency, refinancing of farm mortgages, old-age pensions, increased work relief, and higher taxation of the rich. The leaders were, however, hopelessly divided and quickly split into separate groups. Lemke managed to attract only 882, 479 votes. Despite Lemke's best efforts the party disappeared by 1939.

UNITED NATIONS (UN). The UN is a worldwide organization that was established at the **San Francisco Conference** on 26 June 1945 to protect future generations from "the scourge of war," safeguard "fundamental human rights," and further economic and social welfare. The idea for the UN evolved in the course of **World War II** and became one of the fundamental aims of the **Allies**, who issued a Declaration of the United Nations at the **Arcadia Conference** on 1 January 1942 committing to the principles of the **Atlantic Charter**. The basic organization had been agreed upon by representatives of the United States, **Great Britain**, the **Soviet Union**, and Republic of **China** at the **Dumbarton Oaks Conference** in August 1944. The initial **United Nations Charter**, signed by 50 countries, was ratified by the U.S. Senate on 8 August 1945. It came into force after it had been ratified by the members of the **Security Council** on 24 October 1945. The UN effectively replaced the League of Nations. Its headquarters, built in 1949 and 1950, were established in New York City.

The UN consisted of six principal elements: the **Security Council**, General Assembly, Secretariat, Economic and Social Council, International Court of Justice, and the Trusteeship Council and Secretariat. It was to be headed by the secretary-general, the first of whom was Trygve Lie of Norway from 1946 to 1952. He was succeeded by Dag Hammarskjöld of Sweden from 1953 to 1961. The organization also established specialized agencies with particular functions, like the **United Nations Relief and Rehabilitation Administration, United Nations Educational, Scientific, and Cultural Organization**, World Health Organization, and Food and Agricultural Organization.

The UN had some success in resolving such international disputes as bringing about the withdrawal of Soviet troops from Iran in 1946, settling the conflict in Indonesia in 1948, and bringing peace to **Israel** in 1948 and 1949. In 1950, it approved a "police action" led by the United States in Korea to repulse an invasion from North Korea (*see* KOREAN WAR). In 1956, the UN helped restore peace following the Suez Crisis, and in 1990 UN forces were successfully mobilized in response to the invasion of Kuwait by Iraq under the leadership of Saddam Hussein. However, the organization was often limited due to the conflict between the United States and USSR in the **Cold War**, and later it was less successful in Bosnia, Somalia, and Cambodia in the 1990s and was involved in controversy in the events leading up to the U.S.-led invasion of Iraq in 2003. Agreement in the UN became more difficult as its membership grew to 192 members by 2007, and relationships between the UN and United States have been strained at times.

UNITED NATIONS CHARTER. The United Nations (UN) Charter, signed at the **San Francisco Conference** on 26 June 1945, outlined the principles on which the UN was formed and in 15 chapters provided details of its basic principles, structure, and organization. It came into force following ratification by the **Security Council** on 24 October 1945.

UNITED NATIONS EDUCATIONAL, SCIENTIFIC, AND CULTURAL ORGANIZATION (UNESCO). During **World War II**, a number of nations fighting Nazi **Germany** met to agree to cooperate on educational and scientific initiatives after the war. The United States joined this group, and a conference was convened in London, England, in November 1945. At the end of the meeting, 37 nations joined in the formation of UNESCO, which was formally established in November 1946 with headquarters in Paris, France. West Germany joined in the organization in 1951 and the **Soviet Union** in 1954. The aim of UNESCO is to promote international peace and further human rights through cooperation and collaboration in education, science, and culture. *See also* UNITED NATIONS (UN).

UNITED NATIONS RELIEF AND REHABILITATION ADMINISTRATION (UNRRA). Following a White House conference on 9 November 1943, 44 countries formed UNRRA to provide assistance to liberated and displaced peoples. A steering committee consisting of representatives from the United States, **Great Britain**, the **Soviet**

Union, and France was established with a director-general. The first director-general was **Herbert Lehman**, who was succeeded in 1946 by **Fiorello La Guardia**. In 1947, Major-General Lowell Ward took the post. UNRRA assisted some 8 million people and distributed $3 billion in aid, almost half of it coming from the United States before the program ended in 1949. It was succeeded by the International Refugee Organization. *See also* UNITED NATIONS (UN).

UNITED SERVICE ORGANIZATIONS (USO). Formed in 1941 by presidential order, the USO was established to provide "morale, welfare, and recreation-type services" for the millions of men and women who entered the U.S. armed forces during **World War II**. The USO brought together the work of the Salvation Army, YMCA, YWCA, National Catholic Community Service, National Travelers' Aid Association, and National Jewish Welfare Board to establish centers in some 3,000 towns and cities offering support for service personnel. They provided entertainment at home and abroad and, by 1947, had put on more than 428,000 concerts and shows. The USO continued after the war and is still in existence.

UNITED STATES DEPARTMENT OF DEFENSE. Created on 26 July 1947 under the **National Security Act** and initially known as the National Military Establishment, the Department of Defense was renamed in 1949. It brought the existing War Department and Navy Department together in a unified military establishment housed in the Pentagon.

UNITED STATES EMPLOYMENT SERVICE (USES). Originally established in 1914 on Ellis Island, the U.S. Employment Service was detached from the Bureau of Immigration and expanded during World War I to place workers in war industries. Although reduced in size after the war, USES continued and was reconstituted in 1933. It was initially primarily responsible for directing labor for projects in the **Public Works Administration**. It also placed workers for the **Civil Works Administration** and later for the **Works Progress Administration**. The role of USES expanded after 1935 because all unemployment compensation under the **Social Security Act** was to be paid via USES offices. In 1939, the service was moved to the

Federal Security Agency, and during the war all 1,500 state-run employment offices were taken over by the federal government.

UNITED STATES HOUSING AUTHORITY (USHA). The USHA was established under the **Housing Act** of 1937 to administer federal aid for slum clearance. By 1941, only 120,000 family dwellings had been completed. The functions of the USHA were later taken over by the **Public Housing Administration**.

UNITED STATES MARITIME COMMISSION. Established in 1936 to replace the U.S. Shipping Board created during World War I, the United States Maritime Commission regulated and funded the building of merchant shipping. It was particularly significant in aiding the shipbuilding program during **World War II**, when, through the **War Shipping Administration**, almost 6,000 vessels were constructed under its auspices. The commission ended with its reorganization in 1950, when it was replaced by the **Federal Maritime Board**.

UNITED STATES V. BUTLER **(297 U.S. 1 1936).** On 6 January 1936, the **Supreme Court** ruled in *United States v. Butler* that the processing tax introduced in the **Agricultural Adjustment Act** of 1933 was "a means to an unconstitutional end" that was, to "regulate and control **agriculture**." This was a major setback for President **Franklin D. Roosevelt** and the **New Deal**.

UNITED STATES V. DARBY LUMBER CO. **(312 U.S. 100 1941).** On 3 February 1941, in *United States v. Darby Lumber Co.*, the **Supreme Court** found that the **Fair Labor Standards Act** of 1938 was constitutional. In deciding the case relating to a company in Georgia, the court overturned the decision in *Hammer v. Dagenhart* (1918), in which it was argued that laws relating to conditions of labor were intrastate rather than interstate. In 1941, the court found that even laws affecting intrastate conditions indirectly related to or affected interstate commerce. *See also* NEW DEAL.

UNITED STATES V. PARAMOUNT PICTURES, INC. et al. **(334 U.S. 131 1948).** Also known as the Hollywood Antitrust Case, in

United States v. Paramount Pictures, Inc. et al. on 3 May 1948 the **Supreme Court** ruled by 8–0 in favor of the government and against the film studios in declaring that their control of movie theaters constituted a monopoly. The theaters were subsequently able to show films from whichever studio they wished, further contributing to the decline of the studio system. *See also* CINEMA.

UNITED STATES-JAPANESE SECURITY TREATY, 1951. Agreed upon in San Francisco on 8 September 1951 and ratified by the U.S. Senate on 20 March 1952, the United States-Japanese Security Treaty granted the United States the right to station military forces on or around **Japan**'s islands to maintain peace and security in the Far East. Although the treaty guaranteed U.S. aid if Japan were attacked by a third party, it also provided for assistance to suppress internal disturbances if requested by the Japanese government. Japan was prohibited from granting similar rights to other powers without the consent of the United States. *See also* TREATY OF SAN FRANCISCO.

USSR. *See* SOVIET UNION (USSR).

UTAH BEACH. Utah Beach was one of the two main landing sites of U.S. forces in the **Normandy landings** during **D-Day** on 6 June 1944. It was situated between Pouppeville and La Madeleine in northern France. The landing of 23,000 men was one of the most successful and resulted in only 200 American casualties.

– V –

V-E DAY. V-E Day stood for Victory in Europe Day, which came following the German surrender on 6 May 1945. V-E Day was officially celebrated following the cessation of all hostilities in Europe on 8 May 1945.

V-J DAY. V-J Day was Victory in Japan Day and came with the surrender of **Japan** on 15 August 1945.

V-MAIL. V-mail was the mail of U.S. military personnel during **World War II** that was written on special V-mail letter sheets and then microfilmed and developed once it had reached the mainland. It reduced the space that traditional mail would have otherwise occupied and freed up valuable cargo space on ships.

VALLEE, RUDY (1901–1986). Born Hubert Prior Vallee in Vermont, the singer and musician grew up in Maine, where he learned to play the saxophone and was named "Rudy" after another saxophonist. Vallee enlisted in the navy and served 41 days before it was discovered he was only 16 years old and was discharged. From 1922 to 1923, he was a student at Yale University, but his studies were interrupted by his career as a musician, and he played in an orchestra in London, England, from 1924 to 1925, resuming his studies in 1925 and graduating in 1927. He had already adopted one of his trademark symbols—a raccoon coat—and he also started to use a megaphone to give his voice more depth. Vallee was one of the first of the "crooners"—a style that also influenced **Bing Crosby** and **Frank Sinatra**—and he attracted rapturous audiences. He was enormously popular on the **radio** throughout the 1930s and 1940s with hits like "Life Is Just a Bowl of Cherries." Vallee appeared in his first film, *The Vagabond Lover*, in 1926. Among his other film successes were *The Palm Beach Story* (1942) and *Gentlemen Prefer Brunettes* (1955). During the war, he played with the Coastguard band. His popularity as a singer declined afterward, but he appeared on **television** and in a number of film roles. Although Vallee was still appearing in films as late as the 1980s, his last major film was *How to Succeed in Business without Really Trying* in 1967. *See also* CINEMA; MUSIC.

VAN DEVANTER, WILLIS (1859–1941). Willis Van Devanter was born in Marion, Indiana. He graduated from Cincinnati Law School in 1881 and moved to Wyoming, where he established a legal practice and rose as an important member of the **Republican Party** in state politics. He was a member of the Territorial Legislature, chair of the Judiciary Committee, and in 1889 was appointed chief justice of the Territorial **Supreme Court**. When Wyoming achieved statehood, Van Devanter became the first chief justice of the state Supreme Court but resigned to pursue his private practice.

In 1897, Van Devanter was appointed assistant U.S. attorney general in the Department of the Interior and also taught law at George Washington Law School. In 1910, President William Howard Taft appointed Van Devanter to the Supreme Court, where he became a strong defender of business interests and upholder of laissez faire principles. He was one of the conservatives who consistently ruled against progressive welfare measures in the 1920s. However, he did contribute to the 1925 Judiciary Act improving the efficiency of the court.

During the 1930s, Van Devanter was, with **James McReynolds**, **George Sutherland**, and **Pierce Butler**, one of the "Four Horsemen" who consistently ruled against President **Franklin D. Roosevelt**'s **New Deal** measures. He continued to express dissent even after Roosevelt's **"court packing"** attempt had failed and even though the court began reversing previous anti-New Deal decisions. In 1937, Van Devanter retired and became a judge on the U.S. District Court in the Southern District of New York.

VANDENBERG, ARTHUR HENDRICK (1884–1951). Arthur H. Vandenberg was born in Grand Rapids, Michigan, and after a year at the University of Michigan Law School in 1901, he became a reporter for the *Grand Rapids Herald*. In 1906, he became editor and continued in that role until 1928. Having made a name for himself with his moderate progressive **Republican** views, in 1928 he was appointed to fill the seat in the U.S. Senate for Michigan vacated by Woodbridge N. Ferris upon his death. Vandenberg held the seat until his death. Although he supported some **New Deal** measures, like the **Banking Acts** and public housing legislation, he opposed many of the other measures, including the **Tennessee Valley Authority**, **Agricultural Adjustment Act**, **Works Progress Administration** and 1935 **Revenue Act**. He was also a leading isolationist and active member of the **Nye** Committee.

After **Pearl Harbor** and U.S. entry into **World War II**, Vandenberg modified his position, supporting the war effort, and in 1945 publicly abandoning isolationism in favor of world leadership by the United States. He was a delegate to the **San Francisco Conference** in 1945 and the **United Nations** General Assembly in 1946. Beginning in 1947, Vandenberg chaired the Senate Foreign Relations Committee and worked closely with the **Truman** administration to reach agreement on such major **foreign policy** such as the **Truman Doctrine** and **Marshall Plan**. The **Vandenberg Resolution**, passed by the Senate in June 1948, accepted the necessity of U.S. participation in regional and other collective agreements and paved the way for Senate approval of the **North Atlantic Treaty Organization**. Highly respected in the party, Vandenberg was a possible candidate for the presidential nomination in 1940 and 1944, but he would never campaign openly and so was passed by. Nonetheless, he was an influential figure during this period.

VANDENBERG RESOLUTION, 1948. Introduced in May 1948 by Senator **Arthur H. Vandenberg**, the Vandenberg Resolution was passed in the Senate on 11 June 1948. It approved of action to maintain world security by U.S. participation in the **United Nations** and also through mutual defense treaties or agreements with other nations. It enabled President **Harry S. Truman** to enter into negotiations leading to the **North Atlantic Treaty** in 1949.

VINSON, FREDERICK MOORE (1890–1953). Born in Louisa, Kentucky, Fred Vinson graduated from Center College, Danville, in 1911 and became a lawyer and city attorney in his hometown. After briefly serving in the army during World War I, he returned to law but was elected to the House of Representatives as a **Democrat** in 1924. Although he lost the election in 1928, he was reelected in 1930 and served until 1937. While in Congress, Vinson became a close friend and associate of **Harry S. Truman**. In 1937, he was appointed to the U.S. Court of Appeals on the Washington, D.C., circuit.

Vinson held a number of positions during **World War II**, including director of the Office of Economic Stabilization in 1943 and director of War Mobilization and Reconversion in 1945. After the war, President Truman appointed him secretary of the treasury, where he was responsible for supervising the repayment of **lend-lease** loans, and took part in the meetings at the **Bretton Woods Conference** that led to the creation of the **International Monetary Fund**. In 1946, Truman made him chief justice on the **Supreme Court** as a compromise between choosing either **Robert Jackson** or **Hugo Black**. As a result, Vinson had the task of trying to bring together opposing factions in the court, and he was not very successful. His court was associated with upholding various internal security measures, including the **Smith Act** in *Dennis v. United States* in 1951, and failing to hear the appeal of **Ethel** and **Julius Rosenberg**. None of his decisions were particularly memorable, but he was sympathetic toward **civil rights** issues relating to **African Americans** and wrote the opinion in *Shelley v. Kraemer* in 1948. Vinson died while in office.

VOICE OF AMERICA. The "Voice of America" was created as a **radio** broadcasting service during **World War II** by the **Office of War Information** to transmit to populations under the control of Nazi **Germany**. After the war, an international shortwave radio station was established by the State Department in 1948 to broadcast to countries behind the **Iron Curtain**. Broadcasts were made in 46 languages. This service expanded to reach other parts of the world and eventually included television transmissions. Today it also includes Internet broadcasts.

– W –

WAGE STABILIZATION BOARD (WSB). Established in 1950, the WSB was a board of 18 officials representing public, labor, and management equally with the authority to control wages to limit inflation during the **Korean War**. However, the labor members resigned after the board voted to limit wage increases to 10 percent in February 1951, and the board was reorganized. In March 1952, the board granted wage increases and recognized a union shop in the steel industry. When this was rejected by the steel companies, President **Harry S. Truman** ordered the takeover of the steel mills to avert a strike. When this action was declared unconstitutional by the **Supreme Court** in *Youngstown Sheet & Tube Co. v. Sawyer* in April, the mills were returned to their owners and a strike ensued. After 53 days, a settlement was agreed upon close to that proposed by the WSB. The board was abolished in February 1953. *See also* TRADE UNIONS.

WAGNER ACT. *See* NATIONAL LABOR RELATIONS ACT.

WAGNER-PEYSER ACT. *See* UNITED STATES EMPLOYMENT SERVICE (USES).

WAGNER, ROBERT FERDINAND (1877–1953). Robert F. Wagner was born in **Germany** and immigrated to the United States with his family in 1885. They settled in New York City, where Wagner attended City College of New York and New York Law School. He qualified in law in 1900 and established a law practice. He was elected as a **Democrat** to the New York State Assembly in 1905 and then to the state senate in 1909. He was chairman of the State Factory Investigating Committee from 1911 to 1915 and justice of the **Supreme Court** of New York from 1919 to 1926. Together with **Alfred E. Smith**, Wagner promoted several pieces of reform legislation to improve labor conditions in New York. He was elected to the U.S. Senate in 1926, where he served until his resignation due to ill-health in 1949.

Wagner chaired several committees and sponsored several major pieces of social reform legislation in the **New Deal**, like the **National Industrial Recovery Act** and **Social Security Act**. He was best known as the author of the **National Labor Relations Act**, also known as the Wagner Act, of 1935 that established the **National Labor Relations Board** and recognized workers' rights to free collective bargaining. With Edward Costigan, Democratic senator for Colorado, he was also cosponsor of the unsuccessful **Federal Antilynching Bill** in 1934 and 1935. Wagner also supported passage of the **Housing Act** in 1937. He was a delegate to the United Nations Monetary and Financial Conference at the **Bretton Woods Conference** in 1944. After **World War II**, Wagner saw some of his proposals included in President **Harry S. Truman**'s **Fair Deal**. Poor health forced him to resign his seat in 1949 before much could come to fruition. *See also* TRADE UNIONS.

WALL STREET CRASH, 1929. The greatest financial crash in the history of the United States occurred in October 1929. Following several months during which security prices fell, on "Black Thursday," 24 October, more than 13 million shares were traded on the stock exchange. On 29 October, "Black Tuesday," "the most devastating day in the history of the New York Stock Market," more than

16 million shares were sold, and share prices fell by $40 billion. By July 1933, the decline in value was $74 billion, and the great boom in stocks, the "bull market" of the 1920s, was over.

The speculation boom of the 1920s was fueled by the expansion of manufacturing and growth of consumerism based on such new products as the automobile, **radio**, and other electrical appliances. The mood of optimism was reflected in rising share prices, and shares themselves then became seen as a way of making money quickly, rather than as investments in the country's industrial future. The market, however, was largely unregulated and suffered serious flaws. Investors could buy shares on "margin," that is, paying a fraction—sometimes as little as 10 percent—of the value of the shares and borrowing the rest from brokers. As prices rose, shares could be sold, the balance paid off, and a profit made. When prices fell, panic set in as investors realized the yield would not meet the outstanding balance. Holding companies and investment trusts sprang up offering shares that often bore little relation to industrial assets or profits and sometimes were simply exercises in speculation. Brokers' loans rose from $3.5 million in June 1927 to $8 million in September 1929, and about 4 million Americans owned stock, 1.5 million of them using brokers.

The crash wiped out individual savings and the investments of banks and insurance companies. The loss of confidence in financial institutions due to failure and tales of fraud and embezzlement added to the downward spiral. The rush of savers to withdraw money from banks compounded the crisis that led to a general collapse in financial institutions. By 1932, almost 4,000 banks had failed. This in turn contributed to the onset of the **Great Depression** as investment in industry fell and loans to companies, farms, homeowners, and international banks were called in.

WALLACE, HENRY AGARD (1888–1965). Henry A. Wallace was born in Iowa, the son of Henry C. Wallace, the secretary of **agriculture** in the administrations of Warren Harding and Calvin Coolidge during the 1920s. Like his father, he was interested in farming, and he graduated from Iowa State College of Agriculture in 1910. He then became associate and later senior editor of *Wallace's Farmer*, later *Iowa Homestead and Wallace's Farmer*. He was president of the Hi-Bred Seed Company from 1926 to 1933, and he helped develop the first hybrid seed corn for commercial use. During the 1920s, Wallace supported the unsuccessful McNary-Haugen proposal to have the federal government purchase farm surpluses to sell abroad.

Although a **Republican**, Wallace supported **Alfred E. Smith** in 1928 and **Franklin D. Roosevelt** in 1932. Once elected, Roosevelt appointed Wallace secretary of agriculture, and it was Wallace, assisted by **Rexford Tugwell**, who oversaw the introduction of the **Agricultural Adjustment Act** and other major pieces of farming legislation. His most significant achievement was securing the passage of the second Agricultural Adjustment Act of 1938.

In 1940, Roosevelt chose Wallace as his vice presidential running mate. As vice president during **World War II**, he was chair of the Board of Economic Warfare and the Supply and Allocations Board. He also undertook goodwill visits to Latin America. Wallace's vision of the postwar world was summed up in his *Century of the Common Man* speech and book of the same title in 1942. However, in 1944 he was dropped by the **Democratic Party** in favor of **Harry S. Truman**. Wallace instead was appointed secretary of commerce. He continued in this role under Truman following Roosevelt's death but increasingly found himself at odds with the president over **foreign policy** and relations with the **Soviet Union**. He was dismissed in September 1946 and became editor of the *New Republic*, where he continued to be critical of Truman. In 1948, he ran for the presidency as the candidate for the **Progressive Party** but attracted only 1 million votes. He retired from politics to concentrate on his scientific agrarian work, developing improved strains of vegetables, fruit, and flowers.

WALSH-HEALEY PUBLIC CONTRACTS ACT, 1936. Following the **Supreme Court**'s decision in *Schechter Poultry Corp. v. United States* invalidating the **National Industrial Recovery Act** and its provision for minimum wages and maximum hours for workers, the **Roosevelt** administration responded with several pieces of individual legislation, the "little NRA." Included was the Public Contracts Act, introduced by Senator David I. Walsh, a Democrat from Massachusetts, and Congressman Arthur D. Healey, also a Democrat from Massachusetts, passed on 30 June 1936. The act required that all federal government contractors pay no less than the minimum wage established by the Department of Labor, observe the eight-hour day and 40-hour week, and not employ workers under the age of 18 or use convict labor.

WAR BONDS. War Bonds was the name given to the U.S. Treasury Series E Savings Bonds first issued on 1 May 1941. (U.S. Savings Bonds were first issued in 1935.) After **Pearl Harbor** and U.S. entry into **World War II**, these bonds became known as "war bonds" or "victory bonds." The bonds were sold in eight war loan drives during the war and raised $135 billion.

WAR FOOD ADMINISTRATION (WFA). Established on 21 June 1943 within the Department of **Agriculture** and headed by **Marvin Jones**, the WFA was responsible for ensuring the full production and distribution of food to meet essential needs during **World War II**. Beginning in 1943, the WFA was responsible for the Mexican workers imported under the *bracero* program.

WAR LABOR BOARD (WLB). *See* NATIONAL WAR LABOR BOARD (NWLB).

WAR LABOR DISPUTES ACT, 1943. Known as the Smith-Connally Act and passed over President **Franklin D. Roosevelt**'s veto in May 1943, the War Labor Disputes Act was in response to the wave of strikes affecting the U.S. war industry that year. The act made any strike that took place in a plant or mine on federal contracts before a 30-day "cooling-off" period and secret ballot of workers illegal. It empowered the **National War Labor Board** to adjudicate in such disputes and subpoena the parties involved. Although not particularly effective as a curb to **trade unions**, the act established a precedent for the **Taft-Hartley Act** in 1947.

WAR MANPOWER COMMISSION (WMC). Established by Executive Order 9139 on 18 April 1942 to coordinate and supervise the recruitment of war workers and determine both essential and nonessential industries, the WMC also organized training programs. Headed by **Paul V. McNutt**, the commission did not have powers of enforcement but relied on voluntary cooperation. Beginning in

December 1942 the WMC included **Selective Service**, and in 1943 McNutt issued a "work or fight" order ending deferments for those in nonessential industries but was forced to rescind the order due to congressional opposition. **World War II** ended before proposals to introduce conscription of labor could come into force, and the WMC was incorporated into the Department of Labor.

WAR POWERS ACTS, 1941, 1942. Following the attack on **Pearl Harbor** and U.S. entry into **World War II**, the federal government was granted powers necessary to mobilize the nation for war, first with the War Powers Act of 18 December 1941, enabling the government to assign powers to war agencies or departments, and secondly with the War Powers Act of 27 March 1942. The second act enabled the government to allocate materials or facilities in any way thought necessary to wage war. It provided the power for the **War Production Board** to direct the economy. The act was repealed in March 1947.

WAR PRODUCTION BOARD (WPB). Established on 16 January 1942 to replace the **Office of Production Management**, the WPB was headed by **Donald M. Nelson**. Empowered to oversee the production and distribution of raw materials and manufactured goods and also to award contracts, its powers were increased by the **War Powers Act** in March 1942 to allow it to allocate resources where necessary and provide direction for the nation's economic war mobilization. In 1942, the WPB limited the production of nonessential goods and forbade the use of scarce materials. However, the board was hampered to some extent because the military procurement bodies could still negotiate their own separate contracts and because President **Franklin D. Roosevelt** appointed other leaders with responsibility for such key areas as petroleum, rubber, and manpower. The WPB's plans to allow industry to prepare for reconversion before the end of **World War II** was hotly contested by the military and eventually led to Nelson being replaced in 1944. The WPB ceased to exist as of November 1945.

WAR REFUGEE BOARD (WRB). The WRB was created in January 1944 at the behest of **Henry Morgenthau Jr.** to organize the rescue of racial and religious victims of Nazi persecution and seek the assistance of public and private bodies in the rescue, transportation, and care of refugees. Working with neutral countries, the board helped to effect the movement of refugees to Palestine, Spain, Portugal, and Norway, and it also established a camp for 1,000 Italians in Oswego, New York. It was believed that the WRB had helped save some 200,000 refugees before it was abolished in September 1945.

WAR RELIEF CONTROL BOARD. Established in July 1942, the War Relief Control Board controlled and coordinated the collection and distribution of funds for war relief through charity organizations. It also provided aid for refugees and assistance for U.S. civilians affected by enemy action. By the time it came to an end in June 1945, the board had collected more than $253 million in cash and more than $224 million in kind.

WAR RELOCATION AUTHORITY (WRA). The WRA was established by Executive Order 9102 on 18 March 1942 to relocate and house **Japanese Americans** during **World War II**. The head of the authority was **Milton Eisenhower**. More than 112,000 Japanese Americans were housed in 10 camps under WRA supervision. Locations of the camps included Gila River, Arizona; Granada, Colorado; Heart Mountain, Wyoming; Jerome, Arkansas; Manzanar, California; Minidoka, Idaho; Poston, Arizona; Topaz, Utah; Tule Lake, California; and Rohwer, Arkansas. The camps were basic barrack-style centers, fenced with armed guards in remote areas. Following the **Supreme Court**'s decision in *Endo v. United States*, some inmates were allowed to leave the camps beginning in 1944, and the internment order was rescinded in 1945. The WRA ceased operations on 30 June 1946. *See also HIRABAYASHI V. UNITED STATES; KOREMATSU V. UNITED STATES.*

WAR SHIPPING ADMINISTRATION (WSA). Established on 7 February 1942, the WSA was to acquire and operate all U.S. merchant shipping, allocate ships to the navy, and encourage production of vessels, as well as provide training for merchant seamen. The administration provided for the building of **liberty ships** and Victory ships and saw a massive expansion in the size of the merchant fleet.

It was absorbed back into the **United States Maritime Commission** in September 1946.

WARREN, EARL (1891–1974). Born in Los Angeles, California, Earl Warren worked on the railroads before going to the University of California at Berkeley, where he earned his B.A. in 1912 and his degree from the law school in 1914. After serving in the army during World War I, Warren held a number of positions, including city attorney, country district attorney, and district attorney, in Almeda County. He was elected district attorney in 1926, 1930, and 1934 and in 1938 became attorney general of California. After the attack on **Pearl Harbor**, he was an advocate of the internment of **Japanese Americans**, a decision he subsequently regretted. A **Republican**, in 1942 Warren was elected governor of California and was reelected in 1946. He ran as the vice presidential candidate with **Thomas E. Dewey** in 1948 and was a possible presidential candidate in 1952. When successful candidate **Dwight D. Eisenhower** won the election, he nominated Warren to replace deceased Chief Justice **Fred Vinson** on the **Supreme Court**. It was a choice Eisenhower came to regret as Warren turned out to be one of the most significant figures in court history with the ruling in *Brown v. Board of Education of Topeka* in 1954 declaring segregation in schools unconstitutional. Also significant was the ruling in *Miranda v. Arizona* in 1966 requiring that police officers read individuals their rights before charging them. Warren chaired the committee that investigated the assassination of President John F. Kennedy in 1963. The conclusion that the shooting was the result of a lone gunman, Lee Harvey Oswald, is still regarded as controversial. Warren retired in 1969.

WASHINGTON TREATY, 1949. *See* NORTH ATLANTIC TREATY.

WAVES. *See* WOMEN APPOINTED FOR VOLUNTEER EMERGENCY SERVICE (WAVES).

WAYNE, JOHN (1907–1979). Born Marion Robert (later Mitchell) Morrison in Iowa, actor John Wayne grew up in California, and after two years at the University of Southern California in 1927, he began working in film studios as an extra. In 1930, he appeared as John Wayne in *The Big Trail*. In 1939, he achieved his first major success and began a lifelong working relationship with director **John Ford** in *Stagecoach*.

Exempted from military service during **World War II** due to his age, Wayne made a considerable number of films, including *Reap the Wild Wind* (1942), *The Long Voyage Home* (1940), and *They Were Expendable* (1945). It was after the war that his career really developed with *Fort Apache* (1948), *Red River* (1948), *She Wore a Yellow Ribbon* (1949), *The Sands of Iwo Jima* (1949), and *Rio Grande* (1950). He had the starring role in Ford's *The Quiet Man* in 1952, again in *The Searchers* in 1956, and finally in *The Man Who Shot Liberty Valance* (1962). Wayne produced some of his own films, including *Big Jim McLain* (1952) and *The Alamo* (1960). His conservative political outlook and outspoken patriotism was most obvious in the film he produced, directed, and starred in about Vietnam, *The Green Berets* (1968).

In 1969, Wayne won an Oscar for Best Actor in *True Grit*, but his later films, with the exception of *The Shootist* (1976), were not highly regarded. His place in U.S. film history is best summed up in the inscription on the Congressional Medal of Honor awarded to him shortly before his death: "John Wayne, American." *See also* CINEMA.

WEALTH TAX ACT. *See* REVENUE ACTS, 1935, 1936, 1938.

WEAVER, ROBERT CLIFTON (1907–1997). Robert Weaver was born in Washington, D.C. He obtained his B.A., M.A., and Ph.D. from Harvard, graduating in 1934. From 1933 to 1937, he was an adviser on Negro affairs in the Department of the Interior and a member of President **Franklin D. Roosevelt**'s "**Black Cabinet**." From 1937 to 1940, Weaver was employed as a special assistant for the **United States Housing Authority**. During **World War II**, he was actively involved in mobilizing **African Americans** for the war effort. He worked with the **Office of Production Management** and then was director of Negro Manpower Service in the **War Manpower Commission**.

After the war, Weaver served on the Chicago Mayor's Committee on Race Relations before his specialization in housing matters led to teaching posts at Columbia Teachers College and New York University in 1947 and the J. H. Whitney Foundation in 1949. In 1954, he was appointed deputy commissioner in the New York State Division of Housing. After working for the Ford Foundation from 1959 to 1961, Weaver became an administrator in the Federal Housing and Home Finance Agency until 1966, when he was appointed as the first secretary of housing and urban development by President Lyndon Johnson. His was the first appointment of an African American to a cabinet post. In 1969, he became president of Bernard Baruch College and in 1970 professor of urban affairs at Hunter College. He retired in 1978. Among Weaver's publications were *Negro Labor: A National Problem* (1946) and *The Negro Ghetto* (1948). In 2000, the Department of Housing and Urban Development building in Washington, D. C., was named in his honor.

WEDEMEYER, ALBERT COADY (1897–1989). Born in Omaha, Nebraska, Albert Wedemeyer graduated from the U.S. Military Academy at West Point in 1918. During the 1920s, he served with the infantry in the United States and the Philippines. He became a captain in 1935. Having spent some years training in the German General Staff School in **Berlin**, Wedemeyer was given responsibility for leading the planning for U.S. war mobilization in 1941. In 1943, he was posted to the Southeast Asia Command under British Lord Louis Mountbatten, and he planned the offensives in Sumatra and Malaya. In 1944, he replaced General **Joseph Stilwell** as commander of the U.S. Army forces in **China** and became chief of staff to **Chiang Kai-shek**. Wedemeyer worked to strengthen the nationalist forces, and in 1945, when conflict broke out with the communist groups lead by **Mao Zedong**, he urged support for the nationalists. After a brief return to the United States, in 1947 he was sent on a fact-finding mission to assess the situation in China. He called for massive aid to support the nationalists, but his recommendations were rejected. The failure to follow his proposals was used by the **China lobby** to criticize the **Truman** administration for the "loss" of China.

From 1947 to 1949, Wedemeyer worked in the General Staff, and from 1949 until 1951 he commanded the Sixth Army in San Francisco, California. After he retired from the army, he served as a business executive and was active in the **Republican Party**.

WELLES, ORSON (1915–1985). The **theater**, **cinema**, and **radio** actor, producer, director, and screenwriter was born George Orson Welles in Kenosha, Wisconsin, but grew up in Chicago. He was orphaned at the age of 15 and raised by his stepfather. Welles trained at the Art Institute in Chicago and spent some time touring Ireland, Spain, and Morocco. His first stage appearance was in Dublin in 1931. After his return to the United States in 1933, he worked in the New York Theater and from 1936 was employed by the **Federal Theater Project**, where he produced a memorable all-black *Macbeth* at the American Negro Peoples' Theater in Harlem. He left in 1937 and with John Houseman established the Mercury Theater and produced a contemporary production of *Julius Caesar*. Welles was also acting and writing for radio for CBS. The network gave him a weekly show, the "Mercury Theater on the Air." On 30 October 1938, they performed *War of the Worlds* as a news report of a Martian invasion that was so realistic many listeners believed it was a real event and panicked.

In 1939, Welles began working in Hollywood for RKO Radio Pictures, and in 1941 he directed and starred in *Citizen Kane*, loosely based on the life of **William Randolph Hearst**. It is regarded as one of the greatest films of all time. The following year he directed a second much-admired movie, *The Magnificent Ambersons*, followed by *Journey into Fear*, which he cowrote, directed, and played a leading role for. Welles made several other films in the 1940s, including *Jane Eyre* (1943), *The Stranger* (1946) starring **Edward G. Robinson**, and *Lady from Shanghai* (1947) with **Rita Hayworth**. In 1948, Welles made a low-budget film version of *Macbeth* and then *Othello* in 1951, which was released in the United States in 1955. In the late 1940s, Welles spent most of his time in Europe, perhaps to escape **McCarthyism**. He was among those listed in *Red Channels* in 1950. In 1949, he directed and appeared in *The Third Man*. In 1958, he returned to the United States to direct and act in *A Touch of Evil*, regarded as another film classic. He also made the well-received version of Kafka's *The Trial* in 1963 and played the role of Falstaff in *The Chimes of Midnight* in 1966. Welles made his last film, *F for Fake*, in 1975, and that year he was awarded a Lifetime Achievement Award by the American Film Institute. He is regarded as one of America's greatest filmmakers.

WELLES, SUMNER (1892–1961). Born Benjamin Sumner Welles to a prominent and wealthy family in New York City, Welles went to Groton and then Harvard University. He graduated in 1914 and entered the Foreign Service. Welles spent two years in **Japan** and then in 1919 went to Buenos Aires, Argentina. In 1920, he was appointed assistant chief of the Division on Latin American Affairs. After briefly resigning from the State Department, in 1922 Welles was appointed special commissioner to the Dominican Republic, a post he held for three years, but he resigned from the State Department when President Calvin Coolidge refused to nominate him to another post for personal reasons. Welles had been involved in a messy divorce. In 1933, President **Franklin D. Roosevelt** appointed him assistant secretary of state, and in that capacity he helped shape the **"Good Neighbor" Policy** toward Latin America. In 1933, Welles was involved in trying to bring order to Cuba and, in 1934 he negotiated an agreement ending previous policies giving the United States the right to intervene in Cuban affairs. In 1936, he was instrumental in organizing the **Buenos Aires Conference**.

In 1937, Welles became undersecretary of state, and in 1940 he was sent to Europe to try to secure peace. Although he failed to do so, he obtained much valuable intelligence about the situation. In 1941, he took part in the meeting between Roosevelt and **Winston Churchill** that led to the **Atlantic Charter**. From 1942 onward, he chaired the committee planning for postwar international cooperation that produced the initial ideas for the **United Nations**. In 1944, it seemed likely that widely circulating stories about Welles's homosexuality and heavy drinking would be subject to a Senate hearing, and he resigned. He became a spokesman and authority on U.S. **foreign policy**, writing *Time for Decision* (1944) and *Where Are We Heading* (1946) and editing a series on U.S. **foreign policy** for Harvard.

WEST, MAE (1983–1980). Born Mary Jane West in Brooklyn, New York, actress Mae West began her career as a teenager and appeared in musical reviews in New York from 1911 onward. She also wrote a number of plays and in 1926 appeared in *Sex* as a prostitute. The show was raided by the police, and West was convicted on a morals charge and served 10 days in prison for public obscenity. In 1927, her second play, *The Drag*, focused on homosexuality. In 1928, she explored similar issues and starred once more as a prostitute in *Diamond Lil*. Her next play the same year, *Pleasure Man*, was also raided and closed down by the police.

In 1932, West first appeared in film in *Night After Night*, but it was the film version of *Diamond Lil*, *She Done Him Wrong*, in 1933 costarring **Cary Grant** that brought her stardom and greater notoriety. West's on-screen persona of a liberated, sexually permissive woman famous for sexual innuendo was further established in a string of successful films, including *I'm No Angel* (1933), *Belle of the Nineties* (1934), *Goin' to Town* (1935), *Klondike Annie* (1936), *Go West Young Man* (1936), *Every Day's a Holiday* (1938), and the highly successful *My Little Chickadee* (1940) with **W. C. Fields**. West's famous use of double entendres led to her being banned from the medium after two **radio** appearances in 1937, and she did not reappear on the air until 1949. Her films led to the development of the Motion Picture Production Code and greater censorship of scripts. After appearing in *The Heat Is On* in 1943, she went back to **theater** with *Catherine Was Great*, and she also toured with *Diamond Lil* from 1947 to 1951. During the 1950s, West mainly appeared in nightclub performances but also occasionally on **television**. Her return to film was in *Myra Breckinridge* in 1970, and her last film, also featuring **George Raft**, was *Sextette* in 1978. Her autobiography, using a line from *Night after Night*, was her famous reply to the remark "goodness, what beautiful diamonds"—*Goodness Had Nothing to Do with It* (1959). *See also* CINEMA.

WEST COAST HOTEL V. PARRISH (**300 U. S. 379 1937**). In *West Coast Hotel v. Parrish* on 29 March 1937, the **Supreme Court** suddenly reversed itself when it ruled by a five to four majority that the minimum wage law introduced in Washington in 1932 was constitutional. This decision not only overturned the decision in *Adkins v. Children's Hospital* (1923), but it also saw Chief Justice **Charles Evans Hughes** and Justice **Owen J. Roberts** abandon the conservative majority in what Roberts referred to as a "switch in time that saved nine." The decision to uphold the claim brought by a hotel worker, Elsie Parrish, who had been paid less than the minimum, was based on the argument that liberty of contract could be restricted to protect the community or vulnerable groups, in this case a "class of workers in an unequal position with respect to bargaining power." In changing direction, the court did much to avert the confrontation that had led President **Franklin D. Roosevelt** to attempt to alter the composition of the court through his "**court packing**" proposal.

WEST VIRGINIA STATE BOARD OF EDUCATION V. BARNETTE **(319 U.S. 624 1943).** In *West Virginia State Board of Education v. Barnette* on June 14, 1943, the **Supreme Court** ruled by 8–1 in favor of the Jehovah's Witnesses and against a state law making saluting the flag and pledging allegiance a requirement in schools. In doing so, they overturned their earlier 1940 decision in *Minersville School District v. Gobitis*. The author of the earlier decision, Justice **Felix Frankfurter**, wrote an angry dissenting opinion to the 1943 decision.

WHEELER, BURTON KENDALL (1882–1975). Born in Massachusetts, Burton K. Wheeler worked as a stenographer in Boston before earning his law degree from the University of Michigan in 1905. He then moved to Montana, where he was admitted to the bar. A **Democrat**, Wheeler was elected to the state legislature in 1910 and served for three years before being appointed U. S. attorney for Montana by President Woodrow Wilson. In 1922, he was elected to the U.S. Senate and served four terms.

In 1924, Wheeler ran as **Robert M. La Follette Sr.**'s vice presidential candidate for the Progressive Party, but he returned to the Democratic fold and was a supporter of President **Franklin D. Roosevelt** and the **New Deal** for much of the 1930s. In 1934, he was cosponsor of the **Indian Reorganization Act** linked to the "Indian New Deal." However, he was opposed to the president's "**court packing**" plan and increasingly critical of the administration. As conflict in Europe mounted, Wheeler became an outspoken isolationist. In 1940, he wanted a plank in the Democratic Party platform promising not to send U.S. troops overseas unless attacked. He resisted passage of the **Selective Service Act** in 1940 and tried to prevent revision of the **Neutrality Acts**. Wheeler was one of the leading members of the **America First Committee**, the leading isolationist group in the country. These views cost him renomination in 1946, and he retired from politics to practice law.

WHEELER-RAYBURN ACT, 1935. In 1935, Senator **Burton K. Wheeler** and Congressman **Samuel Rayburn** jointly sponsored the Public Utilities Holding Company Act, which also came to be known as the Wheeler-Rayburn Act. The act gave the federal government the power to regulate rates and business practices of interstate utility companies. Utility holding companies had to register with the **Securities and Exchange Commission (SEC)**, and the SEC had the power to dissolve any company that could not demonstrate its usefulness.

WHITE, WALTER FRANCIS (1893–1955). African American civil rights leader Walter Francis White graduated from Atlanta University in 1916 and worked for two years in insurance. In 1918, he was appointed assistant executive secretary to the **National Association for the Advancement of Colored People (NAACP)**. He held the position until 1929 and then became executive secretary of the organization until his death in 1955. White took advantage of his light color to investigate and report on lynching in the South during the 1920s, and his reports were used in support of the **antilynching bills** in 1922, 1937, and 1940. His book on the subject, *Rope and Faggot: A Biography of Judge Lynch*, was published in 1929. He also wrote two novels, *The Fire in the Flint* (1924) and *Flight* (1926).

White and the NAACP successfully opposed the nomination of John J. Parker to the **Supreme Court** in 1930 because of racist views he expressed during his career. White was also instrumental in initiating the NAACP's legal challenges to discrimination that eventually culminated in the landmark Supreme Court decision in *Brown v. Board of Education of Topeka* in 1954. Through his friendship with **Eleanor Roosevelt**, White gained some influence in the White House, and he helped shape changes in military policy with regard to African Americans in 1940. He supported **A. Philip Randolph**'s campaign against discrimination in defense industries and the threatened **March on Washington** in 1941 that resulted in the creation of a **Fair Employment Practices Committee**. During **World War**

II, White toured U.S. military bases in Europe and Asia to see the treatment of black soldiers firsthand. He published his account in *A Rising Wind* (1945). After the war, he brought details of violence against returning African American servicemen to the attention of President **Harry S. Truman** and was influential in persuading the president to appoint a committee on civil rights in 1946. White was also a consultant to the U.S. Delegation to the **United Nations** in 1945 and 1948.

White's marriage to a white woman in 1949 alienated some white and African American supporters of the NAACP, and he increasingly had differences with fellow activists in the organization because of his anticommunist stance before his death. White's autobiography, *A Man Called White*, was published in 1948.

WHITE HOUSE CONFERENCE ON THE EMERGENCY NEEDS OF WOMEN. Held under the aegis of **Eleanor Roosevelt** in November 1933, the White House Conference on the Emergency Needs of **Women** recognized that the **Great Depression** had an enormously negative impact on women in employment and in the home. Representatives of such women's organizations as the League of Women Voters and Women's Trade Union League, as well as from the Red Cross and National Consumer's League, considered the need for work projects for women and greater federal representation and funding.

WILDER, THORNTON NIVEN (1897–1975). Thornton Wilder was educated at Oberlin College and Yale University and was awarded an M.A. in French literature from Princeton in 1926. Wilder served in the Coast Guard during World War I. He taught French and English at Lawrenceville School and at the University of Chicago from 1930 to 1937. As a writer, he used myth and allegory to explore the meaning of life and the themes of love and tolerance. His best-known book, *The Bridge of San Luis Rey* (1927), won a Pulitzer Prize, as did *Heaven's My Destination* (1935) and the plays *Our Town* (1938) and *The Skin of Our Teeth* (1942). Wilder enlisted during **World War II**, served in the air force, and was awarded the Legion of Merit and the Bronze Star. In the 1950s, he held a chair in poetry at Harvard University and was awarded the National Medal for Literature in

1962. His comedy, *The Matchmaker* (1954), was successfully turned into the film musical *Hello, Dolly!* in 1969. Wilder continued to write until his death. His last book, *Theophilus North*, was published in 1973. *See also* LITERATURE AND THEATER.

WILLIAMS, AUBREY WILLIS (1890–1965). Born to a poor family in Storyville, Alabama, Aubrey Williams left school at the age of nine. He went to Maryville College in Nashville, Tennessee, at the age of 21 in 1911. In 1917, he went to work for the YMCA in Paris and in 1918 joined the U.S. field artillery. After the war, he went to the University of Cincinnati and graduated in 1920. In 1922, Williams became executive secretary to the Wisconsin Conference of Social Work in Madison, and he remained there until 1932. Joining the Public Welfare Association later that year, he worked to help establish relief organizations throughout the South, particularly in Mississippi and Texas. As a result, in 1933 Williams was appointed as a field representative for the **Federal Emergency Relief Administration**, where he also began his association with **Harry Hopkins**.

In 1935, Williams became Hopkins's deputy at the **Works Progress Administration** and executive director of the **National Youth Administration (NYA).** Williams insisted on equal treatment for **African Americans** and was responsible for the appointment of **Mary McLeod Bethune** to the NYA. His outspoken advocacy of **civil rights** and willingness to address radical organizations gave him a reputation that led the U.S. Senate to deny his confirmation as director of the **Rural Electrification Administration** in 1945. He then purchased a journal, the *Southern Farmer*, and in 1948 became president of the Southern Conference Education Fund, a militant civil rights group. His civil rights activities and support for Martin Luther King Jr, in 1955 ultimately led to the withdrawal of advertising revenue from the journal, and it ceased publication in 1959. Williams then moved to Washington, D.C., in 1963.

WILLIAMS, THOMAS LANIER (TENNESSEE) (1911–1983). Playwright Tennessee Williams was born in Columbus, Mississippi. He received the nickname "Tennessee" while in college because of his drawl. The family later moved to Missouri, and in 1929 Williams went to the University of Missouri at Columbia but withdrew to work in a shoe company. He later attended Washington University in St. Louis, Missouri, and Iowa University in Iowa City, where he graduated in 1938. By then, he had already published stories and essays and staged his first play, *Candle to the Sun*, in 1936. It was not until the 1940s, however, that he had major success with plays, exploring the sexual and social tensions of southern society in *The Glass Menagerie* (1944), *A Street Car Named Desire* (1947), *Camino Real* (1953), and *Cat on a Hot Tin Roof* (1955). Both *Street Car* and *Cat on a Hot Tin Roof* won Pulitzer Prizes, and several of Williams's plays were made into movies. His later work included *Suddenly Last Summer* (1958), *Sweet Bird of Youth* (1959), and *The Night of the Iguana* (1961). He also wrote three novels, various short stories, poetry, and his *Memoirs* (1975). He was still writing plays in the 1970s and 1980s but did not repeat his earlier successes. However, along with **Arthur Miller**, Williams was one of the leading dramatists of the 20th century. *See also* CINEMA; LITERATURE AND THEATER.

WILLKIE, WENDELL LEWIS (1892–1944). Born in Elwood, Indiana, Wendell Willkie graduated from Indiana University. After serving in the army during World War I, he established a law practice in Akron, Ohio. In 1929, he became legal counsel for the country's largest utility company, the Commonwealth and Southern Corporation, and by 1933 he was company president. Initially a **Democrat** and supporter of **Franklin D. Roosevelt**, he became increasingly critical of the **New Deal** following the creation of the **Tennessee Valley Authority (TVA)**. He joined the **Republican Party** in 1939 after he was forced to sell Commonwealth and Southern to the TVA. A gifted public speaker, Willkie's combination of criticism of public ownership and nonintervention in Europe won him considerable popular support, and in 1940, with the party convention divided between **Robert A. Taft**, **Arthur H. Vandenberg**, and **Thomas E. Dewey**, he won the Republican presidential nomination on the sixth ballot. Defeated by Roosevelt in the election, he increasingly threw his support behind the president because of the deteriorating situation in Europe. He backed aid to **Great Britain** and in 1941 and 1942 toured Great Britain, the Middle East, the **Soviet Union**, and **China** as Roosevelt's personal representative. His account of his travels,

One World (1943), was a best seller, and his appeal for international cooperation and the creation of an international organizaton of nation states helped win support for the **United Nations**. It did not necessarily win him friends within the Republican Party, and he failed to win the nomination in 1944 and died shortly afterward.

WOMEN. The years of the **Great Depression, World War II**, and the **Cold War** had complicated and often contradictory effects on the position of women in U.S. society. Despite winning the vote in 1920 and the apparent liberation experienced during the "Jazz Age" of the 1920s, the status of women changed very little, as the Depression made all too apparent. In 1930, 10.7 million women were in paid employment. This represented about 22 percent of the labor force and a similar proportion of women over the age of 16. Almost 60 percent of those women were **African Americans** or of immigrant stock. With so many men forced out of work during the Depression, a large numbers of women sought work to support their families. The percentage of the female workforce that was married rose from about 20 percent to 35 percent during the 1930s. However, many people believed that women should not work while men were unemployed, and some employers agreed. They refused to employ married women, and some, particularly schools and banks, dismissed women who married. At the same time, female unemployment rates often rose at a faster rate than those of men. Twenty percent of women were unemployed at the height of the Depression. Women were generally paid less than men, and those who remained in work, already low-paid, often faced wage cuts.

Although the **New Deal** appeared sympathetic to the plight of women and the **Roosevelt** administration held a **White House Conference on the Emergency Needs of Women** in 1933, actions on their behalf were scarce. President Franklin D. Roosevelt appointed a number of women to key positions. **Frances Perkins** was appointed as secretary of labor, and **Ellen Woodward** worked for the **Works Progress Administration (WPA)**. **African American** women were represented by **Mary McLeod Bethune** at the **National Youth Administration**. Women like **Molly Dewson** were organizers for the **Democratic Party**, and equally important was the very public role of the first lady, **Eleanor Roosevelt**. However, women were not as fully included in New Deal agencies as men and were often paid lower rates. Approximately 5,000 women, only two-thirds of whom were eligible, were employed by the WPA in 1938, and the occupations available to them were initially limited to sewing projects and recreation work. Although they benefited from New Deal legislation like the **Fair Labor Standards Act**, many women workers, concentrated as they were in domestic and service industries, were excluded.

The portrayal of women in **cinema**, entertainment, and the visual **arts** tended to reinforce the trends of the 1930s. Although one of the leading photographers of the period was a woman, **Dorothea Lange**, her images, like many others, often suggested that women and the family were the chief victims of the economic crisis and reinforced the centrality of family as an ideal. **Mae West** was probably the only female in movies to challenge the established order, if only in terms of her sexual independence, although the portrayal of Scarlett O'Hara in the film version of **Margaret Mitchell**'s Civil War epic *Gone with the Wind* (1939) also presents a woman who is determined to face and overcome adversity. In **John Steinbeck**'s novel *The Grapes of Wrath* (1939) and its 1940 film version, women move from the periphery to the center as the Joad family disintegrates.

World War II brought a dramatic change to women's situations. During the war, some 6 million women went into war plants encouraged by a massive recruiting drive that produced several iconic images of **Rosie the Riveter** in film and advertising. From 1942 onward, 332,000 women also served in noncombatant roles in the U.S. armed forces in the **Women's Army Corps (WACS)**; **Women Appointed for Volunteer Emergency Services (WAVES)**; the Coast Guard, known as SPARS from "Semper Paratus—Always Ready," the Marine Corps Women Reserves, and the **Women's Air Force Service Pilots**. By 1945, women comprised 36 percent of the labor force and were working in heavy industry, shipyards, and the aircraft industry, as well as in government itself. About 60 percent of the new women workers were married. However, no matter what their marital status, wage rates still tended to be lower than men's, despite "equal pay" agreements, and women were denied an equal share of better-paid and managerial roles.

Throughout the 1930s and the 1940s, women often succeeded in the movies because of their appearance and sexual allure. While Marlene Dietrich and Greta Garbo exuded mystery and sensuality, others like Betty Grable, Rita Hayworth, and Carole Lombard became famous simply as "pin–up girls"—innocent but beautiful sex symbols. They were also very active in morale-boosting tours for troops during the war. Even in movies, women characters portrayed by actresses like Katherine Hepburn could appear as independent career women until they finally capitulated to the man. Women often succeeded in on-screen and sometimes off-screen partnerships, as with Hepburn and Spencer Tracy, Lauren Bacall and Humphrey Bogart, and Veronica Lake and Alan Ladd. There were exceptions to these patterns, as in the case of Bette Davis, but they were rare.

At the end of the war, more than 2 million female workers were laid off, and their percentage in the labor force dropped back down to 29 percent in 1947. Despite this, the pattern of female employment never returned to prewar levels, and by 1950 almost 34 percent of women over the age of 16 were in paid employment. These women constituted just under 30 percent of the labor force, and the trend continued upward through the decade. But the postwar years also seemed to encourage a return to domesticity with an increase in marriage rates and a "baby boom." The best-selling book of the late 1940s and early 1950s was Benjamin Spock's *Baby and Child Care* (1946), which recommended a new cult of domesticity and motherhood. Fashion once more emphasized the feminine shape, and women in the movies were portrayed as loyal wives, dizzy blondes, and sex symbols. *Father Knows Best*, a successful radio sitcom, was transferred equally successfully to television in 1954. Although by 1950 10 million, or 25 percent, of married women were actually in paid employment, during the Cold War the American family unit, which included the working husband and domestic wife raising the children at home, was presented as an ideal alternative to the situation in the communist Soviet Union.

One consequence of these trends was a decline in the proportion of women attending university. In the 1920s, more than 30 percent of students were female. After World War II, this number fell to 20 percent. The results were evident in employment patterns: In 1950, women constituted 30 percent of the workforce but only 1.2 percent of engineers, 4.1 percent of lawyers, and 6 percent of physicians and osteopaths, though 98 percent of registered nurses were women.

See also ALLEN, GRACIE; ANDERSON, MARIAN; BOURKE-WHITE, MARGARET; CARAWAY, HATTIE OPHELIA WYATT; DAVIS, BETTE; DOUGLAS, HELEN GAHAGAN; GARLAND, JUDY; LAMOUR, DOROTHY; RANKIN, JEANNETTE; ROGERS, GINGER.

WOMEN APPOINTED FOR VOLUNTEER EMERGENCY SERVICE (WAVES). WAVES was an auxiliary service of the navy created in August 1942 to free manpower during **World War II**. Some 100,000 women served in WAVES at the height of the war, mainly in communication and clerical capacities. In 1948, the service ceased to exist as women were integrated into the navy and naval reserve.

WOMEN'S AIR FORCE SERVICE PILOTS (WASPS). In 1943, WASPS was established to enable women pilots to assist with the war effort. Although not granted military status, more than 1,000 women served transporting planes from bases to base. Thirty-eight women died in crashes or accidents. WASPS was disbanded in 1945.

WOMEN'S ARMY CORPS (WACS). Originally formed in 1942 as the Women's Army Auxiliary Corps, in 1943 WACS was established as a part of the regular army. Almost 140,000 women served in WACS during **World War II** in a variety of noncombatant roles.

WOOD, GRANT (1892–1942). Grant Wood, regarded as "one of the most American of America's artists," learned his trade at the Minneapolis School of Design and in night classes at the University of Iowa and **Art** Institute of Chicago. He taught in Cedar Rapids, Iowa, but after military service during World War I, he was one of the many artists and writers who spent time in Paris, France. In 1927, he received a commission for a stained glass window commemorating war veterans in Cedar City, Utah. His design, using German glass, caused some controversy, a fact that influenced his satirical painting *Daughters of Revolution* (1932). A number of Wood's paintings shared this ironic view, most famously his austere depiction of a farmer and his wife in *American Gothic* (1930). Other work showing the influence of American folk art and the sense of irony included the *Midnight Ride of Paul Revere* (1931) and *Parson Weems' Fable* (1939).

In the 1930s, Wood became a leading figure in the **regionalist** school of artists, celebrating the richness of the land and offering a vision of hope during the **Great Depression** in work ranging from *Fall Plowing* (1931) and *Birthplace of Herbert Hoover* (1931) to *Iowa Cornfield* (1941). During the 1930s, Wood was head of the Iowa Works Progress Administration Art Project and taught at Iowa University. In 1935, he was elected to the National Academy of Design, and much of his work in the mid-1930s was printmaking and illustration.

WOODRING, HARRY HINES (1887–1967). Harry Woodring was born in Elk City, Kansas. He attended Lebanon Business University in Indiana before starting a career in banking in 1905. He briefly served in the army during World War I and then resumed his career, becoming president and owner of the First National Bank of Neodesha, Kansas. In 1930, Woodring was elected governor of Kansas as a **Democrat**, and he initiated a program of moderate reform, establishing public works and modernizing taxation. He was defeated by **Alf Landon** in 1932. In 1933, President **Franklin D. Roosevelt** appointed him assistant secretary of war, and in 1936 he became secretary of war. He revised the plans for military mobilization and increased the size of the Army Air Corps. However, as an isolationist he increasingly disagreed with Roosevelt's policies, and he resigned when surplus military supplies and aircraft were given to **Great Britain** in 1940. Woodring returned to banking, and his attempt to get reelected as governor failed in 1946 and again in 1956.

WOODWARD, ELLEN (1887–1971). Born Ellen Sullivan in Oxford, Mississippi, but brought up in Washington, D.C., Ellen Woodward was elected to the Mississippi state legislature to succeed her husband, Albert Woodward, upon his death in 1925. After completing the term in 1926, she joined the Mississippi State Board of development, an agency involved in civic and public welfare activity. A supporter of **Franklin D. Roosevelt**, Woodward joined **Harry Hopkins** as an assistant at the **Federal Emergency Relief Administration** in 1933 as director of work relief for **women**. She was particularly active in ensuring not only the participation of women in such agencies as the **Civil Works Administration** and **Works Progress Administration**

but also in expanding the range of employment opportunities for women in the agencies. She was also involved in the **Federal Theater Project**.

In 1938, Woodward joined the Social Security Board, and she remained a member until 1946 when it was replaced by the **Federal Security Agency**. She worked as director of international relations until her retirement in 1954. She was also a member of the U.S. Delegation to the **United Nations Relief and Rehabilitation Administration** between 1945 and 1946.

WORKS PROGRESS ADMINISTRATION (WPA). The Works Progress Administration, which became the Works Project Administration from 1939 onward, was established on 6 May 1935 with an initial appropriation of $4.8 billion to provide federal work relief, the largest single appropriation in U.S. history. Headed by **Harry Hopkins**, the WPA eventually spent more than $8 billion and employed a total of 8 million people, building thousands of public buildings, hundreds of airports, and thousands of miles of road before it came to an end on 4 December 1942.

The WPA also provided work for those in the arts under **Federal One** and the **Federal Writers' Project**, **Federal Theater Project**, **Federal Art Project**, and **Federal Music Project** that together employed 40,000 workers. Critics accused the WPA of encouraging left-wing causes and inefficiency and waste in useless tasks or "boon-doggling." In 1939, the administration was renamed and relocated to the **Federal Works Agency**. Hopkins resigned in 1938 and was replaced by Francis C. Harrington. After 1941, the WPA focused more on war-related projects before it was given what President **Franklin D. Roosevelt** called an "honorable discharge." It was one of the most significant **New Deal** agencies.

WORLD MONETARY AND ECONOMIC CONFERENCE, 1933. *See* LONDON ECONOMIC CONFERENCE.

WORLD WAR II. World War II, often known as the Second World War, began on 1 September 1939 when Nazi **Germany** invaded Poland. However, it had its roots in the situation in Europe after Germany's defeat in 1918 and the Versailles peace settlement. The desire to overthrow the territorial losses and economic burdens of reparations, together with a wish to recover from the psychological humiliation, lay behind the rise of the Nazi Party under **Adolf Hitler** in the late 1920s. The economic impact of the **Great Depression** in Germany further exacerbated the situation and enabled Hitler to become chancellor in 1933 and führer in 1934. His policy of nationalism, militarism, territorial expansion, and racism led to a series of diplomatic crises culminating in the attack on Poland. As **Great Britain** and France had issued guarantees to maintain Polish territorial integrity, this unleashed the world war. Hitler was supported by Italy, led by the fascist dictator Benito Mussolini. Italy had already invaded Ethiopia in 1934 and with Germany had aided General Francisco Franco against the Republican government during the **Spanish Civil War** in 1936.

Alarmed by these developments and fearful that the United States might be drawn into yet another European war, isolationists passed a succession of **Neutrality Acts** aimed at avoiding the mistakes made in 1914 though 1917. However, as the situation in Europe deteriorated after the fall of Poland and the invasion of France in May 1940, President **Franklin D. Roosevelt** increasingly urged support for the Western democracies and also increased military preparedness at home. The arms embargo was replaced in November 1939 with a "cash-and-carry" program that allowed trade without directly endangering U.S. ships. In June 1940, the president called for increases in national defense, and **Selective Service** was introduced in September 1940. That month the president concluded a **Destroyer-for-Bases Agreement** with Great Britain, exchanging 50 out-of-date U.S. warships for access to naval and air bases in the Caribbean and Atlantic. In one of his **"fireside chats"** broadcast on 29 December 1940, Roosevelt told the American people that they had to be "the arsenal of democracy." This was followed in March 1941 by the **Lend-Lease Act** that enabled the president to lend or lease as much material as necessary for the protection of any country deemed vital to the safety of the United States. In August 1941, he and Prime Minister **Winston Churchill** agreed on the **Atlantic Charter** outlining the common international goal. Following the German invasion of the **Soviet Union** in June 1941, lend-lease was extended to include the USSR. As U.S. supply vessels in the Atlantic came under attack and were sunk by German U-boats, war seemed increasingly likely.

In Asia, **Japan** also adopted a policy of extreme nationalism and territorial expansion to stave off the tensions caused by internal economic and social issues. It invaded Manchuria in 1931 and widened the war in 1937 with the invasion of **China**. When Japan ignored diplomatic protests, the United States increasingly applied economic sanctions, with an embargo on scrap metal exports in 1940 and increased aid to China. The embargoes were increased to include other metals in early 1941 and, in the summer of that year, Roosevelt froze all Japanese assets in the United States. In September, all oil shipments to Japan stopped. In August, the president made clear that the United States take any necessary steps if the aggression continued. Faced with the possibility of war, but with negotiations in Washington, D.C., still ongoing, the Japanese struck first, attacking the U.S. fleet stationed in **Pearl Harbor** on the island of Oahu in Hawaii on 7 December 1941. The attack was described by President Roosevelt as "a date which will live in infamy" when he went before Congress to ask for a declaration of war the next day. Congress declared war on Japan with only one vote, that of **Jeannette Rankin**, against the move. On 11 December, in line with the agreements made in 1940 in the Rome–**Berlin**–Tokyo Axis, Germany and Italy declared war on the United States.

The Japanese initially proved unstoppable in the Pacific, and by mid-1942 they had taken Malaya, Singapore, Burma, the Dutch East Indies, Guam, Wake Island, and the **Philippines**, where General **Douglas MacArthur** was forced to abandon his troops to take control of U.S. forces from Australia. After the Japanese defeat of a joint U.S., British, Dutch, and Australian fleet in the Java Sea in February, American naval victories in the Coral Sea in May 1942 and at the Battle of **Midway** in June 1942 halted the Japanese advance, but it was not until August 1942 that the United States was able to go on the offensive, taking **Guadalcanal** and then the Solomon Islands.

The **Allied** policy, agreed upon in Washington, D.C., at the **Arcadia Conference** in January 1942, was to concentrate on "Germany first" and to prevent further Japanese expansion in Asia. As part of the policy of encircling Germany in November 1942, the Allies landed in Morocco and Algeria in North Africa and successfully pushed on to Tunisia. From there, they launched their invasion of Italy on 10 June 1943 in Sicily, and on 8 September Italy surrendered. However,

Rome was not taken until June 1944, and northern Italy remained under German control until 1945. It was on the Eastern Front where the Soviet Union took the offensive against the Germans after the siege of Stalingrad in August 1942 to February 1943 that the Nazi armies initially suffered their biggest defeats. However on **D-Day** on 6 June 1944, Allied troops landed in **Normandy**, France, and by July they had established a beach head allowing for more troops and equipment to land. A breakthrough led by U.S. forces commanded by **Omar Bradley** enabled the Allies to push into northern France toward the German frontier. A southern invasion took place on 15 August near Toulon and Cannes and reached Germany's southern borders by September. The Germans launched a powerful counter-offensive in the **Battle of the Bulge** in the Ardennes in December 1944. The attack was held by the combined Allied forces attacking from north and south, and General **George S. Patton** was able to relieve the U.S. troops holding out at **Bastogne**. It was the German army's last major effort, and in March 1945 the Allied armies crossed the Rhine into Germany. In the east, Soviet forces were also pushing into Germany and reached the capital, Berlin, on 22 April. The U.S. and Soviet forces met on the River Elbe, south of Berlin, on 25 April. Faced with imminent defeat, Hitler committed suicide in his bunker on 30 April, and by May 1945 Berlin had fallen. The war in Europe ended on 8 May 1945.

In the Pacific, the island-hopping campaign continued with the successful capture of New Guinea in January 1943 by combined U.S. and Australian forces. The Marshall Islands followed in February 1944. In June 1944, U.S. forces landed in the Marianas Islands. Their capture provided airfields from which bombing raids could easily be launched on Japan. The Japanese launched a naval response on 19 June culminating in their defeat in the Battle of the Philippine Sea. This was followed by the massive naval battle of **Leyte Gulf** in October 1944 preceding the retaking of the Philippines by forces led by General **Douglas MacArthur** in early 1945. From the Philippines and Guam, the United States was able to launch further attacks, capturing **Iwo Jima** and **Okinawa** after battles that lasted from 1 February to 20 March 1945 and 1 April to 10 June 1945, respectively. From there, U.S. forces were able to launch air raids against Japan, and the dropping of the **atomic bombs** on **Hiroshima** and **Nagasaki** on 6 and 9 August 1945 finally brought the war to an end on 2 September 1945. Formal peace treaties were not signed until 8 September 1951 with Japan and 26 May 1952 with Germany.

More than 15 million people served in the U.S. armed forces during the war, and many more were required in defense industries. During the war, production in U.S. industry reached unprecedented heights as it churned out aircraft, weapons, machinery, and equipment not only for its own forces but also to supply Allied countries, particularly Great Britain and the USSR. Full employment effectively brought the Depression to an end by 1942, and mounting labor shortages brought increased economic opportunity for **women, African Americans**, and **Hispanic Americans**. The demand for war workers also led to enormous population movements as some 15 million people migrated to the defense plants on the west coast and in northern industrial centers. For 112, 000 **Japanese Americans**, migration was involuntary following the executive order issued in February 1942 authorizing their relocation to 10 camps in the West to prevent subversion. This decision was upheld by the **Supreme Court** during the war, but the Japanese Americans were subsequently paid compensation and in 1988 received an official apology.

To mobilize this huge effort, a plethora of war agencies were established replacing many **New Deal** agencies. The number of people employed in the federal government rose from 1.1 million in 1940 to 3.8 million by 1945. Successive **War Powers Acts** in 1941 and 1942 gave the president increased authority, and the war effort was managed by the **War Production Board**. Prices were controlled by the **Office of Price Administration**, which introduced rationing of certain goods and materials from 1942 onward. The **War Manpower Commission** was tasked with the allocation of manpower between the armed forces, defense industry, and **agriculture**, while the **National War Labor Board**, formed in 1942, adjudicated in labor disputes and controlled wage levels. An **Office of War Information** was established to inform and motivate the population, and an **Office of Civilian Defense** was created to prepare for possible enemy attack. Scientists and inventors were mobilized through the **Office of Scientific Research and Development**, part of which included the **Manhattan Project** that produced the atomic bomb. So great was the growth in government that in 1943 the **Office of War Mobilization**, under **James F. Byrnes**, was established to manage the various committees. One consequence of these developments was the reintegration of business interests with government and the rise of a powerful "military-industrial-complex" that grew further during the **Cold War** that followed the peace settlement in 1945.

The war resulted in more than 56 million deaths worldwide. The number of U.S. service personnel who died as a result of battle-inflicted injuries was 292,131, and 671,278 were wounded. For non-battle deaths, the total number of U.S. service personnel who died was more than 400,000. The financial cost of the war for the United States was approximately $300 billion, a large proportion of which was met by money raised through taxation after the **Revenue Act** of 1942 and through **war bonds**. One consequence of the conflict was that the United States abandoned the policy of isolationism and committed itself to the establishment of the **United Nations** to prevent further world conflicts. However, the power vacuums created in Asia and Europe meant that the United States and USSR became the world's major powers, and their opposing political beliefs, mutual suspicion, and international rivalries quickly developed into the Cold War that lasted until 1989. *See also* ANZIO; BATAAN; BOARD OF WAR COMMUNICATIONS; BRETTON WOODS CONFERENCE; CAIRO CONFERENCE; CASABLANCA CONFERENCE; DAVIS, BENJAMIN OLIVER, JR.; DOOLITTLE RAID; EISENHOWER, DWIGHT DAVID; MIDWAY ISLANDS; MILLER, DORIE; MOSCOW CONFERENCE; NIMITZ, CHESTER WILLIAM; NUREMBERG WAR CRIMES TRIALS; OMAHA BEACH; OPERATION HUSKY; OPERATION OVERLORD; OPERATION TORCH; POTSDAM CONFERENCE; TEHRAN CONFERENCE; UTAH BEACH; V-E DAY; V-J DAY; V-MAIL; WAR BONDS; WAR FOOD ADMINISTRATION (WFA); WAR LABOR DISPUTES ACT; WAR REFUGEE BOARD (WRB); WAR RELOCATION AUTHORITY (WRA); WAR SHIPPING ADMINISTRATION (WSA); WOMEN APPOINTED FOR VOLUNTEER EMERGENCY SERVICE (WAVES); WOMEN'S AIR FORCE SERVICE PILOTS (WASPS); WOMEN'S ARMY CORPS (WACS); YALTA CONFERENCE.

WRIGHT, RICHARD NATHANIEL (1908–1960). The grandson of slaves, Richard Wright was born in Mississippi. Abandoned by his father, his family moved to Memphis, Tennessee, and then back to Jackson, Mississippi, where Wright went to school. After leaving school, he worked from 1925 to 1927 for an optical company. He moved to Chicago, Illinois, in 1927, where he worked a number of different jobs, including for the post office. He joined the **Communist Party of the United States of America (CPUSA)** and edited *Left Front* magazine, which the party briefly produced. Wright also contributed to *New Masses* magazine. After a disagreement with some of the CPUSA party members, Wright moved to New York City in 1937 and found work in the **Federal Writers' Project**. He was also the Harlem editor of the newspaper *Daily Worker*. His collection of short stories, *Uncle Tom's Children* (1937), won a Guggenheim Prize that enabled him to write the powerful novel, *Native Son* (1940). It was the first book by an **African American** author selected by the Book-of-the-Month Club and was an immediate best seller. The stage adaptation of the novel, directed by **Orson Welles**, ran on Broadway from 1941 to 1943.

In 1941, Wright produced a photographic history/social study entitled *12 Million Black Voices*. He left the CPUSA in 1942, and his essay "I Tried to be a Communist" was published in the *Atlantic Monthly* magazine in 1944 and reprinted in the book *The God That Failed* in 1949. In 1945, he achieved another major success with the autobiographical account of growing up in the South, *Black Boy*. Disillusioned with life in the United States, Wright moved to Paris in 1946, and having taken French citizenship in 1947, he became a permanent exile. He continued to write, helping to found the magazine *Paris Review* in 1949 and writing among others *The Outsider* (1953), *Savage Holiday* (1954), and his collection of essays and lectures, *White Man, Listen!* (1957). None of these, however, had the success of his earlier writing, but he remained one of the most influential African American authors of his day. *See also* LITERATURE AND THEATER.

WYLER, WILLIAM (1902–1981). Born Willi Weiller to Jewish parents in Mulhausen, Alsace (then part of **Germany**), William Wyler immigrated to the United States in 1920 to take a job in the New

York office of the Universal Film Company. In 1922, he moved to work in their studios in California, and he directed his first film, *Crook Buster*, in 1925. He became one of the great **cinema** directors of the 1930s and 1940s, second only to **John Ford**.

Wyler's first major film was *Hell's Heroes* in 1930. He began working with Samuel Goldwyn in the mid-1930s and achieved critical success with *Dodsworth* in 1936. His first major success, winning him an Oscar for Best Direction, was *Miss Miniver* in 1942, a portrayal of a British family during the war that did much to encourage U.S. support. Once the United States entered **World War II**, Wyler served as a major in the Army Air Corps and made an acclaimed documentary, *Memphis Belle: The Story of a Flying Fortress*, in 1944. After the war, he won a second Oscar for Best Director in 1946 for *The Best Years of Our Lives*, the story of three returning veterans. Wyler went on to make other acclaimed films, including *Roman Holiday* (1953), *The Big Country* (1958), *The Heiress* (1959), and the epic *Ben Hur* (1959), which won 11 Oscars, including Best Director. Wyler's last film was *The Liberation of L.B. Jones* in 1970. Known for his exacting standards and many takes, Wyler's films often stood the test of time. He was awarded a Lifetime Achievement Award by the American Film Institute. *See also* CINEMA.

– Y –

YALTA CONFERENCE, 1945. During **World War II**, the leaders of the "big three"—the United States, **Great Britain**, and the **Soviet Union**—**Franklin D. Roosevelt**, **Winston Churchill**, and **Joseph Stalin** met at Yalta in the Crimea from 3 to 14 February 1945 to coordinate the **Allied** war effort and prepare for the postwar world. With the Red Army 40 miles from **Berlin**, the principal issue was the future of **Germany**, and it was agreed that the Allies would require unconditional surrender, the postwar occupation of Germany by all three plus France, the demilitarization and de-Nazification of Germany, the trial of wartime leaders and war criminals, and a program of reparations, largely to be paid to the USSR. Various territorial concessions were made to the Soviet Union in Asia, including the return of southern Sakhalin and the Kurile Islands and the leasing of Port Arthur as a Soviet naval base. Stalin agreed that the USSR would enter the war against **Japan** within three months of the defeat of Germany.

The Soviet Union was also granted much of eastern Poland as its territory, and Poland was compensated by being given German lands in the west. In return, Stalin accepted the inclusion of a "Declaration on Liberated Europe" that promised "free and unfettered" elections with democratic institutions to be established in Eastern Europe and a broadening of the Provisional Polish Government that had been established by the Soviet forces. No definition of these terms was agreed upon nor was there precise agreement on the amount of reparations to be paid by Germany. These issues were the focus of postwar disagreements and paved the way for the **Cold War**. However, the participants at Yalta did agree on tentative plans for a **United Nations** and a **Security Council** consisting of the United States, Great Britain, France, **China**, and the Soviet Union plus six elected nations on a rotating basis.

YOUNG, OWEN D. (1874–1962). A graduate of Boston Law School and a corporation lawyer, Owen Young joined General Electric (GE) as general counsel and vice president in 1913. He settled strikes in several GE plants during World War I, and in 1919 he served on the Second Industrial Conference. In 1921, he chaired the Subcommittee on Business Cycles and Unemployment of President Warren Harding's Unemployment Conference. From 1925 to 1928, Young chaired the International Chamber of Commerce.

In 1919, GE joined with Westinghouse, American Telephone & Telegraph (AT&T), and Western Electric to form a company to prevent the British Marconi Company from monopolizing long-distance **radio** communication. The result was the Radio Corporation of America (RCA), which with Young as chairman until 1929, pooled U.S. radio technology and equipment. Young entered into agreements with foreign companies dividing the world into radio zones to facilitate communication. Under his leadership, RCA became the largest radio company in the world. In 1926, Young also helped to establish the National Broadcasting Company (NBC) and in 1928 the movie chain Radio-Keith-Orpheum (RKO).

In 1922, Young became chair of the board of GE with **Gerard Swope** as president. The two men were associated with the introduction of programs of "welfare capitalism," which did much to influence labor relations during the 1920s.

Young was a representative to the Reparations Conference in 1924 and was instrumental in securing the acceptance of the Dawes Plan, and in 1929 he chaired the meetings where the Young Plan was agreed upon as a way to scale down German reparations payments. President **Herbert Hoover** appointed Young to the President's Committee on Recent Economic Changes in 1929 and as chair of the Committee on Mobilization of Relief Resources of the President's Unemployment Relief Commission in 1931. He chaired the American Youth Commission from 1936 to 1942 and was a member of the New York Regional Committee of the **War Manpower Commission** in 1942. Having retired from GE in 1939, Young returned as acting chair to supervise the manufacture of war orders in 1942. He finally retired in 1944 but after the war served on President **Harry S. Truman**'s Advisory Committee on Foreign Aid in 1947, helping pave the way for the **Marshall Plan**. Young also chaired the New York Commission on the Need for a State University in 1946. He retired to concentrate on dairy farming.

YOUNGSTOWN SHEET & TUBE CO. V. SAWYER **(343 U.S. 579 1952).** In *Youngstown Sheet & Tube Co. v. Sawyer* on 2 June 1952, the **Supreme Court** found that President **Harry S. Truman** had acted unconstitutionally when he ordered the seizure of steel mills in an industrial dispute and, although such powers were inherent within the authority given the executive, the action had not been expressly approved by Congress. The court upheld an earlier ruling in the U.S. District Court.

– Z –

ZANGARA, GUISEPPE (1900–1933). Born in Italy, Giuseppe Zangara immigrated to the United States in 1923. He worked for a time in New Jersey and California before settling in Miami, Florida. He became a naturalized citizen in 1929. Depressed due to lack of employment and ill-health, Zanagara first blamed President **Herbert Hoover** and then President-elect **Franklin D. Roosevelt**. When Roosevelt visited Florida in February 1933, Zangara fired several shots at him in an attempted assassination. He missed but wounded several onlookers and the mayor of Chicago, Anton Cermak, who was meeting Roosevelt. Initially sentenced to 84 years in prison, after Cermak died from his wounds, Zangara was sentenced to death. He was executed on 20 March 1933.

ZANUCK, DARRYL FRANCIS (1902–1979). Hollywood movie tycoon Darryl Zanuck served in the U.S. Army from 1916 to 1918 before moving to California to establish a career as a writer. He became a screenwriter for Warner Bros. Studios in 1923 and in 1925 became head of production. Following a dispute with Jack Warner, Zanuck left the company in 1933 and began working for 20th Century Films, later 20th Century Fox. In 1935, Zanuck became vice president, and he held the position until 1956. He was responsible for the production of many significant films, including *The Grapes of Wrath* (1940), *Gentlemen's Agreement* (1947), and *The Robe* (1953). During **World War II**, he served with the Signal Corps and made films about the war effort. After breaking with 20th Century Fox in 1956, he returned to take over the company in 1962. The success of his *The Longest Day* (1962) helped get the studio back on its feet, and this was followed with *The Sound of Music* (1965) and *Planet of the Apes* (1968). Internal disputes forced Zanuck to resign in 1971. *See also* CINEMA.

ZEDONG, MAO. *See* MAO ZEDONG (MAO TSE-TUNG).

ZOOT SUIT RIOT. *See* LOS ANGELES RIOT.

Appendix A:
Presidential Administrations, 1933–1953

FRANKLIN D. ROOSEVELT, 1933–1945

Presidential Election Results

		Popular Votes	*Electoral Votes*
1932	Franklin D. Roosevelt	22,809,638	472
	Herbert C. Hoover	15,758,901	59
1936	Franklin D. Roosevelt	27,752,869	523
	Alfred E. Landon	16,674,665	8
1940	Franklin D. Roosevelt	27,307,819	449
	Wendell L. Willkie	22,321,018	82
1944	Franklin D. Roosevelt	25,606,585	432
	Thomas E. Dewey	22,014,745	99

Vice President
John Nance Garner (1933–1941)
Henry A. Wallace (1941–1945)
Harry S. Truman (1945)

Secretary of State
Cordell Hull (1933–1944)
Edward R. Stettinius (1944–1945)

Secretary of the Treasury
William H. Woodin (1933–1934)
Henry Morgenthau Jr. (1934–1945)

Secretary of War
George H. Dern (1933–1936)
Harry H. Woodring (1937–1940)
Henry L. Stimson (1940–1945)

Attorney General
Homer S. Cummings (1933–1939)
Frank Murphy (1939–1940)
Robert H. Jackson (1940–1941)
Francis B. Biddle (1941–1945)

Postmaster General
James A. Farley (1933–1940)
Frank C. Walker (1940–1945)

Secretary of the Navy
Claude A. Swanson (1933–1939)
Charles Edison (1940
Frank Knox (1940–1944)
James V. Forrestal (1944–1945)

Secretary of the Interior
Harold L. Ickes (1933–1945)

Secretary of Agriculture
Henry A. Wallace (1933–1940)
Claude R. Wickard (1940–1945)

Secretary of Commerce
Daniel C. Roper (1933–1938)
Harry L. Hopkins (1939–1940)
Jesse H. Jones (1940–1945)
Henry A. Wallace (1945)

Secretary of Labor
Frances Perkins (1933–1945)

HARRY S. TRUMAN, 1945–1953

Presidential Election Results

		Popular Votes	*Electoral Votes*
1948	Harry S. Truman	24,179,345	303
	Thomas E. Dewey	21,991,291	189
	J. Strom Thurmond	1,176,125	39
	Henry A. Wallace	1,157,326	0

Vice President
Alben W. Barkley (1949–1953)

Secretary of State
Edward R. Stettinius Jr. (1945)
James F. Byrnes (1945–1947)
George C. Marshall (1947–1949)
Dean G. Acheson (1949–1953)

Secretary of the Treasury
Henry Morgenthau Jr. (1945)
Fred M. Vinson (1945–1946)
John W. Snyder (1946–1953)

Secretary of War
Henry L. Stimson (1945)
Robert P. Patterson (1945–1947)
Kenneth C. Royall (1947)

Secretary of Defense
James V. Forrestal (1947–1949)
Louis A. Johnson (1949–1950)
George C. Marshall (1950–1951)
Robert A. Lovett (1951–1953)

Attorney General
Francis Biddle (1945)
Tom C. Clark (1945–1949)
J. Howard McGrath (1949–1952)
James P. McGranery (1952–1953)

Postmaster General
Frank C. Walker (1945)
Robert E. Hannegan (1945–1947)
Jesse M. Donaldson (1947–1953)

Secretary of the Navy
James V. Forrestal (1945–1947)

Secretary of the Interior
Harold Ickes (1945–1946)
Julius A. Krug (1946–1949)
Oscar L. Chapman (1949–1953)

Secretary of Agriculture
Claude R. Wickard (1945)
Clinton P. Anderson (1945–1948)
Charles F. Brannan (1949–1953)

Secretary of Commerce
Henry A. Wallace (1945–1946)
W. Averell Harriman (1946–1948)
Charles W. Sawyer (1948–1953)

Secretary of Labor
Frances Perkins (1945)
Lewis B. Schwellenbach (1945–1948)
Maurice J. Tobin (1948–1953)

Appendix B: Constitutional Amendments

TWENTIETH AMENDMENT

Passed by Congress 2 March 1932; Ratified 23 January 1933.

Section 1. The terms of the President and Vice President shall end at noon on the 20th day of January, and the terms of Senators and Representatives at noon on the 3d day of January, of the years in which such terms would have ended if this article had not been ratified; and the terms of their successors shall then begin.

Section 2. The Congress shall assemble at least once in every year, and such meeting shall begin at noon on the 3d day of January, unless they shall by law appoint a different day.

Section 3. If, at the time fixed for the beginning of the term of the President, the President elect shall have died, the Vice President elect shall become President. If a President shall not have been chosen before the time fixed for the beginning of his term, or if the President elect shall have failed to qualify, then the Vice President elect shall act as President until a President shall have qualified; and the Congress may by law provide for the case wherein neither a President elect nor a Vice President elect shall have qualified, declaring who shall then act as President, or the manner in which one who is to act shall be selected, and such person shall act accordingly until a President or Vice President shall have qualified.

Section 4. The Congress may by law provide for the case of the death of any of the persons from whom the House of Representatives may choose a President whenever the right of choice shall have devolved upon them, and for the case of the death of any of the persons from whom the Senate may choose a Vice President whenever the right of choice shall have devolved upon them.

Section 5. Sections 1 and 2 shall take effect on the 15th day of October following the ratification of this article.

Section 6. This article shall be inoperative unless it shall have been ratified as an amendment to the Constitution by the legislatures of three-fourths of the several States within seven years from the date of its submission.

TWENTY-FIRST AMENDMENT

Passed by Congress 20 February 1933; Ratified 5 December 1933.

Section 1. The eighteenth article of amendment to the Constitution of the United States is hereby repealed.

Section 2. The transportation or importation into any State, Territory, or possession of the United States for delivery or use there in of intoxicating liquors, in violation of the laws thereof, is hereby prohibited.

Section 3. This article shall be inoperative unless it shall have been ratified as an amendment to the Constitution by conventions in the several States, as provided in the Constitution, within seven years from the date of the submission hereof to the States by the Congress.

TWENTY-SECOND AMENDMENT

Passed by Congress 21 March 1947; Ratified 27 February 1951.

Section 1. No person shall be elected to the office of the President more than twice, and no person who has held the office of President, or acted as President, for more than two years of a term to which some other person was elected President shall be elected to the office of the President more than once. But this article shall not apply to any person holding the office of President when this article was proposed by the Congress, and shall not prevent any person who may be holding the office of President, or acting as President, during the term within which this article becomes operative from holding the office of President or acting as President during the remainder of such term.

Section 2. This article shall be inoperative unless it shall have been ratified as an amendment to the Constitution by the legislatures of three-fourths of the several states within seven years from the date of its submission to the states by the Congress.

Bibliography

CONTENTS

I. INTRODUCTION

The literature covering Franklin D. Roosevelt, the New Deal, World War II, Harry S. Truman, and the Cold War is extensive, to say the least, but very few works cover the entire period from 1933 to 1953 other than the most general facts. Among the better surveys are Ralph de Bedts's two volumes, *Recent American History: 1933 through World War II* and *Recent American History: 1945 to the Present*. A readable broad view is found in Godfrey Hodgson's *America in Our Time: From*

World War II to Nixon. An excellent study of the first half of the period is David M. Kennedy's *Freedom from Fear: The American People in Depression and War, 1929–1945*, while a positive interpretation of the war and postwar years can be found in John Patrick Diggins's *The Proud Decades: America in War and Peace, 1941–1960* and William L. O'Neill's *American High: The Years of Confidence, 1945–1960*. A number of useful essays, primarily on labor and politics, can be found in Steve Fraser and Gary Gerstle, eds., *The Rise and Fall of the New Deal Order, 1930–1980*.

There are several major studies of Franklin D. Roosevelt, chief among them being the four-volume study, *Franklin D. Roosevelt*, by Frank B. Freidel, but this ends in 1934. The two volumes by James MacGregor Burns, *Roosevelt: The Lion and the Fox* and *Roosevelt: The Soldier of Freedom*, and Arthur Schlesinger's three-volume set, *The Age of Roosevelt*, remain valuable for style and content, although more critical studies have since appeared. Ted Morgan's *FDR: A Biography* provides a readable comprehensive survey. While the classic single-volume study of the New Deal remains William E. Leuchtenburg's *Franklin D. Roosevelt and the New Deal, 1932–1940*, a recent judicious survey incorporating much of the later writing is Anthony J. Badger's *The New Deal: The Depression Years, 1933–1940*. Critical views of the New Deal are included in Barton J. Bernstein's edited collection *Towards a New Past: Dissenting Essays in American History* and Alonzo L. Hamby's edited *The New Deal: Analysis and Interpretation*. Detailed local studies are provided in John Braeman, Robert H. Bremner, and David Body's second volume of collected essays, *The New Deal: The State and Local Levels*; however, much of the focus has shifted away from the top-down politics to the actual experience of the unemployed and disadvantaged, as evidenced by Robert S. McElvaine in *The Great Depression: America 1929–1941* and Caroline Bird in *The Invisible Scar*. A recent short and clear summary of the causes of the Great Depression and the New Deal can be found in Gene Smiley's *Rethinking the Great Depression*.

A good overall survey of U.S. foreign policy during this period is in Stephen E. Ambrose's *Rise to Globalism: American Foreign Policy, 1938–1980*, and detailed surveys of U.S. foreign policy during the 1930s can be found in Robert H. Ferrell's *American Diplomacy in the Great Depression* and in the more up-to-date study by Robert Dallek,

Franklin D. Roosevelt and American Foreign Policy, 1932–1945. David Reynolds provides a good account of the path to war in *From Munich to Pearl Harbor: Roosevelt's America and the Origins of the Second World War*, while the developing crisis with Japan is well outlined in Jonathan G. Utley, *Going to War with Japan, 1937–1941*. And there has been much debate concerning the Japanese attack on Pearl Harbor, beginning with Charles Beard's *President Roosevelt and the Coming of the War, 1941: A Study in Appearances and Realities*, which appeared in 1948 and suggests that Roosevelt deliberately left the fleet open to attack to engineer U.S. entry into the war. Similar claims are repeated in Charles C. Tansill's *Back Door to War: The Roosevelt Foreign Policy, 1933–1941*, published four years later. These claims have generally been rejected by the historical profession, beginning with Basil Rauch's *Roosevelt, Munich to Pearl Harbor: A Study in the Creation of a Foreign Policy* in 1950, but a revisionist school exemplified by John Toland's *Infamy: Pearl Harbor and Its Aftermath* has found the Roosevelt administration culpable to some extent. A recent survey including Japanese contributions can by found in the symposium edited by Hilary Conroy and Harry Wray, *Pearl Harbor Re-examined: Prologue to the Pacific War*. The Grand Alliance is the subject of many studies, including Simon Berthon's fairly recent *Allies at War: The Bitter Rivalry among Churchill, Roosevelt, and De Gaulle*, the older *Churchill, Roosevelt, and Stalin: The War They Waged and the Peace They Sought* by Herbert Feis, and the useful collection of essays in David Reynolds, Warren F. Kimball, and A. O. Chubarian's volume also entitled *Allies at War: The Soviet, American, and British Experience, 1939–1945*.

The amount of writing on the military campaigns during World War II is enormous. A short overall summary covering the American aspects can be found in Martin Folly's recent study *The United States and World War II: The Awakening Giant*, and A. Russell Buchanan's older *The United States and World War II* is still useful. Several works by Stephen Ambrose and his team of researchers cover many of the aspects of combat in detail. Ambrose's tendency to portray U.S. forces in a generally positive light has been countered by more realistic views of the American wartime experience in the writing of Michael C. C. Adams in *The Best War Ever: America and World War II*, John W. Dower in *War without Mercy: Race and Power in the Pacific War*, Paul Fussell in *Wartime: Understanding and Behavior in the Second World*

War, and Gerald F. Linderman in *The World within War: America's Combat Experience in World War II*. While the campaigns in Europe are well covered by Charles B. MacDonald in *The Mighty Endeavor: The American War in Europe* and Russell F. Weigley in *Eisenhower's Lieutenants: The Campaign of France and Germany, 1944–1945*, the war in the Pacific is addressed by Ronald H. Spector in *Eagle against the Sun: The American War with Japan* and Bernard D. McNalty in *War in the Pacific: Pearl Harbor to Tokyo Bay*. There are many books dealing with particular battles or features of the war, such as the naval campaigns in the Pacific (for example, Dan Van der Vat in *The Pacific Campaign, World War II*), and biographies of individual commanders, such as Stanley P. Hirshson on Patton, Carlo D'Este on Eisenhower, Forrest Pogue on Marshall, and Michael Schaller on MacArthur, can be used to complement the various autobiographies. Studs Terkel's collection of oral memories in *"The Good War": An Oral History of World War Two* includes recollections of combat experiences and also adds the civilian perspective on the war, while Kenneth D. Rose provides an invaluable study of military and civilian experience in his *Myth and the Greatest Generation: A Social History of Americans in World War II*.

The U.S. home front is also a popular topic among historians. Richard D. Polenberg provides one of the first detailed analyses in *War and Society: The United States, 1941–1945*. This was followed by such writers as John Morton Blum in *V Was for Victory: Politics and American Culture during World War II* and John W. Jeffries in *Wartime America: The World War II Home Front*, who tend to point to some of the more negative aspects of the war's domestic impact in terms of labor unrest, race violence, and social and economic disruption. A more positive view of the war years and afterward can be found in William L. O'Neill's *A Democracy at War: American's Fight at Home and Abroad in World War II*.

Debates about the decision to use the atomic bomb in 1945 continue. The various arguments can be found in Gar Alperovitz's *The Decision to Use the Atomic Bomb and the Architecture of an American Myth* and in the collection edited by Kai Bird and Lawrence Lifschultz, *Hiroshima's Shadow: Writings on the Denial of History and the Smithsonian Controversy*, and Michael Hogan, *Hiroshima in History and Memory*.

Harry S. Truman's life and presidency is now well covered in the works of Robert H. Ferrell, especially his *Harry S. Truman: A Life*;

David McCullough's massive *Truman*; and Alonzo L. Hamby's shorter study *A Man of the People: A Life of Harry S. Truman*. Truman's own *Memoirs* also offers readable insights. Domestic politics in the Truman years are covered in various biographies, especially in Robert J. Donovan's two-volume *Conflict and Crisis: The Presidency of Harry S. Truman, 1945–1948* and *Tumultuous Years: The Presidency of Harry S. Truman*. Alonzo L. Hamby provides a useful survey in *Beyond the New Deal: Harry S. Truman and American Liberalism*, while Susan E. Hartmann gives a detailed account of the president's relations with Congress in *Truman and the 80th Congress*. The Fair Deal tends to be overshadowed by the rise of McCarthyism, a subject that has attracted a great deal of attention, ranging from the several biographical studies of McCarthy himself (for example, those by Richard H. Rovere and Thomas C. Reeves), to those dealing with the phenomenon of McCarthyism. Useful studies of this are David Caute's *The Great Fear: The Anti-Communist Purge under Truman and Eisenhower*, Richard Fried's *Nightmare in Red: The McCarthy Era in Perspective*, and Robert Griffith's *The Politics of Fear: Joseph R. McCarthy and the Senate*. Athan G. Theoharis locates the origins of McCarthyism with the Truman loyalty program and Cold War policies in *Seeds of Repression: Harry S. Truman and the Origins of McCarthyism*, while Michael J. Heale provides a useful longer perspective in *American Anticommunism: Combating the Enemy Within, 1830–1970*. A helpful oral history is Griffin Fariello's collection *Red Scare: Memories of the American Inquisition, an Oral History*. The rise of domestic surveillance and the role of the Federal Bureau of Investigation are thoroughly handled in the Rhodri Jeffreys-Jones's recent detailed study *The FBI: A History*.

Much of the focus of the writing on the Truman years is on the history of the Cold War. This has almost come full circle, beginning with the original orthodox views justifying the position of the United States and Harry S. Truman as defenders of liberal democracy in the face of aggressive Soviet expansionism, such as William H. McNeill in *America, Britain, and Russia: Their Co-operation and Conflict, 1941–1946* and Herbert Feis in *From Trust to Terror: The Onset of the Cold War*. Such arguments are also subjected to much critical reappraisal from such writers as Gabriel Kolko, Lloyd Gardner, Daniel Yergin, and others. The latest position—much closer to the original writers but offering a more balanced view recognizing the complexities of wartime and postwar relations—can be found in the several books of John L. Gaddis and those of Thomas G. Paterson and Alonzo L. Hamby. These different interpretations are collected in Thomas G. Paterson and Robert J. McMahon, eds., *The Origins of the Cold War*, while Peter G. Boyle provides a fine overview of the whole subject in *American-Soviet Relations: From the Russian Revolution to the Fall of Communism*.

Although the Korean War often tends to be described as the "forgotten" war, it provoked considerable debate among historians as to its causes and its conduct. Bruce Cumings provides a detailed two-volume account in *The Origins of the Korean War*, and Burton I. Kaufman's more recent study of *The Korean War: Challenges in Crisis, Credibility, and Command* is also useful. Rosemary Foot locates the conflict in the context of broader U.S. polices with regard to China. The conflict between Truman and Douglas MacArthur is well handled in John W. Spanier's *The Truman-MacArthur Controversy and the Korean War*.

The 1930s and 1940s were tumultuous years for different social groups as they were affected in turn by depression, war, ideological conflict, and developing government social welfare policy. While the focus of much of the writing on African American history is on the civil rights movement that appeared from 1955 onward, the significance of the earlier decades has been increasingly recognized. A good overview incorporating much of the new literature can be found in Robert J. Norrell's *The House I Live In: Race in the American Century* and in the useful surveys of the National Association for the Advancement of Colored People by Manfred Berg, *"Ticket to Freedom": The NAACP and the Struggle for Black Political Integration*, and Gilbert Jonas, *Freedom's Sword: The NAACP and the Struggle against Racism in America, 1909–1969*. Studies of the African American experience of the Great Depression and New Deal include Cheryl Lynn Greenberg's study of Harlem, *"Or Does It Explode": Black Harlem in the Great Depression*, the essays in Bernard Sternsher's edited collection, *The Negro in Depression and War: Prelude to Revolution, 1930–1945*, Harvard Sitkoff's *A New Deal for Blacks: The Emergence of Civil Rights as a National Issue*, and Patricia Sullivan's more recent *Days of Hope: Race and Democracy in the New Deal Era*. The political effects of the New Deal on the black population are examined in John B. Kirby's *Black Americans in the Roosevelt Era: Liberalism and Race* and Nancy J. Weiss's *Farewell to the Party of Lincoln: Black Politics in the Age of*

FDR. Studies of such individuals as Walter White by Kenneth Janken and A. Philip Randolph by Paula Pfeffer are also useful for both the 1930s and the war years.

The impact of World War II on race is examined from the military aspect in several works, including Richard M. Dalfiume's detailed *Fighting on Two Fronts: Desegregation of the U.S. Armed Forces, 1939–1953* and Christopher P. Moore's *Fighting for America: Black Soldiers, the Unsung Heroes of World War II*. The overall effects of the war on black life is the subject of Neil A. Wynn's *The Afro-American and the Second World War*, while the significance of the war in terms of changing government policy is the focus of Merl E. Reed's *Seedtime for the Modern Civil Rights Movement: The President's Committee on Fair Employment Practice, 1941—1946* and Daniel Kryder's *Divided Arsenal: Race and the American State during World War II*. Race relations in the postwar period and Truman years are examined in William C. Berman, *The Politics of Civil Rights in the Truman Administration*, Michael R.Gardner, *Harry Truman and Civil Rights: Moral Courage and Political Risks*, and Mary L. Dudziak, *Cold War Civil Rights: Race and the Image of American Democracy*.

The importance of these years for other minority groups has recently gained greater recognition. The treatment of Japanese Americans during World War II, in particular, has come under considerable scrutiny most notably in the work of Roger Daniels, *Concentration Camps USA: Japanese Americans and World War II*; however, more and more writing is being produced by Japanese Americans themselves, including Brian Masaru Hayashi, *Democratizing the Enemy: The Japanese-American Internment*, Gary Y. Okihiro, *Whispered Silences: Japanese Americans and World War II*, and the longer study by David Yoo, *Growing up Nisei: Race, Generation, and Culture among Japanese Americans of California, 1924–1949*. The legal aspects of the relocation of Japanese Americans are discussed fully in Peter H. Irons's scholarly study *Justice at War: The Story of the Japanese-American Internment Cases*.

The history of Mexican Americans during the 1930s and the war years is examined in Abraham Hoffman's *Unwanted Mexican Americans: Repatriation Pressures during the Great Depression*, Erasmo Gamboa's *Mexican Labor and World War II: Braceros in the Pacific Northwest, 1942–1947*, and the collection of essays edited by Maggie Rivas-Rodriguez, *Mexican Americans and World War II*. Several studies also examine Native Americans in this period, chief among them being Kenneth R. Philip's *John Collier's Crusade for Indian Reform, 1920–1954*, Graham D. Taylor's *The New Deal and American Indian Tribalism: The Administration of the Indian Reorganization Act, 1934–1945*, and Alison R. Bernstein's *American Indians and World War II: Toward a New Era in Indian Affairs*. An aspect of the military role played by Native Americans is the subject of Margaret T. Bixler's *Winds of Freedom: The Story of the Navajo Code Talkers of World War II*.

Information on labor history during this period is not as plentiful as for some other subjects. The classic studies are the two volumes by Irving Bernstein, *The Turbulent Years: A History of the American Worker, 1933–1941* and *A Caring Society: The New Deal, the Worker, and the Great Depression*, while a good short overview can be found in Robert H. Zieger, *American Workers, American Unions, 1920–1945*, and his *The CIO, 1935–1955*. Useful essays can be found in the collections by David Brody, *Workers in Industrial America: Essays on the 20th-Century Struggle*, and David Montgomery, *Workers Control in America: Studies in the History of Work, Technology, and Labor Struggles*. Biographies of such key figures as Melvyn Dubofsky and John Van Tine's of John L. Lewis and Nelson N. Lichtenstein's of Walter Reuther are also extremely useful. Lichtenstein's study *Labor's War at Home: The CIO in World War II* and Andrew E. Kersten's *Labor's Home Front: The American Federation of Labor during World War II* are the best detailed treatments of wartime labor policies and their consequences. Truman's relations with trade unions and the labor movement are the subject of Arthur F. McClure's *The Truman Administration and Problems of Postwar Labor, 1945–1948*. More recent perspectives can be found in the essays edited by Robert W. Cherny, William Issel, and Kieran Walsh Taylor, *American Labor and the Cold War: Grassroots Politics and Postwar Popular Culture*.

The experience of women during the 1930s and 1940s has become an increasingly popular area of research. While broad surveys such as Carl N. Degler's *At Odds: Women and the Family in America from the Revolution to the Present* or William H. Chafe's narrower *The Paradox of Change: American Women in the 20th Century* both provide useful starting points, there are now many more specialized studies available. Susan Ware's two books, *Beyond Suffrage: Women in the New Deal* and *Holding Their Own: American Women in the 1930s*, and Lois Scharf in *To Work and to Wed: Female Employment, Feminism, and the Great Depression* both offer useful insights into women's experience of the Great Depression and New Deal.

A great deal of writing exists on the war years, much of it concerned directly or indirectly with the debate about the long-term significance of the war for women and the women's movement. The most important works on this subject are now probably D'Ann Campbell's *Women at War with America: Private Lives in a Patriotic Age*, Sherna Berger Gluck's *Rosie the Riveter Revisited: Women, the War, and Social Change*, and Emily Yellin's *Our Mother's War: American Women at Home and at the Front during World War II*. Susan M. Hartmann takes the story into the postwar with *The Home Front and Beyond: American Women in the 1940s*, as do Eugenia Kaledin in *Mothers and More: American Women in the 1950s* and the contributors to Joanne Meyerowitz's edited collection, *Not June Cleaver: Women and Gender in Postwar America, 1945–1960*. The apparent return of women to domesticity after the war is the subject of Betty Friedan's seminal work, *The Feminine Mystique*, and related issues are dealt with in Elaine Tyler May's fascinating *Homeward Bound: American Families in the Cold War Era*.

The social, demographic, and cultural changes brought about by the successive effects of the Great Depression, World War II, and the Cold War are dealt with in many of the general texts already listed above. The essays in Lawrence W. Levine, *The Unpredictable Past: Explorations in American Cultural History*, are regarded as essential starting points. On the 1930s, McElvaine's *The Great Depression: America 1929–1941* makes many good points on social and cultural history, and some valuable insights can be found in the essays edited by Stephen W. Baskerville and Ralph Willett, *Nothing Else to Fear: New Perspectives on America in the Thirties*. A contemporary view is provided in Frederick Lewis Allen, *Since Yesterday: The 1930s in America*, although some of his observations would be questioned by more recent writers. A key work, particularly with reference to photography, is William Stott's *Documentary Expression in Thirties America*. Film is dealt with in a number of useful studies. John Baxter in *Hollywood in the Thirties* and Charles Higham and Joel Greenberg in *Hollywood in the Forties* provide good basic descriptions of many of the films released during these two decades. Content is discussed more by Robert Sklar in his excellent *Movie-Made America: A Social History of American Movies* and also in the very useful collection of essays edited by Steven Mintz and Randy Roberts in *Hollywood's America: United States History through Its Films.*

The standard work on film during the war years is Clayton R. Koppes and Gregory D. Black's *Hollywood Goes to War: How Politics and Propaganda Shaped World War II Movies*, while Richard R. Lingeman's readable *Don't You Know There's a War On? The American Home Front, 1941–1945* provides a great deal of stimulating detail about the full range of social and cultural matters during the war. Steven J. Whitfield offers a more academic approach in *The Culture of the Cold War*, and the subject of film is the focus of Nora Sayre in *Running Time: Films of the Cold War*. The essays in Elaine McClarnand and Steve Goodson's edited collection *The Impact of the Cold War on American Popular Culture* offer a useful broader view. The effects of the war and postwar years on intellectual thought and ideas are examined in William S. Graebner's *The Age of Doubt: American Thought and Culture in the 1940s*, while Paul Boyer and Margot A. Henriksen focus specifically on the impact of the birth of the atomic age in *By the Bomb's Early Light: American Thought and Culture at the Dawn of the Atomic Age* and *Dr. Strangelove's America: Society and Culture in the Atomic Age*, respectively. A useful broad overview of media and the arts in the postwar period can be found in Richard Alan Schwartz, *Cold War Culture: Media and the Arts, 1945–1990.*

II. PRESIDENTIAL PAPERS

The records of the Roosevelt and Truman administrations are housed at the Franklin D. Roosevelt Library in Hyde Park, New York, and the Harry S. Truman Library in Independence, Missouri. Public papers and speeches of the presidents can also be found at The American Presidency Project at www.presidency.ucsb.edu/ws/. *The Public Papers and Addresses of Franklin D. Roosevelt*, edited by Samuel Rosenman and *Public Papers of the Presidents: Harry S. Truman 1945–1953*, 8 volumes, Washington, D.C.: Government Printing Office, 1961–1966 are a valuable source.

III. BIBLIOGRAPHIES AND ENCYCLOPEDIAS

The most useful source for biographical information is without a doubt John A. Garraty and Mark Carnes, eds., *The American National Biography* (1999), published by Oxford University Press and available online at http://www.anb.org.

Agnew, Jean Christophe, and Roy Rosenzweig, eds. *A Companion to Post-1945 America*. Oxford: Blackwell Publishing, 2005.

Biographical Dictionary of the United States Congress Online. Available from http://bioguide.congress.gov.

Boyer, Paul S., ed. *The Oxford Companion to United States History*. New York: Oxford University Press, 2001.

Carnes, Mark C., ed. *American History*. New York: Simon & Schuster/Macmillan, 1996.

Ciment, James, ed. *Encyclopedia of the Great Depression and New Deal*. Armonk, N.Y.: M. E. Sharpe, 2000.

Graham, Otis L., and Meghan Robinson Wander, eds. *Franklin D. Roosevelt: His Life and Times, An Encyclopedic View*. New York: Da Capo Press, 1985.

Kirkendall, Paul S., ed. *The Harry Truman Encyclopedia*. Boston: G. K. Hall & Co., 1989.

Kort, Michael. *The Columbia Guide to the Cold War*. New York: Columbia University Press, 2001.

Olson, James S. *Historical Dictionary of the 1950s*. Westport, Conn.: Greenwood, 2000.

———. *Historical Dictionary of the Great Depression, 1929–1940*. Westport, Conn.: Greenwood, 2001.

———. *Historical Dictionary of the New Deal: From Inauguration to Preparation for War*. Westport, Conn.: Greenwood Publishing, 1985.

Polmar, Norman B., and Thomas B Allen. *World War II: America at War, 1941–1945*. New York: Random House, 1991.

Smith, Joseph, and Simon Davis. *Historical Dictionary of the Cold War*. Lanham, Md., and London: Scarecrow Press, 2000.

Whitfield, Stephen J., ed. *A Companion to 20th-Century America*. Malden, Mass. and Oxford: Blackwell Publishing, 2004.

IV. GENERAL SURVEYS

Allen, Frederick Lewis. *Since Yesterday: The Nineteen-Thirties in America*. 1940. Reprint, New York: Bantam Books, 1965.

Ambrose, Stephen E. *Rise to Globalism: American Foreign Policy, 1938–1980.* New York: Penguin Books, 1980.

De Bedts, Ralph F. *Recent American History: 1933 through World War II.* Vol. I. Homewood, Ill.: Dorsey Press, 1973.

——. *Recent American History: 1945 to the Present.* Vol. II. Homewood, Ill.: Dorsey Press, 1973.

Diggins, John Patrick. *The Proud Decades: America in War and Peace, 1941–1960.* New York: Norton, 1988.

Goldman, Eric F. *The Crucial Decade—and After: America, 1945–1960.* New York: Vintage, 1961.

Halberstam, David. *The Fifties.* New York: Villard Books, 1993.

Hodgson, Godfrey. *America in Our Time: From World War II to Nixon.* New York: Alfred A. Knopf, 1976.

Hofstadter, Richard. *The Age of Reform: From Bryan to FDR.* New York Alfred A. Knopf, 1955.

Karl, Barry P. *The Uneasy State: The United States from 1915 to 1945.* Chicago: University of Chicago Press, 1983.

Kempton, Murray. *America Comes of Middle Age: Columns, 1950–1962.* Boston: Little, Brown, 1963.

Kennedy, David M. *Freedom from Fear: The American People in Depression and War, 1929–1945.* New York: Oxford University Press, 1999.

Kirkendall, Richard S. *The United States, 1929–1945: Years of Crisis and Change.* New York: McGraw-Hill, 1973.

Leuchtenburg, William E. *A Troubled Feast: American Society since 1945.* Boston: Little, Brown, 1973.

Levine, Lawrence. *The Unpredictable Past: Explorations in American Cultural History.* New York: Oxford University Press, 1993.

Manchester, William. *The Glory and the Dream: A Narrative History of America, 1932–1972.* Boston: Little, Brown, 1974.

Nash, Gerald D. *The Crucial Era: The Great Depression and World War II, 1929–1945.* New York: St. Martins Press, 1992.

O'Neill, William L. *American High: The Years of Confidence, 1945–1960.* New York: Free Press, 1986.

Perrett, Geoffrey. *A Dream of Greatness: The American People, 1945–1963.* New York: Coward, McCann & Geoghegan, 1979.

Polenberg, Richard D. *One Nation Divisible: Class, Race, and Ethnicity in the United States.* New York: Viking Press, 1980.

Sherry, Michael S. *In the Shadow of War: The United States since the 1930s.* New Haven: Yale University Press, 1995.

Susman, Warren I. *Culture as History: The Transformation of American Society in the Twentieth Century.* New York: Pantheon Books, 1984.

Zinn, Howard. *Postwar America: 1945–1971*. Indianapolis: Bobbs-Merrill, 1973.

V. THE CRASH AND THE GREAT DEPRESSION

Bernstein, Irving. *The Lean Years: A History of the American Worker, 1920–1933*. Boston: Houghton Mifflin, 1960.

Bernstein, Michael A. *The Great Depression: Delayed Recovery and Economic Change in America, 1929–1939*. Cambridge: Cambridge University Press, 1987.

Bird, Caroline. *The Invisible Scar*. New York: McKay, 1966.

Bordo, Michael D., Claudia Goldin, and Eugene N. White, eds. *The Defining Moment: The Great Depression and the American Economy in the Twentieth Century*. Chicago: University of Chicago Press, 1998.

Chandler, Lester V. *America's Greatest Depression, 1919–1941*. New York: Harper, 1970.

Daniels, Roger. *The Bonus March: An Episode of the Great Depression*. Westport, Conn.: Greenwood Press, 1941.

Fearon, Peter. *War, Prosperity, and Depression, 1919–1941*. Deddington, Oxfordshire: Philip Allan, 1987.

Fite, Gilbert C. *American Farmers: The New Majority*. Bloomington: Indiana University Press, 1981.

Friedman, Milton, and Anna Jacobson Schwartz. *The Great Contraction, 1929–1933*. Princeton, N.J.: Princeton University Press, 1965.

Galbraith, John Kenneth. *The Great Crash: 1929*. Boston: Houghton Mifflin, 1955.

Garraty, John A. *The Great Depression: An Inquiry into the Causes, Course, and Consequences of the Worldwide Depression of the 1930s*. New York: Harcourt Brace Jovanovich, 1986.

Klingaman, William K. *1929: The Year of the Great Crash*. New York: Harper & Row, 1989.

Lowitt, Richard, and Maurine Beasley, eds. *One Third of a Nation: Lorena Hickok Reports on the Great Depression*. Urbana: University of Illinois Press, 1981.

McElvaine, Robert S. *Down and Out in the Great Depression: Letters from the Forgotten Man*. Chapel Hill: University of North Carolina Press, 1983.

———. *The Great Depression: America 1929–1941*. New York: Times Books, 1984.

Pells, Richard H. *Radical Visions and American Dreams: Culture and Social Thought in the Depression Years*. New York: Harper & Row, 1973.

Rosen, Elliott. *Hoover, Roosevelt, and the Brains Trust: From Depression to New Deal*. New York: Columbia University Press, 1977.

Rothbard, Murray N. *America's Greatest Depression*. Princeton, N.J.: D. Van Nostrand, 1963.

Schlesinger, Arthur M., Jr. *The Age of Roosevelt: The Politics of Upheaval*. Boston: Houghton Mifflin, 1960.

Smiley, Gene. *Rethinking the Great Depression*. Chicago: Ivan R. Dee, 2002.

Sobel, Robert. *The Great Bull Market: Wall Street in the 1920s*. New York: W. W. Norton, 1968.

Terkel, Studs. *Hard Times: An Oral History of the Great Depression*. New York: Pantheon Books, 1970.

Thomas, Gordon, and M. Morgan-Witts. *The Day the Bubble Burst: A Social History of the Wall Street Crash of 1929*. New York: Doubleday, 1979.

Watkins, T. H. *The Great Depression: America in the 1930s*. Boston: Little, Brown, 1993.

Worster, Donald L. *Dust Bowl: The Southern Plains in the 1930s*. New York: Oxford University Press, 1979.

VI. FRANKLIN D. ROOSEVELT AND THE NEW DEAL

Allswang, John. *The New Deal and American Politics: A Study in Political Change*. New York: John Wiley & Sons, 1978.

Amenta, Edwin. *When Movements Matter: The Townsend Plan and the Rise of Social Security*. Princeton, N.J.: Princeton University Press, 2006.

Badger, Anthony J. *The New Deal: The Depression Years, 1933–1940*. New York: Hill & Wang, 1989.

Baskerville, Stephen W., and Ralph, Willett, eds. *Nothing Else to Fear: New Perspectives on America in the Thirties*. Manchester: Manchester University Press, 1985.

Bennett, David H. *Demagogues in the Depression: American Radicals and the Union Party, 1932–1936*. New Brunswick, N.J.: Rutgers University Press, 1969.

Bernstein, Barton J., ed. *Towards a New Past: Dissenting Essays in American History*. New York: Random House, 1987.

Best, Gary Dean. *Herbert Hoover: The Postpresidential Years, 1933–1964*. Stanford, Calif.: Hoover Institution Press, 1983.

——. *Pride, Prejudice, and Politics: Roosevelt versus Recovery, 1933–1938*. New York: Praeger, 1991.

Biles, Roger. *A New Deal for the American People*. DeKalb: Northern Illinois University Press, 1991.

Black, Allida. *Casting Her Own Shadow: Eleanor Roosevelt and the Shaping of Postwar Liberalism*. New York: Columbia University Press, 1996.

———. *Courage in a Dangerous World: The Political Writings of Eleanor Roosevelt*. New York: Columbia University Press, 1999.

Blum, John Morton. *Roosevelt and Morgenthau*. Boston: Houghton Mifflin, 1970.

Braeman, John, Robert H. Bremner, and David Brody, eds. *The New Deal: The National Level*. Vol. 1. Columbus: Ohio State University Press, 1975.

———. *The New Deal: The State and Local Levels*. Vol. 2. Columbus: Ohio State University Press, 1975.

Brewer, Jeutonne P. *The Federal Writers' Project: A Bibliography*. Metuchen, N.H.: Scarecrow Press, 1994.

Brindas, Kenneth J. *All of the Music Belongs to the Nation: The WPA's Federal Music Project*. Knoxville: University of Tennessee Press, 1995.

Brinkley, Alan. *Voices of Protest: Huey Long, Father Coughlin, and the Great Depression*. New York: Alfred A. Knopf, 1982.

Burns, James MacGregor. *Roosevelt: The Lion and the Fox*. New York: Harcourt Brace, 1956.

———. *Roosevelt: The Soldier of Freedom*. New York: Harcourt Brace Jovanovich, 1970.

Clarke, Jeanne N. *Roosevelt's Warrior: Harold Ickes and the New Deal*. Baltimore: Johns Hopkins University Press, 1996.

Cohen, Wilbur J. *The Roosevelt New Deal: A Program Assessment Fifty Years After*. Austin: Lyndon B. Johnson School of Public Affairs, 1986.

Coker, Jeffrey W. *Franklin D. Roosevelt: A Biography*. Westport, Conn.: Greenwood Press, 2005.

Conkin, Paul K. *The New Deal*. 2nd ed. Arlington Heights, Ill.: Harlan Davidson, 1975.

Cook, Blanche Wiesen. *Eleanor Roosevelt: Volume I, 1884–1933*. New York: Viking Press, 1992.

———. *Eleanor Roosevelt: Volume II, 1933–1938*. New York: Viking Press, 1999.

Cushman, Barry. *Rethinking the New Deal Court: The Structure of a Constitutional Revolution*. New York: Oxford University Press, 1998.

Davis, Kenneth S. *FDR, the New Deal Years, 1933–1937*. New York: Random House, 1986.

Dubofsky, Melvyn. *The New Deal: Conflicting Interpretations and Shifting Perspectives*. New York: Garland Publishers, 1990.

Eden, Robert, ed. *The New Deal and Its Legacy: Critique and Appraisal*. Westport, Conn.: Greenwood Press, 1989.

Edsforth, Ronald. *The New Deal: America's Response to the Great Depression.* New York: Blackwell Publishers, 2000.

Einaudi, Mario. *The Roosevelt Revolution.* New York: Harper & Row, 1959.

Finan, Christopher M. *Alfred E. Smith: The Happy Warrior.* New York: Hill & Wang, 2002.

Fraser, Steve, and Gary Gerstle, eds. *The Rise and Fall of the New Deal Order, 1930–1980.* Princeton, N.J.: Princeton University Press, 1989.

Freidel, Frank B. *The Apprenticeship.* Vol. 1 of *Franklin D. Roosevelt.* Boston: Little, Brown, 1952.

———. *The Ordeal.* Vol. 2 of *Franklin D. Roosevelt.* Boston: Little, Brown, 1954.

———. *The Triumph.* Vol. 3 of *Franklin D. Roosevelt.* Boston: Little, Brown, 1956.

———. *Launching the New Deal.* Vol. 4 of *Franklin D. Roosevelt.* Boston: Little, Brown, 1973.

———. *Franklin D. Roosevelt: A Rendezvous with Destiny.* Boston: Little, Brown & Co., 1990.

Garson, Robert A. *The Democratic Party and the Politics of Sectionalism, 1941–1948.* Baton Rouge: Louisiana State University Press, 1974.

Goodwin, Doris Kearns. *No Ordinary Time: Franklin and Eleanor Roosevelt: The Home Front in World War II.* New York: Simon & Schuster, 1995.

Graham, Otis L. *The New Deal.* Boston: Little, Brown, 1973.

Greenbaum, Fred. *Fighting Progressive: A Biography of Edward P. Costigan.* Washington, D.C.: Public Affairs Press, 1971.

Hamby, Alonzo L., ed. *The New Deal: Analysis and Interpretation.* New York and London: Longman, 1981.

Hamilton, David E. *The New Deal.* Boston: Houghton, Mifflin, 1999.

Hawley, Ellis. *The New Deal and the Problem of Monopoly.* Princeton, N.J.: Princeton University Press, 1966.

Hirsh, Jerrold. *Portrait of America: A Cultural History of the Federal Writers' Project.* Chapel Hill: North Carolina Press, 2003.

Hopkins, June. *Harry Hopkins: Sudden Hero, Brash Reformer.* New York: St. Martin's Press, 1999.

Huthmacher, J. Joseph. *Senator Robert F. Wagner and the Rise of Urban Liberalism.* New York: Atheneum, 1971.

Lash, Joseph P. *Eleanor and Franklin.* New York: W.W. Norton & Company, 1971.

Leuchtenburg, William E. *Franklin D. Roosevelt and the New Deal, 1932–1940.* New York: Harper & Row, 1963.

———. *The New Deal: A Documentary History.* New York: Harper & Row, 1968.

———. "The New Deal and the Analogue of War." In *Change and Continuity in Twentieth Century America*, edited by John Braeman, Robert H. Bremner, and Everett Waters. Columbus: Ohio State University Press, 1964.

———. *The Supreme Court Reborn: The Constitutional Revolution in the Age of Roosevelt*. New York: Oxford University Press, 1995.

Levine, Rhonda. *Class Struggle and the New Deal: Industrial Labor, Industrial Capital, and the State*. Lawrence: University Press of Kansas, 1988.

Louchheim, Katie. *The Making of the New Deal: The Insiders Speak*. Cambridge, Mass.: Harvard University Press, 1983.

McCoy, Donald. *Angry Voices: Left-of-Center Politics in the New Deal Era*. Lawrence: University of Kansas, 1958.

———. *Landon of Kansas*. Lincoln: University of Nebraska Press, 1967.

McJimsey, George T. *T. Harry Hopkins: Ally of the Poor and Defender of Democracy*. Cambridge, Mass.: Harvard University Press, 1987.

Mettler, Suzanne. *Dividing Citizens: Gender and Federalism in New Deal Public Policy*. Ithaca, N.Y.: Cornell University Press, 1998.

Morgan, Ted. *FDR: A Biography*. New York: Simon & Schuster, 1985.

Parrish, Michael E. *Felix Frankfurter and His Times: The Reform Years*. New York: Free Press, 1982.

Patterson, James T. *Congressional Conservatism and the New Deal: The Growth of the Conservative Coalition in Congress, 1933–1939*, Lexington: University of Kentucky Press, 1967.

———. *Mr. Republican: A Biography of Robert A. Taft*. Boston: Houghton Mifflin, 1972.

Polenberg, Richard D. *The Era of Franklin D. Roosevelt, 1933–1945: A Brief History with Documents*. Boston and New York: Bedford/St. Martin's Press, 2000.

Reagan, Patrick D. *Designing a New America: The Origins of New Deal Planning, 1890–1943*. Amherst: University of Massachusetts Press, 2000.

Rogow, Arnold. *James Forrestal, a Study of Personality, Politics, and Policy*. New York: Macmillan, 1963.

Romasco, Albert U. *The Politics of Recovery: Roosevelt's New Deal*. New York: Oxford University Press, 1983.

Roosevelt, Eleanor. *The Autobiography of Eleanor Roosevelt*. New York: Da Capo Press, 1992.

Rosenman, Samuel I. *The Public Papers and Addresses of President Franklin D. Roosevelt*. 4 vols. New York: Macmillan, 1941.

Rozell, Mark J., and William D. Pederson, eds. *FDR and the Modern Presidency: Leadership and Legacy*. Westport, Conn.: Praeger, 1997.

Salmond, John. *The Civilian Conservation Corps, 1933–1942*. Durham, N.C.: Duke University Press, 1967.

Saloutos, Theodore. *American Farmers and the New Deal*. Ames: Iowa State University Press, 1982.

Schlesinger, Arthur M., Jr. *The Crisis of the Old Order*. Vol. 1 of *The Age of Roosevelt*. Boston: Houghton Mifflin, 1956.

——. *The Coming of the New Deal*. Vol. 2 of *The Age of Roosevelt*. Boston: Houghton Mifflin, 1958.

——. *The Politics of Upheaval*. Vol. 3 of *The Age of Roosevelt*. Boston: Houghton Mifflin, 1960.

Schwarz, Jordan A. *The New Dealers: Power Politics in the Age of Roosevelt*. New York: Alfred A. Knopf, 1993.

Sternsher, Bernard. *Hope Restored: How the New Deal Worked in Town and Country*. Chicago: Ivan R. Dee, 1999.

Tindall, George Brown. *The Emergence of the New South, 1913–1945*. Baton Rouge: Louisiana State University Press, 1967.

Tugwell, Rexford. *The Brains Trust*. New York: Viking Press, 1968.

Venn, Fiona. *The New Deal*. Edinburgh: Edinburgh University Press, 1998.

Ward, Geoffrey C. *Before the Trumpet: Young Franklin Roosevelt, 1882–1905*. New York: Harper & Row, 1985.

——. *A First Class Temperament: The Emergence of Franklin Roosevelt*. New York: Harper & Row, 1992.

Warren, Donald I. *Radio Priest: Charles Coughlin, the Father of Hate Radio*. New York: Free Press, 1996.

Warren, Frank A. *An Alternative Vision: The Socialist Party in the 1930s*. Bloomington: Indiana University Press, 1976.

White, G. Edward. *The Constitution and the New Deal*. Cambridge, Mass.: Harvard University Press, 2000.

White, Graham, and John Maze. *Harold Ickes of the New Deal: His Private Life and Public Career*. Cambridge, Mass.: Harvard University Press, 1985.

——. *Henry A. Wallace: His Search for a New World Order*. Chapel Hill: University of North Carolina Press, 1995.

Williams, Harry T. *Huey Long*. New York: Alfred A. Knopf, 1969.

Winkler, Allan M. *Franklin D. Roosevelt and the Making of Modern America*. New York and London: Longman, 2006.

Zinn, Howard, ed. *New Deal Thought*. Indianapolis: Bobbs-Merrill, 1966.

VII. ROOSEVELT AND FOREIGN RELATIONS IN PEACE AND WAR

Adler, Selig. *The Isolationist Impulse*. New York: Free Press, 1957.

Berthon, Simon. *Allies at War: The Bitter Rivalry among Churchill, Roosevelt, and De Gaulle*. New York: Carroll & Graf, 2001.

Cashman, Sean D. *America, Roosevelt, and World War II.* New York: New York University Press, 1989.

Cole, Wayne S. *Roosevelt and the Isolationists, 1932–1945.* Lincoln: University of Nebraska Press, 1983.

Dallek, Robert. *Franklin D. Roosevelt and American Foreign Policy, 1932–1945.* New York: Oxford University Press, 1979.

De Conde, Alexander, ed. *Isolation and Security.* Durham, N.C.: Duke University Press, 1957.

Divine, Robert A. *The Illusion of Neutrality.* Chicago: University of Chicago Press, 1962.

——. *The Reluctant Belligerent.* New York: Wiley, 1965.

Feis, Herbert. *Churchill, Roosevelt, and Stalin: The War They Waged and the Peace They Sought.* Princeton, N.J.: Princeton University Press, 1957.

Ferrell, Robert H. *American Diplomacy in the Great Depression.* New Haven, Conn.: Yale University Press, 1957.

Gellman, Irwin F. *Good Neighbor Diplomacy.* Baltimore: Johns Hopkins University Press, 1979.

——. *Secret Affairs: Franklin Roosevelt, Cordell Hull, and Sumner Welles.* Baltimore: Johns Hopkins University Press, 1995.

Jonas, Manfred. *Isolationism in America, 1935–1941.* Chicago: Imprint Publications, 1990.

Kimball, Warren F. *Forged in War: Roosevelt, Churchill, and the Second World War.* New York: W. Morrow, 1997.

Langer, William L., and S. Everett Gleason. *The Challenge to Isolation, 1937–1940.* New York: Harper, 1952.

Marks, Frederick W. *Wind over Sand: The Diplomacy of Franklin Roosevelt.* Athens: University of Georgia, 1988.

Nixon, Edgar B., ed. *Franklin D. Roosevelt and Foreign Affairs.* 3 vols. Cambridge, Mass.: Belknap Press of Harvard University Press, 1969.

Reynolds, David. *From Munich to Pearl Harbor: Roosevelt's America and the Origins of the Second World War.* Chicago: Ivan R. Dee, 2001.

Reynolds, David, Warren F. Kimball, and A. O. Chubarian, eds. *Allies at War: The Soviet, American, and British Experience, 1939–1945.* New York: St. Martin's Press, 1994.

Sainsbury, Keith. *The Turning Point: Roosevelt, Stalin, Churchill, and Chiang-Kai-Shek, 1943: The Moscow, Cairo, and Teheran Conferences.* Oxford: Oxford University Press, 1985.

Schaller, Michael. *The U.S. Crusade in China, 1938–1945.* New York: Columbia University Press, 1979.

Schewe, Donald. *Franklin D. Roosevelt and Foreign Affairs.* 11 vols. New York: Clearwater, 1969.

Wood, Bryce. *The Making of the Good Neighbor Policy*. New York: Columbia University Press, 1961.

Wyman, David S. *The Abandonment of the Jews: America and the Holocaust, 1941–1945*. New York: Pantheon Books, 1984.

VIII. WORLD WAR II

Adams, Michael C. C. *The Best War Ever: America and World War II*. Baltimore: Johns Hopkins University Press, 1993.

Alperovitz, Gar. *The Decision to Use the Atomic Bomb and the Architecture of an American Myth*. New York: Alfred A. Knopf, 1995.

Ambrose, Stephen E. *Band of Brothers: E Company, 506th Regiment, 101st Airborne from Normandy to Hitler's Eagle's Nest*. New York: Simon & Schuster, 2001.

———. *Citizen Soldiers: The U.S. Army from the Normandy Beaches to the Bulge to the Surrender of Germany, June 7, 1944–May 7, 1945*. New York: Simon & Schuster, 1997.

———. *D-Day: June 6, 1944: The Climactic Battle of World War II*. New York: Simon & Schuster, 1994.

———. *Eisenhower and Berlin, 1945: The Decision to Halt at the Elbe*. New York: W. W. Norton, 1967.

———. *Ike: Abilene to Berlin: The Life of Dwight D. Eisenhower from His Childhood in Abilene, Kansas, through His Command of the Allied Forces in Europe in World War II*. New York: Harper & Row 1973.

———. *The Supreme Commander: The War Years of General Dwight D. Eisenhower*. Garden City, N.Y.: Doubleday, 1970.

Beard, Charles, *President Roosevelt and the Coming of War, 1941: A Study in Appearances and Realities*. New Haven, Conn.: Yale University Press, 1948.

Bird, Kai, and Lawrence Lifschultz, eds. *Hiroshima's Shadow: Writings on the Denial of History and the Smithsoniam Controversy*. New York: Pamphleteer's Press, 1997.

Blumenson, Martin. *Patton, the Man behind the Legend, 1885–1945*. New York: Morrow, 1985.

Bradley, James, with Ron Powers. *Flags of Our Fathers*. London: Pimlico, 2000.

Bradley, Omar Nelson, and Clay Blair. *A General's Life: An Autobiography*. New York: Simon & Schuster, 1983.

Brokaw, Tom. *The Greatest Generation*. New York: Random House, 1998.

Buchanan, A. Russell. *The United States and World War II*. New York: Harper, 1964.

Conroy, Hilary, and Harry Wray, eds. *Pearl Harbor Re-examined: Prologue to the Pacific War*. Honolulu: University of Hawaii Press, 1990.

Cray, Ed. *General of the Army: George C. Marshall, Soldier and Statesman*. New York: W.W. Norton, 1990.

Davis, Kenneth S. *FDR: The War President, 1940–1943: A History*. New York: Random House, 2000.

D'Este, Carlo. *Eisenhower: A Soldier's Life*. New York: Henry Holt, 2002.

———. *Patton: A Genius for War*. New York: HarperCollins, 1995.

Doubler, Michael D. *Closing with the Enemy: How GIs Fought the War in Europe, 1944–1945*. Lawrence: University Press of Kansas, 1994.

Dower, John W. *War without Mercy: Race and Power in the Pacific War*. New York: Pantheon Books, 1986.

Feis, Herbert. *The Road to Pearl Harbor: The Coming of the War between the United States and Japan*. Princeton, N.J.: Princeton University Press, 1950.

Folly, Martin. *The United States and World War II: The Awakening Giant*. Edinburgh: Edinburgh University Press, 2002.

Fussell, Paul. *The Boy's Crusade: American GIs in Europe: Chaos and Fear in World War Two*. London: Weidenfeld & Nicolson, 2004.

———. *Wartime: Understanding and Behavior in the Second World War*. New York: Oxford University Press, 1989.

Gambone, Michael D. *The Greatest Generation Comes Home: The Veteran in American Society*. College Station, Tex.: Texas A&M University Press, 2005.

Gelb, Norman. *Desperate Venture: The Story of Operation Torch, the Allied Invasion of North Africa*. New York: W. Morrow, 1992.

Hastings, Max. *Nemesis: The Battle for Japan, 1944–1945*. London: Harper Press, 2007.

Hess, Gary R. *The United States at War, 1941–1945*. Wheeling, Ill.: Harlan Davidson, 2000.

Hirshson, Stanley P. *General Patton: A Soldier's Life*. New York: HarperCollins, 2002.

Hogan, Michael, ed. *Hiroshima in History and Memory*. Cambridge: Cambridge University Press, 1996.

Hoyt, Edwin Palmer. *How They Won the War in the Pacific: Nimitz and His Admirals*. New York: Weybright and Talley, 1970.

Kelly, Orr. *Meeting the Fox: The Allied Invasion of Africa, from Operation Torch to Kasserine Pass to Victory in Tunisia*. New York: John Wiley & Sons, 2002.

Kennett, Lee. *G.I.: The American Soldier in World War II*. New York: Charles Scribner's Sons, 1987.

Lamb, Richard. *War in Italy, 1943–1945: A Brutal Story*. New York: St. Martin's Press, 1993.

Landis, Kenneth, and Rex Gunn. *Deceit at Pearl Harbor: From Pearl Harbor to Midway*. Bloomington, Indiana: 1st Books Library, 2002.

Leckie, Robert. *Challenge for the Pacific: Guadalcanal, the Turning Point of the War*. Garden City, N.Y.: Doubleday, 1965.

Lifton, Robert J., and Greg Mitchell. *Hiroshima in America: Fifty Years of Denial*. New York: Putnam, 1995.

Linderman, Gerald F. *The World within War: America's Combat Experience in World War II*. New York: Free Press, 1997.

Love, Jr., Robert W. *Pearl Harbor Revisited*. New York: St. Martin's Press, 1995.

MacDonald, Charles B. *The Mighty Endeavor: The American War in Europe*. New York: Da Capo Press, 1992.

Maddox, Robert James. *Weapons for Victory: The Hiroshima Decision Fifty Years Later*. Columbia: University of Missouri Press, 1995.

Manchester, William. *American Caesar: Douglas MacArthur, 1880–1964*. Boston: Little, Brown, 1978.

McNalty, Bernard D. *War in the Pacific: Pearl Harbor to Tokyo Bay*. New York: Mayflower, 1978.

Murray, Williamson, and Allan R. Millett. *A War to Be Won: Fighting the Second World War, 1937–1945*. Cambridge, Mass.: Belknap Press of Harvard University Press, 2000.

Perret, Geoffrey. *Old Soldiers Never Die: The Life of Douglas MacArthur*. New York: Random House, 1996

———. *There's a War to Be Won: The United States Army in World War II*. New York: Random House, 1991.

Pogue, Forrest. *George C. Marshall*. 4 vols. New York: Viking Press, 1963–1987.

Potter, Elmer B. *Nimitz*. Annapolis, Md.: Naval Institute Press, 1976.

Prangee, Gordon William, with Donald M. Goldstein and Katherine V. Dillon. *Pearl Harbor: The Verdict of History*. New York: McGraw-Hill, 1986.

Rauch, Basil. *Roosevelt, from Munich to Pearl Harbor: A Study in the Creation of a Foreign Policy*. New York: Creative Age Press, 1950.

Reynolds, David. *Rich Relations: The American Occupation of Britain, 1942–1945*. New York: Random House, 1995.

Rose, Kenneth D. *Myth and the Greatest Generation: A Social History of Americans in World War II*. New York and London: Routledge, 2008.

Schaffer, Ronald. *Wings of Judgment: American Bombing in World War II*. New York: Oxford University Press, 1985.

Schaller, Michael. *Douglas MacArthur: The Far Eastern General*. New York: Oxford University Press, 1989.

Sherwin, Martin. *A World Destroyed: The Atomic Bomb and the Grand Alliance*. New York: Alfred A. Knopf, 1975.

Spector, Ronald H. *Eagle against the Sun: The American War with Japan*. New York: Free Press, 1985.

Stoler, Mark A. *Allies in War: Britain and America against the Axis Powers, 1940–1945*. London: Hodder Arnold, 2005.

Tansill, Charles C. *Back Door to War: The Roosevelt Foreign Policy, 1933–1941*. Chicago: Henry Regnery, 1952.

Toland, John. *Infamy: Pearl Harbor and Its Aftermath*. Garden City, N.Y.: Doubleday, 1982.

Utley, Jonathan G. *Going to War with Japan, 1937–1941*. Knoxville: University of Tennessee Press, 1985.

Van der Vat, Dan. *The Pacific Campaign, World War II: The U.S.-Japanese Naval War, 1941–1945*. New York: Simon & Schuster, 1991.

Weigley, Russell F. *The American Way of War: A History of United States Military Strategy and Policy*. New York: Macmillan, 1973.

——. *Eisenhower's Lieutenants: The Campaign of France and Germany, 1944–1945*. Bloomington: Indiana University Press, 1981.

Whiting, Charles. *Bradley*. New York: Ballantine Books, 1971

Wohlstetter, Roberta. *Pearl Harbor: Warning and Decision*. Stanford, Calif.: Stanford University Press, 1962.

Wright, Derrick. *Battle for Iwo Jima, 1945*. New York: Sutton Publishing, 2000.

IX. WORLD WAR II AT HOME

Bennett, Michael J. *When Dreams Came True: The GI Bill and the Making of Modern America*. Washington, D.C.: Brassey's, 1996.

Bérubé, Allan. *Coming Out under Fire: The History of Gay Men and Women in World War II*. New York: Free Press, 1990.

Blum, John Morton. *V Was for Victory: Politics and American Culture during World War II*. New York: Harcourt Brace Jovanovich, 1976.

Clive, Alan. *State of War: Michigan in World War II*. Ann Arbor: University of Michigan Press, 1979.

Ehrenberg, Lewis A., and Susan E. Hirsch, eds. *The War in American Culture: Society and Consciousness during World War II*. New York: Harcourt Brace Jovanovich, 1976.

Goodwin, Doris Kearns. *No Ordinary Time: Franklin and Eleanor Roosevelt: The Home Front in World War II*. New York: Simon & Schuster, 1994.

Harris, Mark J., Franklin D. Mitchell, and Steven J. Schechter, eds. *The Home Front: America during World War II*. New York: G. P. Putnam, 1984.

Jeffries, John W. *Wartime America: The World War II Home Front*. Chicago: Ivan R. Dee, 1996.

Johnson, Marilynn S. *The Second Gold Rush: Oakland and the East Bay in World War II*. Berkeley: University of California Press, 1993.

Koistinen, Paul A. C. *Arsenal of World War II: The Political Economy of American Warfare, 1940–1945*. Lawrence: University Press of Kansas, 2004.

Lingeman, Richard R. *Don't You Know There's a War On? The American Home Front, 1941–1945*. New York: G. P. Putnam's Sons, 1970.

McMillen, Neil R., ed. *Remaking Dixie: The Impact of World War II on the American South*. Jackson: University of Mississippi Press, 1997.

Mettler, Suzanne. *Soldiers to Citizens: The G.I. Bill and the Making of the Greatest Generation*. New York: Oxford University Press, 2005.

Norrell, Robert J. *Dixie's War: The South and World War II*. Tuscaloosa: University of Alabama Press, 1992.

O'Neill, William L. *A Democracy at War: America's Fight at Home and Abroad in World War II*. New York: Free Press, 1993.

Perrett, Geoffrey. *Days of Sadness, Years of Triumph: The American People, 1939–1945*. Madison: University of Wisconsin Press, 1973.

Polenberg, Richard D. *War and Society: The United States, 1941–1945*. Philadelphia and New York: J. B. Lippincott & Co., 1972.

Reynolds, Clark G. *America at War, 1941–1945: The Home Front*. New York: Random House, 1995.

Ross, Davis R. B. *Preparing for Ulysses: Politics and Veterans during World War II*. New York: Columbia University Press, 1969.

Sparrow, Bartholomew H. *From the Outside In: World War II and the American State*. Princeton, N.J.: Princeton University Press, 1996.

Terkel, Studs. *"The Good War": An Oral History of World War Two*. New York: Pantheon Books, 1984.

Winkler, Alan M. *Home Front, U.S.A.: America during World War II*. Arlington Heights, Ill.: Harlan Davidson, 2000.

——. *The Politics of Propaganda: The Office of War Information, 1942–1945*. New Haven, Conn.: Yale University Press, 1978.

X. HARRY S. TRUMAN, THE FAIR DEAL, AND MCCARTHYISM

Bayley, Edwin R. *Joe McCarthy and the Press*. New York: Pantheon Books, 1982.

Belknap, Michael R. *Cold War Political Justice: The Smith Act, the Communist Party, and American Civil Liberties*. Westport, Conn.: Greenwood Press, 1977.

Bennett, David H. *The Party of Fear: From Nativist Movements to the New Right in American History*. Chapel Hill: University of North Carolina Press, 1988.

Bentley, Eric, ed. *Thirty Years of Treason: Excerpts from Hearings before the House Committee on Un-American Activities, 1938–1968*. New York: Viking Press, 1971.

Berman, William C. *The Politics of Civil Rights in the Truman Administration*. Columbus: Ohio State University Press, 1970.

Carleton, Don E. *Red Scare: Right-Wing Hysteria, Fifties Fanaticisms, and Their Legacy in Texas*. Austin: Texas Monthly Press, 1985.

Caute, David. *The Great Fear: The Anti-Communist Purge under Truman and Eisenhower*. New York: Simon & Schuster, 1978.

Ceplair, Larry, and Stephen Englund. *The Inquisition in Hollywood*. Garden City, N.Y.: Anchor Books, 1980.

Chambers, Whittaker. *Witness*. Chicago: Henry Regnery, 1952.

Crosby, Donald F. *God, Church, and Flag: Senator Joseph R. McCarthy and the Catholic Church, 1950–1957*. Chapel Hill: University of North Carolina Press, 1978.

Davis, David Brion. *The Fear of Conspiracy*. Ithaca, N.Y.: Cornell University Press, 1971.

Donaldson, Gary A. *Truman Defeats Dewey*. Lexington: University Press of Kentucky, 1999.

Donovan, Robert J. *Conflict and Crisis: The Presidency of Harry S. Truman, 1945–1948*. New York: Norton, 1977.

——.*Tumultuous Years: The Presidency of Harry S. Truman*. New York: Norton, 1982.

Fariello, Griffin. *Red Scare: Memories of the American Inquisition, an Oral History*. New York: Avon Books, 1995.

Faulk, John Henry. *Fear on Trial*. New York: Simon & Schuster, 1964.

Ferrell, Robert H. *Harry S. Truman: A Life*. Columbia: University of Missouri Press, 1994.

——. *Harry S. Truman and the Modern Presidency*. Columbia: University of Missouri Press, 1983.

——. *Truman and Pendergast*. Columbia: University of Missouri Press, 1999.

——, ed. *The Autobiography of Harry S. Truman*. Boulder, Colo.: Associated University Presses, 1980.

Freeland, Richard M. *The Truman Doctrine and the Origins of McCarthyism.* New York: Alfred A. Knopf, 1972.

Fried, Albert. *McCarthyism, the Great American Red Scare: A Documentary History.* New York: Oxford University Press, 1997.

Fried, Richard M. *Men against McCarthy.* New York: Columbia University Press, 1976.

——. *Nightmare in Red: The McCarthy Era in Perspective.* New York: Oxford University Press, 1990.

Goldstein, Robert J. *Political Repression in Modern America.* Cambridge, Mass.: Schenkman Books, 1978.

Goodman, Walter. *The Committee: The Extraordinary Career of the House Committee on Un-American Activities.* New York: Farrar, Straus & Giroux, 1968.

Griffith, Robert. *The Politics of Fear: Joseph R. McCarthy and the Senate.* Amherst: University of Massachusetts Press, 1987.

Griffith, Robert, and Athan Theoharis, eds. *The Specter: Original Essays on the Cold War and the Origins of McCarthyism.* New York: Franklin Watts, 1974.

Guttmann, Allen, and Benjamin Munn Ziegler, eds. *Communism, the Courts, and the Constitution.* Lexington, Mass.: D. C. Heath, 1964.

Hamby, Alonzo L. *Beyond the New Deal: Harry S. Truman and American Liberalism.* New York: Columbia University Press, 1973.

——. *A Man of the People: A Life of Harry S. Truman.* New York: Oxford University Press, 1995.

Hartmann, Susan E. *Truman and the 80th Congress.* Columbia: University of Missouri Press, 1971.

Heale, Michael J. *American Anticommunism: Combatting the Enemy Within, 1830–1970.* Baltimore: Johns Hopkins University Press, 1990.

Heller, Francis H., ed. *Economics and the Truman Administration.* Lawrence: Kansas University Press, 1981

——. *The Truman White House: The Administration of the Presidency, 1945–1953.* Lawrence: Kansas University Press, 1980.

Hofstadter, Richard. *Anti-Intellectualism in American Life.* New York: Alfred A. Knopf, 1970.

——. *The Paranoid Style in American Politics and Other Essays.* New York: Vintage Books, 1965.

Holmes, David. *Stalking the Academic Communist.* Hanover, N.H.: University Press of New England, 1989.

Hoover, J. Edgar. *Masters of Deceit: The Story of Communism in America and How to Fight It.* New York: Holt, Rinehart & Winston, 1958.

Howe, Irving, and Lewis A. Coser. *The American Communist Party: A Critical History*. Boston: Beacon Press, 1957.

Jeffreys-Jones, Rhodri. *The FBI: A History*. New Haven and London: Yale University Press, 2007.

Kutler, Stanley I. *The American Inquisition: Justice and Injustice in the Cold War*. New York: Hill & Wang, 1982.

Lacey, M. J., ed. *The Truman Presidency*. Cambridge: Cambridge University Press, 1989.

Martin, John Bartlow. *Adlai Stevenson and the World: The Life of Adlai E. Stevenson*. Garden City, N.Y.: Doubleday, 1976.

Matusow, Allen J., ed. *Joseph R. McCarthy*. Englewood Cliffs, N.J.: Prentice Hall, 1970.

McCoy, Donald R. *The Presidency of Harry S. Truman*. Lawrence: University Press of Kansas, 1984.

McCullough, David. *Truman*. New York: Simon & Schuster, 1992.

McKeever, Porter. *Adlai Stevenson*. New York: William Morrow, 1988.

Miles, Michael. *The Odyssey of the American Right*. New York: Oxford University Press, 1980.

Miller, Merle. *Plain Speaking: An Oral Biography of Harry S. Truman*. New York: Berkley Publishing, 1973.

Muller, Herbert J. *Adlai Stevenson: A Study in Values*. New York: Harper & Row, 1967.

O'Reilly, Kenneth. *Hoover and the Un-Americans*. Philadelphia: Temple University Press, 1988.

Oshinsky, David M. *A Conspiracy So Immense: The World of Joe McCarthy*. New York: Free Press, 1983.

Pemberton, William E. *Harry S. Truman: Fair Dealer and Cold Warrior*. Boston: Twayne Publishers, 1989.

Pessen, Edward. *Losing Our Souls: The American Experience in the Cold War*. Chicago: Ivan R. Dee, 1993.

Phillips, Cabell. *The Truman Presidency: The History of a Triumphant Succession*. New York: Macmillan, 1966.

Powers, Richard Gid. *Secrecy and Power: The Life of J. Edgar Hoover*. New York: Free Press, 1987.

Radosh, Ronald, and Joyce Milton. *The Rosenberg File: A Search for the Truth*. New York: Vintage Books, 1984.

Reeves, Thomas C. *The Life and Times of Joe McCarthy: A Biography*. New York: Stein & Day, 1982.

Rogin, Michael P. *McCarthy and the Intellectuals: The Radical Specter*. Cambridge, Mass.: MIT Press, 1967.

Rovere, Richard H. *Senator Joe McCarthy*. New York: Harcourt, Brace, 1959.

Schlesinger, Arthur M. Jr. *The Vital Center: The Politics of Freedom*. Boston: Houghton Mifflin, 1949.

Schrecker, Ellen W. *The Age of McCarthyism: A Brief History with Documents*. New York: St. Martin's Press, 1994.

——. *No Ivory Tower: McCarthyism and the Universities*. New York: Oxford University Press, 1986.

Selcraig, James Truett. *The Red Scare in the Middle West, 1945–1951*. Ann Arbor: University of Michigan Press, 1982.

Shils, Edward A. *The Torment of Secrecy: The Background and Consequences of American Security Policies*. New York: Free Press, 1956.

Smith, Richard Norton. *Thomas E. Dewey and His Times*. New York: Simon & Schuster, 1982.

Steel, Ronald. *Walter Lippmann and the American Century*. Boston: Little, Brown, 1980.

Steinberg, Peter L. *The Great "Red Menace": United States Prosecution of American Communists, 1947–1952*. Westport, Conn.: Greenwood Press, 1984.

Stern, Philip M. *The Oppenheimer Case: Security on Trial*. New York: Harper & Row, 1969.

Stone, I. F. *The Truman Era*. New York: Monthly Review Press, 1953.

Theoharis, Athan G. *Seeds of Repression: Harry S. Truman and the Origins of McCarthyism*. New York: Times Books, 1971.

Theoharis, Athan G., and John Stuart Cox. *The Boss: J. Edgar Hoover and the Great American Inquisition*. Philadelphia: Temple University Press, 1988.

Truman, Harry S. *Memoirs*. 2 vols. Garden City, N.Y.: Doubleday, 1955, 1956.

——. *Mr. Citizen*. New York: Bernard Geis Associates, 1960.

Truman, Margaret. *Bess W. Truman*. New York: Macmillan, 1986.

——. *Harry S. Truman*. New York: William Morrow & Co., 1973.

Wechsler, James A. *The Age of Suspicion*. New York: Random House, 1953.

Weinstein, Allen. *Perjury: The Hiss-Chambers Case*. New York: Alfred A. Knopf, 1978.

XI. POSTWAR FOREIGN RELATIONS, THE COLD WAR, AND KOREA

Acheson, Dean. *Present at the Creation: My Years in the State Department*. New York: Norton, 1969.

Anderson, Terry H. *The United States, Great Britain, and the Cold War, 1944–1947*. Columbia: University of Missouri Press, 1981.

Boyle, Peter G. *American-Soviet Relations: From the Russian Revolution to the Fall of Communism*. London: Routledge, 1994.

Kaufman, Burton I. *The Korean War: Challenges in Crisis, Credibility, and Command*. 2nd ed. New York : McGraw-Hill, 1997.

Cha, Victor D. *Alignment Despite Antagonism: The United States-Korea-Japan Security Triangle*. Stanford, Calif.: Stanford University Press, 1999.

Clemens, Diane Shaver. *Yalta*. New York: Oxford University Press, 1970.

Crockatt, Richard. *The Fifty Years War: The United States and the Soviet Union in World Politics, 1941–1991*. New York: Routledge, 1995.

Cumings, Bruce. *The Origins of the Korean War*. 2 vols. Princeton, N.J.: Princeton University Press, 1981, 1990.

Dilloway, James. *From Cold War to Chaos? Reviving Humane Development or Remaking Market Man*. Westport, Conn.: Praeger, 1999.

Evangelista, Matthew. *Unarmed Forces: The Transnational Movement to End the Cold War*. Ithaca, N.Y.: Cornell University Press, 1999.

Feis, Herbert. *From Trust to Terror: The Onset of the Cold War*. New York: Norton, 1970.

Fisher, Benjamin F., ed. *At Cold War's End: U.S. Intelligence on the Soviet Union and Eastern Europe, 1989–1991*. Reston, Va.: Central Intelligence Agency, 1999.

Foot, Dorothy. *The Wrong War: American Policy and the Dimensions of the Korean Conflict, 1950–1953*. Ithaca, N.Y.: Cornell University Press, 1985.

Friedman, Norman. *The Fifty-Year War: Conflict and Strategy in the Cold War*. Annapolis, Md.: Naval Institute Press, 2000.

Gaddis, John Lewis. *The Cold War: A New History*. New York: Penguin Press, 2005.

——. *Long Peace: Inquiries into the History of the Cold War*. New York: Oxford University Press, 1987.

——. *Russia, the Soviet Union, and the United States: An Interpretative History*. 2nd ed. New York: McGraw-Hill, 1990.

——. *Strategies of Containment: A Critical Appraisal of Postwar American National Security Policy*. New York: Oxford University Press, 1982.

——. *We Now Know: Rethinking Cold War History*. New York: Oxford University Press, 1997.

——, ed. *Cold War Statesmen Confront the Bomb: Nuclear Diplomacy since 1945*. New York: Oxford University Press, 1999.

Gardner, Lloyd. *Architects of Illusion*. New York: Random House, 1968.

Gillon, Steven M. *Politics and Vision: The ADA and American Liberalism, 1947–1985*. New York: Oxford University Press, 1987.

Harbutt, Fraser J. *The Iron Curtain: Churchill, America, and the Origins of the Cold War*. Oxford: Oxford University Press, 1986.

Hastings, Max. *The Korean War*. New York: Simon & Schuster, 1987.

Heller, Francis E. *The Korean War: A Twenty-Five-Year Perspective*. Lawrence: Kansas University Press, 1977.

Hogan, Michael. *The Marshall Plan*. New York: Cambridge University Press, 1987.

Isaacson, Walter, and Evan Thomas. *The Wise Men: Six Friends and the World They Made: Acheson, Bohlen, Harriman, Kennan, Lovett, and McCloy*. New York: Simon & Schuster, 1986.

Jenkins, Philip. *The Cold War at Home: The Red Scare in Pennsylvania, 1945–1960*. Chapel Hill: University of North Carolina Press, 1999.

Jian, Chen. *China's Road to the Korean War: The Making of the Sino-American Confrontation*. New York: Columbia University Press, 2004.

Johnson, Robert David. *Congress and the Cold War*. Cambridge: Cambridge University Press, 2005.

Karabell, Zachary. *Architects of Intervention: The United States, the Third World, and the Cold War, 1946–1962*. Baton Rouge: Louisiana State University Press, 1999.

Kennan, George F. *Memoirs, 1925–1950*. Boston: Little, Brown, 1967.

Kirkendall, Richard S. *Harry S. Truman, Korea, and the Imperial Presidency*. St. Charles, Miss.: Forum Press, 1975.

Kramer, Hilton. *The Twilight of the Intellectuals: Culture and Politics in the Era of the Cold War*. Chicago: Ivan R. Dee, 1999.

LaFeber, Walter. *America, Russia, and the Cold War, 1945–1992*. 8th ed. New York: McGraw-Hill, 1997.

Lee, Steven Hugh. *The Korean War*. Harlow, England: Pearson Education, 2001.

Leffler, Melvyn. *A Preponderance of Power: National Security, the Truman Administration, and the Cold War*. Stanford, Calif.: Stanford University Press, 1992.

Levering, Ralph, Vladamir Pechatnov, Verena Botzenhart-Viehe, and C. Earl Edmondson. *Debating the Origins of the Cold War*. Baltimore, Md.: Rowman & Littlefield, 2001.

Lucas, Scott. *Freedom's War: The American Crusade against the Soviet Union*. New York: New York University Press, 1999.

MacQueen, Norrie. *The United Nations since 1945: Peacekeeping and the Cold War*. New York: Addison Wesley Longman, 1999.

McNeill, William H. *America, Britain, and Russia: Their Co-operation and Conflict, 1941–1946*. New York: Oxford University Press, 1953.

Millett, Allan R. *The War for Korea, 1945–1950: A House Burning*. Lawrence: University Press of Kansas, 2005.

Miscamble, Wilson D. *From Roosevelt to Truman: Potsdam, Hiroshima, and the Cold War*. Cambridge: Cambridge University Press, 2006.

Mitrovich, Gregory. *Undermining the Kremlin: America's Strategy to Subvert the Soviet Bloc, 1947–1956*. Ithaca, N.Y.: Cornell University Press, 2000.

Nagai, Yonosuke, and Akira Iriye, eds. *The Origins of the Cold War in Asia*. New York: Columbia University Press, 1977.

Ninkovich, Frank. *The Diplomacy of Ideas: U.S. Foreign Policy and Cultural Relations, 1938–1950*. New York: Cambridge University Press, 1980.

———. *Germany and the United States: The Transformation of the German Question since 1945*. Boston: Twayne Publishers, 1988.

Nolan, Janne E. *An Elusive Consensus: Nuclear Weapons and American Security after the Cold War*. Washington, D.C.: Brookings Institution Press, 1999.

Painter, David S., and Melvyn Leffler, eds. *The Origins of the Cold War: An International History*. London: Routledge, 2005.

Paterson, Thomas G. *On Every Front: The Making and Unmaking of the Cold War*. New York: W. W. Norton, 1992.

Paterson, Thomas G., and Robert J. McMahon, eds. *The Origins of the Cold War*. Lexington, Ky.: Heath, 1991.

Pierpaoli, Paul G. Jr. *Truman and Korea: The Political Culture of the Early Cold War*. Columbia: University of Missouri Press, 1999.

Powaski, Ronald E. *The Cold War: The United States and the Soviet Union, 1917–1991*. New York: Oxford University Press, 1998.

Prevots, Naima. *Dance for Export: Cultural Diplomacy and the Cold War*. Middletown, Conn.: Wesleyan University Press, 1998.

Roberts, Geoffrey K. *The Soviet Union in World Politics: Coexistence, Revolution, and Cold War, 1945–1991*. New York: Routledge, 1999.

Schaller, Michael. *The American Occupation of Japan: The Origins of the Cold War in Asia*. New York: Oxford University Press, 1985.

Schonberger, Howard B. *Aftermath of War: Americans and the Remaking of Japan, 1945–1952*. Kent, Ohio: Kent State University Press, 1989.

Sibley, Katherine A. S. *The Cold War*. Westport, Conn.: Greenwood Press, 1998.

Smith, Bradley F. *The Shadow Warriors: O.S.S. and the Origins of the C.I.A.* New York: Basic Books, 1983.

Smith, Joseph. *The Cold War, 1945–1991*. Oxford: Blackwell, 1998.

Snetsinger, John. *Truman, the Jewish Vote, and the Creation of Israel*. Stanford, Calif.: Hoover Institution, 1974.

Spanier, John W. *The Truman-MacArthur Controversy and the Korean War*. Cambridge, Mass.: Belknap Press, 1959.

Trachtenberg, Marc. *A Constructed Peace: The Making of the European Settlement, 1945–1963*. Princeton, N.J.: Princeton University Press, 1999.

Troy, Thomas F. *Donovan and the CIA: A History of the Establishment of the Central Intelligence Agency*. Frederick, Md.: University Publications of America, 1981.

Ulam, Adam B. *Expansion and Coexistence: Soviet Foreign Policy, 1917–1973*. New York: Praeger, 1988.

Westad, Odd Arne. *Cold War and Revolution: Soviet-American Rivalry and the Origins of the Chinese Civil War, 1944–1946*. New York: Columbia University Press, 1993.

Westad, Odd Arne, ed. *Reviewing the Cold War: Approaches, Interpretations, Theory*. London: Frank Cass, 2000.

Williams, William Appleman. *The Tragedy of American Diplomacy*. New York: Dell, 1972.

Yergin, Daniel. *Shattered Peace: The Origins of the Cold War and the National Security State*. Boston: Houghton Mifflin, 1977.

XII. AFRICAN AMERICANS

Anderson, Jervis. *A. Philip Randolph: A Biographical Portrait*. New York: Harcourt Brace Jovanovich, 1973.

Ball, Howard. *A Defiant Life: Thurgood Marshall and the Persistence of Racism in America*. New York: Crown, 1998.

Bates, Beth Tompkins. *Pullman Porters and the Rise of Protest Politics in Black America, 1925–1945*. Chapel Hill: University of North Carolina Press, 2001.

Berg, Manfred. *"Ticket to Freedom": The NAACP and the Struggle for Black Political Integration*. Gainesville: University Press of Florida, 2005.

Berman, William C. *The Politics of Civil Rights in the Truman Administration*. Columbus: Ohio State University Press, 1970.

Borstelmann, Thomas. *The Cold War and the Color Line: American Race Relations in the Global Arena*. Cambridge, Mass.: Harvard University Press, 2001.

Brandt, Nat. *Harlem at War: The Black Experience in World War II*. Syracuse, N.Y.: Syracuse University Press, 1996.

Buchanan, A. Russell. *Black Americans in World War II*. Santa Barbara, Calif.: Clio Books, 1977.

Buckley, Gail L. *American Patriots: The Story of Blacks in the Military from the Revolution to Desert Storm*. New York: Random House, 2001.

Bunche, Ralph. *The Political Status of the Negro in the Age of FDR.* Chicago: University of Chicago Press, 1973.

Cole, Olen. *The African-American Experience in the Civilian Conservation Corps.* Gainesville: University Press of Florida, 1999.

Dalfiume, Richard M. *Fighting on Two Fronts: Desegregation of the U.S. Armed Forces, 1939–1953.* Columbia: University of Missouri Press, 1969.

Dudziak, Mary L. *Cold War Civil Rights: Race and the Image of American Democracy.* Princeton, N.J.: Princeton University Press, 2000.

Egerton, John. *Speak Now against the Day: The Generation before the Civil Rights Movement in the South.* New York: Alfred A. Knopf, 1994.

Fairclough, Adam. *Race and Democracy: The Civil Rights Struggle in Louisiana, 1915–1972.* Athens: University of Georgia Press, 1995.

Gardner, Michael R. *Harry Truman and Civil Rights: Moral Courage and Political Risks.* Carbondale, Ill.: Southern Illinois University Press, 2002.

Greenberg, Cheryl Lynn. *"Or Does It Explode?" : Black Harlem in the Great Depression.* New York: Oxford University Press, 1991.

Hall, Jacquelyn Dowd. *Revolt against Chivalry: Jessie Daniel Ames and the Women's Campaign against Lynching.* New York: Columbia University Press, 1979.

Hill, Robert A., ed. *The FBI's RACON: Racial Conditions in the United States during World War II.* Boston: Northeastern University Press, 1995.

Honey, Maureen, ed. *Bitter Fruit: African American Women during World War II.* Columbia: University of Missouri Press, 1999.

Janken, Kenneth Robert. *White: The Biography of Walter White, Mr. NAACP.* New York: New Press, 2003.

Jonas, Gilbert. *Freedom's Sword: The NAACP and the Struggle against Racism in America, 1909–1969.* New York and London: Routledge, 2007.

Kelley, Robin D. G. *Hammer and Hoe: Alabama Communists during the Great Depression.* Chapel Hill: University of North Carolina Press, 1990.

Kirby, John B. *Black Americans in the Roosevelt Era: Liberalism and Race.* Knoxville: University of Tennessee Press, 1980.

Klinkner, Philip A., with Rogers M. Smith. *The Unsteady March: The Rise and Decline of Racial Equality in America.* Chicago: University of Chicago Press, 1999.

Kryder, Daniel. *Divided Arsenal: Race and the American State during World War II.* Cambridge: Cambridge University Press, 2000.

Lee, Ulysses G. *The Employment of Negro Troops.* Washington, D.C.: Government Printing Office, 1966.

McRae, Donald. *In Black and White: The Untold Story of Joe Louis and Jesse Owens.* London: Scribner, 2003.

Meier, August, and Elliott Rudwick. *CORE: A Study in the Civil Rights Movement, 1942–1968*. New York: Oxford University Press, 1973.

Moore, Christopher P. *Fighting for America: Black Soldiers, the Unsung Heroes of World War II*. New York: One World, 2004.

Morris, Aldon D. *The Origins of the Civil Rights Movement: Black Communities Organizing for Change*. New York: Free Press, 1984.

Motley, Mary Penick, ed. *The Invisible Soldier: The Experience of the Black Soldier in World War II*. Detroit: Wayne State University Press, 1975.

Myrdal, Gunnar. *An American Dilemma: The Negro Problem and Modern Democracy*. New York: Harper, 1944.

Naison, Mark. *Communists in Harlem during the Depression*. Urbana: University of Illinois Press, 1983.

Nalty, Bernard C. *Strength for the Fight: A History of Black Americans in the Military*. New York and London: Free Press, 1986.

Norrell, Robert J. *The House I Live In: Race in the American Century*. New York: Oxford University Press, 2005.

Pfeffer, Paula P. *A. Philip Randolph, Pioneer of the Civil Rights Movement*. Baton Rouge: Louisiana State University Press, 1990.

Plummer, Brenda Gayle. *Rising Wind: Black Americans and U.S Foreign Affairs, 1935–1960*. Chapel Hill: University of North Carolina Press, 1995.

Putney, Martha S. *When the Nation Was in Need: Blacks in the Women's Army Corps during World War II*. Metuchen, N.H.: Scarecrow Press, 1992.

Record, Wilson. *Race and Radicalism: The NAACP and the Communist Party in Conflict*. Ithaca, N.Y.: Cornell University Press, 1964.

Reed, Merl E. *Seedtime for the Modern Civil Rights Movement: The President's Committee on Fair Employment Practice, 1941–1946*. Baton Rouge: University of Louisiana Press, 1991.

Sandler, Stanley. *Segregated Skies: All-Black Combat Squadrons of WWII*. Washington, D.C.: Smithsonian Institution Press, 1992.

Scott, Lawrence P., and William M. Womack, Sr. *Double V: The Civil Rights Struggle of the Tuskegee Airmen*. East Lansing: Michigan State University Press, 1994

Sitkoff, Harvard. *A New Deal for Blacks: The Emergence of Civil Rights as a National Issue, Volume I: The Depression Decade*. New York: Oxford University Press, 1978.

Smith, Graham. *When Jim Crow Met John Bull: Black American Soldiers in World War II Britain*. London: Tauris, 1987.

Sosna, Morton. *In Search of the Silent South: Southern Liberals and the Race Issue*. New York: Columbia University Press, 1977.

Sternsher, Bernard, ed. *The Negro in Depression and War: Prelude to Revolution, 1930–1945*. Chicago: Quadrangle Books, 1969.

Sugrue, Thomas J. *The Origins of the Urban Crisis: Race and Inequality in Postwar Detroit.* Princeton, N.J.: Princeton University Press, 1996.

Sullivan, Patricia. *Days of Hope: Race and Democracy in the New Deal Era.* Chapel Hill: University of North Carolina Press, 1996.

Tushnet, Mark V. *The NAACP's Legal Strategy against Segregated Education, 1925–1950.* Chapel Hill: University of North Carolina Press, 1987.

Weiss, Nancy J. *Farewell to the Party of Lincoln: Black Politics in the Age of FDR.* Princeton, N.J.: Princeton University Press, 1983.

White, Walter. *A Man Called White: The Autobiography of Walter White.* London: Victor Gollancz, 1949.

Wolters, Raymond. *Negroes and the Great Depression: The Problem of Economic Recovery.* Westport, Conn.: Greenwood Publishing, 1970.

Wynn, Neil A. *The Afro-American and the Second World War.* New York: Holmes & Meier, 1993.

Zangrando, Robert L. *The NAACP Crusade against Lynching, 1909–1950.* Philadelphia: Temple University Press, 1980.

XIII. JAPANESE AMERICANS, HISPANICS, AND OTHER MINORITIES

Acu a, Rodolfo. *Occupied America: A History of Chicanos.* New York: Harper & Row, 2000.

Bernstein, Alison R. *American Indians and World War II: Toward a New Era in Indian Affairs.* Norman: University of Oklahoma Press, 1991.

Bérubé, Allan. *Coming Out under Fire: The History of Gay Men and Women in World War II.* New York: Free Press, 1990.

Bixler, Margaret T. *Winds of Freedom: The Story of the Navajo Code Talkers of World War II.* Darien, Conn.: Two Bytes Publishing, 1992.

Collier, John. *Indians of the Americas.* New York: Signet, 1947.

Daniels, Roger. *Concentration Camps USA: Japanese Americans and World War II.* Malabar, Fla.: Krieger, 1993.

Daniels, Roger, Sandra C. Taylor, and Harry H. L. Kitano, eds. *Japanese Americans, from Relocation to Redress.* Seattle: University of Washington Press, 1991.

Franco, Jere Bishop. *Crossing the Pond: The Native American Effort in World War II.* Denton: University of North Texas Press, 1999.

Galarza, Ernesto. *Barrio Boy.* South Bend, Ind.: Notre Dame University Press, 1971.

———. *Farm Workers and Agri-Business in California, 1947–1960.* South Bend, Ind.: Notre Dame University Press, 1977.

———. *Merchants of Labor: The Mexican Bracero Story*. Santa Barbara, Calif.: McNally-Loftin, 1964.

Gamboa, Erasmo. *Mexican Labor and World War II: Braceros in the Pacific Northwest, 1942–1947*. Austin: University of Texas Press, 1990.

Gann, L. H., and Peter J. Duigan. *The Hispanics in the United States: A History*. Boulder, Colo.: Westview Press, 1986.

García, Mario T. *Mexican-Americans: Leadership, Ideology, and Identity, 1930–1960*. New Haven, Conn.: Yale University Press, 1989.

Girdner, Audrie. *The Great Betrayal: The Evacuation of the Japanese-Americans during World War II*. New York: Macmillan, 1969.

Hauptman, Laurence M. *The Iroquois and the New Deal*. Syracuse, N.Y.: Syracuse University Press, 1981.

Hayashi, Brian Masaru. *Democratizing the Enemy: The Japanese American Internment*. Princeton, N.Y.: Princeton University Press, 2004.

Hoffman, Abraham. *Unwanted Mexican Americans: Repatriation Pressures during the Great Depression*. Tucson: University of Arizona Press, 1973.

Irons, Peter H. *Justice at War: The Story of the Japanese-American Internment Cases*. New York: Oxford University Press, 1983.

———, ed. *Justice Delayed: The Record of the Japanese American Internment Cases*. Middleton, Conn.: Wesleyan University Press, 1989

Kawano, Kenji. *Warriors: Navajo Code Talkers*. Flagstaff, Ariz.: Northland Publishing, 1990.

Kitanto, Harry H. L., and Roger Daniels. *Asian Americans: Emerging Minorities*. Upper Saddle River, N.J.: Prentice Hall, 2001.

Meier, Matt S., and Feliciano Rivera. *The Chicanos: A History of Mexican Americans*. New York: Hill & Wang, 1972.

Moore, Joan W., and Harry Pachon. *Hispanics in the United States*. Englewood Cliffs, N.J.: Prentice Hall, 1985.

Myer, Dillon S. *Uprooted Americans: The Japanese Americans and the War Relocation Authority during World War II*. Tucson: University of Arizona Press, 1971.

Okihiro, Gary Y. *Whispered Silences: Japanese Americans and World War II*. Seattle: University of Washington Press, 1996.

Parman, Donald I. *The Navajos and the New Deal*. New Haven, Conn.: Yale University Press, 1976.

Philip, Kenneth R. *John Collier's Crusade for Indian Reform, 1920–1954*. Tucson: University of Arizona Press, 1977.

Reisler, Mark. *By the Sweat of Their Brow: Mexican Immigrant Labor in the United States, 1900–1940*. Westport, Conn.: Greenwood Press, 1976.

Rivas-Rodriguez, Maggie, ed. *Mexican Americans and World War II*. Austin: University of Texas Press, 2005.

Robinson, Greg. *By Order of the President: FDR and the Internment of Japanese Americans.* Cambridge, Mass.: Harvard University Press, 2001.

Sanchez, George J. *Becoming Mexican-American: Ethnicity, Culture, and Identity in Chicano Los Angeles, 1900–1945.* New York: Oxford University Press, 1995.

Servin, Manuel, ed. *The Mexican Americans: An Awakening Minority.* Beverly Hills, Calif.: Glencoe Press, 1970.

Taylor, Graham D. *The New Deal and American Indian Tribalism: The Administration of the Indian Reorganization Act, 1934–1945.* Lincoln: University of Nebraska Press, 1980.

Weglyn, Michi N. *Years of Infamy: The Untold story of America's Concentration Camps.* Seattle: University of Washington Press, 1976.

Yoo, David. *Growing up Nisei: Race, Generation, and Culture among Japanese Americans of California, 1924–1949.* Urbana: University of Illinois Press, 2000.

XIV. LABOR MOVEMENTS

Atleson, James B. *Labor and the Wartime State: Labor Relations and Law during World War II.* Urbana: University of Illinois Press, 1998.

Auerbacj, Jerold S. *Labor and Liberty: The La Follette Committee and the New Deal.* Indianapolis: Bobbs-Merrill, 1966.

Barnard, John. *Walter Reuther and the Rise of the Auto Workers.* Boston: Little, Brown, 1983.

Bernstein, Irving. *A Caring Society: The New Deal, the Worker, and the Great Depression.* Boston: Houghton Mifflin, 1985.

——. *The Turbulent Years: A History of the American Worker, 1933–1941.* Boston: Houghton Mifflin, 1969.

Brody, David. *Workers in Industrial America: Essays on the 20th-Century Struggle.* New York: Oxford University Press, 1993.

Cherny, Robert W., William Issel, and Kieran Walsh Taylor, eds. *American Labor and the Cold War: Grassroots Politics and Postwar Popular Culture.* New Brunswick, N.J.: Rutgers University Press, 2004.

Cochran, Bert. *Labor and Communism: The Conflict That Shaped American Unions.* Princeton, N.J: Princeton University Press, 1977.

Cohen, Lizbeth. *Making a New Deal: Industrial Workers in Chicago, 1919–1939.* Chicago: University of Chicago Press, 1990.

Dubofsky, Melvyn, and John Van Tine. *John L. Lewis: A Biography.* New York: Quadrangle, 1977.

Fones-Wolf, Elizabeth A. *Selling Free Enterprise: The Business Assault on Labor and Liberalism, 1945–1960*. Urbana: University of Illinois Press, 1994.

Freeman, Joshua B. *Working-Class New York: Life and Labor since World War II*. New York: New Press, 2000.

Gordon, Colin. *New Deals: Business, Labor, and Politics in America, 1920–1935*. New York: Cambridge University Press, 1994.

Harris, Howell John. *The Right to Manage: Industrial Relations Policies of American Business in the 1940s*. Madison: University of Wisconsin Press, 1982.

Kersten, Andrew E. *Labor's Homefront: The American Federation of Labor during World War II*. New York: New York University Press, 2006.

Levenstein, Harvey A. *Communism, Anti-Communism, and the CIO*. Westport, Conn.: Greenwood Press, 1981.

Lichtenstein, Nelson N. *Labor's War at Home: The CIO in World War II*. Cambridge: Cambridge University Press, 1982.

———. *The Most Dangerous Man in Detroit: Walter Reuther and the Fate of American Labor*. New York: Basic Books, 1995.

Lipsitz, George. *A Rainbow at Midnight: Labor and Culture in the 1940s*. Champaign: University of Illinois Press, 1994.

McClure, Arthur F. *The Truman Administration and Problems of Postwar Labor, 1945–1948*. Rutherford, N.J.: Fairleigh Dickinson University Press, 1969.

Montgomery, David. *Workers Control in America: Studies in the History of Work, Technology, and Labor Struggles*. Cambridge: Cambridge University Press, 1979.

Nelson, Bruce. *Divided We Stand: American Workers and the Struggle for Black Equality*. Princeton, N.J.: Princeton University Press, 2001.

Schatz, Ronald W. *The Electrical Workers: A History of Labor at General Electric and Westinghouse, 1923–1960*. Urbana: University of Illinois Press, 1983.

Vittoz, Stanley. *New Deal Labor Policy and the American Industrial Economy*. Chapel Hill: University of North Carolina Press, 1987.

Zieger, Robert H. *American Workers, American Unions, 1920–1945*. Baltimore: Johns Hopkins University Press, 1985.

———. *The CIO, 1935–1955*. Chapel Hill: University of North Carolina Press, 1995.

XV. WOMEN

Anderson, Karen. *Wartime Women: Sex Roles, Family Relations, and the Status of Women During World War II*. Westport, Conn.: Greenwood Press, 1981.

Blackwelder, Julia Kirk. *Women of the Depression: Caste and Culture in San Antonio, 1929–1939*. Austin: Texas A&M University Press, 1998.

Campbell, D'Ann. *Women at War with America: Private Lives in a Patriotic Age*. Cambridge, Mass.: Harvard University Press, 1984.

Chafe, William H. *The Paradox of Change: American Women in the 20th Century*. New York and Oxford: Oxford University Press, 1991.

Degler, Carl N. *At Odds: Women and the Family in America from the Revolution to the Present*. New York and Oxford: Oxford University Press, 1980.

Friedan, Betty. *The Feminine Mystique*. New York: W. W. Norton, 1963.

Gluck, Sherna Berger. *Rosie the Riveter Revisited: Women, the War, and Social Change*. Boston: Twayne Publishers, 1981.

Hartmann, Susan M. *The Home Front and Beyond: American Women in the 1940s*. Boston: Twayne Publishers, 1982.

Holm, Jeanne M., ed. *In Defense of a Nation: Servicewomen in World War II*. Arlington, Va.: Vandamere Press, 1998.

Honey, Maureen. *Bitter Fruit: African American Women in World War II*. Columbia: University of Missouri Press, 1999.

Kaledin, Eugenia. *Mothers and More: American Women in the 1950s*. Boston: Twayne Publishers, 1984.

Kessler-Harris, Alice. *Out to Work: A History of Wage-Earning Women in the United States*. New York: Oxford University Press, 1982.

Merryman, Molly. *Clipped Wings: The Rise and Fall of the Women Airforce Service Pilots (WASPs) of World War II*. New York: New York University Press, 1998.

Meyer, Leisa D. *Creating GI Jane: Sexuality and Power in the Women's Army Corps during World War II*. New York: Columbia University Press, 1996.

Meyerowitz, Joanne, ed. *Not June Cleaver: Women and Gender in Postwar America, 1945–1960*. Philadelphia: Temple University Press, 1994.

Milkman, Ruth. *Gender at Work: The Dynamics of Job Segregation by Sex during World War II*. Urbana: University of Illinois Press, 1987.

Morden, Bettie J. *The Women's Army Corps, 1945–1978*. Washington: Center of Military History, United States Army, 1990.

Scharf, Lois. *To Work and to Wed: Female Employment, Feminism, and the Great Depression*. Westport, Conn.: Greenwood Press, 1980.

Wandersee, Winifred D. *Women's Work and Family Values, 1920–1940*. Cambridge, Mass.: Harvard University Press, 1981.

Ware, Susan. *Beyond Suffrage: Women in the New Deal*. Cambridge, Mass.: Harvard University Press, 1981.

———. *Holding Their Own: American Women in the 1930s*. Boston: Twayne Publishers, 1982.

Yellin, Emily. *Our Mother's War: American Women at Home and at the Front during World War II*. New York: Free Press, 2004.

XVI. SOCIAL CHANGE, CULTURE, SPORT, AND ENTERTAINMENT

Aaron, Daniel, and Robert Bendiner, eds. *The Strenuous Decade: A Social and Intellectual Record of the Nineteen-Thirties*. New York: Anchor Books, 1970.

Aronson, James. *The Press and the Cold War*. Indianapolis: Bobbs-Merrill, 1970.

Ashby, Leroy. *With Amusement for All: A History of American Popular Culture since 1830*. Lexington: University Press of Kentucky, 2006.

Barnouw, Erik. *The Image Empire: A History of Broadcasting in the United States*. New York: Oxford University Press, 1970.

Baskerville, Stephen, and Ralph Willett, eds. *Nothing Else to Fear: New Perspectives on America in the Thirties*. Manchester: Manchester University Press, 1985.

Baughman, James. *The Republic of Mass Culture: Journalism, Filmmaking, and Broadcasting in America since 1941*. Baltimore: Johns Hopkins University Press, 1997.

Baxter, John. *Hollywood in the Thirties*. New York: A. S. Barnes & Co., 1980.

Bergman, Andrew. *We're in the Money: Depression America and Its Films*. Chicago: Ivan R. Dee, 1971.

Bernhard, Nancy E. *U.S. Television News and Cold War Propaganda, 1947–1960*. New York: Cambridge University Press, 1999.

Biskind, Peter. *Seeing Is Believing: How Hollywood Taught Us to Stop Worrying and Love the Fifties*. New York: Pantheon Books, 1983.

Blue, Howard. *Words at War: World War II Era Radio Drama and the Postwar Broadcasting Industry Blacklist*. Lanham, Md.: Scarecrow Press, 2002.

Boyer, Paul S. *By the Bomb's Early Light: American Thought and Culture at the Dawn of the Atomic Age*. New York: Pantheon Books, 1985.

Brands, H. W. *The Devil We Knew: Americans and the Cold War*. New York: Oxford University Press, 1993.

Braverman, Jordan. *To Hasten the Homecoming: How Americans Fought World War II through the Media*. Lanham, Md.: Madison Books, 1996.

Brode, Douglas. *The Films of the Fifties: "Sunset Boulevard" to "On the Beach."* Secaucus, N.J.: Citadel Press, 1976.

Burk, Robert F. *Much More Than a Game: Players, Owners, and American Baseball since 1921.* Chapel Hill: University of North Carolina Press, 2001.

Carter, Paul A. *Another Part of the Fifties.* New York: Columbia University Press, 1983.

Ceplair, Larry, and Steven Englund. *The Inquisition in Hollywood: Politics in the Film Community, 1930–1960.* Garden City, N.Y.: Doubleday, 1980.

Chambers, John W., and David Culbert, eds. *World War II, Film, and History.* New York: Oxford University Press, 1996.

Christensen, Terry. *Reel Politics: American Political Movies from "Birth of a Nation" to "Platoon."* New York: Blackwell, 1987.

Clarnand, Elaine, and Steve Goodson, eds. *The Impact of the Cold War on American Popular Culture.* Carrollton: State University of West Georgia, 1999.

Cooney, Terry A. *Balancing Acts: American Thought and Culture in the 1930s.* New York: Twayne Publishers, 1995.

Corber, Robert J. *Homosexuality in Cold War America: Resistance and the Crisis of Masculinity.* Durham: Duke University Press, 1997.

Covert, Catherine L., and John D. Stevens. *Mass Media between the Wars: Perceptions of Cultural Tension, 1918–1941.* Syracuse, N.Y.: Syracuse University Press, 1984.

Culbert, David H. *News for Everyman: Radio and Foreign Affairs in Thirties America.* Westport, Conn.: Greenwood Press, 1976.

Cullen, Jim., ed. *Popular Culture in American History.* Oxford: Blackwell, 2001.

Davies, R. O. *America's Obsession: Sports and Society since 1945.* New York: Harcourt Brace, 1994.

Denning, Michael. *Cultural Front: The Laboring of American Culture in the Twentieth Century.* London: Verso 1998.

Doherty, Thomas. *Projections of War: Hollywood, American Culture, and World War II.* New York: Columbia University Press, 1993.

Doss, Erika. *Twentieth Century American Art.* New York: Oxford University Press, 2002.

Dowdy, Andrew. *The Films of the Fifties: The American State of Mind.* New York: Morrow, 1973.

Engelhardt, Tom. *The End of Victory Culture: Cold War America and the Disillusioning of a Generation.* New York: Basic Books, 1994.

Field, Hermann, and Kate Field. *Trapped in the Cold War: The Ordeal of an American Family.* Stanford, Calif.: Stanford University Press, 1999.

Foreman, Joel, ed. *The Other Fifties: Interrogating Midcentury American Icons.* Urbana: University of Illinois Press, 1997.

———, ed. *American Culture of the 1950s*. Urbana: University of Illinois Press, 1996.

Fried, Richard M. *The Russians Are Coming! The Russians are Coming!: Pageantry and Patriotism in Cold-War America*. New York: Oxford University Press, 1998.

Friendly, Fred W. *Due to Circumstances beyond Our Control . . .* New York: Vintage Books, 1968.

Gans, Herbert J. *The Levittowners: Ways of Life and Politics in a New Suburban Community*. New York: Pantheon Books, 1967.

Gomery, Douglas. *Shared Pleasures: A History of Movie Presentations in the United States*. Madison: University of Wisconsin Press, 1992.

Gorn, Elliott, and Warren Goldstein. *A Brief History of American Sports*. New York: Hill & Wang, 1993.

Graebner, William S. *The Age of Doubt: American Thought and Culture in the 1940s*. Boston: Twayne Publishers, 1991.

Guilbaut, Serge. *How New York Stole the Idea of Modern Art: Abstract Expressionism, Freedom, and the Cold War*. Chicago: University of Chicago Press, 1983.

Henriksen, Margot A. *Dr. Strangelove's America: Society and Culture in the Atomic Age*. Berkeley: University of California Press, 1997.

Higham, Charles, and Joel Greenberg. *Hollywood in the Forties*. New York: A. S. Barnes & Co., 1968.

Hixson, Walter L. *Parting the Curtain: Propaganda, Culture, and the Cold War, 1945–1961*. New York: St. Martin's Press, 1998.

Horten, Gerd. *Radio Goes to War: The Cultural Politics of Propaganda during World War II*. Berkeley: University of California Press, 2002.

Iskstadt, Heinz, Rob Kroes, and Brian Lee, eds. *The Thirties: Politics and Culture Times of Broken Dreams*. Amsterdam, Netherlands: Free University Press, 1987.

Jackson, Kenneth T. *Crabgrass Frontier: The Suburbanization of America*. New York: Oxford University Press, 1985.

Jones, Landon Y. *Great Expectations: America and the Baby Boom Generation*. New York: Coward, McCann & Geoghegan, 1980.

Koppes, Clayton R., and Gregory D. Black. *Hollywood Goes to War: How Politics and Propaganda Shaped World War II Movies*. New York: Free Press, 1987.

Krutch, Joseph Wood. *The American Drama since 1918: An Informal History*. New York: George Braziller, 1957.

Lebow, Richard Ned. *We All Lost the Cold War*. Princeton, N.J.: Princeton University Press, 1993.

Levine, Lawrence W. *Unpredictable Past: Explorations in American Cultural History*. New York: Oxford University Press, 1993.

Lipsitz, George. *Time Passages: Collective Memory and American Popular Culture*. Minneapolis: University of Minnesota Press, 2001.

Loeb, P. *Nuclear Culture: Living and Working in the World's Largest Atomic Complex*. Philadelphia: New Society Publishers, 1986.

MacDonald, J. Fred. *Television and the Red Menace: The Video Road to Vietnam*. New York: Praeger, 1985.

May, Elaine Tyler. *Homeward Bound: American Families in the Cold War Era*. New York: Basic Books, 1988.

May, Lary. *The Big Tomorrow: Hollywood and the Politics of the American Way*. Chicago: University of Chicago Press, 2000.

———, ed. *Recasting America: Culture and Politics in the Age of the Cold War*. Chicago: University of Chicago Press, 1989.

Mintz, Steven, and Randy Roberts. *Hollywood's America: United States History through Its Films*. St. James, N.Y.: Brandywine Press, 2001.

Oakley, Ronald R. *God's Country: America in the Fifties*. New York: Dembner Books, 1986.

Pells, Richard. *The Liberal Mind in a Conservative Age: American Intellectuals in the 1940s and 1950s*. New York: Harper & Row, 1985.

Persico, Joseph E. *Edward R. Murrow: An American Original*. New York: Da Capo Press, 1997.

Roddick, Nick. *A New Deal in Entertainment: Warner Brothers in the 1930s*. London: British Film Institute, 1983.

Rose, Barbara. *American Painting: The Twentieth Century*. New York: Rizzoli Publications, 1986.

Sayre, Nora. *Running Time: Films of the Cold War*. New York: Dial Press, 1982.

Schwartz, Richard Alan. *Cold War Culture: Media and the Arts, 1945–1990*. New York: Facts on File, 1998.

Seidel, Michael. *Streak: Joe DiMaggio and the Summer of '41*. New York: McGraw-Hill, 1988.

Shulman, Holly C. *The Voice of America: Propaganda and Democracy, 1941–1945*. Madison: University of Wisconsin Press, 1990.

Sklar, Robert. *Movie-Made America: A Social History of American Movies*. New York: Random House, 1975.

Solberg, Carl. *Rising High: America in the Cold War*. New York: Mason & Lipscomb, 1973.

Sperber, A.M. *Murrow: His Life and Times*. New York: Freundlich Books, 1986.

Spigel, Lynn. *Make Room for TV: Television and the Family Idea in Postwar America*. Chicago: University of Chicago Press, 1992.

Stott, William. *Documentary Expression in Thirties America*. New York: Oxford University Press, 1973.

Tygiel, Jules. *Baseball's Great Experiment: Jackie Robinson and His Legacy*. New York: Oxford University Press, 1983.

Tyler May, Elaine. *Homeward Bound: American Families in the Cold War Era*. New York: Basic Books, 1988.

Weart, Spencer R. *Nuclear Fear: A History of Images*. Cambridge, Mass.: Harvard University Press, 1988.

Whitfield, Stephen J. *The Culture of the Cold War*. Baltimore: Johns Hopkins University Press, 1991.

Winkler, Allan M. *Life under a Cloud: American Anxiety about the Atom*. New York: Oxford University Press, 1993.

Zolotow, Maurice. *Shooting Star: A Biography of John Wayne*. New York: Simon & Schuster, 1974.

About the Author

Neil A. Wynn was born in 1947 to British parents stationed in The Hague, Holland. When the family returned to Great Britain, he completed his education in Edinburgh, Scotland, where he also attended university from 1965 to 1969. Following his graduation with an M.A. in history, he went to the Open University in England to undertake research for his Ph.D. After four years, including a year as a graduate assistant at State University of New York at Buffalo, Wynn was awarded the first Ph.D. in history at the Open University in 1973 for his thesis on "The Afro-American and the Second World War." In 1979, Wynn was awarded a fellowship by the American Council of Learned Societies and spent a year engaged in research in Washington, D.C.

In 2003, after teaching for 30 years at the University of Glamorgan in Wales, as a senior lecturer, principal lecturer, and reader in history and American studies, he took the appointment of professor in twentieth-century history at the University of Gloucestershire. He has taught on international programs at Central Missouri State University and at the Maastricht Center for Transatlantic Studies in the Netherlands, where he is a director.

Wynn is the author of *Historical Dictionary from the Great War to the Great Depression* (2003); *The Afro-American and the Second World War* (1976, 1993); *From Progressivism to Prosperity: World War I and American Society* (1986); chapters on "The 1940s" and "The 1960s" in *Die Vereinigten Staaten von Amerika [The United States of America]* (1977), and various articles on African American and American history and culture. He also coedited *America's Century: Perspectives on U.S. History since 1900* (1993) and edited *"Cross the Water Blues": African American Music in Europe* (2007). From 1990 to 2003, he reported on events in the United States for the *Annual Register* and has often broadcast on local BBC radio on American current affairs.